resounding

truth

Engaging Culture

WILLIAM A. DYRNESS
AND ROBERT K. JOHNSTON,
SERIES EDITORS

The Engaging Culture series is designed to help Christians respond with theological discernment to our contemporary culture. Each volume explores particular cultural expressions, seeking to discover God's presence in the world and to involve readers in sympathetic dialogue and active discipleship. These books encourage neither an uninformed rejection nor an uncritical embrace of culture, but active engagement informed by theological reflection.

resounding truth

truth

christian wisdom in the world of music

Jeremy S. Begbie

Baker Academic

Grand Rapids, Michigan

Published by Baker Academic
a division of Baker Publishing Group
P.O. Box 6287, Grand Rapids, MI 49516-6287
www.bakeracademic.com

Second printing, September 2008

Printed in the United States of America

Library of Congress Cataloging-in-Publication Data
Begbie, Jeremy.
    Resounding truth : Christian wisdom in the world of music / Jeremy S. Begbie.
        p.   cm. — (Engaging culture)
    Includes bibliographical references and index.
    ISBN 10: 0-8010-2695-4 (pbk.)
    ISBN 978-0-8010-2695-9 (pbk.)
        1. Music—Religious aspects—Christianity. I. Title.
    ML3921.2.B44 2007
    261.5'78—dc22   2007017172

In memory of
MMB and GHB

contents

illustrations

acknowledgments

My interest in music has been lifelong, so it would require many pages to list all those to whom I owe a debt of gratitude. Some, however, must be singled out.

The principal, Christopher Cocksworth, and the staff and students of Ridley Hall, Cambridge, have provided an immensely supportive base and stimulating environment for me to explore the interplay between music and theology. During the writing of this book, I have also been privileged to be associate director at the Institute for Theology, Imagination and the Arts at the University of St. Andrews. The project "Theology through the Arts" is now based there, and an extraordinary community of scholarship, research, and mutual support has developed. From the beginning we have sought to foster an ethos that is unashamedly theological while at the same time does justice to the integrity of the arts. I am very grateful to the institute's director, Professor Trevor Hart, and to my colleagues at St. Andrews for their intellectual courage and practical support during the last few years. Professor Alan Torrance, himself a very fine musician, has been a consistent, loyal, and enthusiastic encourager as well as a constructive critic. Special thanks go to Suzanne McDonald, former research student at St. Andrews, and Steven Guthrie (now at Belmont University), who have both read the entire text with great care and without whose help this would be a much weaker book. In St. Andrews and Cambridge I have also been fortunate to supervise a range of very gifted postgraduate students, whose work has impacted this book in numerous ways. They, and those like them, are the ones who will carry this kind of cross-disciplinary work into the future. In particular I should like to thank Imogen Adkins, Alison Connett, Andy Edwards, Andy McCoy, David McNutt, David Moseley, Steven Prokopchuk, Ed Russell, Paul Scaringi, Chelle Stearns, and Férdia Stone-Davis.

Many members of the Faculty of Divinity at the University of Cambridge have contributed to the shaping of the ideas that appear here; in particular I am indebted to David Ford and Daniel Hardy. The much-lamented Colin Gunton, theologian and musician, provided both intellectual food and musical insight, and my colleague at Ridley Hall, Philip Jenson, provided very helpful comments on the biblical sections. Gratitude goes to many others who have been kind enough to advise on material that has found its way into this book, especially Sam Barrett, David Creese, John Ito, Hyesook Kim, Micky Mattox, Stephen Schoessler, and Robert Sholl.

I am also very grateful for many illuminating conversations with Richard Bauckham, Bruce Benson, Alastair Borthwick, Frank Burch Brown, Graham Cray, Brian Daley, Malcolm Guite, Vanessa Herrick, Simon Howell, Ann Loades, Roger Lundin, David Moseley, Micheal O'Siadhail, David Peacock, John Polkinghorne, Andrew Rumsey, Dal Schindell, Luci Shaw, Janet Martin Soskice, Kevin Vanhoozer, John Walford, Rowan Williams, Tom Wright, Nicholas Wolterstorff, and the late Anthony Monti. Special mention also ought to be made of some distinguished musicians who have had an important influence on my thinking: John Butt, Daniel Chua, Stephen Cleobury, Robert Duerr, Alexander Goehr, Colin Kingsley, James MacMillan, Paul Spicer, Nigel Swinford, John Tavener, and Geoffrey Webber.

Much of the thinking behind this book has arisen through interacting with students and staff of institutions outside the United Kingdom. Regent College, Vancouver, has played a key role, as has Fuller Seminary, Pasadena, California; Wheaton College, Wheaton, Illinois; and Calvin College, Grand Rapids, Michigan; as well as scholars at the universities of British Columbia, Yale, Stanford, Berkeley, Trinity Western, Iowa, and Cape Town. Many chapters were written while a resident member at the Center of Theological Inquiry, Princeton; grateful thanks are due to the former director, Wallace Allston, as well as to Will Storrar and Robert Jenson (a musical theologian if ever there was one) and to the remarkable support staff at that unique gathering place of theological wisdom.

My research assistant, Dan Vaca, provided a huge amount of help, from the mundane to the profound, and Dona McCullagh has proofread the entire manuscript with penetrating wisdom as well as undertaken a hundred other practicalities with grace and good humor—I am indebted to them both. The editors of this series, Robert Johnston and William Dyrness, have given solid and reassuring advice throughout, and Bob Hosack of Baker Academic has been a model of patience, especially as deadlines have frequently been deferred.

The largest expression of gratitude, as always, goes to my wife, Rachel, and our offspring, Helen, Mark, Heather, and Emma—all of whom have taught me much about what it means to seek God's "resounding truth" in music ranging from Palestrina to Michael Jackson.

introduction

Can you imagine a day without music? You wake up. Perhaps a bedside radio brings you a jingle at news time. You take a train to work—easy classics are piped through overhead speakers at the station. Or you drive to work and flick on the radio—cool jazz fills the car, a jeep next to you at the traffic lights throbs with hip-hop. You are at home with children; one of them plays a video game—with synchronized music; they watch a video—most of which is backed by music. In the evening, you put your feet up and watch a sitcom you recorded earlier in the day—the scenes are joined by five-second musical links. Or you go for a beer—and you find a folk band in the bar. Or you go out to a movie—half the sound track is musical. And on Sunday, perhaps you go to church—and about half of the service uses music.

More than ever before in Western society, music is part of our lives, ubiquitously present. Whether we love it or ignore it, play it or shut it out, revel in it or resent it, it is there.

Yet many of us rarely if ever stop to think about what music is, how it works, what it might be doing to us, and what we might be doing with it. Christians are no exception. The last twenty years or so have seen a flood of books on "Christianity and . . . ," covering topics from party politics to biotechnology. And rightly so. In many constituencies in the church, a tendency to retreat into a ghetto and withdraw from culture at large has been superseded by a desire to relate the claims of the faith to every sphere of life. Yet even when the arts are given serious thought, music is often noticeable by its absence.

That is certainly true when it comes to the world of theology. In the last hundred years, serious dialogue between theologians and musicians has been hard to find.[1] In recent times, a flurry of writing on theology and the arts has appeared,[2] but it would be hard to deny that the lion's share of attention has been given to the visual arts (especially painting) and literature. When I attend conferences on "theology and the arts" or "Christianity and the arts," I frequently bump into a default assumption: painting and literature represent art proper, and the rest, including music, will somehow fall into place accordingly.

Why has so little Christian intellectual energy been devoted to music in recent times? Undoubtedly one of the reasons is the sheer difficulty of speaking about it. Elvis Costello once said that writing about music is like dancing about architecture. It may be a cliché to say that the experience of music cannot be grasped in words, but it is no less true for that. Speech always seems to fall painfully short of the reality. George Steiner remarks that "in the face of music, the wonders of language are also its frustrations."[3] Many music critics leave us feeling that we would have gained far more simply by listening to the music. Andrew Solomon writes of his experience of interviewing the Russian virtuoso Evgeny Kissin:

> Watching Kissin perform, one sees a man who seems literally possessed by his music. Though Kissin can speak of music with intellectual clarity, he can no more verbalize how he has arrived at his way of playing the piano than the leopard can explain how he got his spots. "How do you choose your encores?" I asked him. . . . "They come to me," he said. "How do you judge an audience?" "I feel something in the air." "How do you decide when you are ready for a piece?" "This is always very clear to me." "How do you decide which concerts to attend?" "I attend the ones I'm interested in."[4]

Further acute difficulties arise from trying to fathom how it is that music does what it does. It is indisputable that music is one of the most powerful media humans have at their disposal; *how* it mediates and *what* it mediates are notoriously hard to understand or explain.

Moreover, thinking Christians may be inclined to disregard music simply because they believe, with many others, that it does not concern anything objective, anything that could invite claims to truth. Appraisals of music seem to be wholly or largely determined by our own preferences ("I know what I like, and that's all that matters"; "it's all a matter of individual taste, anyway") or by the prevailing currents of our social group. Any conclusion I reach about what makes a piece "good" or "bad" will surely either be arbitrary or die the death of a thousand qualifications. Indeed, some go further and say that there are no universal norms by which music can be interpreted and assessed—an approach intensified in the so-called postmodern ethos, with its "tendency to question the very notion of an original, independent truth or reality to which the arts, morality, or indeed any kind of 'discourse' could refer."[5]

A further reason for neglect is that in comparison with the monumental dilemmas of our age—the ecological crisis, mass starvation, the AIDS pandemic—music will seem for many a thoroughly inconsequential matter. As we shall see, in our culture the most common primary use of music is to create or change moods; it would seem odd to give something so trivial any serious intellectual attention. At best music is a distraction from the urgent and pressing demands of daily living, a luxury for those who have the time and money to use and enjoy it.

Why Bother?

Of course, the chances are that readers of this book already have some interest in music and believe that thinking about it in a Christian way is worthwhile. Nonetheless, in the light of what we have just been saying, it is worth asking: why bother putting our minds to something that is so hard to speak about, so apparently unconcerned with matters of truth, and seemingly so insignificant?

The question of the difficulty of speaking about music and the issue of music's relation to truth will be touched upon many times later in the book. Here we focus on the question: why should music be a significant or important matter for Christians to think about?

Theologically, the most general and basic reason is simply the *lordship of Jesus Christ*. For the follower of Christ, there is no "exclusion zone," no "secular" territory outside the scope of his saving work, no value-free or neutral area of human life. This applies as much to music as to any other cultural activity.

But there are more specific reasons for caring about music. The first we have alluded to already: music is *pervasive* in our culture. Even if we never go near a concert hall, or switch on a radio or TV, or go to films, music will seek us out in airports and train stations, in doctors' clinics and dentists' chairs, at the hairdresser's, and in shopping malls, pubs, and clubs. We do not have to find it; it finds us. A teenager said to a friend of mine recently: "Music is the ocean we swim in." It would be odd if Christians were never to think in depth about something so omnipresent.

Not only that, music seems to be *universal*. We know of no culture without something akin to music. "There have been cultures without counting, cultures without painting, cultures bereft of the wheel or the written word, but never a culture without music."[6] Music spans the full range of wealth and privilege. To think of it as a disposable luxury for the lucky few flies in the face of the evidence. Even the most poverty-stricken peoples will sing. Music may not be necessary for biological survival—on a desert island we could subsist without it—but it does seem vital to human flourishing. Would it not be strange, to say the least, if there were no distinctively Christian comment to make on so prevalent a feature of the human race?

Music also cries out for attention simply because of the *immense power* it can have in many people's lives—something memorably celebrated in movies such as *The Pianist*, *Sister Act*, *Music of the Heart*, and *Les Choristes*. Few doubt that music can call forth the deepest things of the human spirit and affect behavior at the most profound levels. Anyone who has parented a teenager will not need to be told this—study after study has shown that music often plays a pivotal part in the formation of young people's identity, self-image, and patterns of behavior.[7] The commercial sector knows that music can affect, among other things, the time people spend in a shop,[8] the amount of money spent,[9] and the choice of product.[10] Through music, DJs shift the energy levels and social interactions of a club and restaurant managers promote an image and mold our moods. Factory workers are relieved of boredom and fatigue; warriors forget their fear and rush into battle; the mentally ill are helped to health. Polish sacred music played a key role in the solidarities that eventually overturned communism.[11] It is small wonder that some totalitarian regimes have been extremely nervous about music (the Taliban administration in Afghanistan sought to ban virtually all music because of its perceived social dangers) and that others have unashamedly harnessed it precisely because of its influence (the Nazis, for example). Any Christian who cares about the good of human society ought to be concerned with what kind of power music might possess and how such power might be used responsibly.

Another reason for thinking at length about music is *the importance that many people are prepared to grant it in their lives*. George Steiner recounts that for the philosopher Ludwig Wittgenstein, "the slow movement of Brahms' third Quartet pulled him back from the brink of suicide."[12] The singer Sting has said: "I think music is the one spiritual force in our lives that we have access to, really. There are so many other spiritual avenues that are closed off to us, and music still has that, is still important, is important for me. It saved my life. It saved my sanity."[13] Admittedly there are some for whom music possesses little attraction or interest and a few who dislike all music. But they are few. In addition to the music we hear whether we want to or not, a large part of the population spends considerable amounts of time (and money) seeking it out. A glance at the statistics of musical consumption in any Western country will confirm this. The revolution in digital technology and Internet communication availability has played a critical role here, opening up an unprecedented flood of consumer access to music. Again, it would be curious if thinking Christians were to ignore something in which people are prepared to invest so highly.

A further incentive to consider music theologically comes from recognizing what seem to be the *very close links between music and*—for want of a better term—*religious impulses*. An ethnomusicologist comments: "I seriously doubt, in fact, that one could find any religion, large or small, that does not concern itself with the ways 'music' is . . . vital to conveying the word of God. . . . Music," he continues, is "a preferred medium for expressing religious meaning."[14] George Steiner is worth quoting again:

> Music and the metaphysical, in the root sense of that term, music and religious feeling, have been virtually inseparable. It is in and through music that we are most immediately in the presence of the logically, of the verbally inexpressible but wholly palpable energy in being that communicates to our senses and to our

reflection what little we can grasp of the naked wonder of life. . . . It has long been, it continues to be, the unwritten theology of those who lack or reject any formal creed.[15]

In nearly every culture where we encounter phenomena that would normally be categorized as religious, music will not be far behind: the urge to sing, pluck strings, or send air through resonating tubes seems irresistible. Moreover, there are many, as we shall see, who believe music serves a religious or quasi-religious function even when there is no formal or overt recognition of the fact. A good example would be those who see the contemporary club culture as performing, at least in some respects, a religious role in contemporary society.[16]

Care is needed here. There is indeed a kind of intuitive, gut feeling that many have about music: that it is in some special way religiously or theologically "loaded" (or at least particularly well suited to religious purposes) and that this is confirmed by the often intimate links between music and religion in history. Some will want to take this further and claim that just because of this, we have in music a point of contact of immense potential between the church and culture, a bridge across which the church must learn to walk in the interest of engaging effectively with the contemporary world. This might be so in many cases. We would be foolish to deny the possibility of the Spirit's stirrings in music far beyond the church, and the implications of this for the church's mission. Nevertheless, claims of religious experience through music are notoriously hard to evaluate and build upon unless one is prepared to identify at least something of the content of the "religion" in question. The category of "religion" or "religious," after all, is a massively contested one, as is the belief that there is some kind of locatable core or essence of "religious experience." Unless we are willing to clarify what we might mean by asserting that, for example, music puts us in touch with God (for the Christian, as for any theistic faith, this would mean with a quite specific God), we will be powerless in the face of the skeptic, who will see such claims as no more than hyperbole for a fervent emotional experience or as a way of masking our desire to have some kind of ultimate authority to back up our musical tastes! In short, a laudable attempt to connect with musical experience in the culture at large can easily trade away the distinctives of Christian faith, leaving the church more irrelevant than ever.[17]

Nevertheless, the widespread and apparently ineradicable use of music by the world's major faith traditions should at least give us pause for thought. Certainly in the case of Christianity, we only need think of the first stirrings of the church when prayer was quickly wedded to song, or of the centuries of plainsong, the cantatas of Bach, the avalanche of praise music of the last thirty years, the fierce crucifixion symphonies of James MacMillan. The long and strong relationship between Christian faith and music is striking. To be sure, the marriage has not always been a happy one. Currents of suspicion are not hard to find: "Music dulls the intellect and its sensuousness entraps the soul; it offers a world of harmony where no harmony exists, and replaces the real world with the world of entrancing make-believe. So runs the traditional critique of music."[18] But however strong the misgivings, the links between music and Christianity have been persistent and irrepressible, and this deserves attention from the thinking Christian.

Another factor encouraging us to think about music theologically is that *in a wide range of musical genres today*, implicitly and sometimes explicitly, *theological or Christian themes are being explored*, and often in ways that go far beyond using religious words simply for style or surface effect.[19] At times we can find a clear attraction to Jesus Christ along with misgivings about organizational religion (Bono, Moby, Nick Cave), at other times, a far wider "spirituality."[20] A flurry of writing on U2 has highlighted the biblical imagery and Christian resonances of much of their music.[21] A variety of composers with little or no professed religious commitment have been journeying into the theological. Sir Harrison Birtwistle's *Last Supper* (1998–99) is one example; John Adams's oratorio *El Niño* (2000) is another, a two-hour retelling of the nativity story. Significantly, the distinguished director Peter Sellars, who staged the Paris premiere of *El Niño*, comments: "For a number of years, most of the work I've been doing is about conveying a religious or spiritual message. . . . I think in this age of television and Hollywood film, if classical music is going to stick around, there'd better be a very good reason. We have to offer something that is not available other-wise. I think it is spiritual content, which is what's missing from the commercial culture that surrounds us."[22] There are also composers like James MacMillan (discussed in chapter 7) and Sofia Gubaidulina, openly theological in intent and setting overtly Christian texts, who enjoy widespread acclaim.

Of no less interest is the huge commercial success of the so-called New Simplicity music (e.g., John Tavener, Arvo Pärt, Henryk Górecki, and others).[23] In the case of some of these composers, the Christian affiliation is quite overt, and the religious motivation behind their writing very evident. They provoke one writer to talk of "the return of religion" in music.[24] It is hard to miss this music's burgeoning popularity, as well as other music put under the umbrella of "spiritual" or "New Age" in which the interest is not in presenting a musical argument but in creating a kind of "soundscape,"[25] uniform in texture, unhur-ried, with little tension, rhythmic edge, or drive. Again, though, theological caution is needed. The word "spiritual" may be more popular than "religious," but it is no less slippery. Move beyond the language and we find that the depth of engagement with religious (let alone Christian) matters can vary enormously. Nonetheless, whatever our final assessment, there is surely much to be gained from a consciously Christian engagement with such music.

A final reason for Christians to attend to music thoughtfully is, as we have just mentioned, that *music has habitually played a key part in the church's wor-ship*. Despite periods when it has fallen into neglect and even been snubbed altogether, a glance at church history confirms that more often than not, worship has included music and often in copious quantities. Is it not worth asking why this is so? Just what it is about music that has made it so pervasive in the praise of God's people?

Theology and Music

The aim of this Engaging Culture series is "to help Christians respond with theological discernment to our contemporary culture" with a view to "active engagement informed by theological reflection." This book is concerned with music in particular: gaining theological discernment about music with a view to—and, we would want to add, in the midst of—active engagement. It is concerned with how God's truth might "sound" and "re-sound" in the world of music.

Put another way, we are asking: what can Christian theology bring to music?[26] Needless to say, theology is a word that can have hugely negative connotations today. For many, it will suggest at best something harmlessly irrelevant and at worst oppressive dogma imposed on the unwilling. It is commonly associated with abstraction—never touching the ground of day-to-day living and divorced from direct encounter with God (simply thinking *about* God rather than engaging *with* God).

This is hardly the place for a lengthy discussion about the nature of theology; there is much that will have to be assumed. But at least this can be said: I am taking theology to be *the disciplined thinking and rethinking of the Christian gospel for the sake of fostering a wisdom that is nourished by, and nourishes, the church in its worship and mission to the world.* This is worth a little unpacking.

Disciplined thinking and rethinking: Theology entails thinking, intellectual effort, and no apology is made here for the fact that this book will require hard thought. Even if, as we shall see, imagination is a crucial part of this hard thinking, it is no less strenuous for that. However, this is not an isolated type of thinking, cut off at the neck, locked into the mind, unconnected with the rest of what makes us human. Whole streams of writing have attacked the common captivity of theology to this kind of model, epitomized in the indulgently cerebral academic who never leaves his (and it is often assumed to be "his") study. Theology is a form of thinking, certainly, but it is affected by, and ought to affect, every human faculty—including our willing, feeling, sensing, and bodily actions. In the case of theology, it is especially important to recognize that thinking is inextricably bound up with story (the narrative shape of faith), symbols of various sorts (such as the sacraments), and practical action in the world. This rich, multiply-connected kind of thinking is part of what has been made possible through Jesus Christ—the renewal of our minds (Rom. 12:1–2)—and as such, part of an integrated lifestyle in which all of a person's capacities have been liberated by the Holy Spirit to find their true role in relation to God and one another in the world.

Of the Christian gospel: By "the gospel" I mean the announcement that in the life, death, and resurrection of Jesus, the Triune Creator, the God of Israel, has acted decisively to reconcile the world to himself. Here is theology's raison d'être and its lodestar—theology is not free-floating speculation, but it is disciplined by this gospel and seeks to interpret the whole of reality from this center. Just because it is so motivated, the theologian is ultimately responsible to a living God: the God of the gospel is not an inert presence but personally active, continuously at work to transform his creatures and his creation. Hence learning *about* God is undertaken in the context of learning *from* God, as God relates to us and we to God. This means, in turn, that theology is inseparable (though distinct) from prayer and worship—thinking appropriately *about* God means regularly engaging *with* God. It also entails being strenuously faithful to Scripture, since the gospel is testified to and mediated first and foremost through these life-transforming writings, themselves the outcome of God's reconciling work. Thinking theologically about music, then, is gospel-oriented thinking in these senses.

For the sake of fostering a wisdom: Precisely because it relates to the whole of us and concerns the energetic, life-transforming God of the gospel, theology has a practical orientation. One of the best ways to express this is to speak of theology fostering wisdom. In the so-called Wisdom literature of the Bible (for example, the book of Proverbs), gaining wisdom concerns much more than amassing data for the mind's scrutiny. It is practically geared. To be wise means being able to discern what is going on in specific, down-to-earth situations and to judge what it is right to say and do in those situations in a way that is faithful and true to God. We become wise *in order to live well*. As "lived knowledge,"[27] wisdom is directed toward a lifestyle thoroughly "in tune" with God—godly living—that resonates aptly with the Creator's intentions for us and his world. Theology aims at generating and celebrating this kind of wisdom. My hope is that this book will help Christians, and anyone with more than a passing interest in music, to develop a Christian wisdom about music, that is, generate Christian habits of judgment that can form, and perhaps re-form, the practicalities of making and hearing music, whether that means listening to a symphony, composing a song, or playing in a rock band.

Nourished by, and nourishes, the church in its worship and mission to the world: The gospel finds its outworking in a people gathered by God's Spirit to share God's life and make known what he has done in Jesus Christ, a people of worship called to be *in* and *for* the world. Theology that seeks a wisdom true to the gospel, therefore, cannot take flight from this community—fallen, compromised, and shabby as it is and always has been. This is emphatically not to claim that no fruitful Christian or God-honoring thinking can ever take place outside the church, nor is it to claim that theology has no interests outside the Christian community. It is simply to remind ourselves of Christian theology's primary home and where it has its immediate responsibilities, amid the distinctive practices of a distinctive community. Theology's first calling, I would contend, is to help build up the people of God, to shape the Christian community for the sake of its worship and mission to the world. In this book we seek a wisdom about music to this end.

Unfortunately, Christian thinking about music often bypasses the church. Many individual Christian musicians rightly have a strong passion for mission. They are rightly keen to be "salt" in the world and not become closeted in the church or trapped in the worship sanctuary. But mission is no less a corporate affair than worship, and it is unlikely that there can be a transforming Christian musical presence in society until the church refinds its musicians and musicians refind the church. Individual believers are always part of a larger body of Christians, even if during weekdays they may be exercising ministries with few, if any, Christians in sight. Among other things, recovering this corporate sense means being prepared to learn from one another in the body of Christ, to comprehend *with all the saints* (past and present) the breadth, length, height, and depth of the gospel (Eph. 3:18). It also entails a willingness to explore the abundant treasures of Christian wisdom from the past, the way in which God's truth has sounded and re-sounded in the world of music down the centuries. (Chapters 3–7 are concerned with doing just this.)

In the sense I have described it, theology can and should be practiced by all Christians, not only professionally trained academics. All Christians who think intelligently about their faith along these lines are theologians. Certainly, some are called to develop particular theological skills, and some of these may become professionals in an institution (seminary, university, or whatever). But disciplined thought about the Christian faith cannot be the preserve of this latter group alone. Indeed, one of the most encouraging developments in recent years has been the "laicization" of theology: a burgeoning number of laypeople who are not intending to be theological teachers or ordained clergy nonetheless are thinking their faith through rigorously. This book is meant not only for the professional theologian but also for anyone who wants to think seriously about music from a Christian perspective. (Hence I have tried to avoid theological jargon where possible and to confine technicalities to the endnotes.)

Pitfalls

There are serious pitfalls in the kind of enterprise we have in mind, and it is well to be aware of them at the outset. Two of these form a pair, one often leading to the other: *theological imperialism* and *theological aestheticism*. In theological imperialism, theology swells its chest and music is stifled. Out of a concern for doctrinal orthodoxy, music is not given room to be itself, not allowed to glorify God in its own way. Many musicians fear this when they see a theologian approaching on the horizon. To bring Christian theology to bear on music surely means that doctrine and dogma will lay down rules in advance and ignore the way music actually operates. This quickly leads, it is said, to some form of "instrumentalism," where music is treated as the mere carrier of some predetermined theological "message" and as valid only insofar as we can spell out clearly just what that message is. Music becomes an attractive gloss for conceptual truths—secondary and colorful wrapping to be tossed away once the specific "idea" has been grasped. Professor David Ford of Cambridge University rightly notes, "There is often a suspicion that theology in the form of doctrine and argument fails to honor the integrity of [artistic] genres, tending to reduce them to an abstractable didactic content."[28]

Faced with this, many will swing, pendulum-like, to the opposite extreme—theological aestheticism. Here we are told that we must learn to lay aside our Christian presuppositions and, before anything else, listen to music and musicians, try to understand music "on its own terms," with a totally open and value-free mind, and then—and *only* then—begin to understand it (and perhaps evaluate it) with a Christian mind. Embedded in this is a quite understandable desire to recognize and respect music's integrity. But the obvious danger is one that has received much attention in theology and philosophy in recent years: that we will deceive ourselves into thinking that we can interpret something from an entirely neutral standpoint. A specifically Christian perspective can be set aside only by putting something else—regarded by default as more ultimate—in its place. Very often this "something else" is a general and radically undefined concept of religion or religious experience (we have touched on this already). Or, just as questionable, music itself becomes a new theological master, supposedly giving us supreme access to God or perhaps to some (again undefined) "spiritual" realm. (Not so long ago I was at a conference where I was told that music can help us "reconstruct" Christian doctrine from scratch and sweep away the irrelevant clutter of "creedal, word-obsessed church orthodoxy.") Examples of this "religion of music" are not hard to find in modern (and postmodern) times, finding their main precursors in the Romantic movement.

I am generalizing wildly, of course, but only to highlight options that are still very much around. How might we avoid these two extremes? Principally, I believe, by remembering that theology's truthfulness in the last resort is a matter of *orientation*. We have already put the pieces in place to explain this. When we do Christian theology we are *oriented to a living God*. Theology is not chiefly about being true to doctrines, dogma, or propositions (though all these are inescapably part of the enterprise) but about being true to the Triune God of Jesus, who has reached out to us to win us back to himself and through his Spirit transforms us into the likeness of the Son. Because it is true to this God, theology must be true to the gospel—that God has acted decisively in Christ to reconcile the world to himself. Because it is true to this God and this gospel, theology in its fullest form is carried out by those entrusted with the gospel, those being reconciled through Christ by the Spirit, those caught up actively in the dynamic of God's redeeming, revealing activity—the people of God, the church (and this includes the saints of the past). Because it is true to this God and the gospel entrusted to God's people, theology seeks to be faithful to Scripture, for Scripture above all mediates and witnesses to the gospel of Jesus Christ entrusted to the church. In theology, then, we are *oriented* to God by and through the gospel, with the people of God, in truthfulness to Scripture.

With this in mind, we can see that neither of our two extremes have to be followed. Being oriented to God in our thinking need not lead to theological imperialism, debasing music's integrity. Indeed, gaining Christian wisdom about music will mean taking great pains to do justice to the distinctive ways in which music is made and heard. We will make every effort to avoid crude instrumentalism, as if every note of music should conform to every detail of some theological program. But at the same time we will be just as wary of the idea that we can temporarily step outside Christian faith and be oriented nowhere in particular, or that we can allow some superior "ultimate" truth—such as "religion," or even music itself—to guide our thinking. Only God is God. Indeed, we can be more positive: it is just *because* we are oriented to this particular God who desires things and people to flourish in their own integrity (including musical sounds) that we will long to give "room" to the activities of making and hearing music. We can dare to go further: ultimately, it is *only* as we are reconciled by the Spirit to this God—a God who makes possible the flourishing of the world in all its particularity and diversity—that we will be *able* to honor the integrity of music properly.

Another pitfall is to limit the theology-music dialogue to a discussion of *music in worship*. When I speak about music at Christian conferences, even if I never mention worship, I often find most of the discussion after the lecture turns in that direction. This is not surprising. For most Christians, worship is the arena where music and the gospel are brought into closest contact (especially in countries such as my own, where Christian radio and TV channels are scarce and "Christian music" tends to mean "music for worship"). Music in worship also tends to attract prime attention because it provokes such white-hot controversy—no reader of this book will need to be reminded that fights over music can tear a church apart quicker than almost anything else.

Nonetheless, this series of books is about engaging culture, and whether we like to admit it or not, most of the music we experience from day to day does not issue from Christian worship or indeed from any Christian source. Here, in the main, we try to set our sights wider than the sanctuary: asking larger questions about music, the way it operates, and what place it may have in God's purposes for culture at large. Although I do frequently speak of matters of music in worship and hope that the book will have a bearing on such music (directly or indirectly), and although the rejuvenation of worship music is certainly an urgent priority for the church, I am increasingly convinced that many of the dilemmas and difficulties currently plaguing music in worship will begin to be alleviated only when we stand back a little and address broader issues about what kind of medium we are dealing with, how it functions in different settings, and how it links up with God's wider intentions for the world. In any case, one needs to be honest and admit that what is going on musically outside the church is often far more interesting and boundary breaking than what goes on inside it.[29]

A further pitfall is to reduce all theological questions about music to questions of *moral adjudication*. How far should the Christian be involved in popular music? If so, which kinds are acceptable? Is Eminem morally harmful? Is jazz bad for your spiritual health? Doubtless, though the links between music and morality are often hard to trace, they are certainly there. Music is made and used by human beings, and human beings are never morally neutral creatures. If we want to foster wisdom and godly living in the world of music, we cannot escape questions of ethics. However, it is unfortunate if these questions are allowed to dictate the agenda, as they undoubtedly are in some writing. The way we are to act in the world, after all, cannot be considered apart from first considering the identity and activity of the God of Jesus Christ, in whose life and work we are invited to share. Here, therefore, I have tried to shift the center of gravity from questions about what is acceptable or unacceptable to questions about how music might connect with the gospel and its widest implications, in order that ethical issues can be set in this context.[30]

A final pitfall: to turn all talk about music into talk about *words*. This is remarkably common. As a friend of mine recently observed, when Christians start talking about music, they love to change the subject: they speak about lyrics, texts, titles, and the musical sounds are often forgotten.[31] Christian assessments of popular music, for example, have too often focused on scrutinizing lyrics alone—"content analysis" (a term that gives the game away)[32]—as if the musical sounds were no more than a transparent varnish on the words, which alone carry content. This is perhaps not startling, given that for most of history (certainly in the West) music has been linked, directly or indirectly, to words. The vast majority of popular music, it is worth remembering, is vocal. However, the fact remains that musical sounds have characteristics of their own and cannot be treated simply as a subset of words. And in some cases we will find (as in some popular music) that the audibility and references of the words are not crucial—the words being important more for their sound than anything else and as part of a large and varied mix of sounds.

In any case, much of what follows will focus on what musical sounds do in their own way. This is not because I believe music without words is superior to texted music, still less because I believe music can or should be sealed off from everything outside it. Instead it is because I do not want to lose sight of the peculiar properties of musical sounds, the way we make and hear them, and what they might be contributing in different contexts.

———————◆———————

In part 1 we do some scene setting. The first chapter sketches some basic features of the way music is practiced in Western culture and then goes on to examine what that little word "music" might usefully be taken to mean. There follows a chapter on Scripture's references to music.

We then attempt to gain historical perspective on our theme. What Christian thinking there is about music today often looks back no more than half a century, ignoring vibrant streams of Christian wisdom in the past, stretching back many centuries and involving some of the finest minds the church has known. In part 2 we dip into some of these streams—and there is only space to dip in—looking at the "Great Tradition" stemming from Pythagoras and Plato, three Reformation theologians (Luther, Calvin, and Zwingli), and three modern giants in theology (Schleiermacher, Barth, and Bonhoeffer). In this section we have also included the witness of three composers, whose vision of what music is and what music is capable of doing is not embodied in words so much as in music, in tones and semitones, chords and cadences. We devote a chapter to J. S. Bach and another to Olivier Messiaen and James MacMillan.

Part 3 of the book is more constructive—attempting to set music within what I call a Christian "ecology," the basic patterns of beliefs that give the gospel its coherence and, specifically, the doctrine of creation. This part also includes a chapter on some of the distinctive powers of music that make it especially well suited to "re-sounding" Christian truth.

This book is introductory, no more. Its prime aim is to begin to help the reader develop a Christian wisdom that can engage with the extraordinary business of making and hearing music today. There is no attempt to provide any kind of all-inclusive survey of the contemporary musical scene from a Christian perspective (there are many kinds of music that receive little or no mention), but I hope that what is considered will stimulate readers into making connections of their own with music that is not dealt with here. There is also no attempt to provide a comprehensive Christian checklist to judge this or that music acceptable or unacceptable, though part 3 does offer a vision from which judgments about music can be made and makes some evaluative comments in passing. The accent in this book is unashamedly theological—what matters more than anything else for Christians encountering music today is that they are inspired by and live out of a Christian vision of reality, so that over time they develop a wisdom about music with the aroma of Christ that makes a practical difference in the world of music, whatever form that might take. This book is a modest contribution to that end; it is for the reader to take things further.

A final word to preface what follows. The book has emerged in the midst of a very practical interest in music. Music of all sorts has always fascinated and captivated me, and at one stage I was firmly set on course to pursue a career as a practicing musician. After professional training in music, I followed a call to ordination, but my enthusiasm for music making remained undiminished. I soon discovered that remarkably little had been written about the relationship between the gospel and the down-to-earth business of making and hearing music, about how the vibrant truths of the Christian faith might resonate with the world of Beethoven, Mahler, McCartney, Stravinsky, R.E.M, and Pat Metheny. For a number of years I have been trying in various ways to trace and explore these resonances. In doing so, I have never ceased to be practically involved in music—working with choirs, instrumentalists, and worship bands, giving solo concerts, accompanying singers, playing in orchestras, composing, listening to a wide variety of music, leading a course in sacred music, talking with musicians of all sorts, and, not least, teaching and learning from my own children. This, no less than my reading and work in musicology—the history, analysis, and philosophy of music—has provided the setting in which this theological dialogue with music has taken shape. I believe this is right and proper, for, as I shall be arguing, music is best thought of first and foremost not as a theory or a "thing" but as a set of practices: fundamentally, making and hearing sounds. If music can re-sound God's truth, it will be by doing just that before anything else—re-*sounding* it in ways that hold the world enthralled and make us long for the kingdom to come.

part 1

music in action

what are we talking about?

We are committed to pursuing Christian wisdom in the world of music. But what might we mean by "music"? At first glance, this might seem a tiresome and pedantic question. Music is surely a fairly straightforward thing to identify. It is what we play on a guitar, sing in the bath, hear on a CD. If we were pressed for a definition, we might say something to the effect that music is organized sound, or patterns of organized sounds, designed to produce certain effects, and as such, it is different from naturally or randomly occurring sound and from noise. Even if some composers deliberately blur the boundary between the musical and the nonmusical, most people, most of the time, know what music means.

Music and Musics

If we stop to think a little harder, however, we soon find matters are not quite so simple and that much is to be gained by being a little more self-conscious about how we are using this five-letter word. We begin with the plain observation that the English word "music" can be used to cover a huge and diverse range of phenomena across very different cultures. In the 1970s, I lived for a short spell on the Indonesian island of Bali, and there I had my first encounter with gamelan music. On a balmy evening on Kuta Beach, the air was filled with gentle, hovering, transparent sounds. Although I have since come to love this music, on my first hearing I wondered how I was going to endure it for more than a few minutes. None of the musical patterns on which I had been reared seemed to be present—clearly identifiable themes, tension and release, strong closure. It seemed to be little more than a haze of shimmering monotony. As more and more non-Western music is made accessible (so-called world music), we are becoming far more conscious of what anthropologists of music (ethnomusicologists) have long been telling us—that there is no such thing as music, only musics. Finding a definition of music that encompasses Indonesian gamelan and, say, J. S. Bach's *St. John Passion* seems well-nigh impossible.[1] To talk generally of "music" is to turn a tone-deaf ear to the rich diversity of musical practices worldwide. Not only does applying our categories of musical appreciation to other musics often make little sense but the attempt to use even our concept of music in other cultural settings runs into grave difficulties. And, of course, behind the desire to speak globally and monolithically of music there often lies more than a whiff of Western conceit and hegemony: a presumption that our music represents the genuine and most advanced article and any other purported "music" is to be treated as inferior to it.

We need, therefore, to make clear that in this book we are restricting ourselves largely to the broad tradition known as Western "tonal music." This emerged in the seventeenth century in Europe and has been predominant ever since in European culture and in societies shaped by modern Europe. It is the tradition of Beethoven and Bach, Rachmaninoff and the Grateful Dead, Zoltán Kodály and Girls Aloud. It embraces virtually all popular and so-called classical music[2] as well as most music in English-speaking Western churches, and it is spreading worldwide at a remarkable rate. It is constructed out of systems of notes (called keys) that revolve around certain clearly defined centers, and it unfolds in time through building patterns of tension and resolution. We are confining our discussion to this music because, given our limited space, it seems sensible to focus on the tradition of music that will be best known to readers of this book.

To qualify this, however, some points need to be made. First, to restrict ourselves in this way is not to assume that music of this kind is superior to all others; we are not presuming any particular value judgments about music outside the Western tonal tradition. Second, I am not suggesting that this music is the only kind worthy of theological attention. Different kinds of theological conversation are possible with different types of music. Third, Western tonal music cannot be treated as an isolated phenomenon. It has blurred boundaries—it can share many features characteristic of non-Western traditions,[3] and, as it happens, it is currently interacting with many of these traditions worldwide. Fourth, even if we do concentrate on one musical stream, this need not and should not prevent us from being alert to what we can learn from others. Even a minimal awareness of other musics will make us much more self-conscious about our own, of the assumptions we make about what authentic music really is, of the different uses to which music can be put in a society, and so forth. Not least, we will be made much more conscious of the variety of music within our own tradition and the very different ways in which people can think about music. We shall try to keep these perspectives in mind in what follows. Fifth, in chapters 2 and 3 we will be considering music that is not of this tradition (music as referred to in the biblical writings and Western music as it is theorized up until the end of the medieval era). We do this because Western tonal music grew out of a complex history that cannot be ignored if we are to understand it correctly and also because there is a huge amount to learn theologically from this history. In the case of the specifically scriptural material, focused attention will be given to it because any Christian account of music cannot ignore scriptural references to music, scattered and ambiguous as they may be.

Some Features of the Landscape

Attempting to be a little more self-conscious, then, let us draw attention to some key features of the current musical landscape as we experience it in the West and to some of the factors that have shaped it and made it what it is. I am concentrating on features that have a relatively recent history.

Differentiation

A notable feature is what is usually called "differentiation"—the way in which music has become a fairly specific, specialized, and clearly bounded activity, and with this, the way in which quite sharp demarcations between different types of music have developed.[4] As we shall see shortly, there are signs that these differentiations are in the process of breaking up, but they are by no means absent today, so it is worth at least highlighting some of them and the ways they have arisen.

Sociologist Peter Martin observes that so-called primitive music is typically an expression of a collective experience, an inextricable part of everyday social experience, not the work of a single individual. This is in contrast to Western modernity, where the composer emerges as an individual—in the nineteenth century for example, as the heroic, self-expressive artist, externalizing inner thoughts or feelings. Even here, however, composition happens within a social context—it is nourished in society and channeled in ways that acknowledge existing conventions. Martin writes: "We can glimpse here the two contrasting forces from which social order emerges: the active and creative impulse of individuals, and the limitations and constraints which the existing order imposes on them." In the West, what has arisen from these forces is "the differentiation of music from other activities and the gradual emergence of specialised social roles."[5] So, for example, we have become used to a tripartite division of composer, performer, and listener (often very sharply distinguished) and the emergence of "works" of music.

Unremarkable as all this may seem to us now, it is worth recalling that the attribution of pieces to individual composers is relatively recent. It dates from around the fourteenth century, though there are some scattered examples before then. Moreover, for centuries composers in the West were skilled practicing musicians; nowadays composers are often poor practitioners, and few performers are composers. A crucial factor in these differentiations was the development of notation. Again, we may barely stop to think about the fact that so much music is written down, but in the Christian West, notation only emerged around the ninth century and did not reach the level of thoroughness we are used to today until well into the seventeenth century. For most of human history, music has not been written down in any detail. But once it was, the implications were massive, and one of the most important was the emergence of the "work"—an identifiable written piece that could be transported from place to place and whose composer could be identified (and in due course, protected by copyright).[6]

As music came to be perceived increasingly as a distinct, even autonomous sphere of social activity, so the music itself also became increasingly differentiated—we find medieval church music set against folk traditions (i.e., sacred against secular, to use later terms), and so on. In time, this generated the conditions for "art" music (broadly, music to be listened to "for its own sake") as distinct from "devotional" music (music for worship). In the modern age, the proliferation of musical genres was taken further. We witness the burgeoning of instrumental music, a feature that is taken for granted in the contemporary scene, but it generated much controversy when it began to emerge as a force to be reckoned with in the early modern period (fifteenth and sixteenth centuries), not least because it had no words to stabilize its meaning. Even today, the general public shows a very marked preference for vocal music over instrumental music.

More musical differentiation took place in the nineteenth century. By the 1830s, a distinction between "serious" and "light" music emerged. As with many things, music more and more came to be treated as a commodity to be bought and sold, and the consumer took on a new power. The trio of composer/performer/listener is easily mapped onto the producer/distributor/consumer trio of an industrial economy—the "work" being the product. With the substantial growth in domestic music making and the demand for music that could be played and enjoyed quickly, the seeds of the modern music business were sown, and we find a sustained demand for music as entertainment (witness the proliferation of music halls in urban Britain). Further differentiation came with the imperialist period prior to World War I, when the music of other countries was transported to Europe; foreign musical instruments, scales, and rhythms challenged the extent to which Western music could be assumed to be "natural." In the early twentieth century, the most profound differentiation in terms of global influence came from African-American styles—spirituals, ragtime, jazz, and the whole stream of "popular music" that emanated from them, often sharply distinguished from "classical" or "art" music.

I am not attempting any kind of general survey of what are immensely complex processes. But it is worth stressing that these differentiations have shaped not only the practice of music but also the way we think about it. Especially important to underline is the impact of these developments on published theoretical reflection on music. Until very recently, most academic musicology[7] has been largely built on ideas and assumptions that have arisen in the context of art music: the separation of music from life, the focus on a work embodied in a printed score, listening to a work for aesthetic pleasure, and so on. As will become clear later, if we look at tonal music more widely, as it is actually practiced, it is not at all obvious that these ideas and assumptions are always appropriate.

Many academics at work in the study of music are waking up to this. And part of what has shaken up their thinking has been other key developments that have taken place over the last hundred years or so. Again we are dealing with complex matters, and no comprehensive survey is possible. But we should perhaps mention two of these developments in particular: sound technology and the machinery of marketing.

The Technology of Sound

It is hard to overestimate the importance of that CD player on the shelf or iPod in your pocket. Technologies of sound have made music *accessible* as never before. Consider for a moment a composer of the stature of Hector Berlioz (1803–69), a giant of the nineteenth century. The only music he would have heard as a child would have been church music, songs sung in the fields, or occasionally a town band. Compare this with the typical experience of the modern teenager. Music is now available to more people, more of the time, than ever before. The music of virtually all times and places is usually as close as the nearest CD store, and for many of us no further away than our own computers, thanks to broadband and MP3 players. Many of the older differentiations are increasingly out of place. We can now create customized collections of radically different styles with ease: we can have opera buffa on our couches, David Bowie when cycling to work, Miles Davis on our lunchtime jog. We can enjoy the music of practically any culture, from Sri Lankan folk to South American siku.

The sharp separation of music from everyday life, at least as it is exemplified in the invention of the concert hall for classical music, has been dramatically affected. Through sound technology, music has come to *surround* us, some would say invade us, as never before, classical music included. Speaking of the arrival of sound technology in the West, F. A. Biocca writes:

> Three aural technologies—the telephone, the phonograph, and the radio—were about to bombard the ear with more aural information than had ever been expe-

rienced in the history of man. A shift in the technological base was constructing a whole new environment of structured and meaningful sound. . . . Most noticeable to many was the *sudden omnipresence of music*.[8]

Far from having been pushed out by science and technology, "in advanced industrial societies [music] is all around us, a major element in our culture, in contrast to the situation in pre-electronic times when it was a much less pervasive medium, and a much smaller part of most people's experience."[9] To use what is now a cliché, music has become a soundtrack for life. We no longer need to search it out—music will search us out through walls, ceiling speakers, on United Airlines as *Rhapsody in Blue*, through that teenager's earphones on the other side of the bus (which, in Garrison Keillor's memorable words, "emitted a sound like tiny chain saws").[10] The metaphor of "invasion" is not inapt, for our ability to protect ourselves from our aural environment is limited. We can shut our eyes or turn our heads away from the things we do not want to look at, but we cannot do the same with our ears. We have no earlids.

Paradoxically, along with the omnipresence of music, sound and reproductive technology have at the same time given people an unprecedented *control* over their musical environment, and this too has challenged some of the social roles that arose with differentiation (in particular, it relativizes composer and performer). We can turn the music down, skip tracks, fast-forward, move the speakers, compile our own collections of favorite tracks. We can retreat into our own private sound-world and exclude others, via earphones or headphones (a major innovation in musical history, for previously, any music you made or heard would be audible to others near you). But perhaps most important, the appearance of digital technology in the mid-1980s meant not only that sound could be stored and reproduced far more accurately than before but also that it could be sampled: a recorded sound or short musical passage could be extracted and inserted into another context quite effortlessly. Sampling has enabled the manipulation of sound on a scale never possible before and by anyone with a basic computer. The widespread availability of sound-processing software (and MIDI technology)[11] has meant that a burgeoning number of people can create their own music—selecting sounds and mixing them over, say, bass and drum tracks in whatever way they choose. I was once told that in the United States, recording decks outsell guitars by roughly four to one. Moby's album *Play* of 1999, which sold over nine million copies, was recorded entirely by the artist himself in his New York studio. He says: "What I'm not doing is spending my life playing just guitar accompanying my voice. On my records, I'm the composer and the musician and the engineer, but also the plagiarist and thief."[12] The change in the DJ's role is symbolic in this respect; no longer the figure who simply plays prerecorded disks, the DJ in the contemporary club scene is composer, arranger, producer, and performer all in one. Indeed, the DJ can now assume "something of the status, prestige and critical acclaim once reserved for rock artists."[13] In this context, sharp differentiations between composer, performer, and listener are quite out of place.

Further major changes have taken place with regard to performers and listeners and the way they relate. The appearance of recording and digital sound transformation has meant that most music we hear today is *not original*—that is, it does not depend on the physical presence of performers or an audience. We probably take this for granted, but it was unthinkable before recorded sound. At so-called live rock concerts, the music we hear is multiply processed and artificially constructed. And even if the singer is there, he or she is far too small to be seen clearly by all in the vast crowd and has to be projected on vast screens to convey a sense of presence as a physical human being. The very phrase "live recording" is telling: a contemporary oxymoron if ever there were one. Wedded as we have often been to the idea of performers physically present to audiences, we have seen fierce controversies arise about whether we can consider technologized music as bona fide music at all. At a press conference in the summer of 1990 it was announced that the winners of that year's "Best New Artist" award, Milli Vanilli, had had their prize withdrawn because the group's members, Rob Pilatus and Fab Morvan, had not actually performed any of the vocals on their album. This sparked a heated debate about "authenticity" in popular music. The folk-era image of the individual artist communicating directly to her or his listeners, the idea that music without technology is somehow more authentic— these ideas are still very much around, but they are increasingly questioned and challenged in the wake of technologies of sound.

Marketing and Sales

Bound up with sound technology, another hugely powerful force shaping Western music today and the way we think about it is the manner in which it is marketed and sold. Most people are well aware of this in the case of popular music. But it extends much more widely.

The case of classical or art music is especially instructive. It has been argued that classical music is dying in Western culture, and a vigorous dispute has grown up around the issue.[14] Some point to the large number of orchestras (including prestigious ones) struggling to survive financially, dwindling audience figures, the shrinking share of classical recording companies in the overall market, hesitant government funding of classical music, the aging classical music lover, and so on. But in fact classical music is reaching an exponentially larger audience than ever before. Partly this is due to marketing techniques well tried and widely used for other forms of music. Promotional devices associated with popular music have ensured artists like Nigel Kennedy a very wide hearing; the female string quartet Bond has notched up a string of gold and platinum disks (admittedly, playing many styles in addition to classical); and the Three Tenors—Luciano Pavarotti, Placido Domingo, and José Carreras—famously brought Italian opera into the pop charts. In the United Kingdom, every day the radio station Classic FM plays short chunks of classical music (including single movements plucked out of large-scale works). Breaking all predictions of popularity, it has made pieces like Henryck Górecki's Third Symphony known to a huge non-concertgoing public. Moreover, one could point to a revival of interest in opera in most major cities in the West as well as to the use of classical styles in many film scores—Rachmaninoff's Third Piano Concerto in *Shine*, the largely classical score for *The Red Violin*, contemporary classical music for *The Thin Red Line*, Chopin in *The Pianist*, opera excerpts in *Godfather III* and *Pretty Woman*. Developments in sound technology have been drawn into this process. Digital delivery is perhaps the most obvious example. Internet downloads of classical albums grew by nearly 100 percent in the United States in 2005. Radio 3, the United Kingdom's main serious classical music radio station, recorded over 1.3 million downloads when it offered free Beethoven symphonies in 2005 and experienced record numbers of website hits with a recent all-Bach season. The increasingly common fusion of recording and live performance has been another key factor, cutting out high studio expenses: Sir John Eliot Gardiner's label, SDG, has begun to offer concert attendees a freshly pressed recording of the performance they have just witnessed.[15]

It is probably true to say, then, that classical music is not so much dying as changing its social and cultural role. And marketing (allied to rapidly developing sound technology) is likely the most significant factor at work in this shift. A major upshot is that, for many, classical music has come to fulfill the role that is common and basic to most music in our culture today (whatever other functions it may perform at the same time): namely, *managing our mood*. Music creates an ambience, an environment in which we live and move. This is exemplified in the radio station Classic FM, where music is promoted not so much as an aesthetic object as for its ability "to complement and reinforce our existing mood or to help change it."[16] And to this end, like the vast majority of popular music, it will most often be used as a background to some other activity—driving, shopping, jogging, and so on—and become secondary to those other activities, indeed, supposedly helping us to perform them better. Music helps us run better, improves our concentration at work, and so on.

A very noticeable effect of such marketing (together with sound technologies) has been a shaking up of stylistic boundaries and hierarchies on which much musical differentiation in the past has depended. One of the best-selling CDs of the 1990s was *Officium*. An established singing group in the classical world, the Hilliard Ensemble, teamed up with jazz artist Jan Garbarek to produce medieval music intertwined with improvised saxophone. It is instructive to see where such disks get slotted in magazines and stores. Some put them under "fusion," some into "classical," some into "ambient jazz," others into "crossover." The very existence of categories like fusion and crossover tells us much. Many of the old boundaries seem to apply less and less. Paul McCartney composes an oratorio, *Standing Stone*, for chorus and orchestra; Wynton Marsalis is equally at home in Haydn and jazz. At Princess Diana's funeral service in 1997, the congregation at London's Westminster Abbey were treated to music that included the "Libera me" from Verdi's Requiem, sung by the BBC Singers and Lynne Dawson, along with Sir Elton John singing "Candle in the Wind"—something hard to imagine happening twenty years earlier. A recent advertisement for artistic administrator of the Los Angeles Philharmonic listed under "essential functions" serving as part of a team "(including specialists in jazz, world, and pop music) to coordinate and support cross-genre programming."[17] In 2004 the English National Opera's staging of Wagner became the surprise success of the Glastonbury Festival (a youth festival heavily weighted to popular music). The London Sinfonietta worked with Radiohead guitarist Jonny Greenwood in 2005 to produce two sellout concerts at the Royal Festival Hall. Britain has even seen the birth of "classical club nights." A related and no less striking phenomenon is a cross-cultural pollination of music, evident in almost any record store. Not only do we see the availability of so-called world music, but also Damon Albarn of the British band Blur mixing English pop with Malian music, Paul Simon employing the sounds of Soweto in *Graceland*, Talvin Singh creating a fusion of Indian bhangra with drum and bass, and Oxford singing group I Fagiolini collaborating with the South African Sdasa Chorale to produce the album *Simunye*.

Some, especially those in the tradition of the theorist Theodor Adorno, will see most of these developments as deeply worrying.[18] This kind of marketing, it is said, encourages a standardized sound-bite approach to music, superficially consumed by unthinking hearers. It testifies to the homogenizing effects of mass culture. Music is being used in ways foreign to its nature; indeed, it is being not just used but abused. The Three Tenors pleasing the crowds in football stadiums may have brought extracts from opera to millions and swelled the charity accounts, but, as some sports commentators will point out, in creating such superstars—the "Michael Jordaning" of classical music—matters of excellence of practice are quickly forgotten.

Some Christian commentators have followed suit, anxious that questions about quality and standards are getting swamped in the rush for vast sales and quick effect. Mark Hijleh comments: "Art music and popular music have recently been growing closer rather than further apart. . . . For the first time in a long time there is the very real danger that art music will soon be subsumed into pop music culture, and this danger gives even more impetus to the Church for preserving and redeeming art music through Jesus Christ."[19]

Might We Need a Rethink?

Whatever the truth of this, the shifts and changes I have been alluding to have provoked many to question some of the ways we habitually think about music and whether these are appropriate to the way music is actually practiced.[20] This is important for us, since this is a book on thinking about music. As I have pointed out, those in the classical stream have worked with a cluster of assumptions that have dominated academic musicology and that until recently were rarely questioned. But whatever stream we are working in, we tend to assume that the way we think about music is the only way it could ever be thought about. In the 1960s the rock culture encouraged many to think of music as essentially a culturally subversive tool. In the church today, it is not hard to find whole philosophies of music that are co-opted without question. I often encounter what might broadly be called an "expressivist" outlook: that music is fundamentally an outward expression of one's inner life, usually one's emotional life, and that the main value of music in worship is to give vent to inner feeling, albeit under the inspiration of the Holy Spirit. Songs are the outward expression of the songwriter's unique and interior emotion, aimed at provoking in the congregation a corresponding release of emotional energy. I am not claiming that this should be rejected out of hand, but the fact that such beliefs are relatively recent and fairly localized, inherited in large part from nineteenth-century Europe, should at least give us pause for thought.

The key point is this: if we adopt *uncritically* only one particular way of considering music, not only will our vision of the possibilities of music tend to be narrow, but very likely we will not be able to do justice to the diversity of experiences and actions that music involves, even *within* the Western tonal tradition, let alone in other cultures. We will also likely distort our perspective on music as Christians, failing to see that the biblical gospel itself may transform, even overturn, some of our most cherished assumptions about music.

So, still confining ourselves to the broad stream of Western tonal music but alert to the changes and shifts we have just sketched, and with a strong eye to our theological concerns, let us try to do a little rethinking. We are going to propose that to be true to the Western tonal tradition, it is best to think of music primarily as an art of *actions*—the most basic actions being music making and music hearing. These actions nevertheless involve things that have their own particular integrity—*sound-producing materials and sound waves*, the *human body*, the dimension of *time*, and *distinctively musical sound patterns*. We shall also stress that the actions of music are closely intertwined with a rich and complex *context*. In the chapters that follow, all these elements will be viewed and rethought through distinctively Christian perspectives. For the moment, however, let us take a preliminary look at each in turn.

Rethinking Music: Music in Action

First, there is the matter of action. I am proposing that music is best construed first of all not as an object or objects but as something done. So, to pick up Christopher Small's term, we might speak of "musicking" rather than "music."[21]

Not by Works

Obvious as it may seem to stress that music is primarily something human beings do, it contrasts with a very strong stream in musicology that sees music as fundamentally about works, usually written down, treated as self-contained objects that can be understood, to a large extent at any rate, without thinking about what gave rise to them, the composer's circumstances, the way they have been interpreted, the way people react to them, and so on. The work, in other words, is isolated from its context, past and present, and regarded as if it were the "real" music. In many university music departments, achieving a degree still revolves around the study of works understood in this way, analyzed largely in terms of their structural features (as made visible in a score)—"here is the first theme, here is the second, and here is the first theme again, turned upside down," and so on. I remember well when I began music analysis at university how surprised I was that we could talk for two hours in a seminar about a Haydn piano sonata without listening to it or playing it and without ever considering how the first hearers might have perceived it. It was as if the genuine article were somehow too precious to be turned into sound.

This way of conceiving music is bound up with other things we have touched on already and will return to many times: for example, the rise in the nineteenth century of the idea of so-called autonomous music (music without words or any obvious associations, to be listened to purely for its own sake), and with it the conviction that this is a kind of ideal state of music; the development of sophisticated notation, which can preserve "the work" in a fixed form; discrete classes of people—a single "composer" (usually a man, regarded as someone of exceptional talent), "performers" (highly trained and alone qualified to mediate works to us), and "listeners" (who are expected to attend to works with rapt aesthetic attention).

This cluster of ideas, centering around works, insofar as it is regarded as providing the only (or the best) way of thinking about music, has come in for heavy criticism in recent years.[22] It fails to account for the fact that most people's musical experience is far more performance oriented than work oriented, in the sense that the value of music is found chiefly in what is enacted through performance, between the music makers and the music hearers. What is common to different performances of Duke Ellington's "Take the A Train" is a melody and harmonic outline, little more; what we value and enjoy is what the musicians *do* with these relatively simple materials on a specific occasion. Moreover, in everyday life, the music that surrounds us is not normally listened to (or played with the purpose of being listened to) as in a concert hall. Most is heard along with some other activity—dancing, watching a film, or whatever. Much music is never written down, and even when there is a score, quite often it consists of only the loosest of instructions.

This is not to say there is anything intrinsically wrong with writing music down and turning it into a work, or having skillful musicians, or being quiet at concerts! Indeed, later in the book we will devote substantial space to examining works of music (chapters 5 and 7). The danger is in pretending that a focus on works constitutes a universal, or the only, or the best way of conceiving all music, even within Western societies, and thus to lose sight of more fundamental dimensions. In common with many writers today, I would suggest it makes more sense to view music as first and foremost a set of *practices* or *activities* from which works may or may not emerge. As Nicholas Cook expresses it, "Music doesn't just happen, it is what we make it, and what we make *of* it. People *think* through music, decide who they are through it, express themselves through it. . . . It is less a 'something' than a way of knowing the world, a way of being ourselves."[23]

Making and Hearing

What are these practices? I think we can speak of two basic activities closely intertwined with each other: *music making* and *music hearing*.

music making   ⟷   **music hearing**
(performing)

We can speak of music making as *the intentional production of temporally organized patterns of pitched sounds*—a mouthful, maybe, but I hope accurate enough for our purposes. *Intentional* in that someone deliberately puts sounds together, usually with a use in mind; *temporally organized* in that musical sounds occur over time and are very carefully timed in relation to one another; *pitched sounds* in that, at least in the Western tradition, music is dependent on sound-producing bodies—strings, vocal cords, or whatever—vibrating at certain recognizable, discrete, fundamental frequencies. A more common name for music making is, of course, performing, and for the moment I shall assume that performing need not presuppose an audience but can include singing or playing to oneself (the "hearer" can be the performer).

For sound patterns to be called "music," someone needs to hear them not just as sounds but as patterns of notes (or tones) related to one another. We can speak of music hearing as *the perception of temporally organized patterns of pitched sounds as "music."* (This, of course, raises many questions about exactly where the boundaries are to be drawn between mere pitched sounds and "music"—musical patterns of notes—not to mention between noise and music, questions we shall have to leave to one side for the moment.) I take hearing to encompass everything from focused, attentive listening to unfocused, tacit awareness.

This very basic picture can be filled out further. Sometimes a distinct activity precedes the performing—namely, composition, and this may result in "works."

composing → **music making** ←→ **music hearing**
("works")   (performing)

And to this we can add the three characters usually associated with these activities: composer(s), performer(s), and hearer(s).

composer(s) → performer(s) ←→ hearer(s)

composing → **music making** ←→ **music hearing**
("works")   (performing)

Two points need to be made about this scheme. First, the basic realities of music are music making and music hearing (hence the bold lettering above). Before works or identifiable composers appeared, there was music making and music hearing. Second, we should recall our earlier discussion and be careful not to assume too much about our trio of characters (composer/listener/hearer) or about how they relate to one another. In many musical situations there may not be an identifiable composer, there may be no performer physically present, and the role of composer and performer may be fused into one (sometimes along with the hearer). In addition, we should not assume that one of these practices or practitioners is the center around which all else turns. So, for example, much modern discussion of music has tended to presume there is one nameable composer and has poured much energy into unearthing the "creative process," which is often assumed to mean the composer's inner thoughts and strivings, as if this were where the core of music will reside (performance and reception being duly relegated to second and third place). The current enthusiasm for "authentic performance" can lead to an exaggerated interest in what exactly the composer had in mind at the time (which is often hard to recover in any case) and an unwillingness to admit that, for example, performance on modern instruments might be a legitimate extension of a composer's intention![24]

In line with this, it is easy to set up a hierarchy of worth—composer-performer-listener—with the composer at the top and the listener firmly at the bottom. The composer is honored as the music's originator, the performer reproduces what the composer created, a mere servant (in a concert hall, dressed the part in butler's uniform!), and the listener is expected to be silent, still, attentive, and respectful (to both performer and composer). Arnold Schoenberg (1874–1951) gave classic expression to the superiority of composer over listener when he wrote:

> I believe that a real composer writes music for no other reason than that it pleases him. *Those who compose because they want to please others, and have audiences in mind, are not real artists.* They are not the kind of men who are driven to say something whether or not there exists one person who likes it, even if they themselves dislike it. They are not creators who must open the valves in order to relieve the interior pressure of a creation ready to be born. They are merely more or less skilful entertainers who would renounce composing if they could not find listeners.[25]

Harrison Birtwistle, one of the UK's leading composers, once said: "I can't be responsible for the audience: I'm not running a restaurant."[26] We might think the composer-performer-listener hierarchy is limited to classical or art music, but it is not hard to find elsewhere. The distinction between rock music and pop music is often made on the basis that rock musicians perform live and forge their own particular identities, while pop musicians simply reproduce or recycle other people's material as the puppets of market forces, pandering to listeners' (unthinking) tastes.[27] (This is a major subtext in the movie *School of Rock*.) Many traditions of music, however, do not follow the pattern of the composer as king with the performers as mere servants; many folk traditions and much improvised jazz do not work to anything like this model.

Another perspective is to give the lion's share of attention to the hearer and to the activity of appropriating music. Fast-growing currents of musicology urge that we give far more attention to how people actually experience music in particular situations, what they bring to it, and what they do with it (the so-called passive listener is a lot less passive than we often think).[28] This approach has borne much fruit, though sometimes to the detriment of taking adequate account of the integrities of sound, especially musical sound—as we shall shortly stress.

At present I am not adjudicating on the rights or wrongs of these emphases. I am suggesting only that it is good to be aware of them and not assume that the assumptions we have inherited are necessarily going to do justice to the variety of role patterns that can be played out in music.

Social and Cultural Actions

Let us look a little more closely at musical practices. It has become commonplace today to stress that they are *socially and culturally embedded*.[29] The way we make and hear music is shaped by our relations to others—our social setting, all the way from one-to-one relationships to larger social groupings.[30] Because of this, the way we make and hear music is shaped by the patterns of living and thinking that we use to negotiate these relations—patterns that make up "culture." An example to make this clearer: I decide to learn to play the piano. I learn to play by listening to recordings, watching my favorite pianist on TV, and very likely studying with a teacher. In other words, I become an apprentice to a tradition provided by others, a whole set of tried and tested skills, an accumulated knowledge with a very long history. I learn standards of excellence; I submit my choices, preferences, and tastes to standards already held and tested by others. I learn what is considered "musical" and "unmusical," what counts as good phrasing and poor phrasing, what makes a composer "great" rather than mediocre. In time, I may question this stream of convention and wisdom, modify it, enlarge, dispute, and even reject some of it. But I cannot ignore it. This applies not only to making music but to hearing it. Even when I'm plugged into my iPod on my own, the way I hear the music will be affected by what I have been told about it, what I have read in magazines, chats with friends, and so on. I pick up habits of hearing and listening; I do not create them out of nothing. I come to hear music in some ways and not others because of my social and cultural setting.

Obvious as all this may seem, it is often forgotten and even suppressed in our thinking about music. This is similar to the mind-set we have already been speaking about, which thinks of music as if it were a sort of self-contained "object" hovering above the flux of everyday life.[31] It may take someone from outside our culture to shake us out of this. The sociologist Tia DeNora opens her book *Music in Everyday Life* with a telling anecdote:

> On a drizzly Saturday morning in July 1998, I was sheltering under a tree in a North London market, conducting a series of impromptu interviews with women on the topic of "music in their lives." . . . During a lull, the market manager wandered over to ask what I was doing. He told me he was originally from Nigeria, where, he said with emphasis, they "really knew" how to use music. The situation was different in the United Kingdom, he said, where people did not seem to be aware of music's powers, and did not respect its social and physiological force. As he saw it, Europeans merely *listened* to music, whereas in Africa people *made* music as an integral element of social life.[32]

We should underline that the Nigerian was saying not that music was not part of everyday life in the United Kingdom but that British people did not seem to be *aware* that it was part of everyday life—they did not seem to be conscious of what music was doing and could do in their lives.

For our purposes, four further points in particular are worth highlighting about the social and cultural situatedness of music. First, attempts to ignore it can be theologically loaded. Nicholas Wolterstorff puts it sharply: "Anyone who, with open eyes, reads the writing about art from the last two centuries cannot help but be struck by the religiosity of it." Around the notion of the autonomy of art "we have constructed an ideology in which such art is seen as transcending the alienation of everyday society. To immerse oneself in a work of art is to enter a higher realm—a realm of freedom and transcendent universality."[33] We only need think of some CD covers—conductors caught in quasi-religious poses, faces rapt and distant, key figures in the sacred ritual of the performance—or words like "hope," "rebirth," "spiritual," or "sacred moment" appearing in much contemporary writing about music.

Second, seeing music within a social and cultural perspective can alert us to the *enormous variety of roles it can play*—a point repeatedly made by ethnomusicologists.[34] Music "gets into the action" in a hundred ways—we use it to help us work, chill out, go to sleep, stick together, or pray better.[35] Needless to say, speaking about the "roles" of music is bound to make some people nervous. There is a sense that this demeans music in some way, as if any music not intended for concentrated attention, as in a concert hall, were somehow for that reason inferior. But listening to music for its own sake—disinterested and silent aesthetic contemplation—is itself a role, and to insist on it as the sine qua non of musical experience will narrow and distort our vision. The distinction between "functional" music (music composed or used for something external to itself) and "absolute" music (music not so composed and used) is simply confused and bogus, for virtually all music is composed or used for some extramusical end.[36] Having said this, we should restress what we noted earlier, that while recognizing the diversity of roles music can play, in our own culture the most common basic role it seems to be playing (even if it may be playing other roles at the same time) is mood management, usually as a background to, or to serve, some other activity.

Third, music not only reflects and emerges out of our social-cultural world but up to a point it also *constructs* it. Think of the experience of flying.[37] Airlines know that to cram hundreds of people into a tightly sealed metal tube for anything up to thirteen hours with no means of escape is to take a social risk. So they try to find ways to control and order us—to help us behave in ways that reduce the chances of conflict, panic, or riot. They want to keep us seated for most of the time, obedient to instructions, and relaxed. The key attitude to develop is trust: they want us to feel we can give control over to them, that they have things in hand, that they know best, that we can "sit back and enjoy the flight."

On a trip I took to the United States recently, a music video was playing as we boarded the plane, with images of rivers fading into each other, accompanied by slow melodies and whale song. It was all very soothing. The images and music together helped transport me into a world of calm security. The sounds and pictures of the natural world with its slow and ancient rhythms were designed to help me forget the world I was actually entering—a recently built, wholly artificial, and potentially faulty mechanism, which was shortly to project me at over five hundred miles per hour through the thinnest of air, thirty-five thousand feet above any river or whale. While taxiing to the runway, a safety video was introduced with rhythmic and rising brass motifs—clearly calculated to get our attention. And brass instruments have traditionally been associated not only with announcement but also with confidence, success, and achievement. When describing what we had to do if the plane plunged into the ocean, significantly there was no music at all (it would have been tasteless, presumably, to sound upbeat and even more tasteless to play whale music). Upbeat brass music returned toward the end of the video, as we were encouraged to contact one of the attendants if there was anything at all that we should need.

What is going on here? Music, principally through managing our moods, is not only reflecting an existing social reality; it is helping to create and sustain a new one. It is organizing the group, ordering our social world, setting parameters of appropriate reaction, helping to elicit trust and structure desired response.

Another example: In postwar Hong Kong, music played a substantial role in the former colony's search for cultural identity through a combination of Chinese, other East Asian, and international styles of popular and art music. Music not only expressed identity but also played a crucial role in building it. A further example: With its origins in "house" and "techno" music, the club scene since the late 1980s has become a growing urban music culture, in the United Kingdom attracting some five-hundred thousand young people every week. Although various studies reach different conclusions about how youth identity is formed through clubbing, all agree that music is usually crucial in the process. Indeed, Andy Bennett found that although the culture is diverse and the clubs often highly unstable and fleeting, "contemporary dance music, by nature of its attraction for disempowered and disaffected young people, has . . . played a significant role in inspiring a series of proactive socio-political movements."[38] People who ordinarily and outside the club may have little to do with one another are brought together through music to form strategies of resistance. The Exodus Collective is a good example—a group that organized free raves around Britain in the late 1980s and went on to form a major housing cooperative (Housing Action Zone).[39]

A further set of examples of music's social power comes from the way it can demarcate social boundaries. It is well known that émigré communities often hold on to their own music in order to preserve their identity in a foreign country, sometimes with a colossal struggle ("How shall we sing the LORD's song in a strange land?" Ps. 137:4 KJV). A similar phenomenon can be seen in churches. One group will use music to assert itself over against another—there is "our" music and "theirs," choir music and worship-band music, and, of course, each group claims God's approval of its preferences. Spirituals were used by black slaves to delineate their identity over against the white slave owners (with their very different music), complete with coded meanings known only to those who sang them.[40] Similarly, in Northern Ireland the boundary between "Irish" and "British" identities is marked out and enforced by musicians, and this can be done in highly territorial ways. The fife and drum bands of the Protestant Orangemen help to define areas of the Ulster Protestants in Belfast; the Catholic regions of the city are often marked by "Irish traditional" music (associated with Roman Catholicism), widely played in bars and clubs. Here it is not enough to say music is an expression of identity; it is part of the way identity is formed. In short, we do not simply make music, to some extent music makes us. Music organizes its users, creating new forms of life.[41]

A fourth and last point: social and cultural relations are always to some degree intertwined with *power* relations.[42] From the day when a clan leader first sang his people into battle, music has been used in the exercise of power. Virtually every example of music making we have mentioned so far has been implicated in the power of a person or group over others. A worship leader exercises power, as does a DJ in a club or a concert violinist in a recital hall. Power, we should stress, is not intrinsically evil: a mother putting her baby to sleep with a lullaby is not generally regarded as morally questionable, yet she is undoubtedly exercising power through music. That said, there is little doubt that music has often been drawn into destructive power relations. I have just alluded to the way church groups use music to denigrate or distance themselves from others, and we are all aware of times when music has been used manipulatively, to coerce its hearers into particular predetermined responses.

Rethinking Music: The Integrities of the Sonic Order

We have laid great stress on music as an art of actions, socially and culturally embedded. But by now the reader may be getting anxious. Is music to be explained *entirely* in terms of human actions, its social and cultural contexts and uses? Is music no more than the product of this or that social group, this or that culture? Might there not be something, so to speak, "in the notes" and perhaps even in the makeup of all human beings that plays a key part in musical experience?

Indeed there is. And it is a major concern of this book to highlight just this, to see music as a matter not only of human making but also of engaging with the given integrities of what Christians believe is a God-created world. (In part 3 we will develop this at length.) The fashionable rush to account for music (and evaluate it) in social and cultural terms is understandable and quite proper up to a point, but like all academic enthusiasms, it can quickly become a stifling "grand unifying theory" if not held in check. Ironically, those who are unlikely to be sympathetic to such views in other spheres can be found joining hands with the social and cultural constructivists here. Rick Warren in *The Purpose-Driven Life* writes: "Worship has nothing to do with the style or volume or speed of a song. God loves all kinds of music because he invented it all—fast and slow, loud and soft, old and new. . . . If it is offered to God in spirit and truth, it is an act of worship."[43] To put it mildly, this is an unfortunate way of putting things, for although what is offered "in spirit and truth" may be worship, the suggestion here is that the extent to which music is embedded in God-given created integrities is irrelevant to the depth and quality of that worship.

Here much depends on bearing some very obvious (though often forgotten) things in mind about what we might call a "sonic order." That music is not solely about what *we* make and hear is obvious from the fact that it involves physical entities, entities with their own constitution. There are the *materials that directly produce sound*. They have their own given integrities. Pluck a string, and it will vibrate in one way and not another. Send air through a tube, and, if blown in a particular manner, a certain note will sound and not another. Along with sound-producing materials, *sound waves* also have their own integrity: they operate in some ways and not others, they travel at different speeds in different temperatures, they are refracted in particular patterns, and so forth.

Crucial also are the integrities of the *human body*. Music is a very bodily business, whether or not the human voice is used. Our physical, physiological, and neurological makeup shapes the making and hearing of sound to a high degree. George Steiner reminds us that "music is at once cerebral in the highest degree . . . and it is at the same time somatic, carnal and a searching out of resonances in our bodies at levels deeper than will or consciousness."[44] Even when bodily involvement is diminished in music making—when, for instance, the music is largely produced electronically—the body is deeply implicated in hearing and listening to music. Vibrations in the air enter our auditory canals, stimulate microscopic organs, provoke foot tapping and head swaying. Tia DeNora reminds us:

> The human body is (or can itself be thought of as) a musical instrument, and in ways that far exceed the capacity to sing or otherwise make music in the commonsense meaning of the term. And as an instrument, the body "tunes," "clashes," and "resonates with" the sound environment. The "music" of the body includes pulse (heart rate), tempo (speeded or slowed heart rate), fluctuation (a sudden quickening of the pulse). It includes the sounds we make, involuntarily and voluntarily, in the course of simply being; the crying infant and the cooing mother; the rattling of a chest infection; the sounds of conversation—its pitches, rhythms, volumes, and tempos. These things and more are important, if neglected, matters linked to the hearing of music because any sound external to a given human body is in some form of relationship to it.[45]

Indeed, it would seem that music's first appeal (but not necessarily its last) is to the body, and certainly not to the ear alone—the profoundly deaf percussionist, Evelyn Glennie, can perform highly intricate music by sensing floor vibrations through her feet.[46] Our bodies latch onto the perceived properties of the music—we sway our heads, snap our fingers, clap. As DeNora puts it, we "engage in a kind of visceral communion with [the music's] perceived properties."[47] In dancing, especially in its very focused forms like aerobics, music latches onto and then provokes and extends bodily movement. Ghanaian grass cutters work much faster if there is musical accompaniment. The sea shanties of sailors greatly assist the rhythmic coordination needed in sailing.[48] Anthony Storr cites the example of a six-year-old autistic boy who could not tie his shoelaces even after repeated demonstration. A student therapist put the process of tying shoelaces into a song, and the boy succeeded on the second attempt.[49]

Music, then, is mediated through the body, and bodies have their own complex but highly structured means of coping with and deploying musical sounds for bodily purposes. And for all the differences between individuals and ethnic groups, many of these bodily features are shared universally.

The other main element of the sonic order is that of *time*. Sound-producing materials, sound waves, and human bodies have their own time patterns. Strings, for example, vibrate at some frequencies but not others. Sound waves form particular temporal patterns. Our bodies have their own rhythms—the large-scale rhythms, or macrocycles, with their ebb and flow (e.g., sleep and digestion), the smaller-scale kinetic rhythms controlled by the central nervous system (e.g., heartbeat, breathing, pulse), and the very brief rhythms of the brain's electrical impulses. Music intertwines with all of these—which is why we tap our feet to music, bob our heads, gyrate in the aerobics class. (It is worth remembering that the "ideal listener," static and silent, is a relative newcomer on the musical scene. For most of human history, people have moved to music.)

I am suggesting, then, that taken together, the various integrities we have spoken about make up a sonic order—patterns of constraints that exist before any music is actually made. Clearly, this relates to the commonly asked questions: Is music universally or objectively grounded? Does music operate according to "givens" built into the world? Surely, the protest is often made, this cannot be so. To claim that music is a universal language is hyperbole,[50] since musical cultures differ dramatically, and people can respond to music in radically diverse ways. Certainly Chinese, Japanese, and Korean performers have become adept at Western music, but few Western musicians can perform, let alone understand in depth, the music of China, Japan, or Korea. To ascribe some kind of objectivity to music is surely naive; worse still, it inevitably means exalting this or that music as more "natural" than others—a move that should be ruthlessly unmasked as pernicious cultural imperialism.

An enormous and politically loaded controversy lurks in the wings here—the musical version of the nature/nurture debate, which crops up in so many other places. Let us try to refine the questions a little. We can ask: Are musical traditions shaped to a significant extent by universal features of the physical world, including universally shared characteristics of our own bodily makeup (e.g., the operation of the brain and nervous system)? Or can they be accounted for in terms of particular individual and sociocultural factors: idiosyncratic preferences, local customs, as well as broader social and cultural conventions?

The evidence suggests that this is not a simple either-or. Two points should be made. First, to say that different people hear a piece of music in different ways does not *of itself* prove that this music is to be thought of as an entirely human product, wholly contingent for its effect on the variable factors of taste and convention. Similarly, because some patterns of notes are not found universally does not *of itself* say anything about the rooting of these patterns in factors that transcend human making. Second, despite massive variety, it seems that certain constants can be found in the music of almost all cultures—strategies, forms, intervals (stable and unstable), and so forth. Moreover, a plausible case can be made for holding that the basis of at least some of these and of our response to them lies in phenomena I have described under the term "sonic order"—the integrities of the sound-producing materials, sound waves, the human body, time, or temporality—phenomena that are not culture- or individual-specific.[51] This is hardly surprising. Indeed, there is something decidedly odd about insisting that music making and music hearing must be accounted for *solely* in terms of human construction if everyone inhabits essentially the same sonic order.

Thus, since music is something made by humans, it will show the imprint of particular people, social groups, cultures, and their interests. But at the same time, because it is made from given sound-producing materials and sounds and by people who share common physical features and together live in a temporally constituted world, it is not surprising if we find extremely pervasive patterns and procedures in most musics of the world.[52] In short, music seems to be a matter of both nature and nurture, and in gaining a Christian perspective on music, much depends on holding both of these perspectives together. What is at stake theologically here is a full-blooded doctrine of creation that recognizes our embeddedness in a given, common, physical environment—but we must wait until later to expand on this.

Rethinking Music: The Integrity of Musical Sounds

I have spoken of music as fundamentally the actions of music making and music hearing and of these actions as engaging with the integrities of the sonic order: sound-producing materials, sound waves, human bodies, and time. But there is a further, very obvious integrity to mention, which arises from our embeddedness in God's creation: *the patterns of sounds that make up music.* Musical sounds are structured in particular ways and operate in particular ways by virtue of their embeddedness in the sonic order. And some of these structurings and operations are quite unique to music. I go to a jazz concert and hear a virtuosic pianist; I hear the jingle of a cell phone; I hear a U2 song just audible through someone else's MP3 player. What makes me recognize all these as music? The answer is that the sounds are configured, arranged in particular ways, and as such interact with me in particular ways so as to make sense—*musical* sense.[53]

Four points can be made about this. First, typically, most pieces of music regarded as being of any worth possess at least some *aesthetic integrity*. A piece will be formed in such a way so as to give at least some satisfaction if contemplated for aesthetic delight—that is to say, for the pleasure it affords in the way it sounds—even if it is not composed or presented with that purpose in mind.[54] When I listen to a Schumann symphony to appreciate its shapely melodies, the subtlety of its mixture of timbres, the sense of closure the ending affords, and so forth, I am listening to it for aesthetic enjoyment. This aesthetic integrity, from a Christian theological point of view, will be seen as grounded and embodied in God's created order, made and remade in Jesus Christ.

Second, as with any art form, music operates in ways that are best described, I believe, as *metaphorical*, generating a *surplus of meaning*. This may sound obscure and slightly mysterious, but the basic point can be highlighted briefly, even if a full explanation is not possible here. In *Voicing Creation's Praise*, I suggested that common to, and indeed distinctive of, most of what we call "art" (including music) is the process of *metaphor*.[55] A metaphor is a figure of speech whereby we speak of one thing in terms that are suggestive of another. In Shakespeare's metaphor "Juliet is the sun," a person, Juliet, is spoken about in terms that are suggestive of our closest star. We enjoy a metaphor through our ability to fuse two disparate terms (a person and a star) into something that is meaningful for us. The different terms of the metaphor each draw on a whole range of connotations and associations of the words "Juliet" and "sun"; thus a metaphor generates a whole set of new meanings for us, and just because they are generated this way, these meanings can be apprehended only through this metaphor, by being drawn into its life. Thus a metaphor is irreducible: it cannot be translated into another form of language without loss of meaning. As we all know, you cannot convert a metaphor into a literal statement without robbing it of its content and power. ("He is a tiger" must communicate more than "he is ferocious"; otherwise we would likely not bother to use the metaphor.) Moreover, just because we can never exhaustively spell out the range of connotations and associations upon which a metaphor draws and from which it generates a flow of new meanings, there is a very acute sense of a surplus of meaning—a strong impression that the metaphor will always yield more than we can explicitly say and, indeed, more than we can perceive either at once or over many occasions. Each encounter with a good metaphor reveals more or could reveal more; it is multiply evocative. There is potentially always more to a metaphor.[56]

In this light consider, say, the visual arts. The process of metaphor seems to be very much at work. A representational painting may be recognizably "about" something (e.g., an event, a three-dimensional landscape). But it is also an artificial construction: it is flat, two-dimensional, set in a frame, and likely uses artistic techniques (arrangements of subjects and so forth) that make it very obvious we are not dealing with a point-for-point copy of reality. These things set it apart from everyday reality and from the life of the artist (we do not have to share in the personal feelings, memories, and so on of the artist to enjoy a painting). There is something unnatural about bringing together these two elements—the content and the frame. They are disparate, incompatible, yet our imagination manages to fuse them, generating a whole new range of meanings for us. As we are pulled into the painting, as it draws upon our inchoate experience, it evokes more and more for us through its multiple sug-gestiveness; we see more, feel more as we are pulled into its life. Again, we can never sum up what it means in words or any other medium: it is irreducible. Moreover, we can never encapsulate or enclose its meaning: a great painting gives us a sense of an excess or surplus of meaning; its suggestiveness means that its meaning or meanings cannot be grasped, fixed, and finalized by our minds. The most enriching art is suggestion-rich, multiply evocative.[57] (Hilary Brand and Adrienne Chaplin helpfully contrast Van Gogh's famous painting of worn-down shoes—with its evocation of the earth, trudging, a hard day's toil, and so forth—with the two-dimensional picture of a shoe one finds on the side of a shoebox. One is richly suggestive, the other clear and efficient but devoid of allusion.)[58] And, we might add, this sense of surplus will be intensified if there are juxtapositions of unlike elements within the painting itself.

This is not to claim that a painting can mean anything at all, any more than the metaphor "he's a tiger" can mean anything. But it is to say that it can generate multiple meanings, disclose more and more of something, evoke more and more as we are drawn into it, a "more and more" that is potentially inexhaustible.

In much of our day-to-day experience, we do not perceive the world in this way—we often treat the world as an arena of objects that we can manage, control, and speak about reasonably efficiently. Most of the time we do not allow the world to be an arena of suggestiveness—we like to think we have it in our grasp. Art reminds us that in fact the world always *exceeds* our grasp and perception. Art gives us physical objects that can embody the world's excess of meaning with particular potency. Rowan Williams puts it like this: "What is the world that art takes for granted? It is one in which perception is always incomplete. . . .When we are tempted to confine our vision of mental activity to the successful manipulation of defined objects and the solving of practical problems as to how we negotiate with such objects, we need to recognise that this is not all."[59] In other words, we need the arts.

How does all this apply to music? The process of metaphor seems to be at work here as well, generating meaning. Musical sounds are related—whether by nature or convention—to states of affairs outside the music. Music is not wrapped up in itself; as we will explore further below, it makes connections, very strong connections. In particular, it has immense power to gather connotations and associations. At the same time, it is clearly artificial; it is organized through specific procedures, performed over a specific period of time, played by musicians (perhaps on a stage), it begins and ends, and so on. Certainly its consonances and dissonances may relate to features of the physical world, its rhythms to bodily rhythms, but a composer does not replicate these things—he or she reorders them, frames them into something we recognize as music. Through our imagination, we can hold these incompatible things together— its connectedness with the world, and its artificiality—just as we manage to hold the disparate elements of a metaphor together. Moreover, the sound patterns themselves contain a stream of metaphorical devices, combinations of incompatible elements such as antithesis (juxtaposition of contrasting phrases), alliteration (repetition of notes or groups of notes in successive phrases, yet sufficiently modified to produce a violation of expectation), and chiasmus (phrases set against each other in the form ABBA). Meaning in music is "generated by a stream of metaphors."[60]

All this, of course, makes music's meaning irreducible. Who can sum up a piece of music in words? What CD liner notes even come near to the experience of hearing the sounds?[61] It is not that we can say nothing about a piece that is true, only that we cannot translate it without remainder into another form. By the same token, is there any art form that is capable of giving us such a vivid sense of a surplus of meaning? I hardly need point out that a single piece of music can evoke a wide and rich range of significance for people (if not an unlimited range) and that many pieces have the power to provoke an extraordinary wealth of extra significance on repeated hearing.

To return to our main points—third, *different pieces of music are structured in different ways, giving them different capacities*. In their eagerness to see music in terms of its uses and functions, many writers overlook the simple fact that the way musical sounds are put together affects markedly what they can do, and this is because they are embedded in the sonic order we have spoken about. To use current jargon, music is not an "empty sign" to which any meaning can be attached. Marches and lullabies, for example, have very different structural properties, which accounts in large part for their different uses. Marches tend to be loud, regular in tempo, their beats at a marching pace in groups of two or four. A lullaby—one of the most universal forms of music—is usually slow, quiet, and gentle; the melody moves in small steps, often in a rocking pattern, and the sounds are gentle, not angular or harsh. This is music, after all, for comfort and rest.[62]

A fourth point needs to be added. However much music might have in common with other art forms or other things we make, and however bound up with a range of other activities it may be, the fact remains that *its sound patterns are arranged and operate in distinctively musical ways*. Music is still music and not something else. As every lovesick teenager knows, there are times when only a song will do. Those who cherish the ideal of "music alone" (or musical autonomy) may be misguided in many ways, but the concern is valid—musical sounds do their own kind of work in their own kinds of ways.[63] And in chapter 11 we shall be looking at some of these characteristic ways of music, some of its most distinctive powers.

Rethinking Music: Remembering the Context

There is one further dimension of music that we need to bring into relief, one that we have touched on many times already: *music is very context friendly.* We have already talked about music having meaning.[64] It makes sense to us. Otherwise we would not put up with it or bother to buy it. But clearly, it does not mean things in the way that a statement like "There is a brown oak door over there" means something. Musical sounds do not intrinsically point or refer with any precision and consistency to things beyond themselves—objects, events, ideas, and so on—certainly not in ways that command widespread agreement (as with many terms of spoken or written language). It is hard to propose or assert something through music. Music cannot say that Humpty Dumpty sat on a wall, let alone that he had a great fall. This means that many of the models that philosophers and linguists have used to show how language can refer to things tend to break down when applied to music. This has long been recognized and has caused many headaches.[65] In any case, what we value about music rarely seems to center on its ability (such as it is) to direct our attention to specific things in the manner of words.

Just as difficult are attempts to account for musical meaning in terms of representation in the manner of, say, a representational painting.[66] A Dutch landscape painting is recognizable to virtually anyone as a picture of a landscape. But music without words is very hard-pressed to be so unambiguous. More important, the pleasure we get from music rarely seems to come chiefly from its powers (such as they are) to represent things in this sense.

Here someone might reply that music can be used, and has been used, to refer to and represent phenomena "outside" itself, often very specifically. In the second movement of Beethoven's *Pastoral Symphony*, birdsong is depicted by the woodwinds. Music can be composed to correspond to some kind of atmospheric or pictorial reality (Debussy's *La Mer* or Mussorgsky's *Pictures at an Exhibition*) to recount or reflect a story (as in Richard Strauss's *Till Eulenspiegel* or Paul Dukas's *Sorcerer's Apprentice*). And a musical phrase or passage may be linked to a character or event in, say, an opera or a musical (Richard Wagner was perhaps the supreme master of this). This is all true enough, but what is notable about all these instances is that the music in each case would make excellent sense without the particular reference or representation that is given to it. But the statement "There is a brown oak door over there" is meaningless unless its referent is taken seriously, that is, unless it is taken as referring to a particular and recognizable entity (designated by "door"), whether real or imaginary. And in the case of the representational painting, although one could argue that it could make some sense simply as the play of form, light, and color, in a painting of this sort, thoughts about its subject are normally seen as essential to its understanding. This is clearly not the case with a vast amount of music.

Musical notes become meaningful and pleasurable for us, not primarily because they direct our attention to objects that they refer to or represent, but through their relation to one another. Musical sounds are sound patterns in time. Music relies *at every point* on the interrelation of sounds to one another. If we are not clear about this, it is unlikely that serious thinking about music, Christian or not, will get very far. There have been Herculean attempts to show that music operates in a way akin to words that point or pictures that depict. Sometimes this is done to make music respectable, to show it can hold its head up in the halls of meaning and do what any self-respecting language or representative painting can do. But music's celebrated powers do not first of all come from directing our attention to something beyond itself. Before anything else, music pulls us into its own sound patterns, its enticing sonic games, its riffs and cadences, its polyphony and appoggiaturas. This is the secret of its power and the pleasure it affords.

Does this then mean music is wrapped up in itself, in its own little sound game? Not at all. And this brings us to the main point of this section. Musical sound patterns get *related* to a whole range of things that make up the context of our hearing them. Music makes very quick and very close friends with whatever happens to be around.

Let us bring this down to earth and think of an example of hearing music in a context. I have had a hard day at work. I have not eaten. I slump into a chair, and my wife puts on a CD of Samuel Barber's "Adagio for Strings." The way I hear this will depend on a range of factors. Clearly, there are the sounds themselves, generated by sound-producing objects and mediated through my body in time and arranged in particular musical patterns. The piece is slow, its pulse sometimes barely recognizable, its phrases irregular. These and other things about the configuration of its notes mean that it is not generally linked to confidence, joy, and so forth but much more commonly to negative moods and emotions. This music is unlikely to make me dance around the room.

But these sounds are received in a particular context, and this will make a huge difference. When we hear musical sounds, it seems that we pull together and process a diverse range of elements in different ways, whether consciously or not.[67]

1. There is *the particular state of my mind and body*. I hear the Barber while tired and irritable, sitting exhausted in a chair. This affects the way I receive it—on this occasion, I am especially open to its gentle and serene properties. If I were grieving, I would be open to its sad and mournful properties. If I were scrubbing the floor or exercising in the gym, the chances are the piece would do little to help.

2. There are specific *memories* and *associations* linked to this particular piece. (This relates to what we have just been saying about music's metaphorical power—its power to gather associations.)[68] When I first heard this piece—first hearings often make a permanent mark on us—it was part of the sound track to the film *Platoon*, an especially harrowing and barbaric Vietnam drama, which at the time struck me as crude and indulgent. The music has since been colored in a certain way for me. But I also heard this piece a few nights after September 11, 2001, as part of the final concert of the Promenade series at London's Albert Hall. Conducted by the American Leonard Slatkin, the piece was played as a kind of requiem for the victims of the terrorist attack, singularly fitting for those heavy, benumbed days.

There are also memories of words. I have heard and read much about this piece—the fact that it was originally written for string quartet, that it has become immensely popular, that for Americans it has assumed something of the significance that "Nimrod" from Elgar's *Enigma Variations* has for the British. I have heard Barber's own arrangement of this piece for choir, where he sets the words from the Mass, "Agnus Dei" (Lamb of God). I cannot hear the "Adagio" now *without* it evoking the taking away of the world's sin, at least to some extent. All these memories and associations play into my experience of the piece.

3. There is also a vast range of *social and cultural conventions* we bring to the hearing of music. Even if I had never heard the Barber, I would expect its sighing, suspended chords to resolve. I would naturally associate its thick texture with weight and solemnity. We associate a drumroll with anticipation; we expect a rock song to last only a few minutes; we relate certain styles to certain moods, groups, or countries. I have spoken about this already. At a wine store it was once shown that those exposed to classical music tended to buy more expensive items than they did when exposed to popular music, most probably because of the sophisticated, "classy" connotations of classical music.[69] In another experiment, it was found that with French accordion music, French wine sales rose significantly over the German, while German "Bierkeller" had the opposite effect.[70] What we bring from our social group or culture radically affects our hearing of music.

4. There are *the other things I perceive when I hear the musical sounds*. I am aware that my wife is in the next room—I know she is listening, that she likes the piece, and she is probably as moved as I am. As I hear it, I scan family photographs, and poignant memories are triggered. With the Albert Hall rendition on TV, the piece came with images of an ashen-faced American ambassador, a grief-stricken conductor, and tearful students in the front row. All this contributes to the way I hear the music now.

The critical point here is worth underscoring: music never reaches us on its own but always *with* other sensory media. We hear the sounds of a rock band *along with* images projected onto giant screens, recollections of magazine reviews, and thousands of dancing fans. We hear the sounds of Beethoven *along with* the string players' movements we see on stage, the energetic conductor's gesticulations, and so forth. Musical sounds come to us along with other sensory input; they are always part of a multimedia mix, a multisensory experience. "Pure music," Nicholas Cook reminds us, "is an aesthetician's (and music theorist's) fiction."[71] And in Western culture, by far the most common partner of music is the human word—think of a popular song, the rock video, the advertisement, the hymn.

In summary, hearing music (and much of what we have said could apply just as much to making it) is always embedded in complex contexts. Does this mean context is everything? By now the answer should be clear. Context can never be the whole story, for music involves things that have their own integrity regardless of context: the elements that make up the sonic order, as well as musical sound patterns. Nonetheless, we need to bear in mind that particular contexts always play a large part in our experience of music. At the risk of wearisome repetition: music is fundamentally something *done*. Musical sounds do not exist in a vacuum; they are made and heard by real people in real life. Although much of this book will be concentrating on musical sound patterns and their distinctive powers grounded in the sonic order, throughout we need to be alert to the fact that music is very context friendly.

———————◆———————

We have covered much ground in this chapter in an effort to be clearer about that deceptively simple word: music. Concerning ourselves largely with the Western tonal tradition, we have sketched some features of the current musical landscape. Music has been subject to the forces of differentiation, becoming a fairly clearly specialized and bounded activity, and sharp distinctions have arisen between types and styles of music. Nevertheless, many of these differentiations have been challenged by recent developments. Advances in sound technology have had a massive impact on the practice of music and the way we think about it. Music surrounds us as never before, and, at the same time, we have a new ability to control and shape our musical environment. Most of the music we experience is now electronically processed in some manner, raising profound questions about the distancing of music from its physical roots. Along with sound technology, the marketing and selling of music is another hugely influential factor in the contemporary climate, massively affecting the way music is practiced, experienced, and thought about. It has played a major part in developing and reinforcing what is undoubtedly the most common role music plays in our society: the managing of our mood, and to this end, as an accompaniment to some other activity. Boundaries of style have been shaken up also, and numerous forms of crossover music have emerged.

The point of tracing these features of current musical life was to stress that they have affected not only the way we make and hear music but also the way we think about it—the main concern of this book. Being aware of them, and of how recent some of them are, provokes us to ask whether the ways we habitually think about music can do justice to the variety of practices the Western tonal tradition actually involves and, more important, whether they can do justice to a specifically Christian perspective on those practices. So, with an eye to the theological concerns of the book, we attempted the outlines of a "rethink" of music. We have argued that it is best to think of music primarily as an art of *actions*—the most basic actions being music making (the intentional production of temporally organized patterns of pitched sounds) and music hearing (the perception of temporally organized patterns of pitched sounds as "music")—and thus to question the exclusive concentration on works that has dominated much musicology in the West. These actions are socially and culturally embedded; this will remind us that society and culture shape music, that we must be wary of theologically loaded attempts to pull music into some supposedly spiritual sphere; it will remind us of the variety of roles that music can play, that music not only reflects a social-cultural world but also helps to construct it, and that music is inextricably bound up with power relations.

At the same time, social and cultural as it might be, we emphasized that music is embedded in a sonic order—it involves the integrity of the materials that produce sound and of sound waves, the integrities of the human body, and the integrity of time. Moreover, we went on to speak about another integrity—the integrity of musical sound patterns and of the ways they work by virtue of being embedded in the sonic order. We said that pieces of music typically possess an aesthetic integrity, that they operate metaphorically, generating a surplus of meaning. We noted that different sound patterns have different capacities, and however much music may share with other art forms and be bound up with other activities, the sound patterns of music are formed and operate in their own distinctively musical ways.

Finally, we stressed the importance of keeping context in mind: music is very context friendly. Musical notes come to have meaning first and foremost not because of anything they might direct our attention to but because of their relation to one another. Music is "sounds-in-relation" before anything else. However, just because of this, it makes very quick friends with whatever happens to be around. When we hear music, a whole range of elements are pulled together—in particular, our state of mind and body, memories and associations, social and cultural conventions, and other perceptions that come along with the musical sounds. Together, these greatly affect the meaning the music will have for us.

The upshot is a perspective on music that sees it as a matter of *both* nurture *and* nature, both humanly produced *and* grounded in the wider world, both social-cultural *and* embedded in the physical matrices that we all share and of which we are part. In a climate that will want to put most of the weight on the first side of each of these pairs—the constructive, human-made features of music—in this book, without weakening a quite proper sense of music as human action, we shall also be making a conscious effort to do justice to the other side of the matter, music's embeddedness in a cosmos created out of the inexhaustible abundance of the Triune God.

First, however, we must turn to Scripture and its brief and scattered references to music.

music in action
in biblical times

2

A Christian approaching the Bible with strong musical interests may well be disappointed. Scripture provides little direct help in answering the kinds of questions that might readily be asked: What place should music have in human life? How do we go about evaluating different pieces of music? What makes good music? It certainly does not supply anything like a "theology of music." No verses or passages address at any great length how music is to be viewed in relation to God. Moreover, what mention there is of music gives us only a very fragmentary, piecemeal picture of how it was actually practiced in biblical times. The evidence is thin, and many key terms are notoriously ambiguous. We have passing comments, incidental allusions—little more. Gaining theological wisdom about music from Scripture will come more from taking account of the whole sweep of God's creative and redemptive purposes that Scripture recounts than by scrutinizing specific biblical references to music. In part 3 we will turn to that wider task.

Nevertheless, anyone with even a passing knowledge of the Bible will know that references to music do crop up quite frequently—especially to singing and playing instruments—and musical imagery surfaces repeatedly. However much they may need to be set in wider contexts, and however cautious we need to be about reading into them the anachronistic concerns of later times, these specific references can be highly significant and informative, and in this chapter we aim to give them a hearing.

In Ancient Israel

Music in Social Action

One thing is very clear, and it relates closely to the last chapter: when Scripture alludes to music, it is to *music in action*. The music of ancient Israel and of the New Testament church, as part of the music of the ancient world, was not about works or scores; it was something made and heard.

Also linking up with the previous chapter: for ancient Jewish and early Christian culture, music is a social action. Recall the Nigerian's remark to a European sociologist that Europeans merely *listened* to music, whereas in Africa people *made* music as an integral element of social life. For the Israelite, music was part of life. It was interwoven with the fabric of community living, playing a huge range of social roles—to help people work, celebrate, rest, fight, eat, and sleep. In Genesis, the fact that Jubal, "the ancestor of all those who play the lyre and pipe," is mentioned alongside the first smith (Tubal-cain) and the first cattle-breeder (Jabal, Gen. 4:20–22) testifies not only to the importance of music—it is placed alongside more "necessary" occupations—but also to its embeddedness in practical, daily, common life.

Some particular functions of music are worth highlighting. Music was especially prominent at key moments or occasions—at greetings and partings (Gen. 31:27; Luke 15:25), coronations (2 Sam. 15:10; 1 Kings 1:39), processions (2 Sam. 6:5), and the rallying of troops (Judg. 3:27). The link between music and worship, especially praise, is very strong, and we shall return to this below. In many places there is a strong link assumed between music and intense emotional states. This was especially so in the early stages of Israel's life, where we find music accompanying prophecy and associated with ecstatic outpourings. In 1 Samuel 10:1–12, the newly anointed King Saul is told to meet prophets who are using instruments in ecstatic frenzy. David's dancing before the Lord with music (2 Sam. 6:1–2, 5–6, 14–15) may reflect the same circle of ideas, as might Elisha's prophetic release in 2 Kings 3:15: "While the musician was playing, the power of the LORD came on him." Of special note also is the apotropaic use of music—to ward off evil forces and spirits, something very common in the Ancient Near East. It is possible that David's playing for Saul (1 Sam. 16:23) and the frenzied dancing and singing around the golden calf (Exod. 32:17–19) have something of this background.

In any case, the idea of listening to music purely for its own sake—primarily for aesthetic interest or as some kind of object of contemplation (as in a concert hall)—would be unknown in this culture. Quite foreign also would be the modern cult of originality, of a composer attempting to create something novel that self-consciously breaks with the past. Music making was much more about receiving and developing an inherited tradition of shared material than an individual putting his or her unique, creative stamp on the world. Further, sharp lines between composer, performer, and listener were rare. (The major exception to this is the emergence of trained professional guilds of musicians in the Jerusalem temple, although even here the intention was not to perform *to* others but to animate the singing of the congregation.)

One of the first things, then, that a biblical perspective on music can do for us (though we might not have been expecting it) is to reorient us to basic features of music in our own time that we might otherwise forget (the features we were stressing in the last chapter); above all, that music is fundamentally something *done* and done in a social context. By the same token, we will need to resist the temptation to project into the biblical texts things about music that may be familiar to us but quite alien to an ancient Semitic society.

Voice and Instrument

Along with its sheer ordinariness—its interconnectedness with everyday life—the other very obvious thing to note about music in biblical times is *the prominence of singing*. Roughly three quarters of the Bible verses on music refer to song. Ancient Israel was a singing culture, and the variety of songs seems to be as wide as the variety of human activity. So, for example, we read of work songs (Isa. 16:10), military songs (Judg. 5:1–31; 1 Sam. 21:11; 2 Chron. 20:21), songs of instruction, prophecy, and mutual edification (1 Kings 4:32; 1 Chron. 25:1–3), love songs (Isa. 5:1; 23:15–16), songs of entertainment (Job 21:12; Isa. 24:9; Lam. 5:14; Amos 6:5), songs with dance (Exod. 15:20; 1 Sam. 18:6–7), songs of derision (Job 30:9; Ps. 69:12; Lam. 3:14, 63), and songs of mourning and lamentation (2 Chron. 35:25).

What, then, of instruments? Our evidence is scarce, and many of the terms used for instruments in the Hebrew Bible are highly ambiguous.[1] There were instruments that were shaken, struck, flexed, or rubbed—for example, cymbals (*metsiltayim* and *tseltselim*), widely attested in Ancient Near Eastern culture and typically used in ceremonial cultic contexts. "Praise him with clanging cymbals; praise him with loud clashing cymbals!" (Ps. 150:5). David danced before the Lord playing rattles (*mena'an'im*) probably made of clay (2 Sam. 6:5). Closely related are bells (*pa'amon*), cited in Exodus (Exod. 28:33–35; cf. 39:24–26)—platelets or bell-shaped objects hung around the high priest's robe.

Instruments involving the beating of a skin find frequent mention: for example, the wooden-framed drum (*toph*, often translated "tambourine" or "timbrel") associated with festivals, processions, and bands (see fig. 2.1). It seems that women were the only ones who played the *toph* as a solo instrument, the most famous instance being Miriam, who "took a tambourine in her hand" after the Red Sea crossing (Exod. 15:20). Though it played no part in the professional music of the temple, it played a role in cultic dances (1 Sam. 18:6), cultic hymns (Ps. 149:3), feast days (Ps. 81:2), and processions (2 Sam. 6:5). As in other cultures where the drum is associated with women, it appears to have

Fig. 2.1: Pottery figurine of a girl playing the timbrel, from Shikmona, Israel (Iron Age II). Haifa Music Museum and Amli Library

had strong sexual significance (hence its associations with Jephtha's virginity in Judg. 11:34, 37, and with Israel's in Jer. 31:4: "O virgin Israel! Again you shall take your tambourines, and go forth in the dance of the merrymakers").

The most important stringed instruments were the lyre (*kinnor*) and harp (*nebal*). The *kinnor*, essentially a sounding box with arms at each end supporting a yoke from which strings were stretched (fig. 2.2), was widely found in neighboring cultures prior to Old Testament times. It was Jubal's first musical instrument (Gen. 4:21) and came to be especially associated with singing (Gen. 31:27; 2 Sam. 6:5; Isa. 23:16). David soothes Saul with a *kinnor* (1 Sam. 16:23). In second temple worship it becomes an important cultic instrument. Closely related was the *nebal*, or harp, probably very similar to the *kinnor*, and like the latter it seems to have become specific to the Levitical musical guilds (1 Chron. 15:16, 20; 25:1, 6). It was also associated with corrupt and decadent religion (Isa. 5:11–12; Amos 5:23; 6:5).

Wind instruments are cited also. The "pipe" or "flute" (*halil*) probably refers to a double pipe with a double-reed mouthpiece—a sort of double oboe. It is taken up in the festivities of anointing a king (1 Kings 1:40), the celebration of victory (Isa. 30:29), and prophetic ecstasy (1 Sam. 10:5), but it could also symbolize lament (Jer. 48:36) and be associated with excessive revelry (Isa. 5:12). It seems

Fig. 2.2: A *kinnor*, or lyre, reconstructed from a painting on a pottery jug found at Megiddo, Israel (1350–1150 BC). Haifa Music Museum and Amli Library

Fig. 2.3: *Shophars*, or trumpets—A ram's and goat's horn, with silver and gold mouthpieces. Haifa Music Museum and Amli Library

to have had no place in worship. The '*ugabh* (pipe), Jubal's second instrument (Gen. 4:21), is hard to identify with certainty, but it was most likely a long flute of a sort widely attested in neighboring Egypt and Sumeria.

By far the most significant instrument in the Old Testament (and, as we shall see, in the New) is the trumpet.[2] This is not to be confused with the modern instrument played badly by the twelve-year-old next door. *Trumpet* is used as the English translation of two main words—*shophar* and *hatsotserah*. The *shophar*—a long horn (of a goat or ram) with an upturned end (fig. 2.3)—is the most frequently cited instrument in the Old Testament and survives in Jewish liturgy to this day. With its two or three notes, it was used most of all as a signaling instrument in both cultic and noncultic contexts. The *shophar* warns of attack (Jer. 6:1), summons people to war (Job 39:24), proclaims military victory (1 Sam. 13:3), announces kingship (2 Sam. 15:10), and shakes the walls of Jericho (Josh. 6). After the exile it came to be used purely in the cult. The *hatsotserah* is much closer to the modern trumpet—a tube of beaten or hammered silver, about a cubit (40 cm.) long, with a bell-shaped end. Although it could be used in war, following the exile it is mainly a cultic and priestly instrument of the second temple (Num. 10:8; Neh. 12:35, 41).

We have already alluded to the first biblical reference to music, Genesis 4:21, where we are introduced to Jubal, "the ancestor of all those who play the lyre and pipe." This occurs in the midst of a genealogy of Cain's family and offspring, Jubal being one of four children born to Lamech and his wives. The context is one of primeval urbanization and culture (the building of a city, farming, metalworking): "Genesis is making the point that through the (disobedient) line of Cain many of the world's significant cultural discoveries emerged."[3] It has sometimes been concluded that to place music in the line of Cain (the murderer of Abel) and not in the line of Seth (God's substitute for Abel, from whose time people "began to invoke the name of the Lord," Gen. 4:26) is implicitly to paint music (and musical instruments in particular) in decidedly negative colors. But this goes well beyond the evidence. There is no sign that God is visiting the iniquities of the fathers on Cain's descendants; Enoch (Cain's son) was not punished for his father's sin. Nor is there any indication in Genesis 4 of God's displeasure at

Cain's urban enterprise (unlike Genesis 11—the Tower of Babel) or that progress in civilization is being viewed as inherently sinful. Music, along with the other activities mentioned here, "belongs to the basic potential which the creator gave to his creatures and which they are obliged to advance and cultivate."[4]

Nevertheless, musical instruments seem to have played a relatively small role in Israel's culture. Archaeological excavations have unearthed very little evidence of instruments during the biblical period, and compared to some surrounding societies—Mesopotamia, for example—the range of instruments discovered is meager. To be sure, in late Old Testament writings and in the intertestamental literature, there are signs of a more developed instrumental tradition (e.g., the infamous band of King Nebuchadnezzar in Daniel 3:5, 7, 10, 15), and this in turn may reflect new groupings of instruments created during this period elsewhere in the Ancient Near East. But for most of Israel's history, instruments seem to have been fairly marginal.

This is probably due mainly to the prominence of words in Jewish faith, divine and human, and to Israel's attitude toward its neighbors. In the Canaanite cult, for example, with its strong sexual orientation, instruments seem to have played a significant role. But whatever the reason, this relative lack of interest in instruments was greatly exploited and elaborated by later Christian writers (especially in the early church), which in turn has had a deep and lasting impact on Christian attitudes about instruments ever since.

Prophetic Attack

Early Christians also seized on a number of Old Testament passages that appeared openly hostile to instruments.

> Take away from me the noise of your songs;
>   I will not listen to the melody of your harps.
> But let justice roll down like waters,
>   and righteousness like an ever-flowing stream. (Amos 5:23–24)

Amos later cites music in the course of a diatribe against those who indulge in trivia while their country disintegrates around them:

> Alas for those who lie on beds of ivory,
>   and lounge on their couches,
> and eat lambs from the flock,
>   and calves from the stall;
> who sing idle songs to the sound of the harp,
>   and like David improvise on instruments of music;
> who drink wine in bowls,
>   and anoint themselves with the finest oils,
>   but are not grieved over the ruin of Joseph! (Amos 6:4–6)

Set this alongside Isaiah's tirade:

> Ah, you who rise early in the morning
>   in pursuit of strong drink,
> who linger in the evening
>   to be inflamed by wine,
> whose feasts consist of lyre and harp,
>   tambourine and flute and wine,
> but who do not regard the deeds of the LORD,
>   or see the work of his hands! (Isa. 5:11–12)[5]

In the light of many later attacks on music in the church, it is important to see that, fierce as these prophetic denunciations may be, they are not an assault on music or instruments in and of themselves. (Some scholars even think these passages might have been sung!) Music had become an abomination because it was part of an indulgent lifestyle that deafened God's people to the corruption and injustice that surrounded them—a kind of drug that dulled their spiritual senses so that they could no longer discern the deeds of the Lord. The attack is on the abuse of a gift, not the gift itself.

In Corporate Worship

Music's role in worship is alluded to many times in the Hebrew Scriptures, especially in relation to praise (references in the Psalms abound). Liturgical music is reported to have become a regular institution in Israel in the era of David and Solomon, along with the establishment of professional musicians drawn from the Levites. In 1 and 2 Chronicles, David's founding of the temple choir and its patronage by his successors, the organization of the musicians, the instruments used, and the place of music in temple worship are all described at length.

In an important dissertation, John Kleinig has sketched the key dynamics of the way music in worship is presented in Chronicles. He traces a twofold movement, from God to the worshipers and from the worshipers to God.[6] On the one hand, *singing announced, and became a vehicle of, the presence of the Lord to his people* (e.g., 1 Chron. 16:10–11).

> Through the ritual performance of choral music during the oblation of the burnt offering, the singers presented the Lord to his assembled people. They evoked the Lord and announced his presence to the congregation . . . they spoke for God to his people. As they sang their songs of praise, they announced the Lord's acceptance of his people and declared his favorable disposition to them; they also proclaimed the Lord's deliverance of his people and secured his intervention against their enemies.[7]

In this light, it is not hard to see how refusing to sing could be one of the most powerful ways to signal God's absence: "On the willows there we hung up our harps. . . . How could we sing the LORD's song in a foreign land?" (Ps. 137:2, 4). On the other hand, *singing served to articulate a response of the congregation to the Lord's presence with them.* The singers gave thanks, praised, adored, confessed, and interceded on behalf of the king and the people before the Lord. Singing, therefore, both "proclaimed the Lord's gracious presence to his people at the temple and articulated their response to his presence with them there."[8]

And what of instruments? They too seem to have been caught up in this double movement: from God to his people and from the people to God. In temple worship, three groups of instruments were used—trumpets, cymbals, and strings. The trumpets (*hatsotserah*) were signaling instruments, proclaiming the Lord's presence; indeed, the trumpets were so closely associated with the divine presence they were regarded as "holy vessels" and played only by priests. They also served to announce the presentation of the burnt offering and to call the people to prostrate themselves. In the same way, the cymbals proclaimed God's gracious presence and announced his acceptance of the burnt offering; they were also used to introduce the singing, to call the congregation to attend to the performance of sacred song. Stringed instruments (lyres and harps) could announce the Lord's presence and accompany songs of praise and thanksgiving.[9]

It is important to note that the Levites did not see themselves as offering song *instead* of the congregation but on *behalf* of the congregation, even if the congregation were not actually singing. They acted representatively for king and people.[10] Moreover, the congregation could also be invited to sing with them.

> The members of the congregation did not remain passive spectators at the performance of the choral service on their behalf by the Levitical choir. The choir addressed them directly and invited them to join in its praise (1 Chron. 16:8–13). The congregation did so by responding with certain stereotyped words and refrains (1 Chron. 16:36b). It thereby became an active partner in praise.[11]

We might add, anticipating what we shall say later about worship, that the call to praise in 1 Chronicles extends not only to all people but to the whole universe: "Let the heavens be glad, and let the earth rejoice. . . . Let the sea roar, and all that fills it; let the field exult, and everything in it. Then shall the trees of the forest sing for joy before the LORD" (1 Chron. 16:31–33). In Kleinig's words, "Just as the choir offered praise for the congregation, so the congregation with its responses offered praise for all peoples and the whole universe."[12]

It is very hard to judge exactly what words were sung in the temple. We have to be especially careful about assuming that the worshipers sang nothing but the Psalms. There is certainly evidence to suggest that the Psalms were used musically;

the parallelisms and meters in the poetry of the Psalms may well be associated with musical settings. Parallelism is the rhyming or repetition of meaning in a parallel form ("Bless the LORD, O my soul, and all that is within me, bless his holy name. Bless the LORD, O my soul, and do not forget all his benefits," Ps. 103:1–2). Some have claimed to find metrical systems in the Psalms based on the stress of syllables, syllable counting, or word units, but the evidence for this is thin; it may be wiser to find what meter there is in line length and the balance of lines. In any case, the presence of a loose meter of sorts might well reflect or have given rise to musical use.[13] There are also many technical musical expressions scattered in the Psalms: for example, "to the choirmaster" (fifty-five times), "with stringed instruments" (e.g., Psalms 4, 6, 54, 55), "for the flutes" (e.g., Psalm 5), and "Selah" (seventy-one times)—a much-discussed term but probably a musical instruction of some sort, indicating a pause, an instrumental interlude, or perhaps even "louder."[14] And there are frequent references to musical instruments. Nevertheless, although what we know as the Psalter is often described as "the songbook of the temple" and although most scholars would accept that most of the Psalms were closely related to Israel's worship, this is a far cry from saying that all the Psalms, or even most of them, were related to the temple's worship.[15] And as far as singing is concerned, it is probable that many texts besides the Psalms were sung (perhaps psalmlike poems such as the song of Moses, Exod. 15:1–18) and that a number of Psalms were never sung in the temple at all.

Musical Imagery

Along with literal references to music, metaphorical allusions to music abound in the Old Testament. Creation praises the Creator by "singing" (Ps. 96:12; cf. 65:12–13; 98:7–8). The stars sang together with the heavenly beings at the world's creation (Job 38:7)—compare Aslan singing creation into existence in C. S. Lewis's *The Magician's Nephew* or the memorable musical-cosmic introduction to J. R. R. Tolkien's *Silmarillion*.[16] The trees of the forest "sing for joy" (Ps. 96:12; see also 65:12; 98:7–8). This thread is picked up in the Old Testament's apocalyptic literature, looking ahead to God's future salvation: "The mountains and the hills before you shall burst into song" (Isa. 55:12). The singing of a "new song" (Ps. 33:3; 40:3; 96:1; 98:1; 144:9; 149:1; Isa. 42:10) probably refers to literal singing, but it is also a potent image of the impact of salvation: the fresh experience of God's saving grace demands a new song (or a new type of singing?).

In the New Testament Church

Since the first Christians were Jews, much of what applies to pre-Christian Jewish music applies to the music of the New Testament period. Again, music was intertwined with everyday life, and singing seems to have been integral to the emerging Christian community, with little sign of any negative attitude toward music as such.[17] Jesus sings with his disciples before going to the Mount of Olives (Matt. 26:30; Mark 14:26), and Paul and Silas sing in prison (Acts 16:25). Paul writes of singing praise with the spirit and with the mind (1 Cor. 14:15) and singing a hymn to build up the church (1 Cor. 14:26), and he urges the singing of psalms, hymns, and spiritual songs (Eph. 5:19; Col. 3:16). James makes a passing comment about singing songs of praise when "cheerful" (James 5:13), and the Old Testament theme of the "new song" is taken up again in the book of Revelation (Rev. 5:9; 14:3). In Ralph Martin's words: "The Christian Church was born in song."[18]

In the New Testament, instrumental music is neither prohibited nor attacked, and there is no reason to believe that instruments were banned in worship. Nevertheless, references to musical instruments are few and far between, and they are not mentioned in the context of the church's regular worship.[19] The double-reed pipe (Gk. *aulos*) appears again. Jesus finds *aulos* players at the house of the synagogue leader attending his dead daughter (Matt. 9:23).[20] The *kithara* (lyre or harp), mentioned fleetingly in 1 Corinthians 14:7, is God's instrument in the book of Revelation (15:2). It becomes associated with the spiritual power of the "new song" of Christianity (Rev. 14:2–3), the four "living creatures" and "the elders," each holding harps as they sing (Rev. 5:8–10). The trumpet we shall return to shortly.

Again, we need to be careful not to misread passages that might on the surface imply a rejection of instruments. For example, in Paul's famous verse, "If I speak in the tongues of mortals and of angels, but do not have love, I am a noisy gong [*chalkos*] or a clanging cymbal" (1 Cor. 13:1), the *chalkos* he alludes to was probably not a musical instrument at all but a large bronze acoustic amplifier in a theater.[21] The word "cymbal" (*kumbalon*) alludes to the use of cymbals in Jewish worship, which, as we have seen, in addition to announcing the Lord's presence, could introduce sacred song by calling the congregation to attention. Even here, Paul is not suggesting that these instruments are useless or to be banned. Rather, he is using the bronze resonator and the cymbal as illustrations to buttress his point that "no matter how exalted my gift of tongues, without love I am nothing, mere show." And the illustrations are apt, for these devices do no more than make noise, playing a secondary, supportive role—just what Paul wants to say about speaking in tongues.[22]

Music in the Worship of the First Churches

A number of verses and passages testify to the importance of singing in the first Christians' worship.[23] By this time the majority of Jews would have been attending a synagogue rather than the temple (which in any case was destroyed in 70 CE). So it is synagogue worship that provides the major context for understanding worship in the New Testament. There is no sign in these texts of a specialized worship "musician"—this should not surprise us, for there was no office of "cantor" in the synagogue, no group of professionals as in the temple. "Any attempt to speak about 'musicians' in emerging Christianity is an exercise in anachronism."[24] Singing would likely have been relatively informal and involved the whole congregation.[25]

In the text of the New Testament itself, we may well have fragments of the songs of the first churches. Many believe that the great Christ-centered vision of Colossians 1:15–20 was sung as a hymn, and similar passages elsewhere might well bear the marks of singing (e.g., Phil. 2:6–11; 1 Tim. 3:16). It is also likely that a large part of earliest Christian singing "involved the chanting of Old Testament psalms, interpreted christologically," that is, understood as pointing to Jesus Christ.[26] It is also probable that there were fresh compositions inspired by the Spirit, patterned after the biblical Psalms but with a Christ-centered focus—for example, the Magnificat (Luke 1:46–55) or the heavenly songs of Revelation 4:11 and 5:9–10.[27]

The two richest New Testament passages mentioning music are worth quoting in full. It seems safe to assume both are speaking about regular corporate worship.

> Do not get drunk with wine, for that is debauchery; but be filled with the Spirit, addressing one another in psalms and hymns and spiritual songs, singing and making melody to the Lord with all your heart, always and for everything giving thanks in the name of our Lord Jesus Christ to God the Father. (Eph. 5:18–20)

> Let the word of Christ dwell in you richly, teach and admonish one another in all wisdom, and sing psalms and hymns and spiritual songs with thankfulness in your hearts to God. And whatever you do, in word or deed, do everything in the name of the Lord Jesus, giving thanks to God the Father through him. (Col. 3:16–17)

Perhaps the most striking thing here is the lack of any negative comments about music. Both passages come from contexts in which Paul is passionately concerned about resisting and shunning immorality, yet he can speak of music without so much as a hint of its dangers.[28] This contrasts sharply with some later Christian attitudes to music that are much more ready to link music and immorality.

Three Types of Singing?

"Psalms and hymns and spiritual songs." It is tempting to see these as three quite distinct forms of singing, and interpreted in this way the words have often been used to fuel heavy agendas. For example, some will insist that "songs" must refer to spontaneous singing, and because only this word is preceded by "spiritual," spontaneous singing is clearly superior to all other types.

In fact, it is very hard to draw neat lines between the three.[29] Andrew Lincoln believes that "the three terms used here are best seen as [an] example of this writer's fondness for piling up synonyms."[30] The word "psalm" (*psalmos*) could refer to the Old Testament Psalter (as in some other New Testament passages, e.g., Luke 20:42; 24:44; Acts 1:20), but the word can be used more widely, as (probably) in 1 Corinthians 14:26 ("When you come together, each one has a hymn").[31] The term likely means nothing more specific than "a song of praise to God." Much the same goes for the word "hymn" (*humnos*)—in the New Testament, the most probable meaning is a song to or about God (or Christ). "Song" (*hode*) has an even wider interpretation. In the Greek world in Paul's time it could cover a broad range of sung pieces (not only, as with the other two, songs to a divine figure). And we should be careful not to read too much into the placing of the word "spiritual" (*pneumatikos*) before "songs," as if these songs were the exclusive domain of the Spirit. In the Ephesians version of our passage, Paul makes it clear *all* singing is to be inspired by the Spirit—"be filled with the Spirit" (Eph. 5:18) introduces the whole section. Perhaps "spiritual" indicates that these songs were directly generated by the Spirit and thus more spontaneous than psalms and hymns.[32] But this is guesswork, and even if correct, there is no hint that they are being thought of as superior or, indeed, inferior.

Two-Dimensional Song

Much more interesting and significant, however, is the way in which in the Ephesians passage the singing is given a two-dimensional quality. There is singing "to the *Lord*," but in addition, the psalms, hymns, and spiritual songs are means of "addressing *one another*" (Eph. 5:18–19) in edification, instruction, and exhortation. Indeed, much of what is regarded as hymnlike in Paul's writings is not directed immediately to God but is in the form of teaching or encouraging others (e.g., Phil. 2:6–11; Col. 1:15–20). In 1 Corinthians 14:26, the "hymn" (*psalmon*) is intended for the "building up" of the community.

This relates to another strong thread in Paul's argument in 1 Corinthians—public intelligibility, a concern that drives his argument about the place of speaking in tongues in worship.[33] Paul writes:

> The person who prays in a tongue should pray that he or she may put what they have uttered into words. For if I pray in a tongue, my innermost spiritual being prays, but my mind produces no fruit from it. So what follows? I will pray with my deepest spiritual being, but I shall also pray with my mind [i.e., intelligibly]. I will sing praise with the depths of my being, but I will also sing praise with my mind. (1 Cor. 14:14–15)[34]

Some commentators think that ecstatic utterances sometimes took the form of unintelligible chant. Whatever the truth of that, the accent here is clearly on intelligibility and the building up of the congregation.

Although it is often not realized, most of our hymnbooks and songbooks combine these two dimensions: the vertical (Godward) and the horizontal (to one another). Very often as much as half of a hymnbook or songbook will consist of items intended to be addressed to one another, not directly to God or Christ. The most obvious background to this idea is in the Old Testament Psalter, where many of the Psalms extol the greatness of God or celebrate what he has done, inviting others to join in praising him, while also addressing God in the second person. The two seem to go quite naturally together.[35]

Trinitarian Contours

In the Colossians passage, the pattern is *to God* (the Father), *in the name of* as well as *through the Lord Jesus*. In Ephesians we find a similar pattern ("to God the Father . . . in the name of our Lord Jesus Christ," Eph. 5:20), though with the addition of singing *to the Lord*, in this context most likely meaning the exalted Jesus.[36] In any case, the pattern here is not only of Christ as the object of worship, "included in the identity of God" (to use Richard Bauckham's phrase),[37] but also as the one through whom worship is offered. This is filled out in the Epistle to the Hebrews, where once again Jesus, as the eternal Son, belongs to God's identity (Heb. 1:1–4) and is also portrayed as our human High Priest, one of us, tempted yet without sin, supremely qualified to lead God's people in worship (e.g., Heb. 2:17; 3:1; 4:14–5:10). The words of Psalm 22:22 are put onto the lips of Jesus: "I will proclaim your name [i.e., God the Father] to my brothers and sisters, in the midst of the congregation I will praise you" (Heb. 2:12). Jesus himself is pictured as leading the praise of his people in the midst of the congregation.[38]

The Ephesians passage fills out the picture even further, bringing out an unmistakably trinitarian dynamic to worship. Singing is "in the Spirit," and this coheres with what appears to be basic to Paul, that authentic worship is Spirit-led. The personal presence of God the Spirit initiates and sustains the church's worship.[39] Music thus shares in the trinitarian dynamic of worship, which in turn is the dynamic of redemption (cf. Eph. 2:18): the Spirit unites Christ to us and us to him so that with him, as well as through him, we have access to the Father.[40]

Instruments in Worship?

Despite its extensive use of musical instrument imagery and the presence of instruments in everyday life, the New Testament does not explicitly mention instruments in corporate worship. Undoubtedly, one reason was that the very first Christians, all of them Jews, would have been used to worshiping in the synagogue, and even before the destruction of the temple there is next to no evidence that any instruments were used in synagogue worship, with the possible exception of the *shophar*. After the temple had gone, only the *shophar* appears in the synagogue; all other instruments were excluded from worship—in part because of the Pharisees' hostility to instruments, and in part because of deep grief over the temple and the land, and over the loss of the Levitical musical ministry.[41] Another likely factor was the centrality of words in the life of the New Testament church—it was a very specific and urgent *kerygma*, the verbal message of the gospel, known and proclaimed in the Spirit, that provoked faith and led to the formation and mission of the Christian community. None of this, however, need lead us to believe that musical instruments were deliberately banned by some kind of ruling—there is no indication of this.

New Testament Musical Imagery

As we have said, however, instruments provide the New Testament writers with a rich resource of imagery, especially in connection with the final fulfillment of God's purposes, of which we can now have a foretaste through the Spirit. Here the trumpet (*salpinx*) comes into its own.[42] By the time of Jesus, the *salpinx* had a rich range of associations in Jewish faith, especially with the "last days," the things of the end times. As such, it combines a number of the trumpet's functions in the Jewish tradition: summoning, warning, calling to arms, and announcing kingship. So we find the trumpet linked to the final coming of Christ (1 Thess. 4:16, "The Lord himself, with a cry of command, with the archangel's call and with the sound of God's trumpet, will descend from heaven"), the resurrection (1 Thess. 4:16; 1 Cor. 15:52: "the trumpet will sound, and the dead will be raised"), and the gathering of the elect (Matt. 24:31: "And he will send out his angels with a loud trumpet call").

Nowhere is the development of trumpet imagery more striking than in the book of Revelation, in which the instrument plays a leading part in the unfolding dramas of earth and heaven. Beginning in chapter 8, a series of seven trumpets is depicted, six of which announce disasters or judgments, the seventh (Rev. 11:15) signaling Christ's final investiture and rule. Even the one like a son of man (Jesus) speaks with a "voice like a trumpet" (Rev. 1:10; 4:1). Needless to say, these associations have been a gift to composers, and they have been exploited in countless settings—the "Tuba Mirum" from Hector Berlioz's *Requiem* comes to mind as among the most effective.

Whether we treat the imagery of heavenly music *as* imagery or, as many would prefer, in more literal terms as a kind of transformed earthly singing, the metaphor of the "new song" is picked up in the book of Revelation, where it comes to refer to the song of heaven—the "four living creatures" and the "elders" (Rev. 5:9) and the 144,000 on Mount Zion (Rev. 14:3). It is likely that

John is assuming that the singing of Christians in worship is a sharing in that song, or, put differently, that their singing now is a preview of the final song of the new heaven and the new earth they will one day enjoy.

But What Did It Sound Like?

Much scholarly energy has been invested in trying to discern how the sung music of biblical times would have sounded.[43] The evidence is meager—none of the music of either Old Testament or New Testament period was written down (as far as we know). The musical superscriptions in the Psalms (rubrics, cues, and labels of various sorts) are hard to interpret with accuracy; as one scholar puts it, "These expressions are among the most obscure and difficult in the Old Testament."[44] Some believe that Psalms with responses and refrains (e.g., Psalm 136) point to an interplay between different kinds of musicians or between one part of the congregation and another. This is possible, but we are in the realm of conjecture and speculation.

In the case of the New Testament, matters are further confused in that we cannot be sure about the most formative influences on music in the churches of the relevant period. Scholarship is generally agreed that the main influence was Jewish: the first Christians were Jews, and the Jewish community would have been the most obvious place from which to draw their music, adapting it to their own theological needs. But much else is unclear. Given the destruction of the Jerusalem temple in 70 CE and the way in which the earliest church consisted not of regularized formal meetings but of small, informal gatherings, it is unlikely that temple music had any significant impact on early Christian worship. It is possible, however, that they chanted Scripture—a practice that could have been learned from temple traditions.

What of the synagogue? It was once widely believed that the synagogue played a large and direct role in shaping early Christian worship, including its music, but this has been keenly challenged in much scholarship. There is little evidence of an established and uniform synagogue liturgy.[45] It is highly questionable whether the Psalms were commonly part of first-century synagogue worship, for example.[46] This is not to deny the influence of Judaism on the early church's music, but it might not have been of the sort that is often supposed. It may have come indirectly, for example, through family life.[47]

Nonetheless, we are not completely in the dark. Studies by Idelsohn and others have worked on the assumption that Jewish oral (as opposed to written) traditions were passed on for centuries with relatively little change.[48] The singing of some isolated Jewish communities may, then, preserve types of ancient Jewish Psalm singing that predate the rise of the Christian church and thus give us clues as to what the earliest Christian music might have sounded like. If this is so, early Christian singing—and by implication at least some of the singing of the Old Testament period—was almost certainly a form of chant. It would not have included what we call "harmony"—the mixing of notes to make up chords, or different simultaneous melodies. Rather it would consist of a single line of melody to which words were sung, the melody perhaps being repeated a number of times depending on the words set. It would probably have been rhythmical and in some cases might have followed a loose meter in the words. But much more than this it is hard to say with confidence.

———◆———

We will pick up on much of this material in the course of the book, but perhaps the most important thing to note here is the essentially positive impression of music given in Scripture. Admittedly, instrumental music is underdeveloped, and in the prophetic writings we find stern attacks on music when it deafens people to the demands of God, but there is none of the antipathy and hostility toward music itself (especially instrumental music) that we meet in some later periods of the church. Overall, we find a warmhearted acceptance and encouragement of its proper use. This is worth bearing in mind as we turn now from the biblical texts to the ways in which music is approached by the church in the centuries that followed.

part 2

encounters

music and God's cosmic order:
the great tradition

In the last chapter we examined the explicit references to music in Scripture—fragmentary, ad hoc, and ambiguous as many of them are. We stressed that there is nothing approaching a "theology of music" in the Bible, no sustained thinking about how music might fit into God's purposes or how music might resonate with the grand themes of creation and salvation. People, it seems, just got on with singing and playing it. Although on occasion certain types of music and musical instruments were prescribed and some dangers were alluded to, music never seems to have become a burning concern or a matter of fierce contention—certainly not something the Bible's writers felt they needed to address at any length.

However, in postbiblical times a number of thinking Christians, many of them with no practical musical expertise, found themselves provoked into giving music more than a passing ear.[1] And in due course, the number grew. Indeed, as we scan the centuries of church history, we find some of the most astute minds of the church turning their energies toward music. This has been for a variety of reasons—to respond effectively to an issue concerning music in a missionary encounter, for example, or to tackle a controversy over music for worship. Whatever the reason, the result is rich reservoirs of thought that it would be foolish to bypass or ignore. In seeking a Christian wisdom about music, if we cannot learn from the past, we cannot learn.

Here we cannot present anything like a comprehensive story of the theology of music, still less a history of Christian music. The aim is much more modest—to introduce just some of the key figures who engage music with developed and refined Christian minds. Some are theoreticians, some are practicing musicians, some are both. In each case we attempt to enter their world and sit at their feet. We will highlight the pivotal issues their work throws into relief in the hope that this will clarify some of the axes around which a Christian wisdom about music turns. This will provide a context for our attempt in part 3 to set music within a Christian ecology.

Cradled in a Universal Harmony[2]

If I were to walk onto a platform to give a piano recital and introduced the evening by telling the audience that I was about to help them tune into the order of the cosmos, that some of the pieces I was about to play were more cosmically in tune than others, and that the best pieces would help them be finer people and bring them that much closer to the Creator, the audience might well conclude I needed therapy. Most likely I would be told just to get on and play the piano. Today we are so used to linking music to creating moods, entertainment, or immediate pleasure—in other words, we see it in entirely human terms—that it is hard to think of music in any other way, let alone that its fabled powers might be linked to the patterns of the physical world at large and, just because of that, grant some kind of access to God.

Yet for centuries in the West, this thinking, or something like it, was the norm. Indeed, it was so dominant and persistent it is sometimes called "the Great Tradition"—a stream stretching from the half-legendary figure of Pythagoras, through Plato, into the church (via Augustine and Boethius in particular), and in one form or another pervading the entire medieval era.[3] Certainly we should not presume that this tradition completely eclipsed all others of its time, nor that it was monolithic and continuous. As we shall see, there are significant variants of it and at times countertraditions at work. Nonetheless, in one form or another it proved enormously influential. Even when Pythagoreanism waned, the use of musical harmony as a metaphor of cosmic order—as in Henry Vaughan: "The great *Chime* / And *Symphony* of nature"[4]—is carried forward in modern literature and poetry (it can be found in Shakespeare, Milton, Dryden, and many others). The notion that the universe's harmony is a musical one can also be found in ancient myths among the Egyptians, the Indians, and the Chinese. In some versions, the gods are said to sing or play the universe into existence: music composes the world. A modern variation on the idea can be found in the opening of J. R. R. Tolkien's *The Silmarillion*, a spectacular scenario of creation theology elaborated in musical metaphors.[5] No less an important figure than Pope Benedict XVI draws boldly and unashamedly on the tradition:

> The courses of the revolving planets are like melodies, the numerical order is the rhythm, and the concurrence of the individual courses is their harmony. The

music made by man must . . . be taken from the inner music and order of the universe. . . . The beauty of music depends on its conformity to the rhythmic and harmonic laws of the universe. The more that human music adapts itself to the musical laws of the universe, the more beautiful it will be.[6]

Pythagorean Themes

Here we can only sketch some of the broad lines and leading emphases of this venerable current of thought. In its Christian form, the central notion is that musical sound, especially musical harmony, coincides with and gives expression to cosmic order, which in turn reflects and in some manner gives access to the Creator.

Pythagoras (sixth century BCE) emerges as the key ancient figure, credited with having discovered that number underlies musical pitch. Legend has it that he was passing a blacksmith's shop one day and was captivated by what he heard coming from within: every now and then, the clattering from the sounds of the blacksmith's hammering would blend into a harmonious unity. He was determined to find out why. It turned out that each hammer was a different weight and each produced a distinctive pitch; the most "agreeable" musical pitches—that is, pitches that were pleasing to the ear when sounded together— were formed by the simplest mathematical ratios (1:2, 2:3, and so on). Later, away from the blacksmith's workshop, Pythagoras found not only that different lengths of string produced different pitches but also that the most consonant interval, the octave, was produced by string lengths of the ratio 2:1; the next most consonant, the fifth, by lengths of the ratio 3:2; and so on. This led to a vision that was at root numerical, *rational*—the harmony of the universe can be expressed in mathematical ratios or proportions apprehended by the mind, and musical sounds can mediate these ratios.

Pythagoras is also associated with the beguiling notion of the "music of the spheres"—the belief that planets and stars of different sizes emit different pitches, generating a huge, but inaudible, cosmic music. Streams of writers have been charmed by this vision, even when they have been unable to believe it in any literal sense. In the last scene of Shakespeare's *The Merchant of Venice*, the two lovers, Lorenzo and Jessica, gaze into the night sky. Lorenzo is enraptured by the scene:

> How sweet the moonlight sleeps upon this bank!
> Here will we sit and let the sounds of music
> Creep in our ears; soft stillness and the night
> Become the touches of sweet harmony.
> Sit, Jessica. Look how the floor of heaven
> Is thick inlaid with patines of bright gold;
> There's not the smallest orb which thou behold'st
> But in his motion like an angel sings,
> Still quiring to the young-ey'd cherubins.[7]

Moonlight, music, serenity, and love intertwine around the haunting image of the harmony of the spheres. The "touches of sweet harmony" have their source in the rotation of the heavenly orbs. The celestial concord, informing our lives with beauty, finds its counterpart in the human soul, the microcosm of the macrocosm:

> Such harmony is in immortal souls,
> But whilst this muddy vesture of decay
> Doth grossly close it in, we cannot hear it.[8]

Although expressed here in poetry, the Pythagorean vision is nonetheless mathematical through and through: the relationship of planets and stars in motion, the relationship of one part of the creation to another, of soul to body, of one person to another—all these and other relationships were believed to be held together by, and subject to, a single cosmic mathematics. "The whole cosmos, the planetary and stellar spheres with their orderly revolutions, [was] seen as a vast musical instrument with each component attuned according to the same scheme of ratios as obtains in our mortal music."[9] To sing or play music was accordingly a means of being attuned to the universe's harmony. Earthly music sounds the harmony of the universe. It mediates number to the ear and mind.

Platonic Variations

Pythagorean doctrines were a strong influence on the approach to music developed by Plato (427–347 BCE). In the *Republic* Plato elaborates the extraordinary creation myth of Er, alluding to the Pythagorean celestial music: the eight spheres "together combine to produce one single harmony."[10] In his dialogue *Timaeus*—destined to have colossal influence on Christian medieval musical aesthetics—Plato weaves Pythagorean and other traditions in a quite stunning synthesis, encompassing the mathematical proportions of the world soul as well as of the human soul and body. Music gives us not only a model of harmonious balance, unity, and integrity, it actually implants cosmic harmony into the soul of humans. The soul for Plato consists of three parts—the rational, the spirited, and the bodily desires or appetites. Though rationality plays the key role in regulating the soul, true virtue depends on a balance of the soul's elements. Music can help achieve just this; it can be a "means to correct any discord that may have arisen in the courses of the soul . . . our ally in bringing it into harmony and agreement with herself."[11]

In this way, music and morality become closely linked. According to the ancient Greek conception of "ethos," music, through its direct influence on the harmony of the soul, can influence the formation of good character. Critical here were beliefs about certain musical *modes* (*harmoniai*). A mode is essentially a group of notes from which music is made, whose relations to one another generate (as we might say today) a certain "mood."[12] In common with many in his day, Plato linked different modes to different moral effects. Some of them, such as the Phrygian and the Dorian, infused people with courage and temperance, respectively; others, such as the Ionian and the Lydian, soften and weaken the character. By making and taking part in the right kind of music, we find a proper proportion and balance between the parts of our soul and thus come to share in cosmic order. Because Plato's ideal city-state in the *Republic* mirrors the soul's structure, this in turn means that music could play a part in generating harmony in society.

Therefore, heard music for Plato has positive ethical, political, and social potential. The contrast with some dominant present-day attitudes to music—for example, that music is essentially a matter of private individual taste, with little lasting or profound effect—could hardly be greater. But odd as it may seem to us, the power of musical sounds to improve our individual and social behavior was something taken for granted in virtually all ancient Greek musical philosophy and in a vast amount of subsequent Christian thought.

However, there are much darker sides to Plato's assessment of music, repeatedly drawn out in a way that proved pivotal for much of Christianity. Two dimensions of this can be mentioned here. First, music is an imitative art, and of such a kind that it can quickly distance us dangerously from the truth. To summarize (all too crudely): for Plato everything in the world of space, time, and material objects is an imitation—and always a second-rate imitation—of things in the ideal world, the world of Forms. There is a world of objects accessible to our senses, and a higher reality, the reliable, unchanging sphere of Forms—ideals, universals—accessible to the mind. The numerous instances we experience of, say, "mountain" all partake of the ideal "Mountain." Particular things all fall short of the ideal—indeed, they are always less real than the ideal Forms. To discern the true nature of something we must concentrate not on the material world (the realm in which things are constantly changing and never fully manifest their nature) but on the nonmaterial Forms, of which things in this world are only an imitation. In some of his writing, Plato implies that music can partake of ideal truth, beauty, and harmony; elsewhere he makes it clear that musical imitations all too easily misrepresent the ideals, in effect becoming mere imitations of imitations,[13] third-rate copies. Unfortunately, he believes, most musicians are not especially concerned with the truth of their imitations. As a philosopher, we must remember, Plato is chiefly concerned with reliable, rational knowledge of the truly real and ideal, and against that standard, musical imitations can sink to a very low level, leading us far from the true and real.

Second, Plato shows a marked anxiety about music's emotional power. Music can (and ought to) calm the emotions, ridding the body of excess passion. But it can also act in tandem with its imitative function to do just the opposite and disrupt the soul. Highly emotional music that answers to popular taste, claims Plato, appeals more to the appetitive element of the soul than to reason, thus disrupting the soul's harmony. Plato urges that "those who seek for the best kind of song and music ought not to seek for that which is pleasant, but for that which is true."[14]

We should not miss the very strong intellectual thrust here, for it was to be carried forward for centuries, not least in the church. It was embedded in Plato's Pythagorean heritage—the ears might hear musical sound, but only the mind can interpret and grasp their harmony. Though music was given a marked prominence in the curriculum of Greek education, its ultimate significance was in the intellectual grasp of ratios, not in the doing of it.[15] Performers, Plato says, typically adhere to the surface of music—its sonic effects—not to the harmony it reflects. This is why he accords musical science a higher level in musical education than musical practice. It is also why he believed seasoned philosophers were more reliable judges of musical propriety than the composer or the performer.[16]

In this light we can understand Plato's strong desire to subordinate music to words—again something that is taken up by countless Christian writers in the centuries to come. For Plato, rational clarity needs to be ensured above all by the strict subservience of music to words. Without verbal control, music will most likely bypass reason and appeal simply to the baser emotions, with grievous social and political effects.[17] Indeed, much Greek music theory was marked by a suspicion of textless music and a desire to keep instrumental music closely allied to the forms and rhythms of speech. By far the greater part of ancient Greek music consisted of song—either solo or choral. As far as we can tell, these songs were settings of what were often highly sophisticated poetic texts, with little verbal repetition, and it was widely believed that the words should be clearly audible.

The Tradition Baptized

If it never made its way into the Christian world, we would probably not have mentioned the Great Tradition in this book. But it did not die with classical antiquity. It was injected deep into the bloodstream of the church's thinking about music and remained there for centuries. The major figures to contend with here are undoubtedly Augustine and Boethius. But there is a philosopher we must visit first, usually described as a Neoplatonist because of his elaborate variations and transformations of Plato's thought. Living in the early Christian era, though not a Christian, Plotinus (ca. 205–70) acts as an important link between the ancient Greek world and the Christian Middle Ages.

Perhaps most important is Plotinus's softening of Plato's somewhat austere distinction between the real world of eternal ideas or Forms and the less real and subordinate world of material things. Plotinus envisaged a great multileveled hierarchy of being, with what he called "the One" at the highest level—utterly nonmaterial, the infinite cause of all other being—and under the One, a continuum of existence, stretching right down to the plurality of matter, the lowest and least ideal type of being. All things flow from, or emanate from, the One. The first emanation is the Intellect, or Mind (*Nous*), which is the locus of the Platonic Forms (Plotinus's "intellectual world" being roughly equivalent to Plato's ideal world).

For all the complexities, the upshot is a generally more positive estimation of music than Plato's. For music is not merely an imitation of an imitation, but is itself capable of manifesting the music of the ideal realm more directly: music is "the earthly representation of the music there is in . . . the Ideal Realm."[18] This was taken up by many later Christian writers. Nonetheless, this generous outlook is tempered in Plotinus by much more typically Platonic strains. Though not sharing Plato's fascination with the mathematical dimensions of music, he shares his master's wariness of being trapped by sensual experience. Plotinus likens humans to inattentive choir members who get distracted:

> We are like a chorus grouped around a conductor who allow their attention to be distracted by the audience. If, however, they were to turn towards their conductor, they would sing as they should and would really be with him. We are always around the One. If we were not, we would dissolve and cease to exist. Yet our gaze does not remain fixed upon the One. When we look at it, we then attain the end of our desires and find rest. Then it is that, all discord past, we dance an inspired dance around it.[19]

The key point is this: oriented to the One, the musician must make every effort to press *beyond* the sensuous forms of music to the higher beauty "that manifests itself through these forms; he must be shown that what ravishes him was no other than the harmony of the intellectual world and the beauty in that sphere."[20] To get caught up in music's sensuous beauty is to miss the point, to become ensnared in earthly things. The chief value of earthly beauty is to enable an ascent of the soul, to be led by degrees to know the beauty of the immaterial, ideal realm.

Augustine's Struggles

These strands were to be picked up, though certainly not uncritically, by Augustine (350–430), the revered saint of North Africa and bishop of Hippo. At once impassioned and intellectually ruthless, scholar and wordsmith par excellence, devoted to Scripture and philosophically luminous, Augustine was without doubt the most influential Christian theologian in the West until Thomas Aquinas in the thirteenth century. And his reflections on music formed a major stone in the vast mosaic of theology he bequeathed to the church.

The extent of the impact of Platonism and Neoplatonism on Augustine is a much-debated topic. But the overtones of Pythagoras, Plato, and Plotinus are not hard to detect. In Augustine, as Henry Chadwick paraphrases him, we find the notion of God as Absolute Being "from whom descends the great chain or continuum of derived entities, each grade having slightly less being and therefore less goodness than the grade above."[21] In his commentary on the Genesis account of creation, Augustine repeatedly quotes the text from Wisdom of Solomon 11:20: "But you have arranged all things by measure and number." In his commentary on Psalm 42, he alludes to the "intellectual music" of heaven, heard by a man at the point of death.[22] In the relatively early and incomplete *De Musica* (387–91),[23] which contained "a conceptual vocabulary that would be mined for the next one and a half millennia,"[24] we find a deep attraction to the ancient notion that numerical proportions bind the universe together. In Augustine's mind, sounded music must be understood in this context. Audible music can—at least at its best—render these proportions accessible to the ear.

Here we need to underscore something crucial that relates to the numerical and intellectual thrust we have noted in the Greeks. We are used to using the word "music" to refer to something made and heard. In Augustine's world, *musica* was first of all understood not in terms of something you would compose, play, or perform but as a technical subject, a mathematical discipline, and a discipline concerned with number (*numerus*).[25] It was the science of "measuring well" (*bene modulandi*). It involved identifying, classifying, and creating relations between sounds—most often the written or spoken sound of words in poetic rhythm, meter, and verse. It was believed that these numbers-in-relation pervaded the universe: the discipline of music was geared toward the intellectual knowledge of the ratio-embedded character of the cosmos. This is what concerns Augustine in *De Musica*. Music as something made or heard is valuable only insofar as it can enable our apprehension of the mathematics of the universe. We should not be captivated by the pleasure of sounds for their own sake but rather concern ourselves with nonmaterial numerical patterns to which the sounds can direct us.

So in the climax of *De Musica*, the sixth book, Augustine traces out the grades of the various numbers in poetic meters according to a hierarchy (and he includes consideration of a hymn as sung). These numbers derive from the unchanging order of "eternal numbers," which proceed from God himself. As Herbert Schueller explains: "Reason perceives the numbers which, eternal and divine, govern and make perfect everything in rhythms (mensuration) and song, and, having examined them, finds they are eternal and divine."[26] Guided by the hand of divine providence, it is the mind's privilege to rise step by step from the lowest to the highest numbers and thus to the knowledge and love of God, the fount and ground of numerical beauty. Indeed, at the heart of *De Musica* lies the conviction that God actually *is* music in this sense; he is supreme measure, number, relation, harmony, unity, and equality, and all manifestations and embodiments of music in the world are from him. The music of the universe—the harmony, unity, measure, equality, and relation of the music of creation—is but a temporal expression of the eternal music belonging to God.[27] Insofar as we lovingly and obediently turn toward God and acknowledge God as the origin of these manifestations of music, they can reveal God and assist the fallen soul in its return to God.[28]

What more can we say about music as practiced, sung, played, and heard? Here we must remember Augustine's context. In the worship he knew, as in the earliest days of the church, singing played a prominent role, and it consisted of a one-line, unison chant (with no mixing of different pitches as we would know it today, except at the octave).[29] There is evidence that chant was increasingly being used to sing the Psalms and psalmlike material (as well as hymns of various sorts), and there is some evidence that by the time of Augustine, in some places there were song leaders.[30] Instrumental music, however, seems to have had little or no place in worship; indeed, by and large it was vigorously opposed. As we have seen, the Christians of the New Testament period do not seem to have had an antipathy toward instruments, but before long we see the stirrings of what was to become a vehement and sometimes extravagant polemic against instruments among the church fathers of the Western and Eastern churches, most of all because of associations with the music of idolatry and immorality in surrounding society—pagan worship, the theater, feasts, and brothels.[31]

Not surprisingly, given this background and his acute awareness of the danger of being ensnared by an idolatry of the things of this world, Augustine is highly ambivalent about music as made and heard. He writes out of a burning struggle. Yes, music can elevate us toward God, but it can also distract and weaken the soul. It is highly sensuous, after all. We recall Augustine's conversion included a distinctly ascetic renunciation of marriage and a secular career. He never lost his anxiety about the perils of the five senses, that they might trap us in this world and divert our attention from the next. Music's materiality and sensuality, coupled with its emotional power, easily encourage an unhealthy attachment to this life. Augustine thus becomes painfully double-minded about music, an unmistakably Platonic double-mindedness. So in his most famous work, the *Confessions*, Augustine cries to God in rhapsodic terms:

> How I wept during your hymns and songs! I was deeply moved by the music of the sweet chants of your Church. The sounds flowed into my ears and the truth was distilled into my heart. This caused the feelings of devotion to overflow. Tears ran, and it was good for me to have that experience.[32]

He can allude approvingly to Plato's belief in a "hidden affinity" between music and the soul[33] and to musical harmony as a simile of redemption.[34] And he is probably writing about himself when he says that there are "many for whom happiness consists in the music of voices and strings, and who count themselves miserable when music is lacking to their lives."[35] Yet despite all this, pulling in the other direction is a dread of idolatry, of music's sensual pleasures tugging us away from God. He can write of music in worship as a concession to weakness: words help the "weaker mind rise up toward the devotion of worship." And he becomes adamant that music must serve texts: we sing so that "the meaning of the words" can penetrate more deeply, and it is a "sin deserving punishment" if "the music moves me more than the subject of the song."[36] The tussle is captured keenly when he writes: "I fluctuate between the danger of pleasure and the experience of the beneficent effect [of music]."[37] Henry Chadwick sums up the estimation of music expressed here: "Indispensable but dangerous."[38]

Entwined with this ambivalence is a related one concerning the body and the material world—a topic that has become something of a battleground among Augustine scholars. Doubtless, Augustine has often been crudely caricatured. He wanted to do justice to the biblical stress on the God-given value of the physical world, including our bodies. He did not believe the material realm to be basically evil; indeed, he emphatically denied it and held that all material things, to some degree, partake of ideal, perfect beauty. His main concern is with our attitude, the attitude of the soul; we must love things, so to speak, "toward God," not for themselves. This is well put by Carol Harrison:

> As with all temporal manifestations of music (as harmony, unity, order . . .) in the created realm, therefore, whilst appreciating the beauty of music as it is sung in Church, Augustine never ceases to emphasise the need to move beyond and through it: beyond and through the temporal, mutable and bodily towards the eternal, immutable and spiritual. For as long as he is caught up in the sheer beauty, delight and pleasure of the temporal manifestations of music, for that moment he knows that he is distracted from God and risks taking it as an end in itself.[39]

Harrison immediately adds that this is not a rejection or dismissal of music; for one is to move to God both *in* and *through* music, and the same applies to any created reality.

Nonetheless, having said all this, in at least some places in Augustine, some have argued, there is more than a hint of suspicion about the full goodness and reality of created matter, together with suggestions that beauty is not so much something the world embodies as something toward which the world only directs us. Physical beauty is the lowest grade of beauty, being mixed up with many imperfections. We are urged to seek the beauty of the soul and the bodiless beauty that gives form to the mind and through which we judge actions to be beautiful. And above all we are directed toward the supreme beauty, that of God himself.[40]

Boethius's Vision

Important as Augustine was for shaping later medieval thinking about music, it is probably fair to say that his impact was exceeded by one of his own admirers, the philosopher, poet, and politician Boethius (ca. 480–525). More than anyone else, Boethius formed the musical mind of medieval culture. A senator, far and away the best-educated Roman of his generation, with a brilliant command of Greek, he was supremely well placed to gather together the learning of ancient Greece and deliver it to a Latin-speaking empire—an empire Christianized but politically precarious and desperately in need of the treasures of classical wisdom. His reflections on music in *De institutione musica* brought together a huge body of earlier wisdom and gave the Great Tradition the refinement and impetus it needed to dominate musical philosophy for nearly a thousand years.[41]

Boethius's opinion of *musica* could hardly be higher. As Henry Chadwick puts it, for Boethius, "The theory of music is a penetration of the very heart of providence's ordering of things. It is not a matter of cheerful entertainment or superficial consolation for sad moods, but a central clue to the interpretation of the hidden harmony of God and nature in which the only discordant element is evil in the heart of man."[42]

Augustine had identified seven "liberal arts": geometry, arithmetic, astronomy, music, grammar, rhetoric, and dialectic. The first four Boethius designated the quadrivium; the other three eventually became known as the trivium. It is doubtful if these ever evolved into a standard educational curriculum, but the scheme was widely used and highly influential as a framework of knowledge well into the sixteenth century.

Again, we should not forget that the main interest in "music" here is not in how to sing or how to play a lyre. Music is first and foremost a mathematical discipline concerned with the order of the cosmos, something to be *understood* rather than done or experienced in action. To be sure, musical study included such things as the classification of musical instruments according to how they made tones, the moral impact of different modes, and so on. Certainly, the terminology of musical speculation in this period is, to some extent at least, practical in origin, and the Pythagorean harmonics were always there as a standard of correctness. Nonetheless, Boethius's prime interest was in grasping the mathematical ratios and proportions pervading the world, not in encouraging the practical arts of singing and playing.

Boethius speaks of three types or levels of music.[43] *Musica mundana* is cosmic music, subdivided into the harmony of the spheres, the concord of the elements, and the consonance of the seasons. *Musica humana* is the blending or proper proportioning of elements of our humanity—body and soul, different parts of the soul, and different parts of the body. *Musica instrumentalis* is the music we can actually hear. We know Boethius, like Augustine, had a strong love for the physical sound of music, but he saw this as profoundly "instrumental": a first step (and only a first step) toward understanding the higher, universal, unheard harmonies of the soul and the universe, which have their source in the divine realm of unchanging number. At its best, heard music is number made audible.

In keeping with his inheritance, Boethius's account of music takes on a highly intellectual flavor. "The goal of learning *musica* is to ascend to the level of reason. The fundamental principle motivating Platonic music theory is *knowing*, the acquisition of pure knowledge, and Boethius' threefold division of music and three classes of musicians resonate consistently with that principle."[44] Sensuous experience is to be transcended by the mind. The aim of a good education is to develop understanding and wisdom rather than technical or practical skill. Composers and performers thus rank far lower than musical thinkers. This was not just a matter of social convention, of the low status of professional musicians in his time (where, as Chadwick puts it, "most professional pipe-players were negligibly clad girls brought in at dinner parties to entertain the guests").[45] Being able to spin a melody on the *aulos* or sing in tune was nothing to boast about for Boethius. "Practical music . . . was always located in the shadow of cosmic order, *musica mundana*; it had no independent significance or existence of its own."[46] The highest type of musician is thus not the performer, the composer, or the one who merely hears without attending to mathematics, but the philosopher, the *one who reasons*, whose mind ascends beyond sensuous and material ties, the one who can listen with understanding.[47] And as we might expect, this leads directly to ethics. Like his Greek forebears, Boethius believed that because of its embeddedness in divinely grounded cosmic order, heard music could have a profound effect on the harmony of our lives, for good and ill.

How does this relate to the beliefs of Christian orthodoxy? To be fair, in *De institutione musica* Boethius is writing chiefly as a philosopher, not a theologian. Above all he wants to draw together and commend the Pythagorean-Platonic scheme to his culture. Boethius shows himself quite capable of defending Christian theology in other works. And behind his grand vision of music lies a firm belief in the Christian God, the Triune Creator. The God who brought all beauty and number into being is the God who fashioned all things out of nothing; the God to whom we are directed through music is the God who reconciles us to himself through Christ. None of this is in doubt for Boethius.

Still, however, questions are bound to be asked—and have been asked—about how far the distinctives of Christian faith have been allowed to shape Boethius's thinking, about whether (to put it very bluntly) he owes rather too much to Greek thought.[48] To what extent are faith and reason adequately related? Should God's own trinitarian identity shape our understanding of "harmony" rather more than is evident here? To what extent is there due recognition of the biblical conviction that physical reality is both fully real and of intrinsic value, destined for a glorious future previewed in the resurrection of Christ? To what extent is our own physical nature being given its due place in the scheme of things, along with the mind?

Beyond Boethius

Whatever our questions, it is not hard to see how attractive Boethius's theory of music was to an emerging church that was ever widening and strengthening its reach over all facets of life and thought. Here was a vision that could draw on the best of ancient learning and at the same time resonate with a view of the world as created and sustained by the Christian God. Here was a vision that could provide a convincing account of music within an education curriculum. Here was a vision that could provide solid grounds for evaluating music ethically, in a church that would increasingly need ways of adjudicating and controlling its music in worship, as well as ways of assessing music in society at large.

Not surprisingly, then, Boethius's theory proved very durable and survived in one form or another until well into the fifteenth century. In numerous medieval treatises, his classifications and distinctions were drawn out and restated. His notion of cosmic harmony was carried forward in a variety of ways, one of the most notable being found in the work of the Irish monk Johannes Scotus Erigena (810–86), who went beyond Boethius in aligning God's "natural" music (Boethius's *musica mundana* and *musica humana*) with the kind of music sung within the eight church modes that by his day were widely accepted in worship.[49] Boethian doctrines and number symbolism pervade Dante's *Divine Comedy* (early fourteenth century). In visual art, the music of the spheres became a common subject in the Renaissance and beyond.[50] It is no accident that when the first music students were admitted to the universities of Oxford and Cambridge, they were given Boethius as part of their staple diet—at Cambridge, they were even expected to deliver a lecture on him!

The notion that music could help form good character was assumed and taken forward by many. That music could mediate cosmic harmony to humanity was taken for granted by most theoreticians, and the way they typically treat music's emotional powers shows the influence of Boethius's strong intellectual bias: they are generally far more interested in music's ability to tame and calm the mind than in its power to excite the emotions.

Especially notable is the way in which the leading ideas of the Pythagorean tradition are adapted and modified as they are taken into the ecclesiastical environment. In the writings of Pseudo-Dionysius (fifth/sixth century) for example, Plato's harmony of the spheres becomes the harmony of the angelic choirs—a long-lasting and vibrant theme in the medieval era.[51] Another example is the concept of *harmonia*. Used by the Greeks in relation to music only of notes that were heard successively, in the Middle Ages the word is applied to the concord between simultaneously sounding notes. This, of course, is the way the word "harmony" is commonly used today.

Having said all this, we should not assume that music theory, though widespread and influential at the intellectual level, simply trickled down into practice, as if all medieval musicians simply buckled down and sang and played according to the principles of the Great Tradition. In fact, the relation between the theory ("speculation") and the earthy business of singing and playing seems to have been highly complex and by no means always very close. We have noticed how typically the musical thinker (*musicus*), who understood the *why* of music, was seen as far superior to the performing musician (*cantor*), who understood only the *how*. In the words of Guido of Arezzo in the eleventh century:

> Great is the difference between musicians and singers,
> The latter *say*, the former *know* what music comprises.
> And he who does what he does not know is defined as a beast.[52]

In the educational institutions—the monasteries and the schools attached to cathedral churches—many of the musical treatises were oriented strongly to practical matters, especially to the art of singing well, and, as one modern scholar puts it, "Their authors pay their respects to Boethius in an introductory chapter or two and then turn, with evident relief, to more pressing topics."[53] Given the attitudes of some musicians and the sheer complexity of some music theory, it is not surprising to find a gap opening between the music theory of antiquity and those who wanted to focus on the more down-to-earth business of playing and singing.[54]

From around the ninth century, however, there are signs in some places that the links between speculation and practice become noticeably closer, leading to new types of music theory that seem far more interested in paying attention to the musician on the ground. Even when a staunch Pythagorean like Guido offers a division of *musicus* and *cantor*, he sympathizes with the latter when he says that a Boethius treatise is "useful to philosophers but not to singers."[55] A crucial early text in this regard was the ninth-century *Musica enchiridias*, and in the tenth century there seems to have been a number of influential attempts to bring about a fruitful relationship of theory and musical practice.[56]

A number of factors were at play here, but one of the most important was that with the waning of the Carolingian Empire, the musical culture originally associated with the court shifted to the monasteries. Manuscripts preserving the Platonic tradition of *musica* found their way to monastic centers, and central to the worship of these centers was Gregorian chant, which by this time had become the bread and butter of the church's worship diet. This consisted of a single-line melody sung to Latin words in a flexible rhythm— interestingly, this is enjoying a swell of popularity in our own time.[57] Monastic scholars were forced to connect the plainchant they sang in their chapels and churches with the Pythagorean and Platonic learning of their treasured texts: "The task of the scholar of the late ninth and tenth centuries was to adapt the discipline of singing . . . to the quantitative values and pitch collection of Boethius."[58] Resolving the two worlds was not always easy: a fair amount of shoe-horning had to be done to get the chants to "fit" the system, but by the eleventh century there were a number of effective and influential resolutions widely available.[59]

Crucial in this new flowering of music theory was the development of the medieval system of eight modes and the attempt to align these with the ancient Greek modes. This was not a simple process, and because of a vagueness about their meaning, the Greek names were applied to the wrong modes. But their belief that their own modes were basically equivalent to the ancient ones was crucially important because it signaled a concern not only to give intellectual and cultural kudos to plainchant by associating it with classical culture but also to gain God's approval of certain types of sacred music. They needed to be convinced that Gregorian chant was being sung according to those acoustic patterns that ancient wisdom showed were implanted in creation, originating in the Creator himself.[60]

Another factor in pulling theory and practice closer together we have mentioned already: the rise of multipart music—polyphony, the simultaneous singing of different lines of music. Up until this time, unison had been the norm; musicians together would generally all sing the same notes (sometimes at the octave). But from around the ninth century (perhaps before), experiments appear: some sing a chant while others sing the same line five or four notes apart (in addition to the octave), a practice that came to be known as *organum*. By the end of the eleventh century, musicians were able to combine two melodically independent lines—the notes could move in different directions. The emergence of notation made it far easier to compose and produce this more elaborate music and to standardize it in a definitive form. Exactly how (and how deeply) music theorists affected this first flowering of polyphony (and vice versa) is hard to know, but some argue for strong links: for example, the way in which certain intervals between voices (the fourth, the fifth, and the octave) came to play such a leading role in music may well have owed much to the fact that they were Pythagorean consonances.

Questions Arising

We have done no more than outline some of the principal themes of the Platonic-Pythagorean tradition and looked at some of the ways it was adopted by the church. Quite how profoundly it was known and held by (for want of a better term) the average learned person is a moot point. But even if only a matter of general or tacit awareness, it seems to have exercised a considerable sway.

For all its undoubted strengths—and we shall come to what is arguably the main one in a moment—there are some areas where we might naturally ask some critical questions, or, at the very least, register some hesitations. I have hinted at these already; we will come back to them all later in the book.

First, and perhaps most obvious, it is not hard to detect a certain *ambivalence about the goodness and full reality of the physical world under God*, about its inherent value, its ability to glorify God *as* physical, with its own future promised by God. In a way that seems to run counter to so much in the biblical testimony, the repeated thrust of this tradition is to look beyond material sounds to the order or beauty they reflect or point to, to hesitate about honoring them as *embodiments of* order and beauty, to be welcomed and enjoyed as such.

This relates to a second weakness that seems to surface in much of what we have examined—the way in which *the intellectual and the sensual are set off against each other* or, at the least, distinguished very sharply and placed in a hierarchy of value. Need we be quite so embarrassed and cautious about the bodily, sensuous pull of music? Could it be that sensual delight in musical sounds is something to be celebrated as valuable in its own right, however alert we need to be to the risk of idolatry?

These first two difficulties are bound up with a third: the gap that often emerges between *the theoretical and the practical* and *an unwarranted downplaying of the latter*. For all the strenuous efforts often made to weld Pythagorean theory and musical practice, we might still ask: Is the integrity of the practices of making and hearing music being taken seriously enough? Is there not rather too much disdain for the practicing musician and the testimony of the hearer?

A fourth matter, wider and deeper, follows from this: the danger of imposing *too comprehensive a theory of sound (and thus of music) on the physical world*. Is the material world being given enough room to be itself and declare its own kind of order and possibilities? Are the theorists so eager to have their music conform to a supposedly God-given mathematics that they do not allow sufficient space for the realities of sound to reveal themselves as they are and thus open up fresh ways in which music might glorify God? To raise this question is not to downplay for a moment the stupendous glories of, for example, medieval music—as exemplified in the wonders of Pérotin, Philippe de Vitry, Machaut, or Hildegard von Bingen. The point is simply about theories becoming rather too big for their boots. Indeed, the fact that theorists often had to struggle so hard to do justice to the music people were actually making and hearing surely carries its own message.

The issues at stake here came to a head with the emergence of the Reformation and the rise of modern natural science, and we shall return to them later. They can be focused in a question: Is the created world being treated as able to glorify God *in its own way*, by virtue of its own distinctive patterns, rhythms, and movements? Many have argued that the streams of thought that guided much medieval thinking about music did not pay enough attention to the distinctive order and harmony of the universe as it is and as it could be. Out of a keenness to assume direct and necessary correspondences between the created world and God, to preserve (in some cases) a "hierarchy of being," it is debatable whether the structures of creation were always being respected in their full integrity and potential.[61] Many have held that only a vision of creation more strongly rooted in the biblical story of the trinitarian God can orient us in more secure and fruitful directions. It will be our task in part 3 to sketch something of what this might look like.[62]

All this becomes clearer if we examine the waning of the Great Tradition in the sixteenth and seventeenth centuries. Though it could undoubtedly still grip the imagination of poets and creative writers, it found itself struggling to survive in any other form. As the decades passed, musical sound became more and more the object of hard-nosed investigation, according to the canons and methods of the fast-developing natural sciences. Some directly attacked the notion of the unheard heavenly music as fanciful and unconvincing—one of the most notable being Francisco de Salinas in 1577.[63] Others attacked Pythagorean mathematics directly, together with attempts to line up contemporary modes with ancient Greek music: "All tales contrived to confuse loggerheads," snarls Vincenzo Galilei (Galileo's father).[64] In the 1580s, Galilei demonstrated that since different sounding bodies have different configurations, their sounds do not precisely align with one system of perfect numbers. And traditional theory had considerable trouble accounting for the kinds of music that were emerging at the time—especially polyphony, opera, and instrumental virtuosity. Soon we see the growth of "equal temperament," a method of adjusting the tuning of keyboard instruments outside the Pythagorean norms to meet the practical demands of contemporary music. This stoked much ill feeling, since many thought its notes were cosmically "out of tune."[65] Theories creaked and groaned under the weight of what flesh-and-blood musicians were adding to the repertoire. Venerated ancient wisdom could not easily match up to what was being sung, played, and enjoyed in everyday life.

It is here that another current of thinking is worth mentioning, another ancient Greek tradition, less influential and associated not with Plato but with Aristotle, coming to expression in one of his students, Aristoxenus of Tarentum (ca. 354–300 BCE).[66] Aristoxenus sought to give an account of music that grounded it, not in abstract numbers and ratios, but in the way the elements of music actually sound in practice. Preeminently what should concern the theorist is what is audible: for Aristoxenus, we might say, music is "sounds in our ears" before it is "ratios in our minds." This way of thinking by no means died with Aristoxenus—strands of it we have already met in medieval thought. Aristoxenus has his descendants in all who would give priority to the ear in our evaluation and accounts of music (John Calvin is a distinguished example). Certainly, it is a cast of mind that has come to be especially predominant in Western music theory, and as we shall see, it is not without its own problems. But it does at least signal the drawbacks of the overly cerebral outlook of much of the dominant

Pythagorean-Platonic tradition and the way in which the sheer practicalities of making and enjoying music have a habit of disrupting our best theories.

From Cosmos to Anthropos

But we cannot end the chapter here, because in spite of all the critical questions we might ask about it, the combination of Greek and Christian wisdom we have mapped out testifies to something of the utmost importance. Simply put: music is being grounded firmly in a universal God-given order, and thus it is seen as a means through which we are enabled to live more fully in the world that God has made and with the God who made it. This, we shall be arguing, is a perspective sorely needed in a contemporary Christian account of music.

One of the marks of what is called "modernity," or "the modern age" (which for the purposes of argument we can take as beginning with the Italian Renaissance), is that this cosmic perspective has largely been lost; indeed, it is often ridiculed and attacked. To risk gross overgeneralization: thinking about music in modernity has been marked by *a shift from the cosmological to the anthropological*, from justifying music in terms of the cosmos at large to justifying it solely in terms of human needs and aspirations.

These developments began very early. In 1529 the theorist Lodovico Fogliano proposed that sound is an affective quality that exists only in the ear and that the ear, not the mathematician, is thus the final arbiter of consonance and dissonance. It would be hard to find a more pointed sign of the new ethos. Galilei could declare that there was no natural (i.e., physically demonstrable) difference between consonance and dissonance, "that there was an infinity of both kinds of intervals, and that it *was altogether up to the practitioners to decide how to use them according to their own purposes.*"[67] Of almost symbolic significance is a proposal made by Giulio del Bene in 1586 that music be transferred from the quadrivium to the trivium—from the mathematics department, so to speak, to the human arts department.[68] In other words, music is now being seen fundamentally *as a tool of the human will*. Daniel Chua may exaggerate, but his words go to the heart of things: "The harmony of the spheres has collapsed into the song of the self."[69] With this goes a heavy stress on the *verbal*; with music adrift from its cosmic anchoring and grounded firmly in the human sphere, one of the most common ways to show that it was meaningful and valuable was to link it in some way with language. Even if it was not actually tied directly to words (as in the setting of texts), music had to be shown to operate in a way akin to the ways language operates, as a tool of persuasion and communication similar to written and spoken words.

We shall return to these issues many times. The point to note here is that in our own culture, this move from the cosmological to the anthropological is simply taken for granted. The notion of music being embedded in a wider

God-given order will come across as extraordinarily foreign in a modern (and postmodern) environment in which music is typically seen as essentially a human construction and human expression, earthed in nothing bigger than the ideology of a culture, a social group, or the desires of the individual. But as we have seen, music has by no means always been so conceived. In the light of what we have found in this chapter, and remembering all that Scripture says about our calling as humans in relation to creation at large, it might be worth asking: Has something valuable been lost? Some words of musicologist Julian Johnson are worth pondering carefully (and he has no particular theological axes to grind):

> If it now strikes us as amusing that music was once linked to astronomy or natural science, that is only because we fail to recognise *ourselves* there and the historical development of our *own* attempts to understand the world. If we no longer take music seriously as a way of defining our relation to the external world, perhaps we have become not more sophisticated but simply more self-absorbed.[70]

Quite so. For all that we might smile benignly at in the mathematical clumsiness and rhetorical hyperbole of the classical philosopher of music or the intellectual abstractions and tetchy fussiness of the medieval theorist, is there not something in the notion of being "cradled" in God's created *harmonia* that is worth recovering?

a sixteenth-century trio

4

It has long been recognized that major changes in the arts have frequently been intertwined with shifts in theological outlook. In the last chapter we noted that in the sixteenth and seventeenth centuries there was a waning of confidence in the grand Pythagorean scenario that had sustained so much medieval thought about music. The attempt to ground music in some universal cosmic order runs into greater and greater difficulties, and there emerges a far more pointed stress on music as a fundamentally *human* art. This complex story, summed up in the title of a book by John Hollander, *The Untuning of the Sky*,[1] is one of great complexity with many twists and turns. But whatever the intricacies, by the early eighteenth century the venerable tradition had been, if not in all respects abandoned, at least dramatically weakened.

The convulsions that came to be known as the European Reformation of the sixteenth century coincided with this rethinking of music. Indeed, many of the theological currents especially characteristic of the Reformation were closely bound up with currents of thinking about music. Here we shall examine three key theologians of the Reformation period, all of whom engaged with music in one way or another. Though they shared common passions and concerns—most notably a commitment to the priority of God's unconditional grace made known in the gospel of Jesus Christ—they nevertheless adopted quite distinctive angles and emphases, not least as they came to terms with music. Indeed, their differences are as telling as their similarities.

Martin Luther: The Sound of Creation

Music I have always loved. He who knows music has a good nature. Necessity demands that music be kept in the schools. A schoolmaster must be able to sing; otherwise I will not look at him. And before a young man is ordained into the ministry, he should practise music in school.[2]

Fig. 4.1: Portrait of Martin Luther. © Bibliothèque publique et universitaire, Neuchâtel

It is well known that Martin Luther (1483–1546)—leader of the German reform movement and by any reckoning one of the most formidable and influential figures in world history—held music in exceptionally high esteem.[3] His experience of music at home, as a boy in school, in the Augustinian monastery at Erfurt, and as a priest had a profound and lasting effect on him. He became a passionate music lover and, as a singer and lute player, a fine amateur musician.

Luther's writings on music are few, mostly ad hoc, and scattered widely throughout his works. Nowhere did he attempt anything akin to a systematic theology of music. What he does say about music comes in the context of very practical, pragmatic interests. Furthermore, he expressed a wide range of views—so wide that in later debates even those at loggerheads with one another could usually find a quote from Luther to support their views.[4] At any rate, a good place to begin is with Luther's ecstatic acclamation of music:

> I would certainly like to praise music with all my heart as the excellent gift of God which it is and to commend it to everyone. . . . Here it must suffice to discuss the benefit of this great art. But even that transcends the greatest eloquence of the most eloquent, because of the infinite variety of its forms and benefits. We can mention only one point (which experience confirms), namely, that next to the Word of God, music deserves the highest praise.[5]

The essay from which this quote comes is full of assertions about the enormity and diversity of music's benefits and the feebleness of human attempts, especially philosophical attempts, to explain them. In one place, music is even ranked with theology: "I plainly judge, and do not hesitate to affirm, that except for theology there is no art that could be put on the same level with music, since except for theology [music] alone produces what otherwise only theology can do, namely, a calm and joyful disposition."[6]

Perhaps not surprisingly, Luther is scornful of those who have no love of music or who refuse to take it seriously: "Those . . . who are not moved [by music] I believe are definitely like stumps [of wood] and blocks of stone."[7] Luther's energetic promotion of musical education included not only music theory (as part of the quadrivium) but also the training of performers. In time, music became an essential part of the curriculum of the gymnasiums (the schools set up under Luther's direction in Germany), the cantor being second only to the principal (or deputy principal) in importance.[8]

What accounts for this lofty respect for music? Something more seems to be at stake than personal taste. It may be that part of the answer lies in music's *auditory* character. That music shares with the gospel the primacy of the ear—the gospel is something heard—shows it has a kind of built-in suitability for conveying gospel truth.[9] Another factor, more important, lies in the way music embodies *order*. Brian Horne points to Luther's interpretation of the opening chapters of Genesis, where the concept of order plays a very prominent role. The creation of the world's order was a revelation of order in the life and purpose of God himself. "For Luther the entirely non-figurative, non-representational, non-verbal world of sound in which every note and rhythm finds its proper place in the whole, and is indispensable to the whole, was not only a sign of the possibility of order, but was an actual achievement of that order, a sure indication of the stability of God in a shifting and unstable world."[10] In this view, music, the most intensely formal of the arts, the most removed from self-expression, and thus the most dissociated from the untidiness and messiness of life, has, by its grounding in cosmic order, a peculiar power to hold the forces of sin and chaos at bay, to remind us of the fundamental stability God has conferred on the world. So when Luther speaks of music as an "excellent" gift, "noble, wholesome, and cheerful,"[11] this is not hyperbole. Music is a means, granted by God, through which we are given to share in and enjoy the basic God-given order of the world.[12]

Indeed, the cosmos is fundamentally musical through and through. A "natural music" has been implanted in all created things:

> From the beginning of the world it has been instilled and implanted in all creatures, individually and collectively. For nothing is without sound or harmony [literally, "sounding number"]. Even the air, which of itself is invisible and imperceptible to all our senses, and which, since it lacks both voice and speech, is the least musical of all things, becomes sonorous, audible, and comprehensible when it is set in motion. Music is still more wonderful in living things, especially birds.[13]

He contrasts this "natural" music with "artistic" music; the latter, of which the supreme instrument is the human voice, "corrects, develops, and refines the natural music."[14]

This is familiar territory. Luther is alluding to the Great Tradition, schooled as he is in the medieval quadrivium.[15] The stress is, however, rather different from that in some of his more philosophically inclined forebears. His main interest is not in music as a vehicle through which we rise to mathematical comprehension (though he may have believed this). The stress is on music as full and glorious, a *good gift*, with little sense that its physical, material, and sensual nature is a potential hindrance to union with God. Moreover, Luther does not treat practical music making as secondary and inferior to the theoretical discipline of "music"; hence, as we shall see, his massive investment in music as practiced.[16]

Behind this lies a rich and subtle theology of creation that breaks decisively with some streams in Luther's medieval past and relates to questions we raised at the end of the last chapter. Luther shunned any tendency to treat the created world as less than fully real or physical matter as less than fully good.[17] Created things are not copies of eternal paradigms but full-blooded realities in their own right. When he interprets Genesis, to pick up Colin Gunton's words, the "atmosphere is of grace and gratitude,"[18] with a pronounced sense of the world as an expression of God's generosity. Speaking of God's provision for the earth on creation's third day (Gen. 1:11), Luther comments: "It is far better to meditate and wonder at this concern, care, generosity, and benevolence of God . . . than it is to speculate about why God began to equip the earth on the third day."[19] With this goes a stress on the world as utterly distinct from God and *as such* glorifying God: "[Luther's] faith in creation, far from being a taste for the infinite, is on the contrary an affirmation of the finite."[20] The matter is beautifully put in his lectures on Isaiah 40–66: "Reason sees the world as extremely ungodly, and therefore it murmurs. The spirit sees nothing but God's benefits in the world and therefore begins to sing."[21] In this way, music becomes a means by which creation sings its praise to the Creator. In Luther's own words,

> Thanks be first to God, our Lord,
> Who created [the nightingale] by his Word
> To be his own beloved songstress
> And of *musica* a mistress.
> For our dear Lord she sings her song
> In praise of him the whole day long;
> To him I give my melody
> And thanks in all eternity.[22]

We should not find it odd, then, that for Luther, even when not connected directly to words, music has theological power. As is well known, Luther is every inch a theologian of the Word; he believes at the heart of Christian faith there is a verbal gospel to be proclaimed. But this does not prevent him from delighting in music that magnifies the Creator in its own right and in its own way, not least highly elaborate music. In this respect, he stands in sharp contrast to some of his reforming contemporaries, who were much more anxious about the sensual appeal of ornate or complex music. The zealous Andreas Carlstadt, for example, was prepared to allow only unison chant in worship, since it alone embodied unity and avoided the worldly sensuality of multipart harmony. But Luther can positively revel in the polyphony of his time:

> It is most remarkable that one single voice continues to sing the tenor [the fundamental melody within medieval polyphony], while at the same time many other voices play around it, exulting and adorning it in exuberant strains and, as it were, leading it forth in a divine roundelay, so that those who are the least bit moved know nothing more amazing in this world.[23]

The ethical effects of music, which Luther is happy to celebrate, are also seen as flowing from music's participation in and embodiment of natural order: music "makes souls happy, because it drives away the devil, because it awakens innocent joy . . . because it rules in times of peace."[24]

> There cannot be an evil mood
> Where there are singing fellows good,
> There is no envy, hate, nor ire,
> Gone are through me all sorrows dire;
> Greed, care, and lonely heaviness
> No more do they the heart oppress.[25]

Can music be harmful? Although Luther was careful about the modes he adopted for worship, we see nothing to suggest he believed, unlike Plato, that any of them were inherently damaging. Nor does he appear especially concerned about the appeal of music to the senses, as if this necessarily entailed an evasion of the mind. He recognizes that music can be used harmfully—among those not liberated by the Holy Spirit—but he seems more impressed by the ability of music to help free people from the bondage of evil than by its potential hazards. In general, Luther's positive estimation of music is far less qualified than in the majority of the medieval tradition and indeed generally less cautious than many of his Reformation contemporaries.

Music and Preaching

How does this cosmic view of music relate to preaching?[26] Might not this exalted view of music be seen as a threat to the proclamation of the Word?

On the surface at least there is some ambiguity about this in Luther's writings, and it is one that his followers were not slow to exploit.[27] There are the oft-quoted words from *Table Talk*: "God has preached through music, as may be seen in Josquin, all of whose compositions flow freely, gently, and cheerfully, are not forced or cramped by rules, and are like the song of the finch."[28] But this allusion to the Renaissance composer is offered simply as an illustration of the glories of grace in contrast to law; some would say we should not build too much upon it. In his preface to Georg Rhau's *Symphoniae Iucundae* (1538), Luther uses the term *sonora praedicatione* when commending the praise of God through voice and word—a reference, some think, to music as a "sermon in sound."[29] But the meaning of the term is not clear—it could simply be referring to the voice of the preacher.

Following the scholar Oskar Söhngen, many believe that for Luther the office of preaching in the church included music,[30] and that music's preaching role was fulfilled when linked directly to the Word. Its proclamatory role was thus limited to text-based music. Others are not so sure, arguing that Söhngen misinterprets Luther's references to preaching and singing as if they were equivalent rather than serving the two functions of proclamation and praise. Moreover, to identify music's theological role as proclamation would be to confine its positive role to the sphere of worship, whereas Luther regarded all music, both religious and secular, as potentially valuable and God-glorifying.

Is there an unresolved ambiguity here? Perhaps the truth lies along the following lines.[31] First, Luther's view of proclamation is wider than what takes place in the pulpit in the midst of a liturgy. Doubtless, Luther regards the preaching office as the primary means of proclaiming the gospel. But this is not limited to the ordained: each baptized Christian, not only the priest, has a duty to proclaim the Word. Moreover, preaching is not limited to public worship or to a preached sermon; it covers a variety of ways and contexts in which the gospel can be communicated. We have seen that music at large can witness to the unconditional grace of God made known in Jesus Christ. So, when Luther says that God "preached" through Josquin, the point is about his freedom from stifling rules of composition that, like the freedom from religious law, enabled him to express God's grace. The truth of this holds whether we are inside or outside the sanctuary, whether the text is immediately understood or not. Insofar as his music can witness to God's gracious goodness in this way, Josquin is "preaching the gospel."

Nevertheless, second, allowing this wider proclamatory role for music does not in any way downplay the need for the specific and focused Word of the gospel, written and preached. For the ability to see music *as* a good gift of creation, to use it in a way that embodies the freedom of the gospel and expresses an appropriate response to God's goodness, presupposes the faith that comes only through responding to Jesus Christ, and this happens through hearing and receiving the life-changing words of the gospel. (Unless the Creator is known as good, the creation cannot be known as good.) It was, of course, the recovery of this life-changing reality of justification by grace through faith in Christ that was so crucial a part of Luther's own contribution to the church of his time.

Third, it remains true that when music is directly wedded to texts, it grants the words greater power than they would have by themselves. In Söhngen's words, music "can prove its special gift for intensifying the word and thereby making it more forceful."[32] Luther himself urges the singing of hymns and Psalms thus:

> We have so many hymns and Psalms where message and music [sermo et vox] join to move the listener's soul, while in other living beings and [sounding] bodies music remains a language without words. After all, the gift of language combined with the gift of song was only given to man to let him know that he should praise God with both word and music, namely, by proclaiming [the Word of God] through music [the preacher's voice?] and by providing sweet melodies with words.[33]

Music and Emotion

The emotional power of music is for Luther one of music's distinctive contributions to words. In contrast to other streams of Reformation thought, Luther sees music's emotional force in very positive terms:

> [Music] is a mistress and governess of those human emotions—to pass over the animals—which as masters govern men or more often overwhelm them. No greater commendation than this can be found—at least not by us. For whether you wish to comfort the sad, to terrify the happy, to encourage the despairing, to humble the proud, to calm the passionate, or to appease those full of hate—and who could number all these masters of the human heart, namely, the emotions, inclinations, and affections that impel men to evil or good?—what more effective means than music could you find?[34]

We often find Luther telling us of music's power to uplift the gloomy or listless spirit and thus arouse devotion.[35] In at least one place he speaks of music provoking his desire to preach and comments on how his own positive views of music's emotional powers differ from Augustine, adding (less than modestly) that "if he lived in this century, he would be of our opinion."[36]

Supporting this is a view of the human person noticeably more integrated than some of his forefathers—with less distrust of the senses and a greater awareness of the goodness of the physical body. He offers some fascinating reflections on music's effect on the mind; he seems to believe that music can sharpen and intensify the mind's powers, not despite but *through* emotional stimulation. Here he is alluding to part of the superscription of Psalm 4:

> It is the function of music to arouse the sad, sluggish and dull spirit. Thus Elisha summoned a minstrel; that he might be stirred to prophesy (2 Kings 3:15). Hence *menasseah* properly means stimulus, incitement, challenge, and, as it were, a spur to the spirit, a goad, an exhortation. Such were also the heroic songs and

triumphal hymns of the poets, which the Greeks called *epinikia* ("victory songs"), as in the Book of Chronicles (1 Chron. 15:21). For in all these the listless mind is sharpened and kindled, so that it may be alert and vigorous as *it proceeds to the task*. But when they are at the same time sung to artistic music, they kindle the mind more intensely and sharply. And in this manner David here composed his psalm. *Lammenasseah*, that is, as something inciting, stirring, inflaming, so that he might have something to arouse him to stir up the devotion and inclination of the least, and in order that this might be done more sharply, he did it with musical instruments.[37]

Worship in Practice

Luther was resolute in working out his convictions about music in corporate worship. Church music as he first knew it was largely limited to vocal polyphony (in the Renaissance tradition), Gregorian chant, and hymnody in Latin and the vernacular. As is well known, Luther was determined that the Word of God was to be engrained in congregations and—against much medieval tradition—that the whole congregation should sing (though not to the exclusion of a choir) and, ideally, sing in their own language so that all could participate with understanding (though not to the exclusion of Latin in the choral liturgy).[38] He saw congregational hymn-singing in the vernacular as an especially valuable tool for fixing God's Word in people's hearts.

Scholars disagree over the extent of Luther's own achievements as a composer and the strength of his influence on the development of European music.[39] Quite how many and which hymn tunes can safely be ascribed to Luther is not clear. In any case, the first hymnal produced under his guidance was the *Geistliche Gesangbuchlein* of 1524, a collection of motets based on Lutheran chorales (hymns), and this was the first item in a stream of hymn writing throughout Germany.[40] It is worth underlining that Luther's interest in hymn singing was part of a larger concern that the congregation sing in the liturgy. So it is no accident to find a large number of the hymns associated with Luther's name linked to the Ordinary of the Mass (Kyrie, Gloria, Credo, Sanctus, Agnus Dei). "Hymnody for Luther was not simply a means to enable the congregation to participate in worship in a more general sense. It was a means to enable the congregation to participate specifically *in the liturgy* of the Western Catholic tradition, a tradition that he continued to uphold and affirm."[41]

Thus, in Luther's view, choirs were not to be abandoned, not least because they sang the choral Mass, something Luther greatly valued. Organs were certainly not essential, but they were still useful to support and substitute for the choir. The myth of Luther raiding popular music indiscriminately endears him to many, but it has little foundation. He did not adopt any music that would "work" quickly and get the message across. True, the distinction between sacred and secular was much hazier than at later times, and Luther does not seem to have explicitly attacked any musical style. But it is going beyond the evidence to presume he regarded any and every style as suitable for church use. He was quite prepared to distinguish what he felt was appropriate and inappropriate in worship, insisting on material that was crafted and durable, and he had no time for those who would break from the traditions of the Catholic Church thoughtlessly or needlessly.[42] In this connection, Paul Westermeyer cites the case of Luther's own metrical version of the Sanctus: it is derived from Gregorian chant and is neither easy nor "popular."[43] Despite die-hard folklore, the well-known saying, "Why should the devil have all the best tunes?" cannot be traced to Luther. Of all the hymns we can attribute safely to him, only one is secular in origin, "Vom Himmel Hoch," an alteration of a popular song. But he wrote this for a children's pageant, not church worship, and for church use he changed its original tune to one of his own.[44]

Having said this, Luther did combine complex and simple material effectively—what later might be called "high" and "low" art, urban and rural. The chorale itself—the congregational hymn—served this function, appealing very widely, as did the practice of "alternation" (the congregation singing one stanza of a hymn in simple unaccompanied unison, a choir or instruments following this with a stanza set more elaborately, and so on). It should not be forgotten that Luther believed the most sophisticated form of music of his day should be taught to the young and sung in churches *along with* plainer and more straightforward songs (including sacred folk songs). Carl Schalk goes to the heart of the matter: "The Lutheran Reformation, proceeding from Luther's basic understanding of music as a creation and gift of God, successfully encouraged the reciprocal interaction of art music of the most highly developed kind together with simple congregational song."[45] This both-and approach to music (not the same as "anything goes"), along with the variety of music it generated, is undoubtedly one of Luther's greatest legacies. Luther and the tradition he initiated drew on a huge range of material—including Gregorian chant, polyphony, sacred folk songs, and simple unison line singing—and led to an immense wealth of choral and instrumental music ranging from the work of Heinrich Schütz, through Johann Pachelbel and J. S. Bach, to major composers in the nineteenth and twentieth centuries.[46]

John Calvin: Singing in Moderation

To move from Luther to John Calvin (1509–64) is like walking from a rather messy room with bright colors that do not always match into one that is markedly tidier, with subdued shades and tones. Certainly when it comes to music, the mood is far more cautious.[47]

Calvin could not match Luther's musical gifts and expertise, and a quick glance at some of his writings could give the impression that he never gets beyond coldness or antagonism toward music.[48] If we look more closely, how-

Fig. 4.2: Portrait of John Calvin. © Bibliothèque publique et universitaire, Neuchâtel

ever, a rather different picture emerges, at once intriguing and illuminating.[49] As with Luther, Calvin's comments on music must be seen in their practical context. Trained originally in law, Calvin was a man of exceptional intellect, as well as enormous vision and energy, who found himself gripped by what he saw as the heart of the Christian gospel and caught up in the swirling currents of the early sixteenth-century French reform movements in the church. He had an uncanny sense for what was theologically decisive in any situation and a remarkable administrative flair.

As far as music is concerned, everything Calvin said and wrote arose from a deep concern not only to be true to Scripture—his prime authority in all matters of faith and life—but to provide music for the churches under his care, especially for worship (he rarely considers music outside this setting) and especially in Geneva, where from 1541 he settled and built up a center of theology and churchmanship whose influence spread all over Europe. This concern for the practical must never be forgotten: although something of the shape of "a theology of music" can be found in Calvin, it relates at every turn to the very down-to-earth business of church renewal and organization. To echo our first chapter, for Calvin first and foremost music was something *done*.

As is well known, the main practical outcome of Calvin's interest in music was the Genevan Psalter. Its culminating edition appeared in 1562 (with all 150 psalms and 125 tunes). It sold tens of thousands of copies in Calvin's lifetime. It expressed and shaped a quite distinctive spirituality, and it left an indelible mark on subsequent Protestant worship that endures to this day.[50]

A Shift of Attitude

A good entry point for understanding Calvin's approach to music is to note a decisive shift that took place in his thinking. In the first (1536) edition of his major theological work, the *Institutio* (commonly translated *Institutes of the Christian Religion*), he makes passing reference to music in worship, but with little enthusiasm. However, a year later, addressing the organization of the church in Geneva, Calvin believes that singing should be integral to worship: "It is a thing most expedient for the edification of the church to sing some psalms in the form of public prayers by which one prays to God or sings his praises so that the hearts of all may be aroused and stimulated to make similar prayers and to render similar praises and thanks to God with a common love."[51]

Calvin urges that the Psalms alone are to be sung, for only in this way will the heart be appropriately stimulated. We also find an appeal to history—singing Psalms dates from the time of the apostles and now needs to be restored in the vernacular, after centuries in which liturgical music has rendered the Word of God largely unintelligible. The singing of Psalms is thus integrally linked to Calvin's reform program of restoring the face of the ancient church.

All of Calvin's later writings on church music develop these basic points. Charles Garside underlines the change of attitude they represent. Looking ahead to the first edition of the Genevan Psalter, he writes:

> On the basis of what [Calvin] published in 1536 the possibility of a Calvinist liturgy employing music to any considerable degree seemed at best remote. Seven years later, however, he revealed himself as a determined, although by no means uncritical, advocate of psalmody and superintending editor as well of what eventually would be one of the most influential psalters ever created for Christian worship.[52]

Why the change? Garside traces it to the influence of another reformer, Martin Bucer, and also to Calvin's pastoral experience.[53] When Calvin arrived in Geneva for the first time, he came to a church devoid of music and found the situation intolerable. "Certainly at present the prayers of the faithful are so cold that we should be greatly ashamed and confused."[54] He would probably have recalled reports of congregational singing from Roussel and other French evangelicals and been stirred by the singing he had heard while working in Basel. In any case, the remedy for "cold" prayer is psalm-singing: "The psalms can stimulate us to raise our hearts to God and arouse us to an ardour in invoking as well as in exalting with praises, the glory of his name."[55]

What we are witnessing here, then, is a discovery of the *positive* role of music seen as an *integral* part of worship, and without any hint that this need threaten biblical authority. Indeed, Calvin's main justification for his views on music are drawn specifically from Scripture.

And what is it that music contributes to worship? More than anything else Calvin highlights its emotional, affective power. When turned into song, Psalms take on a quality that greatly strengthens communal prayer and praise; the texts are grasped with a heightened intensity, the conjunction of word and music linking mind and emotion in an especially potent way. And this should be read in a thoroughly corporate sense. Calvin's overarching practical interest, we should not forget, is in building up the church: through singing, "the hearts of all may be aroused and stimulated to make similar prayers and to render similar praises and thanks to God *with a common love*."[56]

Calvin and Luther

Sadly, differences between the followers of Luther and Calvin led to painful fractures, eventually resulting in different denominations. Though music was not the culprit, there were marked differences between the two leaders in their attitudes to music, and it is worth pausing to highlight them.

First, like Luther, Calvin sees music as a wonderful gift of God, but the grounding of music in a universal cosmic order and the notion of music as embodying that order do not seem to be anywhere near as strong in Calvin as they are in Luther. In some respects this is strange, given the strong stress on natural order in Calvin's theology. In any case, Calvin traces music to Jubal in Genesis 4:21,[57] describing it as one of the "luculenta . . . divinae bonitatis testimonia"[58]—one of the "shining testaments to divine goodness" that has survived the human fall as an enduring testimony to God's goodness and that was given for our recreation and pleasure. More specifically, it has been given for our "spiritual joy," that we might rejoice and delight in God, which is our "true end."[59] As such it deserves high approval:

> Just as our nature, then, draws us and induces us to seek all means of foolish and vicious rejoicing, so, to the contrary, our Lord, to distract us and withdraw us from the enticements of the flesh and the world, presents to us all possible means in order to occupy us in that spiritual joy which he so much recommends to us. Now among the other things proper to recreate man and give him pleasure, music is either the first or one of the principal, and we must think that it is a gift of God deputed to that purpose.[60]

This stress on music explained chiefly in human terms is linked to a second difference between Luther and Calvin. Though both are keen to stress the distinctiveness of God and creation—God is not the world and the world is not God—Calvin seems especially anxious about anything that might compromise God's utter otherness.[61] He is certainly very wary about granting any human activity too great a role, anything that would diminish God's lordship or suggest that God is not free, that he is somehow at our beck and call. Music must be kept in its place. The different slant in Luther and Calvin here is well illustrated in their treatment of the story in 1 Samuel 16, where David plays his lyre to comfort Saul ("and the evil spirit would depart from him," v. 23). Luther speaks boldly of music as a "tool of God's work" and states explicitly that "*through* music the devil has been driven away."[62] Calvin is much more cautious about linking God and music; music did indeed soothe Saul, but God drove out the spirit in his sovereign freedom. Saul, he says, "had indeed been refreshed by David's harp, but it was really by the Lord's doing and inspiring that power within [David]."[63]

This difference between Luther and Calvin works itself out in many areas of their theology. When it comes to treating the two natures of Christ, Calvin is far more concerned than Luther to stress the distinctiveness of the divine and human in Christ, avoiding any hint of confusion, merger, or compromise of the natures. This in turn profoundly affects Calvin's theology of the Lord's Supper, where his divergence from Lutheranism was to become especially acute and painful: Calvin is passionately keen to retain a sense of communing with the fully human, risen, and corporeally ascended Christ in a way that he felt was being threatened by Luther and the Lutherans.[64]

Not surprisingly, then—and this is the third major difference—Calvin is much more apprehensive than Luther about the negative powers of music. He has an especially vivid sense of the vulnerability of all human activity to sin. Spiritual joy, of which music can be a reminder, was part of our endowment prior to the fall. But the catastrophe of sin has turned music into a very mixed blessing. Music can poison and disfigure the heart as much as uplift it, and it can generate quite disastrous moral consequences. Here Calvin follows Plato closely: "It is true that every bad word (as St. Paul said) perverts good character, but when the melody is added, that word pierces the heart much more strongly and enters within. Just as wine is poured into the vessel through a funnel, likewise venom and corruption are exuded down into the very depths of the heart through melody." He appeals quite openly to the Greek philosopher: "There is hardly anything in the world with more power [than music] to turn or bend, this way and that, the morals of men, as Plato has prudently considered."[65]

Singing from the Heart

Calvin is thus understandably anxious that music be turned to good effect. Crucial here is a proper attitude of the heart, the center of the personality. From Calvin's first musings on music to his last, this theme runs like a leitmotif. Even a fine song, with proper text and music, can be sung to evil purpose if it does not spring from a heart touched and transformed by God's Spirit: "Unless voice and song, if interposed in prayer, spring from deep feeling of heart, neither has any value or profit in the least with God."[66] We also find a repeated accent on the participation of the whole church in worship; the entire congregation must understand what is being sung. Everyone should sing (no specially trained choirs are permitted—though Calvin did allow children to serve as the leaders of singing),[67] and if worship is to edify the whole congregation, the singing must be in the vernacular:

> The heart requires the intelligence, and therein, says Augustine, lies the difference between the singing of men and of birds. For a linnet, a nightingale, a parrot will sing well, but it will be without understanding. *Now the peculiar gift of man is to sing knowing what he is saying.* After the intelligence must follow the heart and the affection, which cannot be unless we have the hymn imprinted on our memory, in order never to cease singing.[68]

By implication, it is also vital that music follows the text. It is, after all, the power of God's Word that will take hold of the church and enable it to worship God from the heart. So the text must have primacy: "We should be careful that our ears be not more attentive to the melody than our minds to the spiritual meaning of the words."[69]

Calvin goes on to allude to Augustine's *Confessions*, specifically to where the early church father speaks of the danger of being more moved by the singing than by what is sung and where he writes of his wish that he could restore the custom of instructing the reader to veer closer to speaking than singing, so that the music might serve the words. Calvin agrees. Music needs to be tempered, or "moderated," by words: "When this moderation is maintained, it is without doubt a most holy and salutary practice."[70] Without such moderation, music is liable to debase and contaminate us, leading to our condemnation;[71] "such songs as have been composed only for sweetness and delight of the ear are unbecoming to the majesty of the Church and cannot but displease God in the highest degree."[72]

And which texts are allowed? Above all the Psalms, or more strictly, poetic reworkings of the Psalms. (From the 1539 Strasbourg Psalter onward, Calvin was prepared to include sung versions of other biblical material—the song of Simeon [Luke 2:29–32] and the Ten Commandments.)[73] Why such a concentration on the Psalms? Because they are the words God gave us to praise him, and nothing can moderate music more effectively—nothing can better curb sin's power.

Every effort must be made to use appropriate music. Here Calvin is far more prescriptive and restrictive than Luther. Music should have a gravity and majesty appropriate to the worship of God, with no lightness or frivolity. Harmony is to be shunned (though this did not stop polyphonic—multipart—settings of the Psalms proliferating *outside* the liturgy).[74] Secular melodies are prohibited; nothing must trivialize worship. There is "a great difference between the music one makes to entertain men at table and in their homes, and the Psalms which are sung in the Church in the presence of God and his angels."[75] Moreover,

Calvin desires the replacement of all secular vocal music with Psalm singing. To the modern reader this will come across as impossibly restrictive, but as John Witvliet points out, it can be read as a blurring of the sacred-secular divide: "Whereas Roman Catholic sensibilities preferred a clear line between liturgy and secular life, the Calvinists freely sang these texts and tunes in their homes and fields."[76] We should also add that one of Calvin's motivations here seems to have been a concern to exclude certain types of obscene song from finding any place in society.[77]

In worship Calvin disallows instrumental accompaniment (though instruments are permitted in homes and schools), for this belonged to the old covenant, which has now been superseded.[78] Here is another point of contrast with Luther. Luther welcomes instruments into the church, appealing to the Old Testament and to long-standing custom in the churches.[79] Calvin stands much closer to the early church fathers, who, as we have seen, generally disapproved of instruments in worship.[80] In any case, the result was an exclusion of instruments from worship—something that can still be found in some church traditions.

Though he did not write any of the melodies in the Psalters, in addition to contributing Psalm paraphrases of his own, Calvin had a considerable influence on the various Psalter editions. The Psalm tunes bear out Calvin's wishes. They consist of one line of notes, they are unaccompanied, generally syllabic (one note to each syllable), and they rarely exceed an octave in range (thus easily singable).[81] The sense of dignity Calvin so longed for was achieved not so much through slow tempi as through the simplicity of the melodies, their uncluttered accessibility. Again, running through this is a corporate concern: that the whole church could readily take part in the act of singing and thus be edified.

A Decisive Turn

We have seen that Calvin has his own distinctive approach to music. Though he shares much with Luther and draws on the Platonic tradition's stress on music's emotional dangers, he develops particular lines of argument and draws them into a theology that gives a highly prominent place to the written and spoken word. It is worth underscoring again the first difference we noted between him and Luther: Calvin approaches music more as a human practice (especially vulnerable to the effects of the fall) than as one integrally embedded in the order of the physical world. This marks a decisive step away not only from Luther but also from the dominant streams of the medieval era. He does not deny that music can articulate the order of the universe, but this seems to play no substantial part in his arguments. And as a human practice, music is linked very closely to the realm of words. Music is seen chiefly as a rhetorical tool intensifying the power of words, and one needing to be held firmly in check by words. Calvin's suspicion of instrumental music without words became very common in Reformation writing. And in the decades that followed, arguments inside and outside the church raged over the relative value of vocal and instrumental music.[82]

Without the cosmos justifying music, some other grounding was needed, and this is provided most often in the realm of language. Here Calvin shows himself to be not only a man of the Bible (a theologian of the written and preached Word) but also a man of the emerging culture, where music is more and more disentangled from the cosmos and aligned with the human sphere and, in many cases, with the human word. Calvin signals a critical turn in European Christian thinking about music. We have moved from the medieval to the modern age.

Huldrych Zwingli: Silence for the Word

The Reformation is full of ironies, and one of the most pointed can be seen in the leading figure of the Swiss Reformation, Huldrych Zwingli (1484–1531). He was by far the most musical of our trio, yet he was also by far the most negative about music in worship.[83]

Fig. 4.3: Portrait of Huldrych Zwingli. © Bibliothèque publique et universitaire, Neuchâtel

Zwingli is probably best known for two things: his "memorialist" view of the Lord's Supper and his recommendation that all music be banned from public worship. From early in his ministry as "people's priest" at the Great Minster in Zurich, Zwingli showed his commitment to a scrupulous reform of the church—a commitment that grew in intensity as the years went by. He preached vigorously against virtually every aspect of traditional medieval Catholic worship, including the veneration of Mary, fasting, and the invocation of the saints. At a large public disputation in 1523, he defended his views so successfully that the city council made his program official policy. By 1525 the Mass was abolished altogether, and with this purging of Roman Catholicism, all vocal and instrumental music was excised from church life.

Yet Zwingli was no music hater. Highly gifted from his earliest days as a singer, player of many instruments, teacher, and composer, Zwingli showed a passion for music that went far beyond the commonplace. A contemporary wrote of him:

> I have never heard about anyone who, in the musical arts—that is, in singing and all the instruments of music, such as lute, harp, large viol, little viol, pipes, German flute—as good as any Swiss—the trumpet, dulcimer, cornett, and waldhorn, and whatever else of such like had been invented and which he saw, could take it to hand as quickly as he and in addition was so learned.[84]

The musical interest was not only practical. Through his university education he became adept in the *musica* of the seven Boethian liberal arts, receiving tuition in Vienna from one of the most distinguished scholars of the day, a poet and keen amateur musician, Conrad Celtis Protucius. Zwingli's love of music is well illustrated in his response to a near-death experience in 1519. Zurich was stricken by a terrible plague, and Zwingli succumbed. Given up for dead by some, he made an astonishing recovery. "Perhaps no other experience in his life was to affect him quite so profoundly or quite so completely."[85] Overwhelmed by a sense that he had been spared for a purpose, he wrote an extended and heartfelt poem, usually referred to as the *Pestlied* ("Plague Song"), revealing his innermost struggles and perplexities as well as his deeply felt gratitude. Although he had written poetry before, this experience demanded something more expressive than words alone. So he set the poem to elaborate four-part polyphony, drawing on his love of music and many years of musical training.

Nevertheless, despite all this, only three years after the *Pestlied*, Zwingli published his recommendation for the prohibition of all music from worship. Why?

Scripture and Worship

We need to sketch some context. Zwingli was trained in institutions that were flourishing centers of that broad movement known as "humanism," which, among other things, laid great stress on going "back to the sources" (*ad fontes*) in the pursuit of learning and wisdom.[86] The writings of Erasmus of Rotterdam (1466–1536) had a significant impact on Zwingli—here he found a yearning for the renewal of Christianity according to the writings of the New Testament and the early church fathers and for a revival of the learning of classical antiquity. Especially important for Zwingli was Erasmus's desire to distance himself from the medieval ecclesiastical environment. Unlike Luther, Zwingli did not come to an evangelical understanding of God's grace amid the philosophical and theological tradition of the late medieval church or within a strong commitment to the ecclesiastical establishment. For him, we find a huge stress on the distinctiveness and utterly unique authority of Scripture as *the* source above all others. "The Bible was at the heart of Zwingli's reformation."[87] It is no accident that at the Wasserkirche in Zurich stands a statue of Zwingli with a sword in his left hand and a Bible held above it in the right hand. Scripture was to be the highest norm in all matters of belief and all outward expressions of belief, including worship (though he did draw extensively on the fathers, church tradition, and non-Christian writers). From this perspective Zwingli urged a root and branch reform of the church, not simply of doctrine but of every dimension of its life.

As far as worship is concerned, his logic is lucid. Worship, Scripture makes plain, is first and foremost an *internal* matter, concerning not outward actions but the inward disposition of the individual. There are basically two forms of worship: one that centers on external forms, the other on internal content. "True worshippers call upon God in spirit and in truth without the clamour before men."[88] Of pivotal importance to Zwingli's account of worship was Christ's teaching on the need for prayer to be private and secret (worship and prayer being inseparable and often synonymous in Zwingli's mind). When we pray we should withdraw into privacy, and there, in secret, call upon our heavenly Father (Matt. 6:6). True, pure worship is private and individual. Outward rituals in worship are thus frowned upon.

> I will confess frankly that I wish to see a considerable portion of the ceremonies and prescriptions abolished. . . . I demonstrated that simple people could be led to recognition of the truth by means other than ceremonies, namely, so far as I was able to learn from Scripture, by those with which Christ and the apostles had led them without ceremonies.[89]

Not surprisingly, Zwingli bemoans what he sees as the empty "babbling" of repeated prayers, phrases recited over and over again, for it encourages a degeneration of worship into hypocrisy and empty exhibition. The choral and instrumental music of the Catholic Church, of course, was full of the repetition of words, and it comes in for some of Zwingli's severest condemnation. Professional choirs are a consummate example of the worst kind of ostentatious display, of "those who perform their deeds to be seen by the world."[90]

Scripture and Singing

The drive of Zwingli's argument is thus fairly plain. Where in Scripture has God commanded choral singing in worship? Nowhere. What of Colossians 3 and Ephesians 5, where Paul seems to speak of singing in worship? For Zwingli, singing "with our hearts" is to be taken to mean "not with our voices" but "in our hearts," in other words, internally and silently. What of the numerous Old Testament verses referring to music in worship? Zwingli replies: nowhere is it clear that singing was actually instituted by God; it is to be seen there as a human initiative, not a divine one. Both in theory and in practice, Zwingli was ruthlessly consistent—the intricacies of Latin polyphony, the sounds of the organ, the chanting of the Psalms, the settings of the Mass, even the unaccompanied unison singing of the Psalms in the vernacular (as Calvin allowed) must all go.

> Farewell, my temple-murmurings! I am not sorry for you. I know that you are not good for me. But welcome, O pious, private prayer that is awakened in the hearts of believing men through the Word of God. Yes, a small sigh, which does not last long, realises itself and goes away again quickly. Greetings to you, common prayer that all Christians do together, be it in Church or in their chambers, but free and unpaid; I know that you are the sort of prayer to which God will give that which He promised.[91]

Just over a year after Zwingli had made public his opposition to song and instrument in church, half of his program had been enacted in Zurich—organs were silenced, and a few years later they were destroyed. Vocal music took a little longer to go: it was not until 1525 that the city council enacted the ban on singing in worship. It was then that "the true stillness of worship had at last been achieved in its entirety."[92]

We should be clear that Zwingli is not resting his case on the dangers of music. His argument is not that music carries some hazards that make it unsuitable for worship. His stance toward music has nothing to do with a prejudice against music as such. Neither has it anything to do with music being worldly or any associations with frivolity or immorality. And it certainly has nothing to do with musical illiteracy on Zwingli's part: he is the last person in the European Reformation one could accuse of being uneducated musically. The heart of his argument is simply that God has not authorized music in worship, and Christ's command is that worship is to be an essentially inward, individual, and private matter.[93]

Theological Accents

We have presented Zwingli very much as a theologian of Scripture, one who believes the exposition and proclamation of the written Word lies at the very core of Christian faith and conduct. All the same, his interpretation of Scripture, and hence his attitude to music, is linked to a number of theological assumptions that predispose him to read the Bible's texts in certain ways and not others and that arguably sit uneasily with the witness of the texts themselves.

There are, for example, assumptions about what kind of book the Bible is. For all three of our reformers, Scripture is the authoritative Word of God, God-given and God-inspired. But for Luther and Calvin, it is concerned first and foremost with the gracious promises of God focusing above all on Christ himself, and its ethics flow out of this center; for Zwingli the center of gravity appears to fall much more on Scripture as the law of God, as a code of conduct adumbrating God's demands.[94] Thus we find a strong drive toward the belief that if God does not explicitly command something in Scripture (e.g., singing in worship), it cannot be allowed today.

There is also an unmistakable streak of Platonism in Zwingli, inherited from his humanist background. This sets up some strong dualities and oppositions, with one side treated as superior to the other—physical and nonphysical, outer and inner, material medium and nonmaterial content, bodily involvement and spiritual commitment, ceremonial piety and inner devotion, and so on. The contrast between the nonmaterial nature of God and the material world is here aligned with the supposedly nonmaterial character of worship:

> The common people think that God is placated by victims of cattle and by corporeal things. But ever since God himself is spirit: mind: not body, it is obvious that like rejoices in like: doubtless he [i.e., God] is above all to be worshipped by purity of mind. And today the mass of Christians worship God through certain corporeal ceremonies: whereas the piety of mind is the most pleasing worship. For the father seeks such worshippers as will worship him in spirit, since he is spirit.[95]

Likewise, Zwingli tends to set flesh and spirit off against each other, in what W. P. Stephens calls "his partially Platonist view" of the human person, which "presupposes a sharp contrast or opposition between the inward and the outward."[96] In his account of baptism and the Lord's Supper, we find a pointed distinction between outward sign and the spiritual reality signified. For him a sacrament does not make present what it signifies; it is a sign that points, witnesses, to the thing signified as something quite other. The physical elements cannot be invested with inherent power or treated as in any sense conveying (or containing) the presence of the risen Christ. With this goes a very strong contrast between Christ's divinity and humanity. The distinction between the divine and human natures that Calvin struggled so hard to maintain against the Lutherans has turned into a severe dichotomy, and a theology of the Lord's Supper emerges that places a huge stress on Christ not being "here"—in a manner very different from both Luther's and Calvin's view of the Lord's Supper. According to his divine nature, says Zwingli, Christ is everywhere; according to his human nature, he is ascended in heaven and, hence, cannot be here at the Lord's Supper. His body can be in only one place. "This is my body," then, means, "this signifies my body." The bread points to Christ's body in heaven. To "eat the flesh" of Christ (John 6:51–58) is to eat spiritually, not bodily, that is, trusting in the mercy and goodness of God shown in Christ. At the Lord's Supper, we do not consume a body present among us; rather, we remember Christ's sacrifice, confess our faith, and pledge our loyalty and love to one another. The sacraments do not create faith; the preaching of the Word does that, and faith should be directed toward Christ who is in heaven, not toward anything earthly or visible. The flesh-spirit contrast of John 6:63 ("It is the Spirit that gives life; the flesh is useless") means that the Spirit of God will raise our hearts above all material and earthly things, bringing our faith to bear on Jesus Christ in heaven.[97]

According to many commentators, propelling many of these concerns is a view of the relation of God to the world that lays a massive stress on God's supreme freedom. Zwingli seems to have been gripped by a forceful sense of the sovereignty of God and of himself as God's instrument under God's providence. God does not need outward physical things, and he is never bound to them. Zwingli repudiates anything that would suggest we could tie the divine hand in some manner or fasten God to physical things. The Creator is utterly free from the created world. We cannot tame or contain or domesticate this freedom, and Zwingli sees a danger of sacramental elements, statues, buildings, ceremonies, and rituals as convincing us that we can. So although he frequently makes reference to biblical texts that speak of God using the visible and outward means to accomplish his purposes, he insists that the power is God's alone and does not dwell in the means: "The ground does not bring forth, nor the water nourish, nor the air fructify, nor the fire warm, nor the sun itself, but rather that power which is the origin of all things, their life and strength, uses the earth as the instrument wherewith to produce and create."[98]

These convictions clearly color his approach to all outward things in worship, including music. Zwingli will give music none of the theological weight we find in Luther, or even Calvin. When it comes to the passage in which David soothes Saul by playing the lyre, we find him even more keen than Calvin to distance God from the music: David's lyre playing *alone* protected Saul from the evil spirit.[99] For Zwingli, music (as we might put it today) is a thoroughly secular matter. To be sure, he played, sang, and enjoyed music until the end of his life. He composed a vigorous battle hymn in 1529 and some incidental music for a performance of Aristophanes's *Plutus* in 1531. He was never in doubt as to the immense psychological and emotional power of music—he sees the capacity to respond to it as basic to human nature. We even find echoes of the Great Tradition cropping up:

> The *ratio* of no other discipline is so profoundly rooted and innate in the souls of all men as that of music. For no men are so stupid that they are not captivated by it, even though they are entirely ignorant of its technique. There are none, on the other hand, who are not offended by the confusion and discord of voices, even those who cannot explain what is dissonant and what is unsuitable.[100]

Yet Zwingli sees music's power purely in psychological and physical rather than theological terms. Music is in the last resort a matter of pleasure and recreation—in the home and school; he has no interest in giving it a theological standing.[101] It is as if the theologian and musician in him were quite separate: after the upheavals of the early 1520s, music becomes "a separate, autonomous activity, divorced from his study and experience of the Word."[102]

Despite Zwingli's strictures, however, music seemed irrepressible. As more and more hymnals and song collections were produced and Zurich became the exception among Swiss cities in banishing music from its liturgy, it was increasingly difficult to say that music could be allowed in schools and homes but not in worship. Eventually music, as it were, had the last laugh. In 1598, more than half a century after Zwingli died, in the Great Minster of Zurich, the congregation was allowed to break into song again: the sounds of music returned.

As we stand back from these three dramatis personae who played such leading roles on the stage of the modern church (and, especially in the case of Luther and Calvin, of Western culture), perhaps most striking is the fact that despite their common allegiance to Scripture, they can differ so markedly, and sometimes very sharply. As the church has often had to learn, a shared commitment to Scripture's authority carries no guarantee of agreement. The differences are due to more than social circumstance and individual taste; as we have seen, most of them can be traced to quite fundamental theological convictions and habits of mind. Even in the case of Zwingli, for all he wanted to distance music from the direct activity of God, his is as much a theologically driven vision of music as Luther's and Calvin's.

We have seen that particularly important were the different ways they viewed the world as God's creation and God's relation (and ours) to the world. The three of them lived during periods when medieval patterns of thinking about these matters were being radically reexamined and reassessed. When it comes to music, it is Luther who seems to retain the strongest grounding of music in God's created order at large, Calvin less so, and Zwingli is suspicious of giving music any kind of theological kudos at all.

It is now time to let a full-time musician give his own testimony.

5

wise beyond
words

Once when visiting the United States, I was invited to dinner at a private house in New Jersey. Having just entered the living room, I glanced behind me and was suddenly confronted with a famous portrait of J. S. Bach[1] (see fig. 5.1). It was as if the composer had startled me from behind, crept up on me with his "commanding though benign presence."[2] The music he held in his right hand—*Canon triplex à 6*—was of the kind that Bach became so adept at writing, full of the unexpected while at the same time meticulously calculated.

With Bach, perhaps more than with any other composer of the last five hundred years, we meet a musician who, if we are prepared to spend time with him, can jolt and shake us and unsettle our musical assumptions and lazy commonplaces, yet in a way that is never arbitrary or bizarre. For he left us music that seems able to provoke a sense of almost inexhaustible surprise while at the same time a sense of profound fittingness. The pianist András Schiff once remarked that he played Bach every day "as a kind of devotional exercise." Compare the cellist Pablo Casals:

> For the past eighty years I have started each day in the same manner. . . . I go to the piano, and I play two preludes and fugues of Bach. . . . It is a sort of benediction on the house. But that is not the only meaning for me. It is a rediscovery of the world of which I have the joy of being part. It fills me with awareness of the wonder of life, with a feeling of the incredible marvel of being a human being. . . . Each day [the music] is something new, fantastic and unbelievable. That is Bach, like nature, a miracle.[3]

Fig. 5.1: Portrait of Johann Sebastian Bach by Elias Gottlob Haussmann (1748). Courtesy of William H. Scheide, Princeton, New Jersey

Certainly, many have discovered that time spent with this man's music, and especially when considered in its context, provokes one to rethink what music might fundamentally be about and—not least—how it might be bound up with Christian faith. An exceptional wisdom seems to be at work here, calling for a dedicated and patient respect.

Johann Sebastian Bach (1685–1750) spent all his adult life as a professional, practicing musician. He served as organist at Arnstadt and Mühlhausen, court organist and concertmaster in the chapel of the Duke of Weimar, music director at the court of the prince of Cöthen, and then finally, from 1723, as cantor at the St. Thomas School and director of music in Leipzig.[4] Though by no means obscure in his lifetime, Bach did not enjoy the popular success of some other baroque composers and would no doubt have been astonished to learn that over 250 years after his death, he would be venerated the world over. The veneration has arisen not because of the man himself but because of his quite astonishing musical output, immense in quantity and unparalleled in its encyclopedic character, embracing a huge variety of genres, combining immense emotional appeal with exquisite technical intricacy.

For our purposes what makes his music so intriguing are its theological resonances—the witness it provides to the Christian gospel and to the created world as perceived through the lens of that gospel. In particular, there is much to be gleaned when we recall that his testimony was forged in a very particular setting—amid one of the major currents of the Protestant Reformation, and at a time of critical turning points in the intellectual and cultural life of modern Europe.

Scene Setting

Pitfalls

Many Bach scholars are suspicious of theologians who turn their attention to this composer (and for that matter, any Christians eager to uncover the theological dimensions of Bach). And not without good reason. The pitfalls for the well-meaning theologian are numerous. Here we pinpoint three.

First, it is common to forget that Bach was a professional musician, not a professional theologian. Undoubtedly he was theologically well informed (his education would have involved reading theological texts in depth). He was raised and educated a Lutheran and was aware of some of the Lutheran debates of his time. But he "never took up a pen to argue a theological point or to support his music with theology."[5] Nor did he offer any theological reflections on his work as a composer. Apart from the music itself, what we know of his theological interests comes from a few scattered and offhand remarks in letters, biblical annotations, and prefaces to pieces.

Second, there is the pitfall of hagiography—imagining Bach as a Christian of exceptional faith and godliness and perhaps also assuming that this explains the superlative quality of his music. Even sympathetic biographers of Bach alert us to his many failings, and his piety was hardly exceptional.[6] He was a serious student of the Bible, demonstrated by the numerous marginal comments in his annotated version of the Bible by the seventeenth-century Lutheran orthodox theologian Abraham Calov.[7] But there is little to suggest he showed unusual Christian com-

mitment for his time and place. The initials "J. J." (*Jesu juva*—"Jesus help!") and
S. D. G. (*Soli deo gloria*—"to God alone be glory"), found in his church compositions and some of the secular pieces, may indicate a strong Christian faith, but he
was hardly alone in writing ascriptions of this sort.[8] A remark very likely made
by Bach—"the ultimate end or final purpose of all music . . . is nothing other
than the praise of God and the recreation of the soul"—has provoked a torrent
of commentary, but the sentiment finds many parallels in German music theory
until well into the eighteenth century.[9] This is not to deny that Bach had a vibrant
and heartfelt faith, only to caution against exaggeration and hyperbole.

Similar comments can be made about a third pitfall: number obsession. There
is little doubt that Bach was fascinated by numbers, that he used some number symbolism in his music,[10] and that some of this symbolism is theological.
The "Sanctus" ("Holy, Holy, Holy") from the *Mass in B Minor*, for example, is
pervaded with threeness.[11] But some have plowed this field almost fanatically,
holding, for example, that Bach frequently employs a "number alphabet" with
each number corresponding to a letter in the alphabet, such that the number
of notes, rests, bars, or whatever carry theological coded messages or allusions.
Many theories of similar intricacy have been proposed.[12] Much of this, however,
should be given a wide berth. The number alphabet thesis has been roundly
criticized, and in any case, the particular connections drawn between numbers
and music in Bach are often of meager theological value.[13] This not to say that
there is no number symbolism in Bach, or that the mathematical dimensions
of his music are of no theological interest at all. But we need to be careful not
to deduce too much from vulnerable data.

Nonetheless, Bach's music still exemplifies a theological engagement with
music that has probably never been surpassed. It was the result not only of a
technical prowess rarely equaled in Western music but also of an extraordinarily
sensitive Christian intelligence, rooted in Scripture, indebted to the Lutheran
tradition, and nourished by regular worship. He may not have left us with a
theological tome. He was not a professional theologian, and his primary skills
were not in words but in tones—melodies and cadences, fugues, trios, arias,
and chaconnes. But the fact remains that he was well informed biblically and
theologically, and his musical output shows he could penetrate the most demanding theological issues with a remarkable acuity, so much so that a growing
number of Bach scholars are prepared to recognize that any serious treatment
of this composer cannot avoid engaging theological issues.[14]

Contexts

As we have noted, Bach was a Lutheran. His schooling was in Lutheran
settings—indeed, he attended the same Eisenach school as Luther himself. Much
of his music was written for the Lutheran liturgies of the day and takes account
of the principles of worship commended by Luther. As a church musician, he

gave formal and written assent to the doctrines enshrined in the *Book of Concord* (1580)—an anthology of documents embracing fundamental Lutheran teaching. An inventory of his library at his death reveals that he owned two sets of Luther's complete works as well as numerous volumes by Lutheran theologians.[15]

It was basic to the Lutheran outlook of Bach's day that men and women are justified on the grounds of what God has done in Jesus Christ, centering on the once-and-for-all achievement of the cross. Christ himself is our righteousness. We are saved *sola fide* ("by faith alone")—a faith that takes hold of Christ, forming an intimate union with him—and through faith we find forgiveness and acceptance. Salvation is from beginning to end *sola gratia*—"by grace alone"; it depends on the utterly undeserved, unconditional love of God, not on our efforts or achievements ("works of the law"). All of this we come to know and experience through the preaching of the gospel and its enactment in the sacraments—the gospel being the message about Christ, the promise of God, to be received in thankful trust and confidence. And since this gospel of Christ is the heart of the message of Scripture, our standing before God depends on respecting the authority of Scripture as unique and superior to the church's authority (*sola Scriptura*, "by Scripture alone").

These themes recur across the full range of Bach's works. We need only think of the way the cross is the culmination and focal point of the *Mass in B Minor* or of the frequent calls to Christ-centered faith in all the mature vocal works. The contrast between law and gospel is basic to the structure of many of the cantatas—an opening chorus exposes the human predicament, our condemnation under God's law; recitatives and arias expand on the theme; and then an aria, perhaps, presents the gospel answer, paving the way for a positive mood taken through to the final chorale. The characteristic Lutheran stress on proclamation of the gospel pervades Bach's music; indeed, Michael Marissen sums up Bach's Leipzig ministry in this way: "It was Bach's job as Cantor at the St. Thomas School of Leipzig to be a musical preacher for the city's main churches."[16] There is good reason to suppose Bach regarded the primary purpose of the cantatas as proclamation of the gospel.[17] It is often forgotten that both the *St. Matthew Passion* and the *St. John Passion* were designed for a preaching service (vespers), the sermon coming during the interval of these works. The Passion setting itself would be understood as a form of preaching—the music intensifying the verbal message, enabling the congregation to appropriate the saving power of the gospel story for themselves as they were drawn to the central figure in the drama, Jesus Christ. The five elements traditionally attributed to a sermon by Lutheran theologians can all be found in the Passions.[18]

Having said all this, Lutheranism was a mixed and fluid movement. If Bach was "orthodox," his was not in all respects the strict orthodoxy of the seventeenth- or eighteenth-century Lutheran theologians. For example, the orthodox defense of elaborate music in worship in the seventeenth century (by theologians) was based on an appeal to a supposedly sharp difference between secular and spiritual music. But Bach adopts a huge variety of styles into his church music, including styles associated with nonchurch culture—dance music, for instance[19]—and mixes them very freely. That Bach could do this is probably due far more to what he held in common with his contemporary musician friends than with any leading theologian—a belief that music needs "space" to do its own kind of theological work.[20]

Further, we should not align Bach too closely with Lutheran Pietism—a strong reform movement within Lutheranism emerging in the second half of the seventeenth century, marked by a call to intense individual devotion and a strong belief that worship should be edifying and comprehensible in all its parts to a congregation and thus should be kept relatively lean and unfussy.[21] Bach experienced Pietism firsthand. He owned Pietist books in his library, and there are sentiments in his works (not least in the texts he uses) that are more typical of Pietism than of any other contemporary movement—for example, a severe awareness of sin in the believer[22] and the need for a direct and unmediated relation with Jesus.[23] However, it is generally agreed that Bach could not have been, as we might say today, a card-carrying Pietist.[24] Among other things, he would be unsympathetic to what could be a quite antiliturgical stance among Pietists, and it is unlikely a composer of his stature would align himself with a movement that could be so antipathetic to music without texts in worship.

Another part of the cultural furniture that Bach could not ignore was the German Enlightenment—a major intellectual and social movement of the late seventeenth and eighteenth centuries, one of whose chief marks was a new confidence in the power of scientific reason, as opposed to acceptance of authority, to discover the truth of things. Bach was not ignorant of these developments, though their significance for him can be overplayed.

Theology in Sound

With the pitfalls and contexts in mind, it is time to look at some music and do some theology.[25] We have space only for a brief exploration of two examples of Bach's "theology in sound," both of them first heard in 1724.

Jesus, der du meine Seele

The first is from his cantata *Jesus, der du meine Seele*,[26] written for the fourteenth Sunday after Trinity. The opening chorus meditates on the death of Jesus and the solace it can bring in the midst of our own suffering; the words are by the seventeenth-century poet Johann Rist.

> Jesus, by whom my soul,
> Through your bitter death

From the devil's dark cave
And heavy affliction of the soul,
Has been forcibly torn out,
And you have let me know this
Through your agreeable Word,
Be even now, O God, my refuge.

The sentiment is typically Lutheran: Christ's suffering and death on the cross has redeemed me; this has been conveyed to me in God's Word and can comfort me in my own suffering.

The bass line slides downward by chromatic steps, as if weighted from below.

etc.

Fig. 5.2: Cantata 78 (BWV78), *Jesus, der du meine Seele* (opening, bass line)

This descending theme is repeated over and over, appropriate to the intensity and relentlessness of Jesus's suffering, and ours. It is not limited to the bass line but permeates virtually every part of the texture, especially the chorus—very likely evoking the way in which suffering wholly engulfed Christ and can be pervasive in our lives.[27] The soprano (top line), however, is free from the suffering, singing not the downward-slipping chromatic line but a chorale melody (the congregational hymn tune for these words) and singing it, as it were, on behalf of the church (fig. 5.3).

Thus identical words—a plea to Christ as God in the midst of suffering—are given two interpretations concurrently: the one underlining the reality, seriousness, and pervasiveness of the sin of the world and the grief that Christ bore; the other, higher line reminding us and assuring us of the freedom that he has, through bearing our sorrows, made possible.

The pattern of keys is also drawn into the theological drama. Roughly halfway through the movement, words about Jesus's salvation are marked by a conspicuous harmonic shift to F major, from the predominantly minor chords of the first part (especially G minor). Here we find grammar, musical structure, and theology intricately interwoven. The words exploit the German syntax. The verb "torn out/pulled out" (*herausgerissen*)—speaking of the divine rescue that makes sense of the first part of the verse—does not appear until the fifth line; the crucial rescue word is delayed. Bach the musician catches this and amplifies it memorably through his change of key.

Just as striking is the extraordinary amalgamation of styles in this piece—something for which Bach is justly renowned. We do not have space here to trace each style, but a commentator sums up Bach's tour de force well:

Fig. 5.3: Cantata 78 (BWV78), *Jesus, der du meine Seele* (bars 17–25)

It is virtually impossible to imagine a grander, more comprehensive, more "universal" synthesis of historical and national styles than Bach has achieved in this movement—incorporating as it does elements of the secular as well as the sacred, the instrumental as well as the vocal; a movement whose frame of reference embraces both the Roman Catholic motet of the sixteenth century and the Lutheran chorale and whose procedures are indebted to the medieval cantus-firmus setting, the variation technique of the seventeenth-century passacaglia, and on to the modern Italian concerto and the French dance suite.[28]

This could hardly be a more appropriate indication of the universal scope and power of Christ's death, extending to all times, all people, and all places.

Es ist Vollbracht

From a cantata to one of the two most celebrated *Passions*. The climactic "It is finished!" of John's Gospel (19:30), Jesus's last words from the cross, takes us to the heart of Luther's crucifixion theology. Far from seeing the cross as a temporary downfall to be reversed by the victory of the resurrection, for Luther the crucifixion is victory; divine glory is focused *here*, in this repugnant, threatening, and puzzling death. Here evil has been endured and overcome, once and for all. Here is God's victorious love revealed in pathetic degradation, God's splendor in ignominy. *Deus absconditus*, as Luther used to say—"God hidden." God's glory revealed under its opposite; God's strength revealed in weakness, his wisdom in apparent folly. God and rejection; God and humiliation—here they can, do, and must go together, for this is how salvation is secured, completed, "finished."[29]

John's Gospel portrays the crucifixion as Jesus's "lifting up," the King's enthronement, the Son's glorification.[30] And in the *St. John Passion*, Bach projects it unflinchingly,[31] nowhere more so than in the alto aria that immediately follows Jesus's "It is finished!"

> It is finished!
> O comfort for the afflicted spirits.
> This night of woe,
> The final hour is passing slow before me.
> Victorious Judah's hero fights
> And ends the strife.
> It is finished!

The aria begins with a winding, haunting theme played by the viola da gamba, an instrument with a very distinctive, reedy sound, and in Bach's day an instrument on its way to obsolescence. This is the only time Bach uses this instrument in the whole of the *Passion*. It was strongly associated with French baroque court music, royalty, and wealth, as were the dotted style rhythms that appear in this aria.

Fig. 5.4: Aria "Es ist vollbracht," from *St. John Passion* (opening)

Yet the aria is marked "molto adagio" (very slow), and most of the notes are slurred with others, rather than being separated or separately articulated—uncharacteristic of the French style. Phrases sigh and fall, limping and almost halting—as with the expiring of a dying man. The atmosphere is unmistakably one of lament: kingly majesty in the midst of sorrow. As Marissen puts it: "Only on the page, which listeners do not see, does the music appear majestic. As Bach's music has it, then, Jesus's majesty is 'hidden' in its opposite."[32] The timbre of the da gamba also makes its own contribution. Wilfrid Mellers comments:

Fig. 5.5: Aria "Es ist vollbracht," from *St. John Passion* (bars 19–23)

"Its tone is heroic yet melancholy, rich yet purged; nothing could be more appropriate to the drooping phrases of this aria."[33]

The alto sings "It is finished" to a variation of the da gamba's theme, until an eruption in the midst of the aria brings another style, with all strings playing along with bassoon and continuo: *stile concitato* ("excited style"—rapidly repeated notes), associated in the Italian baroque with war. B minor lament has turned to D major, a key commonly linked to victory by Bach and his contemporaries. The falling and sighing of the da gamba is answered by the rising, battlelike fanfares. The soloist sings: "Victorious Judah's hero fights and ends the strife" (fig. 5.5).

The powers of evil have met their defeat at the cross; Christ has set the captives free. Yet this section closes with a diminished chord—the most unstable chord in Bach's armory—and resolves back into the lamenting music of the da gamba. Now, however, the lament is heard with the echoes of victory in the memory. The aria draws to a close with the words "Es ist vollbracht" sung over the final cadence.

Standing back a little, we find that this aria itself is set in the midst of a remarkable musical architecture, as if to highlight the centrality of Christ's death to God's victory.[34] It is surrounded by two recitatives and, in turn, two chorales. This structure, called "chiasmus," is very common in Bach.

No. 28   Chorale: "Er nahm alles"
No. 29   Recitative: "Und von Stund an"
No. 30   **Aria: "Es ist vollbracht"**
No. 31   Recitative: "Und neiget das Haupt"
No. 32   Chorale/aria: "Jesus, der du warest tot/Mein teurer Heiland"

If we stand a little farther back, another chiasmus comes into view:

No. 19   Arioso: "Betrachte, meine Seele"
No. 20   Aria: "Erwäge, wie sein blutgefärbter Rücken"
No. 24   Aria/chorus: "Eilt, ihr angefochtnen Seelen"
No. 30   **Aria: "Es ist vollbracht"**
No. 32   Aria/chorale: "Mein teurer Heiland/Jesus, der du warest tot"
No. 34   Arioso: "Mein Herz"
No. 35   Aria: "Zerfliesse, mein Herze"

We should note that the aria "Es ist vollbracht" is the only one that stands on its own in part 2 of the *Passion*; all the others are either linked directly to ariosos[35] or to choral music.

But the chiasmatic design does not stop there. If we take the solo items and all the chorales of part 2 of the *Passion* and lay them out in order, we find they can be arranged as follows (descending from top left, passing through no. 30 "Es ist vollbracht," and continuing from top right).

No. 15 Chorale		
No. 17 Chorale		No. 32 Chorale/aria
No. 19 Arioso		No. 34 Arioso
No. 20 Aria		No. 35 Aria
	No. 30 **Aria: "Es ist vollbracht"**	
No. 22 Chorale		No. 37 Chorale
No. 24 Chorus/aria		No. 39 Chorus
No. 26 Chorale		No. 40 Chorale
No. 28 Chorale		

Each vertical section is framed by chorales (the pairs 15 and 17, 26 and 28; and the single chorales 32 and 40), and each has its central chorale (22 and 37, respectively) framed by an arioso-aria pair and a chorus (19–20/24 and

34–35/39). In short, musically as well as theologically, everything centers on "It is finished."[36]

Significantly, Bach adds a memo of his own to John 19:30 in his Calov Bible: "Christ's Passion is the fulfilment of scripture and the accomplishment of salvation of humankind."[37]

Music, Words, and World

In these cases, of course, words are present. But what can we say about the theological power of music without texts?

It has been argued that in some of Bach's instrumental pieces, quite specific theological meanings can be discerned. Michael Marissen, for example, offers an intriguing theological reading of Bach's *Musical Offering* in relation to some leading themes in Lutheran theology.[38] But here I am more concerned with how, in Bach's outlook, and indeed from a contemporary perspective, his untexted music might be related to theological matters.

Let us pick up some of the threads from the last two chapters. We noted that in much writing about music in the course of the sixteenth and seventeenth centuries, music is tugged ever farther from its cosmological context—out of the grand Pythagorean universe. Accordingly, music increasingly needs a home, a way of validating and justifying it. One of the most common ways to do this was to interpret it in terms of, or link it to, human language. Vocal music was not the main challenge, since it already had words. By the seventeenth and eighteenth centuries, the supremacy of the "verbal paradigm" (as it has been called) meant that by far the majority of theorists in Europe regarded vocal music as superior to instrumental music. Instrumental music was the fly in the ointment, and many believed that it needed to be shown, at the very least, to work in languagelike ways for it to be properly "meaningful" to us. (We saw that Calvin shows himself very much a man of the modern age with his lack of interest in the cosmological tradition but his keenness—doubtless driven mainly by his convictions about the priority of the written and preached Word of God—to tie music to words.)

As we might expect, these shifts were bound up with the development of the natural sciences. In the course of the seventeenth century, musical sound is increasingly being related by theorists to the canons and findings of physics and physiology. By the time we reach the late seventeenth and early eighteenth centuries, the focus of attention is less on the nature of sound "out there" (and our responsibility to the order of sound as part of our responsibility under God to a wider harmony of creation) and far more on what music can do *to us* and *in us*, or—better—what *we can do in and to each other* through music. So for many writers, music comes to be seen as a rhetorical tool, akin to language but working according to physiological laws. One expression of this, as we shall see shortly, is the idea of music as a "language of the emotions," a means through which we can stimulate one another emotionally by virtue of bodily processes amenable to scientific investigation.[39]

Bach was composing at a time when all these issues were very much in the air, though how closely he followed the discussions in any detail is not clear. At any rate, there are good reasons to suppose he knew and was sympathetic to various alliances being made at the time between music and word. Significantly, however, he *also* seems alert to the more ancient cosmic tradition.[40] Let us take each in turn.

Bach and Rhetoric

By the time Bach was active as a composer, there was a fairly well-established tradition in baroque music theory of *musical rhetoric*. Initially, this looked back to ancient Greek and Latin understandings of rhetoric in language. Its proponents wanted to use spoken rhetoric not only to account for how musical compositions worked (especially in relation to texts) but also to establish good practice among composers.

The most important expression of this tradition has come to be known as *Figurenlehre*—the theory or doctrine of "figures."[41] Figures were devices that were thought to give music a greater rhetorical force, analogous to the embellishments orators use to make their speeches more persuasive and drive their points home. For some time composers had enjoyed illustrating textual ideas and words with musical figures. Now the practice assumes a new prominence. If you wanted to "say" something musically, you needed to know your figures.

How deeply Bach was acquainted with (or influenced by) the theoretical attempts to formulate musical rhetoric systematically is hard to say. Nevertheless, he could certainly link rhetorical devices and words in ways that are very much in keeping with his contemporaries. We have just seen one of the most common figures of his time: the falling bass line in "Jesus, der du meine Seele" (see above, fig. 5.2). Known as the *passus duriusculus*, this was stock-in-trade in baroque music as a symbol of lament, in the context of pain and suffering. Essentially the same notes appear in his twelfth cantata (BWV12) in the chorus "Weinen, Klagen, Sorgen, Zagen" ("Weeping, wailing, grieving, fearing")—underlining the distress of those who bear the mark of the crucified Jesus.[42] Most famously it appears in the continuo part of the "Crucifixus" of the *Mass in B Minor* to quite stunning effect (see fig. 5.6).

Some figures are very closely allied to the sounds of speech. Pairs of notes, very close in pitch, were thought to heighten a sense of sighing or lamenting— think of the sound of a sigh. The viola da gamba's sighing in "It is finished" is a good example (see above, fig. 5.4). Sometimes the figures could take the form of word-painting (*hypotyposis*). When Handel in *Messiah* sets "Glory to God in

Fig. 5.6: "Crucifixus," from *Mass in B Minor* (bars 5–9)

the Highest," he uses high, brilliant sounds; for "peace on earth" he uses low, subdued sounds. In Bach's *Mass in B Minor*, in the "Et in unum" we find the words *descendit de coelis* ("came down from heaven") set to a falling melody. Examples of this kind could be multiplied many times over. What we should not miss is that what drives this more than anything else is the assumed link between music and language. Not only did composers believe these devices worked like rhetorical gestures in speech but they also used the devices to drive home a meaning or emotion *already* conveyed by the words.[43]

Closely related to the theory of figures, but developing later, was the theory of affects (*Affektenlehre*), in which specific musical materials and forms—for example, styles, keys, instrumentation, meters, melodic shapes—were correlated with certain affects, or emotional states, such as sadness, hate, joy, and love.[44] The composer, it was thought, can move the affects (i.e., emotions) of the listener. This did not harden into one widely accepted scheme, but some techniques became very common: for instance, wide intervals between notes became associated with joy and confidence, the French overture style with a sense of stately grandeur, trumpets with triumph and elation.

It is not hard to detect such links in Bach. Trumpets, or trumpetlike music, frequently appear in the context of joy (the "Et Resurrexit" of the *Mass in B Minor*); oboes are often associated with love. Keys and key relationships can take on emotional energy and be used to theological effect.[45] D major becomes linked to majesty and splendor (again, the "Et Resurrexit" of the *Mass in B Minor*), E minor to grief and suffering (as in the *St. Matthew Passion*, where E minor plays a critical role). Earlier we saw that in "Jesus, der du meine Seele," language about Jesus's salvation is marked by a shift from minor to major. Again, we should not miss the very close links presumed here between music and the way words operate: indeed, affect theory depends on analogy with rhetoric in language—music can have emotional meaning and power in a way analogous to words; it is a language of the passions.[46]

Thus, as Calvin Stapert explains,

> Baroque composers, unlike those who came under the sway of Romanticism, did not feel a compulsion to be "original." This freed them to "speak" in the commonly understood musical parlance; they could compose with a fair amount of assurance that they would be understood by most of the audience. They were like orators, making use of whatever rhetorical tools they had available to capture the attention of their listeners and then to persuade them of the truth and move them to virtue.[47]

Bach and the Cosmos

Clearly, then, Bach knows and employs these rhetorical traditions. But the question will likely arise: did he believe musical sounds exercise their powers (rhetorical or otherwise) because they themselves have certain properties that are in some way built into the way God created the world? After all, even to claim that some musical sounds are akin to basic speech patterns is to say that music engages with our given bodily makeup, that is, that they transcend particular cultures and conventions.

As it happens, in Lutheranism between Luther and Bach at various times we find much sympathy for that ancient outlook, expressed in Christianized versions of the Great Tradition, in which music is seen as tapping into and bringing to sound the God-given order of the cosmos.[48] Among some church musicians, this current of thinking seems to have been quite lively; for example, when there was a felt need to defend the integrity of music against those who for various reasons were inclined to deny its inherent moral power.[49]

It is likely that Bach knew this stream and had some sympathy with it (though how interested he would have been in the theoretical and philosophical details is hard to determine).[50] There is, for example, a much-quoted saying attributed to Bach ("relatively securely")[51] about the "thoroughbass" (a foundational bass line with accompanying chords, very common in baroque music). It would be hard to overstress the importance of the thoroughbass for Bach. Music theorist Joel Lester goes so far as to say that Bach's "compositions in all genres . . . arise from varying and intensifying the musical materials that emanate from textures that themselves result from elaborations of thoroughbass progressions."[52] Bach refers to the thoroughbass as

> the most perfect foundation of music. It is played with both hands in such a way that the left hand plays the prescribed notes while the right adds consonances and dissonances so that a well-sounding harmony results for the glory of God and the permissible delight of the soul. And so the ultimate end or final purpose of all music and therefore also of the thorough-bass is nothing other than the praise of God and the recreation of the soul. Where this is not taken into account, then there is no true music (*eigentliche Music*), only a devilish bawling and droning.[53]

Note that these words come from a title page to a primer in thoroughbass, not a piece of texted music. Some see echoes here of the Pythagorean vision of well-ordered music embodying world harmony.[54]

Further evidence comes from Johann Abraham Birnbaum's response to an attack on Bach, likely reflecting the views of the composer himself. The critique, launched by Johann Adolf Scheibe in 1737, was that Bach's music was weighed down by an excess of human artifice and as a result sounded "turgid and confused"; it was simply too human, leading us "away from the natural to the artificial."[55] Acting as Bach's mouthpiece, Birnbaum speaks of "the eternal rules of music" and of polyphonous music as an exemplar of the unity and diversity pervading the cosmos.[56] It may be that some ideas prevalent in contemporary Enlightenment philosophy also came into play here about the laws of nature discovered by the scientist being the unalterable laws of God.[57] Also notable is Bach's membership from 1747 in a learned society, the Corresponding Society of the Musical Sciences. The leader of this select group, Lorenz Christoph Mizler, was especially keen to find a mathematical and philosophical basis for music and even wrote at one point: "What is art? An imitation of nature."[58] During the last years of his life, Bach wrote music very much in line with the ideas current in this circle, especially the notion of music as "sounding mathematics"—for example, the *Canonic Variations on "Vom Himmel hoch"* and, most famously, the *Art of Fugue*.[59]

In summary, we can be fairly confident that Bach believed the rules of music are not wholly dependent on culture, fashion, custom, individual taste, or even entirely on our human makeup but to some degree are also established by God in the created world at large, and it is part of the composer's vocation to respect and elicit them. If we are along the right lines, the upshot is that insofar as it shares in the world's harmony—a harmony that testifies to its Maker—music, for Bach, can glorify God in its own way, *even without texts*.

While continuing to direct cantatas and Passions in the Leipzig churches, [Bach] also directed the Collegium Musicum performances at Zimmermann's coffeehouse. And side by side with his work on such great secular works as the Goldberg Variations, Book II of the *Well-Tempered Clavier*, and *The Art of the Fugue*, we find him putting the finishing touches of his great Passions and chorale preludes, composing the Catechism Chorales of *Clavier Übung* III, and completing the *B Minor Mass*. Variations and chorales, fugues and Passions, *all say "Soli Deo Gloria."*[60]

Needless to say, in many quarters these days it is highly unfashionable to give very much weight to a composer's beliefs and intentions. To demonstrate what Bach might or might not have believed about his music does not of itself imply that such beliefs are correct. And as we are constantly reminded, there is no necessary connection between intention and outcome: "The road to hell is paved with authorial intention."[61] Further, it would be very unwise to suggest Bach would have recommended that all music be written with the express and conscious intention of tuning in, and tuning others in, to the world's God-given order or that the musical listener should be constantly thinking about mathematics or harmony, or even God.

Nonetheless, even if we set aside beliefs and intentions, some have held that the musical texts themselves invite a reading that is highly consonant with the view that music can bring to sound a Christian vision of the subtle and supple order of the cosmos. Unfortunately, some scholars have pursued this in ways that are theologically dubious in some respects.[62] But a recent author, David Bentley Hart, has managed to combine secure theology with acute comments on Bach's music in a way that extends the lines we are pursuing here.[63] For Hart, "Bach's is the ultimate Christian music; it reflects as no other human artefact ever has or could the Christian vision of creation."[64] Whether Bach can be singled out in quite so exalted a fashion is a moot point, since much of what Hart points to can be found in the work of other composers. Nevertheless, Hart highlights a number of features of Bach's music that for our purposes are striking. They are all rich with theological resonances and overtones and they can be found, in one way or another, in virtually all his music.

Hart points to *the way in which we are made to hear diversity as intrinsic to unity*. Bach's skill in deriving vast quantities of music from tiny musical units means that he can offer intense experiences of the simultaneous combination of extreme unity and extreme complexity. Even the unifying resolutions in his music rarely neutralize its richness: the reconciliation at the end of the "Dona Nobis Pacem" fugue that closes his *Mass in B Minor*, for example, does not compromise any of that work's immeasurable diversity. Indeed, Bach is adept at helping us perceive rich complexity *in* the apparently simple. In the *Goldberg Variations*, for example, we are given thirty variations on the bass line and chords of a lyrical and stately saraband. After an hour and a quarter of elaboration, Bach asks for the aria to be played at the end, *da capo*, note for note. Now we cannot hear it apart from the memory of all the variations in which it has been imagined. In other words, we now hear the aria *as* varied, replete with diversity. "It has acquired a richness, an untold profundity, of light and darkness, joy and melancholy, levity and gravity; it *is* all its ornamentation and change."[65]

Also, *Bach's elaborations are not subject to an abstract system or logic, a strict premusical idea*; the logic arises from the musical material itself, the character, and motion of the tones. With painstaking care, Laurence Dreyfus has shown that, whatever the precise order in which Bach composed a piece, it is generally inappropriate to envisage him starting with a fixed, precise, and unalterable form and then proceeding to fill it with music; rather, we would be better to understand him searching for material with rich potential and accordingly finding an appropriate form. In other words, this is an art in which the musical substance is not forced into strictly preconceived grids but structured according to the shapes that appear to be latent in it and thus apt for it.[66]

Further, Bach *demonstrates the potential boundlessness of thematic development*. In Christoph Wolff's words, "Characteristic of Bach's manner of composing is a way of elaborating the musical ideas so as to penetrate the material deeply. . . . [The principle of elaboration] determines like nothing else Bach's art and personal style."[67] (Indeed, Bach seems to have had an almost superhuman eye for how relatively simple sets of notes would combine, cohere, and behave in different groupings. His son, C. P. E. Bach, famously testified to how his father used to hear the main theme of a fugue played or sung by someone else, predict what would be done with it, and then elbow his son gleefully when he was proved right.)[68] A simple aria, such as that which starts the *Goldberg Variations*, or the even shorter opening material of the "Ciaccona" from the D minor Partita for solo violin, is, in effect, repeatedly reborn through breathtakingly elaborate variations, but without leaving any impression that the possibilities have been exhausted. The logic is open, the variations unmasterable, as if they were only examples from an infinite range of options.

Further still, we are provoked to hear the *simultaneous presence of radical openness and radical consistency*. Listen to almost any of Bach's unaccompanied pieces for violin, for example, and after a minute or so, press the pause button; it is often hard to predict what will come next. Its internal processes seem astonishingly contingent, free from the laws of necessity. Yet the music is gloriously coherent, full of sense. As Hart puts it, "Each note is an unforced, unnecessary, and yet wholly fitting supplement."[69] An 1805 review of the first edition of Bach's works for solo violin spoke of these pieces as "perhaps the greatest example in any art form of a master's ability to move with freedom and assurance, even in chains."[70] Regular constraint is combined with a kind of tingling, on-the-edge openness. The dynamic is one of constraint and contingency in contrast, interplay, and mutual enhancement. Indeed, much of Bach's music sounds improvised. This was one of the things about Bach that so intrigued the nineteenth-century composer and virtuoso Franz Liszt (1811–86)—who himself transcribed and arranged many of Bach's works[71]—and that captivates many jazz musicians. (It is no accident that Bach was a superb improviser.)

Hart believes that all this helps to open up a distinctively *trinitarian* account of the created world—and this links up with lines we shall be developing much more fully in part 3. The rich diversity to be found within creation's unity derives its "logic" from the irreducible difference within God himself. God is not one and *then* three; he is one as Father, Son, and Spirit from all eternity: "The trinitarian life is always already one of infinite musical richness."[72] The "logic" behind creation is not an abstract idea; creation is rather the result of God's own trinitarian love.[73] Unlike philosophical schemes in which God first creates "ideals" or "forms" and *then* creates the world, we need to affirm that creation is not the product of a principle or structure, but directly a gift of love. Hart rightly insists that "creation can never be understood, in Christian thought, simply as a text that conceals a more fundamental set of abstract meanings. . . . The 'theme' of creation is the gift of the whole."[74] The apparently limitless possibilities of creation's development speak of the utter boundlessness of the triune love, of the uncontainable and infinite "inventiveness" of the Holy Spirit at work in the world. The openness of creation likewise witnesses to the creativity of the Spirit, and creation's consistency, created and redeemed in Christ, is grounded in the reliable, loving order of God's own triune life.[75] Hart presses us further: a vision of the end of creation grounded in the Trinity is not that of one single note ringing into eternity, but "only more and greater harmony, whose developments, embellishments, and movement never 'return' to a state more original than music."[76]

Needless to say, far more space would be needed to justify this way of hearing Bach. But enough has been said to show that it is at least a reasonable reading, and, moreover, one that has historical propriety—that is to say, it would not have been fanciful to Bach himself.

We have, in effect, been pursuing the question: what kind of vision of the cosmos under God might this music stimulate us to imagine? Drawing on Hart in particular, I am suggesting the answer is something like this: a cosmos that reflects and shares in the life and love of a Triune God. And this is the vision we elaborate more fully in part 3.

We should note that along with this vision, in effect, comes a remarkable vision of creativity—again, something we shall say much more about in part 3. If Bach does elicit and bring to sound something of the divinely given order of the cosmos, it is through a process of active making, by means of an astonishing array of highly sophisticated techniques and a dazzling originality and novelty. What an engagement with Bach invites us to envisage is that these two dimensions—the rooting of music in given order and energetic creativity—need not work against each other. Significantly, Bach's obituary spoke of Bach's "ingenious and unusual ideas" *and* his extraordinary grasp of the "hidden secrets of harmony" without so much as a hint that the two need to be at odds.[77]

Bach in a Fracturing Culture

We have seen, then, that Bach is an artist sympathetic to the current traditions of musical rhetoric, and thus to the links between music and language, while at the same time sympathetic to ancient traditions that connect music to the cosmos at large. And we have seen that a good case can be made for hearing his music as bearing out such convictions—at the very least, his music provokes us to think about how music might be linked to the order of the God-given *world* as well as the order of the human *word.*

Bach stands at a critical juncture in Western music, when things that had been held together for centuries were fracturing. Much discussion about music among composers and theorists was molded by a series of antagonisms, tensions, and rivalries—especially between instrumental and vocal music (Italian instrumental versus French vocal), secular and sacred, church and court music (and, in time, concert music). And underneath them all was a waning of the conviction that music in some manner "tunes us in" to the cosmos at large, to a divinely given order to which we are responsible.

After Bach's death, these tensions and fractures proliferate. Instrumental music comes into its own; sonatas, symphonies, and chamber music fill the new purpose-built arena for music without texts—the concert hall. And this is where even Bach's church music migrates in time: today, you are just as likely (or more likely) to hear the *St. Matthew Passion* in a concert hall as in a church. As Joyce Irwin observes,

> [The] emerging trend toward independence of music from religion [was] . . . part of a large cultural change affecting all the arts. From the perspective of secularists it was the beginning of the emancipation of art from religion; for historians of worship, it was the beginning of the decline of liturgy. . . . The divisions between aesthetically-oriented and verbally-oriented worshippers did not originate or terminate during this period, but they reached a critical turning point.[78]

I am not for a moment suggesting we should bemoan all these developments. But what is so intriguing about Bach is that he seems remarkably untroubled by the splits and hierarchies that dogged so many contemporary discussions—he is content to combine secular and sacred styles, to write for church and court, to write vocal music for God's glory and see instrumental music as able to honor the Creator in its own way. His theological outlook is hospitable to both music and word, allowing both to make their contribution, and often together.

It may well be that we need something of this perspective in the contemporary musical climate, but we are unlikely to gain it unless we begin to rediscover the kind of vision of the world to which Bach's music would seem to be pointing us. Once again we are driven back to the doctrine of creation. But for more on this, we will have to wait until part 3.

three musical theologians

6

It is Christmas Eve. We are in the drawing room of a German middle-class home early in the nineteenth century. In the intimate glow of candles and lamps, a couple with their children have invited friends to share in the joy of the season. A sense of expectation and wonder embraces the house, suffused with love and joy. We see presents exchanged and enjoy gentle conversation interspersed with quiet laughter. And we hear music; the sounds of singing and playing mingle and overlap with speech.

Music and Feeling: Friedrich Schleiermacher

It is into such a scene that we are invited by Friedrich D. E. Schleiermacher (1768–1834), and, amid the warmth and conviviality, he asks us to consider music and its powers to expose the heart of true religion. Sometimes called "the father of modern theology," Schleiermacher "is to Christian theology what Newton is to physics, what Freud is to psychology, what Darwin is to biology."[1] Most Christians today have never heard of him; he set up no school and gathered no disciples. But he gave birth to a cast of mind, a way of thinking about the Christian faith that, in one form or another, has proved highly attractive and is anything but dead in today's church.

A man of extraordinary energy, Schleiermacher was a scholar-pastor, an ordained minister of the Reformed Church, and a distinguished academic, his most illustrious post being professor of theology at Berlin University. He was a prolific writer, erudite philosopher, political adviser, and stunning preacher (hundreds flocked to hear him). It is not surprising that by the time he died he had become an international figure—thousands lined the streets of Berlin to see the funeral cortege pass.

Schleiermacher is often regarded as quintessentially *modern* in that he sought to offer a vision of Christianity that was credible and practicable to a culture that had become increasingly suspicious of many of the traditional claims of orthodox faith. By the end of the eighteenth century, among the key challenges to Christian belief emerging in the intellectual world were the growth of modern historical study of the Bible (which seemed to call into question the accuracy of much of Scripture and thus undermine its authority), the advance of the natural sciences with their increasing confidence in scientific reason, and the beginnings of a serious understanding of non-Christian religions such that Christianity came more and more to be interpreted as but one instance of a much wider religious awareness. For Schleiermacher, any restatement of the Christian faith could not ignore these swirling currents of thought and the reactions they set in motion.

What is especially prominent in Schleiermacher, and came to color so much theology of the years to come, was what is sometimes called "the anthropological turn"—the signs of which we have already seen in earlier chapters. Put very simply, in the search for what is authentically and reliably true, we are urged in the first instance to turn to our own immediate experience and perceptions—in religion as much as any other sphere. Religion cannot be justified simply by appealing to some external authority supposedly linked directly to God—such as nature, the Bible, or the church—but chiefly by turning to what is fundamentally and primordially human.

Religion at Christmas

The scene with which I started the chapter opens Schleiermacher's charming *Christmas Eve: Dialogue on the Incarnation*.[2] Written in 1805 when he was thirty-seven,[3] during what is usually seen as the middle period of his intellectual development, it is the nearest Schleiermacher comes to an extended essay on music. Conveniently for us, it also serves as a fine entrée to Schleiermacher's theology. Although he has not yet produced his finest and most developed work, the main lines of thinking here are very consistent with what was to come later, so much so that one commentator has described *Christmas Eve* as "perhaps the most pleasant and painless introduction to the fundamental theological shift that [Schleiermacher] brought about."[4]

That music and theology come together in this book is not accidental. Though Schleiermacher was a pianist and singer of only modest ability, music came to be immensely important to him.[5] Not only do musical analogies and metaphors abound in his writings, but also music is given a quite distinctive religious significance: "it is precisely to the religious feeling that music is most closely related."[6] Let us return to the drawing room to see why.

Eduard, Ernestine, and their children have gathered with friends on Christmas Eve. We are introduced to their precocious ten-year-old, Sophie, who has been given a present in the form of a book of music. A singer and pianist, Sophie "knew how to treat each note aright; her touch and phrasing made each chord sound forth . . . in its own measured strength until it too, like a holy kiss, gives way to the next."[7] In due course she asks that she be allowed to contribute her own Christmas gift to the others. She is not only musical but also fervently devout, and she presents an illuminated Christmas nativity scene, complete with running water, decorations, and Christian symbols. She, her father, and others go through to the music room to sing hymns and chorales.

> Soon the whole company had become their reverent audience. And when they had finished, all remained still, as so often happens with religious music, in a mood of inner satisfaction and retirement. The reaction was followed, however, by a few silent moments in which they all knew that the heart of each person was turned in love toward all the rest and toward something higher still.[8]

Later one of the invited friends, a lawyer and critical rationalist named Leonhardt, wonders aloud: Is it healthy for a child Sophie's age to be quite so devout, to prefer hymn singing and Bible stories to games and toys? "Watch out, my friends. If you don't put a check to this behavior her life is going to go awry."[9] Her parents are quick to defend her. Looking back over the evening, Eduard reflects:

> I feel overflowing with the joy of pure serenity, which I think could withstand anything that might happen to me. . . . A full consciousness of this mood, however, and an apt appreciation of it, I feel I owe in part to the fact that our little one has invited us to express it in music. For every fine feeling comes completely to the fore only when we have found the right musical expression for it. Not the spoken word, for this can never be anything but indirect—a plastic element, if I may put it that way—but a real, uncluttered tone. And it is precisely to religious feeling that music is most closely related. . . . What the word has declared, the tones of music must make alive, in harmony conveying it to the whole inner being of its hearers and holding it fast there."[10]

In the course of the evening, the friends find themselves discussing the true nature of piety and the essence of Christmas celebration. A disparity between the men and the women emerges. Three of the women each offer a story from a Christmas in their own past. Another, Friederike, announces: "I will station myself at the piano, and improvise on your narratives. In this way you can also hear something from me with your finer, heightened ear for music."[11] For the women, the center of the Christmas celebration is seen in the mother-child relationship of Mary and Christ; it is later summed up by one of the men:

Every mother who, profoundly feeling what she has done in bearing a human being, knows . . . that the Spirit of the church, the Holy Spirit, dwells within her. . . . Such a woman also sees Christ in her child—and this is that inexpressible feeling a mother has which compensates for all else. And in like manner each one of us beholds in the birth of Christ his own higher birth whereby nothing lives in him but devotion and love; and in him too the eternal Son of God appears. . . . And this is the very glory of the festival, which you wished also to hear me praise.[12]

The women having finished, one of the men, Ernst, declares: "I think we men owe the ladies something in return." But since "storytelling is not the gift of men,"[13] he suggests they offer discourses, or short lectures. And so they get embroiled in a highbrow debate about the incarnation—the reliability of the Gospels, the historical Jesus, the meaning of redemption, and so forth—hardly the sort of thing likely to liven up a party. As the third concludes, he notices that a late guest has arrived, Josef, and it is to him that Schleiermacher gives the last word. (Some commentators think this is Schleiermacher himself walking, Hitchcock-like, into his own story.)[14]

Josef is dismayed at the way the evening has turned, and he urges them to bring Sophie back in. He wants to draw them all back to the joy of new life and fellowship in Christmas, which no words can encompass but which music is well suited to express. His words are worth quoting at length:

I have not come to deliver a speech but to enjoy myself with you; and I must quite honestly say that it seems to me odd, almost folly even, that you should be carrying on with such exercises; however nicely you may have done them. . . . Your evil principle is among you again: this Leonhardt, this contriving, reflective, dialectical, superintellectual man. No doubt you have been addressing yourselves to him; for your own selves you would surely not have needed such goings on and wouldn't have fallen into them. . . . Now just think what lovely music [the women] could have sung for you, in which all the piety of your discourse could have dwelt far more profoundly. Or think how charmingly they might have conversed with you, out of hearts full of love and joy. Such would have eased and refreshed you differently, and better too, than you could possibly have been affected by these celebratory addresses of yours!

For my part . . . all forms are too rigid, all speech-making too tedious and cold. Itself unbounded by speech, the subject of Christmas claims, indeed creates in me a speechless joy, and I cannot but laugh and exult like a child. Today all men are children to me, and are all the dearer on that account. . . . Come, then, and above all bring the child [Sophie] if she is not yet asleep, and let me see your glories, and let us be glad and sing something religious and joyful![15]

And with this exhortation to song, Schleiermacher's dialogue ends.

Despite the amiable atmosphere, it is hard not to notice the very sharp contrasts being drawn. The musically gifted and pious Sophie is set against the reflective, analytical, intellectual men. Her piety is unforced, spontaneous; her sentiments "come quite naturally"[16] and have "emerged from within" rather than having been "acquired."[17] When Leonhardt presses Sophie as to why she delights in music and piety, her mother interrupts: "I don't think you will get much further with her, Leonhardt. She isn't at all accustomed to sorting out her experiences."[18] Sophie reveals the true nature of piety, for she speaks and acts directly from her immediate awareness. Such is the childlike character of the true believer. "Well," remarks the vivacious Karoline, "She has clearly shown us . . . what that childlike attitude is without which one cannot enter into the kingdom of God. It is simply to accept each mood and feeling for itself and to desire only to have them pure and whole."[19] While Leonhardt is identified as "the evil principle," Sophie embodies kingdom life. While Leonhardt represents learning, Sophie's feeling is marked by "a deep and basic understanding."[20] The women and the men display a similar contrast: the former tell stories, play and sing beautiful music, and penetrate intuitively to the heart of things, while the men give boring speeches. Noticeable too are the contrasts between songs expressing inward piety, on the one hand, and dull and frigid discourses, on the other, between lively and expressive stories and inflexible reasoning.

The very genre Schleiermacher uses is in accord with this. This is not a treatise on the incarnation, a set of abstract pronouncements, but a short story that draws us into an enchanting domestic setting, resonant with the elated love Schleiermacher believes lies at the heart of Christmas. *Christmas Eve*, then, presents us with a portrayal of genuine religion as Schleiermacher saw it, the heart of which is accessed not through heady theoretical reflection, intellectual analysis, and the dissecting spirit of the male mind but through the direct, spontaneous perceptions of a ten-year-old, the intuition of women, and, not least, through the experience of music.

Schleiermacher's Religious Vision

At this point it is worth standing back a little and gaining a wider view of the author's concerns and the way he developed them in the years following *Christmas Eve*. In many ways, Schleiermacher was a man struggling to hold together what so many have failed to hold together in modern times: loosely speaking, piety and intellect, heart and head. Schleiermacher was born in 1768 and brought up in a fervent, evangelical home; his father was a minister of the Reformed Church of Prussia. When very young, Schleiermacher was deeply affected by the warm devotion of the Moravians, who stressed the need for a heartfelt love of Jesus and the availability of direct access to God through him. Somewhere in his early years Schleiermacher began to have doubts about some of the central beliefs of conservative Protestantism (much to the dismay of his father), not least the theory of atonement known as penal substitution. Breathing the air of the Enlightenment during his student years, he drifted further and further from contemporary Protestant orthodoxy, without ever abandoning his deep passion for Jesus. Later as an ordained minister, he was deeply affected by the Romantic movement. Impressed with its reaction to what it saw as the cold rationalism of Enlightenment philosophy, Schleiermacher mixed with some of its leading figures. He warmed to their fascination with the imagination, immediate intuition and feeling, and, indeed, their high regard for music.

The result of this turbulent mix was that he became convinced of the need to persuade his skeptical contemporaries, many of whom had become disdainful of religious faith, that religion was quite different from what they supposed. He longed to commend religion to the "cultured despisers" of his day but in a way that took their suspicions seriously. Religion, he argued, was not rooted in *knowing*: there was little point in trying to prove Christian faith by appealing to reason or to imagine that religious belief was essentially about assenting to creedal propositions. Nor should we think of religion (as some of his contemporaries were suggesting) chiefly as a matter of morality, of *doing*. We will not find the true depth of religion in a set of actions or rules, prescriptions, and codes. Rather, religion is concerned with the infinite, universal wholeness of things. And it concerns a level of human existence lying deeper than knowing or acting—the level of immediate self-consciousness or *feeling* (*Gefühl*). The heart of religion is the *immediate consciousness of all finite things being held in and through the infinite*.[21] In his massive *Christian Faith* (1821–22, 1830–31), Schleiermacher expands on this by speaking of a universal "feeling of absolute dependence" that we all share, which is equivalent to "God-consciousness," an awareness of being in relation to the infinite on which we depend absolutely.[22]

It is easy to misunderstand this. By *Gefühl*, Schleiermacher does not mean merely an emotion. Feeling includes emotion, but it is wider and deeper, for it is a profound sense of the *whole* of us being in relation to the infinite. Moreover, when he speaks of a "feeling of absolute dependence," he is not claiming only that we are all aware of God but that we are all aware of being dependent on God. To claim simply that we are all conscious of God would be to imply that God is some kind of object quite external to ourselves that could, in principle, be considered with a cool and detached mind. For Schleiermacher, it makes no sense to speak of being aware of the infinite apart from a deep-rooted sense of *being dependent on* the infinite. Self-awareness and God-awareness belong together.

We should note the marked inner turn at work here, a preference in much of Schleiermacher's writing for the inward life of piety in contrast to the outer interests of human reason. "You must transport yourselves into the interior of a pious soul and seek to understand its inspiration. . . . I ask . . . that you turn from everything usually reckoned religion, and fix your regard on the inward emotions and dispositions, as all utterances and acts of inspired men direct."[23] Schleiermacher is not commending a religion with no place for the mind. Far from it. He held theology in high esteem and believed it must have its own appropriate intellectual rigor. But theology's first port of call, he insisted, is the life of piety, the religious self-consciousness in action, this primordially human sense of being in relation to the infinite and the way it finds manifold expressions. And in the case of Christian theology, this means the piety of the church, the piety exemplified in Sophie and celebrated by Josef.

For Schleiermacher, then, we are all inherently religious. The claim "I'm not religious" is ultimately vacuous because, if only they will realize it and develop it, at root all human beings have this immediate feeling of absolute dependence that characterizes true religion and that must be nurtured and cultivated for full human flourishing.

Music and Religion

In this primordial religious consciousness, Schleiermacher believed he had found the key to commending religion to his age, making it credible to a European culture increasingly skeptical of Christianity in its traditional forms. He was nothing if not ambitious. In *The Christian Faith* Schleiermacher undertook nothing less than a reworking of the entire gamut of Christian theology, relating every major theme of Christianity to the sense of absolute dependence, specifically as it is found in the corporate piety of the church. We cannot enter into the details of this majestic project here. But we can at least see something of how music finds its place within the outlook expounded in this and Schleiermacher's other works.

Music is given a crucial place among the arts.[24] We have already seen how prominent it is in *Christmas Eve*, which deals with the birth at the heart of Christian faith. Why is it given such a key place? Quite simply because *music has particular powers to open up and express that dimension of human experience that Schleiermacher identifies as distinctively religious.*[25]

There are a number of aspects to this intertwining of music and religion to highlight. First, *music does not speak in words.* From a religious point of view this is not a weakness, for music can tap directly into and give expression to that feeling that by its very nature outstrips what we can do with words. We recall Eduard's assertion that "every fine feeling comes completely to the fore only when we have found the right musical expression for it. Not the spoken word, *for this can never be anything but indirect—a plastic element, if I may put it that way*—but a real, uncluttered tone. *And it is precisely to religious feeling that music is most closely related.*"[26] That is why Eduard believes that we can well dispense with particular words in church music, but not with the singing itself.

> A Miserere, a Gloria, or a Requiem: what special words are required of these? Their very character conveys plenty of meaning and suffers no essential change even though accompanying words may be replaced with others, so long as they fit the timing of the music; and this is true no matter what the language. Indeed,

no one would say that anything of gross importance was lost even if he didn't get the words at all.[27]

In line with this is Josef's plea, against the word-bound men, for the "speechless joy" that Christmas, "unbounded by speech," generates.[28] For Schleiermacher, music is a more basic medium of religious expression than words. It is (to borrow a line from Van Morrison) the "inarticulate speech of the heart."[29] As Karl Barth puts it (with a wry smile), "Words stand opposed to all which Schleiermacher understands as the genuine article of Christmas. . . . How fortunate that when we are disturbed and oppressed by the problems of words we can flee to the realm of music and a musical Christianity!"[30]

Connected with this, while in a sense music may "speak," it does not do so in the concepts we use when we know something through our rational intellects. Barth captures this well: "*Exactly because of its lack of concepts*, music is the true and legitimate bearer of the message of Christmas, the adequate expression for the highest and final dialectical level, a level attainable by singing, by playing on flute and piano."[31]

Second, music for Schleiermacher is the most *inward* of the arts and, because of this, the art most related to our immediate self-consciousness. Music is concerned with the inner world of self-awareness, as distinct from the merely outward. Its "true content is the great chords of our inner nature."[32] Sophie's disposition can be attributed only to "that inner something which takes hold of the child so strikingly [and] has no opportunity to attach itself upon anything merely external."[33]

Third, hearing or listening to music, as with religious experience, is essentially a *receptive* matter. It is not concerned with ordering, organizing, and calculating. It is prior to, and deeper than, making something happen or willing something to happen. Hence the praise for Sophie's youthful, uncluttered receptivity, which Schleiermacher was later to call "the feeling of absolute dependence."[34]

Fourth, music is also religiously significant for Schleiermacher because it offers access to a *universal* plane of experience beneath or underlying *particular* things. Eduard argues that Christianity gives sacred music just enough reference to specific things to be intelligible, yet "without being tied to some mere contingency." For one of the women, it is a *singing* piety "which ascends most gloriously and directly to heaven" because "nothing peculiar or accidental restrains either [singing or piety] . . . never does music weep or laugh over particular circumstances, but always over life itself."[35] This, she suggests, is also the attitude of true piety: it does not rejoice and mourn over the particular, only the universal.

Fifth, another feature that musical experience shares with religious self-consciousness (though Schleiermacher does not bring this out explicitly in *Christmas Eve*) is the way in which musical sounds enter and permeate us. I have touched on this earlier.[36] In the case of what we see, we can shut our eyes.

But we do not have earlids. Musical experience is an experience of permeation, sounds internalize themselves in us—in body and mind—whether we want them to or not. The authentic religious experience, likewise, is not the experience of an object we can shut out at will but of the permeation of our being by the infinite.

Attractions and Questions

If Schleiermacher gave birth to an outlook on religion that has proved long-lasting, the same goes for his account of music, which finds many parallels in current thinking about music. Why might his approach to music be especially appealing in our own day?

At a general level, Schleiermacher will appeal to those who intuitively sense there is some kind of essential kinship between music and religious experience. And, as I said in the introduction, the signs are that this is a widely held perception today. To be more specific: Schleiermacher will be attractive to those who feel acutely the inadequacy of words in speaking of the experience of music. I have a label attached to a key ring that carries a saying attributed to Hans Christian Andersen: "Where words fail, music speaks." Music seems to speak with colossal power, yet our attempts to express *what* it says are usually feeble. And this would seem to explain at least part of the profound kinship between music and religion in history. Religious matters are ineffable: "I can't *say* what I believe or why I believe it, but at a deeper level I have an unmistakable sense of the divine." Further, Schleiermacher will prove appealing to those suspicious of doctrine, those who long for a kind of religion that is less about assenting to dogma and more about the kind of compelling, self-involving experience we often associate with music. For Schleiermacher, although doctrine does arise from reflection on religious feeling, it is not the essence of religion. Only by penetrating to the level of religious consciousness will doctrines come alive, and music has the potential to take us to this deeper level. Further still, Schleiermacher will attract those who wish to relate music to a broad understanding of religious experience. In a multifaith world, to those convinced that discussion of music and religion must not be confined to one particular tradition or, indeed, to organized religion, Schleiermacher's evocation of a common religious awareness not limited to the particularities of time, place, and culture will have much to commend it.

Having said all this, Schleiermacher's alliance of music and religion is open to some serious and searching questions. From the theological side, as we might expect, the most common charge against Schleiermacher is that some of the specifics of Christian faith are in danger of being smothered and distorted by an all-consuming category of religious experience. Certainly, to his dying day Schleiermacher saw himself as a Christian theologian. But many have doubted that he can do full justice to the particularity and finality of Christ, even if he did hold that we require Jesus to assume us into the power of his perfect God-consciousness to be redeemed from sin. In *Christmas Eve* the center of gravity is not a specific birth in the past, a particular happening with decisive significance for the entirety of space and time.[37] What we celebrate at Christmas above all is an experience today—the joy of motherly love, which embodies divine love; the elation of the infinite power of new, untroubled life; the heightened existence in which humanity comes to self-consciousness and fulfillment—in short, the church's experience of redemption.[38] (The particularity of Jesus may seem a marginal issue for us in this book; it is in fact crucial, as we shall see later in part 3.)

Similar things could be said of God's relation to humanity. It is quite proper to insist with Schleiermacher that awareness of God and self-awareness belong together, but only if at some stage we have some convincing means of distinguishing what is *merely* self-consciousness from consciousness of God. What seems so compromised in Schleiermacher is the free agency of God, the notion that God might act to do something particular that we could not anticipate, that God might challenge and even defy some of what we might readily take to be our natural or given innate religious awareness. Critics of Schleiermacher have understandably observed that the "feeling of absolute dependence" does not easily resonate with the biblical notion of responsive fellowship with a personal Creator who, as utterly free and other than the world, can give himself graciously and supremely in Jesus Christ to be the focus of devotion and love.[39]

These problems are not unrelated to Schleiermacher's treatment of music. The heady aroma of Romanticism is not hard to detect. This is pivotal for us to grasp, since so much thinking about music and religion today has been deeply affected by the romantic mood evident in Schleiermacher. In the last chapter, we saw how Bach was living at a time when music, in one way or another, was being aligned with language. Very often a particular model of language was being assumed—that language represents preexisting things in the way a picture might represent or imitate a landscape. With the emergence of the Romantics in the last two decades of the eighteenth century, this view of language—at least as a controlling or all-embracing theory—was in various ways questioned. Indeed, Schleiermacher himself was one of the key questioners. We now find a stress among some on language as *shaping* or constructing what we choose to call "reality." And especially prominent is a sense of the limits of language, not least when it comes to dealing with religious and theological truth.

In his *Aesthetics*, Schleiermacher insists that music is not a referential or representational art: it does not point or refer to extramusical states of affairs, nor can it paint pictures. But we need not worry, he believes, for this makes it all the stronger when it comes to religion. It is wonderfully able to articulate the wordless stirrings of immediate self-consciousness that lie at the heart of religious experience. (We should bear in mind that this is the age when instrumental music proliferates as never before—in the sonatas and symphonies of Haydn and Mozart, for example, and the early symphonies of Beethoven.)

From the Romantics' perspective, we find music being hailed as the art that, as J. N. Forkel expresses it, "begins . . . where other languages can no longer reach."[40] Music without words becomes for many Romantics the highest and most expressive art form, able to convey what can never be expressed in words and concepts. Its movements share in, and bring to sound, not only individual religious feelings but the infinite life of all things that underlie all religious experience and in which the individual's feelings participate. To be fair, Schleiermacher himself was suspicious of a "religion of art" (or music). But many of his contemporaries were less cautious. For E. T. A. Hoffmann, instrumental music, stripped of external trappings such as words, becomes a means of "striving for inner spirituality," for the divine life that resides within. A few years after *Christmas Eve* appeared, Hoffmann wrote in a famous review of Beethoven's Fifth Symphony: "Music opens the door for us to an unknown realm; a world that has nothing in common with the outer world of the senses that surrounds us, one in which we can leave behind all feelings defined by concepts and give ourselves over to the ineffable."[41] Compare Ludwig Tieck in 1822: "Flowing out of every tone is a tragic and divine enthusiasm which redeems every listener from the limitations of earthly existence."[42]

Such ideas certainly did not die with the Romantics. They were developed with colossal power by philosophers such as Arthur Schopenhauer (1788–1860). When Israel Knox summarizes Schopenhauer's philosophy of music, he brings to a head tendencies in the entire romantic stream: "Music peals forth the metaphysics of our own being, the crescendo, the climax, the crisis, the resolutions, of our own striving, impetuosity, peace, and the retardations and accelerations, the surging and passivity, the power and silence of things."[43]

In the introduction, we spoke of currents in contemporary thinking about music that give it a similar religious glow.[44] But for all its appeal, this outlook on music carries with it massive drawbacks, and we have touched on some of them already. Need we assume such a hard-and-fast distinction between musical and intellectual experience? Does music's theological value have to be so divorced from rational knowing? What kind of checks do we have against the idolatry of music? How can we distinguish adequately between encountering the divine and what is no more than an intensely emotional experience conveyed through music?

In addition, there are crucial questions to ask about music and words in this stream of thinking. It may well be that music is stubbornly resistant to being grasped in words. And it may well be that this reminds us of the inability of words to "capture" God and of music's unique powers. But the point can easily be overplayed, especially if music and words are treated as if they are of radically different orders, or if it is suggested that there is a realm of Christian experience that is not in any way responsible to words, to which music can somehow transport us. In the Christian tradition words are not akin to a rocket that gets us into orbit, to be jettisoned once we are enjoying the divine space. Rather, God has graciously used human words as part of the way he has revealed himself; they have become *part of the action*, and to these words we are constantly answerable, even if we recognize that they (like any words) cannot "contain" the things of God (and that there are times when it is proper to be silent). The words of Scripture, and above all the words of Jesus—the words of the Word made flesh—provide the primary criteria of truth for all Christian claims. There never comes a time when we can absolve ourselves of responsibility to these words. And in turn, more words will be needed to explore and pass on the Good News that these words tell. Simply put: though words cannot hold God, through words God can hold us. It is one thing to say words cannot capture or enclose the realities of which they speak and that music has its own ways of accessing those realities; it is quite another to suggest that words by their nature are to be treated as ultimately dispensable, to be superseded by the supposedly "superior" medium of music.[45]

We have strayed a little beyond Schleiermacher to highlight some of the dangers of the broader streams with which he was associated. But that he pushes us to think about these questions in depth is a measure of his greatness. Whatever our final estimate of the theologian himself, he gives potent expression to an approach to music that has proved very resilient; he needs to be taken with utmost seriousness. And in the twentieth century, few acknowledged the greatness of Schleiermacher more than the man who next claims our attention.

Music, Mozart, and God: Karl Barth

> I even have to confess that if I ever get to heaven, I would first seek out Mozart, and only then inquire after Augustine, St. Thomas, Luther, Calvin, and Schleiermacher.
>
> Karl Barth[46]

Revolutionaries are relatively rare in theology, but even his fiercest critics would have to admit that Karl Barth (1886–1968) deserves the epithet. No other twentieth-century theologian has had his impact. In effect, he set out to reorganize the entire discipline of theology, and in a way that is quite impossible to ignore or dismiss. One writer describes his theology as "massive in scale and impressive in architecture, catholic in scope and protestant in perfection"[47]—an intimidating description, but fitting for Barth's vast output and influence.

Barth, the son of a Swiss Reformed minister, gained his university education in Germany. He served as a pastor and from 1921 worked as an academic, first in Germany and from 1935 in Basel, where he remained until he died. It was especially during his years as a pastor in the little Swiss industrial town of Safenwil that Barth came to believe that much of the theology that had flowered in the nineteenth century, and in which he had been reared, had little future. In particular, he became deeply suspicious of any theology that sought to identify the supposed upward progress of "Christian" civilization with the work of the Holy Spirit and, with this, any theology that trivialized or downplayed the darker side of human nature or spoke of some innate human capacity to do good without God. Any assumption that God was simply "given" in what were assumed to be the highest ethical and spiritual values of humankind was anathema to him. Theology cannot be built on the belief in some supposed inner purity of human beings, nor on human inwardness (as with Schleiermacher);[48] theology must rather focus attention rigorously on the way God has actually shown himself to be, which means a resolute attention to God's self-presentation in the person and work of Jesus Christ.

Several elements of this need to be highlighted. According to Barth, we must take with utter seriousness the *Godness of God*—the otherness and the freedom of the Creator. There can be no confusion of God and the created world or God's Spirit and the human spirit and no suggestion that God is bound to the world by some necessity. Nevertheless, this radically other God has not remained mute but has spoken supremely in Jesus Christ, the Word made flesh. God has come in Jesus Christ to claim us as friends and partners, in a way that brings both judgment and mercy. In his mature work, one of Barth's most characteristic emphases is a rigorous concentration on the person of Jesus Christ. It is *in Jesus Christ* that *God's very self has been made known*. Jesus acts out who God is. And the God so revealed is trinitarian through and through; there is no God "behind the back" of the God who reveals himself as Father, Son, and Spirit, no God behind the one who reveals himself as Trinity. Further, in Christ, God has revealed himself *in a reconciling act*—to know God is not to contemplate or consider an inert object but to be changed, transformed, and renewed as we are reconciled to the Father through the Son in the Spirit. Further still, Jesus Christ reveals what it is to be *truly human*—if we are to find out who we are and what we are to be, our ultimate orientation must be to one person, and one person above all others: Jesus Christ, the new Adam.[49]

And where might music find a home in this theologically rich and uncompromising worldview?[50] Throughout his life Barth had an infectious love of music, playing both the piano and violin as well as singing with a fine baritone voice, and he devoted an extended essay to Schleiermacher's *Christmas Eve*.[51] But it is his extravagant devotion to Mozart, amounting almost to an obsession, that is especially striking. He recalls a childhood experience of hearing his father playing on the piano "Tamino mein, o welch ein Glück" from Mozart's *The Magic Flute*. It "thrilled me through and through," Barth recalled, and he mentally noted at the time: "He's the one!"[52] In Barth's adult life, Mozart's music found a place along with his daily prayers. His library included extensive literature on the composer, and in 1956, the two hundredth anniversary of Mozart's birth, he became deeply involved in the festivities, declaring the year more meaningful for this celebration than for the fact it included his own seventieth birthday. He attended many performances of Mozart.

> In one concert at the Basel Musiksaal, at which Clara Hackil was playing the F Major [Piano] Concerto [K.413], I even had a sudden vision of him standing there in front of the piano, so clear that I almost began to cry. That's quite a story isn't it—such a story that even [the Swiss Roman Catholic theologian] Balthasar with his mystical experiences listened respectfully when I told him. At any rate, I know just what Mozart looked like in the last year of his life.[53]

Why this fixation on Mozart? Why did Barth believe this composer deserved a central place in theology, "especially in the doctrine of creation and also in eschatology"?[54] Why was he so certain that when the angels praise God *en famille* they play Mozart and God listens with special pleasure?[55]

As a good entry point to answering that question, we can turn to Barth's treatment of Mozart in volume 3 of his massive *Church Dogmatics*.[56] In a fulsome eulogy to Mozart, he claims that Mozart's music embodies and gives voice to creation praising God, and creation precisely *as* created—limited and finite. This appears in the midst of a discussion of the "shadowside" (*Schattenseite*) of creation. Here it is not entirely clear as to what this shadowside is, but comparison with a later passage[57] makes it probable that he is thinking of finitude and all its effects (including death): leaves fade, humans die, planets burn up, the universe ends.

The shadowside is not evil (*das Nichtige*). God gives things limits, and this is part of their created goodness.[58] It is what God intended from the beginning. Genuine praise can arise only when things and people know they are not God, that they are finite and bounded. In this context, Mozart's music making is presented as a wonderful example of a created person singing praise to God and producing music that sings praise to God in a way that does not try to step out of the limits of this world in a bid for divinity. What does it matter if Mozart died in misery like an "unknown soldier," Barth asks, "when a life is permitted simply and unpretentiously, and therefore serenely, authentically and impressively, to express the good creation of God, *which also includes the limitation and end of man*?"[59] Mozart heard the harmony of creation in which "the shadow is not darkness, deficiency is not defeat, sadness cannot become despair, trouble cannot degenerate into tragedy and infinite melancholy is not ultimately forced to claim undisputed sway."[60] Mozart even acknowledged the limit of death, according to Barth. But Mozart heard even this negative only in and with the positive: in his music, creation praises God *in its very limits, in its finitude,* and in that way it demonstrates authentic praise.

Confirming this, later Barth speaks of the difference between shadowside and evil, when the creature "crosses the frontier" of finitude[61] and tries to outreach itself and play at being God. This is just what Mozart's music does not do, according to Barth. Nor does Mozart: he does not obtrude himself in some "mania for self-expression,"[62] or try to force a message on the listener. He does not "*will* to proclaim the praise of God. He just does it—precisely in that humility in which he himself is, so to speak, only the instrument with which he allows us to hear what he hears: what surges at him from God's creation, what rises in him, and must proceed from him."[63] "He simply offered himself as the agent by which little bits of horn, metal and catgut could serve as the voices of creation."[64] This, for Barth, is what gives Mozart's music its "freedom," its effortless and light quality.[65] It does not take itself too seriously. To pick up a phrase we shall use later, according to Barth, Mozart's music "voices creation's praise," refusing any attempt to be divine.[66]

This can be filled out further if we turn to Barth later in the *Dogmatics*, in which he speaks of parables of God's kingdom in the world at large.[67] Barth claims that Jesus Christ can bear witness to himself and his reconciling work by calling forth parables, not only in the Bible and the church, but in places where Christ is not named. These "secular parables" are not to be confused with Christ; they *point to* Christ, testify to who he is and what has happened in him. And Christ alone has the capacity to call them forth. Barth does not give specific examples here, but it makes very good sense to see music as one such parable. Indeed, David Moseley has convincingly argued that Mozart is the unnamed figure haunting these discussions.[68] The matter is clinched in another place where Barth is quite explicit about the link: "I am not . . . inclined to confuse or identify salvation history with any part of the history of art. But the golden sounds and melodies of Mozart's music have always spoken to me not as gospel but as parables of the realm of God's free grace revealed in the gospel—and they do so again and again with great spontaneity and directness."[69] It would seem, then, that for Barth, Mozart's music embodies the freedom of creation praising God as it should and, by analogy and implication, the freedom that the gospel brings.

We should be quite clear: Barth is not for a moment trying to "prove" God's existence through music, whether Mozart's or anyone else's. He has no interest in building a theology on musical foundations—theology is answerable before anything else to God's self-revealing, reconciling work in Jesus Christ as attested in Scripture. That is the lodestar for all theology that calls itself Christian. Nor do the parables have any power other than the power Christ himself gives them. Moreover, we can hear these parables *as parables*, Mozart's music *as witness*, only insofar as we are reconciled to God through Christ: we need to hear the sounds with redeemed ears.[70] Nonetheless, Barth believes Mozart does bear his own kind of witness to the gospel, and as such, it seems to have helped Barth develop some of his theological thinking. In one place, Barth writes: "Without such music [Mozart], I could not think of that which concerns me personally in both theology and politics."[71]

Is Barth right about Mozart? Can quite so much be loaded onto one composer?[72] These are reasonable questions. However, if we spend too long on them we easily miss what is far more important: the vision that lies at the center of his adulation of Mozart, the vision that Mozart turned into sound for him—"little bits of horn, metal and catgut" praising the Creator in their own particular way, the created world sounding its symphony to the Creator, as God wills it to.[73]

In Barth we see the most pointed effort in modern times to reverse what we have spoken of a number of times already, namely, the trend to treat music as essentially human projection. Barth is attempting to reroot thinking about music in creation at large, specifically a Christ-centered vision of creation, without forgetting its character as humanly made.[74] Some are surprised that a thinker so Protestant and so prolific and enamored with words could have had so much room for music. But, contrary to what many believe about Barth, he had a rich and subtle doctrine of creation and certainly one generous enough to accommodate the very different contributions of both music and word; for him, both can witness to the God of Jesus Christ in their own distinctive ways.

It is fitting that Mozart accompanied one of his greatest devotees out of this world. Barth died peacefully on the night of December 9, 1968. "His wife found him the next morning, while in the background a record was playing the Mozart with which she had wanted to waken him."[75]

Polyphony of Life: Dietrich Bonhoeffer

Words written in jail often provoke fascination. And some have proved seminal—Hitler's *Mein Kampf*, Bunyan's *Pilgrim's Progress*. When a newly engaged theologian and pastor began composing letters and papers in a prison cell, bereft of family, fiancée, and friends, he could hardly have guessed the spell that these writings would cast on subsequent Christian thinking. And he probably never stopped to reflect on the number of times he mentions music.

A German university professor with a doctorate in theology, a Lutheran pastor, a participant in the early ecumenical movement, a prolific writer—Dietrich Bonhoeffer (1906–45) became a central figure in the Protestant church struggle against Nazism. Though he could be highly critical of Barth, he too attempted to wrestle free of much nineteenth-century theology. Like Barth, in the 1930s Bonhoeffer was drawn into the struggles of the Confessing Church, a group opposing both the Nazis and the "German Christians" who colluded with them. Just before the outbreak of World War II, while on a visit to the United States, he sensed God's call to return to Germany: only if he shared in his country's political struggle could he hope to share in its reconstruction. Arrested and imprisoned in 1943 for his part in a plot to assassinate Hitler, Bonhoeffer was hanged at a camp in Flossenbürg on April 9, 1945. He was thirty-nine years old.

Bonhoeffer has captured not only the minds of thousands—most famously a cluster of thinkers of the 1960s sometimes called the "death of God" theologians—but also the imagination of many with little or no interest in theology.

His resilience in the face of a totalitarian state, his determination to live in and build a countercommunity, his fragmentary, provocative, and often mysterious prison writings, and perhaps above all his execution for conspiracy to murder have given him a very wide and devoted following. The literature on Bonhoeffer abounds; he has even inspired a film and an opera.[76]

Music and Life

What is not often appreciated is the place of music in Bonhoeffer's life.[77] If Barth was a passionate amateur, Bonhoeffer was accomplished enough as a pianist to consider a professional career.[78] By the time he was ten he was playing Mozart sonatas, and he soon began composing. As a child he was a fine accompanist, especially to members of his own family, and his musical skills were drawn on as a member of the German branch of the Boy Scout movement. He eventually decided to pursue theology and a church vocation, but not before his parents arranged a performance in front of the virtuoso pianist Leonid Kreutzer.[79]

Bonhoeffer left us with no essay or book on music. Nonetheless, references to music and the other arts are scattered through his writings. He bemoans the Nazis' demonic use of the romantic German tradition (Beethoven, Wagner, and others); he speaks of some music (e.g., Bach) as appropriate to the church and other music as better left outside (the romantic tradition); he warns of music's dangerous power to distract us from God's Word; he alludes to singing serving the struggle for freedom ("only he who cries out for the Jews may sing Gregorian chants");[80] and his discovery of African-American spirituals in the United States affected him deeply. But it was during his last years, especially in his *Letters and Papers from Prison*, that music comes into its own as he struggles with the question of who Jesus Christ is for us today and what it means to be the church in the world.

In prison Bonhoeffer has no radio or gramophone. He had only music in his mind or the music heard distantly in and beyond the prison. At one point he remarks that "the music we hear inwardly can almost surpass, if we really concentrate on it, what we hear physically."[81] An extract from a letter to his parents shows the importance of his musical memory:

> For years now I've associated [Bach's *Mass in B Minor*] with this particular day [Repentance Day, November 17], like the St. Matthew Passion with Good Friday. I remember the evening when I first heard it. I was eighteen, and had just come from Harnack's seminar, in which he had discussed my first seminar essay very kindly, and had expressed hope that some day I should specialise in church history. I was full of this when I went into the Philharmonic Hall; the great *Kyrie Eleison* was just beginning, and as it did so, I forgot everything else—the effect was indescribable. Today I'm going through it, bit by bit, in my mind . . . it's my favorite work of Bach.[82]

Bonhoeffer refers to particular pieces, but music's influence on his thinking goes deeper—music seems to affect the very way he goes about theology. Often he seems to *think musically*. This is why Andreas Pangritz argues that Bonhoeffer's experience of music played a crucial part in preparing the way for his final theological reflections.[83] John de Gruchy believes, "It was music that provided him with most of his aesthetic categories and analogies when engaged in theological reflection. Indeed, his theological thought in prison develops in tandem with his reflection on musical concepts."[84] It is as if, now that he is out of the political maelstrom, a key dimension of his own life, internalized through memory, has a chance to suffuse and inform his thinking.

Music and Aesthetic Existence—Escapism?

To probe this further we can turn to a letter from January 1944 in which Bonhoeffer expresses his wish that "aesthetic existence" finds a proper place in the church. What does this mean? In his earlier *Ethics*, he spoke of Christ's relation to the world in terms of four divine "mandates" or commands: labor, marriage, government, and the church.[85] Music came under the mandate of labor. But in these *Letters* it comes under "the broad area of freedom," which covers art (presumably all the arts), education, friendship, and play. The key passage reads as follows:

> I wonder whether it is possible . . . to regain the idea of the church as providing an understanding of the area of freedom (art, education, friendship, play), so that Kierkegaard's "aesthetic existence" would not be banished from the church's sphere, but would be re-established within it. I really think that it is so, and it would mean that we should recover a link with the Middle Ages.[86]

Bonhoeffer alludes to the Danish nineteenth-century philosopher Søren Kierkegaard (1813–55). Kierkegaard had launched a protest against the "aesthetic," including the view stemming from the romantics that art and the creative imagination, and a life of immediate aesthetic pleasure could heal the brokenness of our lives. This is delusion, Kierkegaard thought. Such an attitude cannot come to terms with ethics, guilt, and suffering, nor with time and the transience of our lives, matters that can be properly engaged only when we know ourselves as wholly answerable to the infinite God of Jesus Christ, when we answer the call of Christ and follow him as disciples in the world.[87] Bonhoeffer is sympathetic to this but wants to stress that this radical call does not mean abandoning the aesthetic.[88] Far from it. He wants to reestablish the aesthetic in the church, and the feature of the aesthetic he has in mind here seems to be its sheer gratuitousness. We do the things in the sphere of freedom—art, education,[89] friendship, play—not to achieve a particular end or goal or because something in the past has made them necessary. We do them just because of the joy of doing them. Hence they do not come under a direct divine mandate. It makes little sense, after all, to *command* anyone to have friends, make art, play, and so on. This is not to say that when we play, or do anything else in the "free" sphere, we shake off all responsibility (playing with loaded weapons in a school playground would presumably be excluded!). The point is that things in this sphere are not bound by tight causes in the past and the future—the past has not made them necessary, and we do not have to do them to achieve a future goal. In this sense, they are free.

So, Bonhoeffer seems to be saying that music, as with all the arts, is significant because it embodies "aesthetic existence," a type of radically free living, and this is something the church badly needs to recover. But the cynic may still want to reply: this is just what we would expect Bonhoeffer to say. Having failed to overthrow Hitler, now incarcerated and isolated, impotent to affect the titanic conflicts tearing his homeland and the church apart, he is bound to become escapist: the church is to flee from the agonies of its life-and-death struggles and take safe refuge in a world-denying aestheticism. But Bonhoeffer cannot be saying this, and to see why, we need to go deeper into his vision of the Christian life that emerged during these prison writings. And music turns out to play a key role in elaborating this vision.

The Art of Fugue *and Polyphonic Life*

The *Mass in B Minor* may have been Bonhoeffer's favorite work of Bach, but it was to another piece in particular that he turned as he reflected on what it means to be a Christian in wartime Germany. In a letter of February 1944 he writes to his friend Eberhard Bethge: "The longer we are uprooted from our professional activities and our private lives, the more we feel how fragmentary our lives are, compared with those of our parents."[90] But this very fragmentariness, this sense of being pulled apart, "may, in fact, point toward a fulfilment beyond the limits of human achievement; I have to keep that in mind, particularly in view of the death of so many of the best of my former pupils. Even if the pressure of outward events may split our lives into fragments, like bombs falling on houses, we must do our best to keep in view how the whole was planned and thought out."[91] He speaks of the individual's life as a fragment:

> The important thing today is that we should be able to discern from the fragment[s] of our life how the whole was arranged and planned, and what material it consists of. . . . There are some fragments that are only worth throwing into the dustbin. . . . [But there are others] whose importance lasts for centuries, because their completion can only be a matter for God, and so they are fragments that must be fragments—I'm thinking, e.g., of the *Art of Fugue*.[92]

The reference here is to Bach dying before completing his tour de force, the *Art of Fugue*. This piece weaves a musical tapestry of fierce intricacy; yet the final closure never arrives. We have no ending. The parts dissipate into an empty page, awaiting completion.

This links up with comments Bonhoeffer makes in earlier letters. He often alludes to Heinrich Schütz (1585–1672), probably the greatest of Germany's seventeenth-century composers, whose music he had come to know well. Writing of Schütz's setting of the hymn "O bone Jesu" (a hymn so important to Bonhoeffer that he wanted it for his funeral), he sketches out some of the musical notes in his letter and asks: "Doesn't this passage, in its ecstatic longing combined with pure devotion, suggest the 'bringing again' of all earthly desire?"[93] The reference is to the gathering up, the recapitulation of all things in Christ envisaged in Ephesians 1:10—"a magnificent conception, full of comfort."[94] Nothing of value on that day will be lost; all things—including our earthly desires, longings, and yearnings—will somehow find their proper transformation, be made transparent, clear.

Bonhoeffer's own adult life, now heading toward death, and the broken-up quality of his prison writings resonate with this poignantly. There is a sense that God will grant a completion and somehow make sense of and ease the anxiety about the unfinished, broken-up character of his life now. Like the *Art of Fugue*,

> If we accumulate, at least for a short time, a wealth of themes and weld them into a harmony in which the great counterpoint is maintained from start to finish, so that at last, when it breaks off abruptly, we can sing no more than the chorale, "I come before thy throne,"[95] we will not bemoan the fragmentariness of our life, but rather rejoice in it.[96]

Bonhoeffer coined the term "polyphony of life" when his own sense of loneliness was at its most acute.[97] In May 1944, at a time of family reunion and celebration (the baptism of Bethge's son, Bonhoeffer's godchild), and feeling intensely his separation from his fiancée, he acknowledges that Bethge (who was a soldier in Italy, on temporary leave) has every right to want to live with and live for his wife and son. But there is a danger: in loving the polyphony of life our love of God might be displaced. Polyphony, we recall, means music with more than one melody played or sung simultaneously, each moving to some extent independently of the others. Bonhoeffer elaborates this by referring to the cantus firmus, the principal or central theme that winds its way through a piece of polyphony, giving coherence and enabling the other parts to flourish.

> God wants us to love him eternally with our whole hearts—not in such a way as to weaken our earthly love, but to provide a kind of *cantus firmus* to which the other melodies of life provide their counterpoint. One of these contrapuntal themes . . . is earthly affection. Even in the Bible we have the Song of Songs; and really one can imagine no more ardent, passionate, sensual love than is portrayed

there (see 7:6). It's a good thing that the book is in the Bible, in face of all those who believe that the restraint of passion is Christian.[98]

If the cantus firmus is secure, we need not fear the other voices: "Where the *cantus firmus* is clear and plain, the counterpoint can be developed to its limits." Bonhoeffer reads the relation between the cantus firmus—love of God—and the surrounding counterpoint—earthly affection—in terms of the divine and human in Christ: "The two are 'undivided and yet distinct' . . . like Christ in his divine and human natures." He asks: "May not the attraction and importance of polyphony in music consist in its being a musical reflection of this Christological fact and therefore of our *vita christiana*?"[99] A diversity of loves and desires can flourish around a firm cantus firmus, everything depending upon having the cantus firmus in place:

> I wanted to tell you to have a good, clear, *cantus firmus*; that is the only way to a full and perfect sound, when the counterpoint has a firm support and can't come adrift or get out of tune, while remaining a distinct whole in its own right. Only a polyphony of this kind can give life a wholeness and at the same time assure us that nothing calamitous can happen as long as the *cantus firmus* is kept going.[100]

In a letter of the next day Bonhoeffer speaks of pain and joy as two elements in life's polyphony. And to Bethge, who was enjoying a good deal more freedom and opportunity at the time, he says: "I do want you to be *glad* about what you have; it really *is* the polyphony of life."[101] The same circle of ideas emerges in later letters. He notices how some of his fellow prisoners find it hard to harbor conflicting emotions at the same time:

> When bombers come, they are all fear; when there is something nice to eat, they are all despair; when they are successful, they can think of nothing else. *They miss the fullness of life* . . . everything objective and subjective is dissolved for them into fragments. By contrast, *Christianity puts us into many different dimensions of life at the same time* . . . life isn't pushed back into a single dimension, but is kept multi-dimensional and polyphonous.[102]

It is hard not to think of Bonhoeffer's own life at this time as richly polyphonic: his engagement to Maria, his contact with friends and family, staff and inmates. He was composing fiction, drama, and poetry, and he was reading history, poetry, science, novels, and philosophy, and—not least—he was writing theology.

Bonhoeffer, then, envisages a polyphonous kind of life for the church in the world, a rich life shot through with joy (a persistent theme in these writings). It is a life of "worldliness"—not the worldliness of the secularist, denying God, nor the worldliness of a certain kind of aesthete, fleeing responsibility, but a fully down-to-earth kind of Christian life that can include free, "aesthetic existence" (friendship, art, etc.) while also being ethically alert and responsible. Or, in de

Gruchy's words, "the 'church for others' is also the sphere of freedom in which a genuinely 'aesthetic existence' becomes possible, affirming the polyphony of life amidst the struggle for justice. The fragments do not fly apart but find their coherence in Christ, in whom the broken themes of praise are restored."[103]

In this chapter we have encountered three major figures of modern theology, all passionate about music and all musically expert to some degree, each interweaving this passion and expertise with the guiding convictions that shape their Christian vision of the world. They may not be the easiest writers to read, but time spent with them has yielded much that we can draw on in the chapters to come.

Before part 3, we turn now from three musical theologians to two theological musicians.

two theological musicians

Evocations of Eternity: Olivier Messiaen

In the early summer of 1940, as Nazi troops moved relentlessly across France, four men were fleeing from Verdun to Nancy. As they reached the end of their journey, a group of German soldiers surrounded and captured them. One of the four, a thirty-one-year-old bespectacled musician working in the medical corps, held a haversack containing a small collection of musical scores. Eventually he found himself a prisoner of war in Stalag 8A at Görlitz in Silesia, about fifty miles east of Dresden. Here he suffered extremes of cold and hunger, but here also his musical imagination was fired, and a masterpiece born.[1]

In the camp with him were a violinist, a clarinetist, and a cellist—all highly competent and experienced players. The first rehearsal of an emerging quartet took place in one of the barrack washrooms, where in the absence of a piano, they could play only through a movement for violin, clarinet, and cello. The first performance of the complete *Quatuor pour la fin du temps* (*Quartet for the End of Time*) on January 15, 1941, is one of the great stories of modern music: for nearly an hour, hundreds of prisoners and soldiers sat in Barrack 27B in the depths of a subzero winter, the wounded lying on stretchers at the front of the audience. They listened to the four performers, the composer in wooden clogs

---

"Theological musician" is the term Halbreich uses of Messiaen (*musicien théologique*) (Harry Halbreich, *Olivier Messiaen* [Paris: Fayard Fondation SACEM, 1980], 17). It can also be used very appropriately of James MacMillan.

Fig. 7.1: Olivier Messiaen. Photo ©1982 Malcolm Crowthers

struggling with a run-down, out-of-tune upright piano. As one of the players later recalled, the music seemed to transfigure the misery of Stalag 8A "into something sublime."[2] The composer himself remarked that he had "never . . . been listened to with such consideration and understanding."[3]

By this time, Olivier Messiaen (1908–92) had managed to publish a number of pieces and had been appointed organist at l'Église de la Trinité in Paris in 1931 (a position he held almost until his death). After his release from confinement, he took up the post of professor of harmony at the Paris Conservatoire, and during decades of teaching there he became the most distinguished and influential French composer of his generation. His pupils included Pierre Boulez, Karlheinz Stockhausen, George Benjamin, as well as the pianist Yvonne Loriod, who became his second wife.[4]

Messiaen's output was huge, and, most important for our purposes, virtually all his pieces bear some form of explicit Christian intent or reference. The titles, the biblical quotations, and the ascriptions he attaches to his scores, his spoken commentaries at performances, and his writings and interviews all evince a devout and passionate Roman Catholic, eager that the often weighty and dense theological symbolism of his music is not missed and that the listener comes to sense something of God's presence in and through it. The driving force behind his composition was never in doubt: "The first idea that I wished to express— and the most important, because it stands above them all—is the existence of the truths of the Catholic faith. . . . This is the first aspect of my work."[5] Paul Griffiths comments: "[Messiaen's] musical imagination became so fixed on theology that, almost immediately, it was impossible for him to compose for any other reason."[6] What is especially evident, not only from his words but also his music, is that Messiaen's faith, though not of the sort that defended itself against skepticism or attack, was nonetheless anything but naive or superficial. He had a quite exceptional theological intelligence, without parallel in twentieth-century music, nurtured through years of reading, prayer, and reflection.

Messiaen is often labeled an eclectic. This is certainly true musically. He was magpielike in drawing on an extensive range of sources, Eastern and Western, among them Gregorian chant (of crucial significance),[7] Debussy, the Russians Rimsky-Korsakov and Stravinsky, his own teacher Paul Dukas, organist and composer Marcel Dupré, as well as Greek meter, church modes, classical Indian rhythms, and—perhaps most famously—birdsong (he was a keen ornithologist). Another key musical influence was Charles Tournemire (1870–1939), a Roman Catholic organist-composer whose use of Greek rhythms, Hindu modes, and a range of sophisticated musical devices created a fusion that blazed a trail for Messiaen's music.

Yet theologically Messiaen could hardly be called eclectic. Aidan Nichols has usefully traced the Catholic strands shaping his work.[8] French Catholicism between 1880 and 1960 was marked by, among other things, a series of revivals: liturgical renewal, a new interest in Scripture both at the scholarly and popular levels, a literary renaissance (Paul Claudel, Ernest Hello, and Léon Bloy), and a fresh enthusiasm for various forms of spirituality (especially that associated with Thérèse of Lisieux, Elizabeth of the Trinity, and St. Francis of Assisi). None of these stirrings departed significantly from mainstream Catholic faith. According to Nichols, it is likely that for Messiaen they came together in a book compiled by Dom Columba Marmion, *Christ in His Mysteries* (*Christ dans ses Mystères*), in which the author, gathering copious quotations from the early church fathers, seeks to show how the whole divine Trinity acts through the events of the life of Jesus of Nazareth, "from Annunciation to Resurrection and the Resurrection's overflow at Pentecost and the final consummation of history in the Second Coming, to heal a fallen world and raise it up to share in the happiness of God."[9]

What seems to have grasped Messiaen, then, was not an eclectic religion or broad spirituality, nor was it mysticism (a label he disliked intensely), but the positive, central teachings of the Catholic Church. "I love the sound, solid gifts of Faith."[10] Messiaen also speaks of the inspiration of the natural world, especially birdsong[11] and human love,[12] but even here the underlying and unifying interest is centered on the church's doctrine, supremely the love of God shown in Christ.[13] Nichols puts it thus: "Messiaen married a traditional Catholicism, colored by particular emphases of the France of the 1920s and 1930s, to a modernist spirit of experimentation and eclecticism in music."[14] Essential to Messiaen's genius was that he could make this marriage work, that he could deploy a very diverse musical toolbox that could catch the attention of his musical contemporaries, but in the service of a focused and orthodox Catholic vision.

Though he was well read in theology,[15] steeped in the Bible,[16] and adored the spiritual classic *The Imitation of Christ*, by Thomas à Kempis, it remains true that Messiaen is first and foremost a musician, and it is in the medium of sound that the subtlety and depth of his theological imagination is most clearly displayed. (The common charge that the theological prefaces to his pieces are crude and elementary is itself naive.)[17] So this is where we must concentrate our attention, highlighting some of the ways in which his music resonates with his devoutly held theological vision.

Time

Comprehensive summaries are out of the question—we are, after all, encountering one of the most sophisticated musical minds of the twentieth century. Although we can accept Messiaen's claim that his Christian convictions converged on the notion of God's love, the theological themes he treats are in fact many and varied, as Siglind Bruhn's helpful summary of them has shown,[18] and Messiaen treats the same theme in different ways at different stages in his life. But we can get a good impression of the flavor of much of his music by concentrating on something dear to his heart, never far from the center of his concerns, involving most of his best-known musical techniques, and very much to the fore in the *Quartet for the End of Time*—his treatment of time and eternity.

To open this up, we need to note something basic to most of the music we know and hear in the West: it is generally marked by a forward-moving dynamic. This, as we shall see in chapter 11, is generated by patterns of tension and relaxation. We hear a sound:

Fig. 7.2: Dominant seventh chord

and we hear it as a tension, something that needs to be resolved. At some stage or level we look for the resolution:

Fig. 7.3: Tension and resolution

Through its multiple tensions and resolutions, encompassing (in principle) every parameter of music, and sometimes stretched over long periods, Western music pulls us into a dynamic of desire. We expect, and usually want, future sounds. Most music of the Western tradition over the last four hundred years or so is directional; it is the music of becoming: we sense it is going somewhere.

Messiaen knows, respects, and loves this tradition. But although the extent to which he departs from it is a matter of some subtlety,[19] it is fair to say that in general he is inclined to distance himself from musical techniques that establish a polemic, pursue conflict, and reach toward fulfillment, the music of implication, irreversible patterns of tension, and resolution. So, for example, in Messiaen's music the chord we have just cited in fig. 7.2—the dominant seventh—will not usually resolve in the way we expect (fig. 7.3); it is likely to be followed by chords (perhaps more dominant sevenths), which themselves seem to require resolution, and these in turn may not resolve in the normal, expected way (fig. 7.4).

Fig. 7.4: "Regard du Père," from *Vingt Regards sur l'Enfant-Jésus* (excerpt)

Some have said that this "lends [Messiaen's] music a static rather than dynamic quality, his harmony existing in a state which is neither tension nor relaxation."[20] Hence Messiaen's fondness for repetitive cycles, verse-refrain forms, and reversible rhythms. Indeed, rhythm became a lifelong interest for him. In the case of traditional Western music, equally spaced beats are grouped in regular bars of twos, threes, or fours, and some beats are more important than others. In Messiaen's music, typically we have beats of irregular length set over an underlying regular pulse of much smaller units, each pulse carrying equal weight—the pulse "insists that all moments are the same, that the past, the present and the future are identifiable."[21]

The underlying pulse can be so slow it is barely discernible. His early organ work *Le Banquet Céleste* (1928) is a good example.

Fig. 7.5: *Le Banquet Céleste* (opening)

There are times here when the music feels as if it has stopped altogether—any sense of being pressed forward, led from one beat to the next, has been radically suppressed. This is heightened by the fact that an organ pipe's sound does not decay but remains relatively steady (unlike, say, a piano string).

Pervasive also in Messiaen's music are heterophonies—that is, distinct threads of music superimposed on each other, often at different speeds and in radical contrast to one another, in Griffiths's words, "the music of many clocks, running fast and slow, forwards and backwards."[22] This is evident in "The Mystery of the Holy Trinity," from *Les Corps Glorieux* (1939), where—appropriately—three distinct musical lines interweave:

Reproduced by kind permission of Editions A. Leduc, Paris/United Music Publishers Ltd.

Fig. 7.6: "The Mystery of the Holy Trinity," from *Les Corps Glorieux* (excerpt)

Eternity in Time?

Messiaen was not the first (and certainly not the last) to write music that questions the dominance and pervasiveness of the forward drive of Western music. But he stands out in two important ways. First, he was the first to do this for Christian theological reasons. Second, his music is quite different from that of some other twentieth-century modernists who took the process very much further than Messiaen and sought to erase any sense of repetition, memory, arrival, or return (as with some of Boulez's music, for example, or Stockhausen's). With Messiaen, not only is there quite often a sense of goal or arrival (at least on the large scale), but his musical language is on the whole far less removed from the dominant Western musical traditions than that of many of his modernist colleagues, and thus it is often a good deal more accessible.

What, then, were the Christian theological reasons that underlay Messiaen's experiments with musical time? Especially crucial, it would seem, was the way he envisioned time in relation to eternity. In Paul Griffiths's words, for Messiaen, "the capacity to speak of God comes only when the march of time is forgotten,"[23] for God's eternity is utterly timeless.

Of course, a composer who believes this and also believes in the ability (and duty) of music to evoke the things of God is plunged into something of a dilemma. For music is a temporal art through and through. It happens in time and it shapes time. It is time-embedded, full of change and motion. What can time-bound music have to do with eternity? Messiaen speaks of the "insuperable obstacle"[24] he faced: how to experience the truth of eternity while still being bound by the world's time. He came to believe that music could indeed offer a taste of life with God in this world's time and thus prepare us for eternity. But critical to this were various musical techniques in which the arrow of time is, if not negated, at least weakened considerably.

From this perspective we can better understand some of the features of Messiaen's music we highlighted earlier. We can also begin to grasp more fully some of the particularly innovative techniques that contribute to the unique character of his music. Three of these are especially important: modes of limited transposition, nonretrogradable rhythms, and symmetrical permutations.

First, *modes of limited transposition*. As Messiaen developed as a composer, he came to rely on a set of modes. We have already spoken of Greek and medieval modes.[25] A mode, for Messiaen, is a series or group of notes taken from the span of an octave (the distance from middle C to the C above) related to each other by certain intervals. Messiaen's modes are arranged symmetrically and center on one or more notes. Moreover, each mode is built in such a way that it can be transposed (translated to another pitch) only a limited number of times before, in effect, it reverts to its original. Hence the phrase "modes of *limited* transposition"—you are soon back to where you started.

Messiaen believed that each mode was associated with a color or group of colors. Indeed, he was fascinated by the connections between sound and color. Like many people, he saw colors in his mind's eye when he heard music ("I see them inwardly"),[26] and he thought everyone needed a sense of some correlation between sounds and colors to appreciate his music.[27] When he was ten years old, he witnessed for the first time the dazzling stained-glass windows of Saint Chapelle in Paris; the effect was overwhelming and life-changing. Through his modes, Messiaen wanted to dazzle the listener as Saint Chapelle's glass had dazzled him. He believed that each mode generated a color palette in sound. A mode's color-character within a piece of music was affected by a whole range of factors: pitch, timbre, volume, time-scales, and so forth, and by the way in which sounds were superimposed on one another. The possibilities of sound-color were thus enormous.

Through his modes and their transpositions, together with their associated colors, Messiaen sought to offer an evocation of eternity of the kind evoked in the multicolored visions of the book of Revelation, thus providing an anticipation here and now of the "perpetual dazzlement" of heaven, which he envisioned as "an eternal music of colors, an eternal color of musics."[28] (He explores this with striking effect in his *Couleurs de la Cité Céleste* [1963] for piano, wind, and percussion.) Indeed, he could speak of his musical language as a "theological rainbow."[29]

In the light of his keenness to reduce the sense of time's direction in music, it is very telling that the link here is with a type of perception that is not dependent on following a temporal sequence but where meaning can be grasped (at least in part) by a glance or gaze, or by roaming freely back and forth with our eyes.

The second innovative technique is *nonretrogradable rhythms*. These are rhythms that sound or play the same backward as they do forward, such as 2, 3, 2:

Messiaen saw these rhythms affirmed everywhere in the world around him—in the other arts, in nature, in the human body[30]—but he also saw them as symbols of eternity. Just because they do not sound different when reversed, they present a kind of fusion of past, present, and future in which beginning and end fold into each other. In "The Almighty Word" from his piano cycle *Vingt regards sur l'enfant-Jésus* (1944), a nonretrogradable rhythm is pounded out by the left hand twenty-one times to symbolize the eternity of the Word. In *Le Corps Glorieux* he uses nonretrogradable rhythms in the course of a movement evoking the power and agility of our resurrection bodies in our future life beyond death:

Fig. 7.7: "Force et Agilité des Corps Glorieux," from *Les Corps Glorieux* (excerpt)

The third technique, *symmetrical permutations*, is an extension of the second. Messiaen lines up note durations with numbers and then manipulates them mathematically into elaborate sequences. Again, this is done in such a way that the number of possible permutations are considerably limited: one soon returns to the sequence with which one started. Symmetrical permutations are used heavily in *Couleurs de la Cité Céleste*, a conjuring up in sound of the kaleidoscopic blaze of the heavenly Jerusalem. As Messiaen puts it, "The work does not end, having never really begun: it turns on itself, interlacing its temporal blocks, like the rose window of a cathedral with its vivid invisible colors."[31]

The upshot of these three techniques should be clear. They give rise to structures that do not flow from tension to resolution, promise to fulfillment, but that fold back on themselves with repeated returns to their origin. Messiaen believed these devices can give music a certain charm or bewitchment, a kind of hypnotic power that he thought was especially appropriate to embodying the truths of the Catholic faith and above all the truth of eternity. We should notice that what the techniques all have in common is symmetry. All three are based on a symmetrical group, each group turning on a central, shared element. Although to some extent they interact with musical elements that do convey a sense of direction (elements of the more standard Western traditions are rarely completely absent in Messiaen), each of these particular devices creates what Jean Marie Wu calls a "closed circuit," and "embodied in the closed circuitry of each innovation, Messiaen found expressions of eternal life."[32]

The End of Time

Now we can return to the *Quartet for the End of Time*, a work whose overall subject is the "ending" of time in eternity. We find the first two of the three symmetrical techniques amply deployed (the third was developed later);[33] indeed, the *Quartet* is in some parts "more blatantly symmetrical than anything outside [Messiaen's] output."[34] Even the number of movements (eight) bears significance. Seven is the biblical perfect number, the number of the Sabbath rest; "the seven of this rest is prolonged into eternity and becomes the eight of everlasting light, of eternal peace."[35] Further, the movements do not follow a sequence; though at the very end the last piece may convey a sense of rest, there is no thrust from one movement to the next, no sense of one succeeding the other.

The work carries the inscription, "In homage to the Angel of the Apocalypse, who raises a hand heavenwards saying: 'There will be no more Time.'" The reference is to Revelation 10:6, and although Messiaen later said he did not see the piece as a commentary on the book of Revelation, he prefaced the first performance with a lecture, explaining to the prisoners that the quartet was not about the end of their time of captivity but "the ending of the concepts of past and future: that is . . . the beginning of eternity, and that in this I relied on the magnificent text of the Revelation."[36] He reflected, "My initial thought was of the abolition of time itself, something infinitely mysterious and incomprehensible to most of the philosophers of time, from Plato to Bergson."[37] The phrase "end of time" also had specifically musical connotations—the end of the traditional, progressive time of Western music.[38]

Nonetheless, though it was not about the end of physical confinement, the piece did give Messiaen a sense of detachment from the camp's harsh conditions: "If I composed this quartet, it was to escape from the snow, from the war, from captivity, and from myself. The greatest benefit that I drew from it was that in the midst of thirty thousand prisoners, I was the only man who was not one."[39]

Here we will concentrate on the fifth and eighth movements—the most famous pieces in the work—and go on to speak of the first. "Louange à l'Éternité de Jésus" (for cello and piano) and "Louange à l'Immortalité de Jésus" (for violin and piano, which ends the whole work) are both serene and exquisitely beautiful. They are strongly rooted in E major, very stable in texture, with undramatic harmonic changes, no disturbing juxtapositions, and little contrast, both fading into silence. They are also radically slow. Most Western music of such a slow pulse would normally have faster harmonic shifts; here the harmony changes very slowly, heightening the already profound quality of unhurried calm. There is an overall goal-directedness of sorts, but in the hands of performers who have the courage to play these pieces at the pace Messiaen stipulates, they generate a mesmerizing aura of stillness rarely equaled in modern music.[40]

"Louange à l'Éternité de Jésus" is said to magnify "with love and reverence the eternity of this powerful and gentle Word, 'which the years can never efface.'"[41] Marked "infinitely slow" in the score, the cello traces a legato melody over the piano's pulsing semiquavers. The piece acts as a sort of prelude to the second half of the *Quartet*, renewing a focus on eternity and involving the gradual removal of chromatic elements from a very simple, fundamental, five-note ("pentatonic") scale. Hence there is a progression, but one toward increasing simplicity. The upper registers of the cello are used extensively; this means that the sound of the player's left hand rubbing on the neck of the instrument is frequently audible. Anthony Pople suggests this may be linked to the physicality of the Word made flesh in Jesus.[42]

The physical humanity of Jesus is the focus of the final movement: "The Word made flesh, resurrected immortally to grant us life. . . . [The violin's] slow ascent to the extreme high register is the ascent of man towards his God, of the child of God towards his Father, of the deified Being towards Paradise."[43] Again a hypnotic pulse is set by the piano over which a violin weaves a soaring melodic line. Messiaen associates the "extremely slow" pace with a state of ecstasy, and it comes as no surprise to discover this movement is a transcription of an early organ work, *Diptyque* (1930), which was subtitled "essay on earthly life and blessed eternity." Here in the *Quatuor*, the focus is resolutely on eternity, the conflicts and tensions of the book of Revelation having finally been resolved.

The last piece does, of course, function as an ending to the whole work. Yet since there are in fact two paeans to Jesus—the two solos we have just examined, both of which are slow solos with piano accompaniment, both in E major, both structured in two parts—and since the first comes in the middle of the work, Messiaen has, in fact, already demonstrated that an apparent conclusion need not be a finale. We are left with a sense that there could have been other movements and more finales. Eternity without end.

Subtler, and harder to listen to, is the opening movement, "Liturgie de cristal." It alludes to the experience of the eternal as it is sensed in our time, in this life. We hear fragmentary imitations of birdsong on the clarinet and violin, played over repeated sequences on the cello and piano. In his own description of the piece, Messiaen tells us of a dawn chorus: "Between three and four in the morning, the awakening of birds: a solo blackbird or nightingale improvises, surrounded by a shimmer of sound, by a halo of trills lost very high in the trees. Transpose this onto a religious plane and you have the harmonious silence of Heaven."[44]

The cello and piano parts (the music of heaven) are carefully constructed to avoid the suggestion of beginning and end. The cello repeats a fifteen-note melody throughout, itself made up of two nonretrogradable rhythms. The sense of just being there, like the expansion of a single point of musical time, is heightened by the way it relates—or does not relate—to the piano part, which itself repeats a different rhythmic sequence over and over, unvaryingly. The two instruments' patterns do not mesh neatly, nor do they ever resolve with respect to each other, and they are both interrupted by the close of the piece—it is as if they could have continued perpetually, ad infinitum. (It has been calculated that it would take many hours for the parts to return to the relation they had at the start.) Further, the piano has a cycle of twenty-nine chords (a harmonic pedal), the cello likewise a cycle of five notes (a melodic pedal), both functioning to create an impression of stasis.

What of the birdsong in this movement? On one level it is the depiction, or near depiction, of birds awakening at sunrise. (Messiaen admitted he could not transcribe birdsong precisely. As Pople puts it, his birds sing with a Messiaen accent!)[45] But inevitably, by being heard along with the cello and piano, the song is set in an eternal context. Or, put another way, we are invited to find a place for the heavenly music in our time, the time of the birdsong. We are offered an evocation in our time of heaven's still presence, the shimmer of eternity discernible at each new dawn. It is worth recalling that Messiaen's interest in birdsong reflects and gives expression to his strong belief that the natural world witnesses to God's glory.[46] Here, then, is a conjunction of heaven and the natural world, a conjunction that comes to fruition in later works such as *Des Canyons aux étoiles* and *Saint François d'Assise*. In Johnson's words, "The eternal is brought into the world, into time, to afford a glance at what is to become the ultimate destiny of mankind."[47]

The idea is extended in "Regard du Fils sur le Fils" from his massive piano work *Vingt regards*, where Messiaen addresses the humanity and deity of Christ, the temporal and eternal in one person. We hear two-chord progressions in different modes, each with different rhythms whose beginnings and endings nevertheless synchronize periodically (the two natures in our time), both supported by the eternal "Thème de Dieu," the theme of God in perfect four-four time.[48] Interestingly, the two upper rhythms are disturbed (their symmetry is interrupted by a directional rhythm)—their perfection disrupted, as it were, by immersion in our time—while the divine theme is consistent and perfectly symmetrical.

It is easy to caricature Messiaen here. On the face of it, it might seem that he thought of the Christian's ultimate destiny as involving the complete absence of time and all we associate with it: a still (and impossibly dull) bliss. In the *Quartet for the End of Time*, the accent is very firmly on created time as we now know it—with its past, present, and future, its transience and decay—being eventually no more. The two cello and violin pieces we looked at point strongly in this direction. Nevertheless, in other pieces it is abundantly clear that he regarded our future life with God to be one in which there is movement: in his *Le Corps Glorieux* he draws on an idea that fascinated him, defended by Thomas Aquinas, that in heaven our bodies will be "agile," mobile as never before,[49] and the music expressing this is dizzyingly fast, full of motion; in *Saint Françoise d'Assise* our future life is a raucous, joyful cacophony of birdsong.[50] Here it is probably best to interpret Messiaen in relation to a concept used by the philosopher Henri Bergson—"duration" (*durée*), an interpenetration of past, present, and future. When we, as temporal creatures, are taken into eternity, this will not mean time's destruction and the end of all movement and dynamism but the *fulfillment* of time, a kind of time in which past, present, and future can no longer be separated. Both Messiaen's joyful "bodily dance" and his exceptionally slow music can be heard as different ways of conveying this.[51] After all, if created time is a good dimension of God's good world, then will it not have a part to play in the final destination of the world—the new heaven and earth—while still being distinct from God's eternity? To say the temporal modes will be no more, that there will be no transience and decay, is not necessarily to say there will be no time at all, that there will be nothing but pure stillness. (Admittedly, Messiaen's radical misunderstanding of Revelation 10:6 hardly helps here. The phrase, "There will be no more time," has nothing to do with time being finished or done away with. It means there will be no more time before God completes his purposes. Hence the NRSV's translation: "There will be no more delay.")

Questions

We have touched on only one central concern in Messiaen's output—eternity and its relation to time—and considered one main work in particular. But even this is enough to show a subtle, refined, and bold theological intelligence at work. And even musicians with no overt Christian conviction have to concede that Messiaen's theological energy played a key part in producing music of such extraordinary interest and novelty. Paul Griffiths remarks: "What cannot be denied . . . is the power and newness of the imagery the music derives from its brush with the things of God."[52]

Nevertheless, we may well want to pose some questions about this "brush" (a rather understated way of putting things), questions that concern matters basic to this book. Again we limit ourselves to his musical treatment of eternity and time. We need to tread carefully here, for as I have hinted already, it is easy to misrepresent Messiaen. Even though he insists that God is without time (in contrast to the created world),[53] he does not espouse a dichotomy between God's eternity and time, as if they have nothing to do with each other—indeed, he wants to convey through music a sense of eternity *in* and *to* the temporal world, the presence of God *in* the world of time. Further, Messiaen does not exalt eternity and abhor time. He could even say: "I love time because it is the starting-point of all creation. Time presupposes change (and therefore Matter) and movement (and therefore Space and Life). . . . Time ought to be the friend of all musicians."[54] And as we saw earlier, though many of his trademark techniques suppress goal-directed temporal movement, they can often be found alongside devices that retain the sense of progression that is so much a part of the Western tradition. Moreover, he does not hold that our future life is without movement, as we have just seen. Nor has he any sympathy with the notion that the time-bound world is to be shunned just because it is physical; he has a vibrant sense of the goodness and harmony of the physical world as God's good creation, a strong belief in the cosmic implications of what happened in Christ, and a vigorous conception of the final remaking of our physical bodies.

Nevertheless, despite all this, we may still feel uneasy about the way the time of this world seems to be regarded. If eternity is fundamentally God's own life, is there enough of a sense that God has secured our final future, our sharing in his eternal life, by directly engaging with the world's evil, and that the gospel thus has singular power to engage now with our temporal world at its worst, with humanity at its most godless? Has Messiaen become so captivated by God's own ecstatic joy[55] that he has downplayed what is so much part of the fabric of the New Testament, that Christ's own life in time, as the eternal Word made flesh, meant undergoing deprivation, fear, anxiety, hunger, loss, frustration, and disappointment, and that all these realities were themselves drawn into—indeed, have become the very material of—salvation, ways in which the eternal God meets us as we are? Why so little of this in his music?

When pressed, Messiaen could be very frank: he said once that while he did tackle themes of suffering in some of his works—for example, in *Visions de l'Amen* and in his very late opera, *Saint François*—he had "no aptitude" for the opposites of joy and glory.[56] "Joy is a great deal more difficult to express than pain . . . if you look at contemporary music, nobody at all expresses joy. There are frightful, sad, sorrowful, black, grey, ominous things, but there's neither joy nor light. That comes with color."[57] In another place: "I've written very few poignant pieces. I'm not made for that. I love Light, Joy, and Glory in the divine sense."[58]

While all this might make a refreshing contrast to the wearisome fixation on the tragic one often finds in the contemporary "serious" music scene, the New Testament's testimony reminds us repeatedly that Christian joy is of a kind that plumbs the depths; it has been forged out of the worst of human degradation at the cross and can therefore speak to us and be given to us at the very darkest of places. It is this that provides perhaps the most striking contrast with the other theological composer of this chapter.

Before we leave Messiaen, however, it is worth quoting the violinist who played for that first performance of the *Quartet* in the prison camp, Jean Le Boulaire.

I'm going to confess something. I am a man who does not believe at all. I don't believe in God. I believe that Christ was a man who existed, but that's all. Yet when I heard Messiaen's music, I suddenly thought that it was possible that there was something. For thousands of reasons: his way of expressing himself, his kindness, his graciousness, his deep studies of music, his love of birds, of wind, of nature. . . . All this made an extraordinary impression on me. I stumbled upon the question of the divine, but with Messiaen's music I suddenly said to myself: "God. . . ."[59]

Engaging the Depths: James MacMillan

In James MacMillan (1959–), we meet another strongly committed Roman Catholic, no less serious about dealing in depth with the doctrinal riches of Christianity and just as vocal about his intention to do so, but not at all convinced that this means suppressing or abandoning the tensions and resolutions that have become so much a part of the Western musical tradition. These very musical techniques, he believes, are a compelling means of keeping a composer in touch with a world that, though created good, has been so severely marred and disfigured.

MacMillan is now recognized as a composer of international stature, his music being commissioned, performed, and recorded extensively all over the world. Born in Ayrshire, he studied music at Edinburgh and Durham Universities, and after lecturing at the University of Manchester, he returned to his homeland in 1988 to settle in Glasgow. Concertos have been commissioned by soloists ranging from the cellist Mstislav Rostropovich (*Cello Concerto* [1996]) to percussionist Evelyn Glennie (*Veni, Veni, Emmanuel* [1992], one of the most widely performed concertos of recent years). Symphonies, choral pieces, operas,

Fig. 7.8: James MacMillan. Photo ©2005 Chris Christodoulou

chamber works, and instrumental pieces have been greeted with wide acclaim. In 2000 MacMillan was appointed composer/conductor with the BBC Philharmonic, and in January 2004 he was awarded a CBE (Commander of the Order of the British Empire).

If we scan the reviews of his music, the same words tend to appear: "lyrical," "raw energy," "emotional directness," "humanity," and, perhaps most common, "accessible." From the late 1980s, MacMillan distanced himself from the severe abstractions of postwar modernism in music and moved toward more humane and approachable styles. Among the key influences he notes in this shift are the Russian composers Alfred Schnittke (1934–98), Sofia Gubaidulina (1931–), and Galina Ustvolskaya (1919–2006), but MacMillan says, "My best teachers were [J. S.] Bach and Palestrina" because they commanded a "complexity of technique but in a way that expresses something that is deeply spiritual as well."[60]

Though his music is undoubtedly demanding on performer and listener, MacMillan seems to be able to resonate with a wide audience at a time when many of his fellow composers struggle for any hearing at all. The London newspaper *The Guardian* once spoke of him as "a composer so confident of his own musical language that he makes it instantly communicative to his listeners."[61]

This accessibility is due in part to the way his music so obviously relates to things beyond itself. Keen that musicians break out of what he sees as self-imposed ghettoes, MacMillan is widely read, with a broad range of interests, and is more than able to engage with professional theologians.[62] His early academic training in the 1970s encouraged him to shun talk of the "extramusical"; music was typically seen as a self-contained art form. The climate in Britain is now somewhat different, and not only does MacMillan admit extramusical influences, he also points them up frequently through titles, the words he sets, the forms he employs, as well as in interviews, lectures, and writing.

Liturgy is one such extramusical connection. Like Messiaen, MacMillan has written relatively little music for worship, but (like Messiaen) he has often employed liturgical models, shaping pieces around forms or ideas drawn from services of worship. In one of his best-known works, *Seven Last Words from the Cross* (1993), the third movement, "Verily, I say unto thee, today thou shalt be with me in Paradise," is structured around a ritual accompanying the unveiling of the cross during the Good Friday liturgy.

His social involvement is another extramusical dimension. His own social and political convictions are strong. Deeply disturbed by what he sees as the commodification of music in contemporary society—the debasement of music in the interests of quick effect and fast money—he has become zealous about bringing a richness of musical experience to people who would not normally darken the doors of a concert hall. Many of his works betray a political edge, as in, for example, *Búsqueda* (1988), a music theater piece inspired by the writings of the "mothers of the disappeared" from Argentina. He comments:

I think art fails when it attempts to be polemical, when it attempts to ally itself with a cause. However, the arts have a proven track record of being able to reflect the concerns and experiences of our fellow human beings throughout history. . . . That's why they speak powerfully to people because they do in many different ways reflect the everyday experiences, the joys as well as the tragedies of our fellow man. In that sense the arts are a great human reflection on everyday realities as well as deep spiritual realities. And therefore I don't think artists and I especially don't think musicians and composers should shrink from these questions and from these subjects. I think they're available potent subjects and material for a composer just as much as they are for a poet or a playwright or a filmmaker.[63]

The other striking extramusical associations are the directly theological ones, where MacMillan tackles specific dimensions of the Christian faith. His Catholic convictions relate to and draw on all the other strands in his writing and are closely bound up with his political interests—he sees the attempt to disconnect religion and politics as thoroughly misguided. Surprisingly, although he is very open about his Christian persuasions and the ways they have shaped his work, this has not resulted in his neglect or marginalization by the musical establishment.

Entering the Extremes

One of the most distinctive features of MacMillan's music is its gritty, conflict-ridden quality, and this relates directly to his theological vision. He is biting in his critique of the sentimentality he detects in much Christian music. Many in his own Catholic Church, he notes, have ignored him; he believes this is in part because "they value the 'folk' quality, the 'music of the people,' which to them is this soupy, sentimental, lowest-common-denominator kind of music."[64] This trivializes the stark reality of human evil, "humanity in all its messiness."[65] Shunning the modernist myth of progress, he remarks bluntly: "I don't think [humanity is] improving. I think this has been the big, misleading mistake of the twentieth century."[66] Speaking of the late music of Richard Strauss (1864–1949), he is especially cutting:

> It is clear that by the time [Strauss] wrote his last work, the *Four Last Songs*, there is a moral flaw in his final gesture of self-pitying regret. The atheist composer gives no hint of realisation that the secular modernity he so assiduously craved has been up to its neck in the major catastrophes of the 20th century. On the other hand, those artists with profound religious sensibilities, such as Ustvolskaya and the rest, have looked into the centre of this abyss and seen it for what it was. In their dark nights of the soul, they recognise the moral blindness at the heart of "progress" and point with their music to its redemption through spiritual renewal.[67]

Certainly, MacMillan's music is marked by an absence of anything like smooth advancement. Though he is far from seeking a simple return to traditional Western techniques (his music does not sound like Beethoven or Brahms), struggle and convergence, conflict and conflict resolution are nonetheless integral to his language. "I love dealing with extremes, with vast ranges of expression."[68] His pieces frequently display the dialectics and juxtaposition of extreme violence and extreme tranquility, the confrontation of dissonance and consonance.

A good example is the work that first brought him major public attention, *The Confession of Isobel Gowdie* (premiered at a London Prom concert in 1990). Gowdie was the hapless victim of religious oppression and was burned at the stake in the seventeenth century. "On behalf of the Scottish people," MacMillan writes, "the work craves absolution and offers Isobel Gowdie the mercy and humanity that was denied her in the last days of her life. . . . The work is the Requiem that Isobel Gowdie never had."[69] Fanatical injustice and mass hysteria are conjured up in a destructive sonic nightmare—clashing, grinding chords; irregular and mutually disrupting rhythms. Toward the end, a sinuous tapestry of strands of Scottish balladry, Gaelic psalm singing, and Gregorian plainsong begin to emerge from the depths, gradually transforming the terror but without trivializing it in the process, the fragments of destruction eventually giving way. As MacMillan says: "It is as if an exorcism is taking place and Isobel Gowdie's soul is traversing the violent passage of death and being released into an eternal light."[70]

From this angle, MacMillan is wary of the "New Simplicity" music of the "holy minimalists" (e.g., Pärt, Tavener, and Górecki).[71] He remarks:

> I find their music very beautiful . . . but it's a music that is deliberately mono-dimensional. It's a music that sets out to be iconic. It sets out to have no sense of conflict. It's a music that's in a kind of a transcendent state and that's why it's beautiful. But that's also why it exists in one level, there is a deliberate avoidance of conflict, and people like Tavener make very convincing claims for why his music should be that way: an avoidance of the dialectical principles that have been in Western music through Beethoven and before.
>
> But that's not what I'm interested in at all. If anything, my whole compositional philosophy thrives on conflict and ambiguity . . . the opposition of extremes and finding space within the same sound space . . . the need for music of different qualities to battle and to create their own dramas. I need that sense of drama and even theatre in my music . . . music that is not mono-dimensional, music which, in a traditional sense I suppose, has a sense of dialogue and dialectic, conflict and resolution; so that there is violence in my music whereas with these other composers there is not, and that sometimes surprises people who think that music of a spiritual dimension should not have violence. . . . Perhaps the downside of the zeitgeist for spirituality in music is this need to retreat from the world. That's never been my concern.[72]

MacMillan identifies another difference:

> We hear music, we experience music; viscerally, physically. It's a sensual experience, the serious listening to music requires the activation of the mind as well as the senses. These are the portals to our spiritual core and for me spirituality is not something you hive off into some kind of aesthetically pure, sanitized environment but it's something that has come out of our natural, physical and corporeal existence. And maybe that's the difference between my music and the music that is very, very popular now.[73]

Circling Three Days

To a large extent, what appears to be driving this critique and MacMillan's concern with visceral antagonism in his own music is something quite specifically Christian: the centrality of three days of Jesus's crucifixion and resurrection; God's direct, flesh-involved engagement with the world in its fallenness.

> I think that a lot of so-called spiritual music can be a monodimensional experience without the sense of sacrifice. . . . I am drawn by the sacrificial aspect of the great Christian narrative, and I seem to be going round and round in circles round the same three days in history. You can't have the Resurrection without the Crucifixion. . . . The best stories are ones which have resolutions of conflict, not just resolution.[74]

It would seem, then, that MacMillan's refusal to give up on the interplay of tension and resolution in Western music does not come from some sort of conservative or cultural nostalgia but from a conviction that this musical dynamic resonates closely with the very core of the Christian story. At the risk of oversimplification, while both Messiaen and MacMillan commit to very similar beliefs, the center of gravity seems to be different in each case: for MacMillan it is God's cross-shaped involvement with this world of time, for Messiaen it is the joyful eternity that the timeless God has promised and secured for us.

MacMillan's orientation is especially clear when he draws together theology, politics, and cultural commentary:

> Important in many [of my] works is the crucifixion narrative. I have traced its territory literally in works like *Seven Last Words from the Cross*; *Visitatio Sepulchri* and *Triduum*, but also obliquely in the theatre works, *Búsqueda* and *Inés de Castro*, where the emblem of the cross is made manifest in the lives of ordinary people. . . .
>
> There is a long tradition of Christian artists feeling the necessity to confront and embrace the harrowing central presence of the crucifixion in the great narrative of sacrifice and redemption. One does not have the resurrection without the crucifixion. By confronting the darkness of this tale one takes the cross into the abyss and redeems it. To retreat from the abyss and focus solely on the tran-

scendent would be to conform with the post-Christian spiritual narcissism of our predominant capitalist culture. We are artists formed in the Christian tradition, and precisely because of this, we bring a radical confrontation and challenge to all that is fashionable and accepted. If our radicalism has a transcendent potential it is because it is rooted in a knowledge of the death of Jesus.

From this position the depths of the human spirit can be probed and plumbed, but not in a spirit of glitzy nihilism that is now so sanctioned by the official arts establishments. The crucifixion is to be found in the here and now, in the turbulence of society's culture wars, in the provocation of its politics, in the dirt and in the mire of the world's dispossessed and in the sorrows as well as the joys of ordinary people.[75]

Interwoven with all this is also an attraction to eclecticism—a mixture of styles and genres. This is in contrast to classic modernism, with its drive toward unity, radical consistency, internal cohesion, and coherence within any piece. The conductor Leonard Slatkin explains: "There's nothing in [MacMillan's] music that would seem to be so radically new. It's the way he puts the devices together that makes it quite unique."[76] Complex atonality faces lush tonality; acerbic and aggressive dissonance is put next to sweetly modal harmony; and often the contrasting materials are superimposed on each other. Part of this eclecticism comes from a desire to relate to different cultures and social groups, but (again) it also serves his theological interests: the need for music of different qualities to battle and to create their own dramas as expressive of that conflict that God came to engage in Jesus Christ.

The contours of MacMillan's outlook find monumental expression in *The Triduum*—three orchestral works relating to the events and liturgies of Maundy Thursday, Good Friday, and the Easter Vigil (respectively, *The World's Ransoming,* the *Cello Concerto,* and *Symphony: Vigil*). The theme of the *Cello Concerto* is Christ's crucifixion, the cello soloist shifting between the roles of protagonist, antagonist, and commentator. In the first movement, vulgar dance-hall music evokes Christ's humiliation, and toward the end the players themselves shout the words of the Good Friday Latin plainsong "Crucem tuam adoremus, Domine." In "The Reproaches," MacMillan quotes "Dunblane Cathedral" (a Protestant hymn), a reference to the shooting of sixteen children and their teacher by a lone gunman in Dunblane, Scotland—an atrocity that occurred as MacMillan worked on the piece. The movement climaxes with brutal percussion blows—nails driven mercilessly into Christ's hands and feet. In the Easter work, *Symphony: Vigil*, the music incorporates ecstatic, irregular dance, and its central movement, *Tuba insonet salutaris* ("Sound the trumpet of salvation"—from the *Exsultet*, sung at the Easter Vigil) is described by MacMillan thus: "The brass quintet, which played unseen at the end of the first movement, now comes into the auditorium and the players position themselves at five different points, representing the trumpets of salvation. The aural perspective takes on new dimensions as music is heard from all angles, and the sounds are bright and startling."[77] The resolution enacted in *Symphony: Vigil* neither effaces the harshness of the memories of the preceding days nor accords them any kind of ultimacy, but through a wide range of carefully controlled musical techniques transfigures the dissonance into a novel and utterly beguiling beauty. Moreover, its beauty is anything but tidy; the forms overlap, material is scattered, dropped, and picked up again; and we are given a concluding section with (in MacMillan's words) "luminous floating chords on high strings accompanying gently soaring trumpet calls and bright percussion."[78]

In this chapter we have examined two composers who have sought to bring a theological wisdom to bear on their work as composers. Their thinking about music—their vision of what music is and what it is capable of doing—is articulated largely in musical terms and is shaped to a very significant extent by the Christian faith in which they stand. We have seen that, for all they have in common, they also bring quite distinctive perspectives to their composition, and we have concentrated on one major divergence between them: God's involvement with time and, as part of this, the centrality and repercussions of the cross.

It is perhaps worth ending, however, by highlighting something crucial they both share. Both have composed a huge amount of music that would readily be associated with a worship setting and have managed to get it taken seriously in the secular contexts of the modern music culture. Messiaen could even say, "My chief originality is to have taken the idea of the Catholic liturgy from the stone building intended for religious services and to have installed it in other buildings not intended for this kind of music and which, finally, have received it very well."[79] The fact that both have done this so effectively is something worth pondering deeply.

part 3

music in a
christian ecology

a christian
ecology

8

We have looked at some key encounters between the world of music and the world of theology. We have turned the spotlight on some of the major figures involved, ranging from Augustine to James MacMillan, highlighting the ways in which they have offered a Christian wisdom in the world of music in different ways at different times and in different contexts. In each case I have tried to draw attention to some of the key axes on which their work turns, to get a little closer to what is critically important for any who seek a distinctively Christian wisdom for music. Now we turn to the more constructive section of the book. Bearing in mind and drawing on the material we have uncovered, in this chapter we attempt to sketch the outline of what I am going to call a "Christian ecology." In the next two chapters we spell out something of what it might mean to think about music within this ecology.

I am using the word "ecology" here in a double sense. First, I have in mind something like "guiding framework," a network of basic beliefs or faith commitments that together shape and pattern our perception of the world. In Christian experience, these faith commitments arise (or ought to arise) under the impact of the gospel itself, as we are reconciled by the Spirit to the Father through Jesus Christ. In theology, they are typically articulated in doctrines. Developing a Christian wisdom about music, then—the purpose of this book—means setting music in the context of the web of faith commitments through which Christians make sense of and live in the world they inhabit. (It needs to be borne in mind that doctrines are manifestations of something much larger—what some call "worldviews," a term referring to precritical, tacit patterns of perception through which people come to terms with reality, typically expressed in stories, key questions, symbols, and forms of practice. Christian wisdom about music entails being alert to the ways in which doctrines express and relate to these different elements of a worldview.)[1]

At the same time, there is a second way I am using the word "ecology"—a more common and concrete sense. When we speak of the "ecological crisis," our interest is in the created world at large as distinct from the human sphere alone. In theology, to talk about a Christian ecology is normally to talk about what would come under the ambit of a "doctrine of creation": an account of God as Creator, what kind of world God creates and relates to, and what our role in relation to the created world at large might be.[2] In short, then, in these three chapters we are concerned with locating music within the wide ecology of Christian belief, while paying special attention to the doctrine of creation.

Why focus on the doctrine of creation? After all, music is surely what *we* do, a human activity. It is not an object just "there" in the physical world. You don't bump into music when you go for a walk in the woods the way you bump into a tree trunk; you *make* music or hear someone make it. (We might speak of birdsong as "music," but only in a very qualified sense.) Why then the special concentration on music as it connects with the created world at large?

The most immediate answer is that music is a form of engagement with the physical world in which we live. We have already stressed this in chapter 1.[3] In Ernst Bloch's striking phrase, music is "moulded sound."[4] Music making involves embodied people taking existing physical objects and making sounds and arranging and combining those sounds into various meaningful patterns. Hearing music involves being caught up in these audible sound patterns as they are mediated through our bodies. I am not suggesting that the pleasures of music can be reduced to nothing but physical components and processes. But a plausible account of music needs to take seriously its fundamental embeddedness in the material world, its deep physicality, as well as our embeddedness as physical creatures in that world. This leads us naturally toward a doctrine of creation.

But this still leaves us with the question: granted that it is important, why give the doctrine of creation *particular* attention? In fact, we have already touched on the matter at stake many times in the previous chapters. Most of the readers of this book live in what is typically called a "late-modern" or "postmodern" setting, characterized by distinctive patterns of thinking and action that have come to mark European and North American society. In the last few chapters, we have discovered some of the major currents that have given birth to these patterns. To risk drastically oversimplifying: for a variety of reasons, since the demise of the medieval scenario in which human beings were seen as inhabiting a God-given order, Western culture has found it increasingly hard to come to terms with the notion of the created world as our intended "home." Music is less and less thought of as tuning into and respectfully developing an order we inhabit as bodily creatures and instead is increasingly identified as a purely human enterprise, a humanly devised means of shaping sounds for our own interests, a tool of human communication, expression, and persuasion. The idea that music might also be able to elicit something of the character of the cosmos (and through that testify to the Creator) will in many quarters today be treated with disdain, with a cynical smile at best.

It is not surprising, then, that one of the most critical questions to emerge in our discussion so far is this: *to what extent is music grounded in or obliged to be faithful to a world we did not make, a world that we did not fashion but that is in some sense given to us?* This is the challenge the Great Tradition puts to us perhaps more strongly than any other; it is the critical question that arises in the shift we noted between Luther and Calvin; it is one of the key questions a close study of Bach throws into relief; it is the question Barth challenges us with in his attempt to reground music cosmologically; and to some extent it arises also with Messiaen's passion to honor what he believed to be the God-given realities of sound and color (and birdsong!). This was not the only important issue to arise in part 2, of course, but it was a prominent and major one, and as we will see, one that is raised acutely in the modern, late-modern/postmodern climate.

Am I recommending we put the clock back? Hardly. As we saw, the Great Tradition, in addition to being very diverse, can also be fraught with problems. But if simplistic nostalgia is one danger, then assuming uncritically that late-modern/postmodern Western habits of thinking about music are the only ones, or the best ones, is another. Without for a moment suggesting that the modern era has brought nothing but ills to music, if we plunge too quickly into asking about *how we should shape the world*, we are much more likely to be sucked into cul-de-sacs when thinking about music than if we begin by asking *how God's shaping of the world might shape our own* (a more biblical approach)—and this is what we are attempting to do here.

Creator, Cosmos, and Calling

How to begin? Bearing in mind our particular interest in the doctrine of creation, by far the most crucial theological question is *what kind of Creator creates?* And from this flow two further questions: *What kind of cosmos does the Creator create and relate to?* And, *what kind of calling do we have in this cosmos?* The answers to these three questions are gathered together in what is usually called the doctrine of creation; this chapter is built around each of them in turn.

In posing these questions, it should be stressed, *imagination* is required. This is not an invitation to uncontrolled fantasy or fiction, as if we should conjure up ideas out of thin air. By imagination here I am speaking of the ability to *perceive connections* between things that are not spelled out, not immediately apparent on the surface, as well as between what we see now in the present and what we could or will see in the future.[5] First and foremost, imagination of this sort should be applied to our reading of Scripture. We need to live inside the world of these texts and inhabit them so deeply that we begin to recognize links, lines of association, and webs of meaning that may not always be laid out explicitly or at any length but that nevertheless give Scripture its coherence, contours, and overall directions. The answers to our three key questions will not come simply by piling up biblical references into a theological edifice. A healthy doctrine of creation emerges when the church reads Scripture imaginatively in the sense just described, trying to perceive broad patterns and unifying threads and to be alert to the themes and counterthemes that crisscross its pages and that together throw into relief guiding convictions about who this Creator God is, what kind of world he has created and relates to, and what our place within this world might be. That is our task in this chapter.[6]

Second, similar imaginative skills need to be applied to our *reading of the world through the doctrine we discover*. Good doctrine jolts our perspectives and shakes up the way we view things; it invites us to perceive the world in a different way and discern connections, not only between the things we perceive in the world but between what we perceive in the world and what we perceive in Scripture. A Christian doctrine of creation that resonates with Scripture says to us, in effect: "try seeing the world we live in . . . *this* way—as a world made, sustained and carried forward to its goal by a Triune God." Arguably, what the church needs urgently today when it comes to music is not so much another course on how to improve its hymns or how to reform the music industry (important as these things may be) but a fresh vision of the created world under God, a renewed imagination, and then the courage to ask, "Why not try thinking about music . . . *this* way?" This we attempt in chapters 9 and 10.

Also in chapters 9 and 10 we aim to exercise the imagination in a third way: we ask what it means to *live in and live out this "reading of the world,"* to ask how life could be (indeed, must be) different and what this means for music. This demands imagination because, of course, the Bible does not spell out the details of Christian behavior for all times, prescribing exact courses of action for every circumstance—and certainly not for music. Because not all is given to us now, imagination is needed. The church needs to *improvise* imaginatively—that is, to be so schooled in these texts and scriptural tradition that it can (out of habit, ideally) act in ways that are true to the texts yet engage with the world as it now is, responding in ever fresh and fruitful ways to whatever life throws at us.[7] So, intertwined with our invitation to "think about music . . . *this way*," in chapters 9 and 10 there is an invitation to practice it in different ways, to dare to make it and hear it in ways perhaps never before envisaged.

What Kind of Creator?

And so to the first question. What kind of God does the creating? Who is the Creator revealed in the gospel of Jesus Christ? The Christian tradition answers:

a trinitarian God who is Father, Son, and Spirit. Everything we will say relates to this claim.

Christ and Creation

Keeping the trinitarian character of God in view depends on maintaining two perspectives. The first concerns Jesus Christ. Christ himself is the entry point to a trinitarian view of the Creator. The links between Christ and creation crop up in many places in the New Testament and seem to have been there from the earliest times.[8] Christ is proclaimed as belonging to the identity of God the Creator. The one who has become flesh (John 1:14)—fully human, who has walked this earth, breathed this air, gone to his death for us—is the one through whom all things were made (John 1:1–3).[9] In 1 Corinthians 8:6, the apostle Paul inserts Christ, so to speak, into the heart of the God of Jewish monotheism as the coagent of creation—Jesus Christ is the one "through whom are all things."[10] Further, Christ is the one through whom all things are upheld (Heb. 1:3) and by whom all things are held together (Col. 1:17). As the one by whose blood all things are reconciled to God (Col. 1:20), Christ is also the one for whom all things are made (Col. 1:16) and in whom all things will finally be gathered up (Eph. 1:10).

To pick up words from James Dunn on Colossians 1:15–20, "The vision is vast. The claim is mind-blowing."[11] At the very least, it is clear that for these writers the Creator God is the God made known in Jesus Christ, and no other. As the Word made flesh, "close to the Father's heart" (John 1:18), Jesus introduces us to the mind and heart of the Father Almighty, maker of heaven and earth. He enacts who God is. He will be the clue as to *why* God created the world. Further, because he belongs to God "on the inside," Christ is the central key to understanding *how* God relates to what he has made. God the Creator will act in a Christlike way and no other way. Further still, the declaration is that in this person God's purposes for all things have found their fulfillment. Christ is not only the instrument of God's plans for creation, he embodies those plans. Where is creation headed? Look at this person, crucified and risen.

Christ himself, then, in whom our reconciliation has been forged, provides the first and supreme benchmark for any theology of creation that dares to call itself Christian, for *he opens up to us the mind and heart of the Creator, revealing the why of creation, the way in which the Creator relates to creation, and the goal for which all things were created.* As the history of theology shows, and as we shall see in due course, all sorts of difficulties arise when a doctrine of creation is built up apart from, or in advance of, a focus on Jesus Christ.[12] To take the New Testament witness seriously means there is no more basic way to think about creation *except* through the prism of Christ.

Spirit and Creation

However, much depends also on giving due attention to the role of the Holy Spirit, along with and in relation to Christ. There is relatively little said in the New Testament about the Spirit at work in creation at large; we have to extrapolate from what we are told about the Spirit's work in the human sphere. Again, this requires imagination. We are going to suggest that the *Spirit's role in creation at large is to bring about in the world what has already been achieved in Christ and in so doing to anticipate the final re-creation of all things.* In the New Testament, the Spirit is the Spirit of the "Age to Come"—what first-century Jews believed would be the final fulfillment of God's purposes for the world. In Christ, that new age, the kingdom, has been embodied and realized. It has yet to come in all its fullness for the world. It is the Spirit's role, as life-giver and transformer, to bring about here and now among us the conditions of the new age, in advance of its final and full coming. The Spirit previews the future.[13]

What Kind of Cosmos?

With this double perspective in mind, we may now move to the second question: What kind of world does the Creator create and relate to?

A World Crafted in Freedom and Love

For the Christian, the world is not the product of chance or random forces. It is not self-created but comes from the personal initiative of a God whose very being is personal through and through. As such, it flows from God's freedom and his love. We can take each in turn.

1. The Christian tradition affirms God's utter *freedom* in creating. There is no internal necessity for God to create—God did not *need* to create the world for his own self-fulfillment or self-realization. Nor is there some external constraint upon God. Contrast the myths of neighboring societies or the philosophies of the early Greek cosmologists, where a god or the gods struggle with some pre-existent material. No such matter predates and restrains Scripture's God. Nor is there another god, a rival deity, provoking this God to create. This God is free from all external compulsions. In the second century the church introduced the phrase "creation out of nothing" (*creatio ex nihilo*) to emphasize this.[14] God did not create the world out of something already existing. There was no "stuff" or primordial material out of which God made the universe (as, classically, in Plato's *Timaeus*), for this would mean that he was prompted, or at least constrained by something beyond himself. Rather, the world is the product of the free will of its Creator.[15]

True as this may be, this could sound arbitrary, as if creation is no more than an act of brute power, a fiat of God's naked will with no rhyme or reason. Many theologies and cosmologies have succumbed to this trap, picturing the repeated command of Genesis 1—"Let there be!"—as little more than an out-of-the-blue declaration, as if the world is just there, a bare given. But creation is a *purposive* act: it is the outcome of God's love, and, just because of that, it has an intended future. We shall talk about the future a little later; here we need to look at what it means to say creation is the outcome of love.

2. The Christian tradition affirms God's *love* in creating. Think of the word "given" I used a moment ago. I might speak of something as a given fact: it is pouring outside; my car is blue. Givens like this are just the way things are. And often the word acquires negative connotations, especially when it is used for boundaries that frustrate us: time, death, our bodies, and so forth. It is easy to treat these as ultimates, on a par with, perhaps even greater than, God.

But this is not the only way of using the word "given." I point to the clock on the shelf and say, "It was given to me by a close friend." The word has connotations of benevolence, warmth, and a concern for my pleasure, and it provokes gratitude on my part. For the writers of Scripture, the created cosmos is never simply there in a neutral sense or a negative sense, and it is not to be seen as some kind of ultimate, on a level with God. It is created out of love with a purpose in mind. This Creator is the God who makes covenants, who reaches out to his people in steadfast love. The Creator is the God of Abraham, Isaac, and Jacob—the saving God of Jesus Christ. His creation is not just a brute fact but the outcome of benevolence; it is given—at least in part—for human delight and flourishing. The same goes for the constraints and limitations we know as creatures; they are not simply there, and they are certainly not to be treated as ultimate (only God and his grace have that privilege); they are there for the good of what is created. We shall return to this point many times when we discuss music.[16]

In the Christian tradition, this love is not something God puts on when he so desires. It is who God is. The steadfast love that the Creator God shows Israel is the love the Father shows for Jesus, climaxing in the cross, which in turn is the love the Father has for the Son from all eternity (John 17:24). Jesus Christ introduces us to a God who is and always has been love in his innermost being—the Father's love for the Son and the Son's love for the Father in the Spirit is an eternal love. It is not simply what God is on the outside but what he is in his very self. Love belongs to who God *is*, to the heart of the Creator.

If we want to make sense of "creation out of nothing"—that is, as creation by the God of Jesus Christ—then we will see it not as an act of arbitrary power but an expression of God's ceaseless love. It *is* an act of power, of course, but as the power of divine love, the power that reaches its acme in the outgoing self-abnegation of Calvary. God "goes beyond himself," renouncing isolation, solitude, and independence. He creates so he can share and enjoy his love with another, both for his own glory and for the good of the reality he establishes. It is love that motivates creation.

We may go further. The love we see acted out for us in Jesus Christ is a love that exposes itself to rejection, to death on a cross. So, tentatively, we might say that creation is an act of suffering or sacrificial love or, at the very least, an act that lays God open to the possibility of rejection. The vulnerability of the stable at Bethlehem and the ignominious death of an alleged criminal is the selfsame vulnerability at the heart of the Creator.[17]

In any case, if this is the world we live in, for all its perplexities and agonies, we can never again regard it as just there. It is given with divine loving intent, and the most fundamental response to such giving will be gratitude, thanksgiving.

A World That Praises God—Good but Not God

There are few places in Scripture where creation's own praise is celebrated quite so compellingly as the opening of Psalm 19.

> The heavens are telling the glory of God;
>   and the firmament proclaims his handiwork.
> Day to day pours forth speech
>   and night to night declares knowledge.
> There is no speech, nor are there words;
>   their voice is not heard;
> yet their voice goes out through all the earth,
>   and their words to the end of the world. (Ps. 19:1–4)

The result of God's "Let there be"—flowing from his free, loving will—is a fabulous cosmos that sings the glory of God in wordless song.

As we are faced with creation's awesome testimony to the Creator, much depends on keeping two cardinal convictions together, both woven into the very fabric of Scripture. The first is about the *goodness* of God's creation. The created world has intrinsic value and worth. Despite being marred by evil, the cosmos is able to glorify God. This is grounded in God's commitment to what he has made; creation is the object of God's attention and dedication, it is cherished by him.[18] And this in turn flows out of what we have just been claiming: God's commitment to what he has made is an expression of that loving commitment within his own trinitarian life, the loving commitment embodied in Jesus Christ.

An oft-heard charge against today's church is that of "anthropocentrism" (or "humanocentrism"): that the church has come to see God's purposes focused solely on humanity and that the nonhuman world is exclusively for our benefit. Consumed with our own self-importance, we have assumed that the only value the nonhuman world has is its "value for us." The modern sorry tale of the rape and pollution of the earth for short-term and selfish gain is closely tied to this.[19] Christians have played a large part in fueling the contemporary ecological tragedy, so the argument goes, by treating creation at best as a mere prelude to a human-centered gospel, as if God had no lasting interest in anything beyond *Homo sapiens*.[20] Nineteenth-century philosopher Ludwig Feuerbach could claim outright that "nature, the world, has no value, no interest for Christians. The Christian thinks only of himself and the salvation of his soul."[21] Tom Wright captures one version of this mind-set well:

> Many Christians . . . have been taught that the "world," usually associated strongly with the physicality of creation, is essentially evil; that God sent his Son from beyond the world to rescue us out of it; that (perhaps) God intends to bring the physical world to a well-deserved end, after which we will finish up either in a nonphysical heaven or a nonphysical hell.[22]

A huge amount of writing in theology has sought to counter this kind of distortion.[23] Many are requiring of us a careful return to the Bible's testimony where, it is urged, we find that God has pledged himself to *all* that he has made and that creation has its own worth, even apart from humans. Scripture presents us with a cosmic drama, tracing the story from the making of *all* things to the remaking of *all* things in the new heaven and earth.[24] There is frequent mention of creation offering praise (or being called to offer praise) to God, without any suggestion that it needs human beings to do so (e.g., Ps. 19:1–6; 69:34; 98:7–8; 104; 148). The notion that the value of things is limited solely to their use by human beings is hard to justify in Scripture. Indeed, the graphic scenario of Job 37–39, in which God draws the attention of Job to his fellow creatures, is designed to decenter humanity quite drastically: "The lesson is to teach him his place as one creature among others in a creation of which he is not the be-all and end-all."[25] Not only are we involved in a common history with the physical world, but we cannot entertain our own redemption in isolation from it. This reaches its supreme confirmation in the appearance of Christ: the eternal Son, through whom the world was made, is born into the world as a physical creature, to bring not only humanity but the entire cosmos to its destiny (Eph. 1:10). Witness the drumbeat of "all things," occurring five times in Colossians 1:15–20; the scope of what has happened in Christ is not one atom less than *ta panta*—all things.

Any hint, therefore, that the created world is somehow shabby or evil just because it includes physical realities has no place in the biblical tradition. Certainly, idolatry is a constant danger—we shall come to this in a moment—but idolatry is a matter not of something evil being treated as good but of something good being treated as the ultimate good. Matter may not *be* God, but it matters *to* God. By the same token, the suggestion that our own physical bodies are to be despised, denigrated, or downplayed just because they are physical should be firmly shunned. We are not disembodied spirits but unities of spirit and matter inhabiting a physical world with which we are intimately bound up. Hence the Christian commitment to the resurrection of the body, based on the resurrection of Christ—my body is not a toy to throw away at death nor a miserable rag, worthless or morally empty. On the contrary, God takes our body so seriously he has promised to bring it out in a new edition (1 Cor. 15:42–49).

Along with this conviction about the goodness of creation goes a second—*the good world is not God*.[26] The biblical tradition assumes an absolute ontological distinction (a distinction of being) between God and the world. This is something else safeguarded by the notion of "creation out of nothing": God did not make the world out of his own self, his own divine being. The world is not a piece or part of God. The world is created; God is not. The world depends on God; God does not depend on the world. The world is finite and transient; God is not. In more biblical language, only the Creator is to be worshiped (the sin of idolatry being denounced in the second commandment and in Romans 1:25). Again, all this is supremely confirmed and exemplified in Jesus Christ, for here Creator and creature meet without subverting or compromising each other—Christ is fully divine and fully human.

So we will want to join Calvin and proclaim that the world is "the theater of God's glory," but this does not make it God. We may join Gerard Manley Hopkins and declare, "The world is charged with the grandeur of God,"[27] but this does not make it God. We rejoice that the heavens announce God's glory (Ps. 19:1), that the nonhuman world displays God's "eternal power and divine nature" (Rom. 1:19–20), that it is upheld and carried forward to its goal by God and pervaded by his intimate presence—but none of this makes creation God.

We can now understand more clearly some of what was going on during that period we looked at toward the end of chapter 3, when the grand medieval worldview, which in one form or another had nourished so much music theory, began to wane.[28] We saw that out of an eagerness to assume direct correspondences between creation and God (perhaps through presuming a "hierarchy of being" between the two), not enough attention was paid to the structures of creation as they actually are, to the way musical sounds, for example, actually operate in practice. Once we realize the world has its *own* character, its *own* ways of functioning, we will begin to attend to it more carefully *as it is* and *as it could be* and will be very wary of projecting onto it a theory of order unthinkingly imported from the philosopher's or the theologian's desk. Indeed, some have argued that the Reformation's insistence on the distinction between God and the world encouraged just this kind of attentiveness and played a key part in the development of modern science.[29] Alan Lewis puts the matter succinctly:

> Precisely because nature was understood not to be divine or supernatural, inhabited and controlled by sacred or diabolical forces, but contingent, secular and profane, it could be studied. Because men and women . . . heard and saw nature

praising God and pointing away from itself, proclaiming its own independence, ordinariness and secularity, they took nature seriously and began to listen to it scientifically also.[30]

In short, the created world is not good *despite* being different from God; it is good *in its very difference and distinctiveness*. It is created, and it will most fully honor God when it fulfills its role as created. This is the paradox we cannot afford to miss—we will see the world as God's world most clearly when we resist treating it as if it were divine. It glorifies God in its own way. As Christopher Smart says,

> Glorious the northern lights a-stream;
> Glorious the song, when God's the theme[31]

Of course, distinctions have a habit of turning into chasms. Especially from the seventeenth century in Europe, a proper concern to preserve the distinctiveness of the creation led in some places to a view of the world as essentially separate from God, as a fundamentally closed mechanism governed by the laws of Newtonian science, with God as the Designer perhaps, but only occasionally intervening (if at all), and human beings dominating and exploiting the nonhuman order with increasing technical prowess, treating it as no more than a resource for human use. Such an outlook (taking many forms) has done immense damage, among other things "disenchanting" the physical world, robbing it of its inherent value. It is not surprising that in time there arose vigorous reactions to this: for example, attempts to "resacralize" the natural order by some of the English and German romantics or in the burgeoning "creation spiritualities" of our own day. Unfortunately, many of these responses, out of an eagerness to recover a sense of the world as upheld and sustained by God, come perilously close to worshiping creation in the process. Arguably, these two extremes—the exploitation of creation and its idolatry—can be avoided only if we keep in mind the double strand so intrinsic to Jewish and Christian faith and life: creation is good, of inestimable worth and value to God, but not thereby divine; it is good precisely in its own finite, created integrity.

A World Made to Flourish toward Its End

In saying that God is committed to what he has made, we are speaking of an active, ongoing commitment. This means abandoning once and for all the popular idea that the role of God the Creator is simply to start things off, to light the firework before standing clear. There may be good reasons to posit an absolute beginning to the world in order to underline that there was nothing before creation—no matter, no primal powers, and no "prior" time.[32] But we should avoid giving the impression that after the Big Bang, God retreated into inactivity, that the world is less dependent on God now than at its first moment of existence.[33] The Christian God is no deistic machine maker, an absentee landlord who merely sets the world running and leaves it to its own devices. In Ruth Etchells's words, God is not "to be understood as having 'made something' and then wondered what to do with it; rather . . . from the first the creative purpose was one of profound and secure relationship, to be felicitous and glorious."[34] In short, God is steadfastly committed to the flourishing of the world, and this is itself an expression of his steadfast love displayed in the crucified and risen Messiah.

This is a commitment with a *future*. The world is made to go somewhere, to prosper toward its end. It has a destiny, promised and embodied in Christ. Its present beauty and glory are not to be worshiped but to be valued as foretastes of the coming glory of God. Indeed, the poignancy of nature's beauty, the fact that its glory is so interlaced with transience (how we long to say to the sunset, "Hold it right there!") can serve to remind us of just this. Creation awaits an end not yet given. Its present beauty is wonderful but not final.

All this entails taking *time* seriously as a real and good dimension of creation. The cosmos is not a timeless lump of matter; it is created with time, with a history. Here we can join hands with a venerable tradition associated with St. Irenaeus of Lyons (ca. 140–202) that holds that the world was created with an intended future.[35] This is not to say that the world was created less than good or corrupt, or that it was created disordered, or that its order is forever changing. Essentially it is to say, in Tom Wright's words: "The Bible always envisages God as having more in store for his creation than has yet been revealed."[36] And the final future has, of course, been previewed in Jesus Christ.

God, then, is actively committed to the flourishing of the world, looking to the end he desires for it.[37] The broad term for the working out of this active commitment of God is "providence." The word carries its own message: God *provides* for the needs of the world, enabling it to achieve the ends for which it was created in the beginning. This takes many forms, all of them to be understood ultimately through Christ. There is *sustenance*—God sustains his world, expressed classically in the "Venite," Psalm 95:4, "In his hand are the depths of the earth; and the heights of the mountains are his also." If no divine hand were there, the world would collapse back into the nothingness. Because the world is directed to a future, however, this upholding must be understood dynamically: God propels the world toward its goal. In Hebrews 1:3, we are told that the Son "sustains" (NRSV alternative reading: "bears along")[38] all things by his powerful word. As part of this, there will be *development*, a bringing about of fresh forms of order: in this connection, mention is often made of the breathtaking and extremely rapid increase in complexity that has marked the history of the universe, and especially the history of biological life on this planet.

Insofar as creation has been held back, infected, and disordered by evil, there will be redemption, a *transfiguration*. This does not mean a return to Eden but a remaking of creation into a new state, purged of death and corruption, a final union with God not given in the beginning. The prototype for this is Jesus Christ himself. The one through whom all things have been created has become one of us. He has entered the depths of cosmic disruption caused by sin. In Jesus's healings, his stilling of the stormy waters, his raising Lazarus from the dead, we see God coming as a creature to demonstrate within the created order his lordship over it, setting it free from the forces of chaos. This is not violating creation but redirecting it toward its true end. At Golgotha, Christ takes on himself the full force of the Father's judgment on creation, absorbing the horrific impact of evil and disorder, and on the third day, with death defeated, created matter reaches its final, glorious form—the uncontainable radiance of Jesus's resurrection body. Easter meets Genesis. Like our bodies, which will be changed from physical to spiritual bodies[39] while still remaining bodies, creation will be remade by the covenant God who promised never to let it go.

The claim celebrated on Easter Sunday, then, is that God's unceasing love for creation has led him to come as a man in Jesus, on the cross to submit to the forces of destruction and chaos, and through the raising of Jesus from the dead, forge out of history's most evil event a resplendent and uncontainable glory. God has not simply destroyed evil (still less explained it), but he has placed himself under its power and disorder in order to wrest out of fallen creation a new creation. In Jesus Christ, crucified and risen, we see our humanity made new; in him, we see physical matter transformed. In him we have a pledge that one day all things will be refashioned afresh, "set free from its bondage to decay" (Rom. 8:21)—such is the dazzling outlook to which even now we are being led, when the thin veil separating heaven and earth will finally be removed and creation made totally transparent to the living God.

The vision is stunning and overwhelming, but the central pivot on which it turns is unmistakable: in the person of Jesus Christ, the Creator has re-created creation within creation, freeing it *from* all that thwarts it (even from death), and freeing it *for* a new future, thus giving us a promise within our world of that day when creation will be flooded with the glory of God and come to its final union with the Creator.

Yet there is a crucial rider here, and it links up with the last section. Union does not mean merger. The world is designed to flourish *in its otherness*. Once again, Christ himself is the prototype. When he rose and ascended, his physical humanity did not dissolve into God; it reached its proper destiny as created matter. Creation is not heading for a dissolution into a sea of divinity, like a drop of wine in an ocean. This is just what we should expect from the covenant love shown in Jesus Christ, a love that respects and is committed to the integrity of the beloved. This love—true love—does not smother the beloved. If I love my wife, I will do all I can to help her flourish in her distinctiveness, as she was made to flourish. This kind of love, embodied supremely in Christ, is the love with which God loves his creation. Ultimately, this is rooted in the Trinity. Simply put: the *way God relates to the world and treats the world reflects who God is in himself.* To be sure, we cannot simply equate the relations between Father, Son, and Spirit with that between God and the world. The created world as a whole cannot love God in return (that is something only humans can do); it is not in God in the same way that the Father is in the Son or the Son in the Father. Nonetheless, the basic and important point should not be missed. The love within God involves radical commitment (the triune persons live for one another) as well as irreducible otherness (Father, Son, and Spirit are distinct from one another). This combination of being radically committed and preserving and promoting otherness is surely what we see time and time again in the Bible's testimony to the way God engages his world.[40]

A World of Ordered Openness

But if the world has its own integrity, what kind of integrity is this? To begin with, we may say the world possesses its own *order*. And we may distinguish here between order of *end* and the order of *kind*—more technically, *teleological* order and *generic* order, respectively. The heart is ordered to pump blood around the body (teleological order); plants and animals are both creatures (generic order). Most of the time we take the order of the world (in these two senses) for granted; we simply assume the world is ordered. The scientist and philosopher Michael Polanyi has written much about this "tacit dimension" in our lives.[41] There is a whole range of things that we assume as we go about our lives, which we do not attend to directly (focally) but which we rely on, draw on (tacitly). When I play a piece on the piano, I am attending (focally) to the sounds I make, but I am also aware of the physical shape of the keys, how much pressure is needed to produce certain sounds, memories of having played the piece before, and so on. These latter things are part of a tacit dimension of which I am subsidiarily aware. I rely on these things to play the piece well.

A scientist's awareness of the world's order is comparable. For example, when scientists come across an unusual chemical reaction, they attempt to link what they find with other reactions they know about, other compounds that behave in similar ways. At that point, they are searching for generic order, and they are tacitly aware of the world as generically ordered, relying on that awareness to advance their knowledge. If every instrument reading in a laboratory were merely a one-off, isolated event that could not be correlated in any intelligible way with other readings, science would be impossible (and pointless).[42] The Christian will want to say that this orderliness (as well as teleological order), while not a knockdown proof of the existence of a Creator, can be read as a witness to the committed faithfulness of God, revealed in its fullness in Christ.

Another part of the scientist's tacit awareness is that the world is *intelligible*. This might seem unremarkable, but it is worth pausing to recall that it might have been different. The physicist and theologian John Polkinghorne points out, "We are so familiar with the fact that we can understand the world that most of the time we take it for granted." But, he continues, "it could have been otherwise. The universe might have been a disorderly chaos rather than an orderly cosmos. Or it might have had a rationality which was inaccessible to us."[43] Our intellectual engagement with the world's order is, of course, only part of the story of being human—there are also physical, emotional, moral, aesthetic interactions with our environment. But in any case, once again, this can be read as a testimony to the givenness of the world. We recall that the world's order is never just there but is God-given, and humans have been created in such a way that they can live in and interact fruitfully with it.

To be sure, this needs to be qualified on two fronts. First, we need to face the stark fact that for many it is anything but clear that the cosmos is benevolently ordered. Victims of malignant illness or natural disaster will not be so ready to see in creation the hand of a faithful God. For them providence seems to turn a blind eye. Nevertheless, whatever we make of the notion of a cosmic "fall," it remains true that the reliable order of the world is not destroyed. Despite the ongoing vulnerability of the earth to destructive forces, the world remains a cosmos, inherently ordered. Life would be quite impossible otherwise.

Second, we need to be careful not to see this order in too closed a sense. One of the most influential worldviews of the modern age, often gripping the popular imagination, is of the cosmos as a self-contained machine, whose movements are no more than the unfolding of its own rigid and built-in laws, a cosmos with no place for God (except perhaps as a first cause or designer). Mainstream Christian thought insists that God is unceasingly interacting with the world. As we have said, it is one thing to stress the world's otherness from God, it is quite another to regard it as a sealed-off, predictable mechanism. Some writers have made much of the behavior of complex dynamic systems in the physical world, which exhibit a supple interplay of stability and unpredictability and suggest that the cosmos is marked by an orderly yet abundant allowance of space, time, and energy through which further abundance can emerge.[44] It is a world, in other words, of untidy outcomes and unexpected twists. Those working at the borderlands of science and theology have not been slow to engage with such ideas. Many have argued for various forms of a metaphysics of flexible openness, where the unpredictability of certain physical systems is not merely a matter of our ignorance but is built in to the way things are.[45]

It is tempting here to align God with one side alone—typically, the "open" element—but God is surely as responsible for the world's stability as for its unpredictable fruitfulness. A stress on both Christ's *and* the Spirit's work in creation can help us here. In the New Testament, Christ is associated especially with the ordering and coherence of the world—all things have already found their end in him, are upheld by him, and will be gathered up in him. But along with this, do we not also need a strong sense of the activity of the Spirit, whose particular ministry is to realize now in ever fresh and unpredictable ways what has already been achieved in the Son?[46] To put it another way, the Spirit is the improviser. Daniel Hardy and David Ford speak of the Spirit as active "to enable new possibilities, to empower freedom to live in the abundance that is given." Speaking of the three "modes" of Father, Son, and Spirit, they go on to write that "the second mode sets the pattern and ideal, and this third mode [the Spirit] is the inspiration and means of achieving and participating in it."[47] This resonates with a theme in the tradition of Basil the Great (ca. 330–79), for whom the Holy Spirit is creation's "perfecter," bringing about in the world particular fulfillments of what has already been secured in Jesus Christ.[48]

A World of Diverse Unity

It is also important not to bypass the Spirit when we turn to think about the world's *unity*. The world has been made by one God, not several. It is not a disconnected and dissipating jumble of isolated objects and events, nor was it ever meant to be. At the same time, the Bible's testimony is that this unity was intended to be a unity of *diversity*. Variety is not a regrettable afterthought. (As we now observe it, there are 750,000 species of insects and 240,000 species of plants.) Not surprisingly, many have related this to the richness of the Triune God, who is not a bland oneness but the abundant life of Father, Son, and Spirit.[49] Irenaeus's ancient wisdom is worth pondering:

> [God] formed [all things] as he pleased, bestowing harmony on all things, and assigning them their own place. . . . In this way he conferred on spiritual things a spiritual and invisible nature, on supercelestial things a supercelestial, on angels an angelical, on animals an animal . . . while he formed all things by his Word that never wearies.[50]

While it is true to say that creation praises God, it is just as true to say that within creation, different things praise God in different ways. This gives different things a *particularity*, their own special character. Few have captured this as well as the poet Gerard Manley Hopkins, who held that each entity has its own "inscape": that which makes it distinctively and uniquely itself.[51] In "As Kingfishers Catch Fire" (1880) we are shown how each thing—whether a bird or insect, a stone thrown down a well, a swinging bell—can express its "self" (inscape) and thus give praise to the Father in its own way:

> As kingfishers catch fire, dragonflies draw flame;
> As tumbled over rim in roundy wells
> Stones ring; like each tucked string tells, each hung bell's
> Bow swung finds tongue to fling out broad its name;

Each mortal thing does one thing and the same:
Deals out that being indoors each one dwells;
Selves—goes its self; *myself* it speaks and spells,
Crying *What I do is me: for that I came.*

I say more: the just man justices;
Keeps grace: that keeps all his goings graces;
Acts in God's eye what in God's eye he is—
Christ. For Christ plays in ten thousand places,
Lovely in limbs, and lovely in eyes not his
To the Father through the features of men's faces.[52]

Magnificent as the words are, we might wish that Hopkins had alluded to the Holy Spirit. For while Christ is undoubtedly the one in whom diverse things cohere and relate in their diversity, is not the Spirit the agent of diversity, and as such the one who particularizes things in their difference—that is, enables them to become more particularly themselves? We recall the day of Pentecost as recounted in Acts 2: the crowds heard the disciples speak in their own tongues; they were not given one language (Acts 2:6, 8–11). Or Paul in 1 Corinthians 12: the Spirit gives different gifts to different people, enabling each to flourish. This is part of what Basil meant when he described the Spirit as the "perfecter"—the Spirit enables all things to be what they were particularly created to be, to praise God in their own fashion. Colin Gunton succinctly writes: "All things hold together in Christ: there is the basis of the wonderful order and unity revealed in the miraculous world of the scientist. But all things are particularised, each in their own way, by the Spirit, who relates them through Christ to God the Father."[53]

What kind of cosmos do we inhabit, then? A world crafted in freedom and love, good but not God, made to flourish toward its end, and of ordered openness and diverse unity. All this is known through, and to be understood supremely in the light of, Jesus Christ, in whom the Triune God's purposes for creation have found their fulfillment, who himself embodies the future of creation, a re-created world to which even now the Spirit is directing us.

What Kind of Calling?

Voicing Creation's Praise

In the midst of this breathtaking praise of creation, the speechless paean of the cosmos to its Creator, the Christian faith dares to affirm that a creature, *Homo sapiens*, is given a singular calling: not simply to acknowledge the cosmic symphony, but also to enable, articulate, and extend it in ever fresh ways. A quite proper concern about human hubris and imperialism toward nature should not be answered by a denial of human uniqueness but by a rediscovery of its true character.[54] In the human being, creation finds a conscious answering voice, a mortal from the dust of the earth who can know and respond to God's love as a creature, love God in return, and as part of this response, "voice creation's praise."[55] To use George Herbert's memorable metaphor, each of us is to be a "secretary" of praise.[56]

We can begin to expand on this by looking at what it means to say humanity is created in the "image of God" (Gen. 1:26–27; 9:6), a metaphor that is scarce in Scripture but that has come to play a huge part in Christian discussions of the uniqueness of human beings.[57] "Then God said, 'Let us make humankind in our image'" (Gen. 1:26). Today there is fairly widespread agreement that, as used in Genesis at least, image does not refer to a possession or endowment (like mind, reason, free will) but is a *relational* term. That is, it makes no sense without considering our relation *to God*—as God's unique "counterpart" or covenant partner (we can know and love God in return)—and because of that, *to other creatures*, human and nonhuman, animate and inanimate. Crucial also is the notion of *representation*: as God's counterparts, human beings are God's earthly representatives, his vice-regents, in the way that an ancient monarch was seen to represent a god or a physical image to represent a king.[58] Bound up with this is the idea of *resemblance* or similarity: as God's partners, humans are in some sense like God (hence the pairing of image with likeness).[59] In short, to say that we are created in God's image is to say that we are created as God's unique counterparts and hence God's representatives on earth, embodying, as creatures and alongside other creatures, the action and presence of God in and to the world.[60]

This brings specific responsibilities or obligations.[61] In Genesis 1:26, God's decision to create humankind in the image of God is followed immediately by his decision that they are to rule, have "dominion" over all living creatures, expanded into a lordship over the created order in Genesis 9:1–3. The theme is picked up in Psalm 8:

> What are human beings that you are mindful of them,
>   mortals that you care for them?
> Yet you have made them a little lower than God,
>   and crowned them with glory and honor.
> *You have given them dominion over the works of your hands*;
>   you have put all things under their feet. (Ps. 8:4–6, italics mine)

We have already alluded to a dangerous misunderstanding of this. Dominion has too often been read as domination—a charter for destruction and plunder.[62] But as God's image bearers, humans are to exercise God's wise and loving rule within the world; to use more modern language, we are to be wise stewards of the earth, caring for it and protecting it in a way that reflects and embodies God's rule over his creation.[63] This is less a "lording over" than a "lording under"[64]—under the loving authority of God. As we shall see shortly, this is what is embodied decisively in Jesus Christ. As the true image of God, in him we see God's dominion in action, the kind of dominion we are meant to share as God's image bearers, the antithesis of selfish manipulation or unbridled coercion.

Nevertheless, it is still a lordship. Adam and Eve were placed in the garden to "be fruitful and multiply, and fill the earth" (Gen. 1:28), to "till it and keep it" (Gen. 2:15; see also 9:1)—what the Dutch Calvinists call the "cultural mandate." (It is always worth remembering that Eden was a garden, not a paradise. In a paradise, fruit falls off the trees onto our tables, but as we all know, a garden needs to be worked at, looked after, tended.) Although caring for the earth may at times mean keeping our hands off it—letting creation get on with praising God in its own way (as when we protect a piece of marshland for the sake of conserving a species of bird), this cannot be the whole story. There is a divine call to direct engagement. Hence the cultural initiatives of Genesis 4 (urban development, tent making, musicianship, and metalworking). We mine coal and convert it to heat; we plough the earth and grow crops; we harvest cocoa pods and make chocolate; we take mold and make penicillin. And we take sounds and make music.

Understandably then, some refer to human beings as "priests of creation." The phrase is apt, for it speaks of a double movement. *On behalf of God*, as God's image bearers, humans are to mediate the presence of God *to the world* and in the world, representing his wise and loving rule. But this is so that *on behalf of creation* humans may gather and focus creation's worship, offering it back *to God*, voicing creation's praise.[65]

Misplaced Praise

The Genesis project has misfired. The catastrophe of Adam is that humanity's vocation as worshiper *in* creation has turned into the worship *of* creation (and that includes self-worship). This is set out with great power and clarity in Romans 1–3, where human idolatry is exposed, stemming from (as one writer puts it) a "refusal to praise God,"[66] and leading to alienation from God and one another and to fruitless and destructive living.

Most poignantly, this is the story of Israel. Israel was called to be God's people in the world and for the world, embodying God's purposes for humanity, the agent of the Creator's healing purposes for creation as a whole. Indeed, Israel was called to be a "kingdom of priests" (Exod. 19:6 RSV). As Wright explains: "If the rest of creation is praising the Creator, however inarticulately, Israel was called to gather up those praises and present them, with clear knowledge and belief, before the Creator. Equally, the process was to flow the other way. Israel, having experienced the rescuing power and love of her God, was to be his means of sharing that powerful love with the rest of the world."[67] (We note the twofold movement, and recall what we said in an earlier chapter about the temple congregation articulating or offering worship on behalf of all creation.)[68] Yet over and over again this calling was deeply compromised: other gods were praised; in one way or another Israel neglected the vocation to be God's people in and for the world.[69]

Moreover, humanity's denial of God has smeared creation at large. God's good *shalom* is spoiled. The disorder of sin has cosmic implications, as Genesis 3 makes clear. We are affected in those dimensions of life we share with the rest of creation as creatures—work becomes sweat and toil; sexuality a source of embarrassment, friction, and dissatisfaction; death the "last enemy" (1 Cor. 15:26). We beat nature into submission and reap the bitter consequences in ecological crises. Nature is enmeshed with us in the corruption of our idolatry; there is cosmic as well as human tragedy. Using musical metaphors, John Milton writes:

> . . . disproportioned sin
> Jarred against nature's chime, and with harsh din
> Broke the fair music that all creatures made
> To their great Lord, whose love their motion swayed
> In perfect diapason, whilst they stood
> In first obedience, and their state of good.[70]

The True Worshiper

But what if someone appeared among us who gave total and undiluted praise to God? And what if there were one who as a fully human being, as an Israelite, acted out God's wise rule in the world? What if we found a creature who exercised true dominion, as one of us, from the dust of the earth, and in whose presence the forces of disorder abated, the waves and seas calmed? What if there were one who bore these chaotic forces to the full and bore them away, so that the great Genesis project could advance again? And what if that person were God's gift to us, perhaps even God giving himself to us?

Such is the miracle played out for us in Jesus Christ. He is our word to God, the word God longed to hear from Israel, and from humanity as a whole—the genuine word of praise from our side. Praise in person. Here creation finds its voice—at last a creature praises God with perfect purity. Here idolatry is at last banished. Here is a true worshiper of the Father, the new and last Adam, from our side offering a life of unbroken, loving obedience to God, even to the point of death on a cross where the root cause of humanity's catastrophe is met and defeated. Here is the one in whom the last enemy, death, has been overcome. In him our humanity has been taken and re-formed, turned around to face God again, remade so that it can say "yes" to the Father Almighty who made heaven and earth.

The double movement of humanity's calling, therefore, comes together in Christ. *He speaks and acts on behalf of God.* He is the image of God in person[71]

(2 Cor. 4:4; Col. 1:15; cf. Col. 3:10—all passages with allusions to Genesis).[72] Here is God's true counterpart (the Son of the Father), imaging the Father ("Whoever has seen me has seen the Father," John 14:9), representing God among us, as one of us. To see him, to see his action and hear him speaking, is to see and hear God. In him we learn the true nature of the human rule over the created order, reflecting God's rule, which was promised in the beginning.[73] At the same time, *he speaks and acts on behalf of us and the whole of creation.* Here God hears and finds a creature who truly honors him, in whom our deepest crisis has been overcome, and in whom we see the very goal of the cosmos. He is the one who perfectly voices creation's praise.

And we are invited to join him. At last, the human project given "in the beginning" can advance and reach forward to a new goal. Our privilege is to find our true place in the world, to be conformed by the Spirit to Christ (2 Cor. 3:18) so we can start to be true image bearers ourselves, reflecting the covenant love of God to the world, part of the new human community, the church, with Christ as our head (Col. 1:18; cf. Rom. 8:29; 1 Cor. 15:49).[74]

Revelation 4 and 5 (consciously echoing Genesis) can be read in this light. Here is a spectacular portrayal of worship: the entire creation pouring forth unending praise before God, and twenty-four elders (the people of God from old and new covenants) falling down and declaring God the Creator as the only one worthy of worship. In chapter 5, God holds a scroll—the scroll of his purposes for the world, the puzzle of history. John weeps bitterly, for there is no one to open it. How can we enter creation's joyful praise when we cannot fathom its story? Only a human being can open the scroll. But who is worthy to do this? The Lamb, the Messiah, who has conquered through his death. He alone can unseal the scroll, and he alone sends the sevenfold Holy Spirit into the world. Creation's worship starts again, with the Lamb at the center alongside God. He, and only he, can carry forward God's mission, not only for humanity but also for the entire creation.

Paul's letter to the Romans can also be read from this perspective. Humanity has fallen into idolatry (Rom. 1:18–32), and in response God has provided the faithful Messiah, Jesus. His dying and rising opens out a new future for humanity, which we can start to share in now as we die and rise with Christ (Rom. 6), and a new future for the cosmos, which we can start to know through the indwelling Spirit (Rom. 8). What is implicit in Revelation's use of Genesis is made explicit in Romans 8. Creation waits for the liberation of the children of God—for human beings to "get their act together," so to speak—so that creation, now aching in bondage to decay, can fully glorify God. In Christ through the Spirit we can recover our calling as God's image bearers, as the people of God exercising wise stewardship. This is part of authentic "spiritual worship" (Rom. 12:1). In Romans 12, because of everything Paul has spelled out in the previous chapters, Romans 1 is turned upside down. Self-destructive, downward-spiraling idolatry (Rom. 1) is transformed into fruitful, God-directed worship, the life of a community centered on Jesus (Rom. 12–15).[75]

To draw some of these themes together, we can turn to a representation of the music of the spheres in visual art, from the eleventh-century Evangeliary of the Abbess Uta of Niedermünster (see fig. 8.1). We see Christ crucified at the center, arms outstretched. The torn temple curtain fills the bottom right-hand corner, and opposite this on the left, believers are being raised from the dead. Along the side borders we find figures representing the church and, probably, the synagogue. Under Christ's arms are a series of inscriptions making up a symbolic diagram of the music of the spheres, and Pythagoras's perfect consonances—commonly used at this time as symbols of the Trinity. Christ, belonging to the Triune God, through his death brings nothing less than cosmic and human harmony.[76]

Fig. 8.1: Symbolic Crucifixion from the Evangeliary of the Abbess Uta of Niedermünster, Codex Monacensis lat.13601, fol.3v. Used by permission of Bayerische Staatsbibliothek

To summarize: our calling in relation to creation as a whole is to extend and elaborate the praise that creation already sings to God. True human praise has been embodied for us in Christ—we do not have to generate it out of our own resources. The one through whom all things were created has became part of a creation whose praise has been corrupted, and in him, crucified and risen, creation is offered back to the Father, redirected toward its goal. At last God receives what he has longed for and is due. And now, through the Spirit, we are given a part to play: made one with Christ, and as members of his new community, we are to bring creation to be more fully what it was created to be, and in so doing we anticipate the final re-creation of all things.

———•◦•———

We have spoken about our responsibility, as God's image bearers, to share in God's dominion. This can never mean simply sitting back and enjoying the status. In the language of Genesis, there is a calling to till the earth. When we speak about music, we are in the realm of culture—we engage with the physical world, ordering and reordering what is given to hand and mind. We turn wilderness into gardens, empty land into housing, wasteland into forests, vibrations in the air into symphonies.

What should this cultural vocation look like? And what shapes it? Here I can do no more than note some of its different dimensions. Later, we fill them out and begin to see what they might mean for music.

Discovering. The first thing to say is that dominion involves discovery. As we have seen, in Genesis 1:28 it does not mean an aggressive exploitation of the earth for purely human ends. God's loving rule, embodied in Jesus Christ, is not one of harshness and force. Having dominion means living in the world with a love that longs for the beloved to thrive, being committed to the flourishing of the other *as other*. In Steven Bouma-Prediger's words, "The proper exercise of dominion yields shalom—the flourishing of all creation."[77] This means developing an attentiveness to the created order as we engage with it, not assuming we know what is there already. It means developing an eye and ear for its distinctive patterns and ways and curiosity as to what is actually in front of us. As Oliver O'Donovan has expressed it, love "achieves its creativity by being perceptive."[78]

Respecting. Bound up with this is respect. If God has endowed his world with a dynamic "open" order of its own, worthy of our trust, then we are to be sensitive to its integrity. The ecological crisis has forced us to learn this afresh: the delicate balances and nuances of our material environment are to be honored. It is the opposite of image bearing to manipulate—to tread and trample, leaving the earth "bleared, smeared with toil";[79] it is of the essence of image bearing to make sure we know our material and act faithfully toward it. Moreover, because the created order is given out of the overflow of God's good abundance, this attentive courtesy or respect must be seen as never grudging subservience but as full of hope, full of expectation that extraordinary and wonderful things will result.

Developing. We are called not only to discover and respect but also to develop. To be an image bearer of the God who himself develops created realities, improvising through his Spirit freely on the given order as he draws things toward their goal, means we will find ourselves bringing about new entities in the world by selecting, re-forming, combining what we are given. We take cocoa pods and transform them into chocolate; we take a blues bass and improvise something never heard before. However small our patch of creativity, we are to enable creation to find fresh, perhaps even richer forms.

Healing. In a world groaning in travail, distorted and spoiled, riven with tragedy and sometimes unspeakable pain, the vocation to be priests of creation is a vocation to be agents of healing and wholeness. This is the "logic"—if we can call it that—of the incarnation, crucifixion, and resurrection of Jesus. The Son of God has become part of his cosmos, immersed himself in its futility, and on the third day the Father raises what was broken, dying flesh to a new and indescribably rich life, the life of the age to come. With Christ, and by the Spirit, our vocation is to be in the midst of this not-yet-redeemed cosmos, in the world and for the world, as those who share in God's healing work. As such, this healing is imbued with hope, a hope rooted in what God has done and promised to do. Alan Lewis writes of ministry in the power of the slain Lamb of Revelation 5:

> Those who serve him and own his lordship, must surely in his name penetrate into the world of decay and suffering as healers of its brokenness and celebrators of its coming wholeness, declaring and demonstrating that the God who raised the slain lamb will raise with him everything that is wounded and bruised, to newness of life.[80]

Anticipating. Running through all this is a momentum toward the future. If, by God's grace, we do play a part in transfiguring the distortions of this life, it will be a mark of the future breaking in, a foretaste of that glorious future promised in the raising of Jesus from the dead. And as such, it will be a mark of the Holy Spirit among us. We embody hope *now* for what *will* be.

Together. This hopeful human vocation is a corporate one. There are no solo priests. To see this, we need only glance back at the passages on creation we have touched on in this chapter. Colossians 1 is as representative as any. What do we find in the midst of Paul's spectacular depiction of Christ as mediator and goal of creation? The affirmation that "He is the head of the body, the Church" (Col. 1:18), the community that fulfills the calling of Israel.[81] The church, grounded and participating in the Son's own communion with the Father (Jesus prays that his followers may be one as he and his Father are one [John 17:22]), and formed through the cross and the outpouring of the Spirit (as John's Gospel goes on to make clear), is the chief agent of culture. Human beings exercise their proper role in God's good earth by being reconciled to one another, bound together in the Spirit with that same self-forgetful love flowing eternally between Father and Son. To image God means to image *in the world* that love that lies at God's very heart in a fellowship or communion (*koinonia*) that will share in and reflect God's own "being as communion."[82]

music in God's world

9

When I started writing the book [*Rumors of Another World*] I would have said that the three things that brought me back to God were not religious things. They were not Billy Graham rallies or gospel tracts. They were the beauty of nature, classical music, and romantic love. When I encountered those three things, suddenly I had this "ding! ding! ding!" experience. I discovered that the world is actually a smiling place, not a scowling place; that God wants me to have a full life, not a half life, not a two-thirds life.

Philip Yancey[1]

"Very few of my students have any possibility of becoming professional artists. My goal is to teach them how to see, so they never have to be bored again."[2]

Where might music find a place in the ecology sketched in the last chapter? In the purposes of a Triune Creator who has created and gathered up all things in Jesus Christ and now perfects all things by his Spirit—what can music contribute? In a world crafted out of freedom and love that praises God in its goodness but is never divine, a world made to flourish toward its end, a world of ordered openness and diverse unity—where do the sounds of singing and playing belong? And in the human vocation to focus and articulate creation's praise, to discover, respect, develop, heal, anticipate, together—how might music play a part?

Again, imagination is needed. As we saw in chapter 2, Scripture's references to music are few and fleeting, and many of them are ambiguous. The links between music and God's cosmic purposes cannot be read off the surface of the biblical text. Pursuing Christian wisdom in the world of music is a far more demanding business. It requires imagination: discerning the unseen and unspoken connections between the kind of vision that has emerged in the last chapter and the beguiling world of tones, chords, melody, and harmony. It is about undergoing those imaginative jolts we spoke about—"try seeing the world we live in . . . *this* way"—and allowing them to work their way out in the sphere of music: "try thinking about music . . . *this* way"—and, intertwined with this, living out the implications in practice: "try hearing and making music . . . *this* way." This is what we are about in this and the next chapter.

We can begin by describing the activity of music at its simplest: music is one of the ways we can voice creation's praise. We work with physical objects in God's good world (our vocal cords, reeds, tubes of bamboo, or whatever) and the sounds that come from them, and we form music. Ideally, we do this in a way that benefits others in some way and brings God glory. Hearing music can likewise be a way in which we can interact fruitfully with our material environment, other people, and, indeed, God, and in so doing, magnify God's name.

But clearly this needs to be filled out, and with an ear alert to some of the particular challenges that our modern, late-modern/postmodern ethos presents. In the previous chapter we asked three questions: What kind of *creator* creates? What kind of *cosmos* does this Creator create and relate to? What kind of *calling* do we have in this cosmos? In what follows, we need to keep in mind the answer to the first question throughout: the creator is the Triune God of Jesus Christ, and none other. However, the implications of this for music will become clearer as we set music in the context of our answers to the second question (our concern in this chapter) and the third question (our concern in the next).

Of course, with limited space there will be numerous themes and issues that I cannot even begin to address. In many places I can do no more than hint at where I think the truth might lie. It is for others to take things much further. Once again, therefore, imagination is needed: to take what is covered here and discern what it might mean for areas that are not covered.

Music—in a World Crafted out of Freedom and Love

We have seen that for the Christian, the world we inhabit can never be seen as just there, a naked fact, to be treated as a neutral boundary or (worse) as something that is basically an impediment to a fulfilling life. The cosmos did not *have* to be. It is made freely, without any prior constraint or necessity superior to God's nature or will. It is given, and given in the rich sense: as an expression of divine love, the love that is God's own trinitarian life.

In his book *Classical and Christian Ideas of World Harmony*, Leo Spitzer puts his finger on the decisive issue here in the context of a discussion about music as a metaphor of the cosmos. "According to the Pythagoreans," he says, "it was cosmic order which was identifiable with music; according to the Christian philosophers, it was love. And in the *ordo amoris* ('loving order') of Augustine we have evidently a blend of the Pythagorean and the Christian themes: henceforth 'order' is love."[3] There is a huge difference between regarding the harmony in which musical sounds are grounded as simply a bare fact or as an outpouring of love.

In chapter 1, we said that music making and music hearing are ways we engage a sonic order: there are sound-producing materials, sound waves, the human body, and the reality of time. These interacting components with which music deals have ultimately arisen through the free initiative of God's love—they are part of the *ordo amoris*. To treat them as given in this full sense has a series of radical implications for understanding music, as we shall see. Here we need only underline that the most basic response of the Christian toward music will be *gratitude*. This does not mean giving unqualified thanks for every bit of music we hear, but it will mean being thankful for the very possibility of music. It will mean regularly allowing a piece of music to stop us in our tracks and make us grateful *that there is* a world where music can occur, *that there is* a reality we call "matter" that oscillates and resonates, *that there is* sound, *that there is* rhythm built into the fabric of the world, *that there is* the miracle of the human body, which can receive and process sequences of tones. For from all this and through all this, the marvel of music is born.[4] None of it *had* to come into being. But it has, for the glory of God and for our flourishing. Gaining a Christian mind on music means learning the glad habit of thanksgiving.

Music—in a World That Is Good but Not God

Brought forth from God's own free love, the cosmos as a whole is value-laden, the object of God's unswerving faithfulness and the theater of God's loving intentions. As such it is able to sing his praise despite the pollution that evil has brought. God, we said, has pledged himself to the world in its physicality—a pledge confirmed in the coming of Jesus, the Word made material flesh.

Sadly, this is often just where the church has been most hesitant about music. It is not hard to trace a double tendency marking much thought about music in the Christian West: a proneness to doubt the full *goodness*, and with it sometimes the full *reality*, of the physical. The outcome is that music, along with the other arts, has frequently been seen as fulfilling its highest function insofar as it denies, shuns, or leaves behind its own materiality.

We have already met this twin tendency. It surfaces prominently in the ancient Greek tradition we examined in chapter 3, and we saw how it worked out in some Platonic music theory: as part of this material world, music can be of serious value only insofar as it directs our attention to the ideal and enduring harmonies beyond the material. And we observed the impact of this on Christian thought: even in Augustine there is a marked ambivalence about physical beauty and the materiality of music (especially in his early writing). In this current of thinking, musical sounds become a vehicle for the contemplation of eternal or ideal beauty, hence the colossal emphasis in much medieval writing on the superiority of intellectual theory over the practical making and enjoyment of music. Commonly, the thrust seems to be to look beyond material sounds to the order or beauty they reflect or point to rather than to welcome them as valuable *embodiments* of God-given order and beauty in their own right, with their physical character intrinsic to that value. We also found related ideas coloring Zwingli's attitude to music: the "spiritual" set against the material and an overplayed fear of anything that might imply an idolatry of music. Some modern evangelical approaches to music (and the other arts) have followed similar tracks: music, bound up as it is so closely with physical things, is regarded as at best irrelevant and at worst dangerous, tugging us away from the more real, nonsensory "spiritual" realities.

In modern times, it is probably fair to say that this reluctance to give lasting value to the physical in music has led to a focus not so much on Platonic-like eternal forms but more on the inner life of the individual, especially the emotional life. What Ernst Kris notes in the development of visual art from the sixteenth century—a shift from the artist as manual worker to the artist as individual creator—could well apply to music: "The work of art is for the first time in human history considered as a projection of an inner image. It is not its proximity to reality that proves its value but its nearness to the artist's psychic life."[5] Perhaps the best-known version of this outlook is the philosophy of "individual expressivism"—the view that music is (or ought to be) the outward expression of inner emotion, an externalizing of emotional urges and surges, sometimes with the aim of stimulating the same emotion in others. The physical elements of music become the mere means to conveying and provoking a (supposedly) nonphysical emotion.[6] This is an immensely popular outlook, often simply assumed by default, not least in Christian churches.

A distinct and modified version of this appeared in the romantic movement of the late eighteenth and early nineteenth centuries—we have touched on this already in discussing Schleiermacher. With some of the romantics, the artist's inner life became linked to the rhythms of the cosmos, the restless, infinite, spiritual momentum of nature. The Great Tradition thus received a new lease on life—music was thought to turn into sound the infinite play of the cosmos, through the strivings and struggles of the romantic composer or performer. It was thought by many that music unencumbered by words could do this best: instrumental music came to be exalted by many as supreme. Rendered marginal for so long in modernity, art (in the form of music) has returned with a vengeance to assume massive proportions as part of a vast cosmology revolving around the human ego.[7] But what we should not miss here is the implicit devaluing of the physical as physical. Indeed, as we shall see in the next chapter, in some versions physical nature, far from being honored and listened to in its own integrity, is seen as *needing* the creative artist to come to fulfillment.

This hesitation to give enduring value to the physical qua physical can take rather different forms, however. In 1910 the painter Wassily Kandinsky (1866–1944) completed what was to become a famous and much-read essay, "On the Spiritual in Art," drawing on ideas from a philosophical movement known as theosophy. Kandinsky is of particular interest here because he pulls in music to buttress his argument. He is anxious about a crass materialism in contemporary culture, a widespread belief that anything not verifiable by our five senses is meaningless: "Only just now awakening after years of materialism, our soul is infected with the despair born of unbelief, of lack of purpose and aim. The nightmare of materialism, which turned life into an evil, senseless game, is not yet passed; it still darkens the awakening soul."[8]

The only effective response is to recognize that all reality has a nonmaterial, spiritual dimension and that to be truly human is to find and resonate with this supersensuous presence. It is the artist's challenge and calling to produce art transparent to the inner soul of humanity and nature. Though the artist is concerned with self-expression, this is only to the end that reality's inner soul may come to expression, and the physical character of the world is a potential stumbling block to this process. Physical forms must be isolated from their everyday contexts and treated with a high level of abstraction so that their inner nonphysical meaning may shine forth, so that their physicality and particularity can be transcended. Hence the move in Kandinsky's own painting toward abstraction. Reality's deepest life can be expressed only if we relinquish the desire to depict objects, to represent the material world in its external, perceivable features. And here, significantly, music is held up as exemplary. Kandinsky was a keen music lover, an amateur pianist, and a cellist. Music is our "best teacher," he claims. Why? Because for some time it

> has been the art which has devoted itself not to the reproduction of natural phenomena, but to the expression of the artist's soul and to the creation of an autonomous life of musical sound. A painter who finds no satisfaction in mere representation, however artistic, in his longing to express his internal life, cannot but envy the ease with which music, the least material of the arts today, achieves this end.[9]

Interestingly, a not dissimilar view emerges from one of the few Christian theologians of modern times to write about music (apart from those we have looked at already), the Congregationalist theologian P. T. Forsyth (1848–1921).[10] Forsyth's basic belief is that music is concerned essentially with releasing us from the bonds and limits of the finite and material order.[11] Music is the least material of the arts (with the sole exception of poetry). Forsyth is struck by its impermanence and insubstantiality (it does not end up as a concrete object), its inwardness (it primarily arises from and is directed toward our emotional life), and its indefiniteness (it cannot refer with any precision to things beyond itself).[12]

A rather more extreme example of pulling apart from physicality is seen in perhaps the most notorious of modern composers, Arnold Schoenberg (1874–1951). As it happens, Kandinsky greatly admired Schoenberg's skill, and they enjoyed an extensive correspondence. The painter writes, "In your works, you have realized what I, albeit in uncertain form, have so greatly longed for in music. The independent progress through their own destinies, the independent life of the individual voices in your compositions, is exactly what I am trying to find in my paintings."[13]

Schoenberg came to believe that music's sensory pleasure—how pleasant it sounds to the ear—is irrelevant to the question of artistic significance (and to this day, much of his music will sound jarring to many). Music should be concerned chiefly with the creation and development of musical ideas; the pleasure it affords should be primarily intellectual. The enduring significance and value of music lies not at the level of the physical at all; we must learn to rise from the mere materiality of sounds, Schoenberg believed, "to be coldly convinced by the transparency of clear-cut ideas."[14]

Whatever form it takes, Trevor Hart sums up well the outlook I have been tracing:

> It is as if the artist must . . . regret the inherent physicality of artistic manifestation in the world, and would prefer it if some direct transmission of the spiritual or intellectual opus between minds could be arranged, short-circuiting the messiness and crudity of mediation through fleshly realities altogether. That it cannot, that some sort of enfleshing of the work of art must occur, is a problem rather than something to be celebrated. . . . The material artefact serves to translate us from the physical world into a spiritual one, to direct our attention quickly away from itself to some other, higher and more pure, object of consideration.[15]

Views of this kind are not, of course, the only ones available in the modern marketplace. But, arguably, they have been influential and in some places dominant. A biblically informed Christian response refuses to apologize for music's embeddedness in material reality and actually may want to recover a fuller sense of it. As we have stressed already, music involves physical entities as part of the sonic order. Sounds, themselves physical vibrations of the air, are produced by regularly constituted material objects. Music comes by pushing air from our lungs through vocal cords, plucking taut wire, drawing rough hair over catgut, depressing a key, stimulating the cone of a loudspeaker. And none of this in and of itself should make music suspect; indeed, it can remind us that goodness, beauty, and truth can be embodied by and expressed in such objects. Here we join hands with numerous Christian writers on the arts of the last few decades.[16] The Calvinist philosopher Nicholas Wolterstorff urges that "the fundamental fact about the artist is that he or she is a worker in stone, in bronze, in clay, in paint, in acid and plates, in sounds and instruments, in states of affairs."[17] This is not to reduce music to the material, to explain it away as something wholly explicable by the physical sciences. But bearing in mind the long-standing legacy of thinking about music we have just considered, which has arguably suppressed a great deal of music and led to unnecessarily negative attitudes toward it (not least in the church), we might do well to regain a sense of music's profound physicality—its embeddedness in God's given material world.

With this will go a retrieval of the significance of the human body, also part of the sonic order. The physical world we inhabit may be known intellectually and emotionally, but it is mediated initially through our bodies. To use Michael Polanyi's language, we "indwell" the physical world.[18] There need be no shame over our bodily involvement in music just because it *is* bodily. Again, given the church's often ambivalent attitude to the body and the part this has played in suspicions about music, we may well need to develop a fuller awareness of its place in music. As we saw in chapter 1, our own bodies—themselves part of the good physical creation—are intrinsically part of musical experience.[19] To insist that Christians are to be spiritual is indeed quite proper, but to be spiritual is not to renounce the body per se (though it is to renounce immoral uses of the body). It is rather to be Holy Spirit inspired, an inspiration that encompasses the body—indeed, liberates the body—and as such grants a foretaste of what it will be like to have a spiritual body beyond death (a body animated by the Spirit, 1 Cor. 15:42–49; cf. Rom. 8:11). There is a proper bodily involvement in the world that enhances the inherent value of our bodies in the process. This outlook has perhaps never been better expressed than by a composer, that virtuoso of the visceral, Igor Stravinsky (1882–1971):

> The very act of putting my work on paper, of, as we say, kneading the dough, is for me inseparable from the pleasure of creation. . . . The word *artist* which, as it is most generally understood today, bestows on its bearer the highest intellectual prestige, the privilege of being accepted as a pure mind—this pretentious term is in my view entirely incompatible with the role of the *homo faber*.[20]

Patrick Shove has suggested that the problems many concertgoers have with "serious" contemporary music may be due in part to its distance from the body:

> Many twentieth-century composers focus on sound qualities or on abstract tonal patterns, and performers of their compositions often neglect whatever kinematic potential the music may have. The absence of natural motion information may be a significant factor limiting the appreciation of such music by audiences. While

compositional techniques and sound materials are subject to continuous change and exploration . . . *the laws of biological motion can only be accepted, negated or violated. If more new music and its performers took these laws into account, the size of the audiences might increase correspondingly.*[21]

In summary, within a Christian ecology there is no need to think of music as necessarily or ideally shifting us beyond the material order or to regard the heart of a musician's work as giving outward expression to inner, nonphysical realities, or to believe that the "real" work is carried out in the sanctuary of the self and the piece of art merely serves to externalize this interior experience. Setting music in the context of a world created by the Triune God of Jesus Christ brings home to us the embeddedness of music in this our God-given home and of this embeddedness being mediated through our own bodies.

Yet for all this we would be foolish to sweep away the ancient suspicion of physicality too hastily. It is easy to read Augustine's vacillation over music in the *Confessions*,[22] for example, in a patronizing way, as if his anxieties could be dismissed as no more than residual Platonism. A considerable danger lurks here, whether we are speaking of the more obviously physical aspects of music or not, and we need the likes of an Augustine—or a Calvin, or indeed a Plato, for that matter—to remind us of it forcibly. It is, of course, the danger of idolatry, the refusal to remember that created realities are good but not God. C. S. Lewis reminisces about his childhood love of Wagner:

To a boy . . . whose highest musical experience has been Sullivan, the *Ride [of the Valkyries]* came like a thunderbolt. From that moment Wagnerian records . . . became the chief drain on my pocket money and the presents I invariably asked for. . . . Asgard and the Valkyries seemed to me incomparably more important than anything else in my experience. . . . Unless I am greatly mistaken *there was in it something very like adoration, some kind of quite disinterested self-abandonment* to an object which securely claimed this by simply being the object it was.[23]

Speaking of his own odyssey through the 1980s, Tom Beaudoin writes, "For a generation of kids who had fragmented or completely broken relationship to 'formal' or 'institutional' religion, pop culture filled the spiritual gaps."[24] And, of course, in many ways music was the heartbeat of that culture and still is. In his book *Generation Ecstasy*, Simon Reynolds comments, "Rave is more than music plus drugs; it's a matrix of lifestyle, ritualised behavior, and beliefs. To the participants, it feels like a religion; to the mainstream observer, it looks more like a sinister cult."[25] To be sure, interpreting these diverse phenomena theologically is a complex and delicate business, and the idolatry doubtless extends beyond the strictly physical, but it is hard to deny at least some substance to Henry Chadwick's words: "For a large number of our contemporaries music is not so much the partner of religion as a substitute for it."[26]

I have taught courses on theology and the arts in many institutions, and very often at least a quarter of any class will have come from a professional career in the arts of some sort. Many of those speak about having been caught up in a kind of total, life-engulfing process, where their art became "incomparably more important than anything else." Many of these, on coming to Christian faith, find the urge to pull out of any involvement with the arts almost irresistible. This is more than understandable, and sometimes people need to be given time to do just that, especially since, in the case of music, the idolatry usually extends far beyond the direct engagement with musical sounds—to performers, careers, salaries, and so on. Nevertheless, the lasting antidote to idolatry is not to spurn what is God-created but to do all in one's power to turn it to the praise of God, to release it to sing the goodness of the Creator.

A swarm of problems arises here, for whether music serves idolatrous ends depends not only on note patterns but also on that cluster of factors we spoke about in chapter 1 that make up the context of music.[27] But I hope by now some positive avenues will have been opened by the preceding chapters. From the perspective of the composer, in chapter 5 I offered a reading of some of Bach's output as an astounding demonstration of how the given raw materials of sound can be fashioned and refashioned into music that sounds the worship of the One who gave us the possibility of sound (though whether they will always be heard in that way is quite another matter). And this was just the way Karl Barth invited us to hear Mozart's music, as part of a good, physical creation giving God praise; a creation testifying to God, magnifying God, but as finite and transient—created, not divine. It is sometimes said Barth was captivated by Mozart's music; it is probably more accurate to say he was captivated by God's goodness through Mozart's music and without needing to escape the created sounds in the process.

Music—in a World Made to Flourish toward Its End

We have said that God is actively committed to the flourishing of the world in its distinctiveness and otherness, a commitment that has in view a glorious future. We can be confident of this commitment because of what has happened in the life, death, and resurrection of the Word made flesh, Jesus Christ—here we see nothing less than the final transfiguration of the fallen cosmos played out for us.

We saw that this means taking *time* seriously. The world is created not *in* time, but *with* time; time is a dimension built in to the way things are. And here music comes into its own, for, more than any art form, it is bound up with time, time being part of the sonic order.[28]

Let us explore this a little further. Music, of course, takes time. To enjoy music is not to experience something in a moment, nor to contemplate a still pattern (the way we might be intrigued by the arrangement of colors on a postage stamp). It is to be carried along, pulled into a movement. The character of a piece of music is not given in an instant, or even a near-instant, but can be discovered only in and through time, and in some pieces only when it reaches a climactic gathering together, the end toward which it travels.

But we need to press the point more strongly. Music is involved in an especially intense way with time, to a degree unparalleled in any other art form. This is because it does not simply take time; notes are critically timed in relation to one another (even in improvised music), creating very specific patterns. If I take a melody like Paul McCartney's "Yesterday" and make only tiny adjustments to the rhythm of the notes, it will not be long before it is unrecognizable. The timing of notes relative to one another is fundamental to what music is. To hear or listen to music is to be drawn into a very carefully timed series of happenings. We recall that at the most basic level, musical notes become meaningful for us, not primarily because of their relation to anything they might be used to point to, but through their relation to one another: *relations* between notes *in time* matter crucially.

Music, Time, and Creation

The fact that music is so time intensive and time involved gives it special powers to disclose something of the nature and character of time. Of course, time is both a complex and controversial topic in contemporary science and philosophy, but there is much to suggest that music has its own important contribution to make to the discussions. It is easy to think that the timing of music is entirely something *we* make—we decide a time signature, we construct its rhythms, accents, and stresses, the length of notes, the length of a piece. But the Austrian musicologist Victor Zuckerkandl has argued that if we examine closely the way musical notes imply and are bound up with one another, we are led to a distinctive view of time (with more than a little support from the natural sciences), in which time is not some kind of absolute container or channel (the bowling alley down which notes roll, so to speak), nor simply something we project from our minds onto the world, but an *intrinsic dimension of the physical world*. Musical experience, in other words, can serve to remind us of what is arguably a profoundly Christian insight: that time belongs to the very fabric of the good creation to which God is committed, something confirmed and sealed in the life, death, and raising of Jesus Christ.[29]

Whatever we make of that particular argument, there is no doubt that music depends for its effect on intertwining to a very high degree with the temporal patterns that govern the physical world. We can link this up with what we said in chapter 1 about music and the sonic order.[30] The physical objects immediately involved in music are embedded in time: built into them are time and temporal patterns. Strings, for example, vibrate at a certain number of beats per second, they take a certain amount of time to decay, and so on. Sound waves operate in particular temporal configurations. Music negotiates and makes use of these features of sound. It taps into the rhythms of these things that belong to the material world we inhabit.

There are also the temporal patterns of our own bodies. Music intertwines with these very closely. This is not to say music always copies nonhuman or bodily rhythms—in fact it rarely does. It interacts with them, highlights them, plays with them, integrates and extends them in ways we are only just beginning to understand.[31]

In any case, what we are driving at should now be clear enough: music can be one of the most powerful and wonderful ways we have of enjoying, discovering, exploring, and interacting with the time and the time patterns God has imprinted in his physical world. And as such, it can play a part in reminding us of the reality and goodness of time (and thus, in turn, of the reality and goodness of physical things in time).

Some Implications

Let us pull out just three implications of this ability of music to throw into relief time's goodness and reality. First, through its intense time involvement, *music can demonstrate that change and order can go together*, that change need not imply chaos—something the church has often tended to forget. From the beginning, there was change in the world; nowhere in Scripture is it suggested that change in itself is harmful or an enemy of order. Yet the fear of change—any change—lurks in many churches: the belief that the less something changes the more valuable it is, that what is truly of worth will endure without change (or at least with relatively little change). So we cling to this committee as it now is, this building and this hymnbook as they now are, because change must mean disorder, chaos. A piece of music, by contrast, is constantly changing, and its notes do not come with precise and stable meanings. Yet at its best it is ordered, beautiful, and stirring. Music demonstrates for us, in and through physical realities, that change need not bring chaos.

Perhaps there is more than a grain of truth in Zuckerkandl's remark that "all fundamental opposition to music . . . is rooted in the same concern: that music may hold the threat of chaos." Music, he believes, can undermine "the dogma that order is possible only in the enduring, the immutably fixed, the substantial." It presents us with "the unprecedented spectacle of an order in what is wholly flux, of a building without matter."[32]

This is of immense significance in the contemporary cultural climate because the postmodern celebration of constant change and flux trades on the belief that flux is incompatible with shape and structure. So in our society we often lurch from uncontrolled change to an authoritarian clamping down on all change.

With music we realize that configurations of things—musical notes—can be in constant motion and yet *as such* be profoundly enriching. Catherine Pickstock draws out the point:

> [Postmodernism's] core belief is that flux and articulation are both necessary to each other and yet mutually cancelling. And yet in music we hear the flux only as articulated, and articulations only in the flux. . . . Neither a pure flow nor pure present moments make any coherent sense. And yet in music we *hear* this impossible reconciliation.[33]

Every church needs to learn that the change God desires is not shapeless, directionless "change for change's sake" but a fruitful, enriching change—of the sort we might hear in the ten-notes-a-second of an Oscar Peterson or an Evgeny Kissin.

Second, *music challenges the belief that the longer something takes, the worse it will be*. Things that happen instantly are better than things you have to wait for—so we often assume. Hence the craving for the instantly accessible, the immediately buyable, here-and-now credit. Music, in a very concentrated way, tells us that something can take time *and* be good. Music takes time to be what it is, and as such can be glorious. It can remind us that it is not a failing of the created world that it reaches its fulfillment only through time. This is part of the way God made things. The created world takes time to be what it is. As the oft-quoted graffito has it: "Time is God's way of not letting everything happen at once."

Following from this, third, *music invites us to enjoy a positive kind of patience and waiting*. Not so long ago a psychiatrist told me that one of the marks of an adult who has never properly grown up is an inability to wait, and a whole therapeutic movement has been built on that one insight alone. Because music takes or demands our time and depends on carefully timed relations between notes, it cannot be rushed. It schools us in the art of patience. Certainly we can play or sing a piece of music faster. But we can do this only to a very limited degree before the piece becomes incoherent. Given today's technology we can cut and paste, we can hop from track to track on the MP3 player, flip from one song to another, and download highlights of a three-hour opera. But few would claim they hear a piece of music in its integrity that way. Music says to us: "There are things you will learn only by passing through this process, by being caught up in this series of relations and transformations."[34] Music requires my time, my flesh, and my blood for its performance and enjoyment, and this means going at *its* speed. Simone Weil described music as "time that one wants neither to arrest nor hasten."[35] In an interview, speaking of the tendency of our culture to think that music is there simply to "wash over" us, the composer James MacMillan remarked: "[Music] needs us to sacrifice something of ourselves to meet it, and it's very difficult sometimes to do that, especially [in] the whole culture we're in. Sacrifice and self-sacrifice—certainly sacrificing *your time*—is not valued any more."[36]

This is why Rowan Williams can claim that music can function as a "moral event": it can remind us that we are not in control of the world, that we do not have the overview, that we are *in* the narrative of the world's history and never above it. Music "tells us what we are and what we are not, creatures, not gods, creators only when we remember that we are not the Creator, and so are able to manage the labour and attention and expectancy that belongs to art."[37] In short, we are liberated from the destructive illusion that we are supposed to be God.

Keeping in Time

We shall say more about musical time patterns in chapter 11.[38] For the moment, we should acknowledge that some will feel uneasy about this heavy stress on time. Indeed, much thinking and writing about music gives the impression of being decidedly uncomfortable about music's alliances with time. We have already talked about the prominence of the notion of works in the Western musical tradition—pieces fixed in a score. This has led not only to a tendency to see a piece of music outside of time, in the sense of outside its historical context, but also—and strict notation encourages this—to think of a piece of music as if it were a kind of immobile object rather than an invitation to a journey.[39] We also saw how the Pythagorean-Platonic tradition was marked by a keenness to see music as pointing us beyond time to timeless patterns or forms.

Also, from the perspective of ordinary listening experiences, it is not hard to see how some would be sympathetic to linking music with "time out." Most of us have listened to music and become unaware of, or radically miscalculated, the time measured by the clock on the wall. ("Is it that time already?") As Thomas Clifton puts it, "There is a distinction between the time which a piece *takes* and the time which a piece presents or *evokes*."[40] Numerous psychological studies have confirmed this.[41] Music can give us a sense of duration, proportions, high points, and low points that differ markedly from the ordinary patterns of our lives. Not surprisingly, this has led some to link music very strongly with timelessness, as if there were something basic to music that reached beyond time.

Moreover, there has been no shortage of experiments by composers in the last hundred years or so in which the regularity and direction of "clock time" is deliberately challenged or erased.[42] This has sometimes gone hand in hand with theological convictions. Some Christian composers today see music's facility to distance itself from ordinary time as potentially very positive: music can and should be harnessed to help us approximate to a time*less* condition, to evoke a world in which there is no time (our future life with God perhaps). As we have seen, some of Messiaen's music moves in this direction, as does some of the (very varied) work of composers such as Tavener, Pärt, Górecki, and others—sometimes grouped together and dubbed "the holy minimalists" or the "New Simplicity."[43]

Three comments are in order here. First, pieces of music do indeed create their own kind of time. But this is not necessarily an experience of timelessness—it may simply be *a different kind of time*. Though some pieces undoubtedly do approximate a kind of stillness that seems to run against, for example, the drivenness of contemporary life, there is nothing intrinsic in the nature of music that need push us away from or apart from time. Second, we need to ask, "Why should the Christian be especially concerned with evoking or approximating timelessness?" Time is a dimension of God's good created world (human and nonhuman), built into the fabric of things, not an afterthought after the fall. It is not at all obvious that a biblically shaped ecology will press us into believing that God's purpose (now or in the future) is to extract us from time; such an ecology rather suggests that his intention is to redeem us within and with time—time as part of a temporal creation that awaits transformation. Third, to bring the last two points together, perhaps music's most valuable strength—as far as time is concerned—is to give us within this world a sense of transformed or "redeemed time," that is, temporal patterns that cohere, make sense, enrich us, and as such offer a foretaste of God's final new creation in the future. This links up with something we said about Messiaen's music: in much of his music he was probably searching not for an eradication of time but for a fullness of time. Arguably, *this* is what we shall enjoy in the age to come. I remember once speaking to a middle-aged woman who had suffered multiple traumas—including the death of her daughter by suicide, her husband's unemployment, and much else besides. She told me that during the darkest hours, the only thing that made any sense and that brought her any comfort was music. Was this escapism, music pulling her *out of* her own "broken" time? Or was it music pulling her into a rich experience *within* time—past, present, and future at peace—bringing a measure of sense and shape to her fragmented world, "recomposing" her?

Some will come back and ask: Nonetheless, is there still not a place for music that calms and quiets us? From a Christian point of view, might it not be perfectly proper to use music to subdue our restlessness, to help us be more attentive to God? "Be still and know. . . ." Could not much of the "holy minimalist" music function in just this way, helping to concentrate our heart and mind, enabling a proper contemplative attitude toward God?

There is certainly a thriving industry today, extending far beyond the world of "serious" composers, turning out huge quantities of music that, in one way or another, are designed to help us "chill out."[44] There are a number of ways to interpret this music in its cultural setting. I have suggested elsewhere that part of its appeal might lie in the way it offers an antidote to much that we find alienating in contemporary urban life, in particular the modernist tyranny of clock time (living by deadlines and timetables) and the postmodernist fragmentation and multiplicity of times (the fact that we have to inhabit so many different times—work, play, home, family, leisure—which leads to the feeling of being "multiply overwhelmed" by the pressures of countless demands).[45] Here is music that does not push us around. It offers a sort of musical decompression, a space amid a temporally compressed culture, a stable place where we are not shoved and driven from here to there. And in a society overloaded with multiple and contradictory communication systems and messages, this music provides a space that is simple—the music is not complex or multilayered. Hearing music like this is like walking into a cool cathedral in a hot, rushed, and overcrowded city.

It would be churlish for Christians to deny the positive potential of this music as a relaxant in an overpressurized culture. And insofar as it is used to help focus us on God, settle our restlessness, and shut out distractions, then this is also to the good. Further, undoubtedly much of it is theologically profound. However, what should be questioned, I suggest, is the assumption that this broad genre of music in some way expresses the heart of a Christian view of our intended relation to time, or indeed God's relation to time. Whatever place there may be for the kind of atmosphere such music generates, Scripture's inescapable testimony is that Christian faith turns on a God of promise, who has secured a future for this world and who calls people on a journey in and through time toward that future. To suppose that curbing all suggestion of this, in the belief that this will somehow evoke the core of the Christian life, is surely questionable.

I have explored these issues much more fully elsewhere[46] and will return to them later. For the moment, the central matter ought to be very evident: I am suggesting that one of music's greatest values for the Christian is to offer experiences of a fruitful interaction with time and the time patterns that we inhabit as physical creatures, the time God has graciously bestowed on the world, and in *this* way bring God glory.[47]

Music—in a World of Ordered Openness

In the last chapter we described the physical world as possessing a reliable and indelible order and humans as made in such a way that they can engage fruitfully with it. We also spoke about this order as an open one, with a rich interplay of regularity and unpredictability, law and circumstance, testifying to the commitment of a faithful Creator who acts through his Son and Spirit.

In what ways is music grounded in this matrix of flexible reliability? We are speaking of a sonic order to which music, to a greater or lesser extent, is bound. Sound-producing materials, sound waves, and the human body all possess inherent shapes, which when working together, embedded in time, form a network of constraints on music. We have been noting ways in which music is affected by these constraints. But now we need to explore a particularly important way in which music is grounded in the sonic order, by examining just one sonic phenomenon: the harmonic series. (This means entering what for many will be very basic acoustics, for others a refresher in high school physics, and for others no doubt an entirely new world.)

Every Note a Sounding Chord: The Harmonic Series

Back to Pythagoras. We saw that he is credited with having discovered that the relative pitch of musical sounds depends on the length of string or pipe and that consonant musical pitches—pitches that are pleasing to the ear when sounded together—are related by whole-number ratios: 1:2, 2:3, 3:4, and so on. It was not until the beginning of the eighteenth century that the basis of this was discovered in something now known as the "harmonic" or "overtone" series.

I play a C on the piano: its hammer strikes a string, the string vibrates, and we hear a tone.

In fact, this string is vibrating not only across its whole length but also in halves, in thirds, in quarters, and so on. Each of these extra vibrations creates an "overtone." These additional vibrations are always present in the sounding string, though we are not usually conscious of them as such. *Every note we hear from a piano is in fact a sounding chord.*

The presence and relative strength of audible overtones in the notes we hear are responsible for us being able to distinguish, say, a clarinet from an oboe when they are playing the same note—an oboe is much richer in overtones than a clarinet, hence its tone is less pure. Low strings on a piano will vibrate with a huge number of audible overtones—hence they sound very thick, and mixing their sounds will create a muddy sound. The top strings have far fewer audible overtones; thus they have a thinner sound and can be mixed much more easily.

The overtones present in a piano note form a series:

The bottom C is called the "fundamental" (f). The first overtone (1), created by the string vibrating across half its length, is also a C—and the interval between them Western musicians call an "octave" expressed in the Pythagorean ratio 1:2.

It is perhaps not surprising that this interval is remarkably pervasive as a kind of basic interval in a vast range of music, past and present.[48] Most musical cultures that name their notes give the octave overtone the same name as the fundamental. In his theological classic *De Trinitate*, Augustine writes with great eloquence about this interval and the way it is fastened into nature and into us. He speaks of

> the power of that consonance of single to double which is found especially in us, and which is naturally so implanted in us (and by whom, except by him who created us?), that not even the ignorant can fail to perceive it, whether when singing themselves or hearing others. For by this it is that treble and bass voices are in harmony, so that anyone who in his note departs from it, offends extremely, not only trained skill, of which the most part of men are devoid, but the very sense of hearing.[49]

Is this interval, then, a "universal"? Here caution is needed. It is a universal in that it is built into the physical world, and the majority of musical systems seem to employ it as a sort of basic component.[50] But we should add the rider: only as far as we know, and some cultures are happy to tolerate octaves that are slightly out of tune, that is, not perfectly in line with the harmonic series. This alerts us to the fact that while music may be grounded in a given physical order, it still involves selecting from and shaping that order, which can take diverse forms.

The second overtone (G) creates an interval with the first called the perfect fifth:

Interestingly, this was one of the first deviations from singing in unison and octaves that the church allowed. Some believe that it was the acoustics of certain stone buildings that made the second overtone audible and that this generated *organum*—the singing of a new tone along with the original.[51] (Some people claim to have heard this overtone clearly when they sing in the bathtub!)

We can continue further up the series. The third overtone is another C, the fourth is an E. The second, third, and fourth overtones—G, C, E—when rearranged, are the constituent notes of the major triad (C major), the building block of much Western music:

We recall: every note on a piano is a sounding chord. *Within* the sounding string (C), a major chord is included.

The most basic intervals to arise in the harmonic series, as we have seen, are the octave and the perfect fifth. The next is the perfect fourth—the interval between the second and the third overtone. The upper note of the fifth resonates with its own harmonic series; likewise in the case of the fourth. Implicit here are the three chords that have shaped the harmony of so much Western tonal music, chords I, IV, and V. (As every beginner guitarist knows, you can tackle a large amount of the popular song repertoire with these three chords alone.) What musicians know as the "pull toward the tonic"—the way in which music seems to gravitate toward the "home" key, or chord I—is grounded in the first overtones of the harmonic series.[52] (In fact, fixed reference pitches are relatively common in music worldwide—pitches that a piece of music circles round or returns to frequently.[53] They often appear in the form of a drone: think of the "held" note in bagpipe music.)

Although the octave may be prevalent in most musical systems, there are many ways to divide it up. Worldwide, studies suggest that the most common divisions are into five, seven, and twelve intervals. If we take the interval of a fifth and continue upward in fifths, we will soon have achieved a five-note scale—C, G, D, A, E—a pentatonic scale. We find scales of this sort in much Chinese music, in Scottish folk tunes, and in the ditties children love to play on the black keys of a piano (these keys play out a pentatonic scale).

If we rise from the C by a fifth, descend by a fourth, rise by a fifth, and so on, we will end up with six notes of the seven-note diatonic scale, part of the staple diet of modern European-derived music. If we start on a C and carry on rising in fifths, in due course we shall end up on C again, and in the process we will have encompassed not only a complete diatonic scale but also a twelve-note or chromatic scale, which forms the repertory of tones for most Western music (the twelve notes within an octave on a piano).

Before our enthusiasm runs away with us, once again, caution is needed. Different kinds of music can be grounded in the harmonic series in different ways. As we stressed in chapter 1, a growing awareness of non-Western traditions has made it clear that musical systems are in fact highly diverse. Stabilizing notes may be common, and the octave may be a "universal" of sorts, but as we have just noted, the octave can vary slightly in pitch in practice, and there are numerous ways in which an octave can be split up.[54] Further, it may well be that groups of five, seven, and twelve tones do comprise a sort of elementary repertoire of much music worldwide, but these by no means exhaust the possibilities, and even within such systems, tones can be tuned in widely divergent ways.

To press the point: the major triad of Western music is indeed derived from the harmonic series, but it would be quite wrong to conclude from this that our Western tonal system is therefore the most "natural," God-given system and that anything that deviates from it is artificial and inferior, running contrary to the divine will stamped into the created order. For the Western musical system itself did not just tumble neatly out of the harmonic series but is based on an adjustment of it. (We have touched on this already in connection with the breakdown of confidence in the Pythagorean system in the sixteenth century.)[55] To give an example: if we play a C and were to go up the keyboard in perfect fifths, with a keyboard big enough we would indeed eventually reach a C again. But if these fifths were tuned *strictly* in accordance with the fifth of the harmonic series, we would not. There would be a slight discrepancy between our last note and a true C (expressed as a fraction called the "Pythagorean comma").[56]

For centuries, Western music was largely content with Pythagorean tuning (strict octaves, fourths, and fifths). But with the development of harmony (the simultaneous singing or playing of different parts at a variety of different intervals) and the advent of the organ and other keyboard instruments, various systems of tuning had to be introduced to enable musicians to keep pace. In due course, for example, they needed to be able to shift from one key (system of notes) to another. So we find what nature had given in the harmonic series was adjusted or "tempered" to fit certain musical needs. Bach's celebrated forty-eight preludes and fugues for *The Well-Tempered Clavier*, each pair in a different key, demonstrated the possibility of playing in all keys on the same instrument, each of them sounding "in tune"—and the instrument had to be specially tuned (tempered) to make this possible.[57]

When we play a major triad on a modern piano, therefore (see the figure on p. 228), we are not hearing a perfectly tuned triad, as found in the harmonic series. We are hearing an approximation of it. The upshot is that the Western system we know so well is, in fact, a good deal more artificial than we might like to think.[58] (Some groups, such as the Hilliard Ensemble, make extensive use of "pure" tuning: it is a hauntingly beautiful sound, especially if one has not heard it before.) To press the point further, some features of *non*-European musics may turn out to be *closer* to the harmonic series than the modern European system, or at least they might allow certain tones in the series to be heard and used more readily. An example can be found in blues music, which includes an overtone quite unplayable on the piano (the sixth overtone, lying between A and B flat):

Albert Blackwell writes of his experience of Javanese music that after initially finding it "alien and impenetrable," he began to hear in it the sixth overtone:

"in music of a traditional Javanese gamelan orchestra, with melodies composed upon a basic five-tone scale . . . I have heard this [overtone] ring out as a sixth melodic tone. The musical effect is tingling."[59]

We should thus be very careful not to privilege Western tonal music (or any other kind of music for that matter) in naive ways. This is not to deny the grounding of this music, or any other, in given acoustical realities; it is only to caution against simplistic ways of understanding this that overlook the fact that music shapes and forms the materials it uses.

Consonance and Dissonance

Similar things can be said of the phenomena known as *consonance* and *dissonance*. When I hear a chord and call it dissonant rather than consonant, what is going on? Am I doing any more than expressing my culture's (or perhaps simply my own) preferences? Is the beauty of consonance all in the ear of the beholder? Or am I, at least in part, reacting to something there in the notes?

To begin with, we need to be clear that consonant and dissonant are best thought of not as neatly bounded boxes. For the sake of argument, we can call those intervals that sound smooth and restful consonant and those that sound clashing and unrestful dissonant.[60] But most people discern *degrees* of dissonance and consonance, often with no sharp divide between them. This means that our question needs to be refined as follows: Is our judgment that this interval or chord is more consonant (or dissonant) than another based on anything more than individual or cultural preference?

The answer is almost certainly yes. Substantial empirical evidence indicates that the widespread use of small-integer frequency ratios (of the octave, fifth, and fourth for instance), and the association of such intervals (and related chords) with stability and rest, can be accounted for at least in part by the harmonic series. It would seem that especially important for the perception of consonance and dissonance is the relative "smoothness" or "roughness" between notes and/ or between their overtones.

Suppose the sound of two different tones, two frequencies, enter the ear. If they are very close to each other, although you cannot hear two pitches, you will likely hear a "beating" between the notes. If we increase the frequency separation, the beating will get faster and produce an unpleasant *roughness* in sound. Increase the separation further and we will begin to hear two separate ("smoother") tones. (All this arises because of the way sounds are dealt with by the structures of the inner ear, but the precise electrical and mechanical processes are unclear and a matter of some controversy.) There is, in other words, a critical bandwidth for roughness (narrower at higher frequencies and wider at lower frequencies). A semitone such as the following will produce roughness, and we might well call it dissonant:

In contrast, two notes an octave apart will be heard as higly consonant ("smooth") because they contain no beating or roughness, being the first two tones of a harmonic series.

Sometimes it is the overtones of the two notes that produce roughness. Take the infamous "tritone":

For some medieval musicians, this was the *diabolus in musica*, the "devil in music," to be strenuously avoided. In Western music, the tritone is frequently used in contexts of strife, unsettledness, instability—as in hundreds of storm sequences in film music or in the theme tune for *The Simpsons*. The interval plays a pivotal part in Benjamin Britten's *War Requiem*, reinforcing many of its ironic tensions and unresolved ambiguities. It seems that the association of this chord with dissonance is due to the roughness between its notes' overtones: the second overtone of the lower note in the tritone is rough against the first overtone of the upper note.[61]

John Pierce, in *The Science of Musical Sound*, sums up well this line of thinking: "To look at experiences of consonance and dissonance as arising from [humanly devised] rules is to look at things the wrong way round. Rather, I believe that the rules and customs [of consonance and dissonance] are based on experiences of consonances and dissonance that are inherent in normal hearing."[62] However, two important qualifications need to be made. First, when we make judgments about consonance and dissonance, we are more often than not talking about intervals and chords as part of a piece of music, not in isolation. So we need to make a distinction between acoustic (or sensory) consonance and musical consonance—the former applying to intervals and chords in isolation, the latter to intervals and chords as they appear in a piece of music.[63] (The same applying to dissonance.) If you are playing an "Amen" at the end of a hymn in G major:

the first chord (C major) sounds consonant on its own but dissonant in relation to the home key, G major. In other words, musical context can make a huge difference to our assessments of consonance and dissonance. In popular song and solo playing, dissonance is used in quite a different way than in, say, Beethoven. In blues music, "blue" notes (see the figure on p. 229) are regarded not as dissonances or distortions of "correct" pitches but as correct within their own system.

The second qualification brings us back again to the importance of understanding music as something *shaped* and *made*. Western music's treatment of dissonance and consonance does not spring fully formed from the head of nature. Our perception of consonance and dissonance is greatly affected by our musical sensitivity, the amount of musical training we have had, and a host of cultural assumptions that can change quite dramatically. (Recall what we said about context in chapter 1.) The tritone, for example, is not now considered to be as dissonant and harmful as it was in much of the medieval era. Some will shrink when they hear certain chord progressions while others find them captivatingly beautiful. Thus, although acoustical factors may be an integral *part* of the story of consonance and dissonance, they are certainly not the whole story.

Major and Minor

Very much the same goes for the way we perceive major and minor keys. I am often asked: What makes minor chords sound sadder than major ones? Why are minor chords so often associated with negative emotions and contexts— anger, grief, death, and so on—while positive situations seem to demand major chords? Is there really something in the chords that accounts for this?

Some believe the attempt to explain acoustically the different effects of major and minor is doomed. Others are less skeptical. The territory is contested, but Donald Hall for one has made a persuasive case for tracing the common associations of major and minor chords to the way in which their triads relate to their respective harmonic series.[64] In brief, the argument runs as follows.

Each triad has an "implied" fundamental (a root tone not actually sounded, but grounding the chord nonetheless). In the case of the major triad, the 4:5:6 ratio of the chord, with its low integers, is relatively simple for the mind to grasp, and this is aided by the presence in a major chord of three of the implied fundamental's earliest harmonics, including at its base a note two octaves above the fundamental. In the case of the minor chord, the lowest integers to express its ratios are 10:12:15—harder to perceive. And the early harmonics of the fundamental are poorly represented in comparison to the major chord (with no tone in the chord directly evoking the fundamental; indeed, the fundamental is an entirely different note). Further, the implied fundamental of the major chord is only two octaves below the chord, whereas the minor chord is over three and a half octaves away from its fundamental. Hall concludes: "(1) there is probably much less tendency to perceive an identifiable root for a minor chord; (2) insofar as we admit the possibility of this weak implied fundamental, it only makes things more complicated instead of reinforcing a simple pattern; and so (3) *the acoustical basis for consonance in minor chords is considerably weaker than in major chords.*"[65] Similar conclusions are reached if we examine the two intervals within major and minor chords and their implied fundamentals.[66]

There would seem to be some grounds, then, to suppose that there is a physical basis for a minor chord being heard as more dissonant than a major chord, and this most likely accounts for its common use in sad, mournful, unresolved contexts. However, immediately we must go on to make the same double qualification we made with consonance and dissonance: much will depend on the context of these chords in a sequence of music (minor chords are not always perceived as particularly dissonant), and much will depend on sensitivity, training, and culture (in many societies joyful music will use predominantly minor chords).

Maybe the Great Tradition Had a Point

In this section on the harmonic series, I have dealt only with the harmonic dimensions of music—notes sounding simultaneously. We do not have space to examine how these harmonic dimensions are played out in time, the extension of music through melody, rhythm, and meter, and the way these also relate to the physical world's givens. But very much the same conclusions would be drawn; namely, that music making and music hearing are a matter of nurture *and* nature, culture and physics, that they arise from "complex interactions of given acoustical laws and contingent cultural histories."[67]

The central point is this: however much particular individual and cultural interests may play a part, by far the majority of music made and heard can be shown to be rooted in given verities that make up what I have called the "sonic order." Of course, this does not *prove* anything theologically, but it can serve to point us in a theological direction: it can help to reorient Christians to something very easy to overlook in a climate overenamored with the notion of music as something we construct, namely, that we have been placed in a world vibrant with its own God-given integrities and with the opportunity of interacting fruitfully with those integrities, and that music is one means we have been given to do just that. The findings of the last section can help deliver one of those imaginative jolts we talked about in the previous chapter: "try thinking about music . . . *this* way," as an engagement with a God-given sonic order intended for our enjoyment and enrichment.

With this in mind, we might well warm to the Great Tradition in its Christian form (see chapter 3) more than we might have done otherwise. No doubt the majestic vision deserved much of the critique it received. From the perspective of mathematics, physics, acoustics, and—not least—theology, it was beset with weaknesses that needed to be exposed in the fires of modern thought. But its broad intuition and its persistent concern to construe the making and hearing of musical sounds as grounded in divinely bestowed matrices of order is surely correct and not to be sacrificed thoughtlessly.

Sharing in a Flexible Order

Before leaving this issue of the givenness of the sonic order, we should, however, remind ourselves that it is not to be understood in inflexible ways. For, as we have just seen, we are able to shape it (and we shall say much more about this in the following chapter). This itself points to the fact that humans are not automatons, bound by iron necessity to their environment, but exercise a freedom, an openness that God has granted them. And this itself can be set in a wider context, for such freedom, presuming it is not an illusion, is part of and testifies to the openness with which God has endowed his entire creation. As we saw in some of Bach's works, music can bear its own kind of witness to this openness, to the subtle interplay between regularity and unpredictability, constraint and contingency that would seem to mark physical process as discovered by the natural sciences and that can be interpreted through Scripture's double witness to the Son and Spirit. Daniel Hardy and David Ford suggest that we should talk not only of order and disorder but also of "nonorder," the "jazz factor" in creation: that spontaneous element in the world and in human life that reaches its apogee in the unforced, unpredictable creativity of Jesus Christ.[68] It is not surprising that some have been keen to use improvisation as a model for integrating theological and scientific accounts of the created world.[69] We pick up on this in the next chapter, but for now the poet Micheal O'Siadhail will say all that is needed:

> Sax and rhythm. The brightness of a reed,
> winding tube and crook are working on
> another hue of the tune that moves
> into its own discourse: *Bud Freeman,*
> *Johnny Hodges, Charlie Parker.* "All right?"
> he drawls, then scats a little as we clap
> a tradition of subversions. But he's off again.
> I watch swarms of dust in the spotlight,
>
> swirls of galaxies, and imagine he's blowing
> a huge balloon of space that's opening
> our world of order. In a waft of creation
> his being becomes a music's happening. . . .
>
> Let the theme return, its mutants echoing
> as a tune balances against its freedom.
> One key—so open-toned and open-stitched.
> A beat poised, a crossgrained rhythm,
> interplays, imbrications of voice over voice,

mutinies of living are rocking the steady
state of a theme; these riffs and overlappings
a love of deviance, our genesis in noise.[70]

Music—in a World of Diverse Unity

And finally, we must not forget the diversity within the sonic order, part of the diversity of the world as a whole. A conductor is faced not with a uniform, homogeneous order but with the different sounds of unique and particular things—strings, vocal chords, pipes. Even within the same categories of instrument, difference is played out in striking ways. We can have a bass, a cello, and a violin all playing middle C, but the sound that meets the ear in each case is quite different. Singers vary dramatically in the color of their voices, even when they try to sing in homogenous unison.

We have already quoted Hopkins extolling the diverse *particularity* of the world in "As Kingfishers Catch Fire." Significantly, the poem evokes not only the way things look, but also the way things sound.

> As kingfishers catch fire, dragonflies draw flame;
> As tumbled over rim in roundy wells
> Stones ring; like each tucked string tells, each hung bell's
> Bow swung finds tongue to fling out broad its name;
> Each mortal thing does one thing and the same:
> Deals out that being indoors each one dwells;
> Selves—goes its self; *myself* it speaks and spells,
> Crying *What I do is me: for that I came*.[71]

Stones and bells have their own sound, expressing their "indoor selves." I speak with this voice and not that—my voice is part of me, the person I am, and not some other. So it is with each and every created entity. Each has a signature of sound; the way it sounds belongs to what it is, its character, its singular identity.

Even before we start thinking about making music, about discrepancies between this interpretation of this lieder and that, this bluegrass guitarist and that, the disparity between music from India and music from Malaysia, it is worth pausing to remember that even *within the sonic order itself*, before we have shaped it into music, we have been granted an extraordinarily diverse order, a multitude of particularities, a multiplicity that is part of creation's God-intended glory. The created things from which music is made, including our bodies, have their own sonic potential, and these are extraordinarily diverse. There is a profound order (held together in Christ), but that order is "flung out" in a dazzling variety of ways (by the Spirit). Insofar as music, then, brings to light—or brings to the ear—the diverse particularity of the one sonic order, it is opening up for us the diverse unity of the created world.

Hearing that diversity may take time and training. In some languages, tiny inflections of the voice can make a huge difference to the meaning of a word; yet in time people learn to distinguish this *a* from that *a*. Just as a painter can learn to notice minute variations in shades of brown in a landscape or a physicist learn to notice minuscule gradations of color in a spectral analysis, so listeners can learn to distinguish the most infinitesimal distinctions between this pitch and that, this chord and a nearly identical chord. To talk about educating the ear in this way will often be dismissed as elitist, as if any music worth its salt must be as free of such subtleties as possible. But is this not to deny ourselves one of the wonders of the cosmos, one of the most extraordinary givens of this, our intended home?

music in
God's calling

Music and silence—how I detest them both! How thankful we should be that ever since Our Father entered Hell . . . no square inch of infernal space and no moment of infernal time has been surrendered to either of those abominable forces, but all has been occupied by Noise—Noise, the grand dynamism, the audible expression of all that is exultant, ruthless and virile—Noise which alone defends us from silly qualms, despairing scruples, and impossible desires. We will make the whole universe a noise in the end. We have already made great strides in this direction as regards the Earth. The melodies and silences of Heaven will be shouted down in the end. But I admit we are not yet loud enough, or anything like it.

Screwtape, in *The Screwtape Letters*, C. S. Lewis[1]

From Cosmos to Calling

Screwtape's devilish venom against music and silence in the name of noise not only throws into relief our propensity to play out our rebellion against God by clattering against God's own givens, but it also calls attention to our true vocation—to make music in the midst of creation's own music, to voice creation's praise. The broad sweep of this calling we have already traced. Our privilege is to extend and elaborate the praise that creation already offers to the Creator.

Sin is the corruption of praise, and it is answered by God in the formation of a people, Israel, and supremely in the sending of his Son. The one through whom all things were made has become part of his creation: in him humanity's refusal to praise is reversed and its consequences borne; in him human flesh is

237

raised and transformed, redirected toward its goal; in him we have a promise for humanity and the whole cosmos. And now, through him, in the power of the Spirit, and as members of the people of God, our original calling can advance again: to enable creation to be more fully what it was created to be, a theater of divine glory, anticipating that final day when all things will fully resound to the Creator's honor.

What could this mean for those who make and those who hear music and for those who do so in a late-modern or postmodern environment? What kind of responsibilities might be appropriate in the world of Brahms and blues, Stravinsky and keyboard playing? I have already spoken of music in the context of a *cosmos* regarded as the creation of a Triune God. Now we can fill this out further by looking at music in the context of our *calling* in this cosmos, and we can use the headings set out in chapter 8—*discovering, respecting, developing, healing, anticipating, together*. It might be thought our headings apply only to the making of music and, hence, that what follows will be relevant solely to composers and performers. In fact, although often the immediate focus will be on the business of music making, it will soon be clear that most of what we say has implications for hearing and listening as well—the way we approach music, use it, react to it, and enjoy it.

Space is limited, so again, imagination is needed: readers will have to take what can be only sketched here and work it out for their own particular contexts.

Discovering

To speak of music as a vehicle of discovery will strike many as decidedly odd, so deeply engrained in many of us is the idea that music can only express, confirm, or perhaps intensify what we already know or feel. As anyone who has tried to raise money for a school music department will know, the suggestion that we might learn something new through music, that music might actually educate us in ways that are enriching and important, is more likely to be greeted with a puzzled frown than a warm welcome.

In fact there are a huge variety of ways in which music can be a vehicle of quite startling and life-changing discoveries, but here we concentrate on one in particular—its ability to open up the wonders of the created, physical world we inhabit. As we saw in chapter 3, for a large part of Western history this would have been a commonplace, and a theologically loaded one at that. And if what we said in the last chapter is true—that because of the sonic order all music is to some extent shaped by the integrity of the physical world—then the idea will be anything but bizarre. This is not to say that music is always (or even very often) composed with the express *intention* that the physical order be explored or that it be perceived in this way. The point is rather that this is one perspective from which the fruitfulness and wonder of music making and music hearing may be usefully understood.

A very particular reason why this idea may appear strange is that we have been schooled to think that we cannot create and discover at the same time.[2] (By discover here I mean "bring to light realities beyond ourselves to which we are subsequently responsible, to which we may have to adapt or change.") To summarize rather crudely, if the main impulse of modernity has been to dominate nature, to understand it in order to master and subjugate it, the inclination of postmodernity is to say that our evaluation of nature is entirely a matter of human choice, that there is no meaning in nature other than what we construct (as with some postmodernist writers, for whom to speak of reality "out there" is entirely vacuous, for we can speak only of what we shape and, indeed, for whom even the stability of the *we* is thrown into question). Accordingly, creativity (in whatever sense) displaces or swallows up the notion of discovery. When I write a song, I am making something, not finding anything, or at least nothing that is not already part of me.

Of course, there is a vital truth to concede here. We never simply receive data like passive containers. All our interaction with the world shapes what we know. We actively affect the content and character of our experience—in this sense we are indeed continually inventive, constructive creatures. This has become a cornerstone of much modern (and some postmodern) philosophy, and not without good reason. What should be questioned, however, is the assumption that constructive human activity necessarily excludes discovery; that the more active we are, the less responsive we can be to anything beyond ourselves; that the more we invent, form new things, the less we can discover. In the musical sphere, this appears as the assumption that *as* we engage with the materials of music—write melodies, make symphonies, improvise jazz—we cannot *at the same time* be eliciting an order that is given to the world (and given to us for our flourishing), to which we are obliged to be responsible.[3]

But need this be accepted? Donald Hall speaks of the way the counterpoint of Bach and the orchestration of the Hungarian composer Béla Bartók (1881–1945) are rooted in certain acoustical realities. Of Bartók he says:

> [There is] good acoustical reason for some traditional rules of orchestration and counterpoint. To keep two musical lines distinct, assign them to instruments of contrasting timbres or attack characteristics, and make the parts move in contrary motion. Smooth and similar timbres (especially on electronic organs) or parallel part motion (especially parallel octaves and fifths) make it too easy for voices to fuse together and lose their individuality.
>
> Occasionally, a composer may want two parts to fuse into a single musical line and so deliberately write for similar instruments in parallel. For a marvellous example, listen to the second movement ("Game of Paris") of Bartók's *Concerto for Orchestra* (1944). I can almost hear each duet as a single melodic line played by some new instrument with a strange, exotic timbre.[4]

Albert Blackwell goes on to comment:

> Hall is arguing—persuasively, I believe—that in setting compositional standards for western counterpoint and orchestration, *Bach and Bartók were at once musical discoverers and inventors*: discoverers of fundamental acoustical verities, given and enduring; inventors within the boundless universe of musical creativity arising out of those verities.[5]

We might want to qualify the word "boundless"—for our creativity is not without limits but is stimulated and made possible *by* limits. But the point about discovery and invention still holds. If we are speaking of a God-given integrity to the sonic world, it will become more apparent (and ought to be made more apparent) *as we engage* vigorously and inventively with it.

Here again it seems we need an imaginative jolt, and few are better qualified to give it than one of the composers just mentioned: Bach. This links with our discussion of Bach in chapter 5.[6] There have been few musicians quite so inventive—in the sense of being able to elaborate a teeming multiplicity of unpredictable music from what seems the most unpromising material, to combine and recombine sounds in a panoply of unprecedented richness. Yet need we think of this in terms of imposition, wresting order out of formless nature? Is there any musician in history who, *in and through* complex elaboration, has explored the properties and contours of key relationships, grounded in the harmonic series, quite so extensively as Bach in *The Well-Tempered Clavier*? I argued that it is likely Bach had substantial sympathy with those streams of thinking that saw music as an exploration and development of the rich order of the cosmos. For Bach himself, to set creativity against discovery, and to do so in the name of "originality" (an infatuation that emerges very soon after Bach's death), would have seemed very puzzling, perhaps even comical. We recall again Bach's obituary, which spoke of Bach's "ingenious and unusual ideas" *and* his extraordinary grasp of the "hidden secrets of harmony."[7] The Bach scholar Christoph Wolff writes:

> Bach, for whom the "invention of ideas" constituted a fundamental requirement ("anyone who has none he advised to stay away from composition altogether," as his son later recounted), understood the elaboration of musical ideas not as an act of free [i.e., unbounded] creation but rather as a process of *imaginative research into the harmonic implications of the chosen subject-matter*.[8]

Of course, just because Bach might have thought along these lines does not itself mean that all his music exemplifies these convictions. But at the very least, can we not allow his music to shake us out of the very parochial and recent assumption that the more active we are in making things the more we will cover up what God has given us? Next time we hear the preludes and fugues of *The Well-Tempered Clavier*, might we not hear it . . . *this way*: as a musician exploring—and thus helping us to discover—God's sonic order, a piece of imaginative research into the glorious richness and fruitfulness of the overtone series?

If there is a key virtue to highlight here on the part of the music maker, it is *attentiveness*. A good composer knows his or her material. As Oliver O'Donovan memorably puts it: love "achieves its creativity by being perceptive"[9]—by attending carefully to a simple chord with its particular resonances, or to the distinctive properties of a rhythmic pattern, and so forth. Improvisers can teach us much here, especially those who improvise regularly with others (and Bach was an astonishing improviser). With a high level of unpreparedness, you have to be exceptionally alert to what is given to you by the other players ("given" in the rich sense). You have to listen intently, constantly monitoring your own and others' sound. Little wonder that improvisers have spoken of their work as an exploration and discovery of sound: "We are *searching* for sounds and for the responses that attach to them, rather than thinking them up, preparing them and producing them. The search is conducted through the medium of sound."[10] The mind is involved, of course, but by thinking *in* notes—not thinking *before* them or *on* to them or simply *through* them, as if the notes were merely tools of ideas, but thinking *in* notes, with an alertness to the intrinsic features of sounds even *as* one shapes them.

Respecting

Closely intertwined with attentiveness is another dimension of our vocation: respect. We can explore and discover the nature of something only if we are prepared to honor it, show it an appropriate courtesy. This applies first and foremost to the medium or material. Nicholas Wolterstorff describes artistic creating as the "fascinating, mysterious, frustrating, exhilarating experience of being led along in conversation with one's material."[11] Recall the improviser just quoted: the search for sounds is conducted "through the medium of sound."

In the last chapter, we saw how a wide variety of music has arisen through a conversation with the given of the harmonic series, musicians working "with the grain of the universe."[12] But the point we are making here can be extended to all the physical realities of the sonic order—musical instruments included and, not least, our bodies. This is easy to underplay, especially if we are bewitched by the idea that the really *great* composer should not need anything so mundane as, say, a keyboard. In fact, probably the majority of composers compose at least in part through an instrument, certainly in popular music. Even the physical process of writing would seem integral to the act of composing. (Some believe Beethoven's sketchbooks show how the movements of his hand on a sheet of paper are intimately bound up with the music that emerges.)[13]

Against the Stream

Strong currents in Western intellectual life over the last two or three hundred years have, of course, pushed us in very different directions. Earlier we traced ancient and deep-seated hesitations about whether the material realm can be seen as itself the bearer of meaning and thus the kind of environment with which we as embodied creatures can have fruitful, enriching relations.[14] Two broad options result. One is to *deny our transcendence over nature*. We are simply dust of the earth; we are not to rule nature in any sense; we are not in any sense superior to other animals. In the world of music, this is a relatively rare attitude, but a good example is in some of the writing and composition of John Cage (we will return to him later).

The other broad route, and the one of particular concern to us here, is to *deny our rootedness in the material world*, to play down our own physical embodiment, and perhaps to see all things physical as essentially problematic. We met a version of this in the thought of Schoenberg. Another sees our relation to the nonhuman world as essentially one of domination, maximum control, and mastery. Both of these are often borne along by and strengthen the belief that the only order our physical environment has is the order we give it. God's unifying will is displaced by ours; nature needs us to be itself. It is not hard to see how this goes hand in hand with a technological mind-set, where the world's resources become mere tools in our quest to achieve dominance over our environment. At various times, these notions have been acted out in the world of music and have affected much modern thinking *about* music. To see this, we can consider one of the most influential views of the artist to emerge in modernity and then turn to one of modernism's most illustrious musical representatives, Pierre Boulez.

Infinite Inner Striving

We have already glanced at the exaltation of music (especially instrumental music) in some romantic writers of the late eighteenth and early nineteenth centuries. Music, many believed, offered a privileged access to a realm far surpassing concepts and words, unknown and ineffable, the world's infinite life. Crucial here is a momentum inward—the composer becomes aware of this infinite life not by stretching outward to God with open arms but through turning inside, through exercising the inner stirrings of the heart in creative activity. This is how contact with the infinite, at work in and through the cosmos, is achieved. As Daniel Chua puts it, "A musical work [becomes] . . . an incarnational glimpse of the God within."[15]

In some respects this is a revised version of the cosmic vision of the Great Tradition. And it chimes in with what is perhaps best known about the Romantics: their ambition to recover a sense of the harmony between humans and nature that they felt had been disrupted by contemporary science and industry. Nature had been robbed of its mystery and beauty, reduced to a cold mechanism for us to observe and control. The Romantic visionaries urged that we imagine nature, with which we are intimately bound up, as a dynamic source of spiritual energy, mediating the infinite or transcendent.[16] Art (and music) becomes a means (for some, the primary means) by which this spiritual reality comes to expression.

But this attempt to resacralize or re-enchant nature was to lead in decidedly different directions from the medieval traditions, and even more so from someone like Luther. In particular, we should note the massive magnetism toward the individual, human self. Charles Taylor charts these developments, noting a steady erosion in the modern age of the belief that our human aspirations and natural realities should correspond. What he calls the "ontic logos" has gradually disappeared as a unifying belief for modern men and women. A major consequence of humanity's "disengagement from cosmic order" was that "the human agent was no longer understood as an element in a larger meaningful order. His paradigm purposes are to be discovered *within*."[17] Thus for all that nature was a source of solace and comfort, there is a deep ambivalence about it in many streams of Romanticism—a strong intuition of the sheer ambiguity of its witness, especially of its limits, fleetingness, and transience.

The impression in some Romantic painting is of human beings at home in nature and yet not at home, a classic example being Caspar David Friedrich's *The Wanderer above the Mists* (1817–18) (see fig. 10.1). The halted traveler—a crucial figure in Romantic painting, especially as a surrogate for the artist—is captivated momentarily by the natural scene; on the edge of the finite, aware not only of nature's grounding in infinity but also of how insubstantial nature is—its aching, misty impermanence. There is order to nature, to be sure, but it is often hidden, opaque, and blurred. As developed by Romantic philosophers (e.g., Novalis), we find an emerging conviction that our access to nature's divine order is found through an inner voice or impulse, that the truth of nature will be found within us. "Das Herz ist der Schlüssel der Welt und des Lebens" ("The heart is the key to the world and life"), Novalis intones.[18] (The links with Schleiermacher, admittedly a far subtler thinker, should not be missed.) And the artist emerges as supreme; the artist becomes "a sacred instrument by which Nature works to surpass herself."[19] The infinite life of the universe, hidden within nature, comes to self-expression in and through the work of the artist.[20] Later, on the other side of the Atlantic, Ralph Waldo Emerson (1803–82) portrayed the truth within the self as a mirror image of the infinite and spiritual truth hidden within nature: the resources to be found deep within the individual will unlock nature's ultimate secrets.[21]

Hence the center of gravity is not in the ingrained and reliable order of the finite materials of nature, calling for our respectful response and trust and giving glory to God in its own created otherness, but it is in what is achieved through the artist—in other words, what is *lacking* in nature is now compensated for by

Fig. 10.1: *The Wanderer above the Mists,* Caspar David Friedrich (1817–18)

the artist. And if nature *is* understood as fundamentally ordered, it has an order to be found not so much by humans looking outward in an effort to allow it to declare itself in its own way but by turning inward.

In this environment, it is hardly surprising if we find the artist assuming gargantuan powers, abilities traditionally attributed to God—an infinitely abundant imagination and the ability to transform the world.[22] Art provides a coherent, safe place in a fragile, unstable, and crumbling world. And artists stand at the center. When Herder claimed, "The artist is become a creator God,"[23] it was wild hyperbole, but not without substance. And later in the nineteenth century, with massive changes in the social, political, and economic position of the artist in society and a further waning of the idea of nature as the source of spiritual life in favor of nature as a mechanism, we find further views of art as "a little island of self-generated meaning from which we heroically defy the ocean of cosmic hostility and meaninglessness that laps around us,"[24] and a much heavier stress on the alienation of the artist from the natural world and society. The artist becomes "a Promethean figure, the rival of Nature and God, cursed with a tragic but glorious doom."[25]

It would be tempting to dismiss all this as the quirky flotsam of a bygone age, extravagant overstatements from those desperate to rescue a sense of mystery in an increasingly science-dominated climate. In any case, the postmodernist will likely tell us we have matured beyond such notions: the lofty romantic and post-romantic artistic genius is surely an offshoot of the modernist self—self-centered and self-reliant, with a unique identity, heroic and driven from inside. To the aficionado of deconstruction and the supposedly decentered self of postmodernity, the idea that a self-directed turn can unlock the secrets of the infinite will sound at best like quaint optimism and at worst perilous hubris. But such distancing of ourselves from these ideas would be unwise. As Roger Lundin and others have shown, the postmodern self of the shopping mall or the Internet cafe, living in the vibrant play of multiple choices and surface images, the self in search of healing through ever more exotic sensory stimulation, is a very obvious descendant of the romantic self:

> The loss of the original utopian hopes of romanticism has not led to an abandonment of the romantic understanding of the self. The postmodernist self is in every way a child of the romantics, one who stands alone in nature, defying demands on the self and searching for that which will satisfy. The difference is that the postmodern self no longer harbors hopes of discovering truth or moral principles. Instead, driven by the ideals of therapy and consumption, it seeks, by whatever means will work, to provide satisfactions for the unencumbered self.[26]

In other words, the much-vaunted "ironic" postmodern self is in many ways the romantic self but stripped of trust, moral obligation, or passion for truth, left with a flux of shifting aesthetic desires that music—along with other devices—is used to satisfy.

What should give us pause for thought is the extent to which the romantic ethos can be discerned in much Christian writing and thinking about music. In some contemporary worship streams, for example, it is not uncommon to find a singer-songwriter revered in ways that bear more than a passing resemblance to the romantic characterization of the priestlike artist, complete with a CD cover picturing him or her a step apart from the ordinary, staring away from the camera in a misty wash. Toward the beginning of a worship service, with the onset of a certain form of music, we are told by the "worship leader" that "worship" can begin, as if music and God were linked not only in a unique but also in a supreme way, all very much in accord with the romantic view that art—for many, music supremely—can provide a kind of sanctuary or refuge, *the* place where human and divine Spirit intertwine in mutually resonant intimacy. ("The Real Presence is in the notes," someone once said to me.)

I have no intention at all of denigrating contemporary worship as a whole or any of those musicians who have been marketed in this way. And it would be quite unfair to suggest that all these notions are driven by a lack of respect for creation's order. But I am suggesting that much of what we too easily accept as Christian attitudes to music may owe far more to Romanticism than to that thrilling vision of the redemption of the cosmos that the New Testament opens up, in whose momentum we are invited to share as embodied creatures. And I am suggesting that if we were rather more determined to resist the idolatry of music and those who make it and rather more keen to allow musicians— including musicians we might not ordinarily listen to—to help us respectfully explore creation's extraordinary order, we might be surprised and delighted.

Pierre Boulez—Control at the Price of Destruction

From time to time in the history of music someone appears who is prepared to push ideas to their very limits, and the French composer and conductor Pierre Boulez (1925–) is one such person. With intense intellectual energy, in the late 1940s and early 1950s he developed a type of composition that in effect probed some of the most profound questions that can ever be asked of music. It came to be known as "total serialism." Although Boulez later moved in very different directions, it is this particular musical adventure we shall concentrate on here.

Total serialism depended on the rigorous organization of music through the use of strict mathematical patterns. Its roots lie principally in Schoenberg, who is probably best known for developing a strategy in which one takes the twelve tones of a chromatic scale (the tones that fill an octave on a piano), arranges them in a particular order or series, and then elaborates a piece of music from various permutations of that series. All the tones are on an equal footing. No one tone dominates the rest (unlike traditional Western music, which gravitates around a central tone). The thrust of this scheme is intellectual through and through: whether the music was pleasant to listen to or easy to play was quite secondary; what mattered above all was adherence to intellectually derived schemes.

Schoenberg's project applied to the arrangement of note pitches. This was not enough for Boulez. He wanted to apply the scheme to *every* musical dimension—volume, note duration, attack, and so on. A whole piece must be mathematically determined from beginning to end, top to bottom—as in his dense and ferociously complex *Structure Ia* (1952), for example. Boulez roundly declares, "Webern [a pupil of Schoenberg] only organised pitch; we organise rhythm, timbre, dynamics; *everything is grist to this monstrous all-purpose mill*."[27] Gerald Bennett comments, "Boulez's composition represents one of the great adventures of music this century: the restructuring of the language by imposing on it relations of absolute logical consistency."[28] And propelling Boulez in large part was a passionate belief that postwar music could advance only if there was a purging of musical memory, an erasing of the past. Not only the memory of past musical pieces, but memory even *within* a piece of music had to be suppressed. Hence he avoids any repetition, anything that might resemble a melody or motif, and with this, any sense of direction or implication.

No one was as perceptive as Boulez himself about the downsides of this exacting enterprise. He realized, for example, that his music was extremely dull, indeed, some of the most tedious ever written. With every element in a constant state of variation, no repetition, no theme or any sense of development, it quickly generates a debilitating sense of boredom in the listener. But it is another weakness that links up especially with our main concerns in this section—it sounds completely chaotic. There was, Boulez reminisces, "a surfeit of order being equivalent to disorder."[29] The music is fiercely organized, but you would not know that by listening to it, even if you had been initiated into its secrets.

The irony is that during this time Boulez was corresponding with John Cage (1912–92), the archpriest of "chance music," and Boulez was deeply perturbed by how close his music sounded to Cage's experiments in making music through random acts such as tossing coins. Listen to the output of Boulez and Cage during these years and it is quite hard to tell the difference. The results of total determinacy and radical indeterminacy sound much the same.

A "surfeit of order being equivalent to disorder." This links up with Ernst Kris's (albeit exaggerated) claim that in artistic modernism "the artist does not 'render' nature, nor does he 'imitate' it, but creates it anew. He controls the world through his work. . . . The unconscious meaning is *control at the price of destruction*."[30] This would seem to resonate with so much that mars the modernist landscape—for example, ruinous histories of violence perpetrated by those keen to impose order on other human beings. What was Nazism if not "control at the price of destruction," "order equivalent to disorder"? Here we have a parable in sound of some of the most disturbing currents in modernity, of what happens when the human will is seen as the center and active source of unity and order.

In an important article, Gerald Bennett observes that increasingly during the 1940s, the more Boulez tries to control his musical material through ever more elaborate schemes, the more the materials resists, and the more he loses control. It becomes more and more inaccessible as music. It is not hard to connect this with the modern ecological crisis: through ever stricter control we lose control of our God-given home and become increasingly alienated from it. Bennett calls Boulez's experiment "one of the most important confrontations in the music of our time—that of a composer determined to force material to obey his complex structural demands on the one hand, on the other the musical material itself, increasingly reluctant to submit gracefully to these demands."

Bennett concludes: "The adventure of Boulez's music is *an examination of the very foundations of composition itself.*"[31]

Indeed it is. For it pushes to the surface the basic question: Can music's order be entirely human-made? Are we the bringers and measure of all order? Applied to Boulez: To what extent does Boulez's computerized passion do violence to the materials of sound? To what extent are the systems that shape this music consonant with the properties of sounds themselves, with their own latent mathematics? To what extent do they honor the way sounds are received and processed by the human body?

It is probably best to be frank at this point and say outright that, as far as I can see, this particular music, in its extreme artificiality, has passed beyond the bounds of what could be enriching for human beings. Certainly, we need to recognize that much music that has appeared impossibly chaotic has, in time, come to be perceived and enjoyed as profoundly ordered. What one generation calls irredeemably ugly, another can find engagingly beautiful. But the issue here is not *whether* this kind of music is ordered—as we have seen, it is some of the most ordered music ever composed—but *what kind of order* it possesses. Does the order on which it is based correspond in any way to the given sonic order (including the order of our own bodies as vehicles of sound), at least in a way that can be perceived, even if only on the intellectual level? Or—as even Boulez came to see—has it reached such a rarefied abstraction that it can no longer relate to or put us in touch with anything that could be recognizably interesting or enjoyable?[32]

Freedom and Constraint

Bound up with the issue of respect is the issue of freedom. The resistance many have to the notion of respect in the arts stems from a pervasive assumption about freedom: in a nutshell, the more we are responsible to some "other" beyond our own construction, the less free we can be. The model is not hard to glean from what we have just surveyed. If the physical world—including our own bodies—is simply there and not given in the rich sense, and if at the same time we see ourselves as in some sense displacing God, or at least assuming God-like powers of creativity, it is not surprising if we start to see our material limits as a curse and burden to be escaped or defeated. Freedom means being free from constraint. The attempt to abstract music from its materiality (as in Schoenberg) is one example of this; the attempt to coerce musical sounds into a particular shape (as in Boulez) is another.

Again, an imaginative jolt is needed. From the vantage point of a Christian ecology, freedom, human flourishing is found *in a responsible relation to constraints* that are worthy of respect, to constraints that are there but in the full sense of given—"there (potentially) for our benefit."[33] Without constraints we cannot flourish. As most parents know, it is only when children "know where they stand" that they start to relax, even more so when they know the limits are set by someone who loves them. The same applies to the physical constraints of music. Albert Blackwell captures this well when he describes the overtone series as "exceedingly hospitable to creative human choices."[34] The attempt to wrestle free from constraints altogether, as even Boulez realized, is ultimately self-defeating. We become imprisoned, not free.[35] This goes not only for phenomena like the harmonic series but also for the scales and systems we derive from them. The Russian twentieth-century composer Igor Stravinsky once wrote:

> I experience a sort of terror when, at the moment of setting to work and finding myself before the infinitude of possibilities that present themselves, I have the feeling that everything is permissible to me. If everything is permissible to me . . . every undertaking becomes futile. . . . I shall overcome my terror and shall be reassured by the thought that I have the seven notes of the scale and its chromatic intervals at my disposal . . . strong and weak accents are within my reach, and . . . in all these I possess solid and concrete elements which offer me a field of experience just as vast as the upsetting and dizzy infinitude that had just frightened me. . . . What delivers me from the anguish into which an unrestricted freedom plunges me is the fact that I am always able to turn immediately to the concrete things that are here in question. . . . *Whatever constantly gives way to pressure, constantly renders movement impossible. . . . Whatever diminishes constraint, diminishes strength.*[36]

Of course there are many constraints that do undermine human freedom—epilepsy, terminal cancer, solitary confinement. The point here, however, is to challenge the belief that we automatically increase freedom by reducing limits or multiplying the options open to us. (Does having thirty brands of yogurt to choose from actually make us any more free?) For the Christian, to be free is not fundamentally to enjoy some supposedly blank space before us, or to increase options, but to be at peace with God and one another and thus at home in a God-given world.[37]

In music, perhaps this is nowhere clearer than in improvised music. For a blues pianist, for example, the chord pattern is there in the full sense of given to enable elaboration. Structure enables freedom. David Sudnow's remarkable study, *Ways of the Hand*, brings the imaginative jolt needed here. He recounts how, as a classically trained pianist, he learned to improvise jazz. Especially significant is the role his body came to play in the process. He found that most teaching manuals on improvisation treat the hands as passive instruments of the mind. The manuals tell you the notes you need to have in your mind and then how to get your hands to play those notes. Sudnow dutifully followed the instructions. But when it came to playing in a trio, it was "like searching for a parking place in a very big hurry. The music was literally 'out of hand.'"[38]

The breakthrough into authentic jazz came when he started to trust his hands to explore their own relation to the physical peculiarities of the keyboard. In other words, he started to respect and trust the constraints. Particular sorts of sound linked with particular hand shapes. In playing blues, for example, one aims not so much for particular notes as for a characteristic sound associated with a distinctive shape of the hand. He had to learn to "hear with the hand." Soon he found that the hand had all sorts of surprises in store; it had ways with the keyboard that opened up fresh music. In playing runs of notes, he learned not to target specific notes but to toss a shaped hand at the keys and then listen and respond to the sound that emerged. Before, he was acutely aware of making mistakes.[39] Now errors could be taken up by the hand. He could relax, knowing that the hand would take care of it: there would always be *something* to play, something "at hand." He made further progress by incorporating the rest of his body—"finger-snapping, head-bobbing, arm-and-shoulder rotating," and, not least, singing: "I sing with my fingers."[40] In all this, he was at the same time exploring and negotiating the shapes of sounds themselves—the properties of chords, the potential of melodies, the possibilities of different harmonic progressions—constantly adjusting his own playing as he heard more. In short, he became free. His body, the instrument, the properties of sounds—these constraints were not impediments to his freedom to be shunned or conquered but the means of discovering and realizing it.

Developing

Let It Be?

Boulez's music may have sounded very similar to that of his transatlantic correspondent, John Cage. But their view of composition was radically different. And the contrast is instructive. If in the late 1940s and early 1950s Boulez is the pioneer of all-encompassing organization, John Cage is the pioneer of "let it be." Cage was an eclectic by nature—summarizing him is hard—but at this stage at least, his fascination with chance and indeterminacy was bound up with a desire to let sounds have their own way rather than make them serve our schemes of organization. Composing, for Cage, was a matter not of linking sounds into a cohesive piece of music but of composing "individual sounds and letting them find their own expressiveness within a blank canvas of empty time."[41] "Where people had felt the necessity to stick sounds together to make a continuity, we . . . felt the opposite necessity to get rid of the glue so that sounds would be themselves."[42] As Paul Griffiths puts it, "The work [is], in the Zen spirit, a vehicle not of thoughts but only events."[43] Composition is about *accepting* rather than *making*. So in *Music for Changes* (1951), coins (or marked sticks) are thrown for chance numbers, hexagrams of thirty-two or sixty-four numbers are formed, and from these the various musical elements proceed. The occurrence of any particular sound was not the outcome of imposing a melodic or harmonic idea "but was now the result of nothing at all but geometry: the sounds simply 'happened.'"[44]

Just as he had no interest in limiting or shaping music, still less was he concerned to convey a message. "Until that time," Cage tells us, "my music had been based on the idea that you had to say something. The charts [of the music of the early 1950s] gave me the indication of the possibility of saying nothing."[45] This notion of emerging sound Cage dubbed "no-continuity," where the ordering of events had nothing to do with any composed relations between them. Each sound is just itself, and any relations among the sounds happen of themselves, not because the composer's mind imposes them. In a letter to Boulez, Cage describes composition as "throwing sounds into silence."[46] Later he could say: "In this new music nothing takes place but sounds: those that are notated and those that are not. Those that are not notated appear in the written music as silences, opening the doors of the music to the sounds that happen to be in the environment."[47] (This is part of the thinking behind his most famous piece, 4'33", which at its first performance consisted of a pianist going to the piano and not playing anything for four minutes and thirty-three seconds. The audience became aware that the "silence" was not silent. Sounds filled the air—shifting in seats, riffling programs, breathing, air conditioning, and so on.) We need not fear the future of music, Cage explains:

> But this fearlessness only follows if . . . where it is realised that sounds occur whether intended or not, one turns in the direction of those [not intended]. This turning is psychological and seems at first to be a giving up of everything that belongs to humanity—for a musician, the giving up of music. This psychological turning leads to the world of nature, where, gradually or suddenly, one sees that humanity and nature, not separate, are in this world together.[48]

It is an intriguing outlook, and in some ways attractive to the Christian, given Cage's desire to honor the integrity of sounds and our own embeddedness in nature. And it is certainly a telling embodiment of the principle of the "death of the artwork." However, although in this vision the composer is not completely passive (for he or she composes the individual sounds that become the material of the composition—when there *are* composed sounds), there seems to be a strong suspicion of the idea that human interaction with the natural world can be fruitful or enriching. Edward Lippman comments: "What clearly is at stake here is the elimination of any distinction between art and nature (or between artistic experience and ordinary experience)."[49] That is probably going too far, but it shows the direction Cage traveled, and it is a direction few have been willing to take since (despite Cage's forecasts about the dissolution of the boundary between noise and music). This, then, represents a virtual denial of any human transcendence over nature, an attitude that, within a Christian ecology at least, needs querying.

It is, then, one thing to spurn the worst of humanity's aggressive imposition on natural order; it is quite another to spurn *any* notion that we are to shape our environment. Put more positively: we have been given the opportunity to *develop* what lies at hand, to fashion things as yet unfashioned. Michelangelo takes the grains of marble and carves *David*; Vivaldi takes catgut, horsehair, and wood and makes *The Four Seasons*. In chapter 1, I contended that especially distinctive to the arts is *metaphor*—the bringing together of unlike elements to create a new whole:[50] Shakespeare combines incompatible words to generate powerful new meaning ("Juliet is the sun"); Coleridge combines a stylized structure (meter, rhyming) with a compelling story (*The Rime of the Ancient Mariner*); Stravinsky sets words of quiet, humble supplication to brusque pistol-shot chords in *Symphony of Psalms*.

What is needed here is a rejection of the suspicion that when we put our hands on something and make something from it we necessarily corrupt it. We will remember that Western music has been based for hundreds of years on an adjustment of the harmonic series; pianos are not tuned precisely in accordance with the series but are tempered to enable us to enjoy playing in a variety of keys and shift from one to another.[51] Many were troubled by this when it first appeared (and some still are), believing it represented an illegitimate departure from what is natural. But could it not be read as *a respectful development of a given order that has led to new, fruitful, and enriching order*? Few would deny the extraordinary music that has been made possible by it (the majority of Western tonal music). The trouble with the phrase "pure tuning" (i.e., in strict accordance with Pythagorean ratios) is that it can suggest that anything else is impure, a distortion, that any interference brings harm. A Christian view of creativity makes no such assumption, believing that it is quite possible to engage respectfully with what is given and *through* this engagement elaborate fresh art that is felicitous and life-enhancing. Indeed, it is more than possible; it is part of our vocation.

Repetition?

To come at this another way, we need to affirm without apology that the calling of the musician includes the making of *new* things. Some will be nervous about the word "new" in this context, and not without good reason. It is rightly said that we do not create "out of nothing." Only God does that. It is rightly said that we cannot jump out of our culture—we always work within a tradition, and the cult of originality is ultimately empty. It is rightly said that composers need to make a living, and to ignore the likes and dislikes of their society is naive—novelty for many is simply not an option if food needs to go on the table the next morning. Nevertheless, at the heart of a faith that takes the resurrection of Jesus and the giving of the Spirit seriously is the conviction that the future does not simply roll out of the past, that we are not locked into a world of tight determinism, that each situation and circumstance is genuinely unique, and that each person is called to respond in the power of the Spirit to each different context in different ways. In short, in music, no less than anywhere else, genuine novelty is possible, indeed, an obligation.

Put another way: we are not given a vocation of identical repetition, replicating the past. Much has been written about the drive to repetition in our consumerist culture, the blandness that mass production generates, not least in music. Indeed, a hefty and much-discussed critique of popular music has been mounted from this angle, and since it raises crucial concerns for the Christian, it is worth giving it some attention here.

The critique is associated especially with the writings of the formidable and influential German theorist Theodor Adorno (1903–69).[52] His views were formed to a significant extent as a reaction to the results of totalitarianism in Germany and Italy in the 1930s, and, interestingly, he saw popular culture as filling the gap left by "spiritual disenchantment" in the West, the waning of the power of religious ideas. He argued that popular music had been swamped by the "culture industry" of global capitalism, a system in which a range of entertainments and pleasures are provided with the goal of producing profit rather than promoting human flourishing. The permeation of musical life by market forces has led to a situation that split music into two main types—first, that which develops new compositional techniques but is usually incomprehensible, being quickly isolated and marginalized by society (the "avant-garde"), and second, the popular music of mass culture, superficially consumed by unthinking hearers, selling in vast quantities but in thrall to the forces of sameness (*Gleichheit*), repetition (*Wiederholung*), and predictability.[53]

In Adorno's eyes, popular music is captive to standardization—heavily dependent on preexisting formulas and norms. He cites as examples the overall structure of pieces (thirty-two-bar chorus), melodic range, song types, harmonic progressions, and so on—forms that amount almost to rules, immediately familiar to listeners and entirely predictable. He directs some of his most pointed invective against jazz.[54] Pieces may be given the appearance of novelty—for example, when a record company makes minor adjustments to songs to create the impression of difference—but this is entirely superficial (hence Adorno's term "pseudo-individualisation"),[55] for just below the surface, the same trite, unchanging formulas are there. There can be no development or progress with this kind of music, only repetition, replication with at best a veneer of difference. Hence this kind of music ages rapidly, fast becoming obsolete. (In "serious" music—and Adorno frequently draws upon Beethoven here—novelty and predictability are held in balance, making each piece unique.)

Linked to this is a picture of consumers as a largely passive mass colluding in their own manipulation, active only in the sense that they "clamor for what they are going to get anyhow."[56] Adorno believes the "culture industries" create, control, and exploit musical desires, and the outcome is a kind of music that functions in ways similar to advertising, creating a demand to which production can subsequently claim to respond. This can breed only immature, psychologically weak individuals. Even when consumers do see through what is happening—as Adorno was prepared to admit could happen—they find themselves powerless to do anything about it. Even if innovative ideas are developed, they are quickly subsumed into the culture industry.[57] This music can offer no effective critique of its society; it offers at one and the same time escape from life's banalities as well as a confirmation of them, its twin functions being distraction (in effect, a kind of drug) and affirmation (it can only maintain the status quo). Adorno would have applauded one recent commentator's observation: "Mirthless promotional photographs betray no sense of irony over rock groups who struggle to project individual disaffection and social non-conformity by endlessly reiterating our musical culture's three most conventional chords [I, IV and V]."[58] He would also not have been surprised to find books such as Jimmy Cauty and Bill Drummond's *The Manual: How to Have a Number One Hit the Easy Way* of 1998, a guide to the standard form and content of successful singles.[59]

Needless to say, Adorno's acidic critique has provoked vigorous responses. It is rightly said that he does not pay enough attention to music's real-life settings, that even in the 1930s and 1940s musical culture was far more diverse than he recognized,[60] that the picture of the largely powerless consumer is too simply drawn. It has been pointed out that however much hype and publicity goes into a product, there can be no guarantee of success—only about 10 percent of all records released actually make money.[61] Also, in popular music, alongside an increase in centralized control there has been persistent dissent of one sort or another (an obvious example is the growth of independent record companies).[62] The Adornian critique cannot easily account for a John Lennon, a Bob Dylan, a Bob Marley, a Merle Haggard, or forms of African-American popular music that offer countercultural perspectives.[63] Even limiting ourselves to popular music of the 1930s and 1940s, there are numerous examples of the adventurous transformation of inherited materials, not only by composers but also by performers.[64] Gordon Lynch points out that "people can make use of 'mass' culture in ways that subvert its intended meanings and challenge socially oppressive ideas."[65] Moreover, it is doubtful if all standardization is regressive or harmful. We should bear in mind that formulaic schemes are not limited to Western popular music but are very common in other musical types and in music worldwide. In a huge amount of Asian and Middle Eastern music we will find relatively fixed or preexisting ideas, adopted and elaborated in performance (e.g., music based on the raga principle), and there is no evidence that such music necessarily encourages uniformity or a duped "mass mind."[66]

Nevertheless, Adorno is not easily dismissed. As Simon Frith puts it: "Adorno's is the most systematic and the most searing analysis of mass culture and the most challenging for anyone claiming even a scrap of value for the products that come churning out of the music industry."[67] It is hard to dispute that the drive for profit has often resulted in a kind of stultifying sameness in musical production. It is not difficult to trace trends toward monopoly and conglomeration and a resulting "conservative appeal to the predictable and universally understood."[68] Richard Middleton believes,

> The force of this theory [of musical production] is undeniable. In an age when a symphony orchestra can appear in uniforms designed to advertise tobacco-industry sponsors; . . . when a small selection of endlessly permutated pop songs provides the background for almost every social activity; when rhythm tracks on disco records can be behavioristically planned and electronically produced, for maximum precision and control: one cannot, at this time, avoid the feeling that if Orwell's "1984" ever arrives, it might well consist of a continuous Eurovision Song Contest.[69]

So-called world music can also be caught up in the forces Adorno identifies, as when the music of an Asian country is sampled and adapted to a drum 'n' bass track from New York. This is the kind of thing hinted at by Philip Bohlman when he speaks of "homogenised global pop, cultural imperialism made sonorous."[70]

Adorno's observations about the often wearisome prevalence of certain musical forms are also difficult to deny, as are his astute comments on manipulation through music. In this connection, James MacMillan has some telling reflections:

> Certainly when I was younger I was hungry for musical experiences from all angles, and popular culture was one of those things which interested me and inspired me. As a teenager I used to play in a little rock band, and in my twenties I used to play Scottish and Irish music around about the folk clubs and pubs in the west of Scotland.

But this enthusiasm waned. He explains:

> I'm alarmed at some of the ubiquitous nature of popular culture, and the way it seems to edge everything else out. It seems to edge out young people's innate curiosity for making discoveries other than the things that are flung at them through the usual popular culture medium. I think popular culture sometimes curtails and limits that natural curiosity, and it can lead to uniformity and conformity, the very things that popular culture claims to be against.[71]

But my purpose here in bringing up Adorno is not to mount an argument against a supposedly monolithic lump of "popular music" (in any case, the forces Adorno identifies are increasingly evident in classical music). Rather, it is to allow this very acute writer to throw a certain danger sharply into relief—that of sidelining, stifling what Christians will want to describe as a God-given calling to develop fresh forms of order in a modern/postmodern culture that is riven with powerful forces of repetition, replication, and homogenization.[72]

To bring this a little closer to home, it is not hard to identify some of these unhealthy trends in Christian music.[73] In North America in particular, Christian Contemporary Music (CCM) is an enormous industry, and some would argue that it has succumbed in an alarming way to the co-opting of religion into the commercial interests of consumption, capitalism, and materialism. In a thorough study, Jay Howard and John Streck have asked some pointed questions about this kind of interpretation, insisting that we should not equate the "authentic" with the noncommercial and also not miss the variety within CCM: some types would seem far more prone to an Adorno-like critique than others.[74]

Nonetheless, some of the pungent remarks of Adorno and his followers would seem very applicable, not least those about sameness and replication. It is disappointing, for example, to find an intense musical conservatism in much of the contemporary worship scene. Granted that simple songs have their place, that accessibility is one of the key merits of this music, and that this is always going to be necessary to some extent, one would have hoped that a movement that can put such weight on the Holy Spirit's renewal could generate somewhat more adventurous material. Many songs are in standard four- and eight-bar phrases, using only a few chords of a basic and very well-worn folk or folk-rock tradition. The questions need to be pressed: Is the church prepared to give its musicians room to experiment (and fail), to juxtapose different styles, to educate themselves in music history, to resist the tendency to rely on formulas that "work" with minimum effort and can quickly guarantee seats filled in church—and all this in order that congregational worship can become more theologically responsible, more true to the God who has given us such abundant potential for developing fresh musical sounds?

It is worth noticing that Howard and Streck distinguish a form of CCM they call "transformational" that, with varying degrees of success, self-consciously struggles against the forces of commercialism.[75] Here music is seen not merely as a tool of communication but as potentially something of artistic and aesthetic worth in its own right. Howard and Streck point to Mark Heard as the "patron saint" of this tradition, but also more recently to Charlie Peacock, and behind them to the Dutch Calvinist tradition (especially Hans Rookmaaker). Among the leading ideas is the notion that "art needs no justification," that music can glorify God without necessarily having an evangelical message tagged on to it, without having to be used consciously and deliberately to communicate a spiritual truth, perhaps simply by having artistic excellence. There is a conviction that the fallenness of the world cannot be evaded, that as God transformed the world through entering and exposing the worst of it, so Christian musicians are called to be honest about the worst they know and yet demonstrate how things could be if God's intentions were honored. These ideas, clearly, are broadly in line with what I am recommending in this book. Even here, however, there will be a struggle; put simply, the pressure to "sell Jesus" leaves transformational artists with the dilemma: "compromise your art or find yourself without the opportunity to produce it."[76]

It may well be that cross-cultural conversation has a crucial part to play here: helping us broaden our vision of "development." Michael Hawn has recently issued a powerful appeal to those engaged in music worship to think globally—to "expand the cultural plurality that is already inherent in worship" by actively encouraging greater cross-cultural encounter. He recommends this as a way of breaking out of the constricting "ethnocentrism" that he believes imprisons much of the debate about music in worship today (e.g., traditional versus contemporary), locking it into circles, and leading to "provincial, partial, and erroneous conclusions."[77] Through the voices of other cultures we are made to rethink many of our fundamental assumptions about the part music plays in worship and thus open up fresh ways for the gospel to be discovered and celebrated more profoundly. To attempt "to create an environment in which worship is experienced only in the most recent normative monocultural terms"[78] will deprive us of many of these possibilities—we will be condemned to repeat what is largely familiar and what simply confirms us in our prejudices.

Healing

Art is not a copy of the real world. One of the damn things is enough.

Virginia Woolf[79]

We have said that music making and music hearing happen in a world marred by misplaced praise and that humans are to be agents of healing, in the confidence that the God who raised the slain Lamb will raise with him everything that is spoiled and injured to a new freedom of life. This means sharing now in the Creator's own redeeming work—in Christ's company and carried by his Spirit, penetrating, judging, and refashioning whatever has been polluted and distorted.

Healing and Hope

In other words, we are called to be agents of hope, witnessing to and embodying the hope that God has given to the world through Christ. To see what this might mean for music, we need to explore a little more closely the theme of hope, which will make clearer the kind of healing that God has set in motion and in which he invites us to share.

It hardly needs saying that the language of hope in many circles today will be greeted with profound misgivings.[80] This is usually seen as very much part of the postmodern ethos, but it is by no means confined to what is commonly put under that label. We can identify at least three closely related strands of suspicion: (1) There is a suspicion of *escapism*. Christian hope evokes for many the attempt to ignore (if not deny) evil, suffering, and pain in the belief that one day believers will be transported to an entirely different place called "heaven," beyond the bright blue sky. This appears to be irresponsible, a sign that we are refusing to face up to the misery so many endure in this life. Worse still, the Marxist will quickly tell us that the prospect of "pie in the sky when you die" will be used by the oppressor to tighten his grip of power and keep his subjects at bay. Urging people to hope in heaven keeps their minds off their plight here and now. (2) Linked to this is a second strand: a suspicion of a *naive optimism in human nature*. Here hope is equated with human-centered confidence, often linked to the modernist myth of human progress, a belief in the steady ascent of humankind to ever-greater heights, the dream of ever-increasing mastery of the world through scientific, technological, and economic advance, and the Eurocentric imperialist dream of spreading these advances worldwide. So many of those hopes have turned out to be empty. Intertwined with the post-Enlightenment wonders of medical advance, increased life expectancy, and the communications revolution, we find weapons of horrific destruction, mass starvation, and ecological devastation. (3) Bound up with this, there is the suspicion of *domination*. Behind the political speeches about hope, the postmodernist sniffs the desire to coerce and oppress, something Nietzsche warned us about long ago. Thus the "hermeneutics of suspicion" seeks to unmask the power plays behind apparently innocent talk of hope, reminding us that so many schemes promising the new heaven end up with the old hell. We need think only of Western "development" and colonization—riding on the rhetoric of hope but so often exploiting other cultures with thoughtless barbarity.

Understandably, Christians today will be quick to respond to these suspicions and insist that all three trade on distortions and misunderstandings of authentic biblical hope. But we should not jump to the defense too quickly. For it is not hard to see that Christians have unwittingly played a massive part in colluding with these distortions. All too often the church has proclaimed an essentially escapist message, all too often displaying a naive trust in the inherent powers of "human nature," and all too often using its own story of hope as a brutal weapon against Hispanics, Maoris, women, African Americans . . . and on the list could go.

Cross-Shaped Hope

It has become increasingly common to stress these signal failures of the church. What is not always seen quite so clearly is the manner in which the gospel itself subverts the false hopes, on the one hand, and paralyzing guilt, on the other. This is the way of the cross. We need to be quite clear: our concern has nothing to do with a Protestant obsession with sin and death but with where the New Testament writers repeatedly direct us when they want to convey and instill hope. God heals the world of its evil in *this* way and no other. God generates hope by *this* route and no other.

Any response to the contemporary threefold suspicion of hope that evades the cross will simply perpetuate the problems and rightly be brushed aside by the cynic as another form of modernist make-believe. Only the cross can meet the suspicion of escapism: God gives hope not by promising to pull us into a different world but by offering us a fresh beginning in this world, by himself coming to a place of the very sort we are tempted to escape, a place where suffering, opposition, and senselessness conspire to make life appear utterly futile and unbearable. Only the cross can meet the suspicion of optimism in human nature: God gives us hope by meeting us not at the lofty summits of human achievement but at the point where all purely human hopes have shrunk and collapsed; it is here that exhausted human hope can be remade out of the inexhaustible possibilities of God's love. Only the cross can meet the suspicion of violent domination: God gives us hope not by defeating the powers of darkness with some equivalent act of violence from above but by submitting to them and bearing their force from below, not by an imperial force that crushes from on high but by a love that absorbs evil in the depths. This is the way of Golgotha, God's wisdom (1 Cor. 1:18–25).

None of this need downplay Easter, as is often thought. Scrupulous care must be taken not to set cross and resurrection against each other in some kind of "balance." Too often we encounter the view that the cross was in some manner cancelled by the resurrection: "The cross was the bad news, but, thankfully, God pulled off a victory on the third day." The New Testament writers never affirm this. The apostle Paul brings things to a head in this respect. For him the victory over the principalities and powers has been won at Golgotha (Col. 2:15). Easter announces to the world God's victory over evil; it is God's great *yes* to what has happened in Jesus, supremely at the cross; it is the pronouncement that evil has been decisively dealt with—the defeat of death confirming the defeat of sin and evil at Calvary (1 Cor. 15:17). And precisely *because* it is that, the resurrection is also a promise that God will one day renew all that has been spoiled by evil—a pledge to his people that he will transform their bodies, in the manner of Jesus's own body, and a pledge that he will re-create the entire cosmos (Rom. 8:19–22; 1 Cor. 15:35–49). The stunning and stupendous Easter hope is possible only because of the crucifixion of Jesus of Nazareth.[81]

Music and God's Healing

If God heals the world this way, and thus brings hope this way, what does it mean to be agents of healing and hope in the world of music? We can use the three contemporary suspicions of hope to shape our discussion.

Escapism. Throughout history, music has often functioned to help people avoid or forget things. Our culture is furnished with vast quantities of music designed to provide a refuge from rush, relief from a heavy responsibility, and so on. Even when not intended by the composer, music is often deployed in this way: soothing sounds greet you at the dentist's reception (distracting you from the torture to come); an iPod plays heavy rock to the depressed student facing exams; a band plays Schubert marches to those arriving at the Nazi death camp.

We have already made some comments on that fast-growing genre of music that includes "New Age," "chill out," and "spiritual" music, frequently marketed to the overpressured and overstressed. Not surprisingly, it contrasts sharply with contemporary postmodern urban life—the music is normally very slow, gentle, unhurried, with blurred boundaries, nothing that jars or stands out. As we have already said, from a Christian point of view, escape or diversion is by no means always to be decried. And in prayer and worship, escape from distraction is essential; if music can aid our being still in order to be receptive to God, all to the good.[82]

Pointed questions, however, need to be asked if music becomes a way of evading responsibility, screening out what needs to be faced, lulling us into a cocoon of false security, or if music's Christian or theological potential is seen as *limited* to providing the solace of escape. The problem becomes especially acute in worship, where music can very easily strengthen a sense that to encounter God is to be sucked into a zone totally unrelated to the world we inhabit from Monday through Saturday, as if to be *in touch* with God through music means being *out of touch* with everything (and everyone) else. While there is of course a need to concentrate on God for God's sake in worship, if it really is *God* on whom we focus, we will be provoked to responsible action in a world for which Christ died that is so obviously still "groaning in labor" (Rom. 8:22). Worship, after all, takes place "in the rhythm of adoration and action."[83] If music does no more than help us forget our obligations or numb us to the world outside, it has become a drug, a dangerous narcotic. We recall Bonhoeffer's words, "Only he who cries out for the Jews may sing Gregorian chants,"[84] and Amos railing against musicians who blind God's people to the cries of the downtrodden (Amos 5:23–24).

William James, musing on a visit to a Christian resort in Chautauqua, New York, tells us of "the atrocious harmlessness of all things" and how he longed for the outside world with its "heights and depths, the precipices and steep ideals, the gleams of the awful and the infinite."[85] We probably need to reckon with the fact that much music that goes under the label "Christian" has been "atrociously harmless"—and I am thinking of a wide variety of styles here—with a relatively small repertoire of easy-to-listen-to chords, with so little sense of the world's dissonance, of the clanking distortions and contradictions of human rebellion, of the clashing and grinding of evil, in short, of the realities that pervade the lives of so many people and that God came to engage directly at Golgotha.

This relates to a concern we have touched on already about the kind of theological claims that have been associated with some of the music of composers such as Tavener and Pärt and similar music from other sources that is characterized by a highly contemplative ambience and often labeled "spiritual." I have suggested one way of accounting for at least part of the immense popularity of this music: it offers a cool sonic cathedral in a hot, rushed, and overcrowded culture. And I spoke of what I think are its potential benefits. But I also questioned the implicit assumptions about God and time that seem to be at work (and are sometimes articulated): in particular, the belief that the more deeply we relate to God, the more we will need to abstract ourselves from time and history.[86] This links up with our concerns about escapism here. If such music is allowed a monopoly on what is to count as spiritual or religious, we could find ourselves with a cast of mind far from that rooted in the coming of God's Word-made-flesh to journey with us in our time and space.

We can press the point further. If Christ has embraced our fallen humanity, including its fear, anxiety, hunger, loss, frustration, and disappointment, and these have been drawn into, indeed, become the very material of salvation, can we be content with a vision of the spiritual that is unable to engage just these realities, with a cool cathedral that bears little relation to the life on the streets? To focus the point further still: God's engagement with our time climaxes in a hideous and ugly death. Any concern for the spiritual cannot evade this (1 Cor. 1:18–25). As we saw, this is what lies behind James MacMillan's suspicion of the New Simplicity movement, that it plays too easily into a world-denying (time-denying) distortion of Christianity in which God's cross-centered involvement with humanity is marginalized.[87]

Naive optimism. This was the second common contemporary suspicion of Christian claims about hope. Again, music in society is often used to generate self-confidence—from the song chanted by the football team to piped music boosting output in a car factory. It has long been known that certain kinds of music can greatly help people to believe in themselves. Music in these contexts will typically be in major keys, upbeat, with a regular pulse, loud, and fairly rapid.

Again, if used to good effect, none of this need be a concern. But questions should be asked if such music becomes a way of effacing or denying the reality of human failure and wickedness, both in us and in others. Again, it is worship that throws the issue into relief most sharply. In the next chapter we will look at delayed gratification in music and the implied superficial confidence evident in some worship music.[88] Rushing over or rushing through tension speaks too easily of evading the plight of the human condition. At Golgotha, godless self-confidence is exposed as dark and deadly. God's most concentrated encounter with us has been at our lowest point in order that he can give us a hope that cannot pivot on our "natural abilities." *This* is the way we are healed. More than that, though the final victory is sealed in Christ, it has not yet arrived in fullness for this world; our lives will not be lives of unqualified triumph. The cross needs to be inscribed into the rhythm of living: there will be a regular dying to sin, for there can be no *living with* Christ without *dying with* him (Rom. 6:8). Frustration, perseverance, endurance, and patience in the midst of opposition are all part of our vocation to share in Christ's sufferings (Rom. 8:17). This is part of what it means to be conformed to the image and likeness of Christ (2 Cor. 3:18), to live in a world not yet fully healed. Can we ever forget that Jesus gave the Spirit to his disciples—commissioning them for their calling— with nail-marked hands (John 20:19–23)?

Domination. Music has undoubtedly often been used as a tool of domination, of manipulation. Dictators have recognized the colossal power of music to help inculcate ideologies, effect group conformity, hold people to a creed. We need only call to mind the Nazis' use of music in the Nürnberg rallies—calculated to capture the hearts of thousands. Painful as it is to acknowledge, the Christian church has often succumbed to similar strategies using music to whip up crowds into mindless enthusiasm, sometimes generating pseudocommunity based on little more than the ability to sing loudly together. Although it is usually simplistic to blame the musical sounds alone for this—as we stressed in chapter 1, it is *people* who use music, and they use it in complex contexts—there is little doubt that some musical sounds are particularly well suited to manipulative use and function, appealing very directly to base instincts.

Anything approaching coercion or duress, the forcing of a response, denies the divine strategy of the cross. God's most concentrated encounter with us has been through an act of noncoercive love. This is the way the world is healed. Most of us, when we are the victims of sin, send the sin back out again; we strike back or pass it on to someone else. God takes the violence of our sin into his own self. It does not get recycled. That is the kind of love that distinguishes those called to be healing agents in the world, in music no less than anywhere else.

A fair amount of this section has been negative in tone. But we should not be deaf to forms of music making that do invite us to experience the kind hope I am speaking about—a hope that without any diminishment of resurrection joy refuses to evade the cross in God's healing strategy. It is not hard to find worship in many African-American Pentecostal Churches, for example, where hopeful praise can intertwine with community renewal, the education of the disadvantaged, legal aid for the downtrodden, and a fight for better housing. Many particular pieces and sections of music also come to mind: Bach's "Crucifixus" and the "Et Resurrexit" from the "Credo" of the *Mass in B Minor*, Duke Ellington's "Come Sunday," some of the liberation songs of South Africa, much of the music of the Iona Community, especially their psalm-settings.[89] And in the world of contemporary art music, the figure who stands out is one we have already examined at length, James MacMillan. The links between MacMillan and what we have been saying hardly need to be spelled out. His music enacts a striking example of a repudiation of false hopes, a refusal to obscure the manner in which "The World's Ransoming" (to use the title of one of his pieces) has been secured, a refusal to articulate hope in any way other than in the manner it has actually been given to us.

Anticipating

This hope, we said in the last chapter, is not of a remote future but of a future tasted now: the remaking of this world and of our own humanity, previewed in the raising of Jesus from the dead, and to be enjoyed now through the Spirit. Implicitly, we have already said much about this. For insofar as music is a vehicle of the kind of discovering, respecting, developing, and healing we have been speaking about (and of the togetherness we shall come to in a moment)—in other words, insofar as it is in line with God's purposes in Christ, which always have a future in view—it will embody that future to some degree. It will be less a "counter-creation" (George Steiner's term) than an anticipation of the new creation.[90] It is the Spirit's role, we said, to bring about in the world what has already been achieved in Christ, and in so doing anticipate the final re-creation of all things.

In chapter 8, we spoke of the importance of imagination in theology, in particular, the ability to perceive connections between things. Included in this, we said, is the ability to connect present and future, to transcend the limits of the present without leaving it behind, to see simultaneously what is and what might be. Richard Bauckham and Trevor Hart speak of this as a basic function of the imagination: "to make present states of affairs which are otherwise absent, not given in what we are currently experiencing of the world," and perhaps sometimes contradicting the facts of the present, as when Martin Luther King imagines a nonracist future ("I have a dream . . .").[91] This kind of imaginative thrust can lead, of course, to empty illusions, but not necessarily, and in any case, survival would be impossible without using the imagination in this way: how would we go on living if we really did believe we were wholly determined by what *now is*, if we did not have some vision of a better future that *could be*?

For centuries, many have seen the arts as crucial to providing such a vision, and we are surely touching on something of inestimable importance for the Christian artist to contribute, not least because he or she lives in the confidence of God's promise—a promise not just about what *could be* but of what *will be*. Within Scripture we can see art functioning this way. The Babylonian exiles settled down to life as they think it has to be, and Isaiah, through oracles bursting with metaphorical energy, jerks their imagination, shakes them out of the flaccid mind-set: "Make straight in the desert a highway for our God. . . . He will feed his flock like a shepherd. . . . Even the nations are like a drop from a bucket."[92] Jesus delivers quirky and unnerving parables, upsetting a worldview that has closed itself to the possibility of God doing "the new thing." It is a theme recently explored by Patrick Sherry: drawing especially on the work of Russian theologians such as Solovyov, Berdyaev, and Bulgakov, he argues that in their highest achievements, the arts, through the Spirit, are capable of granting glimpses of eternal beauty and as such can anticipate and give a foretaste of the transfiguration of the cosmos.[93] As such, the arts can be "scattered acts of [the] recreative anticipation of God's promised future,"[94] or in New Testament terms: signs of the new age of the Spirit in the midst of the old age of sin and death.

But what of music? We have met the idea a number of times already. For example, we saw that Barth dared to suggest that in heaven when the angels play en famille, they play Mozart. No doubt said with a twinkle in his eye, it is a quip with substance, for inasmuch as Mozart's music does voice creation's song to its Creator as God intends, it anticipates his promised future. And if Barth heard Mozart's music as a "parable of the kingdom," then the point is strengthened, for Barth saw such parables as provisional signs, here and now, of the kingdom to come.

Mozart finds just such a place in the movie *The Shawshank Redemption*. Andy, falsely accused for the murder of his wife and her lover, finds himself in a brutal jail. One day, while cleaning the prison office, he manages to lock the guard in the toilet and find a record of a duet from Mozart's *Marriage of Figaro*, "Che soave zeffiretto." He plays it through the prison PA system, and the courtyard full of hardened criminals is suddenly stilled. Andy's friend Red remarks:

> I have no idea to this day what those two Italian ladies were singin' about. . . . I like to think they were singin' about something so beautiful it can't be expressed in words, and makes our heart ache because of it. I tell you those voices soared, higher and farther than anybody in a gray place dares to dream. It was like some beautiful bird flapped into our drab little cage and made these walls dissolve away . . . and for the briefest of moments—every last man at Shawshank felt free.[95]

Andy is thrown into solitary confinement. "Was it worth two weeks in the hole?" asks a friend. "Easiest time I ever did. . . . I had Mr. Mozart to keep me company. Hardly felt the time at all." Andy goes on to say that we need music to remind us that "there are places in this world that aren't made out of stone, and that there's something inside that they can't get to, and that they can't touch. It's yours." "What're you talking about?" asks Red. Andy replies, "Hope." Red responds, "Hope is a dangerous thing. Drives a man insane."[96]

This is not escapism, at least not in the sense that the music transports the prisoners into an unreal world that has nothing to do with the present one. In the film it functions more like an injection of the future into the present. Through this music of startling beauty, they breathe the air not just of the outside world but of the world of the future; indeed, this unexpected taste of freedom is part of what sustains Andy's efforts to chisel away to the outside world, a world—in his case—of justice as well as freedom. Hope becomes "a dangerous thing" precisely because the future has been tasted now.

There are times when a musical piece itself can be deliberately designed to enact or evoke this kind of anticipating hope. Anthony Monti mounts a case for interpreting Beethoven's Ninth Symphony in these terms, as embodying a sense of triumph won out of struggle and as such anticipating in some way an ultimate triumph.[97] To be sure, there are no knockdown cases to be made here, and it would be stretching a point to speak of this symphony as a whole as an expression of orthodox Christian belief, especially bearing in mind the giddy, libertarian optimism of Friedrich Schiller's "Ode to Joy" that crowns the work's choral finale: "Brothers, you should run your course, As joyful as a hero on his way to triumph." Still, Monti convincingly takes issue with the cynicism of some commentators about the apparently ringing affirmations of religious faith. Commenting on Beethoven's setting of "Über Sternen muss er wohnen" ("Above the stars he surely dwells"), Maynard Solomon writes:

> The chorus's measured rhythmic unison disintegrates on the words "muss," which is sounded successively by the basses, the tenors, and altos, and finally by the sopranos, as though by repeated emphasis to query what they dare not acknowledge in reality, that the multitudes have been embracing before an absent deity, *Deus absconditus*.[98]

Solomon believes this signals a profound hesitation in Beethoven, his needing to keep open the question of the "Messianic myth" of the world's redemption at the end of history.

> In Beethoven's re-creation of [the Messianic] myth, history is kept open—as quest for the unreachable, for the as-yet-undiscovered, for the vision of an ultimate felicity. He refuses to accept that history is closed at either its source or its goal, for a perfected order would signal the termination of life and of striving. In the Ninth Symphony, the condition of joy is elusive, even in Elysium. The search continues for a hidden God, a distant beloved, brotherhood.[99]

As Monti points out, this kind of reading is very strained.[100] It is much more straightforward to interpret this section as being on the brink of a revelation to come (the double fugue on the "Joy" theme that follows), combined with an awestruck awareness of the Creator. Monti also proposes seeing the finale as an expression "of childlike joy to be experienced in the new creation—the coming kingdom of God in which all are brothers and sisters as children of a heavenly Father."[101] Indeed, the extraordinary juxtapositions we hear—the majesty of "and the cherub stands before God" next to vulgar Turkish band music, the elaborate cadenza next to the final prestissimo—might better be heard as the wildness and untidiness of a God-centered joy (which is often messy!) rather than (as in Cook's overearnest approach) Beethoven's troubled "irony." Although it would be hard to claim we are being given anything like a fully Christian vision here—for the notion that humanity might actually need a Messiah to be truly free is conspicuous by its absence (certainly in the text)—if baptized into a richer Christian frame of reference, there may well be ample scope for Monti's reading.[102]

The phenomenon of a future anticipated can also sometimes be found in the way a piece is structured, creating a sort of parable in sound of Christian hope—as when, for example, an ending comes "too soon" and transforms a musical argument. According to the New Testament writers, Jesus's resurrection anticipated the grand resurrection finale at the end of history, when all God's people would be raised. It is the final resurrection anticipated in one person, appearing early, too soon. A cheeky example of just this dynamic can be found in the third movement of Mozart's *Jupiter* Symphony no. 41 in C major (1788). Immediately after the end of the minuet section we encounter a "perfect cadence," normally a gesture of closure:[103]

But here this ending gesture serves to kick off the trio section (the middle section of the movement).

Fig. 10.2: Trio, from Mozart, Symphony no. 41 in C Major, K. 551, "Jupiter," third movement.

The perfect cadence (A) turns out to be both an ending *and* a new beginning, an ending serving as a new beginning. The resurrection of Jesus is *the* ending, but found in the midst of history, generating a new beginning. Moreover this cadence, no more than two chords, is developed and elaborated substantially in the extended section that follows. Through the Spirit, according to the New Testament, we can begin to know now the future resurrection life; out of the fresh start of Jesus's resurrection, the Holy Spirit weaves all sorts of novel developments—the story of the church.[104] Mozart—in ways that perhaps not even Barth realized—shows himself to be something of a theologian.

In addition to these examples of anticipation within specific pieces, there are features of music considered more widely that can present and make known this anticipatory dimension of the gospel. This is because music is typically driven by forward-moving patterns of tension and resolution—something we will take up at length in the next chapter.

There is a further dimension of the anticipating power of music that is worth noting also—perhaps most obvious of all—namely, music's ability to offer a foretaste of heavenly music (something we discussed in chapter 2).[105] Some want to treat biblical references to heavenly song (e.g., Rev. 5:9; 14:3) as powerful metaphors of the *shalom* of the new creation but not as literal singing, actual music. But if music is a physical, bodily activity of this life that brings untold delight and pleasure and seems to be part of human flourishing in every age and culture, why should it have no place in the new life of the age to come? Thus, many argue that the references to the music of heaven ought to be understood as audible, temporal sounds, albeit transformed into the conditions of the new heaven and earth. The scientist-theologian John Polkinghorne affirms boldly: "The new creation will not be a timeless world of 'eternity,' but a temporal world whose character is everlasting. (It will contain music, that specifically temporal art.)"[106] Pope Benedict XVI writes eloquently of words and silence eventually yielding to song: "But wherever God's word is translated into human words there remains a surplus of the unspoken and the unspeakable which calls us to silence—into a silence that in the end lets the unutterable become song and also calls on the voices of the cosmos for help so that the unspoken may become audible."[107]

Together

Ethnomusicologist Michael Hawn relates a telling encounter:

In one conversation with my drum instructor, Michael Olanjiwaru, a student at the seminary, I asked a question that seemed so logical to me: "Michael, who do you think is the best drummer in the seminary?" Michael was silent for some time. . . . It turned out that I had not asked the right question. After some further exchange, Michael helped me understand that the question was not "who is the best drummer?" but "which is the best drum ensemble?" As Michael patiently explained to me, an individual drummer cannot be evaluated in isolation, but only in the context of an ensemble—a community of drummers. This was an entirely different philosophy from the one in which I had been trained.[108]

This illustrates well how deeply ingrained certain individualistic habits of mind are in the West. They have complex origins that we cannot trace fully here. But as we might expect, ideas associated with late eighteenth- and nineteenth-century Romanticism have had a large part to play in their development, especially the philosophy of romantic inwardness. For many of the Romantics, we recall, nature's infinite life is discovered and comes to fulfillment through the generative activity of the artist. In this way the act of outward expression through creating a work of art comes to have enormous significance. An artist must be given freedom to perform this act, and in his or her own way. A weighty accent on realizing "individuality" (part of the meaning of *Eigentümlichkeit*, a word used by early Romantics to speak of everything having its own unique potential, existence, and character) leads to a heavy stress on artistic originality, on finding one's own unique voice as a creative agent. Charles Taylor observes, "Expressive individuation has become one of the cornerstones of modern culture. So much so that we barely notice it, and we find it hard to accept that it is such a recent idea in human history and would have been incomprehensible in earlier times."[109]

As we have said already, the contours of the romantic self are anything but absent in writing and teaching about the arts today, music included. Some years ago Jon Stratton showed how pervasive the image is in popular music,[110] but much the same could be said of the Christian arena.[111] Here it is the radical privileging of the inner life that needs to be questioned, encouraged by the often unquestioned assumption that the prime (or sole?) purpose of music is to express inner emotional states. For the Romantics, to be fair, when they spoke of "feeling" they did not generally mean a particular emotional state but a sense shared by all, as Schleiermacher had it, of being dependent on the infinite, on that which underlies the whole of our lives and the life of the cosmos.[112] But in the popular aesthetics of today, feeling in relation to the arts has lost this cosmic reference, and with it a sense of connectedness to others, and becomes often pared down to individual, inner affect. Further, a musician is often construed as most likely to gain his or her deepest visions through distancing himself or herself from others; tradition is before anything else to be distrusted and in some quarters at least, originality and novelty are to be exalted as belonging to the highest artistic virtues. The caricature of the "creative artist," estranged, unconventional, professionally eccentric, anxious about listening too closely to the voices of others in case it deafens him or her to his or her own inner creative urges and surges, is, of course, a caricature, but sadly not without its contemporary representatives.[113] And, as we have seen, the "postmodern self," a descendant of the romantic self, is perhaps most clearly seen in the contemporary consumer of music, for whom music (in fleeting and ever-new forms) becomes, above all, a means to satisfy the desire for immediate sensual stimulation and, through the very act of consumption, a means to establishing at least a minimal sense of identity.

Pentecostal Polyphony

A parable: A few years ago I was part of a group that organized a large celebration event in the University Concert Hall in Cambridge. In one item we asked the whole orchestra to improvise on a given melodic shape and chord structure, in the midst of a giant chorus of praise sung by a sizable congregation. The majority of players were Christian. But some were not, among them a fourteen-year-old in the second violins. Later, she told others that she came to faith during this extravagant extemporization. Normally when she played in an orchestra she would play exactly the same notes as the seven others in a second violin section. Here, for the first time in her musical life, she discovered her own "voice," but she found it through trusting, and being trusted by, others—and in the context of praise.

What was enacted for that girl through music was what the New Testament describes as *koinonia*, variously translated as "fellowship," "communion," "togetherness," "sharing." In Acts 2 we are told that on the day of Pentecost, with the coming of the Spirit, three thousand converts devoted themselves to the apostles' teaching, fellowship (*koinonia*), breaking of bread, and prayers (v. 42) and had all things in common (*koina*, v. 44). Bonhoeffer's metaphor of polyphony comes to mind here. In polyphony, more than one melody is played or sung simultaneously, each moving to some extent independently of the others. A central cantus firmus gives coherence and enables the other parts to flourish in relation to one another. Taking his cue from Bonhoeffer, Micheal O'Siadhail writes of contemporary living:

> Infinities of space and time. Melody fragments;
> music of compassion, noise of enchantment.
> Among the inner parts something open,
> something wild, a long rumour of wisdom
> keeps winding into each tune: *cantus firmus*,
> fierce vigil of contingency, loves congruence.[114]

Bonhoeffer uses the image to speak of the relation between our love of God and the loves and desires that shape the rest of our lives. But we could also use it to speak of the relation of Jesus Christ to his church and to the world, and us to one another. Christ crucified and risen is the cantus firmus, the rumor of wisdom at the heart of things. The Spirit takes human lives and weaves them into a polyphony around this cantus firmus. Moreover, by extension we could say: Christ lives in the polyphony of the Trinity, and by the Spirit we are granted, through him, a share in this trinitarian "enchantment."[115]

Christians are thus polyphonic people. At Pentecost, in opening the disciples and crowds to Jesus Christ and his Father, the Spirit opens people out to one another. Those otherwise closed in on themselves—because of language, culture, race, religion—now find themselves resonating with one another, communicating, and living together in radically new ways. Later, Jew is reconciled to Gentile, the stubborn apartheid of the day subverted. People become responsive to one another, tuned in to one another (the reversal of Babel, where confusion and dissonance reigned). But uniqueness is not erased; the crowds in Jerusalem were not given one language. They heard each other in their "own tongues" (Acts 2:8 KJV, cf. vv. 6, 11; "native languages," NRSV). More than this, as the New Testament makes abundantly clear, the Spirit not only allows difference but also promotes it: in 1 Corinthians 12, where Paul speaks of the church as the body of Christ, the Spirit generates and promotes diversity, allotting "to each one individually just as the Spirit chooses" (1 Cor. 12:11).

The contrast with the romantic model of the artist and with his pale echo, the postmodern aesthete, could hardly be greater. In "Pentecostal polyphony" my relatedness is part of who I truly am. For the contemporary romantic, relations with others are secondary to the process of artistic expression, in which my unique inner life is realized. (Indeed, relations with others are more likely to impede than aid the creative process.) For the modernist self, the first step to discovery of the true self is the individual agent's inward turn; unbounded space *to be* is the key to freedom and fulfillment. And for the postmodern, even this self is shorn of responsibility in the endless play of aesthetic desires and thus is always on the verge of collapse.

In Pentecostal polyphony, by contrast, both the suffocating individualism of modernism and the erasure of personal uniqueness of postmodernism are overcome. True enough, the self is always and already a social product (an important postmodern concern), and yet the self is centered when addressed and treated as a distinct *you* by another person or other persons. I discover who I am in *koinonia*—as I am loved and as I love in the power of the Spirit, with a forgiving love, rooted in God and now opened out to us through Good Friday, Easter, and Pentecost. My identity is discovered not despite but above all *in and through* relationships of this kind. The contemporary Greek Orthodox theologian John Zizioulas is sometimes cited in this connection, in his insistence that my *hypostasis*—my particularity—is discovered in *ekstasis*, "a movement toward communion," as I am turned outward, as I am directed by and toward another person in love.[116] We have all known what it is to greet at the station or airport a very close friend we have not seen for years: we don't care what we look like; we run toward that person with a self-forgetful joy.[117] We recall the father running out to greet the prodigal, and the son discovering who he really is as he is embraced. Such is the ecstatic love at the heart of the Triune God in which we are invited to share.[118]

From Prima Donna to Ensemble

What does this "Pentecostal polyphony" mean for the making and hearing of music? Here we highlight only four things. First, for the musician (and for all Christians engaged with music), *belonging to the church is not an option*. Built into the fabric of Scripture's witness is the conviction that God is forming a people who will demonstrate a new way of being human, to be in the world and for the world, as a foretaste of the final community of the new heaven and earth. In the New Testament we discover that relationships within this community find their source and sustenance in the trinitarian heart of God: the renewed Israel is to be one as the Son and his Father are one (John 17:22). The church is the song of God—God's "breathing out" of his own trinitarian polyphony. It is the way the world hears the music at the heart of God and joins in. The church can therefore never be a choice among others, an "extra" for those of a gregarious nature; it is basic to what God is about in the world. Here we can join hands with many recent writers who insist that in a late-modern/postmodern culture there is nothing as powerful as a community that can embody a kind of mutual commitment that visibly subverts the destructive assumptions on which much of our culture thrives.[119] Sadly, much writing on the Christian's engagement with the arts simply bypasses the concrete reality of the Christian community. But Scripture gives no warrant for such evasion.

To give this more focus, second, *the Christian musician's primary community is the church*. This means a down-to-earth, sustained commitment to a regularly worshiping body of Christians, many of whom will have little interest in music. For some, this will grate. It will be objected that the church "on the ground" is deeply sinful and compromised, that when it comes to handling musicians (let alone other artists), the church's record has all too often been desultory. Sorry tales will be told of the church treating its musicians with everything from indifference to contempt. As an art student once commented poignantly: "My college doesn't understand my faith and my church doesn't understand my art. Where do I fit as a whole person?"[120] I have spent much of my own ministry among ecclesiastically bruised musicians. There are lamentable things for the church to confess here that I do not wish for a moment to trivialize. Indeed, part of the purpose of this book is to expose some of them. But the core point still holds—God calls every Christian into concrete commitment to others who have also been called by him, others we did not choose, and part of our calling is to be dedicated to them in love (and they to us) as God is dedicated to us. This, more than anything else, is how God shapes people into the vessels he wants them to be. Opting out is not an option—and in this, musicians are no different from anybody else.

At the risk of touching on raw sensitivities: there seems to be a residual romanticism in some Christian music circles that encourages alienation from the church, almost as if it were something to be relished (a little like some adolescents, for whom being misunderstood is part of the fun). It can give us a heady sense of superiority to imagine that we are too deep for ordinary people and that our awkwardness is due to our unrecognized profundity or to the fact that we deal in the currency of such a supposedly "spiritual" medium as music. But all too often this is an effective way to avoid costly service to others, especially those who "don't understand us" (but who might well do so if we loved them enough to offer them some time). If we are not careful we will simply perpetuate the sub-Christian images of the artist so beloved of modernity and postmodernity alike. A musician who has learned the discipline of receiving and giving Christlike love will look and sound very different.[121]

Another likely objection to this stress on the church will be that the world is forgotten, that it plays to an image of the church as an inward-looking ghetto of the like-minded, deaf to the cries, needs, and languages of the Monday-to-Saturday world. As far as music is concerned, it will likely result in a fixation on music for worship. These anxieties need to be heard: the church's vocation is indeed to be in the world for the world, sharing in God's mission. However, none of this releases Christian musicians from down-to-earth obligations to a specific community struggling to be just that: God's people in the world for the world. We can put it the other way round: the New Testament would have us believe that the relationships known in a fellowship gathered by the Triune God of Jesus Christ ought to be the most enriching and stimulating we will ever have, renewing and equipping us for practical service far beyond worship services. As we all know, every church is profoundly biblical—that is, marred by hypocrisy and heresy, frictions and factions. But in every church there are also moments when the shaft of *koinonia* breaks through for the musician—a generous check slipped into your hand, an email about a piece you wrote, a good wish for an upcoming concert—undramatic acts, often unrecorded, but bearing the distinctive aroma of Christ.

The other side of this, of course, is that the Christian community needs to learn the art of supporting and encouraging musicians. There is a Herculean agenda here for those in the leadership of the church, and I cannot hope to elaborate on it in detail here. But at the very least it will mean relearning the place and value of music in human life, the way it functions in our society, something of the way it achieves its effects, its delights, and its dangers. It will mean encouraging congregations to gain more sense of the history of music in the church. And then, arising out of this, the church will need to relearn how to uphold musicians—composers, singers, players, arrangers, writers—in their particular callings, whether that be in the worship sanctuary or not.

Thankfully, there are some outstanding examples of Christian communities where these things are happening, where this two-way commitment (musician to church and church to musician) is being worked out, where the radically new relationships made possible by the gospel are making a substantial difference to the way music, along with the other arts, is made and heard. Among many of the more recent that could be mentioned are ARK-T Centre in Cowley, Oxford, England;[122] Hope Chapel in Austin, Texas;[123] The Place Community in Vancouver Island, British Columbia;[124] the Crawl Space at the Vineyard Christian Fellowship of Cambridge, Massachusetts;[125] and the Ecclesia Arts Center at Ecclesia in Houston, Texas.[126]

Third, we need to be prepared to *rethink many of the questions we habitually ask about music in social terms*. Once we get out of the pattern of thinking of music simply as a solo production projected into the world or something merely to satisfy our immediate needs and instead think of it as something that is (potentially) shaped by and can shape groups of interrelated people, new kinds of questions are pushed to the surface. How is this or that music affecting relationships between people? How does a DJ use music in a club? How does a store use music to change customers' spending plans? How does rap help to bind together a neighborhood in the Bronx? Who is paying for this music? What part does economics play in the ways it is being used? How might music serve the renewal of disadvantaged communities, help give a voice to those otherwise unjustly silenced, build lasting trust across radically different cultures? Is music being used in a way that enables people to flourish together? If not, why not? A glance at remarkable projects such as BuildaBridge International—dedicated, among other things, to the Christian transformation of communities through the arts (including music), especially in deprived urban areas—should give us pause for thought.[127]

Questions about responsibility and sensitivity will become increasingly important. A Christian will be concerned that the respect we have spoken about with regard to a musician's materials will apply to those who will hear or listen to music, whether or not they are members of the body of Christ. With characteristic directness, C. S. Lewis writes: "When an artist is in the strict sense working, he of course takes into account the existing tastes, interests and capacity of his audience. These, no less than the language, the marble, the paint, are part of his raw material; to be used, tamed, sublimated, not ignored or defied. Haughty indifference to them is not genius; it is laziness and incompetence."[128] (And, we might add, it shows a lack of love.) It might be that a musician begins to ask far more often: for whom am I speaking, and to whom am I speaking? Albert Camus—hardly a champion of the Christian cause—remarks: "One of the greatest temptations of the artist is to believe himself solitary, and in truth he hears this shouted at him, with a certain base delight. But this is not true. His very vocation . . . is to open the prisons and give voice to the sorrows and joys of all."[129]

Questions about political responsibility will become much more prominent on the agenda. Should the state or government subsidize any music at all? Those inclined to be cynical about subsidizing the arts would do well to recall that in most communities the arts are much more than an optional luxury, whatever the institution of "high art" might suggest—and this includes music. If we believe that the flourishing of music can contribute to the health of society and that the accessibility of a wide range of music is beneficial, then there are going to be occasions when we may want to speak out strongly about a community's responsibility to, and support of, its musicians, whatever precise form that support might take.

Fourth, from the perspective of our calling to be part of God's "Pentecostal polyphony," we will need to speak of *exploring and inhabiting tradition*, the wisdom of the past. To be sure, the suspicion of tradition, so much part of the post-Reformation and post-Enlightenment world, has often been motivated by quite proper concerns—especially the concern to avoid the suffocating effects of unthinking submission to authority. But as a stream of scholarship has been stressing, the suspicion has been drastically overplayed.[130] A Christian account of the human person—embedded in relations, born into communities, baptized into the church—will remind us of the inescapable and potentially positive role of tradition and will link with what we said in chapter 1 about the social and cultural situatedness of music.[131]

Whether we are makers or hearers of music, we are always initiated into a vast range of socially shaped customs and conventions, however we might react against them in due course. I may listen to U2 in the privacy of my living room, but I do so as one who has sat at the feet of others (through reading, studying, and conversations) who are themselves shaped by a lifetime of listening, study, argument, and debate. In other words, I submit myself to traditions that have emerged in a community. The same applies to composing. It is only because we have been so bewitched by the image of the lone creative genius that we neglect the obvious: music is always to some extent a reworking of past music, and some of the most interesting and endlessly fruitful music has come through an intensive engagement with and reworking of established traditions—of the sort found in, for example, Michael Tippett's *Child of Our Time* (1941), Penderecki's *St. Luke Passion* (1966), Peter Maxwell Davies's *Sinfonia* (1968), Judith Weir's *Music, Untangled* (1992), the Orlando Consort's album *Extempore II* (2003).

Related to this, we will be reminded that originality does not come by pursuing originality. Reflecting on Mozart's purported claim: "I really do not study or aim at originality," Keith Johnstone poses the question: "Suppose Mozart *had* tried to be original? It would have been like a man at the North Pole trying to walk north, and this is true of all the rest of us. Striving after originality takes you far away from your true self, and makes your work mediocre."[132]

Trying to be wholly original, to change the metaphor, amounts to sawing off the branch you are sitting on. It is the attempt to climb out of time and achieve what only God has achieved—creation out of nothing. And it is a dream that has enticed numerous artists. It is the attitude summarized in Boulez's pronouncement, "Strong, expanding civilisations have no memory: they reject, they forget the past."[133] In 1919 T. S. Eliot explored this theme with singular insight in what still remains a classic, "Tradition and the Individual Talent." He notes the tendency of the critic to "insist, when we praise a poet, upon those aspects of his work in which he least resembles anyone else. In these aspects or parts of his work we pretend to find what is individual, what is the peculiar essence of the man." Yet, speaking of the writer, Eliot continues, "We shall often find that not only the best, but the most individual parts of his work may be those in which the dead poets, his ancestors, assert their immortality most vigorously." Eliot argues for a strenuous engagement with tradition, for a "historical sense" in the writer that involves "a perception, not only of the pastness of the past, but of its presence" and that "compels a man to write not merely with his own generation in his bones, but with a feeling that the whole of the literature of Europe from Homer and within it the whole of the literature of his own country has a simultaneous existence and composes a simultaneous order." Far from making an artist forgetful of his own particular context, he becomes "acutely conscious of his place in time, of his own contemporaneity."[134] In other words, originality is not so much asserted as discovered, found in the process of allowing a past tradition to speak through us to our present context.

The Christian's *primary* tradition is, needless to say, that dense and varied stream of Christian reflection encompassing the riches of Aquinas and Wesley, Thérèse of Lisieux and Julian of Norwich, as well as sixteenth-century Jesuits in Japan, Spanish missionaries of eighteenth-century America, and underground congregations in former Soviet Russia. To be part of the *koinonia* of the church is to be part of the "communion of saints" stretching back centuries and to be heir to a wisdom that invites our respectful, careful, and critical attention. (A common misunderstanding of Protestantism is that it seeks to rid itself of postbiblical tradition in the quest for *sola Scriptura*, "Scripture alone." In fact, the mainline Reformers never intended to suggest *sola Scriptura* meant *nulla traditio* [no tradition]; their concern was to distinguish between apostolic tradition— that is, Scripture—and postapostolic tradition, and to allow only the former to be the supreme norm for the church.)[135]

When it comes to sustained Christian reflection on music, though in recent years relatively little may have been written, move farther back and, as we have seen, we soon rub shoulders with the likes of Barth, Bonhoeffer, and Schleiermacher, not to mention Augustine and the purveyors of the Great Tradition. Many Christians are not availing themselves of these and other treasures (often through no fault of their own), and it is perhaps small wonder that we are often acutely vulnerable to sub-Christian and pseudo-Christian ideas. It is surely time for many to inhabit this wisdom carefully and gratefully: it is now accessible as never before.

———◆———

In this chapter, I have tried to show something of what a Christian calling with respect to music entails, whether as a music maker or music hearer, drawing upon the material of the preceding chapters. Much has been omitted, much only touched upon, but enough has been said, I hope, to indicate what an extraordinarily rich responsibility this is.

Because we have been speaking of responsibility, much of this discussion has inevitably been couched in the language of task, obligation, duty, and so forth. But I want to end the chapter by stepping back and turning the spotlight on what buoys up and sustains the entire vision I have been sketching—the preeminence of divine grace and the joy it provokes.

Joy is the air the Christian breathes as he or she pursues a vocation. It will be found in at least two forms. First, there is the joy that comes from knowing *we are recipients of an invitation.* We who have misdirected our praise have been invited, against every expectation and everything we deserve, to step back into that role intended for us, to voice creation's praise to the resounding glory of the Creator, and to witness wonders beyond imagining in our own lives and the lives of others. We do indeed have a calling, but it is held aloft by this invitation: to share in the action of the Triune God as he draws all things to himself through his Son and Spirit. While there is a place for talk of task, on its own this can easily conjure up the heavy, deep tones of self-reliance, which so easily muffle the ringing elation that comes from knowing that one is claimed *sola gratia*—by grace alone. Even our worst blunders are answered by forgiveness, and by God reissuing his invitation, over and over again. Christian involvement in music will be marked by the joy of knowing that the dynamic of invitation underwrites all that we are and do.

Second, there is also the joy that comes from knowing *the end is assured.* We have been setting music in the context of a Christian ecology, a vision of the entire cosmos. In much Christian writing on creation, especially if it is alert to our environmental calamities, it is not unusual to find the mood unremittingly bleak—full of regret, guilt by association, a frowning repentance, an earnest determination to act quickly to avert catastrophe. While not for a moment downplaying the seriousness of our situation, for Christians the mandate for any action in the created world (including music) is essentially *evangelical*—grounded in the glad news of God's promise, acted out and guaranteed in Christ, that God has a future for the world he made and that he has a place for his people as part of that future. Any action for good we undertake in the world of music is underwritten by Christ. Any anxiety we have about the sheer enormity of the task facing any Christian in the world of music should be met with the recollection that in Christ the chains of the world's evil have already been snapped. Any dominion we exercise through music—whether crafting a symphony or inventing a rap, conducting an orchestra or playing in a band, or using music in worship—is exercised in the company of Christ, who is already Lord and will one day fully exercise his wise and loving rule over all. A comment by Oliver O'Donovan on a recent document on ecology is especially appropriate here: "One evangelical phrase is missing," he says, " 'Do not be anxious!' "[136]

singular
powers

Music does its own kind of work in its own kinds of ways. Throughout the book I have been assuming that music making and music hearing are first and foremost practices and, as such, are intertwined with all sorts of other activities and interests but that among the integrities that these practices involve is the integrity of musical sounds.[1] At a college commencement, the sound patterns of "The Star-Spangled Banner" are contributing something to the experience of that commencement that nothing else is contributing, or indeed could contribute—however much their effect may be bound up with a host of other elements (the state of our minds and bodies, associations, memories, etc.).

We recall the Nigerian in the North London Market who commented that people in the United Kingdom (in contrast to Africa) "did not seem to be aware of music's powers."[2] Being wise in the world of music, from a Christian or any other perspective, means being aware of these powers—and especially what powers might belong distinctively to music. Here in this chapter we pay particular attention to those distinctive powers that could be of special interest to the Christian, namely, those with strong theological resonances. Can we highlight some features of musical sound patterns as made and heard that are common to a broad range of music and that lend music singular capacities especially well suited to being drawn into the purposes of God? I think we can, and we mention three in particular.

Tensions and Resolutions

It is seven in the morning. You are deep in a dream. The alarm goes off, and your head explodes. After much desperate fumbling, you manage to get your sleepy hand on the right button. A tension is resolved.

Tension-resolution is, of course, one of the most basic psychological patterns governing our lives[3]—from traffic lights on red to lights on green, sexual arousal to orgasm, nerves before the interview to the relief of a job offer. In the kind of music concerning us in this book—Western tonal music—the dynamic of tension and resolution is pervasive. Tensions are set up that demand some kind of release or rest.[4] One of the most important is *harmonic* tension and resolution, easily demonstrated in a chord pattern we have met already, a perfect cadence:

The first chord is expected to resolve on to the second; things cannot be left hanging on that first chord.

Speaking of tension clearly presupposes a prior state of rest, in relation to which we sense something *as* a tension. (We were asleep before the alarm went off.) So the fuller pattern is equilibrium-tension-resolution (ETR). This ETR pattern works in many different ways and at many different levels, potentially engaging every dimension of music. ETR patterns accumulate to give music a forward-moving feel. Western tonal music is teleological, or directional. It is not circular, though it may involve much repetition. It drives toward future rest and closure, often (but not always) leading to some kind of goal or gathering together of a musical process. We sense it is going somewhere. We are made to expect, and often to want, future sounds.[5]

Staying with harmonic ETRs for the moment, let us consider that one of the most common musical structures, seen in thousands of popular songs (as in, e.g., George Gershwin's "I Got Rhythm"), consists of the statement of a melody in a "home" key, followed by a move away from that key, and then a return to the melody in the home key. The homecoming, it should be stressed, is not a simple "back to the beginning." Even if the destination is a note-for-note repetition, it marks the culmination of a kind of sonic journey, so it will be heard as different: as fuller and richer.

Relating this ETR profile to prominent patterns in Scripture is not hard: creation-fall-redemption, promised land-exile-return, "orientation-disorientation-reorientation" in the Psalms (as Walter Brueggemann has expounded it),[6] the journey of the prodigal son to the far country and back again (Luke 15:11–24).

It is perhaps not surprising that the kind of music we are considering emerged and flourished within a predominantly Christian setting. (To be sure, considerable care is needed when making this kind of correlation. There are different types of directionality both in Christian thought and in tonal music. And the theme of displacement from home and subsequent return has been rehearsed in the literature, drama, and music of many cultures not directly affected by the Christian story of salvation. Nevertheless, it seems reasonable to suppose that theological factors have played at least some part in the development of tonal music.)

Let us explore three qualities of tonal music that arise from these patterns of tension and resolution and see how suited they are to embodying some of the dynamics of the Christian gospel.

It Cannot Be Rushed

Not only can music not be rushed in the obvious sense (as we highlighted in chapter 9)—that is, it cannot be rushed *through*, for it can survive only a relatively limited variation in speed before becoming unintelligible[7]—it also cannot be rushed *over*, in the sense that it depends intensely on sequences of tension and resolution. Musical resolutions have no power other than that which they possess *as* the resolutions of tension.

To draw out the resonances between this and the Christian gospel, we might pause to consider Holy Week—Palm Sunday to Easter Sunday—and the way it is celebrated in worship. As the Roman Catholic and Orthodox traditions have known for centuries, and many other churches have discovered too, the only way this extraordinary narrative will yield its meaning is quite simply if we let it and, arguably, if we allow ourselves to play the events at their original speed—God's speed, not ours—living in and through the events day by day: the grieving farewells, the betrayal and denial, the shuddering fear in the garden, the stretched-out day of torture and forsakenness, and the daybreak of wonder, color, and tomb-bursting newborn life. By refusing to skip over these days, with all their dark shadows and turns, we allow ourselves to be led far more profoundly into the story's sense and power. Music is remarkably instructive here, because more than any other art form, it teaches us how not to rush over tension, how to find joy and fulfillment through a temporal movement that *includes* struggles, clashes, and fractures.

The temptation to pass over what needs to be passed through is strongest when confronted with those three days to which MacMillan keeps returning in his music: Good Friday, Holy Saturday, and Easter Sunday. The danger here—and this is surely the root theological error of most Christian sentimentalism[8]—is to succumb to a premature grasp for Easter morning, to refuse to follow the three days of Easter as a threefold, irreversible sequence of victory, to rush *over* what God's own Son has lived *through*.

A very large body of writing in recent years has stressed that the story of Good Friday to Easter needs to be "told and heard, believed and interpreted, *two different ways at once*—as a story whose ending is *known*, and as one whose ending is discovered only *as it happens*. The truth is victim when either reading is allowed to drown out the other; the truth emerges only when both readings are audible, the separate sound in each ear creating, as it were, a stereophonic unity."[9] This is what the New Testament texts themselves offer. We are invited to view the crucifixion in the light of the blazing daybreak of Easter: Sunday morning vindicates the Jesus who was crucified; it announces that he was indeed God's chosen one and that the world's sin has been defeated in him. This is to view the cross from the outside, as it were, with the synoptic gaze we attain when we know the ending: Good Friday is seen to be a saving initiative, "Good." Yet along with this, we are also invited to read the story from the inside, from the perspective of those who lived through the shadows of Friday and Saturday *without* knowing the ending, for whom the Friday was a catastrophic finale to the would-be Messiah's life, a day devoid of victory, a day of shredded hopes, drained of goodness.

Why are we given this inside story? For no other reason than to impress upon us that the healing of the world is achieved in this way and no other. The one whom God vindicates on Easter morning is none other than the one numbered with the lowest of the low, naked, ignominious. The resurrection does not erase the memory of Friday: it confirms the cross as the specific locus where the weight of the world's evil is borne, and borne away. This is how God disarms the principalities and powers and triumphs over them (Col. 2:15); this is how God's idiocy outstrips human wisdom (1 Cor. 1:18–25); this is how "It is finished" (John 19:30). As W. B. Yeats had it: "Love has pitched his mansion in the place of excrement. For nothing can be sole or whole that has not been rent."[10] If we bound over this place to Sunday too quickly in an attempt to seize the music of resolution without tension ("Ah, but we know how the story will end"), we risk losing the very core of the good news that God's love reaches its ultimate intensity at *this* place of excrement, that his decisive victory over sin and evil is won *this* way (where all is "rent"). The resurrection does not erase the memory of the cross: it confirms the cross as *the* place where the world is rescued from its cataclysm, where sin is absorbed away.

It Invites Us to Live on Many Levels

Music is not an art of straight lines. It is never simply a string of ETRs, one after the other, on one level. If it were, we would soon lose interest. Music's ETRs work at many levels simultaneously, and this is one of music's strongest powers, one of the prime ways it gets under our skin and holds us.

We see this most clearly if we delve into the world of meter. Meter is the pattern of beats underlying music. In a score, it is indicated by a time signature

(2/4, 3/4, etc.). When you tap your feet to music, you are tapping to meter. A conductor, whatever else he or she does, is meant to beat meter. When you dance, the chances are you are dancing to meter (whatever else you may be doing as well).[11] Metrical beats are grouped into bars (or measures). In a waltz there are three beats to a bar. These beats are not of the same strength—as anyone who has tried to dance a waltz will know. The first is strongest, the second is weaker, and the third is weaker still, moving toward what will be the first beat of the next bar. A wave of tension and resolution is set up, repeated bar after bar:

Meter does not operate only at this one level. The successive downbeats of each bar are *themselves* of a different strength. In many pieces they are grouped in twos or fours—the first is strongest, the last beat of each group the weakest. Together, then, they build up another wave of tension and resolution at a higher level. And the downbeats of *that* wave are also of a different strength, which make up another wave, and so on. The process continues up, level after level, higher and higher, until the whole piece is covered:

This can be a highly complex process, but this basic multileveled pattern is present in one form or another in virtually all types of Western music, from Bach to Brahms, R.E.M to Eminem.

It will be seen straightaway that music built around these patterns will not (as is so often thought) be linear. Neither is it circular. Indeed, music subverts the common assumption that there are only two types of time: linear and circular. Although directional, musical time is neither linear nor circular—it is multistoried.[12] Making sense of music means perceiving many levels of tension and resolution simultaneously.

Especially important for our purposes is this: every downbeat kicks forward a wave on another level. The momentum of the upper waves is dependent on the tensions and resolutions of the lower waves. One level's return is always another's advance. Every return closes *and* opens, completes *and* extends, resolves *and* intensifies. Music holds our attention because, as long as the piece is running, we are aware that there is at least one wave at a higher level that is not yet closed. And so we expect—and usually want—more. In this way, we are pulled forward by the music and pulled in—kept in the story, so to speak. (Try singing "The Star-Spangled Banner" and stopping after the words "through the perilous fight." The musical phrase has ended [on a lower level], but there is a sense of incompleteness because many upper waves still have to close.)

Put differently: *there is always hope if we live on more than one level.* The God of Jewish and Christian faith moves not just in mysterious ways but in mysterious waves. This God invites people to live on more than one level; that is how God keeps them hoping, keeps them in his story. Frequently in Scripture a promise is made, and the first fulfillment that comes, though genuine, fails to match up in some way to expectation. Take the patriarchal promise of Genesis 12:1–3—the promise to Abraham that he is about to be shown a land, that he will be blessed and be the first of a great nation, and that in time he will be the one through whom all the families of the earth will be blessed. Within Genesis, of course, this only partly transpires. The blessing of the nations, for example, starts, or is foreshadowed, when Jacob brings blessing to Laban, and Joseph to Potiphar, and indeed Jacob to Pharaoh. But all this is very partial. "The theme of the Pentateuch is the *partial* fulfilment—which implies also the partial *non-fulfilment*—of the promise to or blessing of the patriarchs."[13] But does this kill the hope? By no means. The incomplete fulfillments spur on God's people to hope all the more; indeed, the Abrahamic promise of blessing for the nations is picked up elsewhere in the Old Testament.[14] We recall: resolutions at the lower level kick forward higher waves.

Another example is found in Paul's letter to the Romans. Here Christ is portrayed as the central resolution of the story of God's saving his people: he gathers up the multiple hopes and implications of Israel's story, which arch right back to Abraham. In the death and resurrection of Jesus, God has done what he told Abraham he would do—create a worldwide family, while also dealing with the curse that hinders his purpose of blessing the nations. But does this great resolution spell the end of hope? By no means. What has happened in Christ, climactic and utterly decisive as it may be, intensifies and enriches the promise originally made to Abraham. Paul urges his hearers to imagine a higher "wave," to hope *all the* more, *for* more—for a *final* fulfillment of that first promise made to Abraham, when all the nations of the earth will be gathered into one multiethnic community of Jew and Gentile in the new creation. When read in this way, Romans 9–11, often seen as a mind-boggling, intractable detour in Paul's argument, is not only massively clarified but is seen to be the natural outworking of chapters 1–8. Part of what Paul is saying to both Jew and Gentile is if you stay on the one level, the richness and power of the hope God has made possible is lost. Tune into the upper waves of what God is doing, and you will see the grand multileveled sweep of God's purposes for both Jew and Gentile and get caught up in its life-changing momentum.

Time and time again, the Jewish and Christian Scriptures seem to be inviting us into just this kind of multileveled hope. In the contemporary postmodern climate, we are frequently encouraged to live on the lowest level alone—"flat time"—typically with only little short-term microhopes, one day at a time. We dare not hope for anything too great in the long term, nor, many would say, do we know *how* to hope for anything in the long term. With the so-called death of the metanarrative (the big stories that have governed Western culture—for example, Christianity, Marxism, the myth of human progress), we can settle only for microhopes, a lifespan at the most. To be drawn into the waves of God means that our lives are set in the context, not of a linear path (of progress, perhaps?), but of a multileveled hope that covers a huge range of timescales. There may be very small waves at work—the little short-term routines of our lives, for example—but we live in the confidence that even these can be taken up in the longer-reaching purposes of God, the wide and vast waves of God's music.

Even in the church it is easy to go "flat." There is a certain kind of "fundamentalism" that reads Scripture in flat time, where every word of the Bible is treated as if it were literal, plodding prose about events on one level alone, where every prophecy has to come true at only one single time and in one unambiguous way. But if we think on many levels, this habit of thinking dissolves. When God promised to Abraham that he would make "a great nation" (Gen. 12:2), how is that fulfilled? In the people who settled in Canaan? In the kingdom of David? In the community who returned from exile in Babylon? In the church at the end of time? The answer is surely yes, in all of them. A single promise can have many different fulfillments. As long as we limit ourselves to single straight lines, we will struggle hard to conceive of that. But music, with its multiple waves, embodies it for us in even the simplest song.

It Makes Us Wait

We can look at one further form of musical tension with strong gospel overtones: delay—when an expected or desired fulfillment is held up, either in whole or in part. The handling of delay is a crucial musical skill. Musicians are adept at setting up expectations that are deliberately deferred through a myriad of devices: diversions, digressions, pauses, and so on. Indeed, maintaining the "not yet" of resolution through deferred gratification is generally reckoned to be one of the most important things to be learned by any composer, and among the most critical features of musical structure.[15] Be it a rock song or a symphony, a ballet score or a ballad, much depends on handling the space between tensions and postponed resolutions in ways that can satisfy the desire for resolution while also being open-ended enough to sustain the expectation of, and desire for, more.

A simple example can be found in that piece learned by every beginner and encased in millions of telephone answering machines—"Für Elise," by Beethoven. On the first page, the composer inserts two extra bars just before the main melody returns—gratification is deferred, with the result that we are pulled into the piece that much more intensely. (This is one reason why this piece is much harder than its sounds, as many a ten-year-old has found out.) Much more sophisticated is the second movement of Brahms's Second Symphony, where only at the very end are we given the main key chord stably and unambiguously on a strong beat. John Coltrane's *Love Supreme* provides another good example. Leroy Ostransky, in *The Anatomy of Jazz*, observes:

> What distinguishes superior creative musicians from the mediocre ones of all periods is the manner in which they create resolutions, and to create resolutions it is necessary to set up irresolutions. . . . Poor and mediocre jazzmen . . . often do not understand that the quality of their jazz will depend not on any resolution, however elaborate, but rather on the inherent intricacy of the irresolution.[16]

The theme of delay is, of course, very common in Scripture—a sense among the writers that things are being in some manner held back, whether the final fulfillment of God's purposes or the closer, short-term fulfillments. "How long, O Lord?" is not just the wail of the psalmist but the howl of God's people over and over again down through the disillusioned years of Israel's history. When will Yahweh put his world to rights? When will this supposedly just God vindicate his people and scatter their enemies? How can we keep hoping in the midst of unresolved dissonance? And even after the climactic resolution in Christ, a new sense of delay is evident, classically expressed in Romans 8: the whole creation "groans" as it awaits fulfillment (v. 23). The meantime demands *patience*: "If we hope for what we do not see, we wait for it with patience" (v. 25).

Far from being empty or pernicious, however, Paul and others believe this in-between time is potentially rich, enlarging. The raising of Jesus has anticipated the final general resurrection, and through the Spirit we have a foretaste of that dazzling future resurrection age here and now (Rom. 8:9–11). This is the same Spirit who is active deep within creation and the church, struggling to bring about in the world what has already been achieved in Christ (Rom. 8:17–30). The Spirit can enlarge us *in the very waiting*, within and through the apparently circuitous, mysterious, and painful process of deferred fulfillment: "We suffer with [Christ] so that we may also be glorified with him" (Rom. 8:17). In the New Testament, we should recall, patience is often associated with growing in steadfastness and faith through persevering in the midst of difficulty (see, e.g., Hebrews 11). Moreover, human patience can be very closely linked to God's forgiving patience. God's refusal to bring things quickly to a close does not signal his inertia or abandonment (or compliance or indulgence) but can be full of his passion for the world's salvation (2 Pet. 3:9; cf. Rom. 2:4; 3:25).

Of course, delay can at times be anything but enriching or humanizing. Lament and protest are common biblical responses to delay, as they are today, and understandably so. Nonetheless, is there not a patience proper to Christian faith in which *something new is learned of incalculable value* that cannot be learned in any other way? Just because of its multilevel wave structure, just because there is always a wave reaching forward at a higher level, and enough downbeats to remind us of that, music has the power to introduce us to just this kind of enriching meantime and help us understand more deeply what it means to "wait on God." This is most evident in silence. In one of her songs, Alanis Morissette sings about:

> The conflicts, the craziness and the sound of pretences
> Falling all around . . . all around

Then she challenges us:

> Why are you so petrified of silence?
> Here can you handle this?[17]

And the music suddenly stops. Why are we so petrified of silence? Presumably because we think nothing happens in silence. Silence is void, emptiness, blank space. But music's metrical waves extend even through silence. We can sense them even when there is no music. This is how pieces of music can include so much silence; the space is not empty, and a skillful composer will know how to make that very clear. The opening of the theme music of *Jaws* generates its edge-of-the-seat terror largely through silence. The final bars of Sibelius's Fifth Symphony are, in essence, silence punctuated by six chords, creating a remarkably intense longing for resolution. These silences sound charged because of the memory of what has been and the anticipation of what will be, so we are pulled in and held in. Even in the most numbing of silences, when God's absence seems most deadening, the raising of the crucified Jesus from the dead sends a wave arcing through the silence to the final resurrection day, and by the Spirit we can catch it and sense it—and the silence can live. That is how countless Christians have managed to endure in the most hopeless of circumstances—in prison, torture, mental illness, acute loss.

In this light, it is disappointing, to say the least, that deferred gratification is so rare in much of today's music for worship—and I include both "traditional" and "contemporary" music—and in some respects it is also surprising, given music's astonishing powers to embody the kind of delay that is so basic to authentic Christian faith. To be sure, a congregation must be able to grasp new hymns and songs relatively quickly if the music is going to serve their worship, and, certainly, different kinds of music are appropriate at different times. But what are we implying if the music we sing in worship consistently and uniformly demands little in the way of patient waiting, suggests no hindrance, no deferral of the glory to come? What are we saying about the value of all those scriptural passages that remind us it is of the essence of faith that not all is now given, that not all the waves of God's music have found their "end" (real and glorious as the provisional fulfillments are), that to be joint heirs with Christ means patiently suffering with him?

To come at this from a different angle—what if there is little to suggest that we have been given resources in the gospel to resist the overwhelming pressure for instant gratification in our culture? Could music in worship too easily be giving way to the tendency in some Christian quarters to capitulate to the craving for immediate rewards, to live in denial of the realities of frustration and disappointment? Could we be too easily playing into the hands of the postmodernists' justifiable suspicion of quick resolutions, hasty solutions to intractable problems?

Sound Mix

We move on to a second feature of most of the music we make and hear: it mixes sounds—to be more precise, it involves two or more notes sounding simultaneously.[18] This seemingly innocuous phenomenon is in fact one of music's greatest powers, and it is of huge significance from the perspective of Christian faith.

To open this up, we can consider a key difference between aural and visual perception. A painter knows that you cannot have red and yellow on a canvas in the same space and have them visible *as* red and yellow. Either one color hides the other or (if the paint is wet) they merge into some variety of orange. By the same token, you cannot see an object in two places at the same time. Things in our visual field occupy discrete, bounded locations—spaces with edges. The eye tells us that things are either here *or* there; they cannot be in the same place at the same time.

But things are rather different if we consider the world as perceived by the ear. If I play a note on a piano—say, a middle C—

what I hear fills the whole of my heard space. I cannot identify some zone where the heard note is and a zone where it is not. I do not say, "It is here but not there." Unlike the patch of red on a canvas, it is, in a sense, everywhere. To be sure, I can identify the source of the note (the vibrating string), and the source's location ("it is over there"). I can say the sound is "coming from over there." But what I *hear* does not occupy a bounded space with edges. It fills the entirety of my aural space.

If I play a second note along with the middle C—say, the E above it—

that second note *also* fills the whole of my heard space, the same space as the C. Yet I hear the notes as distinct from each other. The notes interpenetrate, occupy the same heard space, but I can hear them as two notes. (Of course, I can play one note so loud that the other is not heard, but the point here is that it is possible to hear them as different notes in the same aural space.)

Some will object that I am using the word "space" metaphorically to speak of the experience of hearing, not the "real" space we can see. This, of course, assumes that what we see, or what is observable visually, should wholly determine what real space is—whereas even a casual glance at the development of modern physics shows much of reality stubbornly defies visualization. But leaving that aside for the moment, we have at least shown that the perception of two notes together makes possible a different conception of space and spaces from that which is typical of, say, two colors together—a different way of thinking about space. Here is a kind of space that is not the space of mutual exclusion but a space that allows for over-lapping and interpenetration. This is tellingly brought out by John Hull when he reflects on the experience of losing his sight. Deprived of sight, he asks:

> What is the world of sound? I have been spending some time out of doors trying to respond to the special nature of the acoustic world. . . . The tangible world sets up only as many points of reality as can be touched by the body, and this seems to be restricted to *one problem at a time*. I can explore the splinters on the park bench with the tip of my finger but I cannot, *at the same time*, concentrate upon exploring the pebbles with my big toe. . . . *The world revealed by sound is so different*. . . . On Holy Saturday I sat in Cannon Hill Park while the children were playing. . . . The footsteps came from both sides. They met, mingled, separated again. From the next bench, there was the rustle of a newspaper and the murmur of conversation. . . . I heard the steady, deep roar of the through traffic, the buses and the trucks. . . . [The acoustic world] *stays the same whichever way I turn my head*. This is not true of the perceptible [i.e., visually perceptible] world. It changes as I turn my head. New things come into view. The view looking that way is quite different from the view looking this way. It is not like that with sound. . . . This is a world which I cannot shut out, which goes on all around me, and which gets on with its own life. . . . *Acoustic space is a world of revelation*.[19]

Let us go back to two notes sounding and consider another feature of vibrating strings that we can hear. Suppose I play middle C and open up the string an octave above by silently depressing the appropriate key.

The upper C string will vibrate even though it has not been struck. This is because its note is the first overtone of the fundamental lower C. The lower string sets off the upper. And the *more* the lower string sounds, the *more* the upper string sounds in its distinctiveness. The strings are not in competition, nor do they simply allow each other room to vibrate. The lower string enhances, brings to life the upper string, frees it to be itself, compromising neither the integrity of the upper string nor its own. Moreover, when certain other strings are opened up alongside both these strings, they too will vibrate in sympathy. And with all these combinations of notes, the sounds mix within our one heard space.

Music has come to depend massively on the interpenetrating and resonating features of sound, and it exploits them to powerful effect. In act 2 of Verdi's *Otello*, for example, there is a famous quartet when what happens in the Shakespeare play at different times—a scene between Desdemona and Othello, a conversation between Emilia and Iago—is brought together. The four voices sing *simultaneously*, in one texture. If spoken, each speech would make good sense on its own but if heard together would sound nonsensical. When the simultaneous words are taken into the order of musical notes, however, nonsense can turn into sense, because the notes can enhance and enrich one another in the same heard space—the effect is intelligible and captivating.[20] Or in U2's song "The Fly": low voices sing of trying to hang on to love like a fly climbing up a wall, while at the same time the upper voice (called, significantly, "gospel" voice) sings in falsetto of love coming down from above. Two very different sets of words are combined through musical interpenetration and resonance.

What particular relevance has this power of music for the Christian faith? The ramifications are considerable; here I highlight only three of them.

First, *music can serve to embody the personal freedom that the gospel proclaims and makes possible.*[21] In the course of the last chapter, we drew a contrast between two types of freedom—on the one hand, that which typifies much writing in modernity, where freedom is seen as freedom *from*, the absence of constraint, maximizing our own "space" and options; on the other hand, the freedom enabled by the Christian gospel—freedom-in-relation, the freedom that emerges from engaging with constraints, including other people.[22] In the first type, persons are understood as self-determining, isolated agents, sovereign over their own bounded space in which completely unconstrained, unfettered choices can be made. But what if I happen to be much stronger and more arrogant than you? You will be crushed. On this model, my freedom is always expressed at the cost of yours.

The perennial dilemma of freedom as it emerges in modernity is that there must be an affirmation of individual human value against the forces of tyranny, but the Enlightenment's belief in the entirely autonomous, self-sufficient choosing individual works against this—indeed, as Richard Bauckham reminds us, it "has led to the asocial, amoral, and isolated individual of contemporary atomized society in the West." Modernity has, in fact, "bequeathed both the idea of the inherent dignity of the individual, entailing the right to freedom *from* domination, and also its contradiction, freedom *as* domination."[23] Fueling this dilemma, I would contend, is a visual model of mutual exclusion—"the more of me, the less of you," and vice versa. (The only other option would seem to be some kind of merger, in which individuals dissolve into each other and thereby lose their identity.)

Applied to our relation to God, a similar picture often crops up, no less troublesome. The more God is active in our lives in all his sovereign freedom, it is assumed, the less room we will have to be ourselves. If God is *here*, he must either force me aside or swallow me up; I cannot be *here* also. "The more of God, the less of us." Again the model is fundamentally competitive: belief in a God who is other than us and freely involved in our lives in his unlimited power can only stifle our true freedom and humanity.[24] Much modern atheism and contemporary suspicion of Christianity has been driven by just such an assumption—there must be hardly a single college campus in North America or Europe where this belief will not be regularly met. The oppressive, tyrannical sovereign God of the Bible, who reduces us to passive objects of his will, must be firmly sent packing so that we can be "free" and assume our displaced dignity. The common conservative reaction to this—"God is everything; we are nothing"—in effect plays the same zero-sum game, presuming God and humanity are fundamentally opposed to each other.[25] (Again, the only other major option is some form of merger—for instance, where humanity is seen as intrinsically part of God, or salvation a process in which we become divine.)

It is clear that ways of thinking derived from music, while not, of course, proving modern atheism to be false, can help to subvert the assumption that has energized much of it. We recall one string setting off another string; the *more* the lower string sounds, the *more* the upper string sounds in its distinctiveness, the more it vibrates in the way it was created to vibrate. Such is the nature of the freedom God grants: the *more* God is involved in our lives, the freer we shall be, liberated to be the distinctive persons we were created to be. And such is the freedom we can share, by virtue of God's gift of freedom, with *others*. Simultaneously sounding notes, and the music arising from them, can witness to a form of togetherness in which there is an overlap of spaces out of which comes *mutual enrichment and enhancement*, and a form of togetherness that can be sensed first and foremost as a gift, not a consequence of individual choices.

During a recent visit to South Africa, a number of times I sang the national anthem, "Nkosi Sikelel' iAfrika." Wherever I sang it, it evoked in me an extraordinary sense of togetherness, even though I hardly knew the hymn and often barely knew the people with whom I was singing. Part of the reason for that, no doubt, was that I knew this song had held thousands together during the fierce decades of apartheid. Part of it was the tremendous welcome I received at most of the assemblies where I sang it. But a large part of it was also its four-part harmony, in which no vocal line predominates over the others (unlike the British national anthem, for example). Sing this in South Africa and, in keeping with a wide range of African music, it will instantly be sung in harmony. (Unlike the Western European tradition, singing in harmony does not need to be taught.) Your voice and all the others fill the same heard space. It is a space not of a hundred separate voices each with their mutually exclusive and bounded place but a space of overlapping sounds, an uncrowded, expansive space without clear edges, where distinct voices mutually establish and enhance one another.

Why was solidarity in South Africa so often expressed in harmonious song during the years of oppression? Among the many reasons, I suggest, is that when crowds met to sing—in townships, churches, marches—the music provided a taste of authentic freedom, when in virtually every other sense they were *not* free. Why is it that freedom and reconciliation have so often been celebrated in this kind of singing? Partly, I believe, because people are experiencing a kind of concord that can embody the kind of freedom-in-relation to others—even our enemies—that God has made possible.

It was in part from African sources that the vast river of jazz emerged. Micheal O'Siadhail writes of jazz improvisation:

> Moody solos. Unique. The stamp of one voice;
> Then pure concert as an ensemble improvises,
>
> Hearing in each other harmonies of cross-purpose,
> As though being ourselves we're more capacious.[26]

Anyone who has experienced "singing in tongues" might well search for similar words—likewise anyone who has either sung in or heard a performance of Thomas Tallis's extravagant forty-part motet, *Spem in Alium* (ca. 1570). Here forty different voices weave their way in and through one another. Tallis's imagination transports the hearer into a fantastical sound-world with freely interweaving counterpoint, antiphonal exchanges in block harmony, and carefully positioned massed outbursts of all forty voices together. Despite the sonic profusion, it never sounds jammed or crowded. There is multiplicity without dissipation, togetherness without mutual overwhelming or fusion, each voice being enabled to become more fully itself: "As though being ourselves we're more capacious."[27]

Freedom is not first of all something we pursue and then struggle to preserve over against others but is essentially a gift. Freedom is not first of all chosen by us, but it is mediated through others, as they give themselves to us and us to them, and never more so than in the community God has provided for just this to happen. In this God-given ensemble, we find we are able to accommodate others we have previously shunned. To be drawn into the hospitable singing of a church can be a powerful enacted metaphor of just this. A complex sound comes to us and envelops us. We do not choose this note or that to be "with";

we are, so to speak, baptized into its notes-in-relation, and through this sound, into a body of flesh-and-blood people. We are not smothered, but we can find our own voice as we are released to listen to and harmonize with others: "being ourselves we're more capacious."

Notice that O'Siadhail writes of "cross-purpose." Not only is God's ensemble a gift, but its power comes from being related to a very particular God—a God who through Golgotha has defeated the very forces that drive us to create our own spaces, exclude others we have not chosen, and displace God; a God who now through his Holy Spirit invites us to share in the fruits of that victory with one another. This is the harmony of "cross-purpose"—the harmony purposed in the cross. Philosophies of individualism and competitive mutual exclusion—as if this represented what we were *really* like and *really* meant to be—will never serve authentic freedom. But experiences in which we are drawn out of ourselves by others, liberated to give ourselves to them, and in the process find our own "voice" enhanced—those we should treasure.

In 1999 a remarkable CD was launched with the title *Simunye*. Two singing groups met in South Africa—a vocal ensemble from the University of Oxford, I Fagiolini, and a church group, the Sdasa Chorale from Soweto. They engaged in an intensive exchange to compare, contrast, and combine their respective musical worlds. They recorded tracks in a township church with a congregation, in the open air and in a studio. Here we find music such as Gibbons's "O Clap Your Hands" and fourteenth-century Machaut combined with South African melodies and cross-rhythms. Perhaps the most striking item is a chant for peace, written during the apartheid era, over which the Oxford singers weave a Gregorian chant setting of the Agnus Dei, the last line being "O Lamb of God who takes away the sins of the world, grant us *peace.*" Here music's very particular way of combining sounds is used to serve three kinds of simultaneity. There is textual simultaneity—a political chant for peace is given fresh gospel depth through the liturgical words, and vice versa; there is stylistic simultaneity—two musical traditions are in conversation without any loss of integrity; and there is ethnic simultaneity—two groups from quite different ethnic backgrounds engage each other. A taste of gospel freedom through musical overlapping.

Second, *music can serve to bring and hold together different dimensions of the gospel.* Because of the manner in which it mixes sounds, music can help us experience and think together quite different strands of the Christian faith, in ways that elude many other media. To return again to Bach, the opening chorus of his immense *St. Matthew Passion*—"Kommt, ihr Töchter" ("Come, you daughters")—is as fine an example as any of this.[28] The chorus is a funeral procession in E minor for a multitude on their way to Jerusalem. And as the words will soon make clear, it also alludes to Jesus carrying his cross—indeed, his journey to Golgotha forms the central momentum of the *Passion*. A sense of heavy distress and undertow is evoked. A repeated note, a thudding E, is played on the lowest string of the basses. The leading upper melodies also begin on

E but soon split, one tugging upward and the other downward, the two held in tension by the steadily pulsating bass E's. This threefold texture generates an immediate sense of strain, the same process being repeated straightaway in the upper voices at a higher pitch. The stress is intensified by a number of other devices, also involving overlapping tones. The upper melodies create, and are interwoven with, an extraordinary succession of chords, with frequent suspended dissonances (when a line of melody is held over a change of harmony underneath, producing an acute tension). Especially pervasive is the tritone—an interval we have already spoken about, heavily associated with strife, precariousness, and instability.[29] These carefully crafted superimpositions give rise to a multitude of tensions, and the fact that many of them are slow to resolve and many create further tensions gives rise to a marked impression of relentless driving against considerable opposition. The appropriateness of this hardly needs to be pointed out.

Into this thickly charged atmosphere, a choir enters. This is the daughter of Zion calling out to the faithful to behold the figure of Christ. "Come, you daughters, help me lament. Behold!" The faithful, on their way to Jerusalem, respond. This is a second choir—apprehensive believers, vaguely aware of impending catastrophe but baffled by this suffering figure. A dialogue ensues:

"Come, you daughters, help me lament. Behold—"
"Whom?"
"The Bridegroom. Behold him—"
"How?"
"Like a lamb."

Over this a third heavenly choir (the "ripieno") sings a chorale, a metrical paraphrase of the "Agnus Dei," which concludes the Good Friday service, the last line echoing the litany ("Have mercy on us, O Jesus"). The key is G major, the key of innocence in this *Passion*, here contrasting with the underlying key of E minor, the key of guilt.[30] This contrast between our guilt and the guiltless Lamb of God who comes to bear our guilt away is in many ways the abiding theme of the work: the One who possessed G major innocence was immersed in E minor tonality for our sakes. And this music surrounds the silent figure on his way to Golgotha—in the manner of the book of Revelation, we witness a particular and unrepeatable death in Jerusalem together with its ultimate significance seen from the perspective of the heavenly choir.

The overlapping goes further still. The bass articulates the pastorale rhythm, associated at this period (and in much music since) with sheep and shepherds. We recall that the "Agnus Dei" would have been sung earlier in the morning service; here the curtain is being drawn back upon the Lamb of God. With this bass, the rhythm of the opening chorus is trochaic, here conveying apprehension and anticipation. It is overlaid with the steady iambic rhythm of the chorale, articulating stability—in this case, the bedrock of faith. These are aligned skillfully and ironically: in the One trudging to his death, identifying with the apprehensive pilgrims, reliable salvation is being worked out.

In this piece, then, deploying music's ability to overlap sounds, Bach manages to combine different levels of meaning in St. Matthew's Gospel, to hold together quite distinct nuances simultaneously, without any merger or confusion. What theologians and others have so often struggled to do, Bach achieves with astonishing ease.

Third, *music can serve to embody the kind of trinitarian space in which we are invited to share.* It is likely that readers will have jumped ahead already to the Trinity. What could be more apt than to speak of the Trinity as a three-note chord, a resonance of life; Father, Son, and Spirit mutually indwelling, without mutual exclusion, and yet without merger, each occupying the same space, "sounding through" one another, yet irreducibly distinct, reciprocally enhancing, and establishing one another *as* other? Early Christians wrote of God's *perichoresis* (co-inherence), the interchange and mutual indwelling of Father, Son, and Spirit, paraphrased by Cornelius Plantinga thus: "Each divine person harbors the others at the centre of his being. In a constant movement of overture and acceptance, each person envelops and encircles the others."[31]

A musicologist writes about a three-note chord: "Three tones sound. . . . None of them is in a place; or better, they are all in the same place, namely everywhere. . . . No difference of places keeps them apart; yet they remain audible as different tones . . . the tones connected in the triad sound *through one another.*"[32] He could almost be speaking of the Trinity. The freedom that we spoke about above, the gospel freedom we are called to receive and share, finds its source and sustenance here, within God. And it is to resound outward. The resonances we enjoy through the Spirit with the Son and the Father, made possible by the cross, catch others up and bind us to them (especially those who are "out of tune"). The church is called to be the song of God's own trinitarian life in the midst of his creation.

It is arguable that a large part of our chronic tendency to treat the Trinity as essentially a problem to be solved—a mathematical conundrum about threeness and oneness to be agonized over on Trinity Sunday—rather than a reality to be enjoyed has been exacerbated by giving pride of place to the eye in telling us what is permissible and impermissible. Then it is hard to avoid the dangers of the supposedly easy ways of solving the problem: imagining God as blandly one (unitarianism), or a celestial committee of individuals (tritheism), or as outwardly three but internally without distinction (modalism). (The next time we hear a Trinity Sunday sermon, there is a good chance that the illustrations will all be visual.)

Of course, clarifications and qualifications are needed. We are not making a covert attack on visual modes of thinking in themselves (a chronic, much-discussed, and much-attacked Protestant tendency),[33] nor are we denying that there have been magnificent visual renderings of the Trinity. The point is rather about refusing to give undue prominence to one sense, one form of perception. Further, we should be careful not to treat the Trinity as a model of harmony that we can simply apply *tout court* to our dealings with others. There are crucial aspects of the life and activity of God that are not transferable—the interpenetrating character of the persons of the Trinity clearly cannot be mapped onto visible human relations in any direct way, for example; nor can the infinite freedom of the Triune God be easily compared to our own finite freedom.[34] Further still, we should be very wary about bypassing the cross and the Spirit—treating the Trinity as an ideal or model of community that we then simply try to reproduce in some manner here on earth. Instead of copying or imitating the Trinity, we would do better to speak of participating in the life and love of the Triune God by virtue of Jesus's death and resurrection and the giving of his Spirit; only within this movement of grace can our relations with others become truly free.[35] Nevertheless, the overlapping of musical sounds, though in important respects dissimilar to the space of Father, Son, and Spirit, can nonetheless serve to embody concretely something of that trinitarian space, the space in which we are invited to share, and embody it in ways that would seem to be unique to this art form.

Emotional Concentration

The emotional power of music is probably its single most controversial feature.[36] As we have seen, it has caused considerable anxiety in much thinking about music—we need think only of the writings of Plato, Augustine, and Calvin—and today it provokes heated debate in discussions about music in worship. Music is undeniably one of the most emotionally potent media we know. Some will speak very readily of music as "a language of the emotions."[37] Psychologists Patrik Juslin and John Sloboda confirm that "some sort of emotional experience is probably the main reason behind most people's engagement with music,"[38] and as we noted in chapter 1, the most pervasive use of music today is to create or change a mood. Vast intellectual energy has been invested in trying to trace the links between music and emotion, and in recent years this has involved many different disciplines—including philosophy, psychology, sociology, and anthropology.[39] Yet despite being one of the most interesting and probably most important fields concerning music, it is also one of the hardest to fathom. The terrain is complex and contested, with a huge number of questions still left unanswered.

Here we are not presenting and defending one theory of music and emotion, nor are we trying to resolve conclusively the major debates. Any who work in this area know that arguments and positions need to be tentative. What follows is exploratory, no more. In any case, our interest in this chapter is theological: we are considering some of the powers of music that have strong Christian resonances. After making some general points about emotional experience and its relation to music, I will focus on just one of music's capacities in the emotional realm of particular theological interest.

Inner States?

Despite much controversy, some things command fairly wide agreement in contemporary writing about emotion, and one of them is that we need to rid ourselves of a fixation on a single person's interior life: thinking about an emotion as merely, or even essentially, an individual's inner state. Emotional states seem to involve a close interplay between various key components (and here I draw especially on the work of David Myers).[40] First, there is *physiological activation*—if you are emotionally aroused you will often sweat, your blood gets diverted from internal organs to the larger muscles, your heart rate increases, and so on. Second, there is *expressive bodily behavior*—when we are irritated, we may tense our shoulders or press our lips together; if we are frightened, our eyebrows often are raised and pulled together. These signs can be quickly read by others. Related to this, many writers stress that emotions are inextricably bound up with our relations to others. Juslin and Sloboda speak of emotions as "intrinsically social"[41] (though this is more apparent with some emotions than others). And third, there is what we might call (for want of a better phrase) a *conscious experience*—we *feel* angry, frightened, sad, or whatever.[42] There is substantial evidence that our emotional involvement with music involves all these factors, and, clearly, this links up with many of the emphases in this book. Whatever terms are used, to think of emotions as exclusively or even chiefly about individuals' interior states—as if the conscious experience aspect were fundamental and all else secondary—is misleading and has skewed much debate.

Emotion and Objects

Immensely influential in our culture have been what we might call "irrationalist" perspectives on emotions, which interpret them as little more than unpredictable, fleeting feelings or animalistic urges, unconnected with the reasoning control of the mind and not intrinsically related to beliefs or judgments about what is true or false. Ironically, both those who are suspicious of the emotions and many who want to give a fuller place to the emotions in, say, the church often share this assumption that emotions are no more than irrational bodily phenomena, more likely to hinder our grasp of reality than aid it.

This has been very widely questioned, and understandably so. Many have demonstrated that, far from necessarily being an impediment to coming to terms with and reacting appropriately to reality, emotions are essential to the process.[43]

Emotions do not happen in a vacuum. The threefold interplay we have been speaking about, in one way or another, relates to objects—things, people, states of affairs not of our own making. I am not angry in the abstract but angry *about* something or angry *at* someone. Fear arises because something has threatened me, joy because I have met something that is good, beautiful, or whatever. Emotions are, we might say, directional states—they are *of* or *about* something. Crucial to grasp here is that emotions involve *beliefs* about and, more important, *evaluations* of a situation. My fear in the face of a bear in the wild involves the belief that it can kill people, and this leads me to evaluate my encounter with the bear as dangerous—it is this that brings about the physiological changes and bodily behavior typical of fear.[44] Further, just because they have this structure, relating to beliefs and judgments, theorists speak of emotions as having "action tendencies"—we *act out of* emotions. Emotions are powerful motivators. Faced with an adult lion, I run! We are moved (often literally!) by the situation we are in—moved toward action: shame moves Adam to hide from God (Gen. 3:8); joy moves David to dance (2 Sam. 6:14); pity moves Jesus to give his disciples authority to exorcise demons and heal the multitudes (Matt. 9:36–10:1).

If this broad perspective is correct, it is clear that emotions can be appropriate and inappropriate, warranted and unwarranted. Emotions can be well founded or ill founded. If a terrorist walks into my office with a gun, my intense fear is justified. If a mouse scuttles across the room and I jump onto the desk shrieking, my response is out of proportion to the reality. Over and over again in Scripture, God's people are told, "Do not fear," not because fear is wrong in itself but because some types of fear are unwarranted—in particular, the fear that amounts to a lack of trust in God.

This insight was developed many years ago by the Scottish philosopher John Macmurray in his concise classic *Reason and Emotion*. Macmurray writes of rational and irrational emotion, emotion that is true to the nature of an object (or, more strictly, based on well-founded beliefs and evaluations about objects in relation to us), and emotion that is untrue (based on ill-founded beliefs and evaluations about objects). He counters the popular notion that emotion is the enemy of reason, that emotion inevitably clouds truth. The danger is not emotion itself, but inappropriate emotion.[45] We recall Jesus urging his disciples: "Do not fear those who kill the body but cannot kill the soul; rather fear him who can destroy both soul and body in hell" (Matt. 10:28). All this is crucial in worship; the danger is not emotion but emotion that is out of sync with the reality we are trying to honor (for example, a joy that is exaggerated, or delight in the face of something that should bring anger).

Music, Emotion, and Objects

Once we take all this into the musical arena, a problem immediately arises, and it is one that has perplexed even the most able music theorists. It is this:

music does not bring its objects with it, yet it moves us. As we have underlined earlier, music itself rarely directs our attention to objects in any very specific, unambiguous, and consistent manner in the way that, say, literature frequently does. When I am moved by a Flannery O'Connor novel, I am moved by what the words refer to. Music does not carry its reference so closely and clearly, and yet it moves us. How?

It would seem that, at the very least, two things are going on here, sometimes simultaneously. First, *we can be moved directly by the aesthetic qualities of the musical sounds*—by their arrangements. We hear a chord sequence, a guitar riff, an intricate elaboration, and its patterning, its formal arrangement generates emotions.[46] But second, very commonly, *music's emotional properties get directed toward and attached to objects that surround it*. As we stressed in chapter 1, we always hear musical sounds in a context. The context provides an arena of potential objects for the music, objects to which we relate the music or to which the music relates us. In Nicholas Cook's words, music is "a bundle of generic attributes in search of an object."[47] Especially important here are memories and associations, and the other phenomena we perceive when we hear the sounds (pictures, words, etc.).

So, for example, we go to a movie. We hear music along with images and words. The music's emotional properties get hooked on to those words and images, drawing us deeper emotionally into the drama. Sometimes the music's general emotional properties are nuanced (focused, made more precise) by words and images. Many know the experience of waking up in the night with a vague sense of anxiety but about nothing in particular. After a while, we remember a sick friend, a difficult meeting next week, or something else. I saw a film recently where music of a vague but disturbing quality accompanied the opening credits, but I saw only those words; the fact the music had nothing to latch on to (apart from names of people) generated a strong sense of anxiety. It was only as images appeared that the anxiety was focused, in this case by a drowning at sea. More commonly, however, this works the other way round: the words and images supply the general emotional properties, and the music nuances them. For example, toward the end of the film *The Mission*, one of the main musical themes returns as the South American mission station is pictured being burned to the ground. The images and words supply the objects; the music's emotional properties draw us into and nuance the emotion in the images and words. In this way, we feel all the more intensely the heartrending poignancy of it all—especially devastating given that the mission station was founded by the priest who played this music's melody on a pipe.

Here music interacts with images. But what about situations in which we hear, say, sad music but where there are no very obvious objects to which we can direct any sadness? People sometimes claim they are saddened by sad music and cheered by happy music but without the presence of any object that comes with the music to be sad or happy *about*. To understand what might be going on here, we can draw on some illuminating reflections by the philosopher Roger Scruton, who speaks about "sympathetic response."[48] If you are afraid of an illness, and I, observing your fear, come to share in your fear while not being threatened by the illness myself, then my response is a sympathetic response. I sympathize with you in your fear. Sympathetic responses are aroused more fully in fictional situations than in nonfictional ones, because fictional characters cannot directly affect my interests; they cannot threaten or impede me, nor can I do anything to change their situation. In the imaginary world, our feelings are freed from the urge to intervene, to do something with or toward somebody, for there are no real, concrete others to be the objects of sympathy. I do not try to rescue King Lear on stage in the play, though I may sense his plight very strongly. By being drawn into a fictional situation like this, my emotional life can be exercised, stretched, widened, and deepened (and in some cases perhaps corrupted)—yet all without a concrete object, and without the immediate need to do anything about the situation.

Among the most remarkable examples of sympathetic response is dancing, when I move with another: I find meaning in the appearance of the other's gestures and respond accordingly with movements of my own, without seeking to change her predicament or share her burden. This is where Scruton draws the analogy with music. When I am deeply moved by, say, joyful music, and in a context where there is no immediate or obvious thing to be joyful about, I am engaged in a kind of latent dancing, an internalized movement, a dancing to or moving with the sounds (even if I remain physically still). I am moved—moved by and with the music.[49]

Is this "emotion without an object" really a full-fledged emotion? Many would think not, and I am inclined to agree. Indeed, it might be better to speak of feeling or mood rather than emotion and reserve the term emotion for situations with an object or objects and with beliefs and evaluations that provoke action. Nevertheless, it is quite plausible to hold that something like sympathetic response—dancing to or with the music—is in fact going on in all our experience of music and is part of what is happening when music is involved in situations of emotional engagement.

Emotional Properties?—Back to the Body

But this still leaves open the question: What is it about the musical sounds, if anything, that makes them appropriate to the expression of emotion that prompts "sympathetic response"? I have talked about "sad music." Does this mean the sounds themselves have emotional properties? Surely this is just naive projection; it is we who make the emotional links between the sounds and objects, and then (falsely) imagine that the sounds have emotional characteristics.

Here we enter another intimidating maelstrom of debate, where firm conclusions are not widely available and much research is still pending. Here I can point only to one especially promising and useful avenue of research, and it links up with our repeated stress on the importance of music's connections with the body. It usually goes under the name of the "contour theory" of musical expressiveness.[50]

This holds that musical sounds can be said to have emotional properties by virtue of their connection with bodily expressive behavior (the second major component of emotional states that I spoke about above). It is claimed that music embodies not emotion as such but *bodily motions associated with emotion*. Music comes to have certain perceptual qualities—heard qualities that we describe in emotional terms because they resonate with certain bodily movements. And among the movements highlighted as particularly important are speech and gesture.[51]

To take speech first: the linking of musical sounds with the vocalization of emotion in speech seems very common in many cultures. Cheerful and ebullient people tend to speak quickly, often in bright and loud tones, in a high register of their voices, and often with a predominance of rising pitch. Music we call "cheerful" will likewise often tend to be fast and use upper registers, phrases will tend to rise in pitch more than they fall, and so forth (e.g., the "Et resurrexit" from Bach's *Mass in B Minor*). Melancholy or grief-ridden people tend to speak softly, slowly, and haltingly; their voices tend to sink at the end of sentences, and they use the lower part of their vocal register. The same often goes for melancholy music (e.g., Chopin's Funeral March). Concerning gesture: typically, sad people walk with a sluggish, tentative gate, with drooping bodies; they speak in a subdued, hesitating voice, with a limited pitch range. Music we call "sad" tends to share similar features (again, just think of funeral music).[52]

Of course, we can always find counterexamples; some emotional states are hard to explain in this way and, needless to say, there is much variation across different cultures. But the theory need not be taken as attempting a complete or global explanation, simply as highlighting something that is likely to be crucial in the emotional experience of music: when music moves us, a significant part of what we are doing is responding to musical embodiments of bodily movements.[53]

It might be that what we spoke about earlier in this chapter—tensions and resolutions in music—can be read in this light. We looked at deferred gratification; some believe that the confirmation or violation of expectancy is "the key to emotional intensity" in Western music[54] and that the emotional power of this device, and of tensions and resolutions more generally, may correlate with bodily movements of one sort or another.[55]

Certainly, if this theory points in the right direction, it has a number of distinct advantages. It avoids the common tendency to limit occurring emotions to states of mind;[56] it attempts to take the bodily dimension of emotional experience seriously (and we recall that bodily movement plays a major part in the experience of music). It also helps us avoid another theory we have touched on a number of times—the "expression theory" of musical emotion.[57] Here the emotional content of music is identified with the composer's emotion; a piece of music expresses the composer's emotional state of mind, and understanding the piece means recovering in some way this mental state at the time of composing. (Among many Christians, something like this is often assumed by default, and it is sometimes turned into an obligation: a songwriter should, first and foremost, strive to convey his or her own emotional state.)

But the flaws in this theory are obvious.[58] Thousands of pieces bear little or no resemblance to the composer's emotional condition at the time of composition.[59] The connection between a composer's emotion and the music he or she composes is nowhere near as natural or transparent as that between emotion and the bodily expressions of emotion. This is not to deny, of course, that a composer *may* directly express a state of mind (intentionally or otherwise), nor that it *may* be possible to surmise things about the composer's state of mind through a piece of music. But as purporting to go to the heart of how and why music moves us, the expression theory is clearly lacking.

The contour theory, by contrast, shows us how a piece of music can be *expressive* of sadness without it *expressing* anyone's sadness, in much the same way that (to use Peter Kivy's celebrated example) a St. Bernard dog can look sad without being sad. O. K. Bouwsma caught this nicely: "The sadness is to the music rather like the redness to the apple, than it is like the burp to the cider."[60]

Further, we avoid the pitfall of "arousal" theories. Here there is an attempt to explain emotional expressiveness in terms of emotions generated *in the hearer or listener*.[61] To say that Elvis Presley's "Lonely Man" expresses sadness is to say that I feel (or ought to feel) sadness when I hear it. But this is clearly not plausible. A piece can express grief without us feeling grief. We can attend a performance of Tchaikovsky's *Pathétique* Symphony and recognize the music as sad yet without feeling sad ourselves. This is not, of course, to deny that music provokes emotional reactions; it is to challenge the notion that it is these reactions that make it true to say that the music is expressive. We generally "have a clear sense of music's expressive character as quite distinct from our (very variable) responses to it."[62] The contour theory has a way of explaining how this is so.

Much more would need to be said to give the contour theory the kind of sturdiness required to service a comprehensive account of musical emotion. In particular, it is likely that the first element of emotional states we highlighted—physiological processes internal to the body—needs to be given greater prominence, for these would seem to have a significant part to play in music's emotional character and impact, perhaps just as significant as overt bodily movement. For example, what we said earlier in chapter 9 about dissonance and consonance suggests that the emotional character we attribute to some sounds may depend to a large extent on the way different sounds stimulate the inner ear. It would be very natural for us to make links between negative emotion and the physical experience of roughness that comes with intervals such as the tritone (or minor chords in contrast to major). Likewise the correlation of certain emotions with tempo and rhythm might well have as much to do with the tempo and rhythm of our heartbeat, blood flow, and so forth as it does with outward bodily motion. Even this, however, only lends support to what we have suggested repeatedly in this book: the bodily mediation of sounds has a highly significant part to play in our engagement with music.

Concentration

Even bearing all this in mind, however, the question still arises: What *benefit* might we gain emotionally from music? Surely it must be doing more than reflecting our emotional life? Is there not a sense in which music *does something with* our emotions?

Typically, our emotional lives are messy. They are often confused and transient; they are tangled, come and go, jump out at us at odd times. Likewise the overt bodily movements associated with them—they will perhaps be sporadic, flaring, out of control. If I am angry, I might throw my arms all over the place, stamp my feet, shout things I only half mean, perhaps grit my teeth and mutter intermittently.

Suppose, however, a dancer wants to display anger. She will likely deploy particular movements—a glare perhaps, a clenched fist, a thrust of the head. Such movements can be described as *concentrated,* and in three senses. First, and most basic, they will be free from irrelevance, pared down and purified, with no off-putting distractions. Second, they might also compress a range of gestures into one; for instance, condensing complex angry states into a single sweep of the arm. Third, they may be nuanced or focused on one type of emotion, specifying *this* emotion rather than *that*; we sense it is *this* anger and not *that*.

Is this not part of what is often going on in the case of music? (And the dancer analogy seems especially fitting here, given music's engagement with bodily movement.) We cited Tchaikovsky's *Pathétique* Symphony earlier. The last movement does not offer grief as we normally experience it but rather concentrated "grief in sound." For all that it may be overwhelming in performance, the music is in fact extremely disciplined; as the dancer uses the formalities of dance, so Tchaikovsky uses the formalities of music: sighing melodic gestures, appoggiaturas (leaning notes), falling chromatic lines, and so on—carefully structured and ordered musical ritual. Through these devices the piece is pared down, focused, highly crafted so as to be shorn of irrelevance. Further, many will testify to a range of feelings of grief compressed into some passages of the piece. And no doubt some would speak of focused or nuanced grief, *this* rather than *that* grief. A good composer knows how to evoke not just sadness but reflective sadness, despairing sadness, fearful sadness, and so on. (This is probably part of what Mendelssohn meant when he said that music is not *less* but *more* precise than words.)[63] In this piece, these different types of grief and others are all present at various stages in the music's unfolding.

It may be that similar grief-ridden music is taken into situations where there is a distinct object or focal point of grief, as when Samuel Barber's "Adagio" was performed at the funeral of President Kennedy. At such occasions, with its power to embody concentrated emotion, music can *represent* us. Not so long ago, a friend of mine led a funeral service for a young mother who had taken her own life, leaving an only son. Immediately after the formalities at the graveside, her son took out a set of bagpipes and played a lament for his mother. My friend said that it was as if he summed up for everyone "what we really wanted to say, deep down." The music took their confused emotions and helped them discover more fully what they really felt. At that funeral, they were *represented*.

We might go a stage further. Was there not something else going on through the music? Many have borne testimony to the fact that music can help us discover more fully not only what we do feel but what we *could* or even *should* feel. To be caught up in the music ("dance with it," in Scruton's sense) is to be caught up in emotional patterns that may be unfamiliar—we may never have felt these things before, or perhaps we have never felt them so deeply. Just as our muscles are toned in a workout in the gym, so some music can, so to speak, give us an emotional workout ("I never knew I had those muscles there"; "I never knew I could feel that way").

To put this another way, music can play its part in *educating, shaping, and reshaping us* emotionally. The central weakness of theories that suggest music simply copies, mirrors, resembles, pictures (or whatever) our emotions is that they overlook the fact that music can do something far more interesting and far more important: it can voice not only what we do feel but what we could or perhaps should feel. Is this not what Bob Dylan did for a whole generation in the 1960s? Is this not what "We Shall Overcome" did for thousands in the civil rights struggle? It changed those who sang it; it helped them find fresh hope and courage. And is this not what the greatest hymns and songs do? They not only help us sing what we already experience emotionally; to some extent they also educate and re-form our emotional experience.

This is why people who grieve often do not want cheerful music, nor something that just plays the chaos of their grief back to them, and not even something that simply concentrates their grief (important as this is). Instead they want something that can both connect with their grief and help them find new forms of grief, perhaps forms that help set their sorrow in a larger, more hopeful emotional context. Is this not just what the best funeral music should be doing?

Christ as Representative

It might seem as if we have wandered far from theology. In fact we have walked right into the middle of it and can now draw the strands of our discussion together. In chapter 8, in sketching a Christian ecology, I spoke of a double movement in the person of Christ. He is God's Word to us; but just as important, he is also a human word, a fully human being, *the* fully human being: our word to God. In him, God has come to engage directly with our spoiled humanity: Christ plunges into our sinful confusion, living a totally God-honoring life in our midst, bearing away the world's sin and rising as the one person now totally liberated from everything that mars the human race. In his earthly life, he embodies what it is to be authentically human, and, in his risen life, he embodies the full human destiny of all those who belong to him. Now, with him, as our representative, and by his Spirit, we can discover what it is to be truly human ourselves.

What might this have to do with our emotions? In short: everything. Easy as it is to forget, our emotional life needs redeeming just as much as any other part of us. When we claim that God was in Christ to reconcile us to himself (2 Cor. 5:18), why exclude our emotions? Jesus of Nazareth, the fully human person, enacted a sinless and perfectly concentrated emotional life, and now, as the risen human, our representative, he can concentrate, shape, and reshape our emotional life in the likeness of his. This is part of what it means to be "saved."

In Jesus, we witness concentrated emotion—emotion cleaned up, shorn of all sin and confusion. In his anger at Chorazin, Bethsaida, and Capernaum (Luke 10:13–15), we see anger made new: an anger purified of revenge and driven by a godly opposition to all that ruins the world God loves. In his joy when praying to the Father (Luke 10:21), we see joy as it is meant to be, an elation completely centered on the one who sent him and at the same time able to engage the worst the world can throw at him. In his grief at the tomb of Lazarus (John 11:35), we see grief as it could be: stinging to the depths and utterly free of sentimentality about death's cruelty. And in these and other cases we find rich emotion compressed and generalized emotion made very specific. The Gospels tell us all this and more so that we can witness our emotional lives as they could or might be. Here we are emotionally represented.

The apostle Paul speaks about us being transformed into the likeness of Christ (2 Cor. 3:18). Through the Spirit, we are given the priceless opportunity of—to put it simply—growing up emotionally: having our emotions purged of sin and stretched, shaped, and reshaped. It is perhaps in worship and prayer, when we engage with God directly and consciously, that this will be (or ought to be) most evident. All too often in the Western church, Christ has become merely the daunting example of worship, or merely the one to whom we direct our worship. But the New Testament also speaks of Christ's active, continuing prayer for us. In Romans 8, and more fully in the Epistle to the Hebrews, Christ is portrayed as the one who prays for us as our representative (Rom.

8:34; Heb. 7:25). He is the High Priest, tempted yet without sin, sympathizing with our weaknesses, unashamed to call us his brothers and sisters, and alive to intercede for us, appearing in God's presence on our behalf. We do not have to "get it right" to be heard by God—we can, as it were, lean on Christ, knowing that he can take our cries before the Father more truly and authentically than we ever could ourselves. Just as ambassadors on foreign trips carry the needs of their country with them, concentrating their people's concerns and speaking as they would speak if they could, so Christ takes our feeble, muddled, and uncontrolled prayers and concentrates them in the presence of *Abba*, Father. Our own prayer is thus purged, compressed, and focused; it is reshaped and renewed, because now it happens with and "through Christ our Lord," in whom we are represented. The educating, shaping, and reshaping of our emotional lives will be part of this process: as we are caught up in Christ's prayer and worship we learn not only what we already feel but also what we could and should feel.[64]

The links between music and emotion are immensely complex, and, as said at the outset, attempts to build all-embracing theories are fraught with danger. I have done no more than highlight one emotional capacity of music in particular—the way in which, through its linking of sounds with emotionally charged bodily movements, it can concentrate our emotional life, thus representing us and in the process educating, shaping, and reshaping us. This dynamic, we have discovered, bears a striking resemblance to a movement at the heart of our transformation in Christ: Christ concentrating and re-forming our emotions as he represents us before the Father, a movement that is integral to Christian prayer and worship.

But music can do more than resemble and model a process. The upshot of what we are saying is that music can be part of the process itself, part of God's work of emotional renewal. If we have argued along the right lines, music would seem to be an especially powerful resource available to the Holy Spirit for remaking us according to the image of Christ's perfected emotional life,[65] not least through prayer and worship. Of course, this power is open to abuse when it is used to stoke emotions that are inappropriate or damaging: manipulation, sentimentality, and emotional self-indulgence are among the ever-present dangers. But emotional abuse should not lead us to run away from emotion. To "grow up" into Christ is to grow up emotionally as much as anything else, and carefully chosen music may have a larger part to play than we have yet imagined.

conclusion

In this book we have been concerned with how God's truth might "sound" and "re-sound" in the world of music. We have been trying to demonstrate what theology—the thinking and rethinking of the Christian gospel in all its height, length, breadth, and depth—can bring to our understanding of the place of music in God's purposes. We have been doing this with practical ends in mind. Our interest has been to help foster a Christian wisdom about music, that is, to generate godly habits of judgment that can form, inform, and re-form the practicalities of making and hearing music (whether listening to Corinne Bailey Rae, composing a fugue, playing in a band, or whatever).

In part 3, drawing on material from parts 1 and 2, we have been seeking this wisdom by setting music within what I have called a "Christian ecology"—that is, in relation to the web of basic faith commitments that emerge from the gospel, with special attention to the doctrine of creation. In chapter 8, we set out three questions to guide us: What kind of *Creator* creates? What kind of *cosmos* does the Creator create and relate to? And what kind of *calling* do we have in this cosmos? We stressed that imagination would be required throughout—to discern the large currents and patterns of meaning in Scripture (chapter 8), and to think about music as well as make and hear it in the light of these currents and patterns (chapters 9 and 10).

In chapters 9 and 10, then, we attempted to situate music within a vision of the purposes of a Triune Creator, who in Jesus Christ has embodied and realized his purposes for creation, who now through his Spirit works to bring all things to their intended end, and who invites us, with Christ and in the Spirit, to "voice creation's praise." In chapter 9 we sought to do this with respect to the created environment in which music is made and heard, the kind of cosmos God has fashioned. If the created world is crafted out of freedom and love, we suggested, the very possibility of music should provoke us to gratitude. If this world is indeed both fully real and good (of enduring value), there is no place for shunning, suspecting, or devaluing music simply because it involves the stuff of the earth and human bodies, reeds and vocal cords, sound waves and eardrums. At the same time, a thoughtless idolatry of the material aspects of music (or any other aspect of it) is equally pernicious, for the created world is neither divine nor heading for divinity. Music praises God in its createdness, in its finite otherness.

Bearing in mind that music takes place in a world made to flourish toward its end, we explored some of the implications of music's intense intertwining with time. We spoke of the "ordered openness" of creation, testifying to the commitment of a Creator working through his Son and Spirit. We stressed that music is embedded in given, ordered, acoustical phenomena (such as the harmonic series), even if the way music negotiates and shapes these phenomena can vary considerably depending on culture, setting, and so on. And the interplay between regularity and unpredictability evident in creation can be powerfully evoked in forms of music in which a high degree of contingency is interlaced with stable constraints. We saw also that the diverse unity of creation, generated and enabled to flourish by the Spirit, is apparent in the remarkable variety of sounds it displays—a variety that can find potent expression and elaboration through music.

In chapter 10 we went on to look at music as part of the human calling: our vocation to extend and elaborate the praise that creation already offers to the Creator, through Christ (in whom our calling is enacted and redeemed), and in the Spirit's power. We spoke of *discovery*—and drew particular attention to the ability of music to elicit and bring to light the wonders of the physical world we inhabit as we engage creatively with it, to make us attentive to the environment God has provided. We spoke of *respect*—and highlighted the importance of a courteous honoring of this environment as embodied creatures, and specifically of sonic order, and seeing artistic freedom as a responsive, responsible relation to given constraints ("given" understood in a rich, benevolent sense). We spoke of *development*—the need in music, as elsewhere, to fashion things as yet unfashioned, respecting and enhancing given order, and of the dangers of the drive toward sameness and repetition in much market-driven contemporary music. We spoke of *healing*—sharing now, in the Creator's own redeeming work; penetrating, judging, and refashioning whatever has been polluted and distorted. In music, as much as anywhere else, this means being agents of hope, and we reflected on the ways in which only a cross-shaped confidence can begin to meet the widespread suspicions of hope in the postmodern climate. We spoke of *anticipation*—the way in which the activities of music can share in the Spirit's previewing of the final remaking of this world, a future promised in the raising of Jesus from the dead. And we spoke of the human vocation as one undertaken *together* with others—within the "Pentecostal polyphony" generated by the gospel itself (against all forms of individualism), and of the potential impact of this on every aspect of music making and music hearing. We added that running through all this will be the heartbeat of joy, born of knowing we are debtors to grace and that the end is assured.

In chapter 11, still working within a Christian ecology, we examined three of the "singular powers" of musical sound patterns, features of a wide range of music that make it especially apt to being employed by the Spirit—its ability to draw us into a multileveled dynamic of tension and resolution, its ability to offer the experience of a distinctive kind of aural space through simultaneous and mutually resonant tones, and its ability to offer us emotional concentration such that our emotional lives can be represented, educated, shaped, and reshaped. We threw into relief the theological potential of each of these features, the ways in which they can help us not only think more deeply and clearly about theological themes but also embody those themes in unique ways. To be wise about music from a Christian perspective means being wise to these and other distinctive powers.

At many points we have sought to relate our argument to the findings of the historical section of the book (part 2). Although those earlier chapters covered a variety of views, and no attempt was made to trace a single line of thought running through the centuries, one issue was brought to the fore more than any other and has been highlighted more than any other in part 3. It is arguably the most important question facing the theology-music conversation in the present climate: *Is music in any way grounded in or obliged to be faithful to a world that we did not make but that is in some sense given to us?* Are music making and music hearing to be understood as embedded in and responsible to an order wider than that which we generate—one that is worthy of respect and trust? As we emerge from modernity into that buzzing and confusing territory of the postmodern, this issue—perhaps more than any other—haunts the debates among those who give music any serious intellectual attention. And if it does so, I suggest it is because of our particular history in the West, a deep ambivalence bequeathed to us from our journey out of late medieval and Renaissance thought into the modern age, an ambivalence about the extent to which our world is to be considered anything more than simply *there* in a bare, neutral sense. Even if not raised with theological concerns in mind, this issue inevitably presses us strongly in a theological direction—if the world is *given*, then by what or whom, and to what end? Here we need not be ashamed of a wealth of fruitful wisdom that the Christian faith and tradition can offer, as we have tried to demonstrate here.

This arches back to points we were making in chapter 1. There we tried to do justice to music as an art of actions—music making and music hearing—but at the same time stressed that music was embedded to a greater or lesser extent in various integrities, principally what I called the "sonic order": sound-producing materials, sound waves, the human body, and time. All this may have seemed glaringly obvious in chapter 1, but we have seen enough since then to understand how this "given" dimension has been marginalized, why it is important, and why Christians, with a very distinctive and extraordinarily rich perception of the world as the "theater of God's glory," have an inestimable contribution to make in helping our culture rediscover it.

Originally, I intended to close this book with a chapter on evaluating music. It would have shown in particular how rethinking music in the light of the broad, creationwide perspective opened up here can help us develop responsible habits of judgment about music as we engage with it in everyday life. It would have sought to take account of the very different kinds of questions one needs to ask about different kinds of music. But to do all this properly and rigorously would require far more than another chapter—another book would be in order, and it is one I hope to write as a follow-up to this one.

As it happens, in the course of these chapters we have in fact made many evaluative judgments about various forms of music making and music hearing, judgments that, I would hope, have been derived from the theological material explored. In any case, as will now be obvious, my main purpose has not been to offer a comprehensive checklist of Christian standards by which we can evaluate any musical experience or a register of prescriptions or prohibitions concerning how exactly music should or should not be made and heard. My prime concern has been—to say it yet again—to jolt the imagination by setting every aspect of music in the context of the breathtaking vision of reality opened up by the gospel of Jesus Christ.

It is perhaps best to close with an opening. John Donne (1572–1631), whose poetry can soar into a word-music of incomparable power, penned "Hymn to God My God, in My Sickness" after a grave illness. He pictures himself just outside heaven's door, tuning up to the sounds of the throng on the other side, just as a child might sneak into the back of an orchestral rehearsal and try tuning her instrument to the sounds of the great ensemble she hopes one day to join. The best Christian wisdom about music, like the best music, attunes us now to the things yet to come.

> Since I am coming to that holy room,
> Where, with thy choir of saints for evermore,
> I shall be made thy music; as I come
> I tune the instrument here at the door,
> And what I must do then, think here before.[1]

notes

Introduction

1. There are, however, some scattered exceptions. There have been some courageous forays into theology by musicologists: e.g., Wilfrid H. Mellers, *Bach and the Dance of God* (Oxford: Oxford University Press, 1981); Mellers, *Beethoven and the Voice of God* (London: Faber, 1983); Eric T. Chafe, *Tonal Allegory in the Vocal Music of J. S. Bach* (Berkeley: University of California Press, 1991); Chafe, *Analyzing Bach Cantatas* (Oxford: Oxford University Press, 2000). And some theologians have ventured into music. Barth's treatment of Mozart will be discussed later. Albert Blackwell's study, *The Sacred in Music* (Cambridge, UK: Lutterworth, 1999), is a sustained theological treatment of music. Other shorter works include Christopher R. Campling, *The Food of Love: Reflections on Music and Faith* (London: SCM, 1997); William Edgar, *Taking Note of Music* (London: SPCK, 1986); Alfred John Pike, *A Theology of Music* (Toledo: Gregorian Institute, 1953); Mark Hijleh, *The Music of Jesus: From Composition to Koinonia* (New York: Writers Club Press, 2001). Heidi Epstein critiques what she sees as sexist theologies of music and outlines her own feminist theology of music in *Melting the Venusberg: A Feminist Theology of Music* (London: Continuum, 2005). A few theological studies of composers have been offered: e.g., Jaroslav J. Pelikan, *Bach among the Theologians* (Philadelphia: Fortress, 1986); Hans Küng, *Mozart: Traces of Transcendence* (London: SCM, 1992); Harold M. Best, *Music through the Eyes of Faith* (San Francisco: HarperSanFrancisco, 1993); Leo Black, *Franz Schubert: Music and Belief* (Woodbridge, Suffolk: Boydell Press, 2003). Looking further back, there are reflections on music by the Congregationalist theologian P. T. Forsyth: see Jeremy S. Begbie, "The Ambivalent Rainbow: Forsyth, Art, and Creation," in *Justice the True and Only Mercy*, ed. Trevor Hart (Edinburgh: T&T Clark, 1995), 197–219. With regard to the potential of music to enrich theology, in addition to Bonhoeffer's enticing discussion of polyphony (see pp. 159–62), see Jeremy Begbie, *Theology, Music, and Time* (Cambridge: Cambridge University Press, 2000); Hans Urs von Balthasar, *Truth Is Symphonic: Aspects of Christian Pluralism* (San Francisco: Ignatius Press, 1987). David Cunningham briefly reflects on the notion of polyphony in theology in *These Three Are One: The Practice of Trinitarian Theology*, Challenges in Contemporary Theology (Oxford: Blackwell, 1998), 127–64. In a number of writings, Jon Michael Spencer has argued that "theomusicology" should be recognized as a legitimate discipline (Jon Michael Spencer, *Theological Music: Introduction to Theomusicology* [London: Greenwood, 1991]; *Theomusicology* [Durham, NC: Duke University Press, 1994]). He contends that theomusicology is "a musicological method for theologizing about the sacred, the secular, and the profane, principally incorporating thought and method borrowed from anthropology, sociology, psychology, and philosophy" (ibid., 3). In *The Art of Performance: Towards a Theology of Holy Scripture* (London: Darton, Longman & Todd, 1990), Frances Young uses musical models to elucidate the process of interpreting the Bible.

2. See, e.g., George Pattison, *Art, Modernity, and Faith: Restoring the Image* (London: SCM, 1998); William A. Dyrness, *Visual Faith: Art, Theology, and Worship in Dialogue* (Grand Rapids: Baker Academic, 2001); Jeremy Begbie, *Voicing Creation's Praise: Towards a Theology of the Arts* (Edinburgh: T&T Clark,

1991); Frank Burch Brown, *Good Taste, Bad Taste, and Christian Taste: Aesthetics in Religious Life* (Oxford: Oxford University Press, 2000); Richard Viladesau, *Theological Aesthetics: God in Imagination, Beauty, and Art* (New York: Oxford University Press, 1999); Viladesau, *Theology and the Arts: Encountering God through Music, Art, and Rhetoric* (New York: Paulist Press, 2000); Hilary Brand and Adrienne Chaplin, *Art and Soul: Signposts for Christians in the Arts* (Carlisle: Solway, 2001); Margaret Miles, *Image as Insight: Visual Understanding in Western Christian and Secular Culture* (Boston: Beacon, 1985); Richard Harries, *Art and the Beauty of God: A Christian Understanding* (London: Mowbray, 2000); Patrick Sherry, *Images of Redemption: Art, Literature, and Salvation* (Edinburgh: T&T Clark, 2003).

3. George Steiner, *Errata: An Examined Life* (London: Phoenix, 1997), 65.

4. Andrew Solomon, "Questions of Genius," *New Yorker*, August 26–September 2, 1996, 114.

5. Anthony Monti, *A Natural Theology of the Arts: Imprint of the Spirit* (Aldershot: Ashgate, 2003), 2. "Major theological figures have typically experienced difficulty negotiating the space between their text-based metaphysical obligations, and an artistic medium habitually described as abstract, non-representational, non-referential, and non-cognitive" (Philip Edward Stoltzfus, "Theology as Performance: The Theological Use of Musical Aesthetics in Friedrich Schleiermacher, Karl Barth, and Ludwig Wittgenstein" [PhD diss., Harvard University, 2000], 6).

6. John D. Barrow, *The Artful Universe Expanded* (Oxford: Oxford University Press, 2005), 223.

7. See, e.g., Andy Bennett, *Popular Music and Youth Culture: Music, Identity, and Place* (New York: Macmillan, 2000). Mark Tarrant, Adrian C. North, and David J. Hargreaves, "Youth Identity and Music," in *Musical Identities*, ed. R. A. R. MacDonald, David J. Hargreaves, and Dorothy Miell (Oxford: Oxford University Press, 2002), 134–50.

8. R. E. Milliman, "Using Background Music to Affect the Behavior of Supermarket Shoppers," *Journal of Marketing* 46 (1982): 86–91.

9. C. S. Areni and D. Kim, "The Influence of Background Music on Shopping Behavior: Classical versus Top-Forty Music in a Wine Store," *Advances in Consumer Research* 20 (1993): 336–40.

10. Adrian C. North and David J. Hargreaves, "Music and Consumer Behaviour," in *The Social Psychology of Music*, ed. Adrian C. North and David J. Hargreaves (Oxford: Oxford University Press, 1997), 274–78. This is not to say that the relation between music and behavior is simply a mechanical one, where a musical stimulus predictably and ineluctably produces a certain effect. See pp. 53–56.

11. According to Adrian Thomas of Cardiff University in an interveiw with Bill Bowder, "The Holy Flame," *Church Times* (May 28, 2004), 19.

12. Steiner, *Errata*, 84.

13. Quoted in Blackwell, *Sacred in Music*, 168.

14. Philip V. Bohlman, "Is All Music Religious?" in *Theomusicology. A Special Issue of Black Sacred Music; A Journal of Theomusicology*, ed. Jon Michael Spencer (Durham, NC: Duke University Press, 1994), 9. See also Philip V. Bohlman, *World Music: A Very Short Introduction* (Oxford: Oxford University Press, 2002), 12–15.

15. George Steiner, *Real Presences: Is There Anything in What We Say?* (London: Faber & Faber, 1989), 216–17, 18.

16. See the lengthy (and critical) discussion of this in Gordon Lynch, *Understanding Theology and Popular Culture* (Oxford: Blackwell, 2005), chap. 8.

17. To take one example: for all its insights and valuable observations, the theological claims made about music in Wilfrid Mellers's study of "religious music" (*Celestial Music* [Woodbridge: Boydell Press, 2002]) are seriously marred by the author adopting a vague and ill-disciplined conception of "religion" (along with equally amorphous related notions). This imprecision, I suspect, will do little to serve the valid and crucial task of discerning the action of the Holy Spirit in music in society at large, and is thus to be regretted.

18. Ivor H. Jones, *Music: A Joy for Ever* (London: Epworth, 1989), 25.

19. See, e.g., Tom Beaudoin, *Virtual Faith: The Irreverent Spiritual Quest of Generation X* (San Francisco: Jossey-Bass, 1998); Robert Wuthnow, *All in Sync: How Music and Art Are Revitalizing American Religion* (Berkeley: University of California Press, 2003); Craig Detweiler and Barry Taylor, *A Matrix of Meanings: Finding God in Pop Culture* (Grand Rapids: Baker Academic, 2003). There are questions some might want

to ask about the theological interpretation these authors offer of music and the arts in contemporary culture, but the quasi-religious phenomena they describe cannot be ignored. For further discussion, see Lynch, *Theology and Popular Culture.*

20. See the discussion of Cave in Detweiler and Taylor, *Matrix of Meanings,* 134–39.

21. E.g., Steve Stockman, *Walk On; The Spiritual Journey of U2* (Lake Mary, FL: Relevant, 2005); Beth Maynard, ed., *Get Up Off Your Knees: Preaching the U2 Catalog* (Cambridge, MA: Cowley, 2003); Mick Wall, *Bono: In the Name of Love* (New York: Thunder's Mouth Press, 2005); Christian Scharen, *One Step Closer: Why U2 Matters to Those Seeking God* (Grand Rapids: Brazos, 2006). Detweiler and Taylor speak of U2 providing for this generation a "postmodern psalmody" (*Matrix of Meanings,* 153).

22. Quoted in Heidi Waleson, "A 'Messiah' for Modern Times," *BBC Music Magazine* (2001): 16.

23. See below, pp. 223–25; see also pp. 179–80, 261.

24. Andreas Andreopoulos, "The Return of Religion in Contemporary Music," *Literature and Theology* 14, no. 1 (2000): 81–95.

25. The precursors of this are in the minimalism of the late 1960s and early 1970s (Steve Reich, Philip Glass, John Adams, and, in the mainstream, Brian Eno); further back, we can see moves in this direction in some of the music of Mahler, Satie, Debussy, Varèse, and others.

26. The question can, of course, move in the other direction: What can music bring to theology? While not shifting our theological bearings—still working within a distinctively Christian worldview—we can ask: How can the practices of music (and reflection on music) help us think more deeply and more faithfully about God, Jesus Christ, and the central realities of the faith? This is not the main concern of this book, but I have developed these interests more fully elsewhere. See, e.g., Jeremy Begbie, ed., *Beholding the Glory: Incarnation through the Arts* (Grand Rapids: Baker Academic, 2000); Begbie, *Theology, Music, and Time.*

27. Kevin J. Vanhoozer, *Is There a Meaning in the Text? The Bible, the Reader, and the Morality of Literary Knowledge* (Leicester: Apollos, 1998), 437. Thiselton believes that the apostle Paul's understanding of the wisdom to be nurtured in the Christian community, as explicated in 1 Cor. 2:6–16, stands in the tradition of Proverbs and the Wisdom literature. He characterizes Paul's "wisdom" among "the mature" of 1 Cor. 2:6 as "*habits of judgement applicable to life.* [Wisdom] concerns *the formation of a Christian mind, which issues in a right action*" (Anthony C. Thiselton, *The First Epistle to the Corinthians: A Commentary on the Greek Text* [Grand Rapids: Eerdmans, 2000], 230).

28. David Ford, "Dramatic Theology: York, Lambeth, and Cambridge," *Sounding the Depths: Theology through the Arts,* ed. Jeremy Begbie (London: SCM, 2002), 88.

29. "It would be unusual to hear anything in . . . churches . . . so ironically and astutely probing as a song on ecological spirituality by James Taylor ('Gaia' from *Hourglass*), or music as alert to alternative spiritualities—African and South-American—as Paul Simon's *Graceland* and *The Rhythm of the Saints* or as achingly yearning in overall effect as k. d. lang's 'Constant Craving' (*Ingénue*) or U2's 'I Still Haven't Found What I'm Looking For' (*Joshua Tree*)" (Frank Burch Brown, "A Matter of Taste?" *Christian Century* [2000]: 904).

30. What is at stake here is the subtle relation between doctrine and ethics—a matter ably dealt with recently in Alan J. Torrance and Michael Banner, eds., *The Doctrine of God and Theological Ethics* (London: T&T Clark, 2006).

31. Paul Westermeyer observes that "the substitution of text for music . . . gives the impression of discussing one thing, while discussing another, rather like discussing hymn texts as if they were tunes. . . . Music is simply avoided in this process, though the impression is given that it has been discussed" ("Reflections on Music and Theology," *Theological Education* 31, no. 1 [1994]: 184).

32. Richard Middleton, *Studying Popular Music* (Milton Keynes: Open University Press, 1990), 227–32.

Chapter 1 What Are We Talking About?

1. Wayne Bowman concludes that "the word 'music' is not the name of any single entity or 'thing' to which we can point in the world; nor is there a single way it all is, or a single end it all serves" (Wayne Bowman, *Philosophical Perspectives on Music* [New York: Oxford University Press, 1998], 16).

2. The terms "popular" and "classical" are notoriously hard to define. "Popular" can take on various shades of meaning—e.g., "of the folk," i.e., homemade, unmediated, and (sometimes) unrefined; "of the mass," i.e., mass-produced and consumed music (the Top 40, for example) to be distinguished sharply from the music of a social elite (usually the "classical" music of "high" culture); "populist," i.e., countercultural, where music becomes a potential or actual form of resistance to the dominant culture within a given society (for example, "punk" when it first appeared). Gordon Lynch urges that we extend the notion of "popular culture" to mean "the shared environment, practices and resources of everyday life" (*Understanding Theology and Popular Culture* [Oxford: Blackwell, 2005], 14). Along similar lines, Anahid Kassabian proposes we should include under popular music studies of the ubiquitous music that is beyond our control—music we do not choose, such as in airports, restaurants, etc. ("Popular," in *Key Terms in Popular Music and Culture*, ed. Bruce Horner and Thomas Swiss [Oxford: Blackwell, 1999], 113–23). As far as "classical" is concerned, historians would generally claim that "classical music" should refer to a type of music written largely in Europe in the second half of the eighteenth century, of which Mozart and Haydn would be the outstanding composers. The word "classical" today is commonly stretched, however, to describe any music in the concert-operatic tradition of the West; it is sometimes called Western "art" music, or even "high art" music.

3. If "tonal" is taken in a very broad sense to refer to any music with fixed reference pitches—tones within a piece that act as stabilizers—then virtually all music could be considered tonal, since these tonal stabilizers are very common in music worldwide (John A. Sloboda, *The Musical Mind: The Cognitive Psychology of Music* [Oxford: Oxford University Press, 1995], 253–54).

4. Here I broadly follow Peter Martin's analysis (Peter J. Martin, *Sounds and Society: Themes in the Sociology of Music* [Manchester: Manchester University Press, 1995], 16–21). Martin's use of the term "differentiation," however, is not entirely consistent. As a sociological term, it appears to describe the way distinct roles and activities emerge and develop within societies, but he also uses it for the appearance of different musical types and styles that are generated by social differentiation. I am assuming both senses here.

5. Ibid., 16.

6. Nicholas Cook highlights three distinct functions of notation. The first is *conservation*: notation gives us a stable, quasi-permanent, visible form to something that—more than any other art form—comes and goes. The second is *communication*: notation enables forms of music to be shared among people, passed on. Third, there is *conception*: notation has had a marked effect on the way we *think* about music. To use Cook's language, it has made many of us conceive music as an "object" (Nicholas Cook, *Music: A Very Short Introduction* [Oxford: Oxford University Press, 1998], chap. 4). For discussion of the issues surrounding the concept of the "work" of music, including pointed debate, see Michael Talbot, ed., *The Musical Work: Reality or Invention?* (Liverpool: Liverpool University Press, 2000). In this collection, Reinhard Strohm mounts a formidable attack on simplistic accounts of the emergence and influence of the "work-concept," pointing out that such accounts by many contemporary writers (e.g., Lydia Goehr in particular) tell us more about our present cultural anxieties than about music history (Reinhard Strohm, "The Problem with the Musical Work-Concept," in Talbot, ed., *Musical Work*, 129–52).

7. In the English-speaking world, the term "musicology" can have different uses. In North America, the name "musicologist" is widely used to refer to the music historian, to be distinguished from the music theorist and the ethnomusicologist. In the United Kingdom, and generally in Australasia, "musicologist" embraces music theorists and ethnomusicologists (music historians calling themselves either that or historical musicologists). Here I use the term in the wide, UK sense.

8. F. A. Biocca, "The Pursuit of Sound: Radio, Perception, and Utopia in the Early 20th Century," *Media, Culture, and Society* 10 (1988): 61–62; italics mine.

9. Martin, *Sounds and Society*, 1. There has been an influential stream of theory—drawing on Max Weber's notion of "disenchantment," which argues that in the modern era the aesthetic has been steadily eroded by a wave of rational administration and bureaucratic, calculative modes of social ordering. The evidence, at least as far as music is concerned, does not bear this out.

10. Garrison Keillor, "Talk Radio," http://prairiehome.publicradio.org/features/deskofgk/971000_atlanticmonthly.shtml.

11. MIDI (Musical Instrument Digital Interface) is a hardware and software standard established in 1983 for the communication of musical data between devices, such as synthesizers, drum machines, and computers.

12. Gerald Marzorati, "All by Himself," 2002, http://www.english.ccsu.edu/barnetts/courses/virtual-culture/TimesMoby.html.

13. A. Bennett, *Cultures of Popular Music* (Buckingham: Open University Press, 2001), 122. The better-known DJs sometimes command their own following, such that hearing *them* is more important than going to a particular club.

14. See, e.g., Norman Lebrecht, *Who Killed Classical Music? Maestros, Managers, and Corporate Politics* (Secaucus, NJ: Carol, 1997); Julian Johnson, *Who Needs Classical Music?* (Oxford: Oxford University Press, 2002).

15. http://www.monteverdi.co.uk/whats_on/news.cfm.

16. Johnson, *Who Needs Classical Music?* 34.

17. http://www.laphil.com/jobs/.

18. For more on Adorno, see below, pp. 253–56.

19. Mark Hijleh, *The Music of Jesus: From Composition to Koinonia* (New York: Writers Club Press, 2001), 41.

20. See Nicholas Cook and Mark Everest, eds., *Rethinking Music* (Oxford: Oxford University Press, 1999).

21. Small points to a potentially misleading bias of the English language: that it has no true verb for musical activity in general. We can say "to paint," but we can't say "to music." Christopher Small, *Music of the Common Tongue: Survival and Celebration in Afro-American Music* (London: J. Calder, 1987), 50–52.

22. See Talbot, *Musical Work*.

23. Cook, *Music: A Very Short Introduction*, vi–vii.

24. For a very illuminating discussion of these issues, see John Butt, *Playing with History: The Historical Approach to Musical Performance* (Cambridge: Cambridge University Press, 2002).

25. Arnold Schoenberg, *Style and Idea*, ed. Leonard Stein, trans. Leo Black (London: Faber & Faber, 1984), 54; italics mine.

26. Quoted in Cook, *Music: A Very Short Introduction*, 40.

27. In the late 1980s and early 1990s, a current of writing in popular music tried to justify the superiority of classic bands in the past (the Beatles being the most obvious example), arguing that they developed innovative styles and compositions out of the distinctive vision of the band members (ibid., 7–14).

28. It has been shown that our emotional involvement in music, for example, is as much due to what *we do* with it—when we link it to our memories, our state of mind at the time—as with the sounds themselves. John A. Sloboda and Patrik N. Juslin, "Music and Emotion: Commentary," in *Music and Emotion: Theory and Research*, ed. Patrik N. Juslin and John A. Sloboda (Oxford: Oxford University Press, 2001), 453–54.

29. See John E. Kaemmer, *Music in Human Life: Anthropological Perspectives on Music* (Austin: University of Texas Press, 1993), chaps. 2 and 3. For a helpful survey of shifts in musical aesthetics, the psychology of music, and ethnomusicology toward seeing music as a human activity embedded in society and culture, see C. Michael Hawn, *Gather into One: Praying and Singing Globally* (Grand Rapids: Eerdmans, 2003), 21–30.

30. See Nicholas Wolterstorff, "The Work of Making a Work of Music," in *What Is Music? An Introduction to the Philosophy of Music*, ed. P. J. Alperson (University Park: Pennsylvania State University Press, 1987), 109–12 for detailed discussion of the concept of "social practices," following Alasdair McIntyre. I am indebted to this article for much in this chapter.

31. The label "essentialism" is sometimes used of the attempt to pull music apart from time and change to discover its true core or enduring heart. The emerging so-called new musicology sets itself against all forms of essentialism. Nicholas Cook explains: "Central to it is the rejection of music's claim to be autonomous of the world around it, and in particular to provide direct, unmediated access to absolute values of truth and beauty. This is on two grounds: first, that there are no such things as absolute

values (all values are socially constructed), and second that there can be no such thing as unmediated access; our concepts, beliefs, and prior experiences are implicated in all our perceptions. The claim that there are absolute values which can be directly known is therefore an ideological one, with music being enlisted to its service. A musicology that is 'critical' in the sense of critical theory, that aims above all to expose ideology, must then demonstrate that music is replete with social and political meaning" (Cook, *Music: A Very Short Introduction*, 117). We should note that one can take the point about the social and cultural situatedness of music without having to adopt the axiom that there are no such things as absolute values.

32. Tia DeNora, *Music in Everyday Life* (Cambridge: Cambridge University Press, 2000), ix.

33. Wolterstorff, "Making a Work of Music," 127–28. See also Tom Wolfe, "The Worship of Art: Notes on the New God," in *The Philosophy of the Visual Arts*, ed. Philip Alperson (Oxford: Oxford University Press, 1992), 357–63.

34. Kaemmer, *Music in Human Life*, chap. 6.

35. For a fine and readable treatment of the variety of roles of music from an ethnomusicological angle, see Andrew H. Gregory, "The Roles of Music in Society: The Ethnomusicological Perspective," in *The Social Psychology of Music*, ed. D. Hargreaves and Adrian C. North (Oxford: Oxford University Press, 1997), 123–40.

36. Nicholas Wolterstorff, "Thinking about Church Music," in *Music in Christian Worship: At the Service of the Liturgy*, ed. Charlotte Kroeker (Collegeville, MN: Liturgical Press, 2005), 5ff. See also Nicholas Wolterstorff, *Art in Action: Toward a Christian Aesthetic* (Grand Rapids: Eerdmans, 1980), passim. I deal with these issues in relation to the arts in general, in Jeremy Begbie, *Voicing Creation's Praise: Towards a Theology of the Arts* (Edinburgh: T&T Clark, 1991), 186–204.

37. I draw extensively on DeNora, *Music in Everyday Life*, 11–14.

38. Bennett, *Cultures of Popular Music*, 130. See also Bennett, *Popular Music and Youth Culture: Music, Identity, and Place* (Basingstoke: Macmillan, 2000), esp. chap. 4.

39. "The Exodus Collective is illustrative of how dance music's capacity for bringing people together in the common space of the rave has functioned to produce a more concrete series of lifestyle strategies through which individuals engage with the social circumstances that confront them" (Bennett, *Cultures of Popular Music*, 131). Comparable proactive movements would be "Reclaim the Streets" and the "Anti-Road Protest" (see G. McKay, ed., *DIY Culture: Party and Protest in Nineties Britain* [London: Verso, 1998]).

40. For discussion of the spirituals as codified songs of protest, see James H. Cone, *The Spirituals and the Blues* (Maryknoll, NY: Orbis, 1998), esp. chaps. 1–5. The former slave and black leader Frederick Douglass wrote of singing these songs as a slave: "A keen observer might have detected in our repeated singing of 'O Canaan, sweet Canaan, I am bound for the land of Canaan,' something more than a hope of reaching heaven. We meant to reach the *North*, and the *North* was our Canaan" (as quoted in ibid., 80).

41. See Frank Burch Brown, *Good Taste, Bad Taste, and Christian Taste: Aesthetics in Religious Life* (Oxford: Oxford University Press, 2000), 162: "We should be careful not to imply that music simply replicates in an audible medium the preexisting social and inner realities of our world. Rap music and the hip-hop culture of which it is an integral part are not just an expression of contemporary African American urban life as it already exists . . . they constitute a new dimension of that life."

42. A stream of "ideological criticism" has laid massive stress on music as the product of power relations in society. See, e.g., L. Kramer, *Classical Music and Postmodern Knowledge* (Berkeley: University of California Press, 1995). Accordingly, "The critic must assume the role of undeceiver, enabling us to perceive truly what has been enchanted, mystified, and hallowed in the interests of power" (Roger Scruton, *The Aesthetics of Music* [Oxford: Clarendon, 1997], 428).

43. Rick Warren, *The Purpose-Driven Life* (Grand Rapids: Zondervan, 2002), 65.

44. George Steiner, *Real Presences: Is There Anything in What We Say?* (London: Faber & Faber, 1989), 217.

45. Tia DeNora, *After Adorno: Rethinking Music Sociology* (Cambridge: Cambridge University Press, 2003), 101.

46. Glennie explains: "For me, music is all about feelings and vibrations. Generally, I sense low sounds in my legs and feet and high sounds in my face and neck. So instead of hearing I am able to sense the

music in order to understand the harmonic makeup" (John Coutts, "Worship: More to It Than Meets the Ear," *Church Times* [2004]: 17). See the Music and the Deaf website: http://www.matd.org.uk.

47. DeNora, *Music in Everyday Life*, 161.

48. Both are discussed in Gregory, "Roles of Music in Society," 125.

49. Anthony Storr, *Music and the Mind* (New York: Ballantine, 1992), 33.

50. For a treatment of this theme by an ethnomusicologist, see John Blacking, *"A Commonsense View of All Music": Reflections on Percy Grainger's Contribution to Ethnomusicology and Music Education* (Cambridge: Cambridge University Press, 1987).

51. The literature on these matters is vast and growing. See, e.g., Jean-Jacques Nattiez, *Music and Discourse: Toward a Semiology of Music* (Princeton, NJ: Princeton University Press, 1990), 62–68; John Blacking, *How Musical Is Man?* (Seattle: University of Washington Press, 1973), 108–9; Sloboda, *Musical Mind*, 253–59; and, more boldly, Scruton, *Aesthetics of Music*, chap. 9. For evidence that demonstrates consistent cross-cultural patterns of response to music, see, e.g., Laura-Lee Balkwill and William Forde Thompson, "A Cross-Cultural Investigation of the Perception of Emotion in Music: Psychophysical and Cultural Cues," *Music Perception* 17, no. 1 (1999): 43–64; Laura-Lee Balkwill and William Thompson, "Recognition of Emotion in Japanese, Western, and Hindustani Music by Japanese Listeners," *Japanese Psychological Research* 46, no. 4 (2004): 337–49; and the useful discussions of musical universals in Nils L. Wallin, Björn Merker, and Steven Brown, eds., *The Origins of Music* (Cambridge, MA: MIT Press, 2001), 425–79.

52. The dead end of trying to explain music *solely* as human construction can be seen clearly in Nicholas Cook's (otherwise very fine) popular primer to music, *Music: A Very Short Introduction*. He insists that music "is *not* a phenomenon of the natural world but a human construction" (131). Yet this claim is made as if it were itself completely objective and impervious to the relativities of human culture—a highly questionable assumption (especially since it is such a recent idea). Not surprisingly, he has to indulge in all sorts of self-defeating positions: for example, with great passion he attacks the idea of "private consciousness" as a bourgeois social construction (128–29) and affirms that "human consciousness [is] something that is irreducibly public" (128). But why assume that this latter position is any less a social creation (thus temporary and in principle revisable) than the former? Or again, he is extremely keen that music becomes a means of social and personal transformation, but is *this* merely a socially constructed desire? What is missing is not only a facing up to the very strong (universal?) moral norms that seem to be assumed in his account but also to what is a remarkably commonsense observation—that music is rooted to some extent in the physical world (including the physicality of our bodies) and that this by no means precludes its being shaped *also* by human intentions, society, and culture. Why see this as an either-or?

53. It is a weakness of some heavily social and cultural theories of music that they are so concerned with actions that they forget the sounds themselves, so keen to point out what people do with and through musical sounds that they lose interest in the patterns of notes that people recognize and value as music.

54. For more detailed discussion, see Wolterstorff, *Art in Action*, 39–45; Jerome Stolnitz, "On the Origins of 'Aesthetic Disinterestedness,'" *Journal of Aesthetics and Art Criticism* (1961): 131–43.

55. Begbie, *Voicing Creation's Praise*, 233–55.

56. This is to be distinguished from ambiguity: a particular metaphor may be ambiguous—that is, capable of being understood in two or more ways—but the quality of metaphor I am getting at here is its inexhaustibility, which gives rise to an intense sense that we cannot spell out everything it could mean. For further discussion of ambiguity, see Kent Bach, "Ambiguity," in *Routledge Encyclopedia of Philosophy*, ed. Edward Craig (London: Routledge, 1998), 98–201.

57. This, I think, is what Calvin Seerveld is getting at when he speaks of art's distinctiveness in terms of "allusivity": "Peculiar to art is a parable character, a metaphorical intensity, an elusive play in its artifactual presentation of meanings apprehended" (Calvin Seerveld, *Rainbows for the Fallen World: Aesthetic Life and Artistic Task* [Toronto: Tuppence, 1980], 27).

58. Hilary Brand and Adrienne Chaplin, *Art and Soul: Signposts for Christians in the Arts* (Carlisle: Solway, 2001), 123.

59. Rowan Williams, *Grace and Necessity: Reflections on Art and Love* (London: Continuum, 2005), 135, 141.

60. Leonard Bernstein, *The Unanswered Question: Six Talks at Harvard* (Cambridge, MA: Harvard University Press, 1976), 131.

61. This is one of the key emphases of George Steiner's provocative study, *Real Presences*.

62. Nicholas Wolterstorff has explored this using the concept of "fittingness." See Wolterstorff, *Art in Action*, 96–121; or more briefly, Wolterstorff, "Thinking about Church Music."

63. Wayne Bowman writes: "I believe that appreciation of the uniquely and distinctly musical is of crucial significance to music students, and that addressing such concerns is among music philosophy's most fundamental obligations" (Bowman, *Philosophical Perspectives on Music*, 3). With a particular interest in cultural theory, Shepherd and Wicke comment: "It can be argued that *no* aspect of music is capable of being understood independently of the wider gamut of social and cultural processes. . . . Yet, *because* of this, it is possible that there are *aspects* of social and cultural processes which are revealed *uniquely* through their musical articulation. The *necessity* of referring to the wider gamut of social and cultural processes in order to explain 'the musical' does not in other words amount to a *sufficiency*. There are aspects of affect and meaning *in culture* that can only be accessed through an understanding of the specific qualities of the signifying practices of music as a cultural form: that is, its sounds" (John Shepherd and Peter Wicke, *Music and Cultural Theory* [Cambridge: Polity, 1997], 33–34).

64. On music meaning, the literature proliferates. For a sample, see Stephen Davies, *Musical Meaning and Expression* (Ithaca, NY: Cornell University Press, 1994); Peter Kivy, *Introduction to a Philosophy of Music* (Oxford: Clarendon, 2002); Scruton, *Aesthetics of Music*; Wilson Coker, *Music and Meaning: A Theoretical Introduction to Musical Aesthetics* (New York: Free Press, 1972); Leonard B. Meyer, *Emotion and Meaning in Music* (Chicago: University of Chicago Press, 1961); John A. Sloboda, *Exploring the Musical Mind: Cognition, Emotion, Ability, and Function* (Oxford: Oxford University Press, 2005), chaps. 7 and 8.

65. As Julian Johnson puts it, music is not a "sublinguistic accompaniment to thinking in words," but "presents specifically music ideas through specifically musical forms" (Johnson, *Who Needs Classical Music?* 61).

66. Davies, *Musical Meaning and Expression*, chap. 2; Scruton, *Aesthetics of Music*, chap. 5.

67. The point is made by many writers, often drawing on the concept of "affordance"—music "affords" resources that we actively appropriate for particular uses. See DeNora, *Music in Everyday Life*, 39–41.

68. Laura Smit writes of the influence of music on our patterns of romantic attraction: "Sometimes music is used not as a tool for moving on but rather as a tool for remaining in the pathos of the painful experience, for reliving the rejection, for keeping alive a fantasy that should have been allowed to die. One woman told of the pain she experienced during her senior year in high school when the boy she was in love with began to date her best friend. She listened to a particular CD over and over, and now, she says, 'I really can't listen to it without feeling like it's the spring of graduation year'" (Laura Smit, *Loves Me, Loves Me Not: The Ethics of Unrequited Love* [Grand Rapids: Baker Academic, 2005], 165).

69. C. S. Areni and D. Kim, "The Influence of Background Music on Shopping Behavior: Classical versus Top-Forty Music in a Wine Store," *Advances in Consumer Research* 20 (1993): 336–40.

70. Adrian C. North, David J. Hargreaves, and Jennifer McKendrick, "In-Store Music Affects Product Choice," *Nature* 390 (1997): 132.

71. Nicholas Cook, *Analysing Musical Multimedia* (Oxford: Clarendon, 1998), 92.

Chapter 2 Music in Action in Biblical Times

1. See the surveys by Ivor H. Jones, "Music and Musical Instruments," in *The Anchor Bible Dictionary*, vol. 4, ed. David Noel Freedman (New York: Doubleday, 1992), 930–39; Joachim Braun, *Music in Ancient Israel/Palestine: Archaeological, Written, and Comparative Sources*, trans. Douglas Stott (Grand Rapids: Eerdmans, 2002), 8–45; Jeremy Montagu, *Musical Instruments of the Bible* (Lanham, MD: Scarecrow, 2002), chap. 1. See also John W. Kleinig, *The Lord's Song: The Basis, Function, and Significance of Choral Music in Chronicles* (Sheffield: JSOT Press, 1993), 79n1. For a useful collation of relevant passages, see David W. Music, *Instruments in Church: A Collection of Source Documents* (Lanham, MD: Scarecrow, 1998).

2. W. S. Smith, *Musical Aspects of the New Testament* (Amsterdam: Have, 1962), chap. 6.

3. Victor P. Hamilton, *The Book of Genesis: Chapters 1–17* (Grand Rapids: Eerdmans, 1990), 239.

4. Claus Westermann, *Genesis 1–11: A Commentary* (Minneapolis: Augsburg, 1984), 332; see also pp. 328, 342–44.

5. Cf. Ezek. 33:32–33, where the inattentiveness of the people to the prophet's message is compared to the attitude of people who listen to a sweet voice and a seductive tune.

6. Kleinig, *Lord's Song*, chap. 5.

7. Ibid., 180–81.

8. Ibid., 181.

9. Ibid., 84–89.

10. Ibid., 91–93. They served in groups, not as individuals. Priests were divided into sections or classes, each of which served duty in the temple, and the same applied to the Levitical musicians. These Levitical musicians were adult males and probably underwent lengthy training.

11. Ibid., 95.

12. Ibid., 96.

13. See the useful survey and discussion in Peter C. Craigie, *Psalms 1–50* (Waco: Word, 1983), 35–39.

14. "Excursus 1: The Meaning of SELAH (סֶלָה) in the Psalms," in Craigie, *Psalms 1–50*, 76–77.

15. Edward Foley, *Foundations of Christian Music: The Music of Pre-Constantinian Christianity* (Bramcote, Nottingham: Grove Books, 1992), 31–32.

16. C. S. Lewis, *The Magician's Nephew* (New York: HarperCollins, 2005); J. R. R. Tolkien, *The Silmarillion* (London: HarperCollins, 2004).

17. J. McKinnon, *Music in Early Christian Literature* (Cambridge: Cambridge University Press, 1987), 12–17.

18. Ralph P. Martin, *Worship in the Early Church* (Grand Rapids: Eerdmans, 1975), 39.

19. See Montagu, *Musical Instruments of the Bible*, chap. 7.

20. The instrument is also mentioned in passing in 1 Cor. 14:7 and Rev. 18:22.

21. See Anthony C. Thiselton, *The First Epistle to the Corinthians: A Commentary on the Greek Text* (Grand Rapids: Eerdmans, 2000), 1035–39.

22. In 1 Cor. 14 Paul picks up on musical instrument imagery in a similar way: in the case of either a flute or a lyre, "If they do not give distinct notes, how will anyone know what is being played? And if the bugle gives an indistinct sound, who will get ready for battle?" (vv. 7–8). Paul clinches the argument: "If in a tongue you utter speech that is not intelligible, how will anyone know what is being said?" (v. 9).

23. Larry Hurtado describes Alan Cabaniss's opinion—that there was no singing in earliest Christian worship—as "bizarre" (Larry W. Hurtado, *At the Origins of Christian Worship: The Context and Character of Earliest Christian Devotion* [Grand Rapids: Eerdmans, 2000], 87n56).

24. Foley, *Foundations of Christian Music*, 52.

25. For the major studies, see Larry W. Hurtado, *Lord Jesus Christ: Devotion to Jesus in Earliest Christianity* (Grand Rapids: Eerdmans, 2003), 147n61.

26. Hurtado, *At the Origins of Christian Worship*, 88; cf. Martin Hengel, "The Song about Christ in Earliest Worship," in *Studies in Early Christology*, ed. M. Hengel (Edinburgh: T&T Clark, 1995), 227–91. Having said this, caution is needed. Although the Psalter is quoted more than any other Old Testament book and very likely played a pivotal part in the reading of early Christian communities, the presence of psalms in Christian worship is not explicitly mentioned before the end of the second century CE. This is not to deny their use, but we should be careful not to assume too much about their prominence (Foley, *Foundations of Christian Music*, 59–60).

27. For further discussion of different types of song, see Foley, *Foundations of Christian Music*, 54–65.

28. I owe this insight to my former colleague at St. Andrews, Dr. Steven Guthrie.

29. Andrew T. Lincoln, *Ephesians* (Dallas: Word, 1990), 345–46; Foley, *Foundations of Christian Music*, 59n5.

30. Lincoln, *Ephesians*, 346. Lincoln points out that they are the three most common terms for religious songs in the Septuagint (the Greek translation of the Old Testament used by the New Testament authors) "and occur there interchangeably in the titles of the psalms" (ibid.).

31. This "likely refers to a song of praise" (Hurtado, *Lord Jesus Christ*, 147). See Thiselton, *First Epistle to the Corinthians*, 1134.

32. Could this be singing in tongues? This is unlikely, given Paul is speaking about "addressing one another" and given his preference for intelligible singing elsewhere. (See 1 Cor. 14:15, where Paul talks about singing with the depths of his being and with his mind.)

33. See esp. 1 Cor. 14:13, 16.

34. Translation from Thiselton, *First Epistle to the Corinthians*, 1081–82.

35. See, e.g., Ps. 30, which addresses God in the second person (vv. 1–3), then others in the congregation (vv. 4–5), before returning to speaking to God (vv. 6–12).

36. Pliny (ca. 112 CE) spoke of Christians who "recited to one another in turns a hymn to Christ as to a god" (*Epistles* 10.96.7). Compare passages in the book of Revelation, where we read of praise and worship—including sung praise—focused on God *and* the Lamb jointly (Rev. 5:8–10, 13–14; 7:9–12). It is likely that the author's own experience of worship influences his choice of language here. The inescapability, and indeed centrality, of Christ in early Christian worship is strongly emphasized by Hurtado, in what is the most thorough treatment of devotion to Christ as divine in the New Testament and early Christianity (see Hurtado, *Lord Jesus Christ*, esp. 148–49, 609–13).

37. Richard Bauckham, *God Crucified: Monotheism and Christology in the New Testament* (Carlisle: Paternoster, 1998), chap. 2.

38. The background to this may very well be the idea of David as the patron of praise (as in Chronicles); David's words are now assumed by Jesus (Kleinig, *Lord's Song*, 185). John Calvin wrote that Christ "is the chief Conductor of our hymns" (*The Epistle of Paul the Apostle to the Hebrews and the First and Second Epistles of St. Peter*, trans. T. H. L. Parker [Edinburgh: Oliver & Boyd, 1963], 27). Cf. John Wesley: "Christ declares the name of God, gracious and merciful, plenteous in goodness and truth, to all who believe, that they also may praise him. 'In the midst of the church will I sing praise unto thee'—as the precentor of the choir. This he did literally, in the midst of his apostles, on the night before his passion. And as it means, in a more general sense, setting forth the praise of God, he has done it in the church by his word and his Spirit; he still does, and will do it throughout all generations" (*Explanatory Notes upon the New Testament* [London: Epworth, 1976], 815–16). For a development of the theme, see Reggie Kidd, *With One Voice: Discovering Christ's Song in Our Worship* (Grand Rapids: Baker Books, 2005).

There is some controversy among scholars about whether the figure singing in Heb. 2:12 is the earthly Jesus, the exalted Jesus, or Jesus at his second coming. My own view is that this is the risen Christ singing in the midst of the church now but as the leader of the music of heaven, in which (through Christ) we can share, and the church's song is a foretaste of the worship of the new heaven and earth to come.

39. "Perhaps most noteworthy from the available evidence is the free, spontaneous nature of worship in Paul's churches, apparently orchestrated by the Spirit himself" (Gordon D. Fee, *Paul, the Spirit, and the People of God* [Peabody, MA: Hendrickson, 1996], 153).

40. For elaborations of this approach to worship, see Alan J. Torrance, *Persons in Communion: An Essay on Trinitarian Description and Human Participation* (Edinburgh: T&T Clark, 1996); Christopher J. Cocksworth, *Holy, Holy, Holy: Worshiping the Trinitarian God* (London: Darton, Longman & Todd, 1997).

41. See Foley, *Foundations of Christian Music*, 48.

42. Even Jesus mentions the trumpet: "So when you give to the needy, do not announce it with trumpets, as the hypocrites do in the synagogues and on the streets, to be honored by men" (Matt. 6:2 NIV). This may allude to a custom of blowing the trumpet when alms were collected or gifts given.

43. On this, see A. Z. Idelsohn, *Jewish Music in Its Historical Development* (New York: Schocken, 1967); W. J. Porter, "Music," in *Dictionary of New Testament Background*, ed. Craig Evans and Stanley E. Porter (Downers Grove, IL: InterVarsity, 2000), 711–19; E. Werner, "Music," in *The Interpreter's Dictionary of the Bible* (Nashville: Abingdon, 1991), 457–69. Suzanne Haèik-Vantoura, a French musicologist, has attempted a reconstruction based on extensive research. Her conclusions, however, remain controversial.

See Suzanne Haëik-Vantoura, *The Music of the Bible Revealed: The Deciphering of a Millenary Notation*, ed. John Wheeler (Berkeley: D. & F. Scott, 1991).

44. Braun, *Music in Ancient Israel/Palestine*, 37.

45. Paul F. Bradshaw, *The Search for the Origins of Christian Worship: Sources and Methods for the Study of Early Liturgy* (New York: Oxford University Press, 1992); Foley, *Foundations of Christian Music*, chap. 3.

46. Foley, *Foundations of Christian Music*, 43–44.

47. J. A. Smith, "The Ancient Synagogue, the Early Church, and Singing," *Music & Letters* 65 (1984): 1–16.

48. Idelsohn, *Jewish Music in Its Historical Development*.

Chapter 3 Music and God's Cosmic Order: The Great Tradition

1. Calvin R. Stapert's book, *A New Song for an Old World* (Grand Rapids: Eerdmans, 2007), on early Christian writing on music, reached me too late to consider in detail.

2. "[T]he fascination that surrounded, and still surrounds, the name of Pythagoras does not come, basically, from specific scientific connotations, or from the rational method of mathematics, and certainly not from the success of mathematical physics. More important is the feeling that there is a kind of knowing which penetrates to the very core of the universe, which offers truth as something at once beatific and comforting, and presents the human being as *cradled in a universal harmony*" (Walter Burkert, *Lore and Science in Ancient Pythagoreanism*, trans. Edwin L. Minar [Cambridge, MA: Harvard University Press, 1972], 482, italics mine).

3. For concise surveys of this tradition, see Wayne D. Bowman, *Philosophical Perspectives on Music* (New York: Oxford University Press, 1998), 19–68; and the entertaining account in Jamie James, *The Music of the Spheres: Music, Science, and the Natural Order of the Universe* (London: Abacus, 1993).

4. From Henry Vaughan, "The Morning-Watch," in *The Oxford Book of English Mystical Verse*, ed. D. H. S. Nicholson and A. H. E. Lee (Oxford: Clarendon, 1916), 58.

5. J. R. R. Tolkien, *The Silmarillion* (London: HarperCollins, 2004).

6. Joseph Ratzinger, *The Spirit of the Liturgy* (San Francisco: Ignatius, 2000), 40.

7. Shakespeare, *The Merchant of Venice* 5.1.54–62.

8. Ibid. 5.1.63–65.

9. M. L. West, *Ancient Greek Music* (Oxford: Clarendon, 1992), 234.

10. Plato, *Republic* 10.617b. This is not to be thought of as a thick eight-note chord but as an agreement of *successive* rather than *simultaneous* sounds. Western music had not yet developed to the point of having chords, or more than one melody sounding at the same time. See Thomas Mathiesen, "Problems of Terminology in Ancient Greek Theory: 'APMONIA," in *Festival Essays for Pauline Alderman*, ed. Burton Karson (Provo, UT: Brigham Young University, 1976), 3–17; Edward A. Lippman, *Musical Thought in Ancient Greece* (New York: Columbia University Press, 1964), 1–44.

11. Plato, *Timaeus* 47d.

12. Although the chief component of a mode was a fixed series of intervals between tones, it seems that other factors could shape its identity—e.g., the relative frequency of notes, rhythmic configurations, and tessitura (the degree to which high or low singing was required). See West, *Ancient Greek Music*, 178–79.

13. Music can, for example, portray bad things in a good light, "imparting an air of pleasantness to things that should not be experienced as such, and habituating people to accept as nature or inevitable things that are not" (Bowman, *Philosophical Perspectives on Music*, 41–42).

14. Plato, *Laws* 2.668.

15. A second-century treatise tellingly depicts Pythagoras as disdainful of the experience of the senses: "The grave Pythagoras rejected the judging of music by the sense of hearing, asserting that its excellence must be *apprehended by the mind*. This is why he did not judge it by the ear, but by the scale based on the proportions, and considered it sufficient to pursue the study no further than the octave" (Plutarch,

Plutarch's Moralia: In Fifteen Volumes, trans. Phillip H. de Lacy and Benedict Einarson [Cambridge, MA: Harvard University Press, 1967], 441; italics mine).

16. Henry Chadwick speaks of the Platonic tradition as regarding musical theory "not so much as a route to the better appreciation of the latest composition in the Lydian mode but rather to the mathematical design and order pervading the universe." He adds, perhaps too strongly: "The theory of music is akin to metaphysics, and the fact that it has something to do with sound is, for ancient theorists, almost an embarrassment" (Henry Chadwick, "Why Music in the Church?" in *Tradition and Exploration: Collected Papers on Theology and the Church*, ed. Henry Chadwick [Norwich: Canterbury Press, 1994], 208).

17. In the third book of the *Republic*, Plato is scathing about musical instruments that offer an excessive number of notes and scales and about the confusion created by complex rhythms. Words must determine mode, rhythm, meter, and melody (*Republic* 3.398–403c).

18. Plotinus, *Fifth Ennead* 9.11.

19. Plotinus, *Fourth Ennead* 9.8.

20. Plotinus, *First Ennead* 3.1.

21. Henry Chadwick, *Boethius: The Consolations of Music, Logic, Theology, and Philosophy* (Oxford: Clarendon, 1981), 249–50.

22. Augustine, *Enarrations on the Psalms* 42.7.

23. Augustine, *On Music (De Musica)*, trans. Robert Catesby Taliaferro, in *The Fathers of the Church: A New Translation*, vol. 4 (New York: CIMA, 1947), 153–379.

24. Nancy van Deusen, "Musica, De," in *Augustine through the Ages: An Encyclopedia*, ed. Allan D. Fitzgerald et al. (Grand Rapids: Eerdmans, 1999), 575. The exact extent of *De Musica*'s influence on subsequent generations is actually quite difficult to assess. For discussion, see Steven Guthrie, "Carmen Universitatis: A Theological Study of Music and Measure" (PhD diss., University of St. Andrews, 2000), 218n24. See also W. F. Jackson Knight, *St. Augustine's "De Musica": A Synopsis* (London: Orthological Institute, 1947). In this section, I am deeply grateful to Dr. Carol Harrison for her very fine article, "Augustine and the Art of Music," in *Musical Theology*, ed. Jeremy Begbie and Steven Guthrie (Grand Rapids: Eerdmans, forthcoming).

25. For a lucid summary of the development and different contexts of *musica*, see Calvin M. Bower, "The Transmission of Ancient Music Theory into the Middle Ages," in *The Cambridge History of Western Music Theory*, ed. Thomas Christensen (Cambridge: Cambridge University Press, 2002), 136–67.

26. Herbert M. Schueller, *The Idea of Music: An Introduction to Musical Aesthetics in Antiquity and the Middle Ages* (Kalamazoo, MI: Medieval Institute Publications, 1988), 250.

27. Harrison, "Augustine and the Art of Music."

28. Augustine, *Eighty-three Different Questions* 83, 46, 2. If this sounds like salvation by intellectual works, we would be mistaken. Augustine is quite clear that we are saved by grace alone. Nonetheless, this does not preclude music—both in the sense of the numerical proportions of creation and in the sense of something made and heard—playing a part in God's gracious, reconciling work.

29. Clement of Alexandria (*Protrepticus* 9, PG 8) famously uses the image of the Word as the leader of the choir, creating "one symphony." The unison song—which would have included singing in octaves, to accommodate men, women, and children—became "an image of the unity and harmony of all Christians" (Johannes Quasten, *Music and Worship in Pagan and Christian Antiquity* [Washington, DC: National Association of Pastoral Musicians, 1983], 67).

30. Paul Westermeyer, *Te Deum: The Church and Music* (Minneapolis: Fortress, 1998), 78–81.

31. This deep antipathy is very evident in, among others, Tertullian (ca. 160–ca. 225), Basil the Great (ca. 330–79), Ambrose (ca. 339–97), and John Chrysostom (ca. 347–407). See ibid., chap. 5; J. McKinnon, *Music in Early Christian Literature* (Cambridge: Cambridge University Press, 1987), 1–4.

32. Augustine, *Confessions* 9.6.14.

33. Ibid. 10.33.49.

34. Augustine, *On the Trinity* 4.2.4.

35. Augustine, *On Free Will* 2.13.35.

36. Augustine, *Confessions* 10.33.50. "I feel that when the sacred words are chanted well, our souls are moved and are more religiously and with a warmer devotion kindled to piety than if they are not so

sung. All the diverse emotions of our spirit have their various modes in voice and chant appropriate in each case, and are stirred by a mysterious inner kinship. But my physical delight, which has to be checked from enervating the mind, often deceives me when the perception of the senses is unaccompanied by reason, and is not patiently content to be in a subordinate place. It tries to be first and in the leading role, though it deserves to be allowed only as secondary to reason. So in these matters I sin unawares, and only afterwards become aware of it" (ibid. 10.33.49).

37. Ibid. 10.33.50.

38. Chadwick, "Why Music in the Church?" 208.

39. Harrison, "Augustine and the Art of Music."

40. The issues are well brought out in Colin E. Gunton, "Creation and Re-creation: An Exploration of Some Themes in Aesthetics and Theology," *Modern Theology* 2, no. 1 (1985): 1–19; see also *The Triune Creator: A Historical and Systematic Study* (Edinburgh: Edinburgh University Press, 1998), 73–86.

41. See Boethius, *Fundamentals of Music*, trans. C. M. Bower (New Haven: Yale University Press, 1989). For an eminently clear account of Boethius's conception of music, see Chadwick, *Boethius*, 78–101. See also John Caldwell, "The *De Institutione Arithmetica* and the *De Institutione Musica*," in *Boethius: His Life Thought and Influence*, ed. Margaret Gibson (Oxford: Blackwell, 1981), 135–54; and the fine dissertation by my former graduate student at Cambridge, Férdia Stone-Davis, "Musical Perception and the Resonance of the Material: With Special Reference to Immanuel Kant and Anicius Manlius Severinus Boethius" (PhD diss., University of Cambridge, 2005).

42. Chadwick, *Boethius*, 101.

43. Boethius, *De institutione musica* 1.2.

44. Bower, "Transmission of Ancient Music Theory," 147.

45. Chadwick, *Boethius*, 86.

46. Quentin Faulkner, *Wiser Than Despair: The Evolution of Ideas in the Relationship of Music and the Christian Church* (Westport, CT: Greenwood, 1996), 186–87.

47. Chadwick, *Boethius*, 85–87.

48. The issues are dealt with deftly in Chadwick, *Boethius*, esp. chaps. 4 and 5.

49. For a magisterial survey of classical and Christian ideas of world harmony, see Leo Spitzer, *Classical and Christian Ideas of World Harmony: Prolegomena to an Interpretation of the Word "Stimmung"* (Baltimore: Johns Hopkins Press, 1963).

50. Kathi Meyer-Baer, *Music of the Spheres and the Dance of Death: Studies in Musical Iconology* (Princeton, NJ: Princeton University Press, 1974).

51. Pseudo-Dionysius the Areopagite, *Celestial Hierarchy* (Leiden: Brill, 1959).

52. Quoted in Bower, "Transmission of Ancient Music Theory," 163.

53. Donald Jay Grout, *A History of Western Music* (London: Dent, 1973), 56.

54. Bower, "Transmission of Ancient Music Theory," 158–59.

55. Quoted in W. Oliver Strunk, *Source Readings in Music History: Antiquity and the Middle Ages* (London: Faber & Faber, 1981), 125.

56. It is noteworthy that although the *Musica enchiriadis* text cites Boethius, and the Pythagorean tradition is known and respected, it also attempts to do justice to the principal work of the monastic calling—the daily singing of the divine office. The tension between the two, and the way in which the author is keen to relate them, is skillfully brought out in C. M. Bower, "'*Adhuc ex parte et in enigmate cernimus . . .*' Reflections on the Closing Chapters of *Musica Enchiriadis*," in *Music in the Mirror: Reflections on the History of Music Theory and Literature for the 21st Century*, ed. Andreas Giger and Thomas J. Mathiesen (Lincoln: University of Nebraska Press, 2002), 21–44.

57. See Richard L. Crocker, *An Introduction to Gregorian Chant* (New Haven: Yale University Press, 2000).

58. Bower, "Transmission of Ancient Music Theory," 159.

59. Ibid., 158–64.

60. For an authoritative treatment, see David Hiley, *Western Plainchant: A Handbook* (Oxford: Clarendon, 1995), 461–63. I am very grateful to Dr. Sam Barrett for clarifying this matter.

61. See Gunton, *Triune Creator*, chap. 5; T. F. Torrance, *Divine and Contingent Order* (Oxford: Oxford University Press, 1981); Alister E. McGrath, *A Scientific Theology*, Vol. 1, *Nature* (Edinburgh: T&T Clark, 2001), esp. part 2.

62. The critical issue at stake here is the vexed question of the *analogia entis* (analogy of being). See below, p. 341n31.

63. Claude V. Palisca, *Humanism in Italian Renaissance Musical Thought* (New Haven: Yale University Press, 1985), 19. Salinas was by no means the first to question the idea of the music of the spheres. Aristotle's doubts (see below n. 66) were echoed, for example, by writers such as Johannes de Grocheio (writing ca. 1300).

64. As in ibid., 346.

65. Daniel K. L. Chua, *Absolute Music and the Construction of Meaning* (Cambridge: Cambridge University Press, 1999), chap. 3. For further explanation, see below, p. 252; see also p. 229.

66. Thomas J. Mathiesen, "Greek Music Theory," in *The Cambridge History of Western Music Theory*, ed. Thomas Christensen (Cambridge: Cambridge University Press, 2002), 109–35. Aristotle (384–322 BCE) had contested Plato's belief that numbers are substances and that the planets emit unheard sounds (*Metaphysics* 985b32–986a2, 1090a20–23, 1093a28–b4; *On the Heavens* 290b21–23).

67. Palisca, *Humanism*, 21; italics mine.

68. The proposal, significantly, comes in the course of commending an educational program based on the notion of "altering" the human personality through the imitative power of the arts (ibid., 337). See Chua, *Absolute Music*, 34–35; Don Hárran, *Word-Tone Relations in Musical Thought: From Antiquity to the Seventeenth Century* (Neuhausen-Stuttgart: American Institute of Musicology, 1986), 72–73.

69. Chua, *Absolute Music*, 3.

70. Julian Johnson, *Who Needs Classical Music?* (Oxford: Oxford University Press, 2002), 13.

Chapter 4 A Sixteenth-Century Trio

1. John Hollander, *The Untuning of the Sky: Ideas of Music in English Poetry, 1500–1700* (New York: Norton, 1970). The phrase comes from the last line of John Dryden's "Song for St Cecilia's Day" (1687)—"and Musick shall untune the sky." Dryden was alluding to the effects of the last trumpet of the day of judgment; Hollander uses the phrase to speak of the early modern demythologizing of music.

2. Martin Luther, *D. Martin Luthers Werke: Kritische Gesamtausgabe*, vol. 30.2 (Weimar: H. Böhlau, 1909), 557, no. 6248.

3. The classic work of Oskar Söhngen in *Theologie der Musik* (Kassel: Johannes Stauda-Verlag, 1967) has been challenged in a number of important respects; see, e.g., Joyce L. Irwin, *Neither Voice nor Heart Alone: German Lutheran Theology of Music in the Age of the Baroque* (New York: Peter Lang, 1993). Other important studies of Luther on music include Paul Nettl, *Luther and Music*, trans. Frida Best and Ralph Wood (New York: Russell & Russell, 1967); Patrice Veit, *Das Kirchenlied in der Reformation Martin Luthers: Eine thematische und semantische Untersuchung* (Stuttgart: Franz Steiner Verlag, 1986); Gracia Grindal, "Luther and the Arts: A Study in Convention," *Word and World* 3 (1983): 373–81; Jean-Denis Kraage, "Luther: Théologien de la Musique," *Études Théologiques et Religieuses* 58 (1983): 449–63; Carl Schalk, *Luther on Music: Paradigms of Praise* (St. Louis: Concordia, 1988).

4. "The danger for modern interpreters . . . has been the desire to focus, for the sake of clarity and simplicity, on one saying of Luther as the key to the whole Luther. To do so is to ignore the tensions with which Luther lives and the paradoxical perspective from which he combined apparent opposites" (Irwin, *Neither Voice nor Heart Alone*, 7).

5. Martin Luther, *Luther's Works*, vol. 53, *Liturgy and Hymns*, ed. Gottfried G. Krodel and Helmut T. Lehman (Philadelphia: Fortress, 1965), 321–23.

6. Martin Luther, *Luther's Works*, vol. 49, *Letters II*, ed. Gottfried G. Krodel and Helmut T. Lehman (Philadelphia: Fortress, 1972), 428.

7. Ibid., 427–28.

8. See John Butt, *Music Education and the Art of Performance in the German Baroque* (Cambridge: Cambridge University Press, 1994); Joe E. Tarry, "Music in the Educational Philosophy of Martin Luther," *Journal of Research in Music Education* 21 (1973): 355–65.

9. Oskar Söhngen, "Music and Theology: A Systematic Approach," in *Sacred Sound: Music in Religious Thought and Practice*, ed. Joyce Irwin (Chico, CA: Scholars Press, 1983), 12–13.

10. Brian L. Horne, "A Civitas of Sound: On Luther and Music," *Theology* 88 (1985): 27.

11. Luther, *Luther's Works*, 53:321, 324.

12. This is not to say that music for Luther has the status of one of the "orders of creation," in his fairly restricted sense, i.e., structures that order and make divine-human and human-human relationships possible (e.g., church, home). I am grateful to Dr. Mickey Mattox for pointing this out to me.

13. Luther, *Luther's Works,* 53:322.

14. Ibid., 324.

15. Rebecca Wagner Oettinger, *Music as Propaganda in the German Reformation* (Aldershot: Ashgate, 2001), 41–44. See also Martin Luther, *Luther's Works*, vol. 1, *Lectures on Genesis Chapters 1–5*, ed. Jaroslav J. Pelikan (Philadelphia: Fortress, 1958), 126: "We do not marvel at the countless other gifts of creation, for we have become deaf toward what Pythagoras aptly terms this wonderful and most lovely music coming from the harmony of the motions that are in the celestial spheres. But because men continually hear this music, they become deaf to it. . . . [The fathers of the church] did not want to be understood as though sound were given off by the motion of the celestial bodies. What they wanted to say was that their nature was most lovely and altogether miraculous, but that we ungrateful and insensible people did not notice it or give due thanks to God for the miraculous establishment and preservation of his creation." Luther, it seems, understands the myth of the harmony of the spheres as a powerful metaphor for the God's ordering of creation.

16. The point is well made in Schalk, *Luther on Music*, 18–30. See Ivor H. Jones, *Music: A Joy for Ever* (London: Epworth, 1989), 71: "This . . . has sometimes been spoken of as Luther's main contribution to aesthetics, an emphasis on music sung and heard which he discovered in the practical music-making of his own education." We should note, however, that Luther did not lose his conviction about the grounding of music in the created order; perhaps his most important contribution to aesthetics is his ability to hold these different interests together.

17. As Gunton notes, the accent falls less on the relation of God to the soul than on the relation of God to the human person as physical creature. Colin E. Gunton, *The Triune Creator: A Historical and Systematic Study* (Edinburgh: Edinburgh University Press, 1998), 149.

18. Ibid., 148.

19. Luther, *Luther's Works*, 1:39.

20. Gunton, *Triune Creator*, 149.

21. Martin Luther, *Luther's Works*, vol. 17, *Lectures on Isaiah 40–66*, ed. Hilton C. Oswald (Philadelphia: Fortress, 1972), 356.

22. Luther, *Luther's Works,* 53:319–20.

23. Ibid., 324.

24. Luther, *D. Martin Luthers Werke*, 30.2:696. The view that music could drive away the devil had many medieval precedents.

25. Luther, *Luther's Works*, 53:319–20.

26. I am particularly grateful to Dr. Joyce Irwin for what follows in this section.

27. Irwin, *Neither Voice nor Heart Alone*, 1–7.

28. Martin Luther, *Luther's Works*, vol. 54, *Table Talk*, ed. Theodore G. Tappert and Helmut T. Lehman (Philadelphia: Fortress, 1967), 129–30.

29. Luther, *Luther's Works*, 53:323.

30. Söhngen, *Theologie der Musik*, 228–29.

31. Here Krummacher's study is significant: Christoph Krummacher, *Musik als Praxis Pietatis* (Göttingen: Vandenhoeck & Ruprecht, 1994).

32. Söhngen, *Theologie der Musik*, 95.

33. Luther, *Luther's Works* 53:323–24; see also 53:316. In his Preface to the *Babst Hymnal* (1545), he declares: "God has cheered our hearts and minds through his dear Son, whom he gave for us to redeem us from sin, death, and the devil. He who believes this earnestly cannot be quiet about it. But he must gladly and willingly sing and speak about it so that others may also come and hear it. And whoever does not want to sing and speak of it shows that he does not believe and that he does not belong under the new and joyful testament, but under the old, lazy, and tedious testament" (ibid., 53:333).

34. Ibid., 53:323.

35. See, e.g., Luther, *Luther's Works*, 49:427–29.

36. Martin Luther, *D. Martin Luthers Werke: Kritische Gesamtausgabe*, vol. 4 (Weimar: H. Böhlau, 1916), 313, no. 4441.

37. Martin Luther, *D. Martin Luthers Werke: Kritische Gesamtausgabe*, vol. 3 (Weimar: H. Böhlau, 1885), 40. It needs to be recognized that in some writings Luther shows signs of a less positive attitude to music, especially in the preface to the *Deutsche Masse* (1526), where he seems to suggest music is a concession to human weakness. Söhngen argues that this is evidence of an unresolved tension in Luther's early years between a liturgical-pedagogical approach and a theological approach, the former corresponding to a tendency to treat music solely within a devotional, psychological framework. In due course, Söhngen sees a shift to a more integrated theological approach: "Where the young Luther spoke psychologically, the mature Luther speaks theologically concerning music" (Söhngen, *Theologie der Musik*, 108).

38. With meticulous attention to the sources, Joseph Herl strongly challenges the popular view that Luther promoted congregational singing at the expense of the choral liturgy and the view that he insisted on the total abandonment of Latin for the sake of the vernacular (Joseph Herl, *Worship Wars in Early Lutheranism* [Oxford: Oxford University Press, 2004], chap. 1). It should be noted that the *German Mass* of 1526 was almost entirely in German, but this was only for villages and towns where Latin was not understood; it was not well received in Wittenberg, where the principal service during Luther's lifetime was the choral mass in Latin.

39. For a balanced assessment, see Schalk, *Luther on Music*, 25–30.

40. For a thorough treatment of the impact of Lutheran hymns on the Reformation, see Christopher Boyd Brown, *Singing the Gospel: Lutheran Hymns and the Success of the Reformation* (Cambridge, MA: Harvard University Press, 2005); see also Robert L. Marshall, *Luther, Bach, and the Early Reformation Chorale* (Atlanta: Pitts Theology Library, 1995).

41. Schalk, *Luther on Music*, 42.

42. "Any view of Luther as a radical liturgical reformer is fundamentally mistaken. While certain new emphases did indeed characterise Luther's reforms . . . what is striking about Luther's approach is its basic conservatism" (Carl Schalk, *Music in Early Lutheranism: Shaping the Tradition (1524–1672)* [St. Louis: Concordia, 2001], 18–19).

43. Paul Westermeyer, *Te Deum: The Church and Music* (Minneapolis: Fortress, 1998), 148. For further discussion, see Irwin, *Neither Voice nor Heart Alone*, 36–37; Erik Routley, *The Music of Christian Hymns* (Chicago: G. I. A., 1981), 21. It needs to be acknowledged, however, that German songs (some of them Luther's own songs, and "popular" in the sense of widely accessible) played a key part in the growth and dissemination of Lutheran Protestantism. See Oettinger, *Music as Propaganda in the German Reformation*.

44. Herl, *Worship Wars in Early Lutheranism*, 21.

45. Schalk, *Luther on Music*, 35. Cf. Herl, *Worship Wars in Early Lutheranism*, chap. 1.

46. See Friedrich Blume, *Protestant Church Music: A History* (New York: Norton, 1974), esp. 3–123.

47. For a fuller version of this material, see Jeremy Begbie, "Music, Word, and Theology Today: Learning from John Calvin," in *Theology in Dialogue: The Impact of the Arts, Humanities, and Science on Contemporary Religious Thought*, ed. Lyn Holness and Ralf Wüstenberg (Grand Rapids: Eerdmans, 2002), 3–27.

48. Buszin, for example, speaks of "Calvin's indifference, or rather hostility, to music" (W. E. Buszin, "Luther on Music," *Musical Quarterly* 32 [1946]: 80).

49. The most useful secondary sources for understanding Calvin's theology of music are Charles Garside, "The Origins of Calvin's Theology of Music: 1536–1543," *Transactions of the American Philo-*

sophical Society 69 (1979): 4–35; Jeffrey T. VanderWilt, "John Calvin's Theology of Liturgical Song," *Christian Scholar's Review* 25, no. 1 (1995): 63–82; John D. Witvliet, "The Spirituality of the Psalter in Calvin's Geneva," in *Worship Seeking Understanding: Windows into Christian Practice* (Grand Rapids: Baker Academic, 2003), 203–29; Frank Burch Brown, "Religious Music and Secular Music: A Calvinist Perspective, Re-formed," *Theology Today* 60 (2006): 11–21. These surpass earlier pieces such as Émile Doumergue, "Music in the Work of Calvin," *Princeton Theological Review* 7 (1909): 529–52; Walter Blankenburg, "Calvin," in *Die Musik in Geschichte und Gegenwart* (Kassel: Bärenreiter-Verlag, 1952), 653–66; and Oskar Söhngen, "Fundamental Considerations for a Theology of Music," in *The Musical Heritage of the Church*, ed. Theodore Hoelty-Nickel (St. Louis: Concordia, 1963), 7–16.

50. For a fine treatment, see Witvliet, "Spirituality of the Psalter in Calvin's Geneva."

51. John Calvin, *Ioannis Calvini Opera Quae Supersunt Omnia*, ed. Guilielmus Baum, Eduard Cunitz, and Eduard Reuss, vol. 10 (Brunsvigae: C. A. Schwetschke, 1871), 6.

52. Garside, "Origins of Calvin's Theology of Music," 6–7.

53. Ibid., 10–14.

54. Calvin, *Opera Quae Supersunt Omnia*, 10:12.

55. Ibid.

56. Ibid., 6; italics mine.

57. "[Jabal's] brother's name was Jubal; he was the ancestor of all those who play the lyre and pipe."

58. John Calvin, *Ioannis Calvini Opera Quae Supersunt Omnia*, ed. Guilielmus Baum, Eduard Cunitz, and Eduard Reuss, vol. 23 (Brunsvigae: C. A. Schwetschke, 1882), 100.

59. John Calvin, "Genevan Psalter: Foreword," in *Source Readings in Music History: From Classical Antiquity through the Romantic Era*, ed. Oliver Strunk (New York: Norton, 1950), 346.

60. Ibid., 347.

61. Carlos Eire notes that the two most commonly used phrases summing up Calvin's main concern for worship are *soli Deo gloria* ("to God alone be the glory") and *finitum non est capax infiniti* ("the finite is not capable of the infinite") (Carlos M. N. Eire, *War against the Idols: The Reformation of Worship from Erasmus to Calvin* [Cambridge: Cambridge University Press, 1986], 197).

62. Luther, *Luther's Works* 53:323; italics mine.

63. John Calvin, *Ioannis Calvini Opera Quae Supersunt Omnia*, ed. Guilielmus Baum, Eduard Cunitz, and Eduard Reuss, vol. 20 (Brunsvigae: C. A. Schwetschke, 1879), 183.

64. Cf. Stephen Edmondson, *Calvin's Christology* (Cambridge: Cambridge University Press, 2004); Alasdair Heron, *Table and Tradition: Towards an Ecumenical Understanding of the Eucharist* (Edinburgh: Handsel, 1983), 122–37; B. A. Gerrish, *Grace and Gratitude: The Eucharistic Theology of John Calvin* (Minneapolis: Fortress, 1993).

65. Calvin, "Genevan Psalter: Foreword," 347.

66. Calvin, *Institutio* 3.20.31. Compare his foreword to the Genevan Psalter: "We must remember what Saint Paul says—that spiritual songs cannot be well sung save with the heart" ("Genevan Psalter: Foreword," 346). See also his comments on Eph. 5:18: "For [Paul] does not enjoin each one to sing inwardly, but then he adds, *singing in your hearts*, it is as if he had said, 'From the heart and not only on the tongue, like hypocrites'" (John Calvin, *The Epistles of the Apostle Paul to the Galatians, Ephesians, Philippians, and Colossians*, trans. T. H. L. Parker [Grand Rapids: Eerdmans, 1980], 203). Compare his comments on Col. 3: "As we ought to stir up others, so also we ought to sing from the heart, that there may not be merely an outward sound with the mouth. Yet we must not understand it as though [Paul] is telling everyone to sing inwardly to himself, but he wants both to be conjoined, provided the heart precedes the tongue" (Calvin, *Galatians, Ephesians, Philippians, and Colossians*, 353).

67. Witvliet, "Spirituality of the Psalter in Calvin's Geneva," 211.

68. Calvin, "Genevan Psalter: Foreword," 348; italics mine.

69. Calvin, *Institutio* 3.20.32.

70. Ibid.

71. Calvin, "Genevan Psalter: Foreword," 347.

72. Calvin, *Institutio* 3.20.32.

73. In the Strasbourg Psalter (1539), Calvin includes a sung creed (the words are arranged by Calvin himself), but he omits it in the 1542 edition.

74. Witvliet, "Spirituality of the Psalter in Calvin's Geneva," 223–25.

75. Calvin, "Genevan Psalter: Foreword," 346.

76. Witvliet, "Spirituality of the Psalter in Calvin's Geneva," 229.

77. Garside, "Origins of Calvin's Theology of Music," 24–25; Witvliet, "Spirituality of the Psalter in Calvin's Geneva," 219–23. For further discussion, see Burch Brown, "Religious Music and Secular Music."

78. Instrumental music was instituted for those "yet tender, like children" being trained under the law; in contrast, "the voice of man . . . assuredly excels all inanimate instruments of music." Purely instrumental music is like the "unknown tongue" that Paul shuns in 1 Cor. 14 (Calvin, "Genevan Psalter: Foreword," 346). What, then, of the references to instruments in worship in the Old Testament? He regards this as God's concession to infirmity—the Jews needed every possible incitement to spirituality. Unlike in the contemporary Roman Church, instruments were employed in a pious, godly way. But the Jews were in religious infancy. With the coming of Christ, all such "external" aids are rendered unnecessary and are more likely to impede rather than assist access to God. See H. P. Clive, "The Calvinist Attitude to Music," *Bibliothèque d'Humanisme et Renaissance* 19 (1957): 91–94. For a useful collection of references to musical instruments in Calvin's works, see David W. Music, *Instruments in Church: A Collection of Source Documents* (Lanham, MD: Scarecrow, 1998), 59–63.

79. See Music, *Instruments in Church*, 55–57.

80. See p. 85.

81. Most of the melodies have their origin in existing models. The roots of most of the Genevan melodies are very likely in medieval church songs; the more immediate models are hard to determine. As far as the first Strasbourg Psalter (1539) is concerned, it seems that a number of the melodies originated in Strasbourg, especially in the work of the musician Matthäus Greitter. See Ford Lewis Battles, *The Piety of John Calvin: An Anthology Illustrative of the Spirituality of the Reformer* (Grand Rapids: Baker Academic, 1978), 144–65. The musician who most influenced the 1562 edition—the first complete version—was Louis Bourgeois, who arrived in Geneva in 1545. See Walter Blankenburg, "Church Music in Reformed Europe," in Blume, *Protestant Church Music*, 520–21.

82. See, e.g., Irwin, *Neither Voice nor Heart Alone*.

83. The classic text on Zwingli and the arts (including music) is Charles Garside, *Zwingli and the Arts* (New Haven: Yale University Press, 1966).

84. Bernhard Wyss, quoted in ibid., 22.

85. Ibid., 23.

86. See Alister E. McGrath, *Reformation Thought: An Introduction* (Oxford: Blackwell, 1999), 44–45.

87. W. P. Stephens, *Zwingli: An Introduction to His Thought* (Oxford: Clarendon, 1992), 30.

88. Quoted in Garside, *Zwingli and the Arts*, 39.

89. Quoted in ibid., 38.

90. Quoted in ibid., 44.

91. Quoted in ibid., 51.

92. Ibid., 58.

93. Zwingli was quite prepared to back up his scriptural case by appealing to nontheological factors, even though he believed the scriptural case could stand quite well on its own.

94. McGrath, *Reformation Thought*, 134.

95. Quoted in Garside, *Zwingli and the Arts*, 37.

96. Stephens, *Zwingli*, 65. For a full account, see W. P. Stephens, *The Theology of Huldrych Zwingli* (Oxford: Clarendon, 1986), chap. 6.

97. Stephens, *Theology of Huldrych Zwingli*, chaps. 9–11; Alasdair Heron, *Table and Tradition*, 114–22.

98. Quoted in Stephens, *Zwingli*, 82.

99. Garside, *Zwingli and the Arts*, 66–67.

100. Ibid., 74.

101. See ibid., 65–69.

102. Ibid., 74.

Chapter 5 Wise beyond Words

1. Painted in 1748 by the court painter at Dresden, Elias Gottlob Haussmann.

2. Boyd's words about Bach in this painting (Malcolm Boyd, *Bach* [Oxford: Oxford University Press, 2000], 228).

3. Quoted in Robert L. Marshall, *The Music of Johann Sebastian Bach: The Sources, the Style, the Significance* (New York: Schirmer, 1989), 70–71.

4. For a particularly fine and readable study of his life and thought, see Boyd, *Bach*. See also Christoph Wolff, *Johann Sebastian Bach: The Learned Musician* (New York: Norton, 2000); Peter F. Williams, *The Life of Bach* (Cambridge: Cambridge University Press, 2004).

5. Joyce L. Irwin, *Neither Voice nor Heart Alone: German Lutheran Theology of Music in the Age of the Baroque* (New York: Peter Lang, 1993), 141.

6. Research in the 1950s and 1960s sought to challenge the dominant view, inherited from the nineteenth century, that—in Friedrich Blume's words—"turned Bach into the great Lutheran cantor, the retrospective champion of tradition, the orthodox preacher of the Bible and the chorale . . . [fostering] the conception of Bach as supremely the church musician, and the ascendancy of the churchman over the musician" (Friedrich Blume, "Outlines of a New Picture of Bach," *Music and Letters* 44 [1963]: 214). Studies of the chronology of Bach's works indicate that Bach ceased to write religious music in the early 1730s (Alfred Dürr, *Zur Chronologie der Leipziger Vokalwerke J. S. Bachs* [Berlin: Evangelische Verlagsanstalt, 1958]; G. von Dadelson, *Beiträge zur Chronologie der Werke Johann Sebastian Bachs* [Trossingen: Hohner Verlag, 1958]). Some have even claimed that Bach's avowed commitment to Lutheranism was a mere convenience. In Blume's oft-quoted words: "Did Bach have a special liking for church work? Was it a spiritual necessity for him? Hardly. There is at any rate no evidence that it was. Bach the supreme cantor, the creative servant of the Word of God, the staunch Lutheran, is a legend. It will have to be buried along with all the other traditional and beloved romantic illusions" (Blume, "Outlines of a New Picture," 218). Since then, however, the discovery of the Calov Bible (see below), research on the contents of Bach's own library, and recognition of the fact that he was composing religious music well after 1730 have, together with other findings, led to a more balanced picture. See C. Trautmann, "J. S. Bach: New Light on His Faith," *Concordia Theological Monthly* 42 (1971): 88–99; Robin A. Leaver, "The Mature Vocal Works and Their Theological and Liturgical Context," in *The Cambridge Companion to Bach*, ed. John Butt (Cambridge: Cambridge University Press, 1997), 36–40; Calvin Stapert, "Bach as Theologian: A Review Article," *Reformed Journal* 37 (1987): 19–27.

7. H. H. Cox, ed., *The Calov Bible of J. S. Bach* (Ann Arbor, MI: UMI Research Press, 1985); Trautmann, "J. S. Bach," 88–99; Robin A. Leaver, *J. S. Bach and Scripture: Glosses from the Calov Bible Commentary* (St. Louis: Concordia, 1985).

8. Irwin, *Neither Voice nor Heart Alone*, 142.

9. Ibid., 143–46. The phrase "for the recreation of the soul" in the quotation probably means no more than what it connotes in English—for leisure. Irwin—*pace* Marti, Eggebrecht, Söhngen et al.—argues there is no indication of anything more theologically profound in mind.

10. Stapert remarks, "If Bach did not use number symbolism, there are a remarkable number of remarkably apt coincidences in his music" (Calvin Stapert, "Christus Victor: Bach's St. John Passion," *Reformed Journal* 39 [1987]: 17).

11. For similar examples, see Robin A. Leaver, "Motive and Motif in the Church Music of Johann Sebastian Bach," *Theology Today* 63 (2006): 42–43.

12. The founding fathers of the movement were the scholars Arnold Schering, Martin Jansen, and Friedrich Smend, though later writers have extended their work. See Ruth Tatlow, *Bach and the Riddle of the Number Alphabet* (Cambridge: Cambridge University Press, 1991); more briefly, Ruth Tatlow, "Number Symbolism," in *J. S. Bach*, ed. Malcolm Boyd (Oxford: Oxford University Press, 1999), 320–22.

13. See Tatlow, *Bach*, passim. So strong was the association of number alphabets with kabbalism and magic that it is likely such devices would have been frowned upon in the Lutheran circles in which Bach moved.

14. See John Butt, ed., *The Cambridge Companion to Bach* (Cambridge: Cambridge University Press, 1997), 2. Michael Marissen comments that the idea that the extramusical, theological dimensions of the *St. John Passion* ought to be ignored "is perhaps like the main character's pleasurable experiences of Italian and Russian in the movie *A Fish Called Wanda*: she is invariably stimulated by their sounds but shows no interest in learning the languages." He stresses that "it is one thing to say that *Bach and religious sentiment* is a story we are not interested in, but another to say that *Bach and pure aesthetic contemplation* is a better and more authentic story" (Michael Marissen, *Lutheranism, Anti-Judaism, and Bach's* St. John Passion: *With an Annotated Literal Translation of the Libretto* [New York: Oxford University Press, 1998], 5).

15. Calvin Stapert, *My Only Comfort: Death, Deliverance, and Discipleship in the Music of Bach* (Grand Rapids: Eerdmans, 2000), 9–10.

16. Marissen, *Bach's St. John Passion*, 7. Stapert holds that Bach's goal "was to write music that would be of use to his church in her worship, to write 'musical sermons' for the edification of her members" (Stapert, *My Only Comfort*, 27).

17. Günther Stiller, *Johann Sebastian Bach and Liturgical Life in Leipzig*, trans. Herbert J. A. Bouman, Daniel F. Poellot, and Hilton C. Oswald (St. Louis: Concordia, 1984), 213.

18. Robin A. Leaver, *Music as Preaching: Bach, Passions, and Music in Worship* (Oxford: Latimer, 1983), 21–27.

19. See Meredith Little and Natalie Jenne, *Dance and the Music of J. S. Bach* (Bloomington: Indiana University Press, 1991).

20. Irwin, *Neither Voice nor Heart Alone*, 149–52.

21. Ibid., esp. chap. 9.

22. E.g., the cantata *Mein Herze schwimmt im Blut* (BWV199) ("My heart is bathed in blood").

23. E.g., the cantata *Mein liebster Jesus ist verloren* (BW154) ("My precious Jesus now hath vanished"). Some would link Bach's theology of death with Pietism. The cantata *Schmücke dich, o liebe Seele* (BWV180) ("Adorn yourself, beloved soul") presents a complex of ideas that are associated by Pietist writers with the foretaste of eternity.

24. Leaver, *Music as Preaching*, chap. 2.

25. For a very accessible and readable way into Bach's theology in music, written for the nonspecialist but with scholarly depth, see Stapert, *My Only Comfort*. Or, for a shorter introduction, see Leaver, "Motive and Motif."

26. BWV78. See http://www.bach-cantatas.com//BWV78.htm. On the cantatas, see Alfred Dürr, *The Cantatas of J. S. Bach*, trans. Richard Jones (Oxford: Oxford University Press, 2005), esp. 523–27; and, with a particularly theological slant, Eric T. Chafe, *Analyzing Bach Cantatas* (Oxford: Oxford University Press, 2000).

27. In bar 9 it appears in the first oboe, immediately after in the second. In bars 25–28 it is found in the alto in contrary motion and then in overlapping canon in the tenor part. The vocal bass then has it in the subdominant. And so on. At bar 89 (end of the section) the sequence ceases, but it leads the sequences of bars 95ff., 107ff., and 136–144.

28. Marshall, *Music of Johann Sebastian Bach*, 79.

29. Alister E. McGrath, *Luther's Theology of the Cross* (Grand Rapids: Baker Academic, 1990), esp. chap. 5.

30. See, e.g., George R. Beasley-Murray, *John* (Waco: Word, 1999), 344.

31. Indeed, it is fair to say, with Pelikan, that the *St. John Passion* is "a celebration of the theme of 'Christus Victor'" (Jaroslav J. Pelikan, *Bach among the Theologians* [Philadelphia: Fortress, 1986], 106).

32. Marissen, *Bach's St. John Passion*, 19.

33. Wilfrid H. Mellers, *Bach and the Dance of God* (Oxford: Oxford University Press, 1981), 137.

34. Stapert, *My Only Comfort*, 123–25.

35. 19 and 20, 34 and 35 are pairs belonging together.

36. I am indebted here to Stapert, *My Only Comfort*, 121–25. For a full discussion of various theories of the chiastic structures of the *Passion*, see Alfred Dürr, *Johann Sebastian Bach: St. John Passion: Genesis, Transmission, and Meaning*, trans. Alfred Clayton (Oxford: Oxford University Press, 1988), 95–107. Dürr

concludes: "It is not the chorale 'Durch dein Gefängnis, Gottes Sohn' which is the climax of the work: it is the death of Christ."

37. Cited in Marissen, *Bach's St. John Passion*, 19.

38. Michael Marissen, "The Theological Character of J. S. Bach's *Musical Offering*," in *Bach Studies 2*, ed. Daniel R. Melamed (Cambridge: Cambridge University Press, 1995), 85–106. In another work, Marissen demonstrates that the now very fashionable social and political interpretations of Bach need not deter those with theological interests; indeed, he shows that in the case of the Brandenburg Concertos they can serve those interests (Michael Marissen, *The Social and Religious Designs of J. S. Bach's Brandenburg Concertos* [Princeton, NJ: Princeton University Press, 1995]).

39. On these developments, see John Neubauer, *The Emancipation of Music from Language: Departure from Mimesis in Eighteenth-Century Aesthetics* (New Haven: Yale University Press, 1986); Daniel K. L. Chua, *Absolute Music and the Construction of Meaning* (Cambridge: Cambridge University Press, 1999), esp. chaps. 10–13.

40. Robert Marshall reaches a similar conclusion, though by means of a slightly different argument; see Robert L. Marshall, "Truth and Beauty: J. S. Bach at the Crossroads of Cultural History," in *A Bach Tribute: Essays in Honor of William H. Scheide*, ed. Paul Brainard and Ray Robinson (Chapel Hill: Hinshaw Music, 1993), 179–88.

41. John Butt, "Figurenlehre," in *J. S. Bach*, ed. Malcolm Boyd (Oxford: Oxford University Press, 1999), 170. The earliest known systematic treatment of figures dates from the end of the sixteenth century (Burmeister's *Hypomnematum musicae poeticae* and his *Musica poetica*). Thereafter they are treated mainly in German sources. Some have claimed to see similar phenomena much earlier, but this is debated territory.

42. It also appears (appropriately) in the cantata "Christ lag in Todesbanden" (BWV4, "Christ lay in death's bondage").

43. This is why we can find the same rhetorical device, even when it is a piece of straightforward word painting, used with different words. It is the *words* that refer to Christ coming down from heaven; the music rides on the back of that reference. It is important, therefore, to distinguish between a "figure" in this baroque sense and, say, a Wagnerian leitmotif; in the latter case, we have a phrase or musical motif specifically intended to designate something that may not be present or may not be designated in any other way. See Butt, "Figurenlehre."

44. For discussion, see Neubauer, *Emancipation of Music*, chap. 3.

45. The classic work on this is Eric T. Chafe's huge (and, some would say, at times tendentious) study, *Tonal Allegory in the Vocal Music of J. S. Bach* (Berkeley: University of California Press, 1991). Much of the same territory is covered in Chafe, *Analyzing Bach Cantatas*.

46. Neubauer argues that we can detect a shift in affect theory, from its alliance with Pythagorean theory in the seventeenth century to one with rhetoric in the eighteenth, Bach belonging principally to the eighteenth century (Neubauer, *Emancipation of Music*, chap. 3). We should nevertheless remember that most eighteenth-century writers on these matters thought that sounds and affects were related by natural laws; there is no particular reason to think Bach would have taken exception to this.

47. Stapert, *My Only Comfort*, 18.

48. Irwin, *Neither Voice nor Heart Alone*, esp. chaps. 4, 11.

49. The cantor George Motz, who believed God created the world harmonically, is one example; the organist and music theorist Andreas Werckmeister is another. See ibid., 112–16; Chafe, *Analyzing Bach Cantatas*, chap. 2.

50. See John Butt, *Music Education and the Art of Performance in the German Baroque* (Cambridge: Cambridge University Press, 1994), 33–35; Wolff, *Johann Sebastian Bach*, 1–11, 465–72.

51. John Butt, "Bach's Metaphysics of Music," in *The Cambridge Companion to Bach*, ed. John Butt (Cambridge: Cambridge University Press, 1997), 52.

52. Joel Lester, *Bach's Works for Solo Violin: Style, Structure, Performance* (New York: Oxford University Press, 1999), 53.

53. Quoted in Butt, "Bach's Metaphysics of Music," 53.

54. John Butt calls it a "late flowering of the Pythagorean view of well composed music as natural harmony" (ibid.).

55. See Boyd, *Bach*, 174–75.

56. For discussion, see Butt, "Bach's Metaphysics of Music," 53–59; Wolff, *Johann Sebastian Bach*, 5–6. Admittedly, there are elements in the Birnbaum document that suggest he believes some things in nature *lack* beauty.

57. Some have tried to align Bach's vision very closely with some of the rationalist cosmologies of the German Enlightenment; see, e.g., John Butt, "'A Mind Unconscious That It Is Calculating'? Bach and the Rationalist Philosophy of Leibniz and Spinoza," in Butt, *Cambridge Companion to Bach*, 60–71; Ulrich Leisinger, "Forms and Functions of the Choral Movements in J. S. Bach's *St. Matthew Passion*," in *Bach Studies 2*, ed. Daniel R. Melamed (Cambridge: Cambridge University Press, 1995), 70–84. We cannot enter the complexities of this case here; I can only register that I find arguments that Bach would have leaned heavily on thinkers such as G. W. Leibniz and Christian Wolff speculative and unconvincing, however commonplace the ideas of harmony, unity, natural laws, and the like might have been in some of Bach's circles. Even Leisinger admits that "no documentary evidence can be presented that Johann Sebastian Bach ever possessed or read any of Leibniz's or Wolff's treatises" (Leisinger, "Forms and Functions," 84). Even if some conceptions of order, drawn from nonbiblical or non-Lutheran sources, did play some part in Bach's composition, there is no indication that he ever stepped outside mainstream Lutheran convictions about the relation between God and the world, and it is these that need to be carefully attended to in the first instance. Laurence Dreyfus has powerfully argued that Bach is better understood as a subtle *critic* of Enlightenment thought than as a staunch supporter of it (Laurence Dreyfus, *Bach and the Patterns of Invention* [Cambridge, MA: Harvard University Press, 2004], chap. 8).

58. Quoted in Wolff, *Johann Sebastian Bach*, 5. Georg Vensky, another member, wrote: "God is a harmonic being. All harmony originates from his wise order and organisation. . . . Where there is no conformity, there is also no order, no beauty, and no perfection. For beauty and perfection consist in the conformity of diversity." Quoted in ibid., 466.

59. Boyd, *Bach*, 205–6.

60. Stapert, *My Only Comfort*, 28; the final italics are mine.

61. The phrase comes from N. T. Wright, *The New Testament and the People of God* (London: SPCK, 1992), 55.

62. E.g., Mellers, *Bach and the Dance of God*. The eminent Bach scholar John Butt characterizes the cosmic view of music (which he calls a "musico-centric" conception) as the belief that "the very substance of music both reflects and *embodies* the ultimate reality of God and the Universe" (Butt, "Bach's Metaphysics of Music," 54; italics mine). He argues that Bach was a believer in the "immanence of God and the sacred in music" and that this would have been "unthinkable within Orthodox Lutheranism. As in most monotheistic religions, God is essentially a figure transcending the imperfect earthly realm, accessible only through specific avenues. . . . To affirm—unequivocally—an immanent sacrality in music is to be open to the charge of pantheism." For evidence, Butt points to remarks in the Calov Bible, especially to Bach's note on 2 Chron. 5:13: "N.B. Where there is devotional music, God with his grace is always present." This, claims Butt, "suggests that the very act of music conjures up the presence of God. Here we have the closest reference to music as a medium through which God becomes immanent, something which would have been heretical to the Pietists and perhaps also somewhat disturbing to many Orthodox thinkers, since it implies that music was on an equal footing with Scripture, officially the only true revelation of the transcendent godhead" (Butt, "Bach's Metaphysics of Music," 46–47, 54–55). This is somewhat questionable. The most natural reading of Bach's comment, especially when seen in relation to the 2 Chron. text, is that where music increases devotion, we can assume God is actively present. Further, to say God is immanent and active in worship is not equivalent to espousing pantheism, nor need it suggest that music is on a par with, or threatening the place of, Scripture. And, we might add, one would be hard-pressed to find a Christian writer in seventeenth- or eighteenth-century Germany, Lutheran or otherwise, who claims that "music both reflects and *embodies* the ultimate reality of God and the Universe." I fear there has been

a failure to distinguish here between (a) the belief that the cosmos has a God-given order, in which music is grounded, and (b) the belief that this cosmic order is to be identified with or equivalent in some manner to God.

63. David Bentley Hart, *The Beauty of the Infinite: The Aesthetics of Christian Truth* (Grand Rapids: Eerdmans, 2003), 282–85. I have developed an overlapping argument myself in Jeremy Begbie, "Created Beauty: The Witness of J. S. Bach," in *The Beauty of God: Theology and the Arts*, ed. Daniel Treier and Mark Husbands (Downers Grove, IL: InterVarsity, forthcoming).

64. Hart, *Beauty of the Infinite*, 283.

65. Ibid.

66. Dreyfus, *Bach and the Patterns of Invention*, esp. chap. 5.

67. Wolff, *Johann Sebastian Bach*, 469.

68. Hans T. David, Arthur Mendel, and Christoph Wolff, eds., *The New Bach Reader: A Life of Johann Sebastian Bach in Letters and Documents* (New York: Norton, 1998), 396.

69. Hart, *Beauty of the Infinite*, 283.

70. Quoted in Wolff, *Johann Sebastian Bach*, 471.

71. See Martin Zenck, "Reinterpreting Bach in the Nineteenth and Twentieth Centuries," in Butt, *Cambridge Companion to Bach*, 228.

72. Hart, *Beauty of the Infinite*, 277.

73. Hart believes that Bach, more than any other composer, is the "most inspired witness to the *ordo amoris* [order of love] in the fabric of being" (ibid., 282).

74. Ibid.

75. The dynamic of structure and openness, constraint and contingency, is a very familiar one in contemporary natural science, and it has been explored extensively by those working at the interface of science and theology. See Jean-Jacques Suurmond, *Word and Spirit at Play: Towards a Charismatic Theology* (Grand Rapids: Eerdmans, 1994), 37–41 and passim; Ann Pederson, *God, Creation, and All That Jazz: A Process of Composition and Improvisation* (St. Louis: Chalice, 2001); A. R. Peacocke, *Theology for a Scientific Age: Being and Becoming—Natural, Divine, and Human* (London: SCM, 1993), 175–77.

76. Hart, *Beauty of the Infinite*, 284.

77. David, Mendel, and Wolff, *New Bach Reader*, 305.

78. Irwin, *Neither Voice nor Heart Alone*, 149–50.

Chapter 6 Three Musical Theologians

1. Stanley Grenz and Roger E. Olson, *20th Century Theology: God and the World in a Transitional Age* (Downers Grove, IL: InterVarsity, 1992), 39.

2. Friedrich Schleiermacher, *Christmas Eve: Dialogue on the Incarnation*, trans. Terrence N. Tice (Richmond: John Knox, 1967). In this section, I am indebted to my former colleague at St. Andrews, Dr. Steven Guthrie, for his work on Schleiermacher.

3. It was revised in 1826.

4. B. A. Gerrish, *A Prince of the Church: Schleiermacher and the Beginnings of Modern Theology* (Philadelphia: Fortress, 1984), 14.

5. For the most substantial treatment of music in Schleiermacher's life and thought, see Philip Edward Stoltzfus, "Theology as Performance: The Theological Use of Musical Aesthetics in Friedrich Schleiermacher, Karl Barth, and Ludwig Wittgenstein" (PhD diss., Harvard University, 2000). See also Gunter Scholtz, *Schleiermachers Musikphilosophie* (Göttingen: Vandenhoeck & Ruprecht, 1981); Albert L. Blackwell, "The Role of Music in Schleiermacher's Writings," in *Internationaler Schleiermacher-Kongress 1984*, ed. Kurt-Victor Selge (Berlin: de Gruyter, 1985), 439–48.

6. Schleiermacher, *Christmas Eve*, 46. Stoltfus sees *Christmas Eve* as containing all the major emphases of Schleiermacher's mature view of music (Stoltzfus, "Theology as Performance," 112).

7. Schleiermacher, *Christmas Eve*, 31.

8. Ibid., 34.

9. Ibid., 42.

10. Ibid., 46.

11. Ibid., 57.

12. Ibid., 84–85.

13. Ibid., 69.

14. "As the painter can be recognised in some corner figure of a mediaeval painting, so we may see in Josef the author's self-portrait" (Karl Barth, *Theology and Church: Shorter Writings, 1920–1928*, trans. Louise Pettibone Smith [London: SCM, 1962], 142). It is probably truer to say that the three men speaking before Josef *all* represent Schleiermacher in their own ways.

15. Schleiermacher, *Christmas Eve*, 85, 86.

16. Ibid., 39.

17. Ibid., 38.

18. Ibid., 52.

19. Ibid., 53.

20. Ibid., 36.

21. "The sum total of religion is to feel that, in its highest unity, all that moves us in feeling is one; to feel that aught single and particular is only possible by means of this unity; to feel, that is to say, that our being is a being and living in and through God" (Friedrich Schleiermacher, *On Religion: Speeches to Its Cultured Despisers*, trans. John Oman [New York: Harper & Row, 1958], 49–50).

22. Friedrich Schleiermacher, *The Christian Faith*, trans. J. S. Stewart (Edinburgh: T&T Clark, 1999), 12–18.

23. Schleiermacher, *On Religion*, 18.

24. Karl Barth believes that "the true theological substance of this little masterpiece [*Christmas Eve*] consists of *music* and '*the divine in woman*'" (Barth, *Theology and Church*, 156). Women, for Schleiermacher, possessed "a unique advantage over men in the capacity to penetrate intuitively to the heart of things. This put [them] on the side of religion as he understood it" (Gerrish, *Prince of the Church*, 16).

25. Stoltzfus argues that the romantic writer Heinrich Wackenroder (1733–98) is a key thinker behind Schleiermacher here (Stoltzfus, *Theology as Performance*, 72–81, 92–97).

26. Schleiermacher, *Christmas Eve*, 46; italics mine.

27. Ibid., 47.

28. Ibid., 85.

29. Van Morrison, *Inarticulate Speech of the Heart*, Polydor 839 604-2. I owe this reference to Steven Guthrie.

30. Barth, *Theology and Church*, 157.

31. Ibid.; italics mine.

32. Schleiermacher, *Christmas Eve*, 47.

33. Ibid., 39. For Schleiermacher, "both musical and religious experience . . . are experiences of *direct self-awareness*, or perhaps we might better say *pre-descriptive* self-awareness" (Blackwell, "Role of Music in Schleiermacher's Writings," 443; italics mine).

34. Schleiermacher, *Christian Faith*, 12–26.

35. Schleiermacher, *Christmas Eve*, 47. Schleiermacher can use music as a metaphor of the universality and particularity of religion; see Schleiermacher, *On Religion*, 51.

36. See above, p. 34.

37. Indeed, the presumed weak historical grounding of the birth narratives, far from being a problem is—according to Leonhardt (who on this point is not opposed)—a positive advantage, for it allows the power of the festival as celebrated today to be known and felt all the more strongly (Schleiermacher, *Christmas Eve*, 73–75).

38. For Schleiermacher, the experience of redemption may have its historical starting point in the historical Jesus, in whom this new life once appeared in its most complete form. But as critics have not been slow to point out, it is not entirely clear here (nor in Schleiermacher's later writings) if Jesus does any more than illustrate or embody our own potential for a higher existence. Is Jesus qualitatively unique?

39. For fuller treatments of these issues, see Gerrish, *A Prince of the Church*; Grenz and Olson, *20th Century Theology*, 39–51; K. W. Clements, *Friedrich Schleiermacher: Pioneer of Modern Theology* (London: Collins, 1987), chap. 2.

40. Cited in Andrew Bowie, *Aesthetics and Subjectivity from Kant to Nietzsche* (Manchester: Manchester University Press, 1990), 31.

41. From an 1810 review, as quoted in Mary Sue Morrow, *German Music Criticism in the Late Eighteenth Century: Aesthetic Issues in Instrumental Music* (Cambridge: Cambridge University Press, 1997), 15.

42. Quoted in Edward A. Lippman, *A History of Western Musical Aesthetics* (Lincoln: University of Nebraska Press, 1992), 207.

43. Israel Knox, *The Aesthetic Theories of Kant, Hegel, and Schopenhauer* (London: Thames & Hudson, 1958), 151.

44. See above, pp. 16–17.

45. I treat these matters much more fully in Jeremy Begbie, *Music, Words, and the Future of Theology* (New York: Oxford University Press, forthcoming). The idea that any language might be directly rooted in the will of God has become increasingly hard to maintain in recent times, especially with the rise of philosophies that massively stress the constructive powers of human language.

46. Karl Barth, *Wolfgang Amadeus Mozart*, trans. Clarence K. Pott (Grand Rapids: Eerdmans, 1986), 16.

47. Nigel Biggar, *Reckoning with Barth: Essays in Commemoration of the Centenary of Karl Barth's Birth* (London: Mowbray, 1988), 1.

48. Barth had enormous respect for Schleiermacher, even if he came to differ from him dramatically with regard to fundamental theological and methodological claims.

49. Among the numerous introductions to Barth, see John Webster, *Barth* (London: Continuum, 2004); George Hunsinger, *How to Read Karl Barth: The Shape of His Theology* (Oxford: Oxford University Press, 1991).

50. For a very thorough treatment of Barth on music, see Stoltzfus, *Theology as Performance*, chap. 4. See also the fine dissertation by David Moseley, my former Cambridge graduate student, to whom I am indebted in this section (David Moseley, "'Parables of the Kingdom': Music and Theology in Karl Barth" [PhD diss., University of Cambridge, 2001]). See also David Moseley, "'Parables' and 'Polyphony': The Resonance of Music as Witness in the Theology of Karl Barth and Dietrich Bonhoeffer," in *Musical Theology*, ed. Jeremy Begbie and Steven Guthrie (Grand Rapids: Eerdmans, forthcoming); and Colin E. Gunton, "Mozart the Theologian," *Theology* 94 (1991): 346–49.

51. Barth, *Theology and Church*, 136–58.

52. Barth, *Wolfgang Amadeus Mozart*, 15; see Eberhard Busch, *Karl Barth: His Life from Letters and Autobiographical Texts* (London: SCM, 1976), 15–16.

53. Karl Barth's letter, April 21, 1956, as quoted in Busch, *Karl Barth*, 409.

54. Karl Barth, *Church Dogmatics*, vol. 3.3, trans. G. W. Bromiley and T. F. Torrance (Edinburgh: T&T Clark, 1960), 298.

55. Barth, *Wolfgang Amadeus Mozart*, 23.

56. Barth, *Church Dogmatics*, 3.3:297–99.

57. Ibid., 349–50.

58. Ibid., 350.

59. Ibid., 298–99; italics mine.

60. Ibid., 298.

61. Ibid., 350.

62. Ibid., 298.

63. Barth, *Wolfgang Amadeus Mozart*, 37–38.

64. Barth, *Church Dogmatics*, 3.3:298.

65. Barth, *Wolfgang Amadeus Mozart*, 47–48. See Jeremy Begbie, *Theology, Music, and Time* (Cambridge: Cambridge University Press, 2000), 93–96. Quoting Barth's comments on Mozart in *Church Dogmatics* 3.3, Albert Blackwell comments that "Barth . . . hears in Mozart's music the immanence of divine goodness in creation" (Albert L. Blackwell, *The Sacred in Music* [Cambridge: Lutterworth, 1999], 33). But this

is just what Barth does *not* say. Barth certainly believes that God is at work in the world, but his point here is that Mozart's music—*in its limited finitude*, as created—honors God.

66. "Surely the playing of musical instruments is a more or less conscious, skilful and intelligent human attempt to articulate before God this sound of a cosmos which is otherwise dumb. Surely the perfect musician is the one who, particularly stirred by the angels, is best able to hear not merely the voice of his own heart but what all creation is trying to say, and can then in great humility and with great objectivity cause it to be heard by God and other men" (Barth, *Church Dogmatics*, 3.3:472).

67. Karl Barth, *Church Dogmatics*, vol. 4.3, trans. G. W. Bromiley and T. F. Torrance (Edinburgh: T&T Clark, 1961), 69.2; see Hunsinger, *How to Read Karl Barth*, 234–80.

68. Barth was writing the material on parables at roughly the same time as he was working on his Mozart bicentenary pieces; the latter use the phrase "parables of the kingdom" to describe the theological status of Mozart's music (Moseley, "'Parables of the Kingdom'"). See Stoltzfus, *Theology as Performance*, 205ff. See also the references to Mozart in Stanley Hauerwas, *With the Grain of the Universe: The Church's Witness and Natural Theology* (Grand Rapids: Brazos Press, 2001), 197n51, 216.

69. Karl Barth, *How I Changed My Mind*, trans. John Godsey (Edinburgh: St. Andrew Press, 1969), 71–72.

70. Secular parables, then, have nothing to do with "natural theology," that is, a theology whose subject and method are shaped according to criteria more ultimate than Scripture's witness to God's self-presentation in Christ (Hunsinger, *How to Read Karl Barth*, 255–56). See Hauerwas, *With the Grain of the Universe*, chaps. 6 and 7. See also Trevor A. Hart, "The Capacity for Ambiguity: Revisiting the Barth-Brunner Debate," in *Regarding Karl Barth*, ed. Trevor A. Hart (Carlisle: Paternoster, 1999), 139–72; Jeremy Begbie, *Theology, Music, and Time*, 274–79.

71. Barth, *How I Changed My Mind*, 72. Some writers have interpreted the structure of his theology in musical terms; see, e.g., Hunsinger, *How to Read Karl Barth*, 28.

72. What of Bach, for example? As a young pastor in Geneva, Barth took part in a performance of the *St. Matthew Passion*, a work he greatly liked (Busch, *Karl Barth*, 56). But later, Barth spoke of Bach's *St. Matthew Passion* as a "tragic ode culminating in a conventional funeral dirge ('Rest softly'). It is neither determined nor delimited by the Easter message, and Jesus never once speaks in it as the Victor"; what we have here is "only an abstraction and not the real passion of Jesus" (Karl Barth, *Church Dogmatics*, vol. 4.2, trans. G. W. Bromiley [Edinburgh: T&T Clark, 1958], 252–53).

73. Using some of his most opulent prose, Barth writes: "What is lacking to the self-attestation of the creature as such . . . they can acquire as and when God Himself begins to speak and claims and uses them in his service. . . . They can blend their voices with that of God. He could hardly be God who has lent them these voices if they could not do this as commanded and empowered by him. What they say can so harmonise with what He Himself says that to hear Him is to hear them, and to hear them to hear Him, so that listening to the polyphony of creation as the external basis of the covenant . . . is listening to the symphony for which it was elected and determined from eternity and which the Creator alone has the power to evoke, yet according to His Word the will also. Nor has He only the will. For when He speaks His one and total Word concerning the covenant which is the internal basis of creation, this symphony is in fact evoked, and even the self-witness of creation in all the diversity of its voices can and will give its unanimous applause" (Karl Barth, *Church Dogmatics*, 4.3:159–60).

74. Stoltzfus is thus right to see Barth as offering a distinctively modern "Pythagorean" project. Stoltzfus, *Theology as Performance*, chap. 4. Stoltzfus believes that Ferruccio Busoni's writings played a key part in Barth's theology of Mozart (ibid., 160ff.).

75. Busch, *Karl Barth*, 498–99.

76. For a very fine introduction to Bonhoeffer, see Stephen Plant, *Bonhoeffer* (London: Continuum, 2004). Eric Till's film is *Bonhoeffer: Agent of Grace* (2000); the opera *Bonhoeffer* (2000) is by Ann Gebuhr, libretto by Robert Hatten.

77. See Andreas Pangritz, *Polyphonie des Lebens: Zu Dietrich Bonhoeffers "Theologie der Musik"* (Berlin: Alektor-Verlag, 1994); Pangritz, "Point and Counterpoint—Resistance and Submission: Dietrich Bonhoeffer on Theology and Music in Times of War and Social Crisis," in *Theology in Dialogue: The Impact of the Arts, Humanities and Science on Contemporary Religious Thought*, ed. Lyn Holness and Ralf Wüstenberg

(Grand Rapids: Eerdmans, 2002), 28–42; John W. de Gruchy, *Christianity, Art, and Transformation: Theological Aesthetics in the Struggle for Justice* (Cambridge: Cambridge University Press, 2001), chap. 4.

78. Eberhard Bethge, *Dietrich Bonhoeffer: Theologian, Christian, Man for His Times; A Biography* (Minneapolis: Fortress, 2000), 25.

79. Ibid., 37.

80. Quoted in de Gruchy, *Christianity, Art, and Transformation*, 139.

81. Dietrich Bonhoeffer, *Letters and Papers from Prison* (London: SCM, 1972), 240.

82. Ibid., 126–27.

83. Pangritz, "Point and Counterpoint."

84. De Gruchy, *Christianity, Art, and Transformation*, 145.

85. Dietrich Bonhoeffer, *Ethics* (London: Macmillan, 1965), 179.

86. Bonhoeffer, *Letters and Papers*, 193.

87. This is the move from the "aesthetic" through what Kierkegaard called the "ethical" to the "religious" stage of life.

88. He is unfair to Kierkegaard in suggesting that the latter is wholly negative toward the aesthetic. See George Pattison, *Kierkegaard: The Aesthetic and the Religious* (London: SCM, 1999).

89. The word *Bildung* (education) can also be translated as "culture" or "cultural formation."

90. Bonhoeffer, *Letters and Papers*, 219.

91. Ibid., 215.

92. Ibid., 219.

93. Ibid., 170.

94. Ibid.

95. The *Art of Fugue* was handed down with this chorale as a conclusion.

96. Bonhoeffer, *Letters and Papers*, 219.

97. Ibid., 303. For expositions of this, see de Gruchy, *Christianity, Art, and Transformation*, 158–60; David Ford, *Self and Salvation: Being Transformed* (Cambridge: Cambridge University Press, 1999), 253–59.

98. Bonhoeffer, *Letters and Papers*, 303.

99. Ibid.

100. Ibid.

101. Ibid., 305.

102. Ibid., 310–11; italics mine.

103. De Gruchy, *Christianity, Art, and Transformation*, 167. Significantly, de Gruchy writes this just before he goes on to sketch what "aesthetic existence" means in postapartheid South Africa. We should acknowledge, however, that despite the use of the polyphony metaphor in the prison letters, in Bonhoeffer's earlier reflections on the nature of Christian community, written in 1938, there is a robust recommendation of unison song as "the essence of all congregational singing." Here his concern is about music distracting us from the meaning of words. He sees singing in church as "bound wholly to the Word." The "soaring tone of unison singing" is supported by the words sung and hence does not need the musical support of other voices, which can be only a distraction. Bonhoeffer is scathing about singers who like the sound of their own voices, especially those who improvise different parts. Nonetheless, this is more than a matter simply of keeping music at bay: unison singing, through its "simplicity and frugality," "humaneness and warmth" can bring a "joy which is peculiar to it alone" (Bonhoeffer, *Life Together*, trans. John W. Doberstein [New York: Harper, 1954], 59–61).

Chapter 7 Two Theological Musicians

1. In fact, the music that was to become the *Quartet for the End of Time* was begun prior to this, after meeting the clarinetist Henri Akoka in Verdun. See Rebecca Rischin, *For the End of Time: The Story of the Messiaen Quartet* (Ithaca, NY: Cornell University Press, 2003), chap. 1.

2. Quoted in ibid., 69.

3. Antoine Goléa, *Rencontres avec Olivier Messiaen* (Paris: Julliard, 1960), 63. For discussions of the piece, its conception and performance, see Rischin, *For the End of Time*; Peter Hill and Nigel Simeone, *Messiaen* (New Haven: Yale University Press, 2005), 97–103; Anthony Pople, *Messiaen: Quatuor pour la fin du Temps* (Cambridge: Cambridge University Press, 1998).

4. For biographies, see Hill and Simeone, *Messiaen*; Christopher Dingle, *The Life of Messiaen* (Cambridge: Cambridge University Press, forthcoming).

5. Claude Samuel, *Conversations with Olivier Messiaen* (London: Stainer & Bell, 1976), 2.

6. Paul Griffiths, *Olivier Messiaen and the Music of Time* (London: Faber & Faber, 1985), 74.

7. Aidan Nichols, "Celestial Banquet: Messiaen's Sacred Music in Context," *Downside Review* 406 (1999): 178–80.

8. Ibid.

9. Ibid., 186. The impact of Marmion is very evident in Messiaen's organ piece *La Nativité du Seigneur* (1935), which follows Marmion's account of the incarnation as God's chosen way of salvation.

10. Quoted in Almut Rössler, ed., *Contributions to the Spiritual World of Olivier Messiaen: With Original Texts by the Composer* (Duisburg: Gilles & Francke, 1986), 89.

11. Messiaen claimed that birds are "the greatest musicians existing on our planet." (Samuel, *Conversations with Olivier Messiaen*, 51).

12. Ibid., 2–3.

13. Indeed, he can speak of all three (Catholic faith, his interest in human love, and his love of nature) being "resolved finally in one and the same idea: Divine Love!" (ibid., 14).

14. Nichols, "Celestial Banquet," 187.

15. For example, Messiaen read for himself the writings of St. Thomas Aquinas (ca. 1225–74), the medieval Dominican scholastic theologian (see, e.g., Messiaen's *Trois Petites Liturgies de la Présence Divine*), and in the last decades of his life he enthusiastically studied the theological aesthetics of the Swiss theologian Hans Urs von Balthasar.

16. Nichols, "Celestial Banquet," 181–82.

17. "The theology of Messiaen's verbal comments is rudimentary, and likely to seem woefully naive by comparison with the examinations of professional theologians" (Griffiths, *Olivier Messiaen*, 64). The judgment is overly harsh; one wonders if it tells us more about the writer's own attitude to theology than about Messiaen.

18. Siglind Bruhn, "Religious Symbolism in the Music of Olivier Messiaen," *American Journal of Semiotics* 13 (Fall 1996): 277–309.

19. Messiaen, for example, by no means abandons musical goals and climaxes: "La Résurrection du Christ" from the *Livre du Saint Sacrement* (1984) is a good example. One can have a sense of rest, closure, and arrival in a piece or work without having to rely on the continuous drama of tension and resolution so typical of Western music.

20. Robert Sherlaw Johnson, *Messiaen* (London: Dent, 1989), 13.

21. Griffiths, *Olivier Messiaen*, 15.

22. Ibid., 16. Messiaen's pupil Pierre Boulez once said, "Messiaen doesn't compose, he juxtaposes." Quoted in Roger Nichols, "Olivier Messiaen (1908–1992): Vingt Regards Sur L'enfant Jésus," note for CD, Collins, 70332 (1996): 4–5.

23. Griffiths, *Olivier Messiaen*, 17.

24. As in Jean Marie Wu, "Mystical Symbols of Faith: Olivier Messiaen's Charm of Impossibilities," in *Messiaen's Language of Mystical Love*, ed. Siglind Bruhn (New York: Garland, 1998), 112.

25. See above, pp. 80–81, 91.

26. Samuel, *Conversations*, 17.

27. Rössler, *Contributions*, 78–79. "Although one doesn't have to see the same colors I see, I do think that one needs a perception of colors when listening to my music" (ibid., 79).

28. Ibid., 66.

29. Wu, "Mystical Symbols of Faith," 103.

30. Samuel, *Conversations*, 44.

31. Quoted in Griffiths, *Olivier Messiaen*, 201.

32. Wu, "Mystical Symbols of Faith," 113.

33. Symmetrical permutations first appear in *Île de feu* (1950), nine years after the *Quartet*. Nevertheless, the *Quartet* was a sort of showpiece for his musical techniques at the time. Soon after, Messiaen wrote his *Technique de mon langage musical* (1944) in which he sets out his principles of composition, and here he cites the *Quartet* more than any other piece.

34. Griffiths, *Olivier Messiaen*, 100–101.

35. Messiaen, as quoted in Pople, *Messiaen*, 11.

36. Goléa, *Rencontres avec Olivier Messiaen*, 64.

37. Ibid., 70.

38. Ibid., 65.

39. Ibid., 67.

40. Some have found these two movements sentimental. Messiaen insisted, "They are not at all luscious nor sweet; they are simply noble, bare, austere" (ibid., 70).

41. Olivier Messiaen, "Preface" to Miniature Score of *Quatuor pour la fin du Temps* (Paris: Durand, 1942), ii.

42. Pople, *Messiaen*, 55.

43. Messiaen, "Preface," ii.

44. Ibid., i.

45. Pople, *Messiaen*, 27.

46. Samuel, *Conversations*, 11. See also Bruhn, "Religious Symbolism," 283.

47. Robert Sherlaw Johnson, "Rhythmic Techniques and Symbolism in the Music of Olivier Messiaen," in *Messiaen's Language of Mystical Love*, ed. Siglind Bruhn (New York: Garland, 1998), 126.

48. Bruhn, "Religious Symbolism," 295–96.

49. St. Thomas Aquinas, *Summa Theologica*, trans. Fathers of the English Dominican Province, vol. 5 (Allen, TX: Christian Classics, 1981), qu. 84, pp. 2907–12. See Messiaen's comments on *Les Corps Glorieux* in Rössler, ed., *Contributions*, 28–29.

50. We could also cite works such as *La Transfiguration de Notre Seigneur Jésus-Christ* (1965–69) and *Éclairs sur l'Au-delà* (1988–92), in which we are given rich and subtle musical explorations of time and eternity.

51. In *Diptyque* (1930) there are two movements, one about this earthly life and one about eternity. The main theme from the first is transformed in the second—a possible allusion to creaturely time being transformed in the future life.

52. Griffiths, *Olivier Messiaen*, 64.

53. "Time is one of God's strangest creatures because it is totally opposed to Him who is Eternal by nature, to Him who is without beginning, end, or succession" (Samuel, *Conversations*, 11). In the course of a description of his organ masterpiece *Méditations sur le Mystère de la Sainte Trinité* (1969), Messiaen writes: "Then comes eternity: God is eternal; he has neither beginning nor end nor succession. I treated this notion like a glittering flash of color. God is immutable, which is to say, no change can occur in him" (Messiaen, *Music and Color: Conversations with Claude Samuel*, trans. E. Thomas Glasgow [Portland, OR: Amadeus, 1994], 126).

54. Rössler, *Contributions*, 40.

55. "Messiaen's God is ecstatically happy, filled with a bliss that can reach intensities to resemble drunken frenzy, and His creatures are loved without exception or bounds" (Bruhn, "Religious Symbolism," 277).

56. Rössler, ed., *Contributions*, 52.

57. Ibid., 91.

58. Ibid., 92.

59. Quoted in Rischin, *For the End of Time*, 44.

60. S. Ratcliffe, "MacMillan," *Choir and Organ* 7, no. 3 (1999): 38.

61. Quoted on the Boosey & Hawkes website: http://www.boosey.com/pages/cr/composer/composer_main.asp?composerid=2799.

62. For example, he collaborated with the theologian Rowan Williams and poet Michael Symmons Roberts to produce *Parthenogenesis* (2000)—a venture on which all three reflect in Jeremy Begbie, ed., *Sounding the Depths: Theology through the Arts* (London: SCM, 2002), 17–53. Williams invited MacMillan to write a piece for his enthronement as Archbishop of Canterbury (*To My Successor*, 2002), and Mac-Millan dedicated his *A Deep and Dazzling Darkness* (2001–2) to the Archbishop.

63. From an interview with Tom Regan, October 15, 2002, http://www253.pair.com/coralleg/html/interview_macmillan.html.

64. Quoted in Mark Hijleh, *The Music of Jesus: From Composition to Koinonia* (New York: Writers Club Press, 2001), 96.

65. Interview at http://www.thetablet.co.uk/sample17.shtml.

66. Quoted in Hijleh, *Music of Jesus*, 96.

67. "Unholier Than Thou," *Guardian*, October 11, 2003, accessed at http://books.guardian.co.uk/review/story/0,1059182,00.html#article_continue.

68. Quoted in Stephen Johnson, "Harnessing Extremes," *Gramophone* (May 1995): 17.

69. James MacMillan, "Composer's Notes," *The Confession of Isobel Gowdie*, accessed at http://www.boosey.com/pages/cr/catalogue/cat_detail.asp?musicid=3115.

70. Interview at http://www.thetablet.co.uk/sample17.shtml.

71. See p. 18.

72. Interview with James MacMillan, June 1998, during the 2nd Annual Vancouver New Music Festival. Accessed at http://www.sfu.ca/twentieth-century-ltd/macmillan1.html.

73. Ibid.

74. Quoted in Jolyon Mitchell, "Sound of Heart," *Third Way* 22, no. 5 (1999): 19.

75. James MacMillan, "Parthenogenesis," in Begbie, *Sounding the Depths*, 35, 37.

76. Quoted in Robert Schwarz, "James MacMillan: A Composer Finds Favor without Courting Fashion," *New York Times*, March 3, 1996, 29.

77. James MacMillan, "Composer's Notes," *Symphony: Vigil*, accessed at http://www.boosey.com/pages/cr/catalogue/cat_detail.asp?musicid=771.

78. Ibid.

79. Samuel, *Conversations*, 4.

Chapter 8 A Christian Ecology

1. The literature on "worldview" and theology is vast, but for a sample, see J. Richard Middleton and Brian J. Walsh, *Truth Is Stranger Than It Used to Be: Biblical Faith in a Postmodern Age* (Downers Grove, IL: InterVarsity, 1995); N. T. Wright, *The New Testament and the People of God* (London: SPCK, 1992), 122–26; David K. Naugle, *Worldview: The History of a Concept* (Grand Rapids: Eerdmans, 2002); and J. P. Moreland and William Lane Craig, *Philosophical Foundations for a Christian Worldview* (Downers Grove, IL: InterVarsity, 2003).

2. Here I am using "creation" rather than "nature" to speak of the whole cosmos, to stress that it is God's handiwork, not simply existing in a neutral sense. See Alister E. McGrath, *A Scientific Theology*, vol. 1, *Nature* (Edinburgh: T&T Clark, 2001), chap. 3. In general, I shall use the word "nature" when I want to distinguish our nonhuman environment from creation as a whole (without meaning to suggest that we are dealing with something alien, quite foreign to us, set over against us problematically).

3. See above, pp. 46–49.

4. Ernst Bloch, *Essays on the Philosophy of Music*, trans. Peter Palmer (Cambridge: Cambridge University Press, 1985), 138.

5. Of course, there is much more to the imagination than this. On the imagination in theology, see, among many studies, Trevor A. Hart, "Imagining Evangelical Theology," in *Evangelical Futures: A Conversation on Theological Method*, ed. John G. Stackhouse (Grand Rapids: Eerdmans, 2000), 191–207; Garrett Green, *Imagining God: Theology and the Religious Imagination* (San Francisco: Harper & Row, 1989); Green, *Theology, Hermeneutics, and Imagination: The Crisis of Interpretation at the End of Modernity* (Cambridge: Cambridge University Press, 2000); Paul D. L. Avis, *God and the Creative Imagination:*

Metaphor, Symbol, and Myth in Religion and Theology (London: Routledge, 1999); John McIntyre, *Faith, Theology, and Imagination* (Edinburgh: Handsel, 1987); David Tracy, *The Analogical Imagination: Christian Theology and the Culture of Pluralism* (New York: Crossroad, 1981).

6. To put this another way, we are exercising a form of what in some circles is being called variously "biblical theology" or "a theological interpretation of Scripture"—an approach to the Bible's texts that arises out of the conviction that the governing interest of the Bible's authors, of the text itself, and of the original community of readers is *theological*: coming to hear, know, and be transformed by the Triune God. Such a reading of Scripture proposes that there are irreducibly *theological matters*, arising from the sense and reference of the biblical text itself, that demand to be taken seriously as such and that in due course can lead to the substantive claims that the doctrinal theologian will want to advance. It also takes seriously the *ecclesial context* of Scripture's reading, past and present, and it avoids the imposition of a "general hermeneutic" on Scripture—the notion that the Bible is to be read "like any other book," according to principles of interpretation derived externally and fixed in advance of reading the texts. The literature on this is burgeoning, but especially helpful examples and discussions include Richard Bauckham, *The Theology of the Book of Revelation* (Cambridge: Cambridge University Press, 1993); Frances M. Young and David Ford, *Meaning and Truth in 2 Corinthians* (Grand Rapids: Eerdmans, 1987); Christopher R. Seitz, *Word without End: The Old Testament as Abiding Theological Witness* (Grand Rapids: Eerdmans, 1998); Markus Bockmuehl, "Reason, Wisdom, and the Implied Disciple of Scripture," in *Reading Texts, Seeking Wisdom: Scripture and Theology*, ed. D. F. Ford and G. N. Stanton (London: SCM, 2003), 53–68; Francis Watson, *Text and Truth: Redefining Biblical Theology* (Grand Rapids: Eerdmans, 1997); L. Gregory Jones and James Joseph Buckley, *Theology and Scriptural Imagination* (Oxford: Blackwell, 1998); Craig G. Bartholomew and Elaine Botha, *Out of Egypt: Biblical Theology and Biblical Interpretation* (Grand Rapids: Zondervan, 2004); Stephen E. Fowl, *Engaging Scripture: A Model for Theological Interpretation* (Oxford: Blackwell, 1998); Kevin J. Vanhoozer, *First Theology: God, Scripture, and Hermeneutics* (Downers Grove, IL: InterVarsity, 2002); Vanhoozer, ed., *Dictionary for Theological Interpretation of the Bible* (Grand Rapids: Baker Academic, 2005), esp. 19–25.

7. For the fullest and most convincing use of the metaphor of improvisation for understanding a biblical ethics for the church, with much attention to the imagination, see the excellent study by Samuel Wells, *Improvisation: The Drama of Christian Ethics* (London: SPCK, 2004). Wells significantly revises N. T. Wright's earlier use of the improvisation metaphor (our role being to improvise the fifth act of a five-act divine drama) (Wells, *Improvisation*, 53–57). Cf. Wright, *New Testament and the People of God*, 139–43; Middleton and Walsh, *Truth Is Stranger Than It Used to Be*, 182–87. In the same circle of ideas, see Jeremy Begbie, *Theology, Music, and Time* (Cambridge: Cambridge University Press, 2000), chaps.7–9.

8. See Richard Bauckham, *God Crucified: Monotheism and Christology in the New Testament* (Carlisle: Paternoster, 1998). For a very clearheaded way into this theme, see Cornelius Plantinga, *Engaging God's World: A Christian Vision of Faith, Learning, and Living* (Grand Rapids: Eerdmans, 2002), chap. 2.

9. Note the allusions here to Gen. 1; cf. Heb. 1:2; Col. 1:16.

10. Bauckham, *God Crucified*, 37–40.

11. James D. G. Dunn, *The Epistles to the Colossians and to Philemon: A Commentary on the Greek Text* (Grand Rapids: Eerdmans, 1996), 104.

12. It is, of course, essential to take the order of the Bible's narrative seriously and to respect the integrity and particularity of Old Testament texts such as Genesis 1. But it is just as essential to respect the integrity of Scripture as a whole, which means taking the centrality of Christ for Scripture's interpretation with full seriousness.

13. The Spirit is the "firstfruits" of the final harvest (Rom. 8:23) and the "down payment" (2 Cor. 1:22; 5:5; Eph. 1:14) and as such is both the *evidence* that the final future has invaded the present and the *guarantee* that the future fulfillment will come (Gordon D. Fee, *God's Empowering Presence: The Holy Spirit in the Letters of Paul* [Peabody, MA: Hendrickson, 1994], 805–8). Irenaeus of Lyons (ca. 140–202 CE) used the image of God creating through the two "hands" of his Son and Spirit (*Adversus haereses* 5.6.1). For development of the significance of this, see Colin E. Gunton, *The Triune Creator: A Historical and Systematic Study* (Edinburgh: Edinburgh University Press, 1998), 52–56.

14. The idea is not explicitly stated in canonical Scripture (though it can be found in 2 Macc. 7:28). For discussion, see David Fergusson, *The Cosmos and the Creator: An Introduction to the Theology of Creation* (London: SPCK, 1998), 23–36; Gunton, *Triune Creator*, chap. 4; Gerhard May, *Creatio Ex Nihilo: The Doctrine of "Creation out of Nothing" in Early Christian Thought* (Edinburgh: T&T Clark, 1994); Paul Copan and William Lane Craig, *Creation out of Nothing: A Biblical, Philosophical, and Scientific Exploration* (Grand Rapids: Baker Academic, 2004).

15. This is one of the things the Christian tradition has meant when it has described the world as "contingent." The word "contingent" can have a number of meanings in theology. Two broad senses can be highlighted: (a) it can mean "dependent upon"—the world is dependent upon God; (b) it can mean "not necessary," "not bound by some necessity." This second sense itself fans out into a number of meanings, of which we can mention three. The first we have just encountered: (i) It can be used to say that the *world need not have existed*. Creation did not have to happen. (ii) It can be used to say *the world could have been a different kind of world* from the kind of world it actually is. This conviction seems to have had a profound impact on the development of modern science. (iii) It can also be used to *distinguish certain kinds of events in the world*, the unpredictable as distinct from the predictable.

16. Samuel Wells draws attention to the way in which much Christian ethics has treated a series of boundaries (death, time, space, the body, etc.) as ultimates, with the result that the Christian life becomes seen as little more than damage limitation—we negotiate as best we can these "overbearing and sometimes competing superpowers of brute reality" (Wells, *Improvisation*, 122). In conversation with John Milbank, Wells points out that the gospel itself subverts this supposed ultimacy. Properly speaking, "God takes the place in Christian ethics normally reserved for time, death, sin, bodily limitation, and so on—the conventional boundaries. The only boundary, in other words, is the boundary of God. And meanwhile the place that God conventionally takes in Christian ethics—that of a perhaps helpful but largely peripheral and certainly not essential figure—in other words, a gift, a 'bonus'—should be taken by those familiar perennial so-called 'givens.' So what seemed given—the conventional boundaries— becomes gift; and what seemed to be gift—God—becomes the given" (ibid., 124).

17. A swarm of controversy opens up at this point, much of it not directly relevant for us here. Some see creation as an act of self-limitation and God's ongoing relation to the created world in similar kenotic terms. This picks up on Paul's language of self-emptying in Phil. 2:7. There is a danger here of becoming ensnared by spatial metaphors (as if God "pulls out" of some previously existing place). God's refusal to violate the created order is better construed as an expression of his unswerving faithfulness to it rather than as a retreat into some kind of self-imposed impotence; God's faithfulness to the created order is better seen as founded in, and nothing other than, the faithfulness of God to the reality of who he is in himself, his triune love now turned outward toward us. (I owe this wording to my colleague, Suzanne McDonald.) For further discussion, see Alan J. Torrance, "Creatio ex Nihilo and the Spatio-Temporal Dimensions, with Special Reference to Jürgen Moltmann and D. C. Williams," in *The Doctrine of Creation*, ed. Colin E. Gunton (Edinburgh: T&T Clark, 1997), 82–103; John Polkinghorne, ed., *The Work of Love: Creation as Kenosis* (Grand Rapids: Eerdmans, 2001).

18. Genesis 1:31 is sometimes used to make this point; here God expresses satisfaction with everything that he has made: "and indeed, it was very good" (1:31), summing up the repeated refrains of verses 4, 9, 12, 18, 21, and 25. Care is needed here, however. While these verses certainly disallow any notion of the prehuman created world as evil, corrupt, without value, or something from which we should try to escape, the main thrust of "good" is probably not about affirming the value of this world in itself so much as its appropriateness as an *ordered setting* for human and animal life. "Good" here has a forward-looking dimension—"good for achieving its purpose." Rogerson comments: "This understanding of 'good' . . . enables us to say that, in spite of the curse, the flood and the compromise (9:1–7) [the Noah story], the creation is still 'good' in that it provides the order and stability in which the life given by God can be lived out" (J. W. Rogerson, *Genesis 1–11* [Sheffield: JSOT Press, 1991], 61).

19. Steven Bouma-Prediger, *For the Beauty of the Earth: A Christian Vision for Creation Care* (Grand Rapids: Baker Academic, 2001), chap. 2.

20. The case was classically put, albeit in exaggerated and sometimes questionable terms, by the medievalist Lynn White in "The Historical Roots of Our Ecological Crisis," *Science* 155 (1967): 1203–7. See Bouma-Prediger, *Beauty of the Earth*, chap. 3.

21. Ludwig Feuerbach, *The Essence of Christianity*, trans. George Eliot (New York: Harper & Row, 1957), 287.

22. N. T. Wright, *New Tasks for a Renewed Church* (London: Hodder & Stoughton, 1992), 9.

23. See, for example, Bouma-Prediger, *Beauty of the Earth*; Fergusson, *Cosmos and the Creator*; Alister E. McGrath, *The Re-enchantment of Nature: Science, Religion, and the Human Sense of Wonder* (London: Hodder & Stoughton, 2002); Gunton, *Triune Creator*; Jürgen Moltmann, *God in Creation: An Ecological Doctrine of Creation* (London: SCM, 1985); Richard Bauckham, *God and the Crisis of Freedom* (Louisville: Westminster John Knox, 2002), chap. 7.

24. Revelation 21 has in mind not the obliteration of creation but its remaking. Bauckham, *Theology of the Book of Revelation*, 49–50; G. K. Beale, *The Book of Revelation: A Commentary on the Greek Text* (Grand Rapids: Eerdmans, 1999), 1040. The objection can be made that 2 Pet. 3:8–10 speaks of the burning up of the earth, and this would seem to undermine a hope in creation's renewal. In fact, though a purging of creation certainly seems to be envisaged in this passage, the most likely meaning of the last phrase is: the evil done on earth will be *disclosed*, open to judgment. For a full explanation, see Richard Bauckham, *Jude, 2 Peter* (Dallas: Word, 1983), 314–22.

Some will justifiably object that, seen in purely scientific terms, the universe seems condemned to utter futility. Either the universe will expand to the point where it will simply run down, or else the present expansion of the universe will be halted and everything will contract through the force of gravity, ending in a "big crunch." This certainly puts a question mark beside evolutionary optimism—hope for a fulfillment solely within the confines of the unfolding of present physical processes. But it need not threaten Christian hope, which is based not on the world's immanent processes but on God, who raises Jesus from the dead. The problem is essentially no different from that of our own human death. For further discussion, see J. C. Polkinghorne and Michael Welker, *The End of the World and the Ends of God: Science and Theology on Eschatology* (Harrisburg, PA: Trinity Press International, 2000).

25. Richard Bauckham, "Stewardship and Relationship," in *The Care of Creation: Focusing Concern and Action*, ed. R. J. Berry (Leicester: Inter-Varsity, 2000), 104.

26. "The first proposition [of a doctrine of creation]: that God creates means that there is other reality than God *and that it is really other than he*" (Robert W. Jenson, *Systematic Theology*, vol. 2, *The Works of God* [New York: Oxford University Press, 1999], 5; italics mine.)

27. From Gerard Manley Hopkins, "God's Grandeur" in *Poems and Prose* (London: Penguin, 1985), 27.

28. See pp. 92–94.

29. See the discussions by McGrath, *Scientific Theology*, vol. 1, esp. part 2; Gunton, *Triune Creator*, chap. 5.

30. Alan E. Lewis, *Theatre of the Gospel* (Edinburgh: Handsel, 1984), 10.

31. Christopher Smart, "A Song to David," 1763. The mammoth issue lurking in the wings here is that of the *analogia entis*—"analogy of being," that is, the extent to which we can assume an ontological continuity (continuity of being) between the divine and the created realms that grounds our knowledge of, and speech about, God. The analogy of being is given different interpretations by different theologians and has become a matter of fierce controversy, especially in light of Karl Barth's famous (and often misunderstood) opposition to some versions of it. We do not have space to enter the debate in detail here, but our own approach rejects (1) any continuity between divine and created being that is assumed *in advance of* and *apart from* attention to the reconciling self-disclosure of God in Jesus Christ; (2) any theology that proceeds on the supposition of some supposed *necessity* of created rationality to resemble uncreated (divine) rationality, and resemble it in particular ways, rather than on the basis of what God makes possible by virtue of his gracious, dynamic presence to the world as revealed in Jesus Christ; and with this, (3) any theology that would forget or downplay the fallout from human sinfulness—i.e., that redeemed eyes and ears are necessary to apprehend the true relatedness of the world to God. None of this precludes the participation of human and nonhuman created reality in God's

life, and thereby "analogously" corresponding to it, but everything depends on how such "analogy" is believed to be grounded and perceived. For an especially illuminating and lucid discussion, see Alan J. Torrance, *Persons in Communion: An Essay on Trinitarian Description and Human Participation* (Edinburgh: T&T Clark, 1996), chap. 3.

32. As Augustine put it, addressing God: "You have made all times; and before all times only you are, nor does time antecede itself" (*Confessions* 9.6.14).

33. "Creation out of nothing" is not an event situated at a point on some kind of timeline. It is not temporally (or spatially) located. To affirm that all things were created out of nothing is (among other things) to say that the totality of the created order is contingent upon God's creative act, which in turn implies that all things (in all times and places) are equally present to God (Torrance, "Creatio ex Nihilo," 90–93).

34. Ruth Etchells, *A Model of Making: Literary Criticism and Its Theology* (Basingstoke: Marshall, Morgan & Scott, 1983), 50. At the same time, care is needed not to allow the doctrine of creation to be sucked into that of providence, as in the popular but, I believe, confused notion of "continuous creation" (*creatio continua*). A distinction needs to be made between (a) God establishing a world (not "in time" but "with time"), which posits (but is not reducible to) an absolute beginning, and (b) the Creator's interaction with that world, guiding it to its intended destiny. The first speaks of ontological origination (the world has its source solely in God's will) and serves to remind us of the Creator/creature distinction and the establishment of a stable order; the second speaks of God's engagement with the created world, serving to remind us of God's unswerving determination to see the world flourish toward its end. It is important not to let these be driven apart or to see the distinction as a crudely temporal one (*first* God creates and *then*, later, does something with what he creates). But to merge them into each other can encourage a view of the world as eternal or in shapeless flux, or of God as a prisoner of the world and its time, or some combination of these. Whatever form it takes, the integrity of both God and world is threatened. See Oliver O'Donovan, *Resurrection and Moral Order: An Outline for Evangelical Ethics* (Leicester: Inter-Varsity, 1994), chap. 3. Some argue that Jürgen Moltmann in his Gifford Lectures (*God in Creation*) falls into just this kind of trap (see Watson, *Text and Truth*, 227–32; Torrance, "Creatio Ex Nihilo").

35. Irenaeus held that although the world was created good, it was created to reach its final perfection in and through time. Similarly with Adam—he was created incomplete, needing to grow. Unfortunately, Irenaeus's thought has been severely misunderstood by some writers who align him quite wrongly with certain kinds of evolutionary progressivism, ignoring his marked stress on the devastating effects of the fall. See the helpful discussions by Gunton, *Triune Creator*, 202–3; Douglas Farrow, *Ascension and Ecclesia: On the Significance of the Doctrine of the Ascension for Ecclesiology and Christian Cosmology* (Edinburgh: T&T Clark, 1999), 44–58, 74–85.

36. Wright, *New Tasks*, 12.

37. This is why we find some biblical writers using covenant language and creation language in the same breath. God pledges himself to the created world as he pledges himself in covenant love to people. To be sure, apart from passing references in Jer. 33:19–25, the Bible does not explicitly speak of God's relationship with creation as a whole in terms of covenant. And in Genesis, creation "in the beginning" is best understood as providing the foundation or ordered environment for God entering into covenants with people, beginning with Abraham (Watson, *Text and Truth*, 227–41). Having said this, in the Old Testament the covenant God is the creator God, and it is clear in many places that God's radical, unconditional commitment to his people finds its counterpart in his radical, unconditional commitment to all creation: for example, in Ps. 136, where God's enduring "steadfast love" is used of God's activity toward creation *and* of the exodus. Again, the strong link is clinched by reading creation through the lens of Jesus Christ. The New Testament makes it plain that in Christ, God's covenant purposes have reached their fulfillment, and these purposes include a future for creation. Prior to Moltmann, few have pressed the link between creation and covenant harder than Karl Barth. For Barth, creation is the "external basis for the covenant" and the covenant the "internal basis of creation" (Karl Barth, *Church Dogmatics*, vol. 3.1, trans. G. W. Bromiley and T. F. Torrance, vol. 3.1 [Edinburgh: T&T Clark, 1958], 34–329).

38. F. F. Bruce glosses this: "[Christ] upholds the universe not like Atlas supporting a dead weight on his shoulders, but as one who carries all things forward on their appointed course" (F. F. Bruce, *The Epistle to the Hebrews* [Grand Rapids: Eerdmans, 1990], 49).

39. When Paul writes about us receiving a "spiritual body" (e.g., 1 Cor. 15:44) he means not a nonphysical body but one animated by the Holy Spirit, fit for the future new heaven and new earth. See N. T. Wright, *The Resurrection of the Son of God* (London: SPCK, 2003), 312–61.

40. Pannenberg is one of many who want to trace the roots of the distinctiveness of the created world from God in the differentiation of God's intratrinitarian life (Wolfhart Pannenberg, *Systematic Theology*, vol. 2, trans. Geoffrey W. Bromiley [Grand Rapids: Eerdmans, 1994], 20–35). See also David Bentley Hart, *The Beauty of the Infinite: The Aesthetics of Christian Truth* (Grand Rapids: Eerdmans, 2003), 249–73.

41. Michael Polanyi, *The Tacit Dimension* (Gloucester, MA: Peter Smith, 1983).

42. McGrath, *Scientific Theology*, vol. 1, 218–32.

43. John Polkinghorne, *Science and Creation: The Search for Understanding* (London: SPCK, 1988), 20.

44. For a very succinct overview, see John Polkinghorne, *Science and Theology: An Introduction* (London: SPCK, 1998), 39–44.

45. See, for example, the different approaches evident in Moltmann, *God in Creation*; A. R. Peacocke, *Creation and the World of Science* (Oxford: Clarendon, 1979); Polkinghorne and Welker, *End of the World*. The lively debate about "open theism" has tackled these issues in different ways. To those familiar with this movement, it will be clear by now that I would distance myself from some of what it stresses. See Clark H. Pinnock, *Most Moved Mover: A Theology of God's Openness* (Grand Rapids: Baker Academic, 2001); Gregory A. Boyd, *God of the Possible: A Biblical Introduction to the Open View of God* (Grand Rapids: Baker Books, 2000); John M. Frame, *No Other God: A Response to Open Theism* (Phillipsburg, NJ: P&R, 2001); William Hasker, *Providence, Evil, and the Openness of God* (London: Routledge, 2004).

46. See, e.g., Jean-Jacques Suurmond, *Word and Spirit at Play: Towards a Charismatic Theology* (Grand Rapids: Eerdmans, 1994), 37–41 and passim.

47. Daniel W. Hardy and David Ford, *Praising and Knowing God* (Philadelphia: Westminster, 1985), 119–20.

48. For discussion of related ideas, see Patrick Sherry, *Spirit and Beauty: An Introduction to Theological Aesthetics* (London: SCM, 2002), chap. 7. This does not mean that the world was created "imperfect" in the sense of not being good or of being tainted with evil. The world's journey is not one from an initial evil to a final good but, I am contending, one from an incomplete perfection, through a broken perfection, to a final perfection. In other words, perfection should not be understood in a static sense of ruling out change. Jesus was perfect at every point in his life, but it was a perfection lived out in different ways at different times, indeed, a perfection realized by the Spirit. For a recent treatment of the Holy Spirit as the one who frees creation, see Sigurd Bergmann, *Creation Set Free: The Spirit as Liberator of Nature*, trans. Douglas Stott (Grand Rapids: Eerdmans, 2005).

49. See, e.g., Hart, *Beauty of the Infinite*, esp. 249–88.

50. Irenaeus, *Adversus haereses* 2.2.4.

51. Here Hopkins stands very close to the Franciscan philosopher Duns Scotus (ca. 1266–1308). One of Scotus's key terms was *haecceitas* ("thisness"), denoting the uniqueness of things. He believed entities are what they are because God wants them to be so; *this* and not *that*.

52. Gerard Manley Hopkins, "As Kingfishers Catch Fire, Dragonflies Draw Flame," in *Poems and Prose* (London: Penguin, 1985), 51.

53. Colin E. Gunton, *The Christian Faith: An Introduction to Christian Doctrine* (Oxford: Blackwell, 2002), 35.

54. While this book was being written, London Zoo put on an exhibit titled "Human Zoo," parading a group of men and women with only fig leaves to cover their modesty, "to demonstrate the basic nature of man as an animal." If this means "no more than animals," then questions need to be asked. For a concise and exceptionally lucid discussion of human uniqueness from a biblical perspective, highlighting the ease with which Christians can locate it in the wrong place, see Joel B. Green, "What Does It Mean to Be Human? Another Chapter in the Ongoing Interaction of Science and Scripture," in *From Cells to Souls and Beyond*, ed. Malcolm Jeeves (Grand Rapids: Eerdmans, 2004), 179–98.

55. Jeremy Begbie, *Voicing Creation's Praise: Towards a Theology of the Arts* (Edinburgh: T&T Clark, 1991).

56. "Of all the creatures both in sea and land / Only to Man thou hast made known thy ways, / And put the pen alone into his hand, / And made him Secretary of thy praise" (George Herbert, "Providence," in *The Temple* [1633]).

57. For one of the best recent treatments of the theme, see Stanley Grenz, *The Social God and the Relational Self: A Trinitarian Theology of the Imago Dei* (Louisville: Westminster John Knox, 2001).

58. Ibid., 200.

59. Watson, *Text and Truth*, 288–93.

60. Grenz, *Social God*, 197–203.

61. Obligations *flow from* imaging. Dominion, for example, is a *consequence* of creation in the divine image, not constitutive of it (ibid., 197).

62. Bauckham provides an especially illuminating summary of the fateful turn from dominion to domination (Bauckham, "Stewardship and Relationship"). Dominion imagery is almost certainly royal (as in Ps. 72): humankind is commissioned to rule nature as a benevolent king, acting as God's representative. See Gordon J. Wenham, *Genesis 1–15* (Waco: Word, 1987), 33.

63. Stewardship, although not an image Scripture uses to describe the proper human relation to the rest of creation, has become a very widely used term. For a helpful history (and critique) of the concept, see Bauckham, *God and the Crisis of Freedom*, 168–72.

64. Plantinga, *Engaging God's World*, 31.

65. Some are nervous of the language of priesthood in this context. In an essay that helpfully draws attention to the weaknesses of the term "stewardship" (that it overplays our vertical relation to creation, pandering to our hubris and underplaying our continuity with other creatures), Richard Bauckham points to similar drawbacks with the language of priesthood. "There is no indication in the Bible," he writes, "of the notion that the other creatures need us to voice their praise for them. This idea, that we are called to act as priests to nature, mediating, as it were, between nature and God . . . intrudes our inveterate sense of superiority exactly where the Bible will not allow it" (Bauckham, *God and the Crisis of Freedom*, 177). In other words, creation is quite capable of praising God without us; in fact, it is often rather better at it! Nevertheless, I am not convinced the language of priesthood need be rejected. Our claim that we are called to "voice creation's praise" as priests of creation is not to be taken as implying that creation is unable to praise God without us; it is only to call attention to the character of our role in relation to that praise: to articulate it in unique ways, to extend and elaborate it.

66. Alistair McFadyen, "Sins of Praise: The Assault on God's Freedom," in *God and Freedom: Essays in Historical and Systematic Theology*, ed. Colin E. Gunton (Edinburgh: T&T Clark, 1995), 32–56.

67. Wright, *New Tasks*, 59.

68. See above, pp. 65–67.

69. For a very concise and readable account of Israel's vocation, and its outworking in Christ, see Richard Bauckham, *Bible and Mission: Christian Witness in a Postmodern World* (Carlisle: Paternoster, 2003).

70. From John Milton, "At a Solemn Music," in *John Milton: Complete Shorter Poems*, ed. John Carey (London: Longman, 1971), 164.

71. Language about the image of God in Genesis, therefore, along with other passages that speak (daringly) of a visual similarity of God and man (Ezek. 1:26), can be read as anticipating and pointing forward to the incarnation, the coming of Jesus Christ, the truly human person who perfectly images God.

72. Watson, *Text and Truth*, 281–82. It would be hard to better Joel Green's encapsulation of the theology of human uniqueness: our uniqueness lies not in the possession of a "soul," he writes, but "in the human vocation, given and enabled by God, to relate to God as God's partner in covenant, and to join in companionship within the human family and in relation to the whole cosmos in ways that reflect the covenant love of God. 'Humanness,' in this sense, is realised in and modeled by Jesus Christ" (Green, "What Does It Mean to Be Human?" 197).

73. Hebrews 2:5–9 brings this out clearly, where Ps. 8 is interpreted with Jesus at its center. Christ, who is far above all angels, belonging to the identity of God (the thrust of the first part of chapter 1), was for a while made a "little lower than the angels" (a reference to his earthly life), but is now "crowned with glory and honor"—that is, exalted to the right hand of the Father. And the description of human transcendence over the created world in Ps. 8 is now implicitly applied to Jesus.

74. This is why Stanley Grenz rightly insists that the image of God, understood in light of the entire biblical witness, is an eschatological metaphor—that is, it is embodied preeminently in Christ, who is the goal, the destination to which we are heading. We are to be conformed by the Spirit to his image (2 Cor. 3:18) and become image bearers on earth (Rom. 8:29 and 1 Cor. 15:49). Grenz goes on to comment that, seen from this perspective, the image of God is something we are growing into, through a process of becoming (Grenz, *Social God*, chap. 6).

75. See Michael B. Thompson, *Clothed with Christ: The Example and Teaching of Jesus in Romans 12.1–15.13* (Sheffield: JSOT Press, 1991), 124–27.

76. Kathi Meyer-Baer, *Music of the Spheres and the Dance of Death: Studies in Musical Iconology* (Princeton, NJ: Princeton University Press, 1974), 83–86.

77. Bouma-Prediger, *Beauty of the Earth*, 74.

78. O'Donovan, *Resurrection and Moral Order*, 26.

79. From Hopkins, "God's Grandeur," 27.

80. Lewis, *Theatre of the Gospel*, 31.

81. Compare Eph. 1:22–23: "[God] has put all things under his feet and has made him the head over all things for the church, which is his body, the fullness of him who fills all in all." It would be hard to find a higher view of the church than this.

82. See John Zizioulas, *Being as Communion: Studies in Personhood and the Church* (London: Darton, Longman & Todd, 1985); James Torrance, *Worship, Community, and the Triune God of Grace* (Carlisle: Paternoster, 1996).

Chapter 9 Music in God's World

1. Philip Yancey, interview with *Sojourners* magazine, "Sex, Lies, and Life on the Evangelical Edge," http://www.sojo.net/index.cfm?action=magazine.article&issue=soj0402&article=040224.

2. An art professor at a major university quoted in Ellen F. Davies, *Wondrous Depth: Preaching the Old Testament* (Louisville: Westminster John Knox, 2005), xiii.

3. Leo Spitzer, *Classical and Christian Ideas of World Harmony: Prolegomena to an Interpretation of the Word "Stimmung"* (Baltimore: Johns Hopkins University Press, 1963), 19–20. Some might want to ask whether Augustine developed this line of thinking far enough himself. In any case, David Bentley Hart adds, "Such a change in emphasis was natural: for Christian dogma all beauty and order belong eminently to the order of the trinitarian relations, and so have no basis profounder than love" (David Bentley Hart, *The Beauty of the Infinite: The Aesthetics of Christian Truth* [Grand Rapids: Eerdmans, 2003], 276).

4. To sidestep into the world of painting: Philip Blond speaks of Van Gogh's *The Sower* (1888) as "bringing to the particular and undissolved phenomena of what we actually see an evermore wondrous realisation *that they are*" (Philip Blond, "Perception: From Modern Painting to the Vision in Christ," in *Radical Orthodoxy: A New Theology*, ed. John Milbank, Graham Ward, and Catherine Pickstock [London: Routledge, 1998], 230).

5. As in Brandon Taylor, *Modernism, Post-Modernism, Realism: A Critical Perspective for Art* (Winchester: Winchester School of Art Press, 1987), 36.

6. Leo Tolstoy gave classic expression to this view when he said, "Art is a human activity consisting in this, that one man consciously by means of certain external signs, hands on to others feelings he has lived through, and that others are infected by these feelings and also experience them" (quoted in Gordon Graham, *Philosophy of the Arts: An Introduction to Aesthetics* [London: Routledge, 2000], 24).

7. For explanation and discussion, see Edward A. Lippman, *A History of Western Musical Aesthetics* (Lincoln: University of Nebraska Press, 1992), 203–38.

8. Wassily Kandinsky, *Concerning the Spiritual in Art, and Painting in Particular* (New York: Wittenborn, 1947), 24.

9. Ibid., 40.

10. For a much fuller treatment, see Jeremy S. Begbie, "The Ambivalent Rainbow: Forsyth, Art, and Creation," in *Justice the True and Only Mercy*, ed. Trevor Hart (Edinburgh: T&T Clark, 1995), 197–219.

11. In his book *Christ on Parnassus* (1911) Forsyth wants to show that "Christian art" has followed a distinct course of development from painting through music to poetry, and he interprets this as a procession of increasing spiritualization, a "progressive attenuation of the material." He believes this reflects the impact of a religion that hinges chiefly on a spiritual, moral reconciliation between humanity and God, and the broader context is his conviction that the divine Spirit is "entombed within material Nature" and comes to self-realization through the artist (P. T. Forsyth, *Christ on Parnassus: Lectures on Art, Ethic, and Theology* [London: Hodder & Stoughton, 1911], 259–60).

12. For Forsyth, music's indefiniteness is a danger as well as a strength, since music can quickly lead to an undisciplined flight from truth and goodness. Here poetry has the edge over music, with its power for precise reference to things in the world. Forsyth sees the entrance of the choir in the last movement of Beethoven's Ninth Symphony as poetry breaking in, cavalry-like, to deliver music from its dangerous ambiguities: "Poetry comes to the rescue of music" in order "to save it from inadequacy and collapse" (P. T. Forsyth, "Music and Worship," *Congregational Quarterly* 33 [1955]: 344). A key figure behind Forsyth here is the seminal German philosopher G. W. F. Hegel (1770–1831). See Begbie, "Ambivalent Rainbow," 206n32.

13. Kandinsky, in a letter to Schoenberg, January 18, 1911. In Arnold Schoenberg, Wassily Kandinsky, and Jelena Hahl-Koch, eds., *Arnold Schoenberg, Wassily Kandinsky: Letters, Pictures, and Documents* (London: Faber & Faber, 1984), 21.

14. Arnold Schoenberg, *Style and Idea*, ed. Leonard Stein, trans. Leo Black (London: Faber & Faber, 1984), 235.

15. Trevor Hart, "Through the Arts: Seeing and Touching the Truth," in *Beholding the Glory: Incarnation Through the Arts*, ed. Jeremy Begbie (Grand Rapids: Baker Academic, 2000), 14–15.

16. See, e.g., John W. Dixon, *Nature and Grace in Art* (Chapel Hill: University of North Carolina Press, 1964); George Pattison, *Art, Modernity, and Faith: Restoring the Image* (London: SCM, 1998); Nicholas Wolterstorff, *Art in Action: Toward a Christian Aesthetic* (Grand Rapids: Eerdmans, 1980).

17. Wolterstorff, *Art in Action*, 91.

18. Michael Polanyi, *The Tacit Dimension* (Gloucester, MA: Peter Smith, 1983).

19. See above, pp. 47–48.

20. Igor Stravinsky, *Poetics of Music in the Form of Six Lessons*, trans. Arthur Knodel and Ingolf Dahl (Cambridge, MA: Harvard University Press, 1947), 51.

21. Patrick Shove and Bruno H. Repp, "Musical Motion and Performance: Theoretical and Empirical Perspectives," in *The Practice of Performance: Studies in Musical Interpretation*, ed. John Rink (Cambridge: Cambridge University Press, 1995), 78–79; italics mine; see also 55–83.

22. See above, pp. 85–86.

23. C. S. Lewis, *Surprised by Joy* (London: Collins, 1955), 64; italics mine.

24. Tom Beaudoin, *Virtual Faith: The Irreverent Spiritual Quest of Generation X* (San Francisco: Jossey-Bass, 1998), 21.

25. Simon Reynolds, *Generation Ecstasy: Into the World of Techno and Rave Culture* (Boston: Little Brown, 1998), 9.

26. Henry Chadwick, "Why Music in the Church?" in *Tradition and Exploration: Collected Papers on Theology and the Church*, ed. Henry Chadwick (Norwich: Canterbury Press, 1994), 215.

27. See above, pp. 53–56.

28. For a much fuller treatment of this field, see Jeremy Begbie, *Theology, Music, and Time* (Cambridge: Cambridge University Press, 2000); Jonathan D. Kramer, *The Time of Music: New Meanings, New Temporalities, New Listening Strategies* (New York: Schirmer, 1988).

29. See Begbie, *Theology, Music, and Time*, chap. 2.

30. See above, pp. 46–49.

31. See above, pp. 47–48.

32. Victor Zuckerkandl, *Sound and Symbol: Music and the External World* (London: Routledge & Kegan Paul, 1956), 241–42.

33. Catherine Pickstock, "Soul, City, and Cosmos after Augustine," in *Radical Orthodoxy: A New Theology*, ed. John Milbank, Catherine Pickstock, and Graham Ward (London: Routledge, 1999), 269.

34. Rowan Williams, "Keeping Time," in *Open to Judgement: Sermons and Addresses* (London: Darton, Longman & Todd, 1994), 247.

35. Simone Weil, *The Note Books of Simone Weil*, vol. 1, trans. Arthur Wills (London: Routledge & Kegan Paul, 1956), 39.

36. Quoted in Daniel Jaffé, "High Priest of Music," *Classic CD* 111 (1999): 28; italics mine.

37. Williams, "Keeping Time," 249.

38. See below, pp. 278–86.

39. Much musicology has struggled to find "kinetic" ways of analyzing music, ways that do justice to the fact that music cannot be experienced "at a glance."

40. Thomas Clifton, *Music as Heard: A Study in Applied Phenomenology* (New Haven: Yale University Press, 1983), 81.

41. Kramer, *Time of Music*, chap. 11.

42. Ibid., chap. 12.

43. See Mark J. Prendergast, *The Ambient Century: From Mahler to Trance. The Evolution of Sound in the Electronic Age* (London: Bloomsbury, 2000), 91–177; Piers Dudgeon, *Lifting the Veil: The Biography of Sir John Tavener* (London: Portrait, 2003); Geoffrey Haydon, *John Tavener: Glimpses of Paradise* (London: Gollancz, 1995); John Tavener, *The Music of Silence: A Composer's Testament*, ed. Brian Keeble (London: Faber & Faber, 1999); Paul Hillier, *Arvo Pärt*, Oxford Studies of Composers (Oxford: Clarendon, 1997); Oliver Kautny, *Arvo Pärt zwischen Ost und West: Rezeptionsgeschichte* (Stuttgart: Metzler, 2002); Adrian Thomas, *Górecki* (Oxford: Clarendon, 1997); Josiah Fisk, "The New Simplicity: The Music of Górecki, Tavener and Pärt," *Hudson Review* 47, no. 3 (1994): 394–412; Andreas Andreopoulos, "The Return of Religion in Contemporary Music," *Literature and Theology* 14, no. 1 (2000): 81–95.

44. To generalize, this music is characterized by exceptional slowness, simplicity as opposed to complex multiplicity, a restraint of a sense of direction or goal orientation as articulated through patterns of tension and resolution (basic to most Western music), and with this a suppression of driving change and motion, the evasion of clearly defined beginnings and endings (the music can emerge out of silence and drift seamlessly back into silence, giving the impression of being in the midst of previously—and subsequently—unheard music), and uniform texture (the same kind of "thickness" of sound over long periods).

45. Begbie, *Theology, Music, and Time*, 74, 144. On "multiply overwhelming," see David Ford, *The Shape of Living: Spiritual Directions for Everyday Life* (Grand Rapids: Baker Books, 1997). For another perspective on this music, see Andreopoulos, "Return of Religion," 81–95.

46. See, e.g., Begbie, *Theology, Music, and Time*, chap. 5, where I also explore the implications of this for our understanding of God's eternity as dynamic.

47. Stravinsky may be overstating the case, but he is worth citing: "The phenomenon of music is given to us with the sole purpose of establishing an order in things, including, and particularly, *the co-ordination between man and time*" (Igor Stravinsky, *Igor Stravinsky: An Autobiography* [London: Calder & Boyars, 1975], 54; italics mine).

48. John E. Kaemmer, *Music in Human Life: Anthropological Perspectives on Music* (Austin: University of Texas Press, 1993), 83–84.

49. Augustine, *On the Trinity* 4.2.4.

50. A psychologist of music writes, "The octave appears to be a particularly privileged interval" (John A. Sloboda, *The Musical Mind: The Cognitive Psychology of Music* [Oxford: Oxford University Press, 1995], 254).

51. See above, p. 91.

52. Donald Hall demonstrates the acoustical rootedness of a number of Western music's most common harmonic progressions (Donald Hall, *Musical Acoustics* [Pacific Grove, CA: Brooks/Cole, 2002], 438–43).

53. Sloboda, *Musical Mind*, 253–54.

54. For a summary of factors influencing such differences, see Albert L. Blackwell, *The Sacred in Music* (Cambridge: Lutterworth, 1999), 75.

55. See above, p. 93.

56. For fuller treatments, see Hall, *Musical Acoustics*, 418–21; Stuart Isacoff, *Temperament: How Music Became a Battleground for the Great Minds of Western Civilization* (New York: Alfred A. Knopf, 2001).

57. In fact, for Bach "well-tempered" was probably not the "equal" temperament as on a modern piano (the division of the octave into exactly equal parts) but an arrangement such that some keys were more equally tuned than others. In this way, different keys would come to acquire different characteristic features or qualities (Malcolm Boyd, *Bach* [Oxford: Oxford University Press, 2000], 105–9).

58. This is why we need to be cautious of comments like the following from the composer Paul Hindemith: "The intervals which constitute the building material of melodies and harmonies fall into tonal groupments, necessitated by their own physical structure and without our consent. . . . It seems to me that attempts at avoiding them are as promising as attempts at avoiding the effects of gravitation" (Paul Hindemith, *A Composer's World: Horizons and Limitations* [Cambridge, MA: Harvard University Press, 1952], 55, 24). The sentiment—respect for given order—is fine, but the point is overplayed.

59. Blackwell, *Sacred in Music*, 74.

60. Hall, *Musical Acoustics*, 412.

61. "The dissonance of seconds, sevenths, and tritones may be attributed to the roughness of the beating associated with the nearness to unisons, octaves, and fifths, respectively" (ibid., 415).

62. John R. Pierce, *The Science of Musical Sound* (New York: Scientific American Library, 1983), 74–75.

63. Hall, *Musical Acoustics*, 443.

64. Ibid., 439–41.

65. Ibid., 440; italics mine.

66. Ibid. It may also be that the minor third sets up "difference tones" (a frequency equal to the difference in frequency between the two sounding tones) that colors it in a particular way. See Blackwell, *Sacred in Music*, 139–40.

67. Blackwell, *Sacred in Music*, 135. For a very open recognition of the importance of "universal acoustic phenomena" shared by all music making and music hearing, which does not thereby downplay the role of social and cultural shaping, see Kaemmer, *Music in Human Life*, chap. 4. Kaemmer is writing as an ethnomusicologist. Blackwell's sustained argument against Susan McClary's extreme "constructivism" is also worth alluding to in this context. See Blackwell, *Sacred in Music*, 105–12.

68. Daniel W. Hardy and David Ford, *Praising and Knowing God* (Philadelphia: Westminster, 1985), 20, 142.

69. A. R. Peacocke, *Theology for a Scientific Age: Being and Becoming—Natural, Divine, and Human* (London: SCM, 1993), 175; Ann Pederson, *God, Creation and All That Jazz: A Process of Composition and Improvisation* (St. Louis: Chalice, 2001).

70. From Micheal O'Siadhail, "Cosmos," in *Poems 1975–1995* (Newcastle upon Tyne: Bloodaxe Books, 1999), 154.

71. Hopkins, "As Kingfishers Catch Fire, Dragonflies Draw Flame," in *Poems and Prose* (London: Penguin, 1985), 51.

Chapter 10 Music in God's Calling

1. C. S. Lewis, *The Screwtape Letters* (New York: Macmillan, 1961), 102–3.

2. For a subtle treatment of these issues, see George Steiner, *Grammars of Creation* (London: Faber, 2001).

3. The crucial philosopher here is undoubtedly Immanuel Kant (1724–1804), who has set the stage for so much modern philosophical thought, especially in epistemology (the theory of knowledge). For him, the nature of our knowledge cannot be understood so long as we think of it simply as fed to us from outside ourselves, and of ourselves as passive recipients of information. Our experience and understanding are shaped by our own minds. Even the most fundamental categories we use to supply the framework of our knowledge, space and time, are provided by the mind. As many have argued, this pushes one strongly toward the view that form and order are essentially created and imposed by the mind on the plurality of the (unknown) world. This in turn too easily "generates what can only be called a technocratic attitude to the world about us, encouraging attitudes of dominance and disparaging receptivity" (Colin E. Gunton, *Enlightenment and Alienation: An Essay Towards a Trinitarian Theology* [Grand Rapids: Eerdmans, 1985], 25). Applied to aesthetics: for Kant, the crucial factor in the experience of beauty is the "form of purposiveness," and the "form" is given by the subject's mind. Despite his belief that it is the aesthetic object that evokes aesthetic pleasure, this pleasure is derived primarily from those powers that enable *us* to arrange the plurality of sense data. What gives us satisfaction is "the mere form of the purposiveness in the representation by which an object is *given* to us, so far as we are conscious of it" (Immanuel Kant, *Critique of Judgement*, trans. J. H. Bernard [New York: Hafner, 1968], 56). What should be challenged here is Kant's stress on the mind's imposition of a *fixed* order on essentially *unknown* reality. I discuss these themes much more extensively in *Voicing Creation's Praise: Towards a Theology of the Arts* (Edinburgh: T&T Clark, 1991), 186–204.

4. Donald Hall, *Musical Acoustics* (Pacific Grove, CA: Brooks/Cole, 2002), 412.

5. Albert L. Blackwell, *The Sacred in Music* (Cambridge: Lutterworth, 1999), 70; italics mine.

6. See above, pp. 135–39.

7. See pp. 137–38. For more extensive discussion, see Jeremy Begbie, "Created Beauty: The Witness of J. S. Bach," in *The Beauty of God: Theology and the Arts*, ed. Daniel J. Treier and Mark Husbands (Downers Grove, IL: InterVarsity, forthcoming).

8. Christoph Wolff, *Johann Sebastian Bach: The Learned Musician* (New York: Norton, 2000), 468; italics mine.

9. Oliver O'Donovan, *Resurrection and Moral Order: An Outline for Evangelical Ethics* (Leicester: Inter-Varsity, 1994), 26.

10. Cornelius Cardew, *Treatise Handbook* (London: Edition Peters, 1971), xviii.

11. Nicholas Wolterstorff, *Art in Action: Toward a Christian Aesthetic* (Grand Rapids: Eerdmans, 1980), 95.

12. The phrase is John Howard Yoder's, though he uses it with a particular slant to the crucifixion: "People who bear crosses are working with the grain of the universe." This is picked up by Stanley Hauerwas in ways that overlap with many of the concerns of this book (Stanley Hauerwas, *With the Grain of the Universe: The Church's Witness and Natural Theology* [Grand Rapids: Brazos Press, 2001], 17 and passim).

13. See the fascinating discussion in Victor Zuckerkandl, *Man the Musician* (Princeton, NJ: Princeton University Press, 1973), 282, and the whole section 274–85.

14. See above, pp. 81–86.

15. Daniel K. L. Chua, *Absolute Music and the Construction of Meaning* (Cambridge: Cambridge University Press, 1999), 185.

16. Alister E. McGrath, *The Re-enchantment of Nature: Science, Religion and the Human Sense of Wonder* (London: Hodder & Stoughton, 2002), chap. 6.

17. Charles Taylor, *Sources of the Self: The Making of the Modern Identity* (Cambridge: Cambridge University Press, 1996), 193; italics mine.

18. Quoted in ibid., 371.

19. Monroe C. Beardsley, *Aesthetics from Classical Greece to the Present: A Short History* (Tuscaloosa: University of Alabama Press, 1977), 262.

20. See Taylor, *Sources of the Self*, chaps. 20, 21; esp. the notion of "nature as source."

21. Roger Lundin, *The Culture of Interpretation: Christian Faith and the Postmodern World* (Grand Rapids: Eerdmans, 1993), chap. 5. See the immensely illuminating discussion of Emerson in Roger

Lundin, *From Nature to Experience: The American Search for Cultural Authority* (Lanham, MD: Rowman & Littlefield, 1993), chap. 2.

22. We should note that the notion of the artist as a creator analogous to God as Creator has roots very much further back in European thought. See E. N. Tigerstedt, "The Poet as Creator: Origins of a Metaphor," *Comparative Literature Studies* 5 (1968): 455–88.

23. Quoted in Taylor, *Sources of the Self*, 378.

24. I borrow the words from John Polkinghorne and Michael Welker, *Faith in the Living God* (London: SPCK, 2001), 16.

25. Beardsley, *Aesthetics*, 262. See Taylor, *Sources of the Self*, 456–66.

26. Lundin, *Culture of Interpretation*, 75.

27. Pierre Boulez, *Stocktakings from an Apprenticeship* (Oxford: Oxford University Press, 1991), 16; italics mine.

28. Gerald Bennett, "The Early Works," in *Pierre Boulez: A Symposium*, ed. William Glock (London: Eulenburg, 1986), 84.

29. Pierre Boulez, *Conversations with Célestin Deliège* (London: Eulenburg, 1976), 57.

30. Quoted in Brandon Taylor, *Modernism, Post-Modernism, Realism: A Critical Perspective for Art* (Winchester: Winchester School of Art Press, 1987), 36–37; italics mine.

31. Bennett, "The Early Works," 41, 84; italics mine.

32. Some would say that the new and burgeoning technologies of production and reproduction make many of these questions redundant by taking us into radically new musical territory. Electronic music, for example, would seem to be distanced to an unprecedented degree from nature, involving a hitherto unimaginable artificiality. But whether a computer or a human being generates mathematical sequences, whether a vocal cord or a speaker cone vibrates, the fact remains that musical sound is produced by physical objects, mediated through the air and through our bodies, and as such is governed by certain integrities that can be respected and honored, as well as ignored and effaced.

33. Constraint here refers not so much to "confinement" as to "specificity" or "particular shape." The terms are John Webster's (John Webster, *Barth's Ethics of Reconciliation* [Cambridge: Cambridge University Press, 1995], 71). Constraints are structures that prevent us from being amorphous creatures and that give us our identity. There are constraints internal to the person (genetic makeup, physiological processes, etc.) and those that are external (e.g., other persons, the extrahuman material world).

34. Blackwell, *Sacred in Music*, 76.

35. "[The business of the artist] is not to escape from his material medium or bully it, but to serve it; but to serve it he must love it. If he does so, he will realise that in its service is perfect freedom" (Dorothy L. Sayers, *The Mind of the Maker* [London: Methuen, 1941], 53).

36. Igor Stravinsky, *Poetics of Music in the Form of Six Lessons*, trans. Arthur Knodel and Ingolf Dahl (Cambridge, MA: Harvard University Press, 1947), 63–65; italics mine.

37. For a compelling account of the approach to freedom I have in mind, see Richard Bauckham, *God and the Crisis of Freedom* (Louisville: Westminster John Knox, 2002). On freedom and constraint in relation to music, see Jeremy Begbie, *Theology, Music, and Time* (Cambridge: Cambridge University Press, 2000), chaps. 7 and 8.

38. David Sudnow, *Ways of the Hand: A Rewritten Account* (Cambridge, MA: MIT Press, 2001), 35.

39. Ibid., 49.

40. Ibid., 92, 130.

41. James Pritchett, *The Music of John Cage* (Cambridge: Cambridge University Press, 1993), 74.

42. Quoted in Reginald Smith Brindle, *The New Music: The Avant-Garde since 1945* (Oxford: Oxford University Press, 1987), 126.

43. Paul Griffiths, *Cage* (London: Oxford University Press, 1981), 27. Cage later spoke of the purpose of music as being "to sober and quiet the mind, thus making one susceptible to divine influence" (quoted in Richard Fleming and William Duckworth, *John Cage at Seventy-Five* [Lewisburg, PA: Bucknell University Press, 1989], 23).

44. Pritchett, *Music of John Cage*, 66.

45. Quoted in Griffiths, *Cage*, 24.

46. Jean-Jacques Nattiez, *Music and Discourse: Toward a Semiology of Music* (Princeton, NJ: Princeton University Press, 1990), 78.

47. John Cage, *Silence* (London: Calder & Boyars, 1973), 7–8.

48. Ibid., 8.

49. Edward A. Lippman, *A History of Western Musical Aesthetics* (Lincoln: University of Nebraska Press, 1992), 436.

50. See above, pp. 50–52.

51. See above, p. 229; see also p. 93.

52. For fine treatments, see Gordon Lynch, *Understanding Theology and Popular Culture* (Oxford: Blackwell, 2005), 70–77; R. Witkin, *Adorno on Popular Culture* (London: Routledge, 2003); Max Paddison, *Adorno's Aesthetics of Music* (Cambridge: Cambridge University Press, 1993).

53. Theodor Adorno, "On Popular Music," in *On Record: Rock, Pop, and the Written Word*, ed. John Storey (New York: Pantheon, 1990), 301–14.

54. Theodor Adorno, "Perennial Fashion—Jazz," in *Prisms* (London: Neville Spearman, 1967), 119–32.

55. Adorno, "On Popular Music," 307–9.

56. Ibid., 310.

57. As contemporary examples of this, Lynch cites the commodification of rap music and the music of the "acid house" scene in Britain (Lynch, *Theology and Popular Culture*, 75–76).

58. Blackwell, *Sacred in Music*, 69.

59. J. Cauty and B. Drummond. *The Manual: How to Have a Number One Hit the Easy Way* (London: Ellipsis, 1998).

60. Richard Middleton, *Studying Popular Music* (Milton Keynes: Open University Press, 1990), chap. 2.

61. Simon Frith, *Sound Effects: Youth, Leisure, and the Politics of Rock 'n' Roll* (New York: Pantheon, 1981), 147.

62. Middleton, *Studying Popular Music*, 37–39.

63. See, e.g., Robert Beckford, *Jesus Is Dread: Black Theology and Black Culture in Britain* (London: DLT, 1998); Beckford, *Jesus Dub: Theology, Music and Social Change* (London: Routledge, 2006).

64. Middleton, *Studying Popular Music*, 51–54.

65. Lynch, *Theology and Popular Culture*, 75.

66. Indeed, it seems the underlying repeated schemes can be the vehicle of enriching and subtle social activities (Middleton, *Studying Popular Music*, 55).

67. Simon Frith, *The Sociology of Rock* (London: Constable, 1978), 195.

68. Middleton, *Studying Popular Music*, 37.

69. Ibid.

70. Philip V. Bohlman, *World Music: A Very Short Introduction* (Oxford: Oxford University Press, 2002), 147. Bohlman, however, goes on to say that the suspicion of such phenomena is often based on misinterpretation.

71. Quoted in Mark Hijleh, *The Music of Jesus: From Composition to Koinonia* (New York: Writers Club Press, 2001), 97.

72. See Colin E. Gunton, *The One, the Three, and the Many: God, Creation, and the Culture of Modernity* (Cambridge: Cambridge University Press, 1993); Rowan Williams, "Making It Strange: Theology in Other(s') Words," in *Sounding the Depths*, ed. Jeremy Begbie (London: SCM, 2002), 19–32.

73. For discussion, see William Romanowski, "Evangelicals and Popular Music: The Contemporary Christian Music Industry," in *Religion and Popular Culture in America*, ed. Bruce David Forbes and Jeffrey H. Mahan (Berkeley: University of California Press, 2000), 165–79.

74. Jay R. Howard and John M. Streck, *Apostles of Rock: The Splintered World of Contemporary Christian Music* (Lexington: University Press of Kentucky, 1999), 154–58.

75. Ibid., chap. 4. This is set alongside "Separational CCM" and "Integrational CCM."

76. Ibid., 160.

77. C. Michael Hawn, *Gather into One: Praying and Singing Globally* (Grand Rapids: Eerdmans, 2003), 4.

78. Ibid., 13.

79. Quoted in Wolterstorff, *Art in Action*, 54.

80. For a fine treatment of these themes, see Richard Bauckham and Trevor A. Hart, *Hope against Hope: Christian Eschatology at the Turn of the Millennium* (Grand Rapids: Eerdmans, 1999).

81. For a thorough and moving presentation of the relation between cross and resurrection that I am commending here, see Alan E. Lewis, *Between Cross and Resurrection: A Theology of Holy Saturday* (Grand Rapids: Eerdmans, 2001).

82. See above, pp. 224–25.

83. Miroslav Volf, "Worship as Adoration and Action: Reflections on a Christian Way of Being-in-the-World," in *Worship: Adoration and Action*, ed. D. A. Carson (Grand Rapids: Baker Books, 1993), 203–11.

84. Quoted in John W. de Gruchy, *Christianity, Art, and Transformation: Theological Aesthetics in the Struggle for Justice* (Cambridge: Cambridge University Press, 2001), 139.

85. Quoted in William Edgar, *Taking Note of Music* (London: Third Ways, SPCK, 1986), 18.

86. See above, pp. 224–25.

87. See above, pp. 179–80.

88. See below, pp. 283–86.

89. Hawn, *Gather into One*, chaps. 4 and 6.

90. Anthony Monti, *A Natural Theology of the Arts: Imprint of the Spirit* (Aldershot: Ashgate, 2003), 139. See George Steiner, *Real Presences: Is There Anything in What We Say?* (London: Faber & Faber, 1989), esp. 200–216.

91. Bauckham and Hart, *Hope against Hope*, 85–86.

92. Isaiah 40:3, 11, 15. See Walter Brueggemann, *Israel's Praise: Doxology against Idolatry and Ideology* (Philadelphia: Fortress, 1988), 45–51.

93. Patrick Sherry, *Spirit and Beauty: An Introduction to Theological Aesthetics* (London: SCM, 2002), chap. 7.

94. Bauckham and Hart, *Hope against Hope*, 70.

95. *The Shawshank Redemption*, directed by Frank Darabont (Columbia Pictures, 1994).

96. Ibid.

97. Monti, *Natural Theology of the Arts*, 148–51.

98. Maynard Solomon, "The Ninth Symphony: A Search for Order," in *Beethoven Essays* (Cambridge, MA: Harvard University Press, 1988), 3–32. Cf. Nicholas Cook, *Beethoven: Symphony No. 9* (Cambridge: Cambridge University Press, 1993), 100–105.

99. Solomon, "The Ninth Symphony," 32.

100. Even Nicholas Cook, sympathetic to this line of argument, has to admit that to hear this passage as evidence of an absent deity may well require a twentieth- or twenty-first-century listener (Cook, *Beethoven*, 104).

101. Monti, *Natural Theology of the Arts*, 151.

102. Quite unwittingly, by insisting that Beethoven is being "ironical" (profoundly hesitant about what he also affirms), Cook highlights the crucial theological matter to be raised: Is Schiller's dream of universal brotherhood realizable without a divine engagement with the worst of humanity's predicament? Cook's less than secure grasp of basic Christian teaching will not help him here. In the course of his discussion he claims, extraordinarily, that "like Christianity, [Wagner's] *Parsifal* asserts that only man can help himself, and that only God can help man; and yet the two assertions are at loggerheads with each other" (Cook, *Beethoven*, 100).

103. See p. 278.

104. For more detail, see Begbie, *Theology, Music, and Time*, 111–14.

105. See above, pp. 72–73.

106. J. C. Polkinghorne, *The God of Hope and the End of the World* (London: SPCK, 2002), 177.

107. From Joseph Ratzinger, *A New Song for the Lord* (New York: Crossroad, 2005), 137. I owe this reference to Michael O'Connor, who has amended the translation.

108. Hawn, *Gather into One*, 272.

109. Taylor, *Sources of the Self*, 376.

110. See Middleton, *Studying Popular Music*, 39.

111. Roger Lundin has argued that contemporary evangelicalism's debt to romanticism has, directly and indirectly, been considerable: "It seems quite logical that when evangelical students of culture begin to emerge from the dusky passageways of fundamentalism, their eyes should be dazzled by the enchanting romantic tradition. Because of its skepticism about the relevance of the past and because of its sense of being alienated both from unadorned nature and from mass culture, romantic theory has offered an appealing sight to those whose aesthetic lenses have been ground in the shop of American fundamentalism" (Lundin, *Culture of Interpretation*, 235).

112. "Most of the great Romantic poets saw themselves as articulating something greater than themselves: the world, nature, being, the word of God. They were not concerned primarily with an expression of their own feelings" (Taylor, *Sources of the Self*, 427).

113. The comment from a worship leader, "I must express what is on my heart," usually indicates a concern for authenticity: the worship leader must be totally committed and involved. This is quite proper. The danger of such "heart" language, however, is that it becomes captive to our culture's love of the "inner turn," and that worship inadvertently becomes a function of the feeling state of the leader on that particular day, which the congregation is invited to share. See Pete Ward, *Selling Worship: How What We Sing Has Changed the Church* (Bletchley: Paternoster, 2005), 152–55.

114. From Micheal O'Siadhail, "Motet," in *Poems 1975–1995* (Newcastle upon Tyne: Bloodaxe Books, 1999), 129.

115. The image of polyphony has been much used in recent theology. See, e.g., David Ford, *Self and Salvation: Being Transformed* (Cambridge: Cambridge University Press, 1999), 245–59; David S. Cunningham, *These Three Are One: The Practice of Trinitarian Theology*, Challenges in Contemporary Theology (Oxford: Blackwell, 1998), chap. 4.

116. John Zizioulas, *Being as Communion: Studies in Personhood and the Church* (London: Darton, Longman & Todd, 1985), 91–92, 106–7.

117. When Moses came down from the mountain, he did not even know his face was shining (Exod. 34:29).

118. The literature on "relational" views of the person is now vast. For a way into the field from a philosophical angle, see Calvin O. Schrag, *The Self after Postmodernity* (New Haven: Yale University Press, 1997); Taylor, *Sources of the Self*. From a theological perspective, see Anthony C. Thiselton, *Interpreting God and the Postmodern Self: On Meaning, Manipulation, and Promise* (Edinburgh: T&T Clark, 1995); J. Richard Middleton and Brian J. Walsh, *Truth Is Stranger Than It Used to Be: Biblical Faith in a Postmodern Age* (Downers Grove, IL: InterVarsity, 1995), chap. 6; Stanley Grenz, *The Social God and the Relational Self: A Trinitarian Theology of the Imago Dei* (Louisville: Westminster John Knox, 2001); Christoph Schwöbel and Colin E. Gunton, eds., *Persons, Divine and Human: King's College Essays in Theological Anthropology* (Edinburgh: T&T Clark, 1991).

In recent years, some have voiced strong concern about the language of "sharing" or "participation" used of our redeemed relation to the Triune God, fearing (among other things) that it will lead us to compromise the Creator/creature distinction, lose sight of the priority of God's covenantal action, and neglect the necessity of the cross. See, e.g., John Webster, "The Church and the Perfection of God," in *The Community of the Word: Toward an Evangelical Ecclesiology*, ed. Mark Husbands and Daniel J. Treier (Downers Grove, IL: InterVarsity, 2005), 75–95; cf. Bruce L. McCormack, "What's at Stake in Current Debates over Justification?" in *Justification: What's at Stake in the Current Debates*, ed. Mark Husbands and Daniel J. Treier (Downers Grove, IL: InterVarsity, 2004), 81–117. Properly qualified, however, I see no compelling reason to abandon the language of participation as an appropriate way of conveying at least part of the meaning of *koinonia*. For an exceptionally fine discussion of the critical issues, see Julie Canlis, "Calvin, Osiander, and Participation in God," *International Journal of Systematic Theology* 6, no. 2 (2004): 169–84.

119. The examples are legion but see, e.g., Stanley Hauerwas, *After Christendom? How the Church Is to Behave if Freedom, Justice, and a Christian Nation Are Bad Ideas* (Nashville: Abingdon, 1991); Lesslie Newbigin, *The Gospel in a Pluralist Society* (Grand Rapids: Eerdmans, 1989); N. T. Wright, *New Tasks for a Renewed Church* (London: Hodder & Stoughton, 1992); Miroslav Volf, *After Our Likeness: The Church as the Image of the Trinity* (Grand Rapids: Eerdmans, 1998). See also "The Ekklesia Project," http://www.ekklesiaproject.org. In recent years, this concern has led to extensive discussions, not least among many Protestant evangelical communities, about the forms of "being church" that are appropriate to this cultural engagement. See http://www.theooze.com and http://www.emergentvillage .com. Significantly, the arts, including music, figure prominently in much of this conversation, as does the recovery of pre-Protestant tradition. For representative literature, see Ian Stackhouse, *The Gospel Driven Church: Retrieving Classical Ministries for Contemporary Revivalism* (Carlisle: Paternoster, 2004); Robert Webber, *The Younger Evangelicals: Facing the Challenges of the New World* (Grand Rapids: Baker Books, 2002); Webber, *Ancient-Future Evangelism: Making Your Church a Faith-Forming Community* (Grand Rapids: Baker Books, 2003); Michael Moynagh, *Emergingchurch.Intro* (Oxford: Monarch, 2004); Duncan MacLaren, *Mission Implausible: Restoring Credibility to the Church* (Bletchley: Paternoster, 2004); MacLaren, *Mission-Shaped Church: Church Planting and Fresh Expressions of Church in a Changing Context* (London: Church House, 2004); Eddie Gibbs and Ryan K. Bolger, *Emerging Churches: Creating Christian Community in Postmodern Cultures* (Grand Rapids: Baker Academic, 2005); Mark Husbands and Daniel J. Treier, eds., *The Community of the Word: Toward an Evangelical Ecclesiology* (Downers Grove, IL: InterVarsity, 2005). A pointed critique of much of the emerging church movement can be found in D. A. Carson, *Becoming Conversant with the Emerging Church: Understanding a Movement and Its Implications* (Grand Rapids: Zondervan, 2005).

120. Quoted in Hilary Brand and Adrienne Chaplin, *Art and Soul: Signposts for Christians in the Arts* (Carlisle: Solway, 2001), 25.

121. Madeleine L'Engle's words are worth chewing over carefully: "It's a sad commentary on our world that 'integrity' has slowly been coming to mean self-centeredness. Most people who worry about their integrity are thinking about it in terms of themselves. It's a great excuse for not doing something you really don't want to do, or are afraid to do: 'I can't do that and keep my integrity.' Integrity, like humility, is a quality which vanishes the moment we are conscious of it in ourselves" (Madeleine L'Engle, *A Circle of Quiet* [New York: Farrar, Straus & Giroux, 1972], 130).

122. http://www.ark-t.org.

123. http://www.hopearts.org.

124. http://www.theplacelite.blogspot.com.

125. http://www.cambridgevineyard.org/offerings/arts/index.htm.

126. http://www.ecclesiahouston.org.

127. http://www.buildabridge.org.

128. C. S. Lewis, *Screwtape Proposes a Toast and Other Pieces* (London: Fontana, 1965), 118–19.

129. Albert Camus, *The Myth of Sisyphus* (Harmondsworth: Penguin, 1975), 191–92.

130. For a very fine recent treatment of the theme, see Kevin J. Vanhoozer, *The Drama of Doctrine: A Canonical-Linguistic Approach to Christian Theology* (Louisville: Westminster John Knox, 2005), chap. 5. See also Bauckham, *God and the Crisis of Freedom*, chap. 5; Newbigin, *Gospel in a Pluralist Society*, chap. 4; Stephen R. Holmes, *Listening to the Past: The Place of Tradition in Theology* (Grand Rapids: Baker Academic, 2002); Trevor Hart, "Living with Diversity: Scripture, Tradition and the Present," http://www .anglicancommunioninstitute.org/articles/livingwithdiversity.htm.

131. See pp. 42–46.

132. Keith Johnstone, *Impro: Improvisation and the Theatre* (London: Faber, 1979), 88.

133. Boulez, *Conversations*, 33.

134. T. S. Eliot, "Tradition and the Individual Talent," in *Selected Essays* (London: Faber & Faber, 1932), 14, see also 13–22.

135. See Vanhoozer, *Drama of Doctrine*, 231–36. For a fine popular treatment of this theme, see D. H. Williams, *Retrieving the Tradition and Renewing Evangelicalism: A Primer for Suspicious Protestants* (Grand Rapids: Eerdmans, 1999).

136. Oliver O'Donovan, "'Where Were You . . . ?'" in *The Care of Creation: Focusing Concern and Action*, ed. R. J. Berry (Leicester: Inter-Varsity, 2000), 92.

Chapter 11 Singular Powers

1. See chap. 1, pp. 49–53, esp. 52–53.

2. Tia DeNora, *Music in Everyday Life* (Cambridge: Cambridge University Press, 2000), ix.

3. The material here is much more fully elaborated in Jeremy Begbie, *Theology, Music, and Time* (Cambridge: Cambridge University Press, 2000), esp. chaps. 2 and 4.

4. I am using the word "tension" in a very wide sense to describe any musical event that arouses in us a sense that matters cannot be left as they are. The tension may arise through some kind of conflict or antagonism between two or more musical elements. But this is not necessarily so. All that is necessary is the generation of a sense of incompleteness, implying later closure. "Resolution" is accordingly understood in a broad sense to describe any musical event that dissipates tension.

5. For the ways in which this concurs (and does not concur) with the theorists Leonard Meyer and Heinrich Schenker, see Begbie, *Theology, Music, and Time*, 38n28, 39n30.

6. Walter Brueggemann, *The Message of the Psalms* (Minneapolis: Augsburg, 1984).

7. See pp. 222–23.

8. For much fuller discussion, see Jeremy Begbie, "Beauty, Sentimentality, and the Arts," in *The Beauty of God: Theology and the Arts*, ed. Mark Husbands and Daniel J. Treier (Downers Grove, IL: InterVarsity, forthcoming).

9. Alan E. Lewis, *Between Cross and Resurrection: A Theology of Holy Saturday* (Grand Rapids: Eerdmans, 2001), 33. Lewis goes on to suggest that "the multiple meaning of the story will only emerge as we hold in tension what the cross says on its own, what the resurrection says on its own, and what each of them says when interpreted in the light of the other." Lewis recommends that the second day (Holy Saturday) be seen as the vantage point from which this may be done, for it "serves both to keep the first and third days apart in their separate identities and to unite them in the indivisibility" (ibid., 33–34).

10. W. B. Yeats, "Crazy Jane Talks with the Bishop," in *The Collected Poems of W. B. Yeats* (London: Macmillan, 1933), 295.

11. It is important to distinguish meter and rhythm. Meter is a patterned succession of beats; rhythm refers to the variegated pattern of durations given in a succession of notes. Strictly speaking, we do not hear meter directly; we hear tones that make up rhythmic patterns, and the meter is implied and sensed through the rhythm of tones. Rhythm and meter may coincide very closely, but they can be out of step, sometimes quite radically.

12. Begbie, *Theology, Music, and Time*, esp. 58–61.

13. David J. A. Clines, *The Theme of the Pentateuch* (Sheffield: Sheffield Academic Press, 1994), 29.

14. Ps. 72:17; Isa. 19:24–25; Jer. 4:2; Zech. 8:13.

15. By far the most important scholar in this connection is Leonard B. Meyer. Adopting an information-theoretic approach, and focusing especially on tension and release, Meyer believes that musical processes appeal directly to the logic and flux of mental and psychological processes. See Leonard B. Meyer, *Emotion and Meaning in Music* (Chicago: University of Chicago Press, 1961); Meyer, *Explaining Music: Essays and Explorations* (Berkeley: University of California Press, 1973). For careful critiques, see Wayne D. Bowman, *Philosophical Perspectives on Music* (New York: Oxford University Press, 1998), 166–95; Stephen Davies, *Musical Meaning and Expression* (Ithaca, NY: Cornell University Press, 1994), 27–29, 287–89.

16. Leroy Ostransky, *The Anatomy of Jazz* (Seattle: University of Washington Press, 1960), 83.

17. Alanis Morissette, "All I Really Want," from *Jagged Little Pill*, Maverick Records, 1995.

18. Much of this material appears in a fuller form, with special attention to the person of Christ, in Jeremy Begbie, ed., *Beholding the Glory: Incarnation through the Arts* (Grand Rapids: Baker Academic, 2000), 138–54. For a very illuminating discussion of musical space in relation to Christology, see Colin E. Gunton, *Yesterday and Today: A Study of Continuities in Christology* (Grand Rapids: Eerdmans, 1983), chap. 6, esp. 111–19.

19. John Hull, *Touching the Rock: An Experience of Blindness* (London: SPCK, 1990), 61–64; italics mine.

20. See Victor Zuckerkandl, *Sound and Symbol: Music and the External World* (London: Routledge & Kegan Paul, 1956), 331–35.

21. For an excellent and concise treatment of the theological issues concerning freedom relevant to this section, see Richard Bauckham, *God and the Crisis of Freedom* (Louisville: Westminster John Knox, 2002).

22. See pp. 248–50.

23. Bauckham, *God and the Crisis of Freedom*, 197, 198.

24. The theologian Karl Rahner speaks of the tendency in some quarters to presume mistakenly that God can only "become greater and more real by the devaluation and cancellation of the creature" (Karl Rahner, *Theological Investigations*, vol. 1 [London: Darton, Longman & Todd, 1961], 188).

25. See David S. Cunningham, *These Three Are One: The Practice of Trinitarian Theology, Challenges in Contemporary Theology* (Oxford: Blackwell, 1998), 129. Also see the illuminating discussion in Alistair McFadyen, "Sins of Praise: The Assault on God's Freedom," in *God and Freedom: Essays in Historical and Systematic Theology*, ed. Colin E. Gunton (Edinburgh: T&T Clark, 1995), 32–56.

26. From Micheal O'Siadhail, "That in the End," in *Our Double Time* (Newcastle upon Tyne: Bloodaxe Books, 1998), 96.

27. This is not to say that unison singing cannot make its own kind of witness to Christian unity. It is worth remembering that oft-quoted passages from the early church fathers about the power of singing to weld many people into one (e.g., in Ignatius and Clement of Alexandria) have unison singing in mind (or singing at the octave), not what we would call "harmony." And in this connection we recall Bonhoeffer permitting only unison singing in *Life Together*; see the discussion on p. 335n103.

28. For a fuller treatment, see Jeremy S. Begbie, "Music, Mystery, and Sacrament," in *The Gestures of God: Explorations in Sacramentality*, ed. Geoffrey Rowell and Christine Hall (London: Continuum, 2004), 181–84.

29. See above, p. 231.

30. Eric T. Chafe, *Tonal Allegory in the Vocal Music of J. S. Bach* (Berkeley: University of California Press, 1991), 368–71. Strictly speaking, this is not superimposition (G major sung directly over E minor), but the two keys are nevertheless in immediate juxtaposition and very close association.

31. Cornelius Plantinga, *Engaging God's World: A Christian Vision of Faith, Learning, and Living* (Grand Rapids: Eerdmans, 2002), 20–21.

32. Zuckerkandl, *Sound and Symbol*, 297, 298, 299.

33. For an attempt to rehabilitate the virtues of "optics" in the face of some of the critics of "ocularcentrism," see Robert Paul Doede and Paul Edward Hughes, "Wounded Vision and the Optics of Hope," in *The Future of Hope*, ed. Miroslav Volf and William Katerberg (Grand Rapids: Eerdmans, 2004), 170–99. For strong treatments of the visual in Protestantism, see especially William A. Dyrness, *Reformed Theology and Visual Culture: The Protestant Imagination from Calvin to Edwards* (Cambridge: Cambridge University Press, 2004); Paul Corby Finney and James Lomax, eds., *Seeing Beyond the Word: Visual Arts and the Calvinist Tradition* (Grand Rapids: Eerdmans, 1999); David Morgan, *Protestants and Pictures: Religion, Visual Culture, and the Age of American Mass Production* (New York: Oxford University Press, 1999); and Morgan, *The Sacred Gaze: Religious Visual Culture in Theory and Practice* (Berkeley: University of California Press, 2005).

34. Bauckham, *God and the Crisis of Freedom*, 198–209.

35. For exceptionally fine and nuanced accounts of this "participation," see Julie Canlis, "Calvin, Osiander, and Participation in God," *International Journal of Systematic Theology* 6, no. 2 (2004): 169–84; Alan J. Torrance, *Persons in Communion: An Essay on Trinitarian Description and Human Participation* (Edinburgh: T&T Clark, 1996), 307–71.

36. The material in this section is developed much more fully in my "Music, Emotions, and Worship," in *Musical Theology*, ed. Jeremy Begbie and Steven Guthrie (Grand Rapids: Eerdmans, forthcoming).

37. The most famous defense of this is Deryck Cooke's classic tour de force, *The Language of Music* (New York: Oxford University Press, 1959). Cooke argues that a musical lexicon can be devised that

assigns emotive meanings to basic terms of musical vocabulary. Cooke points to numerous correlations between emotions and particular patterns of melodies, rhythms, and harmonies that have been used to convey these emotions in Western music since 1400. Such evidence suggests that music is a means of communicating moods and feelings. The sheer number of musical patterns that Cooke identifies in similar expressive contexts, across a wide historical spread of music, is impressive. Nonetheless, the weaknesses of his case are considerable, most of them hinging on the weight he is prepared to put on the music-language comparison—he too quickly assumes linguistic principles are operating in music, underplays the malleability and context-dependent character of musical expression, places too much stress on music as a means of emotional communication, pays little attention to large-scale musical form, and is not clear about whether he believes expressiveness to be a property of the music or an emotional state to which it refers. For discussions of Cooke, see Davies, *Musical Meaning and Expression*, 25–26; Roger Scruton, *The Aesthetics of Music* (Oxford: Clarendon, 1997), 203–8; Jeremy S. Begbie, *Voicing Creation's Praise: Towards a Theology of the Arts* (Edinburgh: T&T Clark, 1991), 243–44.

38. Patrik N. Juslin and John A. Sloboda, "Music and Emotion: Introduction," in *Music and Emotion: Theory and Research*, ed. Patrik N. Juslin and John A. Sloboda (Oxford: Oxford University Press, 2001), 3.

39. Among the most important studies available are Juslin and Sloboda, eds., *Music and Emotion*; Aaron Ridley, *Music, Value, and the Passions* (Ithaca, NY: Cornell University Press, 1995); Malcolm Budd, *Music and the Emotions: The Philosophical Theories* (London: Routledge & Kegan Paul, 1985); Davies, *Musical Meaning and Expression;* Wilson Coker, *Music and Meaning: A Theoretical Introduction to Musical Aesthetics* (New York: Free Press, 1972); Frank Burch Brown, "Music, Religion, and Emotion," in *Oxford Handbook of Religion and Emotion*, ed. John Corrigan (forthcoming). For older, "classic," and much-discussed accounts, see Meyer, *Emotion and Meaning in Music*; Meyer, *Explaining Music*; Susanne Langer, *Feeling and Form* (New York: Scribner's, 1953); Langer, *Philosophy in a New Key* (Cambridge, MA: Harvard University Press, 1957); Nelson Goodman, *Languages of Art* (Indianapolis: Bobbs-Merrill, 1968); Cooke, *Language of Music*; Eduard Hanslick, *The Beautiful in Music*, trans. Gustav Cohen (New York: Da Capo, 1957). See also Tia DeNora, *After Adorno: Rethinking Music Sociology* (Cambridge: Cambridge University Press, 2003), chap. 4.

40. David G. Myers, *Psychology* (New York: Worth Publishers, 2004), chap. 13. See also Patrik N. Juslin and John A. Sloboda, "Psychological Perspectives on Music and Emotion," in Juslin and Sloboda, *Music and Emotion*, 84–85.

41. Juslin and Sloboda, "Psychological Perspectives on Music and Emotion," 86.

42. K. R. Scherer has called these three together the classic "reaction triad" (K. R. Scherer, "Neuroscience Projections to Current Debates in Emotion Psychology," *Cognition and Emotion* 7 [1993]: 3). Some like to think of the elements we have outlined as occurring in sequence, but there is much dispute about this.

43. For a fine popular presentation, see Jamie Dow, *Engaging Emotions: The Need for Emotions in the Church* (Cambridge: Grove Books, 2005). See also John Macmurray, *Reason and Emotion* (London: Faber & Faber, 1995). Broadly, what I am outlining in this section would be an example of a cognitive account of emotion. The category, in fact, holds together a number of perspectives, the common element being that cognition is given a crucial role in accounting for emotion. Our particular interest here, however, is in cognitive theories that give belief and evaluation a central and determinative place in emotional theory. For useful accounts, see K. T. Strongman, *The Psychology of Emotion* (Chichester: Wiley, 1996), chap. 6; William E. Lyons, *Emotion* (Cambridge: Cambridge University Press, 1993), esp. chap. 2. Within the disciplines of psychology at least, it is fair to say that the tide has turned strongly in favor of cognitive theories (paralleling the ascendancy of cognitive psychology).

44. Even if this basic point holds, the matter of objects in emotional experience is nonetheless one of considerable complexity. The account offered by William Lyons is the most convincing I have found: Lyons, *Emotion*, chap. 6.

45. Macmurray, *Reason and Emotion*, chaps. 1–3.

46. Sloboda and Juslin point out that psychological research has "embarrassingly little to say" about this kind of aesthetic response (Juslin and Sloboda, "Psychological Perspectives on Music and Emotion," 81–82).

47. Nicholas Cook, *Analysing Musical Multimedia* (Oxford: Clarendon, 1998), 23.

48. Scruton, *Aesthetics of Music*, 354–57.

49. Scruton writes: "The great triumphs of music . . . involve this synthesis, whereby a musical structure, moving according to its own logic, compels our feelings to move along with it, and so leads us to rehearse a feeling at which we would not otherwise arrive" (ibid., 359).

50. See Davies, "Philosophical Perspectives on Music's Expressiveness," 34–37; Peter Kivy, *Sound Sentiment: An Essay on the Musical Emotions, including the Complete Text of the Corded Shell* (Philadelphia: Temple University Press, 1989); Kivy, *Introduction to a Philosophy of Music* (Oxford: Clarendon, 2002), esp. chaps. 3–7. For critique, see A. H. Goldman, "Emotion in Music (a Postscript)," *Journal of Aesthetics and Art Criticism* 53 (1995): 59–69; Jerrold Levinson, "Emotion in Response to Art: A Survey of the Terrain," in *Emotion and the Arts*, ed. M. Hjort and S. Laver (Oxford: Oxford University Press, 1997), 20–34; Geoffrey Madell, *Philosophy, Music, and Emotion* (Edinburgh: Edinburgh University Press, 2002), chap. 1.

51. See Juslin and Sloboda, "Psychological Perspectives on Music and Emotion," 93–94; P. N. Juslin and P. Laukka, "Emotional Expression in Speech and Music: Evidence of Cross-Modal Similarities," in *Emotions Inside Out: 130 Years after Darwin's "The Expression of the Emotions in Man and Animals,"* ed. P. Ekman et al. (New York: New York Academy of Sciences, 2003), 279–82; Manfred Clynes, *Sentics: The Touch of Emotions* (Garden City, NY: Doubleday, 1977).

52. For further examples of the correlation between bodily states and emotional properties ascribed to music, see DeNora, *After Adorno*, 99–104.

53. It is important to emphasize that this is not a "representational" theory or a "theory of reference." The claim is not that we hear musical sounds as representative of melancholy and cheerfulness, or as referring to these properties, any more than we see a yellow car as representative of, or as referring to, yellowness. The theory maintains that we hear melancholy and cheerfulness *as properties of the musical sounds*; we will often (usually?) be quite unaware of hearing them *as* such. For further discussion, see Kivy, *Introduction to a Philosophy of Music*, chap. 3.

54. Juslin and Sloboda, "Psychological Perspectives on Music and Emotion," 92.

55. E.g., Kivy, *Introduction to a Philosophy of Music*, 43–45.

56. This is one of the weaknesses of Susanne Langer's much-discussed theory of musical emotion. She speaks of an analogy of dynamic structure between emotion and music and argues that music is an iconic symbol of mental states. Music conveys not the content of specific feelings but the *form* of feelings (Langer, *Feeling and Form*). For her, music is an example of "presentational" symbolism. A presentational symbol does not symbolize by means of fixed units of meaning as in the case of language or discursive symbolism. The elements of a presentational symbol are understood only through the meaning of the whole symbol as its elements interrelate with one another. A presentational symbol is a dynamic instrument of discovery and clarification rather than a purveyor of static references; it does not so much assert as articulate (Langer, *Philosophy in a New Key*, chap. 4). A piece of music, Langer believes, is a nonlinguistic presentational symbol. It symbolizes human feelings, not by ostensive denotation, but through possessing the same temporal structure as some segment or segments of emotional life. The dynamic structure of a musical work and the form in which emotions are experienced can resemble each other in their patterns of motion and rest, tension and release, fulfillment, excitation, sudden change, etc. Music, and indeed all art, "is the creation of forms symbolic of human feeling" (Langer, *Feeling and Form*, 40). For extensive criticism of Langer, see Davies, *Musical Meaning and Expression*, 123–34.

57. E.g., see above, p. 38.

58. For criticism, see, e.g., Scruton, *Aesthetics of Music*, 144–45.

59. Mozart was thoroughly depressed when he wrote the last movement of his *Jupiter* Symphony, but it is widely heard as thoroughly joyful. It might be replied that his composing was a kind of therapy to offset his depression, but this shows only the weakness of the "expression of composer's emotion" theory.

60. O. K. Bouwsma, "The Expression Theory of Art," in *Philosophical Analysis*, ed. M. Black (Englewood Cliffs, NJ: Prentice-Hall, 1950), 94.

61. See D. Matravers, *Art and Emotion* (Oxford: Clarendon, 1998).

62. Davies, "Philosophical Perspectives on Music's Expressiveness," 33. Some, unable to connect effectively music's expressiveness to real persons through expression and arousal theories, introduce the idea of *imaginary or fictional* persons. According to one version of this, in experiencing expressiveness in music we sometimes imagine a "persona" who is the subject of a narrative in the music (Jenefer Robinson, "The Expression and Arousal of Emotion in Music," *Journal of Aesthetics and Art Criticism* 52, no. 52 [1994]: 13–22). In the theory's stronger forms, there is the suggestion that this way of listening is always required if we are to appreciate music's expressiveness (Jerrold Levinson, *The Pleasures of Aesthetics: Philosophical Essays* [Ithaca, NY: Cornell University Press, 1996], chap. 6). Martha Nussbaum speaks of an "implied composer"—"the voice or presence or sense of life that animates the work taken as a whole" (Martha C. Nussbaum, *Upheavals of Thought: The Intelligence of Emotions* [Cambridge: Cambridge University Press, 2001], 252–53). But it is far from clear that those we could regard as "qualified listeners"—those capable of recognizing music's expressiveness—do in fact in all cases imagine such a persona, or indeed need to do so to recognize the expressive character of the music. Further, the parallel drawn between musical persona and the characters of narrative fiction (on which some versions of the persona theory rely) is flawed. For a critique, see Kivy, *Introduction to a Philosophy of Music*, 113–19.

63. As in Nussbaum, *Upheavals of Thought*, 251.

64. For a very full treatment of prayer in relation to Christ's priesthood, see Graham Redding, *Prayer and the Priesthood of Christ: In the Reformed Tradition* (London: T&T Clark, 2003).

65. I owe this way of expressing the point to Steven Guthrie.

Conclusion

1. John Donne, "Hymn to God My God, in My Sickness," in *John Donne: The Major Works Including Songs and Sonnets and Sermons* (Oxford: Oxford University Press, 1990), 332.

bibliography

Abbate, Carolyn. *Unsung Voices: Opera and Musical Narratives in the Nineteenth Century.* Princeton, NJ: Princeton University Press, 1991.

Adorno, Theodor. "On Popular Music." In *On Record: Rock, Pop, and the Written Word*, edited by John Storey, 301–14. New York: Pantheon, 1990.

———. "Perennial Fashion—Jazz." In *Prisms*, 119–32. London: Neville Spearman, 1967.

Alperson, Philip. *What Is Music? An Introduction to the Philosophy of Music.* University Park: Pennsylvania State University Press, 1994.

Andreopoulos, Andreas. "The Return of Religion in Contemporary Music." *Literature and Theology* 14, no. 1 (2000): 81–95.

Aquinas, Thomas. *Summa Theologica.* Vol. 5. Translated by the Fathers of the English Dominican Province. Allen, TX: Christian Classics, 1981.

Areni, C. S., and D. Kim. "The Influence of Background Music on Shopping Behavior: Classical versus Top-Forty Music in a Wine Store." *Advances in Consumer Research* 20 (1993): 336–40.

Augustine. *On Music (De Musica).* Translated by Robert Catesby Taliaferro. The Fathers of the Church: A New Translation, vol. 4, 153–379. New York: CIMA Publishing, 1947.

Avis, Paul D. L. *God and the Creative Imagination: Metaphor, Symbol, and Myth in Religion and Theology.* London: Routledge, 1999.

Bach, Kent. "Ambiguity." In *Routledge Encyclopedia of Philosophy*, edited by Edward Craig. London: Routledge, 1998.

Bailey, Adrienne Thompson. "Music in the Liturgies of the Reformers: Martin Luther and Jean Calvin." *Reformed Liturgy and Music* 21 (1987): 74–79.

Balkwill, Laura-Lee, and William Forde Thompson. "A Cross-Cultural Investigation of the Perception of Emotion in Music: Psychophysical and Cultural Cues." *Music Perception* 17, no. 1 (1999): 43–64.

———. "Recognition of Emotion in Japanese, Western, and Hindustani Music by Japanese Listeners." *Japanese Psychological Research* 46, no. 4 (2004): 337–49.

Ballantine, Christopher. *Music and Its Social Meanings.* New York: Gordon and Breach, 1984.

Balthasar, Hans Urs von. *Truth Is Symphonic: Aspects of Christian Pluralism*. San Francisco: Ignatius, 1987.

Barber, John. "Luther and Calvin on Music and Worship." *Reformed Perspective Magazine* 8, no. 26 (2006): 1–16.

Barker, Andrew. *Greek Musical Writings*. Vol. 1, *The Musician and His Art*. Cambridge: Cambridge University Press, 1989.

———. *Greek Musical Writings*. Vol. 2, *Harmonic and Acoustic Theory*. Cambridge: Cambridge University Press, 2004.

Baron, Carol K., ed. *Bach's Changing World: Voices in the Community*. Rochester, NY: University of Rochester Press, 2006.

Barrow, John D. *The Artful Universe Expanded*. Oxford: Oxford University Press, 2005.

Barth, Karl. *Church Dogmatics*. Vol. 3.1. Translated by G. W. Bromiley and T. F. Torrance. Edinburgh: T&T Clark, 1958.

———. *Church Dogmatics*. Vol. 3.3. Translated by G. W. Bromiley and T. F. Torrance. Edinburgh: T&T Clark, 1960.

———. *Church Dogmatics*. Vol. 4.2. Translated by G. W. Bromiley and T. F. Torrance. Edinburgh: T&T Clark, 1958.

———. *Church Dogmatics*. Vol. 4.3. Translated by G. W. Bromiley and T. F. Torrance. Edinburgh: T&T Clark, 1961.

———. *How I Changed My Mind*. Translated by John Godsey. Edinburgh: Saint Andrew Press, 1969.

———. *Theology and Church: Shorter Writings, 1920–1928*. Translated by Louise Pettibone Smith. London: SCM, 1962.

———. *Wolfgang Amadeus Mozart*. Translated by Clarence K. Pott. Grand Rapids: Eerdmans, 1986.

Bartholomew, Craig G., and Elaine Botha. *Out of Egypt: Biblical Theology and Biblical Interpretation*. Bletchley: Paternoster; Grand Rapids: Zondervan, 2004.

Barton, Stephen C. *Invitation to the Bible*. London: SPCK, 1997.

———. "New Testament Interpretation as Performance." *Scottish Journal of Theology* 52, no. 2 (1999): 179–208.

———, ed. *Where Shall Wisdom Be Found? Wisdom in the Bible, the Church, and the Contemporary World*. Edinburgh: T&T Clark, 1999.

Basney, Lionel. "Who Killed Classical Music?" *Books and Culture* (2001): 8–9, 40–42.

Battles, Ford Lewis. *The Piety of John Calvin: An Anthology Illustrative of the Spirituality of the Reformer*. Grand Rapids: Baker Academic, 1978.

Bauckham, Richard. *Bible and Mission: Christian Witness in a Postmodern World*. Carlisle: Paternoster, 2003.

———. *The Climax of Prophecy: Studies on the Book of Revelation*. Edinburgh: T&T Clark, 1993.

———. *God and the Crisis of Freedom*. Louisville: Westminster John Knox, 2002.

———. *God Crucified: Monotheism and Christology in the New Testament*. Carlisle: Paternoster, 1998.

———. *Jude, 2 Peter*. Dallas: Word, 1983.

———. "Stewardship and Relationship." In *The Care of Creation: Focusing Concern and Action*, edited by R. J. Berry, 99–106. Leicester: Inter-Varsity, 2000.

———. *The Theology of the Book of Revelation*. Cambridge: Cambridge University Press, 1993.

Bauckham, Richard, and Trevor A. Hart. *Hope against Hope: Christian Eschatology at the Turn of the Millennium*. Grand Rapids: Eerdmans, 1999.

Beale, G. K. *The Book of Revelation: A Commentary on the Greek Text*. Grand Rapids: Eerdmans, 1999.

Beardsley, Monroe C. *Aesthetics from Classical Greece to the Present: A Short History*. Tuscaloosa: University of Alabama Press, 1977.

Beasley-Murray, George R. *John*. Waco: Word, 1999.

Beaudoin, Tom. *Virtual Faith: The Irreverent Spiritual Quest of Generation X*. San Francisco: Jossey-Bass, 1998.

Beckford, Robert. *Jesus Dub: Theology, Music and Social Change*. London: Routledge, 2006.

———. *Jesus Is Dread: Black Theology and Black Culture in Britain*. London: DLT, 1998.

Begbie, Jeremy S. "The Ambivalent Rainbow: Forsyth, Art, and Creation." In *Justice the True and Only Mercy*, edited by Trevor Hart, 197–219. Edinburgh: T&T Clark, 1995.

———, ed. *Beholding the Glory: Incarnation through the Arts*. Grand Rapids: Baker Academic, 2000.

———. "Music, Mystery, and Sacrament." In *The Gestures of God: Explorations in Sacramentality*, edited by Geoffrey Rowell and Christine Hall, 173–91. London: Continuum, 2004.

———. "Music, Word, and Theology Today: Learning from John Calvin." In *Theology in Dialogue: The Impact of the Arts, Humanities, and Science on Contemporary Religious Thought*, edited by Lyn Holness and Ralf Wüstenberg, 3–27. Grand Rapids: Eerdmans, 2002.

———, ed. *Sounding the Depths: Theology through the Arts*. London: SCM, 2002.

———. *Theology, Music, and Time*. Cambridge: Cambridge University Press, 2000.

———. *Voicing Creation's Praise: Towards a Theology of the Arts*. Edinburgh: T&T Clark, 1991.

Begbie, Jeremy, and Steven Guthrie, ed. *Musical Theology*. Grand Rapids: Eerdmans, forthcoming.

Benjamin, Walter. *Illuminations: Essays and Reflections*. Translated by Harry Zohn. New York: Shocken, 1968.

Bennett, A. *Cultures of Popular Music*. Buckingham: Open University Press, 2001.

Bennett, Andy. *Popular Music and Youth Culture: Music, Identity, and Place*. New York: Macmillan, 2000.

Bennett, Gerald. "The Early Works." In *Pierre Boulez: A Symposium*, edited by William Glock, 41–84. London: Eulenburg, 1986.

Bergmann, Sigurd. *Creation Set Free: The Spirit as Liberator of Nature*. Translated by Douglas Stott. Grand Rapids: Eerdmans, 2005.

Berliner, Paul. *Thinking in Jazz: The Infinite Art of Improvisation*. Chicago: University of Chicago Press, 1994.

Bernstein, Leonard. *The Unanswered Question: Six Talks at Harvard*. Cambridge, MA: Harvard University Press, 1976.

Best, Harold M. *Music through the Eyes of Faith*. San Francisco: HarperSanFrancisco, 1993.

Bethge, Eberhard. *Dietrich Bonhoeffer: Theologian, Christian, Man for His Times; A Biography*. Minneapolis: Fortress, 2000.

Biggar, Nigel. *Reckoning with Barth: Essays in Commemoration of the Centenary of Karl Barth's Birth*. London: Mowbray, 1988.

Biocca, F. A. "The Pursuit of Sound: Radio, Perception, and Utopia in the Early 20th Century." *Media, Culture, and Society* 10 (1988): 61–80.

Black, Leo. *Franz Schubert: Music and Belief*. Woodbridge, Suffolk: Boydell Press, 2003.

Blacking, John. *"A Commonsense View of All Music": Reflections on Percy Grainger's Contribution to Ethnomusicology and Music Education*. Cambridge: Cambridge University Press, 1987.

———. *How Musical Is Man?* Seattle: University of Washington Press, 1973.

Blackwell, Albert L. "The Role of Music in Schleiermacher's Writings." In *Internationaler Schleiermacher-Kongress 1984*, edited by Kurt-Victor Selge, 439–48. Berlin: de Gruyter, 1985.

———. *The Sacred in Music*. Cambridge: Lutterworth, 1999.

———. "Schleiermacher on Musical Experience and Religious Experience: What Hath Vienna to Do with Jerusalem?" In *Friedrich Schleiermacher and the Founding of the University of Berlin*, edited by Herbert Richardson, 121–39. Lewiston, NY: Edwin Mellen, 1991.

Blankenburg, Walter. "Calvin." In *Die Musik in Geschichte und Gegenwart*, 653–66. Kassel: Bärenreiter-Verlag, 1952.

———. "Church Music in Reformed Europe." In *Protestant Church Music: A History*, edited by Friedrich Blume, 509–90. New York: Norton, 1974.

———. "Johann Sebastian Bach und die Aufklärung." In *Bach Gedenkschrift 1950*, edited by K. Matthaei, 25–34. Freiburg im Breisgau: Atlantis Verlag, 1950.

Bloch, Ernst. *Essays on the Philosophy of Music*. Translated by Peter Palmer. Cambridge: Cambridge University Press, 1985.

Blond, Philip. "Perception: From Modern Painting to the Vision in Christ." In *Radical Orthodoxy: A New Theology*, edited by John Milbank, Graham Ward, and Catherine Pickstock, 220–42. London: Routledge, 1998.

Blume, Friedrich. "Outlines of a New Picture of Bach." *Music and Letters* 44 (1963): 214–27.

———. *Protestant Church Music: A History*. New York: Norton, 1974.

Bockmuehl, Markus. "Reason, Wisdom, and the Implied Disciple of Scripture." In *Reading Texts, Seeking Wisdom: Scripture and Theology*, edited by D. F. Ford and G. N. Stanton, 53–68. London: SCM, 2003.

Boethius. *The Consolation of Philosophy*. Oxford: Clarendon, 1999.

———. *Fundamentals of Music*. Translated by C. M. Bower. New Haven: Yale University Press, 1989.

Bohlman, Philip V. "Is All Music Religious?" In *Theomusicology. A Special Issue of Black Sacred Music; A Journal of Theomusicology*, edited by Jon Michael Spencer, 3–12. Durham, NC: Duke University Press, 1994.

———. *World Music: A Very Short Introduction*. Oxford: Oxford University Press, 2002.

Bonhoeffer, Dietrich. *Ethics*. London: Macmillan, 1965.

—————. *Letters and Papers from Prison*. London: SCM, 1972.

—————. *Life Together*. Translated by John W. Doberstein. New York: Harper, 1954.

Boulez, Pierre. *Conversations with Célestin Deliège*. London: Eulenburg, 1976.

—————. *Stocktakings from an Apprenticeship*. Oxford: Oxford University Press, 1991.

Bouma-Prediger, Steven. *For the Beauty of the Earth: A Christian Vision for Creation Care*. Grand Rapids: Baker Academic, 2001.

Bouwsma, O. K. "The Expression Theory of Art." In *Philosophical Analysis*, edited by M. Black, 71–96. Englewood Cliffs, NJ: Prentice-Hall, 1950.

Bowder, Bill. "The Holy Flame." *Church Times*, May 28, 2004, 19.

Bowen, William. "St. Augustine in Medieval and Renaissance Musical Science." In *Augustine on Music: An Interdisciplinary Collection of Essays*, edited by Richard R. La Croix, 29–51. Lewiston, NY: Edwin Mellen, 1988.

Bower, Calvin M. "'Adhuc Ex Parte Et in Enigmate Cernimus . . .' Reflections on the Closing Chapters of *Musica Enchiriadis*." In *Music in the Mirror: Reflections on the History of Music Theory and Literature for the 21st Century*, edited by Andreas Giger and Thomas J. Mathiesen, 21–44. Lincoln: University of Nebraska Press, 2002.

—————. "The Transmission of Ancient Music Theory into the Middle Ages." In *The Cambridge History of Western Music Theory*, edited by Thomas Christensen, 136–67. Cambridge: Cambridge University Press, 2002.

Bowie, Andrew. *Aesthetics and Subjectivity from Kant to Nietzsche*. Manchester: Manchester University Press, 1990.

Bowman, Wayne D. *Philosophical Perspectives on Music*. New York: Oxford University Press, 1998.

Boyd, Gregory A. *God of the Possible: A Biblical Introduction to the Open View of God*. Grand Rapids: Baker Books, 2000.

Boyd, Malcolm. *Bach*. Oxford: Oxford University Press, 2000.

—————, ed. *J. S. Bach*. Oxford: Oxford University Press, 1999.

Bradley, Ian. *You've Got to Have a Dream: The Message of the Musical*. London: SCM, 2004.

Bradshaw, Paul F. *The Search for the Origins of Christian Worship: Sources and Methods for the Study of Early Liturgy*. New York: Oxford University Press, 1992.

Brand, Hilary, and Adrienne Chaplin. *Art and Soul: Signposts for Christians in the Arts*. Carlisle: Solway, 2001.

Braun, Joachim. *Music in Ancient Israel/Palestine: Archaeological, Written, and Comparative Sources*. Translated by Douglas Stott. Grand Rapids: Eerdmans, 2002.

Brindle, Reginald Smith. *The New Music: The Avant-Garde since 1945*. Oxford: Oxford University Press, 1987.

Brown, Christopher Boyd. *Singing the Gospel: Lutheran Hymns and the Success of the Reformation*. Cambridge, MA: Harvard University Press, 2005.

Brown, David. *Tradition and Imagination: Revelation and Change*. Oxford: Oxford University Press, 1999.

Brown, Royal S. *Overtones and Undertones: Reading Film Music*. Berkeley: University of California Press, 1994.

Bruce, F. F. *The Epistle to the Hebrews*. Grand Rapids: Eerdmans, 1990.

Brueggemann, Walter. *Israel's Praise: Doxology against Idolatry and Ideology*. Philadelphia: Fortress, 1988.

———. *The Message of the Psalms*. Minneapolis: Augsburg, 1984.

Bruhn, Siglind. "Religious Symbolism in the Music of Olivier Messiaen." *American Journal of Semiotics* 13 (Fall 1996): 277–309.

Budd, Malcolm. "Aesthetic Attitude." In *Routledge Encyclopedia of Philosophy*, edited by Edward Craig. London: Routledge, 1998.

———. *Music and the Emotions: The Philosophical Theories*. London: Routledge & Kegan Paul, 1985.

Burch Brown, Frank. *Good Taste, Bad Taste, and Christian Taste: Aesthetics in Religious Life*. Oxford: Oxford University Press, 2000.

———. "A Matter of Taste?" *Christian Century* (2000): 904–11.

———. "Music, Religion, and Emotion." In *Oxford Handbook of Religion and Emotion*, edited by John Corrigan, forthcoming.

———. "Religious Music and Secular Music: A Calvinist Perspective, Re-Formed." *Theology Today* 60 (2006): 11–21.

Burkert, Walter. *Lore and Science in Ancient Pythagoreanism*. Translated by Edwin L. Minar. Cambridge, MA: Harvard University Press, 1972.

Busch, Eberhard. *Karl Barth: His Life from Letters and Autobiographical Texts*. London: SCM, 1976.

Buszin, W. E. "Luther on Music." *Musical Quarterly* 32 (1946): 80–97.

Butler, Christopher. *After the Wake: An Essay on the Contemporary Avant-Garde*. Oxford: Clarendon, 1980.

Butt, John. *Bach: Mass in B Minor*. Cambridge: Cambridge University Press, 1991.

———. "Bach's Metaphysics of Music." In *The Cambridge Companion to Bach*, edited by John Butt, 46–71. Cambridge: Cambridge University Press, 1997.

———, ed. *The Cambridge Companion to Bach*. Cambridge: Cambridge University Press, 1997.

———. "Figurenlehre." In *J. S. Bach*, edited by Malcolm Boyd, 170. Oxford: Oxford University Press, 1999.

———. "'A Mind Unconscious That It Is Calculating'? Bach and the Rationalist Philosophy of Leibniz and Spinoza." In *The Cambridge Companion to Bach*, edited by John Butt, 60–71. Cambridge: Cambridge University Press, 1997.

———. *Music Education and the Art of Performance in the German Baroque*. Cambridge: Cambridge University Press, 1994.

———. *Playing with History: The Historical Approach to Musical Performance*. Cambridge: Cambridge University Press, 2002.

Cage, John. *Silence*. London: Calder & Boyars, 1973.

Caird, G. B. *A Commentary on the Revelation of St. John the Divine*. London: Black, 1966.

Caldwell, John. "The *De Institutione Arithmetica* and the *De Institutione Musica*." In *Boethius: His Life, Thought, and Influence*, edited by Margaret Gibson, 135–54. Oxford: Blackwell, 1981.

Calvin, John. *The Epistle of Paul the Apostle to the Hebrews and the First and Second Epistles of St. Peter.* Translated by T. H. L. Parker. Edinburgh: Oliver and Boyd, 1963.

———. *The Epistles of the Apostle Paul to the Galatians, Ephesians, Philippians, and Colossians.* Translated by T. H. L. Parker. Grand Rapids: Eerdmans, 1980.

———. "Genevan Psalter: Foreword." In *Source Readings in Music History: From Classical Antiquity through the Romantic Era,* edited by Oliver Strunk, 345–48. New York: Norton, 1950.

———. *Ioannis Calvini Opera Quae Supersunt Omnia.* Vol. 10. Edited by Guilielmus Baum, Eduard Cunitz, and Eduard Reuss. Brunsvigae: C. A. Schwetschke, 1871.

———. *Ioannis Calvini Opera Quae Supersunt Omnia.* Vol. 20. Edited by Guilielmus Baum, Eduard Cunitz, and Eduard Reuss. Brunsvigae: C. A. Schwetschke, 1879.

———. *Ioannis Calvini Opera Quae Supersunt Omnia.* Vol. 23. Edited by Guilielmus Baum, Eduard Cunitz, and Eduard Reuss. Brunsvigae: C. A. Schwetschke, 1882.

———. *Ioannis Calvini Opera Quae Supersunt Omnia.* Vol. 30. Edited by Guilielmus Baum, Eduard Cunitz, and Eduard Reuss. Brunsvigae: C. A. Schwetschke, 1886.

Campling, Christopher R. *The Food of Love: Reflections on Music and Faith.* London: SCM, 1997.

Camus, Albert. *The Myth of Sisyphus.* Harmondsworth: Penguin, 1975.

Canlis, Julie. "Calvin, Osiander, and Participation in God." *International Journal of Systematic Theology* 6, no. 2 (2004): 169–84.

Cardew, Cornelius. *Treatise Handbook.* London: Edition Peters, 1971.

Carpenter, Nan Cooke. *Music in the Medieval and Renaissance Universities.* New York: Da Capo, 1972.

Carson, D. A. *Becoming Conversant with the Emerging Church: Understanding a Movement and Its Implications.* Grand Rapids: Zondervan, 2005.

Casetti, P. "Funktionen der Musik in der Bibel." *Freiburger Zeitschrift für Philosophie und Theologie* 24 (1977): 366–89.

Cauty, J., and B. Drummond. *The Manual: How to Have a Number One Hit the Easy Way.* London: Ellipsis, 1998.

Chadwick, Henry. *Boethius: The Consolations of Music, Logic, Theology, and Philosophy.* Oxford: Clarendon, 1981.

———. "Why Music in the Church?" In *Tradition and Exploration: Collected Papers on Theology and the Church,* edited by Henry Chadwick, 203–16. Norwich: Canterbury Press, 1994.

Chafe, Eric T. *Analyzing Bach Cantatas.* Oxford: Oxford University Press, 2000.

———. *Tonal Allegory in the Vocal Music of J. S. Bach.* Berkeley: University of California Press, 1991.

Chamberlain, D. S. "Philosophy of Music in the *Consolation* of Boethius." *Speculum* 45 (1970): 80–97.

Charry, Ellen. *By the Renewing of Your Minds: The Pastoral Function of Christian Doctrine.* Oxford: Oxford University Press, 1997.

Chua, Daniel K. L. *Absolute Music and the Construction of Meaning.* Cambridge: Cambridge University Press, 1999.

————. "Vincenzo Galilei, Modernity, and the Division of Nature." In *Music Theory and the Natural Order from the Renaissance to the Early Twentieth Century*, edited by Suzannah Clark and Alexander Rehding, 17–29. Cambridge: Cambridge University Press, 2001.

Clements, K. W. *Friedrich Schleiermacher: Pioneer of Modern Theology*. London: Collins, 1987.

Clifton, Thomas. *Music as Heard: A Study in Applied Phenomenology*. New Haven: Yale University Press, 1983.

Clines, David J. A. *The Theme of the Pentateuch*. Sheffield: Sheffield Academic Press, 1994.

Clive, H. P. "The Calvinist Attitude to Music." *Bibliothèque d'Humanisme et Renaissance* 19 (1957): 80–102.

Clynes, Manfred. *Sentics: The Touch of Emotions*. Garden City, NY: Doubleday, 1977.

Cocksworth, Christopher J. *Holy, Holy, Holy: Worshiping the Trinitarian God*. London: Darton, Longman & Todd, 1997.

Coker, Wilson. *Music and Meaning: A Theoretical Introduction to Musical Aesthetics*. New York: Free Press, 1972.

Coleridge, Samuel Taylor. *Biographia Literaria*. Vol. 2. Princeton, NJ: Princeton University Press, 1983.

Cone, Edward T. *The Composer's Voice*. Berkeley: University of California Press, 1974.

Cone, James H. *The Spirituals and the Blues*. Maryknoll, NY: Orbis, 1998.

Cook, Nicholas. *Analysing Musical Multimedia*. Oxford: Clarendon, 1998.

————. *Beethoven: Symphony No. 9*. Cambridge: Cambridge University Press, 1993.

————. *Music: A Very Short Introduction*. Oxford: Oxford University Press, 1998.

————. *Music, Imagination, and Culture*. Oxford: Oxford University Press, 1990.

Cook, Nicholas, and Mark Everest, eds. *Rethinking Music*. Oxford: Oxford University Press, 1999.

Cooke, Deryck. *The Language of Music*. New York: Oxford University Press, 1959.

Copan, Paul, and William Lane Craig. *Creation out of Nothing: A Biblical, Philosophical, and Scientific Exploration*. Grand Rapids: Baker Academic, 2004.

Coutts, John. "Worship: More to It Than Meets the Ear." *Church Times* (2004): 17.

Cox, H. H., ed. *The Calov Bible of J. S. Bach*. Ann Arbor, MI: UMI Research Press, 1985.

Craigie, Peter C. *Psalms 1–50*. Waco: Word, 1983.

Cray, Graham. "Justice, Rock, and the Renewal of Worship." In *In Spirit and in Truth: Exploring Directions in Music in Worship Today*, edited by R. Sheldon, 1–27. London: Hodder & Stoughton, 1989.

Crocker, Richard L. *An Introduction to Gregorian Chant*. New Haven: Yale University Press, 2000.

Cunningham, David S. *These Three Are One: The Practice of Trinitarian Theology, Challenges in Contemporary Theology*. Oxford: Blackwell, 1998.

Dadelson, G. Von. *Beiträge zur Chronologie der Werke Johann Sebastian Bachs*. Trossingen: Hohner Verlag, 1958.

Dahlhaus, Carl. *Esthetics of Music*. Cambridge: Cambridge University Press, 1982.

————. *The Idea of Absolute Music*. Chicago: University of Chicago Press, 1989.

Dalferth, Ingolf. "Representing God's Presence." *International Journal of Systematic Theology* 3, no. 3 (2001): 237–56.

Daniel, Reuning. "Luther and Music." *Concordia Theological Quarterly* 48 (1984): 17–21.

Darbyshire, Ian. "Messiaen and the Representation of the Theological Illusion of Time." In *Messiaen's Language of Mystical Love*, edited by Siglind Bruhn, 35–52. New York: Garland, 1998.

David, Hans T., Arthur Mendel, and Christoph Wolff, eds. *The New Bach Reader: A Life of Johann Sebastian Bach in Letters and Documents*. New York: Norton, 1998.

Davies, Ellen F. *Wondrous Depth: Preaching the Old Testament*. Louisville: Westminster John Knox, 2005.

Davies, John Booth. *The Psychology of Music*. London: Hutchinson, 1978.

Davies, Stephen. *Musical Meaning and Expression*. Ithaca, NY: Cornell University Press, 1994.

———. "Philosophical Perspectives on Music's Expressiveness." In *Music and Emotion: Theory and Research*, edited by Patrik N. Juslin and John A. Sloboda, 23–44. Oxford: Oxford University Press, 2001.

Day, Thomas. *Why Catholics Can't Sing: The Culture of Catholicism and the Triumph of Bad Taste*. New York: Crossroad, 1990.

De Gruchy, John W. *Christianity, Art, and Transformation: Theological Aesthetics in the Struggle for Justice*. Cambridge: Cambridge University Press, 2001.

DeNora, Tia. *After Adorno: Rethinking Music Sociology*. Cambridge: Cambridge University Press, 2003.

———. *Music in Everyday Life*. Cambridge: Cambridge University Press, 2000.

Detweiler, Craig, and Barry Taylor. *A Matrix of Meanings: Finding God in Pop Culture*. Grand Rapids: Baker Academic, 2003.

Deutsch, D., ed. *The Psychology of Music*. San Diego: Academic Press, 1999.

Dingle, Christopher. *The Life of Messiaen*. Cambridge: Cambridge University Press, forthcoming.

Dixon, John W. *Nature and Grace in Art*. Chapel Hill: University of North Carolina Press, 1964.

Doede, Robert Paul, and Paul Edward Hughes. "Wounded Vision and the Optics of Hope." In *The Future of Hope*, edited by Miroslav Volf and William Katerberg, 170–99. Grand Rapids: Eerdmans, 2004.

Donne, John. "Hymn to God My God, in My Sickness." In *John Donne: The Major Works Including Songs and Sonnets and Sermons*, 332. Oxford: Oxford University Press, 1990.

Doumergue, Émile. "Music in the Work of Calvin." *Princeton Theological Review* 7 (1909): 529–52.

Dow, Jamie. *Engaging Emotions: The Need for Emotions in the Church*. Cambridge: Grove Books, 2005.

Dreyfus, Laurence. *Bach and the Patterns of Invention*. Cambridge, MA: Harvard University Press, 2004.

Dudgeon, Piers. *Lifting the Veil: The Biography of Sir John Tavener*. London: Portrait, 2003.

Dunn, James D. G. *The Epistles to the Colossians and to Philemon: A Commentary on the Greek Text.* Grand Rapids: Eerdmans, 1996.

Durant, Alan. *Conditions of Music.* London: MacMillan, 1984.

Dürr, Alfred. *The Cantatas of J. S. Bach.* Translated by Richard Jones. Oxford: Oxford University Press, 2005.

———. *Johann Sebastian Bach, St. John Passion: Genesis, Transmission, and Meaning.* Translated by Alfred Clayton. Oxford: Oxford University Press, 1988.

———. *Zur Chronologie der Leipziger Vokalwerke J. S. Bachs.* Berlin: Evangelische Verlagsanstalt, 1958.

Dyrness, William A. *Reformed Theology and Visual Culture: The Protestant Imagination from Calvin to Edwards.* Cambridge: Cambridge University Press, 2004.

———. *Visual Faith: Art, Theology, and Worship in Dialogue.* Grand Rapids: Baker Academic, 2001.

Edgar, William. *Taking Note of Music.* London: Third Ways, SPCK, 1986.

Edmondson, Stephen. *Calvin's Christology.* Cambridge: Cambridge University Press, 2004.

Eire, Carlos M. N. *War against the Idols: The Reformation of Worship from Erasmus to Calvin.* Cambridge: Cambridge University Press, 1986.

Eliot, T. S. "Tradition and the Individual Talent." In *Selected Essays*, edited by T. S. Eliot, 13–22. London: Faber & Faber, 1932.

Engel, Mary Potter. *John Calvin's Perspectival Anthropology.* Atlanta: Scholars Press, 1988.

Epstein, Heidi. *Melting the Venusberg: A Feminist Theology of Music.* London: Continuum, 2005.

Etchells, Ruth. *A Model of Making: Literary Criticism and Its Theology.* Basingstoke: Marshall, Morgan & Scott, 1983.

Farley, Edward. *Faith and Beauty: A Theological Aesthetic.* Aldershot: Ashgate, 2001.

Farrow, Douglas. *Ascension and Ecclesia: On the Significance of the Doctrine of the Ascension for Ecclesiology and Christian Cosmology.* Edinburgh: T&T Clark, 1999.

Faulkner, Quentin. *Wiser Than Despair: The Evolution of Ideas in the Relationship of Music and the Christian Church.* Westport, CT: Greenwood, 1996.

Fee, Gordon D. *God's Empowering Presence: The Holy Spirit in the Letters of Paul.* Peabody, MA: Hendrickson, 1994.

———. *Paul, the Spirit, and the People of God.* Peabody, MA: Hendrickson, 1996.

Fergusson, David. *The Cosmos and the Creator: An Introduction to the Theology of Creation.* London: SPCK, 1998.

Feuerbach, Ludwig. *The Essence of Christianity.* Translated by George Eliot. New York: Harper & Row, 1957.

Finney, Paul Corby, and James Lomax, eds. *Seeing beyond the Word: Visual Arts and the Calvinist Tradition.* Grand Rapids: Eerdmans, 1999.

Fisk, Josiah. "The New Simplicity: The Music of Górecki, Tavener, and Pärt." *Hudson Review* 47, no. 3 (1994): 394–412.

Fleming, Richard, and William Duckworth. *John Cage at Seventy-Five.* Lewisburg, PA: Bucknell University Press; London: Associated University Presses, 1989.

Foley, Edward. *Foundations of Christian Music: The Music of Pre-Constantinian Christianity.* Bramcote, Nottingham: Grove Books, 1992.

———. *Worship Music: A Concise Dictionary.* Collegeville, MN: Liturgical Press, 2000.

Ford, David. "Dramatic Theology: York, Lambeth, and Cambridge." In *Sounding the Depths: Theology through the Arts,* edited by Jeremy Begbie, 71–91. London: SCM, 2002.

———. *Self and Salvation: Being Transformed.* Cambridge: Cambridge University Press, 1999.

———. *The Shape of Living: Spiritual Directions for Everyday Life.* Grand Rapids: Baker Books, 1997.

Forsyth, P. T. *Christ on Parnassus: Lectures on Art, Ethic, and Theology.* London: Hodder & Stoughton, 1911.

———. "Music and Worship." *Congregational Quarterly* 33 (1955): 339–44.

Fowl, Stephen E. *Engaging Scripture: A Model for Theological Interpretation.* Oxford: Blackwell, 1998.

Frame, John M. *No Other God: A Response to Open Theism.* Phillipsburg, NJ: P & R Publishing, 2001.

Frith, Simon, ed. *The Cambridge Companion to Pop and Rock.* Cambridge: Cambridge University Press, 2001.

———. *Performing Rites: On the Value of Popular Music.* Oxford: Oxford University Press, 1996.

———, ed. *Popular Music: Critical Concepts in Media and Cultural Studies.* 4 vols. London: Routledge, 2004.

———. *The Sociology of Rock.* London: Constable, 1978.

———. *Sound Effects: Youth, Leisure, and the Politics of Rock 'n' Roll.* New York: Pantheon, 1981.

———. "Towards an Aesthetic of Popular Music." In *Music and Society: The Politics of Composition, Performance, and Reception,* edited by Richard Leppert and Susan McClary, 133–50. Cambridge: Cambridge University Press, 1997.

———. "Why Do Songs Have Words?" In *Lost in Music: Culture Style and the Musical Event,* edited by A. L. White, 105–28. London: Routledge & Kegan Paul, 1987.

Garside, Charles. "Calvin's Preface to the Psalter: A Re-appraisal." *Musical Quarterly* 37 (1951): 566–77.

———. "The Origins of Calvin's Theology of Music: 1536–1543." *Transactions of the American Philosophical Society* 69 (1979): 4–35.

———. *Zwingli and the Arts.* New Haven: Yale University Press, 1966.

Gerrish, B. A. *Grace and Gratitude: The Eucharistic Theology of John Calvin.* Minneapolis: Fortress, 1993.

———. *A Prince of the Church: Schleiermacher and the Beginnings of Modern Theology.* Philadelphia: Fortress, 1984.

Gibbs, Eddie, and Ryan K. Bolger. *Emerging Churches: Creating Christian Community in Postmodern Cultures.* Grand Rapids: Baker Academic, 2005.

Gilbert, Shirli. *Music in the Holocaust: Confronting Life in the Nazi Ghettos and Camps.* Oxford: Oxford University Press, 2006.

Gill, Theodore A. "Barth and Mozart." *Theology Today* 43 (1986): 403–11.

Goeser, Robert. "Luther: Word of God, Language, and Art." *Currents in Theology and Mission* 18 (1991): 6–11.

Goldman, A. H. "Emotion in Music (a Postscript)." *Journal of Aesthetics and Art Criticism* 53 (1995): 59–69.

Goléa, Antoine. *Rencontres avec Olivier Messiaen*. Paris: Julliard, 1960.

Goodman, Andrew. *Dancing in the Distraction Factory: Music Television and Popular Culture*. Minneapolis: University of Minnesota Press, 1992.

Goodman, Nelson. *Languages of Art*. Indianapolis: Bobbs-Merrill, 1968.

Graham, Gordon. *Philosophy of the Arts: An Introduction to Aesthetics*. London: Routledge, 2000.

———. "The Theology of Music in Church." *Scottish Journal of Theology* 57, no. 2 (2004): 139–45.

Green, Garrett. *Imagining God: Theology and the Religious Imagination*. San Francisco: Harper & Row, 1989.

———. *Theology, Hermeneutics, and Imagination: The Crisis of Interpretation at the End of Modernity*. Cambridge: Cambridge University Press, 2000.

Green, Joel B. "What Does It Mean to Be Human? Another Chapter in the Ongoing Interaction of Science and Scripture." In *From Cells to Souls and Beyond*, edited by Malcolm Jeeves, 179–98. Grand Rapids: Eerdmans, 2004.

Gregory, Andrew H. "The Roles of Music in Society: The Ethnomusicological Perspective." In *The Social Psychology of Music*, edited by D. Hargreaves and Adrian C. North, 123–40. Oxford: Oxford University Press, 1997.

Grenz, Stanley. *The Social God and the Relational Self: A Trinitarian Theology of the Imago Dei*. Louisville: Westminster John Knox, 2001.

Grenz, Stanley, and Roger E. Olson. *20th Century Theology: God and the World in a Transitional Age*. Downers Grove, IL: InterVarsity, 1992.

Griffiths, Paul. *Cage*. London: Oxford University Press, 1981.

———. *Olivier Messiaen and the Music of Time*. London: Faber & Faber, 1985.

Grindal, Gracia. "Luther and the Arts: A Study in Convention." *Word and World* 3 (1983): 373–81.

Grout, Donald Jay. *A History of Western Music*. London: Dent, 1973.

Gunton, Colin E. *A Brief Theology of Revelation: The 1993 Warfield Lectures*. Edinburgh: T&T Clark, 1995.

———. *The Christian Faith: An Introduction to Christian Doctrine*. Oxford: Blackwell, 2002.

———. "Creation and Re-creation: An Exploration of Some Themes in Aesthetics and Theology." *Modern Theology* 2, no. 1 (1985): 1–19.

———. "The End of Causality? The Reformers and Their Predecessors." In *The Doctrine of Creation*, edited by Colin E. Gunton, 63–82. Edinburgh: T&T Clark, 1997.

———. *Enlightenment and Alienation: An Essay towards a Trinitarian Theology*. Grand Rapids: Eerdmans, 1985.

———. "Mozart the Theologian." *Theology* 94 (1991): 346–49.

—————. *The One, the Three, and the Many: God, Creation, and the Culture of Modernity.* Cambridge: Cambridge University Press, 1993.

—————. *The Triune Creator: A Historical and Systematic Study.* Edinburgh: Edinburgh University Press, 1998.

—————. *Yesterday and Today: A Study of Continuities in Christology.* Grand Rapids: Eerdmans, 1983.

Guthrie, Steven. "Carmen Universitatis: A Theological Study of Music and Measure." PhD diss., University of St. Andrews, 2000.

Haëik-Vantoura, Suzanne. *The Music of the Bible Revealed: The Deciphering of a Millenary Notation.* Edited by John Wheeler. Berkeley: D. & F. Scott, 1991.

Halbreich, Harry. *Olivier Messiaen.* Paris: Fayard Fondation SACEM, 1980.

Hall, Donald. *Musical Acoustics.* Pacific Grove, CA: Brooks/Cole, 2002.

Hall, Douglas John. *Imaging God: Dominion as Stewardship.* Grand Rapids: Eerdmans, 1986.

Halter, Carl, and Carl Schalk. *A Handbook of Church Music.* St. Louis: Concordia, 1978.

Hamilton, Victor P. *The Book of Genesis: Chapters 1–17.* Grand Rapids: Eerdmans, 1990.

Hanslick, Eduard. *The Beautiful in Music.* Translated by Gustav Cohen. New York: Da Capo, 1957.

Hardy, Daniel W., and David Ford. *Praising and Knowing God.* Philadelphia: Westminster, 1985.

Hárran, Don. *Word-Tone Relations in Musical Thought: From Antiquity to the Seventeenth Century.* Neuhausen-Stuttgart: American Institute of Musicology, 1986.

Harries, Richard. *Art and the Beauty of God: A Christian Understanding.* London: Mowbray, 2000.

Harrison, Carol. "Augustine and the Art of Music." In *Musical Theology*, edited by Jeremy Begbie and Steven Guthrie. Grand Rapids: Eerdmans, forthcoming.

Hart, David Bentley. *The Beauty of the Infinite: The Aesthetics of Christian Truth.* Grand Rapids: Eerdmans, 2003.

Hart, Trevor. "The Capacity for Ambiguity: Revisiting the Barth-Brunner Debate." In *Regarding Karl Barth*, edited by Trevor A. Hart, 139–72. Carlisle: Paternoster, 1999.

—————. "Imagining Evangelical Theology." In *Evangelical Futures: A Conversation on Theological Method*, edited by John G. Stackhouse, 191–207. Grand Rapids: Eerdmans, 2000.

—————. "Through the Arts: Seeing and Touching the Truth." In *Beholding the Glory: Incarnation through the Arts*, edited by Jeremy Begbie, 1–26. Grand Rapids: Baker Academic, 2000.

Hasker, William. *Providence, Evil, and the Openness of God.* London: Routledge, 2004.

Hauerwas, Stanley. *After Christendom? How the Church Is to Behave If Freedom, Justice, and a Christian Nation Are Bad Ideas.* Nashville: Abingdon, 1991.

—————. *With the Grain of the Universe: The Church's Witness and Natural Theology.* Grand Rapids: Brazos, 2001.

Hawn, C. Michael. *Gather into One: Praying and Singing Globally.* Grand Rapids: Eerdmans, 2003.

Haydon, Geoffrey. *John Tavener: Glimpses of Paradise.* London: Gollancz, 1995.

Hegel, G. W. F. *Aesthetics*. Translated by T. M. Knox. London: Oxford University Press, 1975.

Hengel, Martin. "The Song about Christ in Earliest Worship." In *Studies in Early Christology*, edited by M. Hengel, 227–91. Edinburgh: T&T Clark, 1995.

Heninger, S. K. *Touches of Sweet Harmony: Pythagorean Cosmology and Renaissance Poetics*. San Marino, CA: Huntington Library, 1974.

Herl, Joseph. *Worship Wars in Early Lutheranism*. Oxford: Oxford University Press, 2004.

Heron, Alasdair I. C. *A Century of Protestant Theology*. Philadelphia: Westminster, 1980.

———. *Table and Tradition: Towards an Ecumenical Understanding of the Eucharist*. Edinburgh: Handsel, 1983.

Higgins, Kathleen Marie. *The Music of Our Lives*. Philadelphia: Temple University Press, 1991.

Hijleh, Mark. *The Music of Jesus: From Composition to Koinonia*. New York: Writers Club Press, 2001.

Hiley, David. *Western Plainchant: A Handbook*. Oxford: Clarendon, 1995.

Hill, Peter. *The Messiaen Companion*. London: Faber & Faber, 1995.

Hill, Peter, and Nigel Simeone. *Messiaen*. New Haven: Yale University Press, 2005.

Hillier, Paul. *Arvo Pärt*. Oxford Studies of Composers. Oxford: Clarendon, 1997.

Hindemith, Paul. *A Composer's World: Horizons and Limitations*. Cambridge, MA: Harvard University Press, 1952.

Hollander, John. *The Untuning of the Sky: Ideas of Music in English Poetry, 1500–1700*. New York: Norton, 1970.

Holmes, Stephen R. *Listening to the Past: The Place of Tradition in Theology*. Grand Rapids: Baker Academic; Carlisle: Paternoster, 2002.

Holze, Heinrich. "Luther's Concept of Creation. Five Remarks on His Interpretation of the First Article in the Large Catechism (1529)." In *Concern for Creation*, edited by Elizabeth Bettenhausen, 49–52. Uppsala: Tro & Tanke, 1995.

Hopkins, Gerard Manley. "As Kingfishers Catch Fire, Dragonflies Draw Flame." In *Poems and Prose*, 51. London: Penguin, 1985.

———. "God's Grandeur." In *Poems and Prose*, 27. London: Penguin, 1985.

Horne, Brian L. "A Civitas of Sound: On Luther and Music." *Theology* 88 (1985): 21–28.

Howard, Jay R., and John M. Streck. *Apostles of Rock: The Splintered World of Contemporary Christian Music*. Lexington: University Press of Kentucky, 1999.

Hughes, Robert. *The Shock of the New: Art and the Century of Change*. London: Thames & Hudson, 1993.

Hull, John. *Touching the Rock: An Experience of Blindness*. London: SPCK, 1990.

Hunsinger, George. *Disruptive Grace: Studies in the Theology of Karl Barth*. Grand Rapids: Eerdmans, 2000.

———. *How to Read Karl Barth: The Shape of His Theology*. Oxford: Oxford University Press, 1991.

Hurtado, Larry W. *At the Origins of Christian Worship: The Context and Character of Earliest Christian Devotion*. Grand Rapids: Eerdmans, 2000.

———. *How on Earth Did Jesus Become a God? Historical Questions about Earliest Devotion to Jesus*. Grand Rapids: Eerdmans, 2005.

———. *Lord Jesus Christ: Devotion to Jesus in Earliest Christianity*. Grand Rapids: Eerdmans, 2003.

Husbands, Mark, and Daniel J. Treier, eds. *The Community of the Word: Toward an Evangelical Ecclesiology*. Downers Grove, IL: InterVarsity, 2005.

Idelsohn, A. Z. *Jewish Music in Its Historical Development*. New York: Schocken, 1967.

Irwin, Joyce L. *Neither Voice nor Heart Alone: German Lutheran Theology of Music in the Age of the Baroque*. New York: Peter Lang, 1993.

Isacoff, Stuart. *Temperament: How Music Became a Battleground for the Great Minds of Western Civilization*. New York: Alfred A. Knopf, 2001.

Ito, John. "Looking for Bach." *Books and Culture* (2003): 8–9, 40–41.

Jaffé, Daniel. "High Priest of Music." *Classic CD* 111 (1999): 28–31.

James, Jamie. *The Music of the Spheres: Music, Science, and the Natural Order of the Universe*. London: Abacus, 1993.

Jenson, Robert W. *America's Theologian: A Recommendation of Jonathan Edwards*. New York: Oxford University Press, 1988.

———. *Systematic Theology*. Vol. 1, *The Triune God*. New York: Oxford University Press, 1997.

———. *Systematic Theology*. Vol. 2, *The Works of God*. New York: Oxford University Press, 1999.

Johnson, Julian. *Who Needs Classical Music?* Oxford: Oxford University Press, 2002.

Johnson, Robert Sherlaw. *Messiaen*. London: Dent, 1989.

———. "Rhythmic Techniques and Symbolism in the Music of Olivier Messiaen." In *Messiaen's Language of Mystical Love*, edited by Siglind Bruhn, 121–40. New York: Garland, 1998.

Johnson, Stephen. "Harnessing Extremes." *Gramophone* (May 1995): 14, 17.

Johnston, Robert K. *Reel Spirituality: Theology and Film in Dialogue*. Engaging Culture. Grand Rapids: Baker Academic, 2000.

Johnstone, Keith. *Impro: Improvisation and the Theatre*. London: Faber, 1979.

Jones, Ivor H. *Music: A Joy for Ever*. London: Epworth, 1989.

———. "Music and Musical Instruments." In *The Anchor Bible Dictionary*. Vol. 4, edited by David Noel Freedman, 930–39. New York: Doubleday, 1992.

Jones, L. Gregory, and James Joseph Buckley. *Theology and Scriptural Imagination*. Oxford: Blackwell, 1998.

Juslin, Patrik N., and John A. Sloboda. "Music and Emotion: Introduction." In *Music and Emotion: Theory and Research*, edited by Patrik N. Juslin and John A. Sloboda, 3–20. Oxford: Oxford University Press, 2001.

Juslin, Patrik N., and P. Laukka. "Emotional Expression in Speech and Music: Evidence of Cross-Modal Similarities." In *Emotions Inside Out: 130 Years after Darwin's "The Expression of the Emotions in Man and Animals,"* edited by P. Ekman, J. Campos, R. J. Davidson, and F. De Waal, 279–82. New York: New York Academy of Sciences, 2003.

Kaemmer, John E. *Music in Human Life: Anthropological Perspectives on Music*. Austin: University of Texas Press, 1993.

Kalb, F. *Theology of Worship in 17th-Century Lutheranism*. Translated by H. P. A. Hamann. St. Louis: Concordia, 1965.

Kallas, Endel. "Martin Luther in Praise of Music." *Journal of Church Music* 25 (1983): 13–16.

Kandinsky, Wassily. *Concerning the Spiritual in Art, and Painting in Particular*. New York: Wittenborn, 1947.

Kant, Immanuel. *Critique of Judgement*. Translated by J. H. Bernard. New York: Hafner, 1968.

———. *Immanuel Kant's Critique of Pure Reason*. Translated by Norman Kemp Smith. London: Macmillan, 1929.

Kassabian, Anahid. "Popular." In *Key Terms in Popular Music and Culture*, edited by Bruce Horner and Thomas Swiss, 113–23. Oxford: Blackwell, 1999.

Kautny, Oliver. *Arvo Pärt zwischen Ost und West: Rezeptionsgeschichte*. Stuttgart: Metzler, 2002.

Kenny, Anthony. *Action, Emotion, and Will*. London: Routledge & Kegan Paul, 1963.

Kidd, Reggie. *With One Voice: Discovering Christ's Song in Our Worship*. Grand Rapids: Baker Books, 2005.

Kivy, Peter. *The Corded Shell: Reflections on Musical Expression*. Princeton, NJ: Princeton University Press, 1980.

———. *The Fine Art of Repetition: Essays in the Philosophy of Music*. Cambridge: Cambridge University Press, 1993.

———. *Introduction to a Philosophy of Music*. Oxford: Clarendon, 2002.

———. *Music Alone: Philosophical Reflections on the Purely Musical Experience*. Ithaca, NY: Cornell University Press, 1990.

———. *Sound and Semblance: Reflections on Musical Representation*. Princeton, NJ: Princeton University Press, 1984.

———. *Sound Sentiment: An Essay on the Musical Emotions, Including the Complete Text of the Corded Shell*. Philadelphia: Temple University Press, 1989.

Kleinig, John W. *The Lord's Song: The Basis, Function, and Significance of Choral Music in Chronicles*. Sheffield: JSOT Press, 1993.

Knight, W. F. Jackson. *St. Augustine's "De Musica": A Synopsis*. London: Orthological Institute, 1947.

Knox, Israel. *The Aesthetic Theories of Kant, Hegel, and Schopenhauer*. London: Thames & Hudson, 1958.

Kraage, Jean-Denis. "Luther: Théologien de la Musique." *Études théologiques et religieuses* 58 (1983): 449–63.

Kramer, Jonathan D. *The Time of Music: New Meanings, New Temporalities, New Listening Strategies*. New York: Schirmer, 1988.

Kramer, L. *Classical Music and Postmodern Knowledge*. Berkeley: University of California Press, 1995.

———. *Music as Cultural Practice, 1800–1900*. Berkeley: University of California Press, 1990.

Krummacher, Christoph. *Musik als Praxis Pietatis*. Göttingen: Vandenhoeck & Ruprecht, 1994.

Küng, Hans. *Mozart: Traces of Transcendence*. London: SCM, 1992.

La Croix, Richard R., ed. *Augustine on Music: An Interdisciplinary Collection of Essays*. Lewiston, NY: Edwin Mellen, 1988.

Langer, Susanne. *Feeling and Form*. New York: Scribner's, 1953.

———. *Philosophy in a New Key*. Cambridge, MA: Harvard University Press, 1957.

Langlois, T. "Can You Feel It? DJs and House Music Culture in the UK." *Popular Music* 11, no. 2 (1992): 229–38.

Lanza, Joseph. *Elevator Music: A Surreal History of Muzak, Easy-Listening, and Other Moodsong*. London: Quartet, 1994.

Lash, Nicholas. "Performing the Scriptures." In *Theology on the Way to Emmaus*, 37–46. London: SCM, 1986.

Leaver, Robin A. *J. S. Bach and Scripture: Glosses from the Calov Bible Commentary*. St. Louis: Concordia, 1985.

———. "Lutheranism." In *J. S. Bach*, edited by Malcolm Boyd, 277–78. Oxford: Oxford University Press, 1999.

———. "The Mature Vocal Works and Their Theological and Liturgical Context." In *The Cambridge Companion to Bach*, edited by John Butt, 86–122. Cambridge: Cambridge University Press, 1997.

———. "Motive and Motif in the Church Music of Johann Sebastian Bach." *Theology Today* 63 (2006): 38–47.

———. "Music and Lutheranism." In *The Cambridge Companion to Bach*, edited by John Butt, 35–45. Cambridge: Cambridge University Press, 1997.

———. *Music as Preaching: Bach, Passions, and Music in Worship*. Oxford: Latimer, 1983.

Lebrecht, Norman. *Who Killed Classical Music? Maestros, Managers, and Corporate Politics*. Secaucus, NJ: Carol, 1997.

Leisinger, Ulrich. "Forms and Functions of the Choral Movements in J. S. Bach's *St. Matthew Passion*." In *Bach Studies 2*, edited by Daniel R. Melamed, 70–84. Cambridge: Cambridge University Press, 1995.

L'Engle, Madeleine. *A Circle of Quiet*. New York: Farrar, Straus & Giroux, 1972.

Lester, Joel. *Bach's Works for Solo Violin: Style, Structure, Performance*. New York: Oxford University Press, 1999.

Levinson, Jerrold. "Emotion in Response to Art: A Survey of the Terrain." In *Emotion and the Arts*, edited by M. Hjort and S. Laver, 20–34. Oxford: Oxford University Press, 1997.

———. *The Pleasures of Aesthetics: Philosophical Essays*. Ithaca, NY: Cornell University Press, 1996.

Lewis, Alan E. *Between Cross and Resurrection: A Theology of Holy Saturday*. Grand Rapids: Eerdmans, 2001.

———. *Theatre of the Gospel*. Edinburgh: Handsel, 1984.

Lewis, C. S. "On Church Music." In *Christian Reflections*, edited by Walter Hooper, 94–99. London: Bles, 1967.

———. *The Screwtape Letters*. New York: Macmillan, 1961.

———. *Screwtape Proposes a Toast and Other Pieces*. London: Fontana, 1965.

————. *Surprised by Joy*. London: Collins, 1955.

Lewis, Michael, and Jeannette M. Haviland-Jones, eds. *Handbook of Emotions*. New York: Guilford, 2000.

Lincoln, Andrew T. *Ephesians*. Dallas: Word, 1990.

Lippman, Edward A. *A History of Western Musical Aesthetics*. Lincoln: University of Nebraska Press, 1992.

————. *Musical Thought in Ancient Greece*. New York: Columbia University Press, 1964.

Little, Meredith, and Natalie Jenne. *Dance and the Music of J. S. Bach*. Bloomington: Indiana University Press, 1991.

Loades, Ann. "On Music's Grace: Trying to Think Theologically about Music." In *Truth, Religious Dialogue, and Dynamic Orthodoxy*, edited by Julius J. Lipner, 25–38. London: SCM, 2005.

Lomax, A. *Folksong, Style, and Culture*. Washington, DC: American Association for the Advancement of Science, 1968.

Lundin, Roger. *The Culture of Interpretation: Christian Faith and the Postmodern World*. Grand Rapids: Eerdmans, 1993.

————. *From Nature to Experience: The American Search for Cultural Authority*. Lanham, MD: Rowman & Littlefield, 1993.

Luther, Martin. *D. Martin Luthers Werke: Kritische Gesamtausgabe*. Vol. 3. Weimar: H. Böhlau, 1885.

————. *D. Martin Luthers Werke: Kritische Gesamtausgabe*. Vol. 4. Weimar: H. Böhlau, 1916.

————. *D. Martin Luthers Werke: Kritische Gesamtausgabe*. Vol. 30.2. Weimar: H. Böhlau, 1909.

————. *Luther's Works*. Vol. 1, *Lectures on Genesis Chapters 1–5*. Edited by Jaroslav J. Pelikan. Philadelphia: Fortress, 1958.

————. *Luther's Works*. Vol. 17, *Lectures on Isaiah 40–66*. Edited by Hilton C. Oswald. Philadelphia: Fortress, 1972.

————. *Luther's Works*. Vol. 49, *Letters 2*. Edited by Gottfried G. Krodel and Helmut T. Lehman. Philadelphia: Fortress, 1972.

————. *Luther's Works*. Vol. 53, *Liturgy and Hymns*. Edited by Gottfried G. Krodel and Helmut T. Lehman. Philadelphia: Fortress, 1965.

————. *Luther's Works*. Vol. 54, *Table Talk*. Edited by Theodore G. Tappert and Helmut T. Lehman. Philadelphia: Fortress, 1967.

Lynch, Gordon. *Understanding Theology and Popular Culture*. Oxford: Blackwell, 2005.

Lyons, William E. *Emotion*. Cambridge: Cambridge University Press, 1993.

MacIntyre, Alasdair C. *After Virtue: A Study in Moral Theory*. Notre Dame, IN: University of Notre Dame Press, 1984.

MacLaren, Duncan. *Mission Implausible: Restoring Credibility to the Church*. Bletchley: Paternoster, 2004.

MacMillan, James. "Parthenogenesis." In *Sounding the Depths*, edited by Jeremy Begbie, 33–38. London: SCM, 2002.

Macmurray, John. *Reason and Emotion*. London: Faber and Faber, 1995.

Macquarrie, John. *In Search of Humanity: A Theological and Philosophical Approach.* London: SCM, 1982.

Madell, Geoffrey. *Philosophy, Music, and Emotion.* Edinburgh: Edinburgh University Press, 2002.

Marissen, Michael. *Lutheranism, Anti-Judaism, and Bach's St. John Passion.* New York: Oxford University Press, 1998.

———. *The Social and Religious Designs of J. S. Bach's Brandenburg Concertos.* Princeton, NJ: Princeton University Press, 1995.

———. "The Theological Character of J. S. Bach's *Musical Offering.*" In *Bach Studies 2,* edited by Daniel R. Melamed, 85–106. Cambridge: Cambridge University Press, 1995.

Marshall, Robert L. *The Compositional Process of J. S. Bach: A Study of the Autograph Scores of the Vocal Works.* Princeton, NJ: Princeton University Press, 1972.

———. *Luther, Bach, and the Early Reformation Chorale.* Atlanta: Pitts Theology Library, 1995.

———. *The Music of Johann Sebastian Bach: The Sources, the Style, the Significance.* New York: Schirmer, 1989.

———. "Truth and Beauty: J. S. Bach at the Crossroads of Cultural History." In *A Bach Tribute: Essays in Honor of William H. Scheide,* edited by Paul Brainard and Ray Robinson, 179–88. Basel: Bärenreiter Kassel; Chapel Hill, NC: Hinshaw Music, 1993.

Martin, Peter J. *Sounds and Society: Themes in the Sociology of Music.* Manchester: Manchester University Press, 1995.

Martin, Ralph P. *Worship in the Early Church.* Grand Rapids: Eerdmans, 1975.

Mathiesen, Thomas J. "Greek Music Theory." In *The Cambridge History of Western Music Theory,* edited by Thomas Christensen, 109–35. Cambridge: Cambridge University Press, 2002.

———. "Problems of Terminology in Ancient Greek Theory: 'APMONIA." In *Festival Essays for Pauline Alderman,* edited by Burton Karson, 3–17. Provo, UT: Brigham Young University, 1976.

Matravers, D. *Art and Emotion.* Oxford: Clarendon, 1998.

May, Gerhard. *Creatio ex Nihilo: The Doctrine of "Creation out of Nothing" in Early Christian Thought.* Edinburgh: T&T Clark, 1994.

Maynard, Beth, ed. *Get Up Off Your Knees: Preaching the U2 Catalog.* Cambridge, MA: Cowley, 2003.

McClary, Susan. "The Blasphemy of Talking Politics during Bach Year." In *Music and Society: The Politics of Composition, Performance, and Reception,* edited by Richard D. Leppert and Susan McClary, 13–62. Cambridge: Cambridge University Press, 1987.

———. *Feminine Endings: Music, Gender, and Sexuality.* Minneapolis: University of Minnesota Press, 1991.

McCormack, Bruce L. "What's at Stake in Current Debates over Justification?" In *Justification: What's at Stake in the Current Debates,* edited by Mark Husbands and Daniel J. Treier, 81–117. Downers Grove, IL: InterVarsity, 2004.

McDonnell, Kilian. *John Calvin, the Church, and the Eucharist.* Princeton, NJ: Princeton University Press, 1967.

McFadyen, Alistair. "Sins of Praise: The Assault on God's Freedom." In *God and Freedom: Essays in Historical and Systematic Theology*, edited by Colin E. Gunton, 32–56. Edinburgh: T&T Clark, 1995.

McGann, Mary E. *Exploring Music as Worship and Theology: Research in Liturgical Practice.* Collegeville, MN: Liturgical Press, 2002.

McGrath, Alister E. *Luther's Theology of the Cross.* Grand Rapids: Baker Academic, 1990.

———. *The Re-enchantment of Nature: Science, Religion, and the Human Sense of Wonder.* London: Hodder & Stoughton, 2002.

———. *Reformation Thought: An Introduction.* Oxford: Blackwell, 1999.

———. *A Scientific Theology.* Vol. 1, *Nature.* Edinburgh: T&T Clark, 2001.

McIntyre, John. *Faith, Theology, and Imagination.* Edinburgh: Handsel, 1987.

McKay, G., ed. *DIY Culture: Party and Protest in Nineties Britain.* London: Verso, 1998.

McKinnon, J. *Music in Early Christian Literature.* Cambridge: Cambridge University Press, 1987.

McLelland, J. *Prometheus Rebound: The Irony of Atheism.* Waterloo, ON: Wilfrid Laurier University Press, 1988.

Mellers, Wilfrid H. *Bach and the Dance of God.* Oxford: Oxford University Press, 1981.

———. *Beethoven and the Voice of God.* London: Faber, 1983.

———. *Celestial Music.* Woodbridge: Boydell, 2002.

Messiaen, Olivier. *Music and Color: Conversations with Claude Samuel.* Translated by E. Thomas Glasgow. Portland, OR: Amadeus, 1994.

———. "Preface" to Miniature Score of *Quatuor pour la fin du temps.* Paris: Durand, 1942.

———. *The Technique of My Musical Language.* Paris: Alphonse Leduc, 1956.

Mestrovic, Stjepan Gabriel. *Postemotional Society.* London: Sage, 1997.

Meyer, Leonard, B. *Emotion and Meaning in Music.* Chicago: University of Chicago Press, 1961.

———. *Explaining Music: Essays and Explorations.* Berkeley: University of California Press, 1973.

Meyer-Baer, Kathi. *Music of the Spheres and the Dance of Death: Studies in Musical Iconology.* Princeton, NJ: Princeton University Press, 1974.

Middleton, J. Richard, and Brian J. Walsh. *Truth Is Stranger Than It Used to Be: Biblical Faith in a Postmodern Age.* Downers Grove, IL: InterVarsity, 1995.

Middleton, Richard. *Studying Popular Music.* Milton Keynes: Open University Press, 1990.

Miles, Margaret. *Image as Insight: Visual Understanding in Western Christian and Secular Culture.* Boston: Beacon, 1985.

Milliman, R. E. "Using Background Music to Affect the Behavior of Supermarket Shoppers." *Journal of Marketing* 46 (1982): 86–91.

Milton, John. "At a Solemn Music." In *John Milton: Complete Shorter Poems*, edited by John Carey, 161–65. London: Longman, 1971.

Mitchell, Jolyon. "Sound of Heart." *Third Way* 22, no. 5 (1999): 18–21.

Moltmann, Jürgen. *God in Creation: An Ecological Doctrine of Creation.* London: SCM, 1985.

Montagu, Jeremy. *Musical Instruments of the Bible.* Lanham, MD: Scarecrow, 2002.

Monti, Anthony. *A Natural Theology of the Arts: Imprint of the Spirit*. Aldershot: Ashgate, 2003.

Moore, Allan F., ed. *Analyzing Popular Music*. Cambridge: Cambridge University Press, 2003.

Moreland, J. P., and William Lane Craig. *Philosophical Foundations for a Christian Worldview*. Downers Grove, IL: InterVarsity, 2003.

Morgan, David. *Protestants and Pictures: Religion, Visual Culture, and the Age of American Mass Production*. New York: Oxford University Press, 1999.

———. *The Sacred Gaze: Religious Visual Culture in Theory and Practice*. Berkeley: University of California Press, 2005.

Morrison, Richard. "An Afternoon with James MacMillan." *Times*, September 20–26, 1997, 10–11.

Morrow, Mary Sue. *German Music Criticism in the Late Eighteenth Century: Aesthetic Issues in Instrumental Music*. Cambridge: Cambridge University Press, 1997.

Moseley, David. "'Parables of the Kingdom': Music and Theology in Karl Barth." PhD diss., University of Cambridge, 2001.

———. "'Parables' and 'Polyphony': The Resonance of Music as Witness in the Theology of Karl Barth and Dietrich Bonhoeffer." In *Musical Theology*, edited by Jeremy Begbie and Steven Guthrie. Grand Rapids: Eerdmans, forthcoming.

Moynagh, Michael. *Emergingchurch.Intro*. Oxford: Monarch, 2004.

Music, David W. *Instruments in Church: A Collection of Source Documents*. Lanham, MD: Scarecrow, 1998.

Myers, David G. *Psychology*. New York: Worth, 2004.

Nattiez, Jean-Jacques. *Music and Discourse: Toward a Semiology of Music*. Princeton, NJ: Princeton University Press, 1990.

Naugle, David K. *Worldview: The History of a Concept*. Grand Rapids: Eerdmans, 2002.

Nebelsick, Harold P. *The Renaissance, the Reformation, and the Rise of Science*. Edinburgh: T&T Clark, 1992.

Nettl, Paul. *Luther and Music*. Translated by Frida Best and Ralph Wood. New York: Russell & Russell, 1967.

Neubauer, John. *The Emancipation of Music from Language: Departure from Mimesis in Eighteenth-Century Aesthetics*. New Haven: Yale University Press, 1986.

Newbigin, Lesslie. *The Gospel in a Pluralist Society*. Grand Rapids: Eerdmans, 1989.

Nichols, Aidan. "Celestial Banquet: Messiaen's Sacred Music in Context." *Downside Review* 406 (1999): 173–90.

Nichols, Roger. *Messiaen*. Oxford: Oxford University Press, 1986.

———. *Olivier Messiaen (1908–1992): Vingt Regards Sur L'enfant Jésus*. Note for CD, Collins, 70332, 1996.

Nkeita, J. H. K. *The Music of Africa*. London: Gollancz, 1988.

North, Adrian C., and David J. Hargreaves. "Music and Consumer Behaviour." In *The Social Psychology of Music*, edited by Adrian C. North and David J. Hargreaves, 268–89. Oxford: Oxford University Press, 1997.

North, Adrian C., David J. Hargreaves, and Jennifer McKendrick. "In-Store Music Affects Product Choice." *Nature* 390 (1997): 132.

Nussbaum, Martha C. *Love's Knowledge: Essays on Philosophy and Literature*. New York: Oxford University Press, 1990.

———. *Upheavals of Thought: The Intelligence of Emotions*. Cambridge: Cambridge University Press, 2001.

O'Donovan, Oliver. *Resurrection and Moral Order: An Outline for Evangelical Ethics*. Leicester: Inter-Varsity, 1994.

———. " 'Where Were You . . . ?' " In *The Care of Creation: Focusing Concern and Action*, edited by R. J. Berry, 90–93. Leicester: Inter-Varsity, 2000.

Oettinger, Rebecca Wagner. *Music as Propaganda in the German Reformation*. Aldershot: Ashgate, 2001.

O'Siadhail, Micheal. *Poems 1975–1995*. Newcastle upon Tyne: Bloodaxe Books, 1999.

———. *Our Double Time*. Newcastle upon Tyne: Bloodaxe Books, 1998.

Ostransky, Leroy. *The Anatomy of Jazz*. Seattle: University of Washington Press, 1960.

Paddison, Max. *Adorno's Aesthetics of Music*. Cambridge: Cambridge University Press, 1993.

Palisca, Claude V. *Humanism in Italian Renaissance Musical Thought*. New Haven: Yale University Press, 1985.

Pangritz, Andreas. "Point and Counterpoint—Resistance and Submission: Dietrich Bonhoeffer on Theology and Music in Times of War and Social Crisis." In *Theology in Dialogue: The Impact of the Arts, Humanities and Science on Contemporary Religious Thought*, edited by Lyn Holness and Ralf Wüstenberg, 28–42. Grand Rapids: Eerdmans, 2002.

———. *Polyphonie des Lebens: Zu Dietrich Bonhoeffers "Theologie der Musik."* Berlin: Alektor-Verlag, 1994.

Pannenberg, Wolfhart. *Systematic Theology*. Vol. 2. Translated by Geoffrey W. Bromiley. Grand Rapids: Eerdmans, 1994.

Pattison, George. *Art, Modernity, and Faith: Restoring the Image*. London: SCM, 1998.

———. *Kierkegaard: The Aesthetic and the Religious*. London: SCM, 1999.

Peacocke, A. R. *Creation and the World of Science*. Oxford: Clarendon, 1979.

———. *Theology for a Scientific Age: Being and Becoming—Natural, Divine, and Human*. London: SCM, 1993.

Pederson, Ann. *God, Creation, and All That Jazz: A Process of Composition and Improvisation*. St. Louis: Chalice, 2001.

Pelikan, Jaroslav J. *Bach among the Theologians*. Philadelphia: Fortress, 1986.

Pickstock, Catherine. "Soul, City, and Cosmos after Augustine." In *Radical Orthodoxy: A New Theology*, edited by John Milbank, Catherine Pickstock, and Graham Ward, 243–77. London: Routledge, 1999.

Pierce, John R. *The Science of Musical Sound*. New York: Scientific American Library, 1983.

Pike, Alfred John. *A Theology of Music*. Toledo: Gregorian Institute, 1953.

Pinnock, Clark H. *Most Moved Mover: A Theology of God's Openness*. Grand Rapids: Baker Academic, 2001.

Plant, Stephen. *Bonhoeffer*. London: Continuum, 2004.

Plantinga, Cornelius. *Engaging God's World: A Christian Vision of Faith, Learning, and Living*. Grand Rapids: Eerdmans, 2002.

Plutarch. *Plutarch's Moralia: In Fifteen Volumes*. Translated by Phillip H. de Lacy and Benedict Einarson. Cambridge, MA: Harvard University Press, 1967.

Polanyi, Michael. *The Tacit Dimension*. Gloucester, MA: Peter Smith, 1983.

Polkinghorne, John. *The God of Hope and the End of the World*. London: SPCK, 2002.

——. *Reason and Reality: The Relationship between Science and Theology*. London: SPCK, 1991.

——. *Science and Creation: The Search for Understanding*. London: SPCK, 1988.

——. *Science and Theology: An Introduction*. London: SPCK, 1998.

——, ed. *The Work of Love: Creation as Kenosis*. Grand Rapids: Eerdmans, 2001.

Polkinghorne, John, and Michael Welker. *The End of the World and the Ends of God: Science and Theology on Eschatology*. Harrisburg, PA: Trinity Press International, 2000.

——. *Faith in the Living God*. London: SPCK, 2001.

Pople, Anthony. *Messiaen: Quatuor pour la fin du temps*. Cambridge: Cambridge University Press, 1998.

Porter, W. J. "Music." In *Dictionary of New Testament Background*, edited by Craig Evans and Stanley E. Porter, 711–19. Downers Grove, IL: InterVarsity, 2000.

Prendergast, Mark J. *The Ambient Century: From Mahler to Trance. The Evolution of Sound in the Electronic Age*. London: Bloomsbury, 2000.

Prendergast, Roy M. *Film Music, a Neglected Art: A Critical Study of Music in Films*. New York: Norton, 1992.

Pritchett, James. *The Music of John Cage*. Cambridge: Cambridge University Press, 1993.

Pseudo-Dionysius the Areopagite. *Celestial Hierarchy*. Leiden: Brill, 1959.

Quasten, Johannes. *Music and Worship in Pagan and Christian Antiquity*. Washington, DC: National Association of Pastoral Musicians, 1983.

Rahner, Karl. *Theological Investigations*. Vol. 1. London: Darton, Longman and Todd, 1961.

Ratcliffe, S. "Macmillan." *Choir and Organ* 7, no. 3 (1999): 38–42; 7, no. 4 (1999): 39–42.

Ratzinger, Joseph. "Liturgy and Sacred Music." *Communion* 13 (1986): 377–91.

——. *A New Song for the Lord*. New York: Crossroad, 2005.

——. *The Spirit of the Liturgy*. San Francisco: Ignatius, 2000.

Redding, Graham. *Prayer and the Priesthood of Christ: In the Reformed Tradition*. London: T&T Clark, 2003.

Reimann, Henry W. "Luther on Creation: A Study in Theocentric Theology." *Concordia Theological Monthly* 24 (1953): 26–40.

Reynolds, Simon. *Generation Ecstasy: Into the World of Techno and Rave Culture*. Boston: Little, Brown, 1998.

Richard, L. "Bach as Religious Interpreter." In *The Universal Bach: Lectures Celebrating the Tercentenary of Bach's Birthday, Fall 1985*. Philadelphia: American Philosophical Society, 1985.

Ridley, Aaron. *Music, Value, and the Passions*. Ithaca, NY: Cornell University Press, 1995.

Rischin, Rebecca. *For the End of Time: The Story of the Messiaen Quartet*. Ithaca, NY: Cornell University Press, 2003.

Rivera, Benito V. *German Music Theory in the Early 17th Century: The Treatises of Johannes Lippius*. Rochester, NY: University of Rochester, 1980.

Robinson, Jenefer. "The Expression and Arousal of Emotion in Music." *Journal of Aesthetics and Art Criticism* 52, no. 1 (1994): 13–22.

Rogerson, J. W. *Genesis 1–11*. Sheffield: JSOT Press, 1991.

Romanowski, William. "Evangelicals and Popular Music: The Contemporary Christian Music Industry." In *Religion and Popular Culture in America*, edited by Bruce David Forbes and Jeffrey H. Mahan, 165–79. Berkeley: University of California Press, 2000.

Rössler, Almut, ed. *Contributions to the Spiritual World of Olivier Messiaen: With Original Texts by the Composer*. Duisburg: Gilles & Francke, 1986.

Routley, Erik. *Church Music and Theology*, Philadelphia: Fortress, 1965.

————. *The Music of Christian Hymns*. Chicago: G. I. A., 1981.

Samuel, Claude. *Conversations with Olivier Messiaen*. London: Stainer & Bell, 1976.

Savage, Edward B. "The St. Matthew Passion as a Drama of Conversion." *Church Music* 80 (1980): 56–69.

Sayers, Dorothy L. *The Mind of the Maker*. London: Methuen, 1941.

Schalk, Carl. *Luther on Music: Paradigms of Praise*. St. Louis: Concordia, 1988.

————. *Music in Early Lutheranism: Shaping the Tradition (1524–1672)*. St. Louis: Concordia, 2001.

Scharen, Christian. *One Step Closer: Why U2 Matters to Those Seeking God*. Grand Rapids: Brazos, 2006.

Scherer, K. R. "Neuroscience Projections to Current Debates in Emotion Psychology." *Cognition and Emotion* 7 (1993): 1–41.

Schleiermacher, Friedrich. *The Christian Faith*. Translated by J. S. Stewart. Edinburgh: T&T Clark, 1999.

————. *Christmas Eve: Dialogue on the Incarnation*. Translated by Terrence N. Tice. Richmond: John Knox, 1967.

————. *On Religion: Speeches to Its Cultured Despisers*. Translated by John Oman. New York: Harper & Row, 1958.

Schoenberg, Arnold. *Style and Idea*. Translated by Leo Black. Edited by Leonard Stein. London: Faber & Faber, 1984.

Schoenberg, Arnold, Wassily Kandinsky, and Jelena Hahl-Koch, eds. *Arnold Schoenberg, Wassily Kandinsky: Letters, Pictures, and Documents*. London: Faber & Faber, 1984.

Scholtz, Gunter. *Schleiermachers Musikphilosophie*. Göttingen: Vandenhoeck & Ruprecht, 1981.

Schrag, Calvin O. *The Self after Postmodernity*. New Haven: Yale University Press, 1997.

Schueller, Herbert M. *The Idea of Music: An Introduction to Musical Aesthetics in Antiquity and the Middle Ages*. Kalamazoo, MI: Medieval Institute Publications, 1988.

Schulenberg, David. "Affektenlehre." In *J. S. Bach*, edited by Malcolm Boyd, 6. Oxford: Oxford University Press, 1999.

Schwarz, Robert. "James MacMillan: A Composer Finds Favor without Courting Fashion." *New York Times*, March 3, 1996, 29.

Schwöbel, Christoph, and Colin E. Gunton, eds. *Persons, Divine and Human: King's College Essays in Theological Anthropology*. Edinburgh: T&T Clark, 1991.

Scruton, Roger. *The Aesthetics of Music*. Oxford: Clarendon, 1997.

Seerveld, Calvin. *Rainbows for the Fallen World: Aesthetic Life and Artistic Task*. Toronto: Tuppence, 1980.

Seitz, Christopher R. *Word without End: The Old Testament as Abiding Theological Witness*. Grand Rapids: Eerdmans, 1998.

Shepherd, John, and Peter Wicke. *Music and Cultural Theory*. Cambridge: Polity, 1997.

Sherry, Patrick. *Images of Redemption: Art, Literature, and Salvation*. Edinburgh: T&T Clark, 2003.

———. *Spirit and Beauty: An Introduction to Theological Aesthetics*. London: SCM, 2002.

Shove, Patrick, and Bruno H. Repp. "Musical Motion and Performance: Theoretical and Empirical Perspectives." In *The Practice of Performance: Studies in Musical Interpretation*, edited by John Rink, 55–83. Cambridge: Cambridge University Press, 1995.

Shuker, Roy. *Understanding Popular Music*. London: Routledge, 2001.

Sloboda, John A. *Exploring the Musical Mind: Cognition, Emotion, Ability, and Function*. Oxford: Oxford University Press, 2005.

———. *Generative Processes in Music: The Psychology of Performance, Improvisation, and Composition*. Oxford: Clarendon, 1988.

———. *The Musical Mind: The Cognitive Psychology of Music*. Oxford: Oxford University Press, 1995.

Sloboda, John A., and Patrik N. Juslin. "Music and Emotion: Commentary." In *Music and Emotion: Theory and Research*, edited by Patrik N. Juslin and John A. Sloboda, 453–62. Oxford: Oxford University Press, 2001.

———. "Psychological Perspective on Music and Emotion." In *Music and Emotion: Theory and Research*, edited by Patrik N. Juslin and John A. Sloboda, 71–104. Oxford: Oxford University Press, 2001.

Small, Christopher. *Musicking: The Meanings of Performing and Listening*. Hanover, NH: University Press of New England, 1998.

———. *Music of the Common Tongue: Survival and Celebration in Afro-American Music*. London: Calder, 1987.

Smallman, Basil. *The Background of Passion Music: J. S. Bach and His Predecessors*. London: SCM, 1957.

Smit, Laura. *Loves Me, Loves Me Not: The Ethics of Unrequited Love*. Grand Rapids: Baker Academic, 2005.

Smith, J. A. "The Ancient Synagogue, the Early Church, and Singing." *Music & Letters* 65 (1984): 1–16.

Smith, W. S. *Musical Aspects of the New Testament*. Amsterdam: Have, 1962.

Söhngen, Oskar. "Fundamental Considerations for a Theology of Music." In *The Musical Heritage of the Church*, edited by Theodore Hoelty-Nickel, 7–16. St. Louis: Concordia, 1963.

———. "Music and Theology: A Systematic Approach." In *Sacred Sound: Music in Religious Thought and Practice*, edited by Joyce Irwin, 1–19. Chico, CA: Scholars Press, 1983.

———. *Theologie der Musik*. Kassel: Johannes Stauda-Verlag, 1967.

Solomon, Andrew. "Questions of Genius." *New Yorker*, August 26–September 2, 1996, 113–23.

Solomon, Maynard. "The Ninth Symphony: A Search for Order." In *Beethoven Essays*, 3–32. Cambridge, MA: Harvard University Press, 1988.

Spencer, Jon Michael. *Theological Music: Introduction to Theomusicology*. London: Greenwood, 1991.

———, ed. *Theomusicology*. Durham, NC: Duke University Press, 1994.

Spitzer, Leo. *Classical and Christian Ideas of World Harmony: Prolegomena to an Interpretation of the Word "Stimmung."* Baltimore: Johns Hopkins University Press, 1963.

Stackhouse, Ian. *The Gospel Driven Church: Retrieving Classical Ministries for Contemporary Revivalism*. Carlisle: Paternoster, 2004.

Stapert, Calvin. "Bach as Theologian: A Review Article." *Reformed Journal* 37 (1987): 19–27.

———. "Christus Victor: Bach's St. John Passion." *Reformed Journal* 39 (1989): 17–23.

———. *My Only Comfort: Death, Deliverance, and Discipleship in the Music of Bach*. Grand Rapids: Eerdmans, 2000.

———. *A New Song for an Old World: Musical Thought in the Early Church*. Grand Rapids: Eerdmans, 2007.

Steiner, George. *Errata: An Examined Life*. London: Phoenix, 1997.

———. *Grammars of Creation*. London: Faber, 2001.

———. *Real Presences: Is There Anything in What We Say?* London: Faber & Faber, 1989.

Steinitz, Paul. *Bach's Passions*. Masterworks of Choral Music. London: Elek, 1979.

Stephens, W. P. *The Theology of Huldrych Zwingli*. Oxford: Clarendon, 1986.

———. *Zwingli: An Introduction to His Thought*. Oxford: Clarendon, 1992.

Stevenson, Robert. "Bach's Quarrel with the Rector of St. Thomas School." *Anglican Theological Review* 33 (1951): 219–30.

Stiller, Günther. *Johann Sebastian Bach and Liturgical Life in Leipzig*. Translated by Herbert J. A. Bouman, Daniel F. Poellot, and Hilton C. Oswald. St. Louis: Concordia, 1984.

Stockman, Steve. *Walk On: The Spiritual Journey of U2*. Lake Mary, FL: Relevant, 2005.

Stolnitz, Jerome. "On the Origins of 'Aesthetic Disinterestedness.'" *Journal of Aesthetics and Art Criticism* (1961): 131–43.

Stoltzfus, Philip Edward. "Theology as Performance: The Theological Use of Musical Aesthetics in Friedrich Schleiermacher, Karl Barth, and Ludwig Wittgenstein." PhD diss., Harvard University, 2000.

Stone-Davis, Férdia. "Musical Perception and the Resonance of the Material: With Special Reference to Immanuel Kant and Anicius Manlius Severinus Boethius." PhD diss., University of Cambridge, 2005.

Storr, Anthony. *Music and the Mind*. New York: Ballantine, 1992.

Stravinsky, Igor. *Igor Stravinsky: An Autobiography*. London: Calder & Boyars, 1975.

————. *Poetics of Music in the Form of Six Lessons*. Translated by Arthur Knodel and Ingolf Dahl. Cambridge, MA: Harvard University Press, 1947.

Strohm, Reinhard. "The Problem with the Musical Work-Concept." In *The Musical Work: Reality or Invention?* edited by Michael Talbot, 129–52. Liverpool: Liverpool University Press, 2000.

Strongman, K. T. *The Psychology of Emotion*. Chichester, UK: Wiley, 1996.

Strunk, W. Oliver. *Source Readings in Music History: Antiquity and the Middle Ages*. London: Faber & Faber, 1981.

————. *Source Readings in Music History from Classical Antiquity through the Romantic Era*. New York: Norton, 1950.

Sudnow, David. *Ways of the Hand: A Rewritten Account*. Cambridge, MA: MIT Press, 2001.

Suurmond, Jean-Jacques. *Word and Spirit at Play: Towards a Charismatic Theology*. Grand Rapids: Eerdmans, 1994.

Talbot, Michael, ed. *The Musical Work: Reality or Invention?* Liverpool: Liverpool University Press, 2000.

Tarrant, Mark, Adrian C. North, and David J. Hargreaves. "Youth Identity and Music." In *Musical Identities*, edited by R. A. R. MacDonald, David J. Hargreaves, and Dorothy Miell, 134–50. Oxford: Oxford University Press, 2002.

Tarry, Joe E. "Music in the Educational Philosophy of Martin Luther." *Journal of Research in Music Education* 21 (1973): 355–65.

Tatarkiewicz, Wladyslaw. "The Great Theory of Beauty and Its Decline." *Journal of Aesthetics and Art Criticism* 31 (1972): 165–80.

Tatlow, Ruth. *Bach and the Riddle of the Number Alphabet*. Cambridge: Cambridge University Press, 1991.

————. "Number Symbolism." In *J. S. Bach*, edited by Malcolm Boyd, 320–22. Oxford: Oxford University Press, 1999.

Tavener, John. *The Music of Silence: A Composer's Testament*. Edited by Brian Keeble. London: Faber & Faber, 1999.

Taylor, Brandon. *Modernism, Post-Modernism, Realism: A Critical Perspective for Art*. Winchester: Winchester School of Art Press, 1987.

Taylor, Charles. *Sources of the Self: The Making of the Modern Identity*. Cambridge: Cambridge University Press, 1996.

Terry, Richard. *Calvin's First Psalter*. London: Benn, 1932.

Thiselton, Anthony C. *The First Epistle to the Corinthians: A Commentary on the Greek Text*. Grand Rapids: Eerdmans, 2000.

————. *Interpreting God and the Postmodern Self: On Meaning, Manipulation, and Promise*. Edinburgh: T&T Clark, 1995.

Thomas, Adrian. *Górecki*. Oxford: Clarendon, 1997.

Thompson, Michael B. *Clothed with Christ: The Example and Teaching of Jesus in Romans 12.1–15.13*. Sheffield: JSOT Press, 1991.

Tigerstedt, E. N. "The Poet as Creator: Origins of a Metaphor." *Comparative Literature Studies* 5 (1968): 455–88.

Tolkien, J. R. R. *The Silmarillion*. London: HarperCollins, 2004.

Torrance, Alan J. "Creatio ex Nihilo and the Spatio-Temporal Dimensions, with Special Reference to Jürgen Moltmann and D. C. Williams." In *The Doctrine of Creation*, edited by Colin E. Gunton, 82–103. Edinburgh: T&T Clark, 1997.

———. *Persons in Communion: An Essay on Trinitarian Description and Human Participation*. Edinburgh: T&T Clark, 1996.

Torrance, Alan J., and Michael Banner, eds. *The Doctrine of God and Theological Ethics*. London: T&T Clark, 2006.

Torrance, James. *Worship, Community, and the Triune God of Grace*. Carlisle: Paternoster, 1996.

Torrance, Thomas Forsyth. *Divine and Contingent Order*. Oxford: Oxford University Press, 1981.

———. *Theological Science*. London: Oxford University Press, 1969.

Tracy, David. *The Analogical Imagination: Christian Theology and the Culture of Pluralism*. New York: Crossroad, 1981.

Trautmann, C. "J. S. Bach: New Light on His Faith." *Concordia Theological Monthly* 42 (1971): 88–99.

Vanderwilt, Jeffrey T. "John Calvin's Theology of Liturgical Song." *Christian Scholar's Review* 25, no. 1 (1995): 63–82.

Van Deusen, Nancy. "Music, Rhythm." In *Augustine through the Ages: An Encyclopedia*, edited by Allan D. Fitzgerald et al., 572–74. Grand Rapids: Eerdmans, 1999.

———. "Musica, De." In *Augustine through the Ages: An Encyclopedia*, edited by Allan D. Fitzgerald et al., 574–76. Grand Rapids: Eerdmans, 1999.

Vanhoozer, Kevin J., ed. *Dictionary for Theological Interpretation of the Bible*. Grand Rapids: Baker Academic, 2005.

———. *The Drama of Doctrine: A Canonical-Linguistic Approach to Christian Theology*. Louisville: Westminster John Knox, 2005.

———. *First Theology: God, Scripture, and Hermeneutics*. Downers Grove, IL: InterVarsity, 2002.

———. *Is There a Meaning in the Text? The Bible, the Reader, and the Morality of Literary Knowledge*. Leicester: Apollos, 1998.

Vaughan, Henry. "The Morning-Watch." In *The Oxford Book of English Mystical Verse*, edited by D. H. S. Nicholson and A. H. E. Lee, 58. Oxford: Clarendon, 1916.

Veit, Patrice. *Das Kirchenlied in der Reformation Martin Luthers: Eine thematische und semantische Untersuchung*. Stuttgart: Franz Steiner Verlag, 1986.

Viladesau, Richard. *Theologial Aesthetics: God in Imagination, Beauty, and Art*. New York: Oxford University Press, 1999.

———. *Theology and the Arts: Encountering God through Music, Art, and Rhetoric*. New York: Paulist Press, 2000.

Volf, Miroslav. *After Our Likeness: The Church as the Image of the Trinity*. Grand Rapids: Eerdmans, 1998.

———. "Worship as Adoration and Action: Reflections on a Christian Way of Being-in-the-World." In *Worship: Adoration and Action*, edited by D. A. Carson, 203–11. Grand Rapids: Baker Books, 1993.

Waleson, Heidi. "A 'Messiah' for Modern Times." *BBC Music Magazine* (2001): 16.

Walhout, Donald. "Augustine on the Transcendent in Music." *Philosophy and Theology* 3, no. 3 (1989): 283–92.

Wall, Mick. *Bono: In the Name of Love*. New York: Thunder's Mouth Press, 2005.

Wallace, Ronald S. *Calvin, Geneva, and the Reformation: A Study of Calvin as Social Reformer, Churchman, Pastor, and Theologian*. Edinburgh: Scottish Academic Press, 1988.

———. *Calvin's Doctrine of the Word and Sacrament*. Edinburgh: Oliver and Boyd, 1953.

Wallin, Nils L., Björn Merker, and Steven Brown, eds. *The Origins of Music*. Cambridge, MA: MIT Press, 2001.

Walton, Kendall L. *Mimesis as Make-Believe: On the Foundations of the Representational Arts*. Cambridge, MA: Harvard University Press, 1990.

Ward, Pete. *Selling Worship: How What We Sing Has Changed the Church*. Bletchley: Paternoster, 2005.

Warren, Rick. *The Purpose-Driven Church*. Grand Rapids: Zondervan, 2002.

Watson, Francis. *The Open Text: New Directions for Biblical Studies?* London: SCM, 1993.

———. *Text and Truth: Redefining Biblical Theology*. Grand Rapids: Eerdmans, 1997.

———. "Theology and Music." *Scottish Journal of Theology* 51 (1998): 435–63.

Webber, Robert. *Ancient-Future Evangelism: Making Your Church a Faith-Forming Community*. Grand Rapids: Baker Books, 2003.

———. *The Younger Evangelicals: Facing the Challenges of the New World*. Grand Rapids: Baker Books, 2002.

Webster, John. *Barth*. London: Continuum, 2004.

———. *Barth's Ethics of Reconciliation*. Cambridge: Cambridge University Press, 1995.

———. "The Church and the Perfection of God." In *The Community of the Word: Toward an Evangelical Ecclesiology*, edited by Mark Husbands and Daniel J. Treier, 75–95. Downers Grove, IL: InterVarsity, 2005.

Weil, Simone. *The Note Books of Simone Weil*. Vol. 1. Translated by Arthur Wills. London: Routledge & Kegan Paul, 1956.

Wells, Samuel. *Improvisation: The Drama of Christian Ethics*. London: SPCK, 2004.

Wencelius, Léon. *L'esthétique de Calvin*. Paris: Belles Lettres, 1979.

———. "L'idée de Modération dans la Pensée de Calvin." *Evangelical Quarterly* 7 (1935): 87–94, 295–317.

Wenham, Gordon J. *Genesis 1–15*. Waco: Word, 1987.

Werner, E. "Music." In *The Interpreter's Dictionary of the Bible*, 457–69. Nashville: Abingdon, 1991.

———. "Musical Instruments." In *The Interpreter's Dictionary of the Bible*, 469–76. Nashville: Abingdon, 1991.

Wesley, John. *Explanatory Notes upon the New Testament*. London: Epworth Press, 1976.

West, M. L. *Ancient Greek Music*. Oxford: Clarendon, 1992.

Westermann, Claus. *Genesis 1–11: A Commentary*. Minneapolis: Augsburg, 1984.

Westermeyer, Paul. "Grace and the Music of Bach." *Christian Century* 102, no. 1 (1985): 291–94.

———. "Reflections on Music and Theology." *Theological Education* 31, no. 1 (1994): 183–89.

———. *Te Deum: The Church and Music*. Minneapolis: Fortress, 1998.

White, Lynn. "The Historical Roots of Our Ecological Crisis." *Science* 155 (1967): 1203–7.

Wieninger, Fritz. "Die Musik im pastoralen Konzept Martin Luthers." *Diakoni* 14 (1983): 372–77.

Williams, D. H. *Retrieving the Tradition and Renewing Evangelicalism: A Primer for Suspicious Protestants*. Grand Rapids: Eerdmans, 1999.

Williams, Peter F. *Bach: The Goldberg Variations*. Cambridge: Cambridge University Press, 2001.

———. *The Life of Bach*. Cambridge: Cambridge University Press, 2004.

Williams, Rowan. *Grace and Necessity: Reflections on Art and Love*. London: Continuum, 2005.

———. "Making It Strange: Theology in Other(s') Words." In *Sounding the Depths*, edited by Jeremy Begbie, 19–32. London: SCM, 2002.

———. *Open to Judgement: Sermons and Addresses*. See especially "Keeping Time," 247–50. London: Darton, Longman & Todd, 1994.

Willis, Paul E. *Profane Culture*. London: Routledge & Kegan Paul, 1978.

Wilson-Dickson, Andrew. *The Story of Christian Music: From Gregorian Chant to Black Gospel*. Oxford: Lion, 1992.

Witkin, R. *Adorno on Popular Culture*. London: Routledge, 2003.

Witvliet, John D. "Images and Themes in John Calvin's Theology of Liturgy." In *Worship Seeking Understanding: Windows into Christian Practice*, 127–48. Grand Rapids: Baker Academic, 2003.

———. *Worship Seeking Understanding: Windows into Christian Practice*. See especially "The Spirituality of the Psalter in Calvin's Geneva," 203–29. Grand Rapids: Baker Academic, 2003.

Wolfe, Gregory. "Editorial Statement: The Painter of Lite™." *Image* 34 (2002): 3–6.

Wolfe, Tom. "The Worship of Art: Notes on the New God." In *The Philosophy of the Visual Arts*, edited by Philip Alperson, 357–63. Oxford: Oxford University Press, 1992.

Wolff, Christoph. *Johann Sebastian Bach: The Learned Musician*. New York: Norton, 2000.

Wolterstorff, Nicholas. *Art in Action: Toward a Christian Aesthetic*. Grand Rapids: Eerdmans, 1980.

———. "Thinking about Church Music." In *Music in Christian Worship: At the Service of the Liturgy*, edited by Charlotte Kroeker, 3–16. Collegeville, MN: Liturgical Press, 2005.

———. "The Work of Making a Work of Music." In *What Is Music? An Introduction to the Philosophy of Music*, edited by P. J. Alperson, 103–29. University Park: Pennsylvania State University Press, 1987.

Wright, N. T. *New Tasks for a Renewed Church*. London: Hodder & Stoughton, 1992.

———. *The New Testament and the People of God*. London: SPCK, 1992.

———. "Poetry and Theology in Colossians 1:15–20." In *The Climax of the Covenant: Christ and the Law in Pauline Theology*, 99–119. Edinburgh: T&T Clark, 1991.

————. *The Resurrection of the Son of God*. London: SPCK, 2003.

Wu, Jean Marie. "Mystical Symbols of Faith: Olivier Messiaen's Charm of Impossibilities." In *Messiaen's Language of Mystical Love*, edited by Siglind Bruhn, 84–120. New York: Garland, 1998.

Wuthnow, Robert. *All in Sync: How Music and Art Are Revitalizing American Religion*. Berkeley: University of California Press, 2003.

Yeats, W. B. "Crazy Jane Talks with the Bishop." In *The Collected Poems of W. B. Yeats*, 294–95. London: Macmillan, 1933.

Young, Frances M. *The Art of Performance: Towards a Theology of Holy Scripture*. London: Darton, Longman & Todd, 1990.

Young, Frances M., and David Ford. *Meaning and Truth in 2 Corinthians*. Grand Rapids: Eerdmans, 1987.

Zenck, Martin. "Reinterpreting Bach in the Nineteenth and Twentieth Centuries." In *The Cambridge Companion to Bach*, edited by John Butt, 226–50. Cambridge: Cambridge University Press, 1997.

Zizioulas, John. *Being as Communion: Studies in Personhood and the Church*. London: Darton, Longman & Todd, 1985.

Zuckerkandl, Victor. *Man the Musician*. Princeton, NJ: Princeton University Press, 1973.

————. *The Sense of Music*. Princeton, NJ: Princeton University Press, 1971.

————. *Sound and Symbol: Music and the External World*. London: Routledge & Kegan Paul, 1956.

scripture index

name index

subject index

References to the principal treatment of a subject are in **boldface**. Page numbers in *italics* denote illustrations.

absolute music, 39, 44
aesthetic existence, 158–59, 162
aestheticism, theological, 21–23
affects, theory of, 132–33
affordance, 316n67
alliteration, 52
analogy of being, 322n62, 341n31
anthropocentrism, 192–93
anticipation, 190, 207, 208, 238, **263–67**. *See also* hope
antithesis, 52
arousal theories, 300
art, 51, 213, 215, 219, 244, 346n11
    and music, 13–14, 147, 151, 216
    and theology, 13–14, 263–64
    visual arts, 50–51, 206, 211, 286, 293–94, 345n4
        and meaning or representation, 50–51, 53–54
art music, 32, 37, 42, 262, 312n2. *See also* classical music
artist. *See* self, artistic
attentiveness, 207–8, **241**
authenticity. *See under* music
autonomous music. *See* absolute music; autonomy, musical
autonomy, musical, 52–53, 215. *See also* absolute music
avant-garde music, 253

baroque music, 127, 128, 131, 133
beauty, 83, 84, 86, 182, 196, 214, 216–17

Bible, 20, 23, chapter 2 passim, 123, 187–88, 211–12, 283
    biblical theology, 339n6
    musical imagery in, 67, 68, 72–73
    musical instruments in, **61–64**, *62–63*, 66, 72
        perceived hostility towards, 63–65, 68, 74
    music and daily life in, 60
    music and worship in, 65, 67, 71–74
    singing in, 61, 66, 70–71
birdsong, 53, 165, 172–73, *174*
blues, 229, 232, 249, 250
body, human. *See under* emotion; music
boundlessness, 136–37, 240
brokenness, 158–60, 162, 208, 224

cadence, 266–67, 278
calling. *See under* humankind
cantus firmus, 160–61, 269
Catholicism, Roman, 112–13, 114, 164–65, 170, 176, 178
chance music, 247, 250–52
change, 221–22, 244, 245
chant, 71, 74, 85, 101, 115
    Gregorian, 90, 91, 104, 105, 165, 179, 291
    plainchant, 91, 181
chaos, 199, 221
chiasmus, 52, 129–30
chill out music, 224, 260
Christian Contemporary Music. *See* contemporary worship music
Christian faith, 149–50, 155, 178
Christmas, 142–45
chromaticism, 125
church, 20–21, 158–59, 271–72, 293
    and music, 17 (*see also under* worship)

Jeremy S. Begbie (PhD, University of Aberdeen) is honorary professor of theology at the University of St. Andrews; associate principal of Ridley Hall, Cambridge; and an affiliated lecturer in the Faculty of Divinity at the University of Cambridge. A notable pianist, he has lectured widely in the UK, the US, and South Africa. He is the author of *Voicing Creation's Praise: Towards a Theology of the Arts* and *Theology, Music, and Time* and the editor of *Beholding the Glory: Incarnation through the Arts* and *Sounding the Depths: Theology through the Arts*.